THE
LONGMAN WRITER

Rhetoric, Reader, Research Guide,
and Handbook

NINTH EDITION

JUDITH NADELL
JOHN LANGAN

with contributions from

DEBORAH COXWELL-TEAGUE
Florida State University

PEARSON

Boston   Columbus   Indianapolis   New York   San Francisco   Upper Saddle River
Amsterdam   Cape Town   Dubai   London   Madrid   Milan   Munich   Paris   Montréal   Toron
Delhi   Mexico City   São Paulo   Sydney   Hong Kong   Seoul   Singapore   Taipei   Tokyo

SENIOR ACQUISITIONS EDITOR: Lauren A. Finn
DIRECTOR OF DEVELOPMENT: Mary Ellen Curley
SENIOR DEVELOPMENT EDITOR: Linda Stern
EXECUTIVE MARKETING MANAGER: Roxanne McCarley
SENIOR SUPPLEMENTS EDITOR: Donna Campion
SENIOR MEDIA PRODUCER: Stefanie Snajder
MEDIA PROJECT MANAGER: Sara Gordus
PROJECT MANAGER: Eric Jorgensen
PROJECT COORDINATION, TEXT DESIGN,
AND ELECTRONIC PAGE MAKEUP: Integra
COVER DESIGN MANAGER: Wendy Ann Fredericks
COVER DESIGNER: Nancy Sacks
SENIOR MANUFACTURING BUYER: Dennis J. Para
PRINTER/BINDER: R.R. Donnelley/Crawfordsville GT 31
COVER PRINTER: Lehigh-Phoenix Color/Hagerstown

Credits and acknowledgments borrowed from other sources and reproduced, with permission, in this textbook appear on the appropriate page within text [or on page 591].

Library of Congress Control Number: 2013953435

10 9 8 7 6 5 4 3 2—DOC—16 15 14

Student ISBN 10:   0-321-91413-9
ISBN 13: 978-0-321-91413-2
A la Carte ISBN 10:   0-321-91419-8
ISBN 13: 978-0-321-91419-4

PEARSON

www.pearsonhighered.com

Contents

Part III
The Patterns of Development

Part IV
The Research Essay

Part VI
A Concise Handbook

Preface

The Longman Writer brings together equal parts product and process. We describe possible sequences and structures to stress the connection between reading and writing and emphasize that these steps and formats should be viewed as strategies, not rigid prescriptions, for helping students discover what works best for them. This flexibility ensures that *The Longman Writer* can fit a wide range of teaching philosophies and learning styles.

The Longman Writer includes everything that students and instructors need in a one- or two-semester, first-year composition course: (1) a comprehensive *rhetoric*, including chapters on each stage of the writing process and discussions of the exam essay and literary paper; (2) a *reader* with *professional selections* and *student essays* integrated into the rhetoric; (3) a *research guide*, with information on writing and properly documenting a research paper; and (4) a concise, easy-to-use *handbook.* Throughout the text, we aim for a supportive, conversational tone that inspires students' confidence. Numerous *activities* and *writing assignments—more than 500 in all—*develop awareness of rhetorical choices and encourage students to explore a range of composing strategies.

What's New in the Ninth Edition

The ninth edition of *The Longman Writer* has been fully updated to provide helpful advice on the writing process, more in-depth coverage of the research process, and examples of student writing throughout.

> **Eight new professional readings are research-based and cited in MLA style**, modeling how to synthesize the ideas of others with the writer's own, include supporting detail effectively, use signal phrases skillfully, and cite accurately (Part 3).
>
> **Six new professional readings incorporate images into text** and illustrate how to use images to support a paper's thesis (Part 3).
>
> **Sixteen selections, including many of the new readings, are written from the third person** point of view in order to more closely reflect the kinds of writing students are asked to produce in college (Part 3).

Research coverage has been streamlined to focus on the essentials of writing a researched essay, integrating sources, and documenting sources. Updated MLA and APA citations for electronic sources include ebooks on iPad and Kindle as well as postings on social media.

New end-of-chapter writing activities include "Assignments Using Visuals" and offer opportunities to practice incorporating images and graphs into writing in ways that are both appropriate and effective (Part 3).

New chapter opening images and an updated design increase contemporaneity and improve visual appeal for today's readers (throughout).

The Book's Plan

Part I, "The Reading Process," provides guidance in a three-step process for text and images, in which students learn the importance of developing critical reading skills.

Part II, "The Writing Process," takes students, step by step, through a multi-stage composing sequence. Each chapter presents a stage of the writing process and includes:

- Checklists that summarize key concepts and keep students focused on the essentials as they write.
- Diagrams that encapsulate the writing process, providing at-a-glance references as students compose their own essays.
- Activities that reinforce pivotal skills and involve students in writing from the start, showing them how to take their papers through successive stages in the composing process.

Part III, "The Patterns of Development," cover nine patterns: description, narration, illustration, division-classification, process analysis, comparison-contrast, cause-effect, definition, and argumentation-persuasion. Each chapter contains a detailed explanation of the pattern, as well as the following:

- *Checklists* for prewriting and revising summarize key concepts and keep students focused on the essentials as they write.
- *Diagrams* encapsulate the patterns of development, providing at-a-glance references as students compose their own essays.
- *Annotated student essays* clearly illustrate each pattern of development. Commentary following each essay points out the blend of patterns in the paper and identifies both the paper's strengths and areas that need improvement.
- *Prewriting* and *Revising Activities* ask students to generate raw material for an essay, help them to see that the essay may include more than one pattern of development, and allow students to rework and strengthen paragraphs and examine and experiment with rhetorical options.

- *Professional selections* represent not only a specific pattern of development, but also showcase a variety of subjects, tones, and points of view. Extensive apparatus accompanies each professional selection.
  - *Biographical notes* provide background on every professional author and create an interest in each piece of writing.
  - *Pre-Reading Journal Entries* prime students for each professional selection by encouraging them to explore their thoughts about an issue.
  - *Diagrams* outline the structure of professional readings and provide students with an easy reference for identifying each pattern of development.
  - *Questions for Close Reading* help students to interpret each selection, while *Questions About the Writer's Craft* ask students to analyze a writer's use of patterns.
  - *Writing Assignments* ask students to write essays using the same pattern as in the selection, to write essays that include other patterns, and to conduct research.
- End-of-chapter *General Assignments, Assignments Using Visuals,* and *Assignments with a Specific Purpose, Audience, and Point of View* that provide open-ended topics for students to explore and applications of rhetorical context to real-world settings.

Part IV, "The Research Essay," discusses how to locate, evaluate, analyze, synthesize, integrate, and document electronic and print sources for a research paper and includes the following:

- *Checklists* summarize key concepts and keep students focused on essentials as they select a research topic, evaluate sources, write and revise a research essay, and create their bibliography.
- *Source Samples* provide concrete examples of how students can locate all the necessary components of an MLA citation by presenting the actual source and its corresponding citation.
- *Activities* ensure mastery of key research skills.

Part V, "The Literary Essay and Exam Essay," shows students how to adapt the composing process to fit the requirements of two highly specific writing situations.

Part VI, "A Concise Handbook," provides easy-to-grasp explanations of the most troublesome areas of grammar, punctuation, and spelling that students encounter.

Marginal icons alert students and instructors to unique elements of this book:

- In Part II, student writing-in-progress is indicated with 🖋.
- In Part III, assignments that are conducive to using the library or Internet are indicated with 🌣.
- In Parts II–V, ethical issues are indicated with ⚖.
- In Parts II, III, and V, combined patterns of development are indicated with 🌿.

Supplements

MyWritingLab™ **Integrated solutions for writing.** MyWritingLab is an online homework, tutorial, and assessment program that provides engaging experiences for today's instructors and students. New features designed specifically for composition instructors and their course needs include a new writing space for students, customizable rubrics for assessing and grading student writing, multimedia instruction on all aspects of composition, and advanced reporting to improve the ability to analyze class performance.

Adaptive learning. For students who enter the course underprepared, MyWritingLab offers preassessments and personalized remediation so they see improved results and instructors spend less time in class reviewing the basics.

Visit www.mywritinglab.com for more information.

Pearson eText. An online version of *The Longman Writer* brings together the many resources of MyWritingLab with the instructional content of this successful book to create an enhanced learning experience for students.

CourseSmart eTextbook. Students can subscribe to *The Longman Writer* at CourseSmart.com. The format of the eText allows students to search the text, bookmark passages, save their own notes, and print reading assignments that incorporate lecture notes.

Android and iPad eTextbooks. Android and iPad versions of the eText provide the complete text and the electronic resources described above.

Instructor's Manual. A comprehensive Instructor's Manual includes a thematic table of contents; pointers about using the book; suggested activities; a detailed syllabus; and in-depth responses to the end-of-chapter activities, Questions for Close Reading, and Questions about the Writer's Craft.

PowerPoints. Ideal for hybrid or distance learning courses, the PowerPoint presentation deck offers instructors slides based on learning objectives to adapt to their own course needs.

Accelerated Composition. Support for acceleration or co-requisite courses in MyWritingLab focuses on three fundamental areas: reading, writing, and grammar. Additional questions for professional and student readings help students understand, analyze, and evaluate the strategies writers employ. For each of the text's major writing assignments, additional activities and prompts encourage students to break down the tasks involved in writing a paper into manageable chunks. Grammar support includes diagnostic, practice, instruction, and mastery assessment.

Michelle Zollars, Associate Professor and Coordinator of the Accelerated Learning Program at Patrick Henry Community College, authors the reading and writing support for accelerated co-requisite courses. She has been teaching the accelerated composition model for over five years; has presented on acceleration at National Association for Developmental Education, the Council on Basic Writing conferences, and the Conference on Acceleration; and has served on the Developmental English Curriculum Team of the Virginia Community College System.

Acknowledgments

Many writing instructors have reviewed *The Longman Writer*, and their practical comments guided our work every step of the way. To the following reviewers we are indeed grateful: Nina Beaver, Crowder College; Ken Bishop, Itawamba Community College; Ann Bukowski, Bluegrass Community and Technical College; Philip Wayne Corbett, South University Columbia; Denise Dube, Hill College; Wynora W. Freeman, Shelton State Community College; Virginia Armiger Grant, Gaston College; Carolyn Horner, South University; Rick Kmetz, South University; Jacquelyn Markham, South University; Jeannine Morgan, St. Johns River State College.

We are most indebted to Deborah Coxwell-Teague of Florida State University for her significant, conscientious, and expert contributions to the ninth edition, including the selection of new and contemporary readings; new questions and activities; a new emphasis on incorporating visuals and sources; a thoroughly reimagined treatment of the research process with expanded discussion of analyzing, evaluating and synthesizing sources; and even new chapter opening images.

Many thanks go to our editor Lauren Finn for her fresh perspective and sound guidance as well as to Linda Stern.

To both sides of Judy Nadell and John Langan's family go affectionate thanks for being so supportive of our work. Finally, we're grateful to our students. Their candid reactions to various drafts of the text sharpened our thinking and kept us honest. We're especially indebted to the students whose work is included in this book. Their essays illustrate dramatically the potential and the power of student writing.

JUDITH NADELL
JOHN LANGAN

Becoming a Critical Reader

In this chapter, you will learn:

1.1 To read, annotate, and evaluate texts
1.2 To read, annotate, and evaluate visuals

Why don't more people delight in reading? After all, most children feel great pleasure and pride when they first learn to read. As children grow older, though, the initially magical world of books is increasingly associated with home-work, tests, and grades. Reading can turn into an anxiety-producing chore. No wonder people can end up avoiding it.

Nevertheless, people with this kind of negative experience can still come to find reading gratifying and enjoyable. The key is to be an ac-tive participant as a reader. Even a slick best seller requires the reader to decode and interpret what's on the page. In addition, many readings include visuals—images and graphics—that need to be ex-plored and evaluated. So effective reading takes a little work, but the satisfactions of reading, whether for pleasure or information, more than reward any effort involved.

The three-stage approach dis-cussed in the pages ahead will help you get the most out of the read-ings in this book, as well as any other readings, including those with

visuals. See in particular the checklists for each stage that follow here and the material on reading visuals, on pages 4–7.

Stage 1: Get an Overview of the Selection

Ideally, you should get settled in a quiet place that encourages concentration. If you can focus your attention while sprawled on a bed or curled up in a chair, that's fine. But if you find that being too comfortable is more conducive to daydreaming and dozing off than it is to studying, avoid getting too relaxed. If you're reading on a computer screen, tablet, or e-book reader, make sure you've adjusted the type size, font, and other features so that you're comfortable.

Once you're settled, it's time to read the selection. To ensure a good first reading, try the following hints.

☑ FIRST READING: A CHECKLIST

☐ Get an overview of the essay and its author. Start by checking out the author's credentials. If a biographical note precedes the selection, as in this book, you'll want to read it for background that will help you evaluate the writer's credibility, as well as his or her slant on the subject. For other materials, do a computer search for information on the author and the publication or Web site where the reading appears.

☐ Consider the selection's title. A good title often expresses the essay's main idea, giving you insight into the selection even before you read it.

☐ Read the selection straight through purely for pleasure. Allow yourself to be drawn into the world the author has created. Because you bring your own experiences and viewpoints to the piece, your reading will be unique.

☐ If a reading has visuals, ask yourself these questions: Who created the visual? Is the source reliable? What does the caption say? If the visual is an image, what general mood, feeling, or other impression does it convey? If it is a graphic, is information clearly labeled and presented?

☐ After this initial reading of the selection, briefly describe the piece and your reaction to it.

Stage 2: Deepen Your Sense of the Selection

At this point, you're ready to move more deeply into the selection. A second reading will help you identify the specific features that triggered your initial reaction.

There are a number of techniques you can use during this second, more focused reading. Mortimer Adler, a well-known writer and editor, argued passionately for marking up the material we read. The physical act of annotating, he believed, etches the writer's ideas more sharply in the mind, helping readers grasp and remember those ideas more easily. Adler also described various annotation techniques he used when reading. Several of these techniques, adapted somewhat to reflect our reading of both print and digital texts, are presented in the following checklist.

☑   **SECOND READING: A CHECKLIST**

Using a pen (or pencil) and highlighter for print texts—or digital commenting and highlighting features if you're reading online—you might . . .

- ☐ Underline or highlight the selection's main idea, or thesis, often found near the beginning or end. If the thesis isn't stated explicitly, write down your own version of the selection's main idea. If you're reading the selection online, you might add a digital sticky note or comment with your version of the thesis.
- ☐ Locate the main supporting evidence used to develop the thesis. Number the key supporting points by writing in the margin or adding digital sticky notes.
- ☐ Circle or put an asterisk next to key ideas that are stated more than once.
- ☐ Take a minute to write "Yes" or "No" or to insert these comments digitally beside points with which you strongly agree or disagree. Your reaction to these points often explains your feelings about the aptness of the selection's ideas.
- ☐ Return to any unclear passages you encountered during the first reading. The feeling you now have for the piece as a whole will *probably* help you make sense of initially confusing spots. You may possibly discover that the writer's thinking isn't as clear as it could be.
- ☐ Use a print or online dictionary to check the meanings of any unfamiliar words.
- ☐ Take some quick notes about any visuals. If you're reading online, you might choose to make digital comments. What is the author's purpose? Do images such as photos tell a story? Do they make assumptions about viewers' beliefs or knowledge? What elements stand out? How do the colors and composition (arrangement of elements) work to convey an impression? Are any graphs and similar visuals adequately discussed in the text? Is the information current and presented without distortion? Is it relevant to the text discussion?
- ☐ If your initial impression of the selection has changed in any way, try to determine why you reacted differently on this reading.

Stage 3: Evaluate the Selection

Now that you have a good grasp of the selection, you may want to read it a third time, especially if the piece is long or complex. This time, your goal is to make judgments about the selection's effectiveness. Keep in mind, though, that you shouldn't evaluate the selection until after you have a strong hold on it. Whether positive or negative, any reaction is valid only if it's based on an accurate reading.

To evaluate the selection, ask yourself the following questions.

☑ **EVALUATING A SELECTION: A CHECKLIST**

☐ *Where does support for the selection's thesis seem logical and sufficient? Where does support seem weak?* Which of the author's supporting facts, arguments, and examples seem pertinent and convincing? Which don't?

☐ *Is the selection unified? If not, why not?* Where are there any unnecessary digressions or detours?

☐ *How does the writer make the selection move smoothly from beginning to end?* Are any parts of the essay abrupt and jarring? Which ones?

☐ *Which stylistic devices are used to good effect in the selection?* How do paragraph development, sentence structure, word choice *(diction)*, and tone contribute to the piece's overall effect? Where does the writer use figures of speech effectively? (Consult the index to see where these devices are explained.)

☐ *How do any visuals improve the reading and support the writer's main points?* Are the visuals adequately discussed in the text? Are images such as photos thought-provoking without being sensationalistic? Do graphs and similar visuals give relevant, persuasive details?

☐ *How does the selection encourage further thought?* What new perspective on an issue does the writer provide? What ideas has the selection prompted you to explore in an essay of your own?

Assessing Visuals in a Reading

Writers may use visuals—images and graphics—to help convey their message. You can incorporate your "reading" of these visuals into the three-stage process you use for reading text: In stage 1, *preview* the visuals at the same time that you get an overview of the text. In stage 2, *analyze and interpret* the visuals as a means of deepening your sense of the reading. Finally, in stage 3, *evaluate* the visuals as part of your evaluation of the entire selection.

Some kinds of visuals you are likely to find are listed below. Following this list are two examples of assessing visuals using the three-stage process.

Illustrations

- Photographs, paintings, drawings, and prints — Illustrate a particular scene, time period, activity, event, idea, person, and so on.
- Cartoons and comics — May make a joke, comment on a situation, or tell a story.

Graphics

• Tables	Use columns and rows to present information, especially specific numbers, concisely.
• Bar graphs	Use rectangular bars of different sizes to compare information about two or more items.
• Line graphs	Use horizontal lines moving from point to point to show changes over time.
• Pie charts	Use a circle divided into wedges to show proportions.
• Charts and diagrams	Use different shapes and lines to show flow of information, organization of a group, layouts such as room plans, or assembly instructions.
• Maps	Present information by geographical location.

Photos, paintings, and similar illustrations may appear in Web pages, periodicals, books, and advertisements. Graphics regularly appear in academic, technical, and business writing. You can evaluate all these visuals just as you would text.

Assessing an Image: An Example

Suppose a reading aims to persuade readers that the international community must set up an organization that stands ready to implement an immediate and coordinated response to natural diasters, no matter where they occur. The reading includes a photo (see page 6) taken in the aftermath of the magnitude 7 earthquake that hit Haiti on January 12, 2010. How can we evaluate this image and its effectiveness for the reader?

1. **Previewing the Photo.** We see that the photo was found at *Time* magazine online and was taken by a photographer for the Associated Press (AP)—both reliable sources that we can trust. The author of the essay has written a caption that clearly explains the image, and the phrase "Using whatever implements are at their disposal" supports the author's point that an immediate response is needed. We also notice, however, that the caption uses strong language, for example, "catastropic" and "devastated." Information in the reading will have to support the use of these terms. Still, our first response to the photo would be one of sympathy and perhaps compassion for the people of Haiti.

2. **Analyzing and Interpreting the Photo.** The photo tells a story of people coming together to help one another in the aftermath of the earthquake. The elements in the photo are arranged so that we first see people silhouetted against clouds, working with hand tools. Then we realize the people are standing atop a collapsed building, and we see the startling image of cars crushed beneath that structure. Now we understand the scope of the wreckage. The vivid blue,

Using whatever implements are at their disposal, Haitians searched for survivors—
and victims—of the catastrophic earthquake that devastated Port-au-Prince and many
surrounding areas on January 12, 2010.

red, and silver of the ruined cars and the hopeful brightness of the sky are
overshadowed by the dark, massive bulk of the collapsed structure. Though
we cannot see people's faces, we can imagine their determination. But we can
also tell that their tools are unlikely to be adequate for the urgent task of finding those buried in the rubble.

3. **Evaluating the Photo.** The photo powerfully illustrates the scale of the work
facing Haiti and the probable inadequacy of the country's resources. The
contrast between the crushed cars and building and the determined workers
conveys a sense of the hopefulness of the human spirit even in dire situations.
Many readers will feel an emotional response to these people, will see that
they need help, and will want to help them. The photo and caption together,
therefore, successfully support the idea that some countries may not have the
means to cope effectively with huge natural disasters. The text of the reading
will have to convince the reader that setting up an international organization
to coordinate responses to these crises is the right solution.

Assessing a Graph: An Example

Imagine that a reading's purpose is to show that people need to do more to eradi-
cate disease in the poorest countries and that the article includes the pie chart
in Figure 1.1 on the next page. How can we approach this graphic element and
assess its usefulness to the reader?

FIGURE 1.1

Distribution of the 219 Million Cases of Malaria Reported Worldwide in 2010

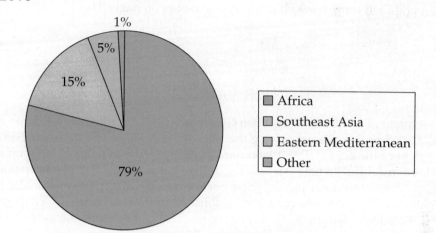

Source: From data reported in the *World Malaria Report, 2012*. World Health Organization.

1. **Previewing the Graph.** We see right away that the author has created a pie chart comparing cases of malaria in regions of the world. The chart is clearly labeled, and a full caption tells us the information is from a reliable source—the World Health Organization, which is part of the United Nations.

2. **Analyzing and Interpreting the Graph.** The source's date tells us that the information is not only reliable, but also current. The chart clearly shows that the greatest percentage of malaria cases reported in 2010 occurred in Africa. However, percentages can be misleading. If there were only 1,000 malaria cases altogether, 85 percent would not represent a very big number of cases. But because the caption gives us the number of cases—and that number is very large (219 million)—we can conclude that malaria is a serious health problem in Africa.

3. **Evaluating the Graph.** Without being sensationalistic, the chart is striking. It effectively dramatizes the point that the poorest regions of the world suffer substantially more from certain diseases than the developed regions do. The chart appeals to our sense of fairness. After all, if we can do more to prevent malaria in poor regions, shouldn't we? The author must still persuade us that it's really possible to do more, but the graph strongly supports at least part of the author's main idea.

A Model Annotated Reading

To illustrate the multi-stage reading process, we've annotated the professional essay that follows: Ellen Goodman's "Family Counterculture." As you read Goodman's essay, try applying the three-stage sequence. You can measure your ability to dig into the selection by making your own annotations on Goodman's essay and then comparing them to ours. You can also see how well you evaluated the piece by answering the questions in "Evaluating a Selection: A Checklist" on page 4 and then comparing your responses to ours on pages 11–12.

Ellen Goodman

The recipient of a Pulitzer Prize, Ellen Goodman (1941–) worked for *Newsweek* and *The Detroit Free Press* before joining the staff of *The Boston Globe* in the mid-1970s. A resident of the Boston area, Goodman wrote a popular syndicated column that provided insightful commentary on life in the United States. Her pieces appeared in a number of national publications, including *The Village Voice* and *McCall's*. Collections of her columns have been published in *Close to Home* (1979), *At Large* (1981), *Keeping in Touch* (1985), *Making Sense* (1989), and *Value Judgments* (1993). The following selection is from *Value Judgments*.

Pre-Reading Journal Entry

Television is often blamed for having a harmful effect on children. Do you think this criticism is merited? In what ways does TV exert a negative influence on children? In what ways does TV exert a positive influence on youngsters? Take a few minutes to respond to these questions in your journal.

FAMILY COUNTERCULTURE

Interesting take on the term *counterculture*

Time frame established

Light humor. Easy, casual tone

Sooner or later, most Americans become card-carrying members of the   1
counterculture. This is not an underground holdout of hippies. No beads are required. All you need to join is a child.

Time frame picked up

Thesis, developed overall by cause-effect pattern

At some point between Lamaze and the PTA, it becomes clear that one   2
of your main jobs as a parent is to counter the culture. What the media delivers to children by the masses, you are expected to rebut one at a time.

First research-based example to support thesis

The latest evidence of this frustrating piece of the parenting job descrip-   3
tion came from pediatricians. This summer, the American Academy of Pediatrics called for a ban on television food ads. Their plea was hard on the heels of a study showing that one Saturday morning of TV cartoons contained 202 junk-food ads.

4   The kids see, want, and nag. That is, after all, the theory behind advertising to children, since few six-year-olds have their own trust funds. The
end result, said the pediatricians, is obesity and high cholesterol.

5   Their call for a ban was predictably attacked by the grocers' association.
But it was also attacked by people assembled under the umbrella marked
"parental responsibility." We don't need bans, said these "PR" people, we
need parents who know how to say "no."

6   Well, I bow to no one in my capacity for naysaying. I agree that it's a
well-honed skill of child raising. By the time my daughter was seven, she
qualified as a media critic.

Relevant paragraph?
Identifies Goodman as
a parent, but interrupts
flow

7   But it occurs to me now that the call for "parental responsibility" is
increasing in direct proportion to the irresponsibility of the marketplace.
Parents are expected to protect their children from an increasingly hostile
environment.

Transition doesn't work
but would if ¶6 cut.

8   Are the kids being sold junk food? Just say no. Is TV bad? Turn it off.
Are there messages about sex, drugs, violence all around? Counter the
culture.

Series of questions and
brief answers consistent
with overall casual tone

9   Mothers and fathers are expected to screen virtually every aspect of their
children's lives. To check the ratings on the movies, to read the labels on the
CDs, to find out if there's MTV in the house next door. All the while keeping
in touch with school and, in their free time, earning a living.

Brief real-life examples
support thesis.

Fragments

10   In real life, most parents do a great deal of this monitoring and just-
say-no-ing. Any trip to the supermarket produces at least one scene of a
child grabbing for something only to have it returned to the shelf by a
frazzled parent. An extraordinary number of the family arguments are
over the goodies—sneakers, clothes, games—that the young know only
because of ads.

More examples

11   But at times it seems that the media have become the mainstream culture in children's lives. Parents have become the alternative.

Another weak
transition—no contrast

Restatement of thesis

12   Barbara Dafoe Whitehead, a research associate at the Institute for
American Values, found this out in interviews with middle-class parents.
"A common complaint I heard from parents was their sense of being overwhelmed by the culture. They felt their voice was a lot weaker. And they
felt relatively more helpless than their parents.

Second research-based
example to support
thesis

Citing an expert rein-
forces thesis.

Restatement of thesis   →   "Parents," she notes, "see themselves in a struggle for the hearts and   13
minds of their own children." It isn't that they can't say no. It's that
there's so much more to say no to.

Comparison-contrast   Without wallowing in false nostalgia, there has been a fundamental   14
pattern—signaled by   shift. Americans once expected parents to raise their children in accor-
Today, *Once*, and *Now*   dance with the dominant cultural messages. Today they are expected to
raise their children in opposition.

                         Once the chorus of cultural values was full of ministers, teachers, neigh-   15
bors, leaders. They demanded more conformity, but offered more support.
Now the messengers are Ninja Turtles, Madonna, rap groups, and celebrities pushing sneakers. Parents are considered "responsible" only if they
are successful in their resistance.

Restatement of thesis   → It's what makes child raising harder. It's why parents feel more isolated.   16
It's not just that American families have less time with their kids. It's that
we have to spend more of this time doing battle with our own culture.

Conveys the challenges   It's rather like trying to get your kids to eat their green beans after   17
that parents face   they've been told all day about the wonders of Milky Way. Come to think
of it, it's exactly like that.

Thesis: First stated in paragraph 2 ("…it becomes clear that one of your main jobs as a parent is to counter the culture. What the media delivers to children by the masses, you are expected to rebut one at a time.") and then restated in paragraphs 11 ("the media have become the mainstream culture in children's lives. Parents have become the alternative."); 13 (Parents are frustrated, not because "…they can't say no. It's that there's so much more to say no to."); and 16 ("It's not just that American families have less time with their kids. It's that we have to spend more of this time doing battle with our own culture.").

First Reading: A quick take on a serious subject. Informal tone and to-the-point style get to the heart of the media versus parenting problem. Easy to relate to.

Second and Third Readings:

1. Uses the findings of the American Academy of Pediatrics, a statement made by Barbara Dafoe Whitehead, and a number of brief examples to illustrate the relentless work parents must do to counter the culture.
2. Uses cause-effect overall to support thesis and comparison-contrast to show how parenting nowadays is more difficult than it used to be.
3. Not everything works (reference to her daughter as a media critic, repetitive and often inappropriate use of *but* as a transition), but overall the essay succeeds.
4. At first, the ending seems weak. But it feels just right after an additional reading. Shows how parents' attempts to counter the culture are as commonplace as their attempts to get kids to eat vegetables. It's an ongoing and constant battle that makes parenting more difficult than it has to be and less enjoyable than it should be.

5. Possible essay topics: A humorous paper about the strategies kids use to get around their parents' saying "no" or a serious paper on the negative effects on kids of another aspect of television culture (cable television, MTV, tabloid-style talk shows, and so on).

The following answers to the questions on page 4 will help crystallize your reaction to Goodman's essay.

1. **Where does support for the selection's thesis seem logical and sufficient? Where does support seem weak?** Goodman begins to provide evidence for her thesis when she cites the American Academy of Pediatric's call for a "ban on television food ads" (paragraphs 3–5). The ban followed a study showing that kids are exposed to 202 junk-food ads during a single Saturday morning of television cartoons. Goodman further buoys her thesis with a list of brief "countering the culture" examples (8–10) and a slightly more detailed example (10) describing the parent-child conflicts that occur on a typical trip to the supermarket. By citing Barbara Dafoe Whitehead's findings (12–13) later on, Goodman further reinforces her point that the need for constant rebuttal makes parenting especially frustrating: Because parents have to say "no" to virtually everything, more and more family time ends up being spent "doing battle" with the culture (16).

2. **Is the selection unified? If not, why not?** In the first two paragraphs, Goodman identifies the problem and then provides solid evidence of its existence (3–4, 8–10). But Goodman's comments in paragraph 6 about her daughter's skill as a media critic seem distracting. Even so, paragraph 6 serves a purpose because it establishes Goodman's credibility by showing that she, too, is a parent and has been compelled to be a constant naysayer with her child. From paragraph 7 on, the piece stays on course by focusing on the way parents have to compete with the media for control of their children. The concluding paragraphs (16–17) reinforce Goodman's thesis by suggesting that parents' struggle to counteract the media is as common—and as exasperating—as trying to get children to eat their vegetables when all the kids want is to gorge on candy.

3. **How does the writer make the selection move smoothly from beginning to end?** The first two paragraphs of Goodman's essay are clearly connected: The phrase "sooner or later" at the beginning of the first paragraph establishes a time frame that is then picked up at the beginning of the second paragraph with the phrase "at some point between Lamaze and the PTA." And Goodman's use in paragraph 3 of the word *this* ("The latest evidence of *this* frustrating piece of the parenting job description…") provides a link to the preceding paragraph. Other connecting strategies can be found in the piece. For example, the words *Today*, *Once*, and *Now* in paragraphs 14–15 provide an easy-to-follow contrast between parenting in earlier times and parenting in this era. However, because paragraph 6 contains a distracting aside, the contrast implied by the word *But* at the beginning of paragraph 7 doesn't work. Nor does Goodman's use of the word *But* at the beginning of paragraph 11 work; the point there emphasizes rather than contrasts with the one made in paragraph 10. From this point on, though, the essay is tightly written and moves smoothly along to its conclusion.

4. Which stylistic devices are used to good effect in the selection? Goodman uses several patterns of development in her essay. The selection as a whole shows the *effect* of the mass media on kids and their parents. In paragraphs 3 and 12, Goodman provides *examples in the form of research data* to support her thesis, whereas paragraphs 8–10 provide a series of *brief real-life examples.* Paragraphs 12–15 use a *contrast,* and paragraph 17 makes a *comparison* to punctuate Goodman's concluding point. Throughout, Goodman's *informal, conversational tone* draws readers in, and her *no-holds-barred style* drives her point home forcefully. In paragraph 8, she uses a *question and answer format* ("Are the kids being sold junk food? Just say no.") and *short sentences* ("Turn it off" and "Counter the culture") to illustrate how pervasive the situation is. And in paragraph 9, she uses *fragments* ("To check the ratings . . ." and "All the while keeping in touch with school . . .") to focus attention on the problem. These varied stylistic devices help make the essay a quick, enjoyable read. Finally, although Goodman is concerned about the corrosive effects of the media, she lightens her essay with dashes of *humor.* For example, the image of parents as card-carrying hippies (1) and the comments about green beans and Milky Ways (17) probably elicit smiles or gentle laughter from most readers.

5. How does the selection encourage further thought? Goodman's essay touches on a problem most parents face at some time or another—having to counter the culture in order to protect their children. Her main concern is how difficult it is for parents to say "no" to virtually every aspect of the culture. Although Goodman offers no immediate solutions, her presentation of the issue urges us to decide for ourselves which aspects of the culture should be countered and which should not.

Following are some sample questions and writing assignments based on the Goodman essay; all are similar to the sort that appear later in this book. Note that the final writing assignment paves the way for the successive stages of a student essay presented in Part II, "The Writing Process." (The final version of the essay appears on pages 120–121.)

Questions for Close Reading

1. According to Goodman, what does it mean to "counter the culture"? Why is this harder now than ever before?

2. Which two groups, according to Goodman, protested the American Academy of Pediatric's ban on television food ads? Which of these two groups does she take more seriously? Why?

Questions About the Writer's Craft

1. What audience do you think Goodman had in mind when she wrote this piece? How do you know? Where does she address this audience directly?

2. What word appears four times in paragraph 16? Why do you think Goodman repeats this word so often? What is the effect of this repetition?

Writing Assignments

1. Goodman believes that parents are forced to say "no" to almost everything the media offer. Write an essay supporting the idea that not everything the media present is bad for children.

2. Goodman implies that, in some ways, today's world is hostile to children. Do you agree? Drawing upon but not limiting yourself to the material in your pre-reading journal, write an essay in which you support or reject this viewpoint.

2

Getting Started Through Prewriting

In this chapter, you will learn:

2.1 To use prewriting to generate ideas before composing a first draft
2.2 To organize your ideas into an outline that will help to make the writing process more manageable

When you read a piece of writing, you see only the finished product. Not being privy to the writer's effort to convey meaning, you may hold a romanticized notion of what it means to be a writer. So you shouldn't be surprised if you feel some apprehension when it's time to write a paper.

Your uneasiness may stem in part from your belief that some people are born writers and others are not—and that you're one of the latter. However, learning to write well is a challenge for everyone. In practice, most writers do not spontaneously pour out well-formed thoughts. Shaky starts and changes in direction aren't uncommon. Although there's no way to eliminate the work needed to write effectively, certain approaches can make the process more manageable and rewarding. In Chapters 2–9, we describe a sequence of steps for writing essays. During the sequence, you do the following:

- Prewrite
- Identify your thesis
- Support the thesis with evidence
- Organize the evidence
- Write the paragraphs of the first draft
- Revise meaning, structure, and paragraph development
- Revise sentences and words
- Edit and proofread

14

Even though we present the sequence as a series of steps, it's not a formula that you must follow rigidly. Some writers mull over a topic in their heads and then move quickly into a promising first draft; others outline their essays in detail before beginning to write. Between these two extremes are any number of effective approaches. We urge you to experiment with the strategies we present. Try them, use what works, discard what doesn't. And always feel free to streamline or alter the steps in the sequence to suit your individual needs and the requirements of specific writing assignments.

Use Prewriting to Get Started

Prewriting refers to strategies you can use to generate ideas *before* starting the first draft of a paper. (See Figure 2.1.) Because prewriting techniques encourage imaginative exploration, they also help you discover what interests you most about your subject. Having such a focus early in the writing process keeps you from plunging into your initial draft without first giving some thought to what you want to say. Prewriting thus saves you time in the long run by keeping you on course.

FIGURE 2.1

Process Diagram: Prewriting

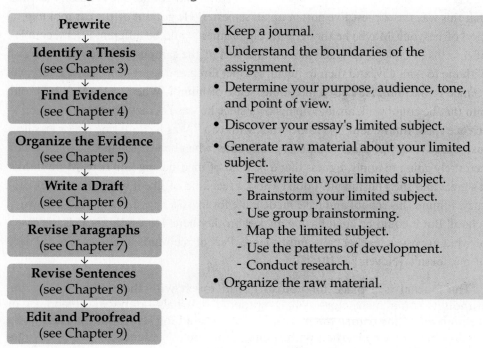

Prewrite	• Keep a journal.
↓	• Understand the boundaries of the assignment.
Identify a Thesis (see Chapter 3)	• Determine your purpose, audience, tone, and point of view.
↓	
Find Evidence (see Chapter 4)	• Discover your essay's limited subject.
↓	• Generate raw material about your limited subject.
Organize the Evidence (see Chapter 5)	- Freewrite on your limited subject.
↓	- Brainstorm your limited subject.
Write a Draft (see Chapter 6)	- Use group brainstorming.
↓	- Map the limited subject.
Revise Paragraphs (see Chapter 7)	- Use the patterns of development.
↓	- Conduct research.
Revise Sentences (see Chapter 8)	• Organize the raw material.
↓	
Edit and Proofread (see Chapter 9)	

Prewriting can help in other ways, too. When we write, we often sabotage our ability to generate material because we continually critique what we put down on paper. During prewriting, you deliberately ignore your internal critic. Your purpose is simply to get ideas down on paper or on a computer screen *without evaluating* their effectiveness.

One final advantage of prewriting: The random associations typical of prewriting tap the mind's ability to make unusual connections. You may stumble upon an interesting idea. Prewriting helps you appreciate—right from the start—this element of surprise in the writing process.

Keep a Journal

Of all the prewriting techniques, keeping a **journal** (daily or almost daily) is the one most likely to make writing a part of your life. No matter what format your journal takes—notebook or computer file—be sure to date all entries.

Some journal entries focus on a single theme; others wander from topic to topic. Your starting point may be a dream, a conversation, a video on YouTube, a political cartoon, an issue raised in class or in your reading—anything that surprises, interests, angers, depresses, confuses, or amuses you. You may also use a journal to experiment with your writing style—say, to vary your sentence structure if you tend to use predictable patterns.

Here is a fairly focused excerpt from a student's journal:

Today I had to show Paul around school. He and Mom got here at 9. I didn't let on that this was the earliest I've gotten up all semester! He got out of the car looking kind of nervous. Maybe he thought his big brother would be different after a couple of months of college. I walked him around part of the campus and then he went with me to Am. Civ. and then to lunch. He met Greg and some other guys. Everyone seemed to like him. He's got a nice, quiet sense of humor. When I went to Bio., I told him that he could walk around on his own since he wasn't crazy about sitting in on a science class. But he said "I'd rather stick with you." Was he flattering me or was he just scared? Anyway it made me feel good. Later when he was leaving, he told me he's definitely going to apply. I guess that'd be kind of nice, having him here. Mom thinks it's great and she's pushing it. I don't know. I feel kind of like it would invade my privacy. I found this school and have made a life for myself here. Let him find his own school! But it could be great having my kid brother here. I guess this is a classic case of what my psych teacher calls ambivalence. Part of me wants him to come, and part of me doesn't. (November 10)

The journal is a place for you to get in touch with the writer inside you. Although some instructors collect students' journals—done in notebooks or through an online course management system or a blog set up for the class—you needn't be overly concerned with spelling, grammar, sentence structure, or organization. Although journal writing is typically more structured than freewriting (see page 25), your entries needn't be mini-essays. On the contrary, sometimes you may find it helpful to use a simple list (see the journal entry at the bottom of this page) when recording your thoughts. You may leave loose ends, drift to new topics, and evoke the personal and private without fully explaining or describing. The most important thing is to let your journal writing prompt reflection and insights.

The Pre-Reading Journal Entry

To reinforce the value of journal writing, we've included a *Pre-Reading Journal Entry* assignment before every selection. These exercises get you ready for the piece by encouraging you to explore—in a tentative fashion—your thoughts about an issue that will be raised in the selection. Here, once again, is the *Pre-Reading Journal Entry* assignment that precedes Ellen Goodman's "Family Counterculture" (see page 8):

> Television is often blamed for having a harmful effect on children. Do you think this criticism is merited? In what ways does TV exert a negative influence on children? In what ways does TV exert a positive influence on youngsters? Take a few minutes to respond to these questions in your journal.

The following journal entry shows how one student, Harriet Davids, responded to the journal assignment. A thirty-eight-year-old college student and mother of two young teenagers, Harriet was understandably intrigued by the assignment. As you'll see, Harriet used a listing strategy to prepare her journal entry. She found that lists were perfect for dealing with the essentially "for or against" nature of the journal assignment.

TV's Negative Influence on Kids	TV's Positive Influence on Kids
Teaches negative behaviors (violence, sex, swearing, drugs, alcohol, etc.)	Teaches important educational concepts (*Sesame Street*, shows on The Discovery Channel, etc.)
Cuts down on imagination and creativity	Exposes kids to new images and worlds (*Dora, Word Girl*)
Cuts down on time spent with parents (talking, reading, playing games together)	Can inspire discussions (about morals, sexuality, etc.)
Encourages parents' lack of involvement with kids	Gives parents a needed break from kids
Frightens kids by showing images of violence	Educates kids about the painful realities in the world

(Continued)

TV's Negative Influence on Kids	TV's Positive Influence on Kids
Encourages isolation (watching screen rather than interacting with other kids)	Creates common ground among kids, basis of conversations and games
De-emphasizes reading and creates need for constant stimulation	Encourages kids to slow down and read books based on a TV series or show (the *Arthur* and the *Clifford* series, etc.)
Promotes materialism (commercials)	Can teach kids that they can't have everything they see

As you've just seen, journal writing can stimulate thinking in a loose, unstructured way; journal writing can also prompt the focused thinking required by a specific writing assignment. When you have a specific piece to write, you should approach prewriting in a purposeful, focused manner.

Understand the Boundaries of the Assignment

Sometimes a professor will indicate that you can write on a topic of your own choosing; other times you may be given a highly specific assignment. Most assignments, though, will fit somewhere in between. In any case, you shouldn't start writing a paper until you know what's expected. First, clarify the *kind of paper* the instructor has in mind. If you're not sure about an assignment, ask your instructor to make the requirements clear. Most instructors are more than willing to provide an explanation.

Second, find out *how long* the paper is expected to be. Many instructors will indicate the approximate length of the papers they assign. If no length requirements are provided, discuss with the instructor what you plan to cover and indicate how long you think your paper will be.

Determine Your Purpose, Audience, Tone, and Point of View

Once you understand the requirements for a writing assignment, you're ready to begin thinking about the essay.

Purpose

Start by clarifying to yourself the essay's broad **purpose**. What do you want the essay to accomplish? Essays are usually meant to *inform* or *explain*, to *convince* or *persuade*, and sometimes to *entertain*. In practice, writing often combines purposes. You might, for example, write an essay trying to *convince* people to support a new trash recycling program in your community. But before you win readers over, you most likely would have to *explain* something about current waste-disposal technology.

When purposes blend in this way, the predominant one influences the essay's content, organization, pattern of development, emphasis, and language. Assume you're writing about a political campaign. If your primary goal is to *entertain*, to take a gentle poke at two candidates, you might use the comparison-contrast pattern to organize your essay. You might, for example, start with several accounts of one candidate's "foot-in-mouth disease" and then describe the attempts of the other candidate, a multimillionaire, to portray himself as an average Joe. Your language, full of exaggeration, would reflect your objective. But if your primary purpose is to *persuade* readers that the candidates are incompetent and shouldn't be elected, you might adopt a serious, straightforward style. Selecting the argumentation-persuasion pattern to structure the essay, you might use one candidate's gaffes and the other's posturings to build a case that neither is worthy of public office.

Audience

Writing is a social act and thus implies a reader or an **audience**. To write effectively, you need to identify who your readers are and to take their expectations and needs into account.

If you forget your readers, your essay can run into problems. Consider what happened when one student, Roger Salucci, submitted a draft of his essay to his instructor for feedback. The assignment was to write about an experience that demonstrated the value of education. Here's the opening paragraph from Roger's first draft:

When I received my first page as an EMT, I realized pretty quickly that all the weeks of KED and CPR training paid off. At first, when the call came in, I was all nerves, I can tell you. When the heat is on, my mind tends to go as blank as an unplugged computer screen. But I beat it to the van right away. After a couple of false turns, my partner and I finally got the right house and found a woman fibrillating and suffering severe myocardial arrhythmia. Despite our anxiety, our heads were on straight; we knew exactly what to do.

Roger's instructor found his essay unclear because she knew nothing about being an EMT (emergency medical technician). When writing the essay, Roger neglected to consider his audience; specifically, he forgot that college instructors are no more knowledgeable than anyone else about subjects outside their specialty. Roger's instructor also commented that she was thrown off guard by the paper's casual, slangy approach ("I was all nerves, I can tell you"; "I beat it to the van right away"). Roger used a breezy, colloquial style—almost as though he were chatting about the experience with friends—but the instructor had expected a more formal approach.

The more you know about your readers, the more you can adapt your writing to fit their needs and expectations. The accompanying checklist will help you analyze your audience.

☑ ■ **ANALYZING YOUR AUDIENCE: A CHECKLIST**

- ☐ What are my readers' ages, sex, and educational levels? How do these factors affect what I tell and don't tell them?
- ☐ What are my readers' political, religious, and other beliefs? How do these beliefs influence their attitudes and actions?
- ☐ What interests and needs motivate my audience?
- ☐ How much do my readers already know about my subject? Do they have any misconceptions?
- ☐ What biases do they have about me, my subject, and my opinion?
- ☐ How do my readers expect me to relate to them?
- ☐ What values do I share with my readers that will help me communicate with them?

Tone

Just as your voice may project a range of feelings, your writing can convey one or more **tones**, or emotional states: enthusiasm, anger, resignation, and so on. Tone is integral to meaning. It permeates writing and reflects your attitude toward yourself, your purpose, your subject, and your readers.

In writing, how do you project tone? You pay close attention to *sentence structure* and *word choice*. In Chapter 8, we present detailed strategies for finetuning sentences and words during the revision stage. Here we simply want to help you see that determining your tone should come early in the writing process because the tone you select influences the sentences and words you use later.

Sentence structure refers to the way sentences are shaped. Although the two paragraphs that follow deal with exactly the same subject, note how differences in sentence structure create sharply dissimilar tones:

> During the 1960s, many inner-city minorities considered the police an occupying force and an oppressive agent of control. As a result, violence grew against police in poorer neighborhoods, as did the number of residents killed by police.

> An occupying force. An agent of control. An oppressor. That's how many inner-city minorities in the '60s viewed the police. Violence against police soared. Police killings of residents mounted.

The first paragraph projects a neutral, almost dispassionate tone. The sentences are fairly long, and clear transitions ("During the 1960s"; "As a result") mark the progression of thought. The second paragraph seems intended to elicit a strong emotional response; its short sentences, fragments, and abrupt transitions reflect the turbulence of earlier times.

Word choice also plays a role in establishing the tone of an essay. Words have **denotations**, neutral dictionary meanings, as well as **connotations**, emotional associations that go beyond the literal meaning. The word *beach*, for instance, is defined in the dictionary as "a nearly level stretch of pebbles and sand beside a body of water." This definition, however, doesn't capture individual responses to the word. For some, *beach* suggests warmth and relaxation; for others, it calls up images of a once-clean stretch of shoreline ruined by an oil spill.

Because tone and meaning are tightly bound, you must be sensitive to the emotional nuances of words. Think about some of the terms denoting an adult human female: *woman, chick, broad, member of the fair sex.* While all of these words denote the same thing, their connotations—the pictures they call up—are sharply different. Similarly, in a respectful essay about police officers, you wouldn't refer to *cops, narcs,* or *flatfoots;* such terms convey a contempt inconsistent with the tone intended. Your words must convey tone clearly; otherwise, meaning is lost.

Point of View

When you write, you speak as a unique individual to your audience. **Point of view** reveals the person you decide to be as you write. Like tone, point of view is closely tied to your purpose, audience, and subject. Imagine you want to convey to students in your composition class the way your grandfather's death—on your eighth birthday—impressed you with life's fragility. To capture that day's impact on you, you might tell what happened from the point of view of a child: "Today is my birthday. I'm eight. Grandpa died an hour before I was supposed to have my party." Or you might choose instead to recount the event speaking as the adult you are today: "My grandfather died an hour before my eighth birthday party." Your point of view will affect the essay's content and organization.

The most strongly individualized point of view is the **first person** (*I, me, mine, we, us, our*). The first-person point of view is appropriate in narrative and descriptive essays based on personal experience. It also suits other types of essays (for example, causal analyses and process analyses) when the bulk of evidence presented consists of personal observation. In such essays, avoiding the first person often leads to stilted sentences like "There was strong parental opposition to the decision" or "Although organic chemistry had been dreaded, it became a passion." In contrast, the sentences sound much more natural when the first person is used: "*Our* parents strongly opposed the decision" and "Although *I* had dreaded organic chemistry, it became *my* passion."

In essays voicing an opinion, most first-person expressions ("I believe that…" and "In my opinion…") are unnecessary and distracting; the point of view stated is assumed to be the writer's unless another source is indicated.

In some situations, writers use the **second person** (*you, your, yours*), alone or in combination with the first person. For instance, "If *you're* the kind of person who doodles while thinking, *you* may want to try mapping…" rather than "If a *writer* is the kind of person who doodles while thinking, *he* or *she* may want to try mapping.…" The second person simplifies style and involves the reader in a more personal way. You'll also find that the *imperative* form of the verb ("*Send* letters of protest to the television networks") engages readers in much the same way. The implied *you* speaks to the audience directly and lends immediacy to the directions. Despite these advantages, the second-person point of view isn't appropriate in many college courses, where more formal, less conversational writing is usually called for.

The **third-person** point of view is by far the most common in academic writing. The third person gets its name from the stance it conveys—that of an outsider or "third person" observing and reporting on matters of primarily public rather than private importance. In discussions of historical events, scientific phenomena, works of art, and the like, the third-person point of view conveys a feeling of distance and objectivity. Be careful not to adopt such a detached stance that you end up using a stiff, artificial style: "On this campus, approximately two-thirds of the student body is dependent on bicycles as the primary mode of transportation to class." Aim instead for a more natural and personable quality: "Two-thirds of the students on campus ride their bikes to class." (For a more detailed discussion of levels of formality, see pages 103–104 in Chapter 8.)

Discover Your Essay's Limited Subject

Once you have a firm grasp of the assignment's boundaries and have determined your purpose, audience, tone, and point of view, you're ready to focus on a **limited subject** of the general assignment. Too broad a subject can result in a rambling essay, so be sure to restrict your general subject before starting to write.

The following examples show the difference between general subjects that are too broad for an essay and limited subjects that are appropriate and workable.

General Subject	Less General	Limited Subject
Education	Computers in education	Computers in elementary school arithmetic classes
Transportation	Low-cost travel	Hitchhiking
Work	Planning for a career	College internships

How do you move from a general to a narrow subject? Imagine that you're asked to prepare a straightforward, informative essay for your writing class.

The assignment, prompted by Ellen Goodman's essay "Family Counterculture" (pages 8–10), is an extension of the writing assignment on page 13.

> Goodman implies that, in some ways, today's world is hostile to children. Do you agree? Drawing upon but not limiting yourself to the material in your pre-reading journal, write an essay in which you support or reject this viewpoint.

Keeping your purpose, audience, tone, and point of view in mind, you may **question** or **brainstorm** the general subject. Although the two techniques encourage you to roam freely over a subject, they also help restrict the discussion by revealing which aspects of the subject interest you most.

Question the General Subject

One way to narrow a subject is to ask a series of *who, how, why, where, when,* and *what* questions. The following example shows how Harriet Davids, the mother of two young teenagers, used this technique to limit the Goodman assignment.

Before reading Goodman's essay, Harriet used her journal to explore TV's effect on children (see pages 17–18). After reading "Family Counterculture," Harriet concluded that she essentially agreed with Goodman; she felt that parents nowadays are indeed forced to raise their children in an "increasingly hostile environment."

Harriet had to narrow the Goodman assignment, so she started by asking a number of pointed questions about the general topic. She used the table feature on her computer to create boxes that she filled in. As she proceeded, she was aware that the same questions could have led to different limited subjects—just as other questions would have.

General Assignment: We live in a world that is difficult, even hostile, toward children.

Question	Limited Subject
<u>Who</u> is to blame for the difficult conditions under which children grow up?	Parents' casual attitude toward child rearing
<u>How</u> have schools contributed to the problems children face?	Not enough counseling programs for kids in distress
<u>Why</u> do children feel frightened?	Divorce
<u>Where</u> do kids go to escape?	TV; makes the world seem even more dangerous
<u>When</u> are children most vulnerable?	The special problems of adolescents
<u>What</u> dangers or fears should parents discuss with their children?	AIDS, drugs, alcohol, war, terrorism, school shootings

Brainstorm the General Subject

Another way to focus on a limited subject is to list quickly everything about the general topic that pops into your mind. Note brief words, phrases, and abbreviations that capture your free-floating thoughts. Writing in complete sentences will slow you down. Don't try to organize or censor your ideas. Even the most fleeting, random, or seemingly outrageous thoughts can be productive.

Here's an example of the brainstorming that Harriet Davids decided to do in an effort to gather even more material for the Goodman assignment.

General Subject: We live in a world that is difficult, even hostile toward children.

TV—shows corrupt politicians, casual sex, sexually explicit videos, drugs, alcohol, foul language, violence

Real-life violence on TV, esp. terrorist attacks, war, and school shootings, scares kids—have nightmares!

Kids babysat by TV

Not enough guidance from parents

Kids raise selves

Too many divorces

Parents squabbling over material goods in settlements

Money too important

Kids feel unimportant

Families move a lot

Rootless feeling

Drug abuse all over, in little kids' schools

Pop music glorifies drugs

Kids not innocent—know too much

Single-parent homes

Abuse of little kids in day care

TV coverage of daycare abuse frightens kids

Perfect families on TV make kids feel inadequate

As you can see, questioning and brainstorming suggest many possible limited subjects. To identify especially promising ones, reread your material. What arouses your interest, anger, or curiosity? What themes seem to dominate and cut to the heart of the matter? Star or highlight ideas with potential. Pay close attention to material generated at the end of your questioning and brainstorming. Often your mind takes a few minutes to warm up, with the best ideas popping out last.

After marking the material, write or type several phrases or sentences summarizing the most promising limited subjects. These, for example, are just a few that emerged from Harriet Davids's questioning and brainstorming the Goodman assignment:

TV partly to blame for children having such a hard time

Relocation stressful to children

Schools also at fault

The special problems that parents face raising children today

Harriet decided to write on the last of these limited subjects. This topic, in turn, is the focus of our discussion on the pages ahead.

Generate Raw Material About Your Limited Subject

When a limited subject strikes you as having possibilities, your next step is to begin generating material about that topic. If you do this now, in the prewriting stage, you'll find it easier to write the paper later on. Because you'll already have amassed much of the material for your essay, you'll be able to concentrate on other matters—say, finding just the right words to convey your ideas. Taking the time to sound out your limited subject during the prewriting stage also means you won't find yourself halfway through the first draft without much to say.

To generate raw material, you may use *freewriting, brainstorming, mapping,* and other techniques.

Freewrite on Your Limited Subject

Although freewriting can help you narrow a general subject, it's more valuable once you have limited your topic. **Freewriting** means jotting down (whether on paper or on a computer) in rough sentences or phrases everything that comes to mind.

To capture this continuous stream of thought, write or type nonstop for ten minutes or more. Don't reread, edit, or pay attention to organization, spelling, or grammar. If your mind goes blank, repeat words until another thought emerges.

Consider part of the freewriting that Harriet Davids generated about her limited subject, "The special problems that parents face raising children today":

Parents today have tough problems to face. Lots of dangers. The Internet first and foremost. Also crimes of violence against kids. Parents also have to keep up with cost of living, everything costs more, kids want and expect more. Television? Another thing is *Playboy*, *Penthouse*. Sexy ads and videos on TV, movies deal with sex. Kids grow up too fast, too fast. Drugs and alcohol. Witness real-life violence on TV, like terrorist attacks and school shootings. Little kids can't handle knowing too much at an early age. Both parents at work much of the day. Finding good day care a real problem. Lots of latchkey kids. Another problem is getting kids to do homework, lots of other things to do. Especially like going to the mall or chatting with friends online! When I was young, we did homework after dinner, no excuses accepted by my parents.

Brainstorm Your Limited Subject

Let your mind wander freely, as you did when narrowing your general subject. This time, though, list every idea, fact, and example that occurs to you about your limited subject. Use brief words and phrases, so you don't get bogged down writing full sentences. For now, don't worry whether ideas fit together or whether the points listed make sense.

To gather additional material on her limited subject for the Goodman assignment ("The special problems that parents face raising children today"), Harriet brainstormed the following list:

Trying to raise kids when both parents work

Prices of everything outrageous, even when both parents work

Commercials make everyone want <u>more</u> of everything

Clothes so important

Day care not always the answer—cases of abuse

Day care very expensive

Sex everywhere—TV, movies, magazines, Internet

Sexy clothes on little kids. Absurd!

Sexual abuse of kids

Violence on TV, esp. images of real-life terrorist attacks and school shootings—scary for kids!

Violence against kids when parents abuse drugs

Acid, Ecstasy, heroin, cocaine, AIDS

Schools have to teach kids about these things

Schools doing too much—not as good as they used to be

Not enough homework assigned—kids unprepared

Distractions from homework—Internet, TV, cellphones, MP3s, computer games, malls

Use Group Brainstorming

Brainstorming with other people stretches the imagination, revealing possibilities you may not have considered on your own. Group brainstorming doesn't have to be conducted in a formal classroom. You can bounce ideas around with friends and family anywhere.

Map the Limited Subject

If you're the kind of person who doodles while thinking, you may want to try **mapping**, sometimes called **diagramming** or **clustering**.

Begin by expressing your limited subject in a crisp phrase and placing it in the center of a blank sheet of paper. As ideas come to you, put them along lines or in boxes or circles around the limited subject. Draw arrows and lines to show the relationships among ideas. Don't stop there, however. Focus on each idea; as subpoints and details come to you, connect them to their source idea, again using boxes, lines, circles, or arrows to clarify how everything relates.

Figure 2.2 is an example of the kind of map that Harriet Davids could have drawn to generate material for her limited subject based on the Goodman assignment.

Use the Patterns of Development

Throughout this book, we show how writers use various **patterns of development**, singly or in combination, to develop and organize their ideas. Because each pattern has its own distinctive logic, the patterns encourage you to think about a limited subject in surprising new ways.

The various patterns of development are discussed in detail in Chapters 10–18 of Part III. At this point, though, you should find the chart on pages 27–28 helpful. It not only summarizes the broad purpose of each pattern but also shows the way each pattern could generate different raw material for the limited subject of Harriet Davids's essay.

FIGURE 2.2

Mapping the Limited Subject

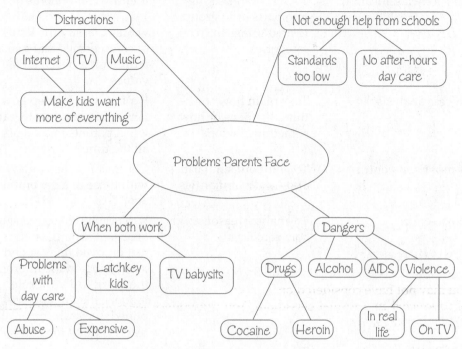

Limited Subject: The special problems that parents face raising children today.

Pattern of Development	Purpose	Raw Material
Description	To detail what a person, place, or object is like	Detail the sights and sounds of a glitzy mall that attracts lots of kids
Narration	To relate an event	Recount what happened when neighbors tried to forbid their kids from going online
Illustration	To provide specific instances or examples	Offer examples of family arguments nowadays: Will permission be given to go to a party where alcohol will be served? Can parents block certain Web sites?

(Continued)

Pattern of Development	Purpose	Raw Material
Division-classification	To divide something into parts or to group related things into categories	Identify components of a TV ad that distorts kids' values Classify the kinds of commercials that make it difficult to teach kids values
Process analysis	To explain how something happens or how something is done	Explain step by step how family life can disintegrate when parents must work all the time
Comparison-contrast	To point out similarities and/or dissimilarities	Contrast families today with those of a generation ago
Cause-effect	To analyze reasons and consequences	Explain the consequences of absentee parents: Kids feel unloved; they spend long hours on the Internet; they turn to TV for role models; they're undisciplined; they take on adult responsibility too early
Definition	To explain the meaning of a term or concept	What is meant by "tough love"?
Argumentation-persuasion	To win people over to a point of view	Convince parents to work with schools to develop programs that make kids feel safer

(For more on ways to use the patterns of development in different phases of the writing process, see pages 36, 42–43, 48, and Part III.)

Conduct Research

Some limited subjects (for example, "Industry's daycare policies") can be developed only if you do some research. You may conduct **primary research**, in which you interview experts, conduct your own studies, compile your own statistics, and the like. Or you may conduct **secondary research**, in which you visit the library and/or go online to identify books and articles about your limited subject. At this point, you don't need to read closely the material you find. Just skim and perhaps take a few brief notes on ideas and points that could be useful.

In researching the Goodman assignment, for instance, Harriet Davids could look under the following headings and subheadings:

Day care	Parent-child relationships
Drug abuse	Child abuse
Family	Children of divorced parents
School and home	Children of working mothers

Organize the Raw Material

Some students prefer to wait until after they have formulated a thesis to shape their prewriting material. (For information on thesis statements, see Chapter 3.) But if you find that imposing a preliminary order on your prewriting provides the focus needed to devise an effective thesis, you'll probably want to prepare a **scratch list** or **outline** at this point. In Chapter 5, we talk about the more formal outline you may need later on in the writing process (pages 51–54). Here we show how a rough outline or scratch list can help shape the tentative ideas generated during prewriting.

As you reread your exploratory thoughts about the limited subject, keep the following questions in mind: What *purpose* have you decided on? What are the characteristics of your *audience?* What *tone* will be effective in achieving your purpose with your audience? What *point of view* will you adopt? Record your responses to these questions at the top of your prewriting material.

Now go to work on the raw material itself. Cross out anything not appropriate for your purpose, audience, tone, and point of view; add points that didn't originally occur to you. Star or circle compelling items that warrant further development. Then draw arrows between related items, your goal being to group such material under a common heading. Finally, determine what seems to be the best order for the headings. If you are creating your scratch outline on a computer, cut and paste; move items around as you try to figure out the order that might work best for presenting your ideas.

By giving you a sense of the way your free-form material might fit together, a scratch outline makes the writing process more manageable. You're less likely to feel overwhelmed once you start writing because you'll already have some idea about how to shape your material into a meaningful statement. Remember, though, the outline can, and most likely will, be modified along the way.

Harriet Davids's handwritten annotations on her brainstormed list (pages 25–26) illustrate the way Harriet began shaping her raw prewriting material. Note how she started by recording at the top her limited subject as well as her decisions about purpose, audience, tone, and point of view. Next, she crossed out the material she didn't want to use. For instance, Harriet decided that the example of violence, such as terrorism, on TV was too complex to include it in her essay, so she crossed it out. Note how clear supporting points emerged after she grouped together similar ideas.

Purpose: To inform

Audience: Instructor as well as class members, most of whom are 18–20 years old

Tone: Serious and straightforward

Point of view: Third person (mother of two teenage girls)

Limited subject: The special problems that parents face raising children today

① Day Care

Trying to raise kids when both parents work

Prices of everything outrageous, even when both parents work

Commercials make everyone want more of everything

Clothes so important problems—before and after school

Day care not always the answer—cases of abuse

Day care very expensive

③ Sexual material everywhere

Sex everywhere—Internet, TV, movies, magazines

Sexy clothes on little kids. Absurd!

Sexual abuse of kids

④ Dangers

Violence on TV, esp. images of real-life terrorist attacks and school shootings—scary for kids!

Violence against kids when parents abuse drugs

Acid, Ecstasy, heroin, cocaine, AIDS—also drinking

Schools have to teach kids about these things

Schools doing too much—not as good as they used to be

Not enough homework assigned—kids unprepared

② Homework distractions

Distractions from homework—Internet, TV, cellphones, MP3s, computer games, malls

The following scratch outline shows how Harriet began to shape her prewriting into a more organized format. (If you'd like to see Harriet's more formal outline and her first draft, turn to pages 53 and 72–74.)

Purpose: To inform

Audience: Instructor as well as class members, most of whom are 18–20 years old

Tone: Serious and straightforward

Point of view: Third person (mother of two teenage girls)

Limited subject: The special problems that parents face raising children today

1. Day care for two-career families
   - Expensive
   - Before-school problems
   - After-school problems

   2. Distractions from homework
       • Internet, televisions, MP3s, cell phones
       • Places to go—malls, movies, fast-food restaurants
   3. Sexually explicit materials
       • Internet
       • Magazines
       • Television shows
       • Movies
   4. Life-threatening dangers
       • Drugs
       • Drinking
       • AIDS
       • Violence against children (by sitters, in day care, etc.)

Continues on page 38

ACTIVITIES: GETTING STARTED THROUGH PREWRITING

1. Number the items in each set from 1 (*broadest subject*) to 5 (*most limited subject*):

    Set A   **Set B**

    Abortion   Business majors

    Controversial social issue   Students' majors

    Cutting state abortion funds   College students

    Federal funding of abortions   Kinds of students on campus

    Social issues   Why students major in business

2. Which of the following topics are too broad for an essay of three to five type-written pages: soap operas' appeal to college students; day care; trying to "kick" junk food; male and female relationships; international terrorism?

3. Assume you're writing essays on two of the topics given here. For each one, explain how you might adapt your purpose, tone, and point of view to the audiences indicated in parentheses. (You may find it helpful to work with others on this activity.)

    a. Overcoming shyness (ten-year-olds; teachers of ten-year-olds; young singles living in large apartment buildings)

    b. Telephone solicitations (people training for a job in this field; homeowners; readers of a humorous magazine)

    c. Smoking (people who have quit; smokers; elementary school children)

4. Choose one of the following general topics for an essay. Then use the prewriting technique indicated in parentheses to identify several limited topics. Next, with

the help of one or more patterns of development, generate raw material on the limited subject you consider most interesting.

a. Friendship (*journal writing*)
b. Malls (*mapping*)
c. Leisure (*freewriting*)
d. Television (*brainstorming*)
e. Required courses (*group brainstorming*)
f. Manners (*questioning*)

5. For each set of limited subjects and purposes that follows, determine which pattern(s) of development would be most useful. (Save this material so you can work with it further after reading the next chapter.)

a. The failure of recycling efforts on campus
   Purpose: to explain why students and faculty tend to disregard recycling guidelines
b. The worst personality trait that a teacher, parent, boss, or friend can have
   Purpose: to poke fun at this personality trait
c. The importance of being knowledgeable about national affairs
   Purpose: to convince students to stay informed about current events

6. Select *one* of the following limited subjects. Then, given the purpose and audience indicated, draft a paragraph using the first-, second-, or third-person point of view. Next, rewrite the paragraph two more times, each time using a different point of view. What differences do you see in the three versions? Which version do you prefer? Why?

a. American fantasy movies like *Avatar* and the *Twilight Saga* series
   Purpose: to defend the enjoyment of such films
   Audience: those who like foreign "art" films
b. Senioritis
   Purpose: to explain why high school seniors lose interest in school
   Audience: parents and teachers
c. Television commercials aimed at teens and young adults
   Purpose: to make fun of the commercials' persuasive appeals
   Audience: advertising executives

7. Select *one* of the following general subjects. Keeping in mind the indicated purpose, audience, tone, and point of view, use a prewriting technique to limit the subject. Next, by means of another prewriting strategy, generate relevant information about the restricted topic. Finally, shape your raw material into a scratch

outline—crossing out, combining, and adding ideas as needed. (Save your scratch outline so you can work with it further after reading the next chapter.)

a. Hip-hop music
   Purpose: to explain its attraction
   Audience: classical music fans
   Tone: playful
   Writer's point of view: a hip-hop fan

b. Becoming a volunteer
   Purpose: to recruit
   Audience: ambitious young professionals
   Tone: straightforward
   Writer's point of view: head of a volunteer organization

c. Sexist attitudes in music videos
   Purpose: to inform
   Audience: teenagers of both sexes
   Tone: objective but with some emotion
   Writer's point of view: a teenage male

3

Identifying a Thesis

In this chapter, you will learn:

3.1 To find and write an effective thesis
3.2 To place your thesis in an essay

The process of prewriting—discovering a limited subject and generating ideas about it—prepares you for the next stage in writing an essay: identifying the paper's *thesis,* or controlling idea.

What Is a Thesis?

The **thesis**, which presents your position on a subject, should focus on an interesting and significant issue, one that engages your energies and merits your consideration. Your thesis determines what does and does not belong in the essay. The thesis, especially when it occurs early in an essay, also helps focus the reader on the piece's central point and thus helps you achieve your writing purpose.

Finding a Thesis

Sometimes the thesis emerges early in the prewriting stage, particularly if a special angle on your limited topic sparks your interest or becomes readily apparent. Often, though, you'll need to do some library research or other work to determine your thesis. The best way to identify a promising thesis may be to look

FIGURE 3.1

Process Diagram: Identifying a Thesis

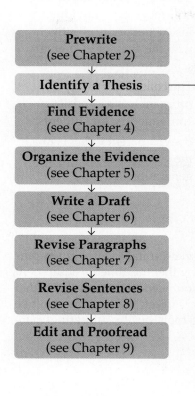

- Develop a point of view or attitude about your limited subject.
- Write a statement expressing your limited subject and point of view.
- Think of patterns of development that best serve your purpose.
- Optional: Include a plan of development presenting the essay's main points.
- Avoid thesis statements that are
    - Highly opinionated statements.
    - Neutral announcements.
    - Simply factual statements.
    - Broad statements.
- Find an effective placement for your thesis statement:
    - At the middle or end of the introductory paragraph for most essays.
    - After background paragraphs if your subject is complex.
    - Early on, for a direct approach.

through your prewriting and ask yourself: What statement does all this prewriting support? What aspect of the limited subject is covered in most detail? What is the focus of the most provocative material? (See Figure 3.1.)

For a look at the process of finding the thesis within prewriting material, glance back in Chapter 2 at the annotated brainstorming (page 30) and the resulting scratch outline (pages 30–31) that Harriet Davids prepared for her limited subject. (To see how Harriet arrived at her thesis, see page 38.)

Writing an Effective Thesis

What makes a thesis effective? The thesis statement, generally expressed in one or two sentences, has two parts. One part presents your paper's *limited subject;* the other presents your *point of view,* or *attitude,* about that subject. In each thesis statement on the next page, the limited subject is underlined once and the attitude twice.

General Subject	Limited Subject	Thesis Statement
Education	Computers in elementary school arithmetic classes	Computer programs in arithmetic <u>can individualize instruction more effectively than the average elementary school teacher can</u>.
Work	College internships	The college internship program <u>has had positive consequences for students</u>.
Our anti-child world	Special problems that parents face raising children today	Being a parent today <u>is much more difficult than it was a generation ago</u>.

Tone and Point of View

An effective thesis establishes a tone and point of view suitable for a given purpose and audience. If you're writing an essay arguing that multimedia equipment can never replace a live teacher in the classroom, you need to frame a thesis that matches your and your readers' concerns about the subject: "Education won't be improved by purchasing more electronic teaching tools but by allocating more money to hire and develop good teachers."

Implied Pattern of Development

On pages 18–19, we show how an essay's purpose may suggest a pattern of development. In the same way, an effective thesis may point the way to a pattern of development that would be appropriate for developing the essay. Consider the thesis statements in the preceding list. The first thesis might use *comparison-contrast*; the second *cause-effect*; and the third *argumentation-persuasion*. (For more information about the relationship between an essay's purpose and its pattern of development, see the chart on pages 27–28.)

Including a Plan of Development

Sometimes a thesis will include a **plan of development**: a concise *overview of the essay's main points in the exact order* in which those points will be discussed. To incorporate a plan of development into your thesis, use single words or brief phrases that convey—in a nutshell—your essay's key points; then add those summarized points to the end of the thesis, being sure to present them in the order in which they will appear in the essay. Note, for example, the way a plan of development (in italics) is included in the following thesis: "An after-school job develops *responsibility, human-relations skills, and an awareness of career options*."

A thesis with a plan of development is effective in keeping readers focused on an essay's main points. Be careful, though, not to overload it with too much information.

If the essay's key points resist your efforts to reduce them to crisp phrases, you can place the plan of development in a separate sentence, directly *after* the thesis. Consider the plan of development (in italics) that comes after the following thesis: "Many parents have unrealistic expectations for their children. These parents want their children to *accept their values, follow their paths, and succeed where they have failed.*" Note that the points in a plan of development are expressed in grammatically parallel terms, for example, verb phrases ("accept their values," "follow their paths," "succeed where they have failed").

Because preparing an effective thesis is such a critical step in writing a sharply focused essay, you need to avoid the following four common problems.

1. Don't Write a Highly Opinionated Statement

Although your thesis should express your attitude toward your subject, don't go overboard and write a dogmatic, overstated thesis: "With characteristic clumsiness, campus officials bumbled their way through the recent budget crisis." A more moderate thesis can make the same point, *without alienating readers:* "Campus officials had trouble managing the recent budget crisis effectively."

2. Don't Make an Announcement

Some writers use the thesis statement merely to announce the limited subject of their paper and forget to indicate their attitude toward the subject. Such statements are announcements of intent, not thesis statements. Compare the following:

Announcement	Thesis Statement
My essay will discuss whether a student pub should exist on campus.	This college should not allow a student pub on campus.
The legislating of assault weapons will be the subject of my paper.	Banning assault weapons is the first step toward controlling crime in America.

3. Don't Make a Factual Statement

Your thesis, and thus your essay, should focus on an issue capable of being developed. If a fact is used as a thesis, you have no place to go; a fact generally doesn't invite much discussion. Notice the difference between the factual statements and thesis statements on page 38.

Factual Statement

Many businesses pollute the environment.

Movies nowadays are often violent.

Thesis Statement

Tax penalties should be levied against businesses that pollute the environment.

Movie violence provides a healthy outlet for aggression.

4. Don't Make a Broad Statement

Broad statements make it difficult for readers to grasp your essay's point. If you start with a broad thesis, you're saddled with the impossible task of trying to develop a book-length idea in an essay that runs only several pages.

Broad Statement

Nowadays, high school education is often meaningless.

Nobody reads newspapers any more.

Thesis Statement

High school diplomas have been devalued by grade inflation.

With the growth of online sources, fewer and fewer people depend on print newspapers for news.

Arriving at an Effective Thesis

On pages 34–35 we discussed finding a thesis; we also pointed out how Harriet Davids identified her paper's thesis: "Being a parent today is much more difficult than it was a generation ago." But Harriet went through several stages before she came up with the final wording.

- Harriet started with her limited subject ("The special problems that parents face raising children today"). She tentatively worded her thesis to read "My essay will show that raising children today is a horror show compared to how it was when my parents raised me."
- Harriet asked herself, "Is my thesis *highly opinionated*? an *announcement*? a *factual statement*? a *broad statement*?" She realized that she had prepared an *announcement* rather than a thesis.
- Harriet rewrote her statement so that she would not be making an *announcement*. She came up with the following: "Raising children today is a horror show compared to how it was when my parents raised me."
- As she read over her revised statement, Harriet realized that although she had eliminated the *announcement,* the rephrasing highlighted two problems she hadn't detected previously: her statement was *highly opinionated* and *slangy* ("horror show"). She also realized that the statement *misrepresented*

Continues
on page 43

what she intended to do by suggesting—incorrectly—that she was going to (1) discuss the child-rearing process and (2) contrast her parents' and her own child-raising experiences. She planned to do neither. Instead, she intended to (1) emphasize parenthood's challenges and (2) address—in a general way—the difference between parenting today and parenting years ago.

- Harriet revised her statement one more time to eliminate these problems and arrived at the final wording of her thesis: "Being a parent today is much more difficult than it was a generation ago."

Placing the Thesis in an Essay

The thesis is often at the middle or end of the introduction, but audience, purpose, and tone should always guide your decision about its placement. For example, if you feel readers would appreciate a direct, forthright approach, you might place the thesis early, even at the very beginning of the introduction.

Sometimes the thesis is reiterated—using fresh words—in the essay's conclusion or elsewhere. If done well, this repetition keeps readers focused on the essay's key point. You may even leave the thesis implied, relying on strong support, tone, and style to convey the essay's central idea.

One final point: Once you start writing your draft, some feelings, thoughts, and examples may emerge that modify, even contradict, your initial thesis. Don't resist these new ideas. Keep them in mind as you revise the thesis and move toward a more valid and richer view of your subject.

ACTIVITIES: IDENTIFYING A THESIS

1. For the following limited subject, four possible thesis statements are given. Indicate whether each thesis is an announcement (A), a factual statement (FS), too broad a statement (TB), or an acceptable thesis (OK). Revise the flawed statements. Then, for each effective thesis statement, identify a possible purpose, audience, tone, and point of view.

   Limited subject: Privacy and computerized records

   - Computers raise some significant questions for all of us.
   - Computerized records keep track of consumer spending habits, credit records, travel patterns, and other personal information.
   - Computerized records have turned our private lives into public property.
   - In this paper, the relationship between computerized records and the right to privacy will be discussed.

2. Turn back to activity 5 on page 32. For each set of limited subjects, develop an effective thesis. Select *one* of the thesis statements. Then, keeping in mind the purpose indicated and the pattern of development you identified earlier, draft a paragraph developing the point expressed in the thesis.

3. Following are three pairs of general and limited subjects. Generate an appropriate thesis for each pair. Select one of the thesis statements, and determine which pattern of development would support the thesis most effectively. Use that pattern to draft a paragraph developing the thesis.

General Subject	Limited Subject
Psychology	The power struggles in a classroom
Health	Doctors' attitudes toward patients
Work	Minimum-wage jobs for young people

4. Following are key points for an essay. Based on the information provided, prepare a possible thesis for each essay. Then propose a possible purpose, audience, tone, and point of view.

    - We do not know how engineering new forms of life might affect the earth's delicate ecological balance.
    - Another danger of genetic research is its potential for unleashing new forms of disease.
    - Even beneficial attempts to eliminate genetic defects could contribute to the dangerous idea that only perfect individuals are entitled to live.

5. Keep a journal for several weeks. Then reread a number of entries, identifying two or three recurring themes or subjects. Narrow the subjects and, for each one, generate possible thesis statements. Using an appropriate pattern of development, draft a paragraph for one of the thesis statements.

6. Return to the scratch outline you prepared in response to activity 7 on pages 32–33. Identify a thesis that conveys the central idea behind most of the raw material. Then, ask others to evaluate your thesis in light of the material in your scratch outline. Finally, keeping the thesis—as well as your purpose, audience, and tone—in mind, refine the scratch outline by deleting inappropriate items, adding relevant ones, and indicating where more material is needed.

Supporting the Thesis with Evidence

In this chapter, you will learn:

4.1 To find evidence using the patterns of development
4.2 To know the characteristics of evidence

After identifying a preliminary thesis, you should develop the evidence needed to support that central idea. This supporting material grounds your essay, showing readers you have good reason for feeling as you do about your subject. Your evidence also adds interest and color to your writing.

In college essays of 500 to 1,500 words, you usually need at least three major points of evidence to develop your thesis.

What Is Evidence?

By **evidence**, we mean a number of different kinds of support. *Reasons* are just one option. To develop your thesis, you might also include *examples, facts, details, statistics, personal observation* or *experience, anecdotes,* and *expert opinions* and *quotations* (gathered from a variety of both print and digital sources that might include Web sites, books, articles, interviews, documentaries, and the like). Imagine you're writing an essay with the thesis "People normally unconcerned

about the environment can be galvanized to constructive action if they feel personally affected by an environmental problem." You could support this thesis with any
combination of the following types of evidence:

- *Reasons* why people become involved in the environmental movement: they
  believe the situation endangers their health; they fear the value of their homes
  will plummet; they feel deceived by officials' empty assurances.
- *Examples* of successful neighborhood recycling efforts.
- *Facts* about residents' efforts to preserve the quality of well water in a commu-
  nity undergoing widespread industrial development.
- *Details* about steps one can take to get involved in environmental issues.
- *Statistics* showing the growing number of Americans concerned about the
  environment.
- A *personal experience* telling about the way you became involved in an effort to
  stop a local business from dumping waste into a neighborhood stream.
- An *anecdote* about a friend who protested a commercial development.
- A *quotation* from a well-known scientist about the impact that well-organized,
  well-informed citizens can have on environmental legislation.

How Do You Find Evidence?

Where do you find the examples, anecdotes, details, and other types of evidence
needed to support your thesis? As you saw when you followed Harriet Davids's
strategies for gathering material for an essay (pages 22–31), a good deal of information is generated during the prewriting stage. The library and the Internet are
also rich sources of supporting evidence. (For information on using the library
and the Internet, see Chapter 19.)

How the Patterns of Development Help Generate Evidence

In Chapter 2, we discussed how the patterns of development could help generate
material about Harriet Davids's limited subject (pages 26–28). The same patterns
also help develop support for a thesis. The chart below shows how they generate
evidence for this thesis: "To those who haven't done it, babysitting looks easy. In
practice, though, babysitting can be difficult, frightening, even dangerous." (For
further discussion of ways to use the patterns of development in different phases
of the writing process, see pages 27–28, 36, 48–49 and 60–61.)

Pattern of Development	Evidence Generated
Description	Details about a child who, while being babysat, was badly hurt playing on a backyard swing.
Narration	Story about a child who became ill and whose con-dition was worsened by the babysitter's remedies.

Illustration	Examples of potential babysitting problems: infant rolls off a changing table; toddler sticks objects into an outlet; child is bitten by a neighborhood dog.
Division-classification	A typical babysitting evening divided into stages: playing with the kids; putting them to bed; dealing with nightmares.
	Classifying kids' nightmares: monsters under their beds; bad dreams; being abandoned.
Process analysis	Step-by-step account of what a babysitter should do if a child becomes ill or injured.
Comparison-contrast	Contrast between two babysitters: one well-prepared, the other unprepared.
Cause-effect	Why children have temper tantrums; the effect of such tantrums on an unskilled babysitter.
Definition	What is meant by a *skilled* babysitter?
Argumentation-persuasion	A proposal for a babysitting training program to be offered by the local community center.

Characteristics of Evidence

No matter how it is generated, all types of supporting evidence share the characteristics described in the following sections. As you'll see shortly, Harriet Davids focused on many of these issues as she worked with the evidence she collected during the prewriting phase.

The Evidence Is Relevant and Unified

All the evidence in an essay must clearly support the thesis. Irrelevant material can weaken your position. It also distracts readers from your controlling idea, thus disrupting the paper's overall unity.

Early in the writing process, Harriet Davids was aware of the importance of relevant evidence. Review Harriet's annotated prewriting (page 30). Even though Harriet hadn't yet identified her thesis, she realized she should delete a number of items on the reshaped version of her brainstormed list.

The Evidence Is Specific

When evidence is vague and general, readers lose interest in what you're saying, become skeptical of your ideas' validity, and feel puzzled about your meaning. In contrast, *specific, concrete evidence* provides sharp *word pictures* that engage your readers, persuades them that your thinking is sound, and clarifies meaning.

FIGURE 4.1

Process Diagram: Finding Evidence

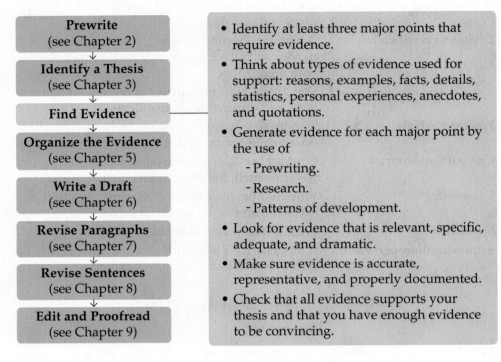

   Look at the annotations Harriet Davids entered on her prewriting material (page 30). Note the way she jotted down new details to make her prewriting more specific. For instance, to the item, "Distractions from homework," she added the example "malls." And once Harriet arrived at her thesis ("Being a parent today is much more difficult than it was a generation ago"), she realized that she needed to provide even more specifics. With her thesis firmly in mind, she expanded her prewriting material—for instance, the point about sexuality on television. To develop that item, she specified three kinds of TV programming that depict sexuality offensively: soap operas, R-rated comedians, R-rated cable movies. And, as you'll soon discover, Harriet added many more specific details when she prepared her final outline (page 53) and her first and final drafts (pages 72–74 and 120–121).

The Evidence Is Adequate

Readers won't automatically accept your thesis; you need to provide *enough specific evidence* to support your viewpoint. On occasion, a single extended example will suffice. Generally, though, you'll need a variety of evidence: facts, examples, reasons, personal observations, expert opinion, and so on.

Now take a final look at Harriet's annotations on her prewriting (page 30). Harriet realized she needed more than one block of supporting material to develop her limited subject; that's why she identified four separate blocks of evidence (day care, homework distractions, sexual material, and dangers). As soon as Harriet formulated her thesis, she reexamined her prewriting to see if it provided sufficient support for her essay's central point. Luckily, Harriet recognized that these four blocks of evidence needed to be developed further. Harriet's final outline (page 53) reflects these decisions. She added so many specific and dramatic details when writing her first and final drafts (pages 72–74 and 120–121) that her evidence was more than sufficient.

Continues on page 52

The Evidence Is Dramatic

The most effective evidence enlarges the reader's experience by *dramatizing reality.* Say you plan to write an essay with the thesis, "People who affirm the value of life refuse to wear fur coats." If, as support, you state only that most animals killed for their fur are caught in leg-hold traps, your readers will have little sense of the suffering involved. But if you write that steel-jaw, leg-hold traps snap shut on an animal's limb, crushing tissue and bone and leaving the animal to die, in severe pain, from exposure or starvation, your readers can better envision the animal's plight.

The Evidence Is Accurate

When you have a strong belief and want readers to see things your way, you may be tempted to overstate or downplay facts, disregard information, misquote, or make up details. Suppose you plan to write an essay making the point that dormitory security is lax. You begin supporting your thesis by narrating the time you were nearly mugged in your dorm hallway. Realizing the essay would be more persuasive if you also mentioned other episodes, you decide to invent some material. Yes, you've supported your point—but at the expense of truth.

The Evidence Is Representative

Using *representative* evidence means that you rely on the *typical,* the *usual,* to show that your point is valid. Contrary to the maxim, exceptions don't prove the rule. Perhaps you plan to write an essay contending that the value of seat belts has been exaggerated. To support your position, you mention a friend who survived a head-on collision without wearing a seat belt. Such an example isn't representative because the facts and figures on accidents suggest your friend's survival was a fluke.

Borrowed Evidence Is Documented

If you include evidence from outside sources (books, Web sites, articles, interviews), you need to *acknowledge* where that information comes from. The rules for crediting sources in informal writing are less established than they are for formal research. Follow the guidelines your instructor provides, and try to keep your notations as simple as possible.

Strong supporting evidence is at the heart of effective writing. Without it, essays lack energy and fail to project the writer's voice and perspective. Take the time to accumulate solid supporting material. (For more on the characteristics of strong evidence, see pages 61–66. For suggestions on organizing an essay's evidence, see Chapter 5.)

ACTIVITIES: SUPPORTING THE THESIS WITH EVIDENCE

1. Imagine you're writing an essay with the following thesis in mind. Which of the statements in the list support the thesis? Label each statement acceptable (OK), irrelevant (IR), inaccurate (IA), or too general (TG).

    Thesis: Colleges should put less emphasis on sports.

    a. High-powered athletic programs can encourage grade fixing.
    b. Too much value is attached to college sports.
    c. Competitive athletics can lead to extensive and expensive injuries.
    d. Athletes can spend more time on the field and less time on their studies.

2. For each of the following thesis statements, list at least three supporting points that convey vivid word pictures.

    a. Rude behavior in movie theaters seems to be on the rise.
    b. Recent television commercials portray men as incompetent creatures.
    c. The local library fails to meet the public's needs.

3. Turn back to the paragraphs you prepared in response to activity 2, activity 3, or activity 5 in Chapter 3 (page 40). Select one paragraph and strengthen its evidence, using the guidelines presented in this chapter.

4. Choose one of the following thesis statements. Then identify an appropriate purpose, audience, tone, and point of view for an essay with this thesis. Using freewriting, mapping, or the questioning technique, generate at least three supporting points for the thesis. Last, write a paragraph about one of the points, making sure your evidence reflects the characteristics discussed in this chapter. Alternatively, you may go ahead and prepare the first draft of an essay having the selected thesis. (If you choose the second option, you may want to turn to Figure 6.2 on page 72 for a diagram showing how to organize a first draft.) Save whatever you prepare so you can work with it further after reading the next chapter.

    a. Winning the lottery may not always be a blessing.
    b. All of us can take steps to reduce the country's trash crisis.
    c. Drug education programs in public schools are (or are not) effective.

5. Select one of the following thesis statements. Then determine your purpose, audience, tone, and point of view for an essay with this thesis. Next, use the patterns of development to generate at least three supporting points for the thesis. Finally, write a paragraph about one of the points, making sure that your evidence demonstrates the characteristics discussed in this chapter. Alternatively, you may go ahead and prepare a first draft of an essay having the thesis selected. (If you choose the latter option, you may want to turn to Figure 6.2 on page 72 for a diagram showing how to organize a first draft.) Save whatever you prepare so you can work with it further after reading the next chapter.

   a. Teenagers should (or should not) be able to obtain birth-control devices without their parents' permission.
   b. The college's system for awarding student loans needs to be overhauled.
   c. E-mail has changed for the worse (or the better) the way Americans communicate with each other.

6. Look at the thesis and refined scratch outline you prepared in response to activity 6 in Chapter 3 (page 40). Where do you see gaps in the support for your thesis? By brainstorming with others, generate material to fill these gaps. If some of the new points generated suggest that you should modify your thesis, make the appropriate changes now. (Save this material so you can work with it further after reading the next chapter.)

(For more activities on generating evidence, see pages 74–77 in Chapter 6 as well as pages 112–115 in Chapter 8.)

5

Organizing the Evidence

In this chapter, you will learn:

5.1 To use the patterns of development in your essay

5.2 To organize the evidence in one of four ways: chronologically, spatially, emphatically, or simply-to-more complex

5.3 To create an outline to assist in writing a first draft of your essay

Once you've generated supporting evidence, you're ready to *organize* that material. When moving to this stage, you should have in front of you your scratch outline (pages 31–32) and thesis, plus any supporting material you've accumulated since you did your prewriting.

Use the Patterns of Development

As you saw on pages 27–28 and 42–43, the patterns of development (definition, narration, process analysis, and others) can help you develop prewriting material and generate evidence for a thesis. In the organizing stage, the patterns provide frameworks for presenting the evidence in an orderly, accessible way. Here's how.

Each pattern of development has its own internal logic that makes it appropriate for some writing purposes but not for others. (You may find it helpful at this point to turn to pages 27–28 so you can review the broad purpose of each pattern.) Imagine that you want to write an essay *explaining why* some students drop out of college during the first semester. If your essay consisted only of a lengthy narrative of two friends floundering through the first month of college, you wouldn't achieve your purpose. A condensed version of the narrative might be appropriate at some point in the essay, but—to meet your objective—most of the paper would have to focus on *causes and effects*.

Once you see which pattern (or combination of patterns) is implied by your purpose, you can block out your paper's general structure. For instance, in the preceding example, you might organize the essay around a three-part discussion of the key reasons that students have difficulty adjusting to college: (1) they miss friends and family, (2) they take inappropriate courses, and (3) they experience conflicts with roommates. As you can see, your choice of pattern of development significantly influences your essay's content and organization.

Some essays follow a single pattern, but most blend them, with a predominant pattern providing the piece's organizational framework. In our example essay, you might include a brief *description* of an overwhelmed first-year college student; you might *define* the psychological term *separation anxiety;* you might end the paper by briefly explaining a *process* for making students' adjustment to college easier. Still, the essay's overall organizational pattern would be *cause-effect* because the paper's primary purpose is to explain why students drop out of college. (See pages 60–61 for more on how patterns often mix.)

Although writers often combine the patterns of development, your composition instructor may ask you to write an essay organized according to a single pattern. Such an assignment helps you understand a particular pattern's unique demands. Keep in mind, though, that most writing begins not with a specific pattern but with a specific *purpose*. The pattern or combination of patterns used to develop and organize an essay evolves out of that purpose.

Select an Organizational Approach

No matter which pattern(s) of development you select, you need to know four general approaches for organizing the supporting evidence in an essay: chronological, spatial, emphatic, and simple-to-complex. (See Figure 5.1.)

Chronological Approach

When an essay is organized **chronologically**, supporting material is arranged in a clear time sequence, usually from what what happened first to what happened last. Occasionally, the order can be resequenced to create flashback or flashforward effects, two techniques discussed in Chapter 11 on narration.

Essays using narration (for example, an experience with prejudice) or process analysis (for instance, how to deliver an effective speech) are most likely to be organized chronologically. (For examples of chronologically arranged student essays, turn to pages 164–165 in Chapter 11 and pages 259–261 in Chapter 14.)

FIGURE 5.1

Process Diagram: Organizing the Evidence

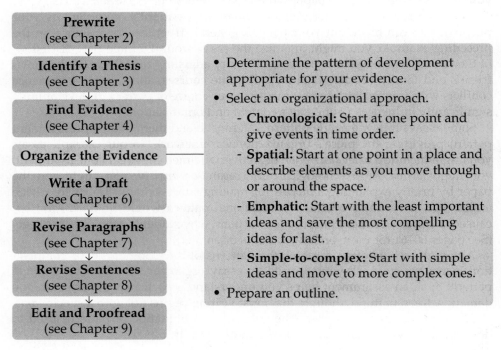

Spatial Approach

When you arrange supporting evidence **spatially**, you discuss details as they occur in space, or from certain locations. This strategy is particularly appropriate for
description. Although spatial arrangement is flexible, you should always proceed
systematically. And once you select a particular spatial order, you should usually
maintain that sequence throughout the essay; otherwise, readers may get lost along
the way. (A spatially arranged student essay appears in Chapter 10 on pages 133–135.)

Emphatic Approach

In **emphatic** order, the most compelling evidence is saved for last. This arrangement is based on the psychological principle that people remember best
what they experience most recently. Emphatic order has built-in momentum
because it starts with the least important point and builds to the most significant. This method is especially effective in argumentation-persuasion essays,
in papers developed through examples, and in pieces involving comparison-
contrast, division-classification, or causal analysis. (The student essays on
pages 193–194 in Chapter 12, pages 292–294 in Chapter 15, and pages 357–359
in Chapter 17 all use an emphatic arrangement.)

Simple-to-Complex Approach

A final way to organize an essay is to proceed from relatively **simple** concepts to more **complex** ones. By starting with easy-to-grasp, generally accepted evidence, you establish rapport with your readers and assure them that the essay is firmly grounded in shared experience. (See pages 324–325 in Chapter 16 for an example of a student essay using the simple-to-complex arrangement.)

Depending on your purpose, any one of these four organizational approaches might be appropriate. For example, assume you planned to write an essay developing Harriet Davids's thesis: "Being a parent today is much more difficult than it was a generation ago." To emphasize that the various stages in children's lives present parents with different difficulties, you'd probably select a *chronological* sequence. To show that the challenges parents face vary depending on whether children are at home, at school, or in the world at large, you'd probably choose a *spatial* sequence. To stress the range of problems that parents face (from less to more serious), you'd probably use an *emphatic* sequence. Finally, to illustrate today's confusing array of theories for raising children, you might take a *simple-to-complex* approach, moving from the basic to the most sophisticated theory.

Prepare an Outline

Do you, like many students, react with fear and loathing to the dreaded word *outline?* The outline helps you organize your thoughts, and it guides your writing as you work on the draft. Even though ideas continue to evolve during the draft, an outline clarifies how ideas fit together, which points are major, which should come first, and so on. An outline may also reveal places where evidence is weak, prompting you to eliminate the material altogether, retain it in an unemphatic position, or do more prewriting to generate additional support.

To prepare an effective outline, you should reread and evaluate your scratch list and thesis as well as any other evidence you've generated since the prewriting stage. Then decide which pattern of development (description, cause-effect, and so on) is suggested by your evidence. Also determine whether your evidence lends itself to a chronological, a spatial, an emphatic, or a simple-to-complex order. Now you're ready to identify and sequence your main and supporting points.

> ### ☑ OUTLINING: A CHECKLIST
>
> ☐ Type or write your purpose, audience, tone, point of view, and thesis at the top of the outlining page.
>
> ☐ Below the thesis, enter the pattern of development that seems to be implied by the evidence you've accumulated.
>
> ☐ Record which of the four organizational approaches would be most effective in sequencing your evidence.

☐ Reevaluate your supporting material. Delete anything that doesn't develop the thesis or that isn't appropriate for your purpose, audience, tone, and point of view.

☐ Add any new points or material.

☐ Group related items together. Give each group a heading that represents a main topic in support of your thesis.

☐ Label these main topics with roman numerals (I, II, III, and so on). Let the order of numerals indicate the best sequence.

☐ Identify subtopics and group them under the appropriate main topics. Indent and label them (A, B, C, and so on).

☐ Identify supporting points (often reasons and examples) and group them under the appropriate subtopics. Indent and label them (1, 2, 3, and so on).

☐ Identify specific details (secondary examples, facts, statistics, expert opinions, quotations) and group them under the appropriate supporting points. Indent and label them (a, b, c, and so on).

☐ Examine your outline, looking for places where evidence is weak. Where appropriate, add new evidence.

☐ Double-check that all content develops some aspect of the thesis. Also confirm that all items are arranged in the most logical order.

The amount of detail in an outline will vary according to the paper's length and the instructor's requirements. A scratch outline consisting of words or phrases (such as the one on pages 30–31 in Chapter 2) is often sufficient, but for longer papers, you'll probably need a more detailed and formal outline. In such cases, the suggestions in the accompanying checklist will help you develop a sound plan. Feel free to modify these guidelines to suit your needs.

The sample outline on page 53 develops the thesis "Being a parent today is much more difficult than it was a generation ago." You may remember that this is the thesis that Harriet Davids devised for the essay she planned to write in response to the assignment on page 23. Harriet's scratch list, based on her brainstorming, appears on pages 31–32. (You may want to review pages 44 and 45 to see how Harriet later reconsidered material on the scratch list in light of her thesis.) Harriet's outline contains more specifics (for instance, the details about sexually explicit materials—on the Internet, in magazines, in movies, and on television). On the other hand, the outline doesn't include all the material in the scratch list. For example, after reconsidering her purpose, audience, tone, point of view, and thesis, Harriet decided to omit from her outline the section on day care and the point about AIDS.

Harriet's **topic outline** uses phrases, or topics, for each entry. (See pages 258, 291–292, and 403 for other examples of topic outlines.) For a more complex paper, a **sentence outline** might be more appropriate (see pages 192–193).

You can also mix phrases and sentences (see page 322), as long as you are consistent about where you use each.

Purpose: To inform
Audience: Instructor as well as class members, most of whom are 18–20 years old
Tone: Serious and straightforward
Point of view: Third person (mother of two teenage girls)
Thesis: Being a parent today is much more difficult than it was a generation ago.
Pattern of development: Illustration
Organizational approach: Emphatic order

I. Distractions from homework – *Topic Sentence*
   A. At home – *Example 1*
      1. MP3 players
      2. Computers—Internet, computer games
      3. Television
   B. Outside home – *Example 2*
      1. Malls
      2. Movie theaters
      3. Fast-food restaurants

II. Sexually explicit materials – *Topic Sentence*
   A. Internet
      1. Easy–to-access adult chat rooms
      2. Easy–to-access pornographic Web sites
   B. In print and in movies
      1. Sex magazines—*Playboy, Penthouse*
      2. Casual sex
   C. On television
      1. Soap operas
      2. R–rated comedians
      3. R–rated movies on cable

III. Increased dangers
   A. Drugs—peer pressure
   B. Alcohol—peer pressure
   C. Violent crimes against children

(If you'd like to see the first draft that resulted from Harriet's outline, turn to pages 72–74. Hints for moving from an outline to a first draft appear on pages 56–57. For additional suggestions on organizing a first draft, see Figure 6.2 on page 72.)

Before starting to compose your first draft, show your outline to several people (your instructor, friends, classmates). Their reactions will indicate whether your proposed organization is appropriate for your thesis, purpose, audience, tone, and point of view. Their comments can also highlight areas needing additional work. After making whatever changes are needed, you're in a good position to go ahead and write the first draft of your essay.

ACTIVITIES: ORGANIZING THE EVIDENCE

1. The following thesis statement is accompanied by a scrambled list of supporting points. Prepare a topic outline for a potential essay, being sure to distinguish between major and secondary points.

   Thesis: Our schools, now in crisis, could be improved in several ways.

Teacher certification requirements	Merit pay for teachers
Schedules	Better textbooks
Teachers	Longer school days
Longer school year	More challenging courses

2. For each of the following thesis statements, there are two purposes given. Determine whether each purpose suggests an emphatic, chronological, spatial, or simple-to-complex approach. Note the way the approach varies as the purpose changes.

   a. *Thesis:* Traveling in a large city can be an unexpected education.
      Purpose 1: To explain, in a humorous way, the stages in learning to cope with the city's cab system
      Purpose 2: To describe, in a serious manner, the vastly different sections of the city as viewed from a cab

   b. *Thesis:* Supermarkets use sophisticated marketing techniques to prod consumers into buying more than they need.
      Purpose 1: To inform readers that positioning products in certain locations encourages impulse buying
      Purpose 2: To persuade readers not to patronize those chains using especially objectionable sales strategies

3. Return to the paragraph or first draft you prepared in response to activity 4 or activity 5 in Chapter 4 (pages 46–47). Applying the principles discussed in Chapter 5, strengthen the organization of the evidence you generated. (If you rework a first draft, save the draft so you can refine it further after reading the next chapter.)

4. The following brief essay outline consists of a thesis and several points of support. Which pattern of development would you probably use to develop the overall organizational framework for each essay? Which pattern(s) would you use to develop each point of support? Why?

   Thesis: Friends of the opposite sex fall into one of several categories: the pal, the confidante, or the pest.

   Points of Support

   - Frequently, an opposite-sex friend is simply a "pal."
   - Sometimes, though, a pal turns, step by step, into a confidante.
   - If a confidante begins to have romantic thoughts, he or she may become a pest, thus disrupting the friendship.

5. For the thesis statement given in activity 4, identify a possible purpose, audience, tone, and point of view. Then, use one or more patterns to generate material to develop the points of support listed. Get together with someone else to review the generated material, deleting, adding, combining, and arranging ideas in logical order. Finally, make an outline for the body of the essay. (Save your outline. After reading the next chapter, you can use it to write the essay's first draft.)

6. Look again at the thesis and scratch outline you refined and elaborated in response to activity 6 in Chapter 4 (page 47). Reevaluate this material by deleting, adding, combining, and rearranging ideas as needed. Then, in preparation for writing an essay, outline your ideas. Consider whether an emphatic, chronological, spatial, or simple-to-complex approach will be most appropriate. Finally, ask at least one other person to evaluate your organizational plan. (Save your outline. After reading the next chapter, you can use it to write the essay's first draft.)

6

Writing the Paragraphs in the First Draft

In this chapter, you will learn:

6.1 To move from outline to first draft
6.2 To develop strategies for moving forward if you get bogged down
6.3 To use a sequence for writing the first draft

After prewriting, deciding on a thesis, and developing and organizing evidence, you're ready to write a first draft—a rough, tentative version of your essay.

How to Move from Outline to First Draft

There's no single right way to prepare a first draft. However you choose to proceed, consider the suggestions in the following checklist when moving from an outline or scratch list to a first draft.

 TURNING OUTLINE INTO FIRST DRAFT: A CHECKLIST

☐ Make the outline's *main topics* (I, II, III) the *topic sentences* of the essay's supporting paragraphs. (Topic sentences are discussed later in this chapter.)

☐ Make the outline's *subtopics* (A, B, C) the *subpoints* in each paragraph.

- ☐ Make the outline's *supporting points* (1, 2, 3) the *key examples* and *reasons* in each paragraph.
- ☐ Make the outline's *specific details* (a, b, c) the *secondary examples,* facts, statistics, expert opinion, and quotations in each paragraph.

(To see how one student, Harriet Davids, moved from outline to first draft, turn to pages 72–74.)

General Suggestions on How to Proceed

Although outlines and lists are valuable for guiding your work, don't be so dependent on them that you shy away from new ideas that surface during your writing of the first draft. It's during this time that promising new thoughts often pop up; as they do, jot them down in the margins of your draft. If you're typing your draft on a computer, you can easily use digital commenting features to help you keep track of ideas that come to you as you're composing. Then, at the appropriate point, go back and evaluate the ideas that came to you as you were writing your draft: Do they support your thesis? Are they appropriate for your essay's purpose, audience, tone, and point of view? If so, go ahead and include the material in your draft.

It's easy to get stuck if you try to edit as you write. Remember: A draft isn't intended to be perfect. For the time being, adopt a relaxed, noncritical attitude. Working as quickly as you can, don't stop to check spelling, correct grammar, or refine sentence structure. Save these tasks for later.

If You Get Bogged Down

All writers get bogged down now and then. The best thing to do is accept that sooner or later this will happen to you. Just include a reminder to yourself in the margin ("Fix this," "Redo," or "Ugh!") to fine-tune the section later. Or leave a blank space for the right words when they finally break loose. It may also help to reread—out loud is best—what you've already written. Regaining a sense of the larger context is often enough to get you moving again.

If a section of the essay strikes you as particularly difficult, don't spend time struggling with it. Move on to an easier section, write that, and then return to the challenging part. If you're still getting nowhere, take a break. While you're relaxing, your thoughts may loosen up. If an obligation such as a class or an appointment forces you to stop writing when the draft is going well, take a few seconds to make notes in the margin to remind yourself of your train of thought.

A Suggested Sequence for Writing the First Draft

Because you read essays from beginning to end, you may assume that writers work the same way. Often, however, this isn't the case. In fact, because an introduction depends so heavily on everything that follows, it's usually best to write the introduction *after* the essay's body. (See Figure 6.1.)

When preparing your first draft, you may find it helpful to follow a four-step sequence.

FIGURE 6.1

Process Diagram: Writing a Draft

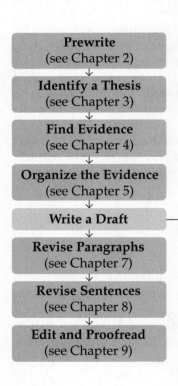

Prewrite (see Chapter 2)

Identify a Thesis (see Chapter 3)

Find Evidence (see Chapter 4)

Organize the Evidence (see Chapter 5)

Write a Draft

Revise Paragraphs (see Chapter 7)

Revise Sentences (see Chapter 8)

Edit and Proofread (see Chapter 9)

- Write the supporting paragraphs.
  - Use topic sentences.
  - Use patterns of development.
  - Make paragraphs unified.
  - Make paragraphs specific.
  - Provide adequate support.
  - Use signal devices—transitions, bridging sentences, repeated words, synonyms, and pronouns—to make paragraphs coherent.
- Write background and transitional paragraphs.
- Write the introduction, which may include:
  - A broad statement narrowing to a limited subject.
  - A brief anecdote.
  - The opposite of the idea you actually develop.
  - A series of short questions.
  - A quotation.
  - Some brief background.
  - Refutation of a common belief.
  - A dramatic fact or statistic.
- Write the conclusion; include a summary, prediction, quotation, statistic, or call for action.

1. Write the Supporting Paragraphs

Before starting to write the essay's **supporting paragraphs**, enter your thesis at the top of the page. You might even underline key words in the thesis to keep yourself focused on the central ideas you plan to develop. Also, now that you've planned the essay's overall organization, you may want to add to your thesis a **plan of development**—a brief *overview* of the essay's *major points in the exact order* in which you will discuss those points—if you didn't do so when you developed your thesis statement. (For more on plans of development, see pages 36–37.)

In a long complex essay, a plan of development helps readers follow the progression of main points in the supporting paragraphs. Whether or not you include a plan of development, always keep in mind that writing the draft often leads to new ideas; you may have to revise your thesis, plan of development, and supporting paragraphs as the draft unfolds.

Drawn from the main sections in your outline or scratch list, each supporting paragraph should develop an aspect of your essay's thesis or plan of development. Although there are no hard-and-fast rules, strong supporting paragraphs are (1) often focused by topic sentences, (2) organized around one or more patterns of development, (3) unified, (4) specific, (5) adequately supported, and (6) coherent. Aim for as many of these qualities as you can in the first draft.

Use Topic Sentences

Usually, each supporting paragraph in an essay is focused by a **topic sentence**. This sentence usually states a main point in support of the thesis.

The topic sentence usually appears at or near the beginning of the paragraph. However, it may also appear at the end, in the middle, or—with varied wording—several times within the paragraph. In still other cases, a single topic sentence may state an idea developed in more than one paragraph. When a paragraph is intended primarily to clarify or inform, you may want to place its topic sentence at the beginning; that way, readers are prepared to view everything that follows in light of that main idea. If, though, you intend a paragraph to heighten suspense or to convey a feeling of discovery, you may prefer to delay the topic sentence until the end.

Regardless of its length or location, the topic sentence states the paragraph's main idea. The other sentences in the paragraph provide support for this central point in the form of examples, facts, expert opinion, and so on. Like a thesis statement, the topic sentence *signals the paragraph's subject* and frequently *indicates the writer's attitude* toward that subject. In the topic sentences that follow, the subject of the paragraph is underlined once and the attitude toward that subject is underlined twice:

Topic Sentences

Some students select a particular field of study for the wrong reasons.

The ocean dumping of radioactive waste is a ticking time bomb.

As you work, you may find yourself writing paragraphs without paying too much attention to topic sentences. That's fine, as long as you remember to evaluate the paragraphs later on. When revising, you can provide a topic sentence for a paragraph that needs a sharper focus, recast a topic sentence for a paragraph that ended up taking an unexpected turn, and even eliminate a topic sentence altogether if a paragraph's content is sufficiently unified to imply its point.

Use the Patterns of Development

As you saw on page 48, an entire essay can be organized around one or more patterns of development. These patterns can also provide the organizational framework for an essay's supporting paragraphs. Assume you're writing an article for your town newspaper with the thesis, "Year-round residents of an ocean community must take an active role in safeguarding the seashore environment." As the following examples indicate, your supporting paragraphs could develop this thesis through a variety of patterns, with each paragraph's topic sentence suggesting a specific pattern or combination of patterns.

Of course, each supporting paragraph in an essay doesn't have to be organized according to a different pattern of development; several paragraphs may use the same pattern. Nor is it necessary for any one paragraph to be restricted to a single pattern; supporting paragraphs often combine patterns. (For more on using the patterns of development in the writing process, see pages 27–28, 36, 42–43, and 48–49.)

Topic Sentence	Possible Pattern of Development
In a nearby ocean community, signs of environmental damage are everywhere.	*Description* of a seaside town: polluted waters, blighted trees, diseased marine life
Typically, residents blame industry or tourists for such damage.	*Narration* of a conversation among seaside residents
Residents' careless behavior is also to blame, however.	*Illustrations* of residents' littering the beach, injuring marine life while motor boating, walking over fragile sand dunes
Even environmentally concerned residents may contribute to the problem.	*Cause-effect* explanation of the way Styrofoam packaging and plastic food wrap, even when properly disposed of in a trash can, can harm scavenging seagulls
Fortunately, not all seaside towns are plagued by such environmental problems.	*Comparison-contrast* of one troubled shore community with another more ecologically sound one
It's clear that shore residents must become "environmental activists."	*Definition* of an *environmental activist*

Residents can get involved in a variety of pro-environmental activities.	*Division-classification* of activities at the neighborhood, town, and municipal levels
Moreover, getting involved is an easy matter.	*Process analysis* of the steps for getting involved at the various levels
Such activism yields significant rewards.	A final *argumentation-persuasion* pitch showing residents the benefits of responsible action

Make the Paragraphs Unified

Just as overall evidence must support an essay's thesis (pages 41–42), the facts, opinions, and examples in each supporting paragraph must have *direct bearing* on the paragraph's topic sentence. If the paragraph has no topic sentence, the supporting material must be *consistent* with the paragraph's *implied focus*. A paragraph is **unified** when it meets these requirements.

Consider the following sample paragraph. The paragraph lacks unity because it contains points (underlined) unrelated to its main idea given in the topic (first) sentence. To present a balanced view of cable versus network television, the writer should discuss these points, but in *another paragraph*.

Nonunified Support

Many people consider cable TV an improvement over network television. For one thing, viewers usually prefer the movies on cable. Unlike network films, cable movies are often only months old, they have not been edited by censors, and they are not interrupted by commercials. Growing numbers of people also feel that cable specials are superior to the ones the networks grind out. Cable viewers may enjoy such performers as Usher, Adele, or Chris Rock in concert, whereas the networks continue to broadcast tired, look-alike reality shows and boring awards ceremonies. There is, however, one problem with cable comedians. The foul language many of them use makes it hard to watch these cable specials with children. The networks, in contrast, generally present "clean" shows that parents and children can watch together. Then, too, cable TV offers viewers more flexibility because it schedules shows at various times over the month. People working night shifts or attending evening classes can see movies in the afternoon, and viewers missing the first twenty minutes of a show can always catch them later. It's not surprising that cable viewership is growing while network ratings have taken a plunge.

Make the Paragraphs Specific

If your supporting paragraphs are vague, readers will lose interest, remain unconvinced of your thesis, even have trouble deciphering your meaning. In contrast, paragraphs filled with **concrete, specific details** engage readers, lend force to ideas, and clarify meaning, as in the following example.

Specific Support

More and more companies have begun to realize that flex-time scheduling offers advantages over a rigid 9-to-5 routine. Along suburban Boston's Route 128, such companies as Compugraphics and Consolidated Paper now permit employees to schedule their arrival any time between 6 a.m. and 11 a.m. The corporations report that the number of rush-hour jams and accidents has fallen dramatically. As a result, employees no longer arrive at work weighed down by tension induced by choking clouds of exhaust fumes and the blaring horns of gridlocked drivers. Studies sponsored by the journal *Business Quarterly* show that this more mellow state of mind benefits corporations. Traffic-stressed employees begin their workday anxious and exasperated, still grinding their teeth at their fellow commuters, their frustration often spilling over into their performance at work. By contrast, stress-free employees work more productively and take fewer days off. They are more tolerant of co-workers and customers, and less likely to balloon minor irritations into major confrontations. Perhaps most important, employees arriving at work relatively free of stress can focus their attention on working safely. They rack up significantly fewer on-the-job accidents, such as falls and injuries resulting from careless handling of dangerous equipment. Flex-time improves employee well-being, and as well-being rises, so do company profits.

Five Strategies for Making Paragraphs Specific. How can you make the evidence in your paragraphs specific? The following techniques should help.

1. **Provide examples that answer** *who, which, what,* **and similar questions.** The preceding paragraph provides examples that answer basic questions. Instead of the general comment "Several companies outside Boston" (*which* companies?), the author provides specific names "Compugraphics and Consolidated Paper." Similarly, "on-the-job accidents" (*which* accidents?) is illustrated with "falls and injuries resulting from careless handling of dangerous equipment."

2. **Replace general nouns and adjectives with precise ones.** In the following sentences, note how much sharper images become when exact nouns and adjectives replace imprecise ones:

General	More Specific	Most Specific
A *man* had trouble lifting the *box* out of the *old car.*	A *young man, out of shape,* struggled to lift the *heavy crate* out of the *beat-up sports car.*	*Joe, only twenty years old but more than fifty pounds overweight,* struggled to lift the *heavy wooden crate* out of the *rusty* and *dented Mustang.*

3. **Replace abstract words with concrete ones.** Notice the way the example on the right, firmly grounded in the physical, clarifies the intangible concepts in the example on the left:

Abstract	Concrete
The fall day had great *beauty*, despite its *dreariness*.	*Red, yellow,* and *orange* leaves *gleamed wetly* through the *gray mist.*

(For more on making abstract language concrete, see page 105 in Chapter 8.)

4. **Use words that appeal to the five senses (sight, touch, taste, smell, sound).** The sentence on the left lacks impact because it fails to convey any sensory impressions; the sentence on the right, though, gains power through the use of sensory details:

Without Sensory Images	With Sensory Images
The computer room is eerie.	In the computer room, keys *click* and printers *grate* while row after row of students stare into screens that *glow without shedding any light.* (sound and sight)

(For more on sensory language, see pages 130–131 in Chapter 10.)

5. **Use vigorous verbs.** Linking verbs (such as *seem* and *appear*) and *to be* verbs (such as *is* and *were*) paint no pictures. Strong verbs, however, create sharp visual images. Compare the following examples:

Weak Verbs	Strong Verbs
The spectators *seemed* pleased and *were* enthusiastic when the runners *went* by.	The spectators *cheered* and *whistled* when the runners *whizzed* by.

(For more on strong verbs, see pages 106–107 in Chapter 8.)

Provide Adequate Support

Each supporting paragraph should also have **adequate support** so that your readers can see clearly the validity of the topic sentence. At times, a single extended example is sufficient; generally, however, an assortment of examples, facts, personal observations, and so forth is more effective.

The following paragraph offers examples, descriptive details, and dialogue—all of which make the writing stronger and more convincing.

Adequate Support

Gas stations are a good example of this impersonal attitude. At many stations, attendants have even stopped pumping gas. Motorists pull up to a combination convenience store and gas island where an attendant is enclosed in a glass booth with a tray for taking money. The driver must get out of the car, pump the gas, and walk over to the booth to pay. Even at stations that still have "pump jockeys," employees seldom ask, "Check your oil?" or wash windshields, although they may grudgingly point out the location of the bucket and squeegee. And customers with a balky engine or a nonfunctioning heater are usually out of luck. Why? Many gas stations have eliminated on-duty mechanics. The skillful mechanic who could replace a belt or fix a tire in a few minutes has been replaced by a teenager in a jumpsuit who doesn't know a carburetor from a charge card and could care less.

Make the Paragraphs Coherent

Paragraphs can be unified, specific, and adequately supported, yet—if internally disjointed or inadequately connected to each other—leave readers feeling confused. Readers need to be able to follow with ease the progression of thought within and between paragraphs. One idea must flow smoothly and logically into the next; that is, your writing must be **coherent**.

To avoid incoherent paragraphs, use two key strategies: (1) a clearly *chronological, spatial,* or *emphatic order* and (2) *signal devices* to show how ideas are connected.

Chronological, Spatial, and Emphatic Order. As you learned in Chapter 5, an entire essay can be organized using chronological, spatial, or emphatic order (pages 49–51). These strategies can also be used to make a paragraph coherent.

Imagine you plan to write an essay showing the difficulties many immigrants face when they first come to this country. Let's consider how you might structure the supporting paragraphs, particularly the way each paragraph's organizational approach can help you arrange ideas in a logical, easy-to-follow sequence.

One paragraph, focused by the topic sentence "The everyday life of a typical immigrant family is arduous," might be developed through a **chronological** account of the family's daily routine: purchasing, before dawn, fruits and vegetables for their produce stand; setting up the stand early in the morning; working there for ten hours; attending English class at night. Another paragraph might develop its topic sentence,"Many immigrant families get along without the technology that others take for granted," through **spatial** order, taking readers on a brief tour of an immigrant family's rented home: the kitchen lacks a dishwasher or microwave; the living room has no computer or phone, only a small TV; the basement has just a washtub and clothesline instead of a washer and dryer. Finally, a third paragraph, with the topic sentence "A number of worries typically beset immigrant families," might use an **emphatic** sequence, moving from less significant concerns (having to wear old, unfashionable clothes) to more critical issues (having to deal with isolation and discrimination).

TRANSITIONS

Time	Addition or Sequence	Comparison

Time

after, afterward

at the same time

before, earlier,
      previously

finally, eventually

first, next

immediately

in the meantime

meanwhile

simultaneously

subsequently, later

then, now

Space

above, below

next to, behind

Examples

for instance, for
      example

namely, specifically

to illustrate

Addition or Sequence

and, also, too

besides

finally, last

first,...second,...third

furthermore

moreover, in addition

next

one...another

Contrast

although, though

but, however

conversely

despite, even though

in contrast

nevertheless,
      nonetheless

on the contrary, whereas

on the one (other) hand

otherwise

yet, still

Comparison

also, too

likewise

in comparison

in the same way

similarly

Cause or Effect

as a result

because, since

consequently

in turn

so

therefore, then

Summary or Conclusion

in conclusion

in short

therefore

thus

Signal Devices. Once you determine a logical sequence for your points, you need to make sure that readers can follow the progression of those points within and between paragraphs. **Signal devices** provide readers with cues, reminding them where they have been and indicating where they are going.

Try to include some signals—however awkward or temporary—in your first draft. If you find you *can't,* that's probably a warning that your ideas may not be arranged logically—in which case, it's better to find that out now rather than later on. Keep in mind, though, that a light touch should be your goal with such signals. Overuse can make the essay mechanical and plodding.

1. **Transitions.** Words and phrases that ease readers from one idea to another are called **transitions.** The following chart lists a variety of such signals. (You'll notice that some transitions can be used for more than one purpose.)

Note how the underlined transitions in the following paragraph provide clear cues to readers, showing how ideas fit together:

Although the effect of air pollution on the human body is distressing, its effect on global ecology is even more troubling. In the Bavarian, French, and Italian Alps, <u>for example</u>, once magnificent forests are slowly being destroyed by air pollution. Trees dying from pollution lose their leaves or needles, allowing sunlight to reach the forest floor. <u>During</u> this process, grass prospers in the increased light and pushes out the native plants and moss that help hold rainwater. The soil <u>thus</u> loses absorbency and becomes hard, causing rain and snow to slide over the ground instead of sinking into it. This, <u>in turn</u>, leads to erosion of the soil. <u>After</u> a heavy rain, the eroded land <u>finally</u> falls away in giant rockslides and avalanches, destroying entire villages and causing life-threatening floods.

2. **Bridging sentences.** Although **bridging sentences** may be used within a paragraph, they are more often used to move readers from one paragraph to the next. Look again at the first sentence in the preceding paragraph on pollution. Note that the sentence consists of two parts: The first part reminds readers that the previous discussion focused on pollution's effect on the body; the second part tells readers that the focus will now be pollution's effect on ecology.

3. **Repeated words, synonyms, and pronouns.** The **repetition** of important words maintains continuity, reassures readers that they are on the right track, and highlights key ideas. **Synonyms**—words similar in meaning to key words or phrases—also provide coherence, while making it possible to avoid unimaginative and tedious repetitions. Finally, **pronouns** (*he, she, it, they, this, that*) enhance coherence by causing readers to think back to the original word (antecedent) the pronoun replaces. When using pronouns, however, be sure there is no ambiguity about antecedents.

    The following paragraph uses repeated words (underlined once), synonyms (underlined twice), and pronouns (underlined three times) to integrate ideas:

<u>Studies</u> have shown that color is also an important part of the way <u>people</u> experience <u>food</u>. In one <u>study</u>, <u>individuals</u> fed a rich red tomato sauce didn't notice <u>it</u> had no flavor until <u>they</u> were nearly finished eating. Similarly, in another <u>experiment</u>, <u>people</u> were offered strangely colored <u>foods</u>: gray pork chops, lavender mashed potatoes, dark blue peas, dessert topped with yellow whipped cream. Not one of the <u>subjects</u> would eat the strange-looking <u>food</u>, even though <u>it</u> smelled and tasted normal.

2. Write Other Paragraphs in the Essay's Body

Paragraphs supporting the thesis are not necessarily the only kind in the body of an essay. You may also include paragraphs that give background information or provide transitions.

Background Paragraphs

Usually found near the essay's beginning, **background paragraphs** provide information that doesn't directly support the thesis but that helps the reader understand or accept the discussion that follows. Such paragraphs may consist of a definition, brief historical overview, or short description. For example, in the student essay "Salt Marsh" on pages 133–135, the paragraph following the introduction defines a salt marsh and summarizes some of its features. This background information serves as a lead-in to the detailed description that makes up the rest of the essay. Since you don't want to distract readers from your essay's main point, background paragraphs should be kept as brief as possible.

Transitional Paragraphs

Another kind of paragraph, generally one to three sentences long, may appear between supporting paragraphs to help readers keep track of your discussion. Like the bridging sentences discussed earlier in the chapter, **transitional paragraphs** usually sum up what has been discussed so far and then indicate the direction the essay will take next.

While too many such paragraphs make writing stiff and mechanical, they can be effective when used sparingly, especially in essays with sharp turns in direction.

3. Write the Introduction

Many writers don't prepare an **introduction** until they have started to revise; others feel more comfortable if their first draft includes in basic form all parts of the final essay. No matter when you prepare it, keep in mind how crucial the introduction is to your essay's success. The introduction serves three distinct functions: It arouses readers' interest, introduces your subject, and presents your thesis. Remember, the introduction's style and content should flow into the rest of the essay.

The length of your introduction will vary according to your paper's scope and purpose. Most essays you write, however, will be served best by a one- or two-paragraph beginning. To write an effective introduction, use any of the following methods, singly or in combination. The thesis statement in each sample introduction is underlined. Note, too, that the first thesis includes a plan of development, whereas the last thesis is followed by a plan of development (see pages 36–37).

Broad Statement Narrowing to a Limited Subject

For generations, morality has been molded primarily by parents, religion, and schools. Children traditionally acquired their ideas about what is right and wrong, which goals are important in life, and how others should be treated from these three sources collectively. But in the past few decades, a single force—television—has undermined the beneficial influence that parents, religion, and school have on children's moral development. Indeed, <u>television often implants in children negative values about sex, work, and family life.</u>

Brief Anecdote

At a local high school recently, students in a psychology course were given a hint of what it is like to be the parents of a newborn. Each "parent" had to carry a raw egg around at all times to symbolize the responsibilities of parenthood. The egg could not be left alone; it limited the "parents'" activities; it placed a full-time emotional burden on "Mom" and "Dad." This class exercise illustrates a common problem facing the majority of new mothers and fathers. <u>Most people receive little preparation for the job of being parents.</u>

Starting with an Idea That Is the Opposite of the One Actually Developed

We hear a great deal about divorce's disastrous impact on children. We are deluged with advice on ways to make divorce as painless as possible for youngsters; we listen to heartbreaking stories about the confused, grieving children of divorced parents. Little attention has been paid, however, to a different kind of effect that divorce may have on children. <u>Children from divorced families may become skilled manipulators, playing off one parent against the other, worsening an already painful situation.</u>

Series of Short Questions

What happens if a child is caught vandalizing school property? What happens if a child goes for a joyride in a stolen car and accidentally hits a pedestrian? Should parents be liable for their children's mistakes? Should parents have to pay what might be hundreds of thousands of dollars in damages? Adults have begun to think seriously about such questions because the laws concerning the limits of parental responsibility are changing rapidly. <u>With unfortunate frequency, courts have begun to hold parents legally and financially responsible for their children's misbehavior.</u>

Quotation

Educator Neil Postman believes that television has blurred the line between childhood and adulthood. According to Postman, "All the secrets that a print culture kept from children . . . are revealed all at once by media that do not, and cannot, exclude any audience." <u>This media barrage of information, once intended only for adults, has changed childhood for the worse.</u>

Brief Background on the Topic

For a long time, adults believed that "children should be seen, not heard." On special occasions, youngsters were dressed up and told to sit quietly while adults socialized. Even when they were alone with their parents, children were not supposed to bother adults with their concerns. However, beginning with psychologist Arnold Gesell in the 1940s, child-raising experts began to question the wisdom of an approach that blocked communication. In 1965, Haim Ginott's ground-breaking book *Between Parent and Child* stressed the importance of conversing with children. More recently, two of Ginott's disciples, Adele Sager and Elaine Mazlish, wrote a book on this subject: *How to Talk So Children Will Listen and Listen So Children Will Talk.* <u>These days, experts agree, successful parents are those who encourage their children to share their thoughts and concerns.</u>

Refutation of a Common Belief

Adolescents care only about material things; their lives revolve around brand-name sneakers, designer jeans, the latest fad in electronics. They resist education, don't read, barely know who is president, are plugged into their music 24/7, experiment with drugs, and exist on a steady diet of Ring-Dings, nachos, and beer. This is what many adults, including parents, seem to believe about the young. <u>The reality is, however, that young people today show more maturity and common sense than most adults give them credit for.</u>

Dramatic Fact or Statistic

Seventy percent of the respondents in a poll conducted by columnist Ann Landers stated that, if they could live their lives over, they would choose not to have children. This startling statistic makes one wonder what these people believed parenthood would be like. <u>Many parents have unrealistic expectations for their children.</u> Parents want their children to accept their values, follow their paths, and succeed where they failed.

4. Write the Conclusion

A strong **conclusion** is an important part of an effective essay. However important conclusions may be, they're often difficult to write. When it comes time to write one, you may feel you've said all there is to say. To prevent such an impasse, you can try saving a compelling statistic, quotation, or detail for the end. Just make sure that this interesting item fits in the conclusion and that the essay's body contains sufficient support without it.

Occasionally, an essay doesn't need a separate conclusion. This is often the case with narration or description. For instance, in a narrative showing how a crisis can strengthen a faltering friendship, your point will probably be made with sufficient force without a final "this is what the narrative is all about" paragraph.

Usually, though, a conclusion is necessary. Generally one or two paragraphs in length, the conclusion should give the reader a feeling of completeness and finality. One way to achieve this sense of "rounding off" is to return to an image, idea, or anecdote from the introduction.

Because people tend to remember most clearly the points they read last, the conclusion is also a good place to remind readers of your thesis, phrasing this central idea somewhat differently than you did earlier in the essay. You may also use the conclusion to make a final point. This way, you leave your readers with something to mull over. Be careful, though, not to open an entirely new line of thought at the essay's close. If you do, readers may feel puzzled and frustrated, wishing you had provided evidence for your final point. And, of course, always be sure that concluding material fits your thesis and is consistent with your purpose, tone, and point of view.

In your conclusion, it's best to steer away from stock phrases like "In sum," "In conclusion," and "This paper has shown that..." Also avoid lengthy conclusions. As in everyday life, prolonged farewells are tedious.

Following are examples of some techniques you can use to write effective conclusions. These strategies may be used singly or in combination. The first strategy (*summary*) can be especially helpful in long, complex essays because readers may appreciate a review of your points. Tacked onto a short essay, though, a summary conclusion often seems boring and mechanical.

Summary

Contrary to what many adults think, most adolescents are not only aware of the important issues of the times but also deeply concerned about them. They are sensitive to the plight of the homeless, the destruction of the environment, and the pitfalls of rampant materialism. Indeed, today's young people are not less mature and sensible than their parents were. If anything, they are more so.

Prediction

The growing tendency on the part of the judicial system to hold parents responsible for the actions of their delinquent children can have a disturbing impact on all of us. Parents will feel bitter toward their own children and cynical about a system that holds them accountable for the actions of minors. Children, continuing to escape the consequences of their actions, will become even more lawless and destructive. Society cannot afford two such possibilities.

Quotation

The comic W. C. Fields is reputed to have said, "Anyone who hates children and dogs can't be all bad." Most people do not share Fields's cynicism. Viewing childhood as a time of purity, they are alarmed at the way television exposes children to the seamy side of life, stripping youngsters of their innocence and giving them a glib sophistication that is a poor substitute for wisdom.

Statistic

Granted, divorce may, in some cases, be the best thing for families torn apart by parents battling one another. However, in longitudinal studies of children from divorced families, psychologist Judith Wallerstein found that only 10 percent of the youngsters felt relief at their parents' divorce; the remaining 90 percent felt devastated. Such statistics surely call into question parents' claims that they are divorcing for their children's sake.

Recommendation or Call for Action

It is a mistake to leave parenting to instinct. Instead, we should make parenting skills a required course in schools. In addition, a nationwide hotline should be established to help parents deal with crises. Such training and continuing support would help adults deal more effectively with many of the problems they face as parents.

Write the Title

Some writers say that they often begin a piece with only a title in mind. But for most, writing the **title** is the finishing touch. Although creating a title is usually one of the last steps in writing an essay, it shouldn't be done haphazardly. It may take time to write an effective title—one that hints at the essay's thesis and snares the reader's interest.

Good titles may make use of the following techniques: *repetition of sounds* ("The Sanctuary of School"), *humor* ("Becoming a Videoholic"), and *questions* ("What Are Friends For?"). More often, though, titles are straightforward phrases derived from the essay's subject or thesis: "The Toxic Truth About Sugar" and "Why We Flirt," for example.

Pulling it All Together

Now that you know how to prepare a first draft, you might find it helpful to examine Figure 6.2 to see how the different parts of a draft can fit together. Keep in mind that not every essay you write will take this shape. As your purpose, audience, tone, and point of view change, so will your essay's structure. The basic

FIGURE 6.2

Structure of an Essay

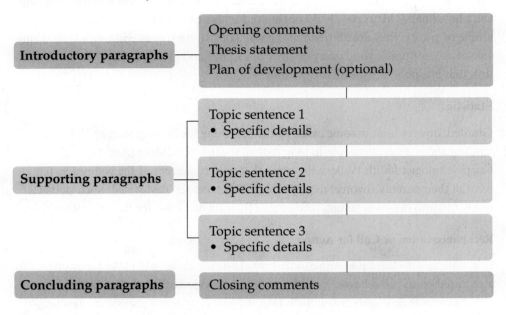

format presented here offers a strategy for organizing a variety of writing assignments. Once you feel comfortable with the structure, you have a foundation on which to base your variations.

Sample First Draft

Here is the first draft of Harriet Davids's essay. (You saw Harriet's prewriting scratch list on pages 30–31, her thesis on page 38, and so on.) Harriet wrote the draft in one sitting. Working at a computer, she started by typing her thesis. Then, following the guidelines on pages 56–57, she moved the material in her outline (page 53) to her draft. Harriet worked rapidly; she started with the first body paragraph and wrote straight through to the last supporting paragraph.

By moving quickly, Harriet got down her essay's basic text rather easily. Once she felt she had captured in rough form what she wanted to say, she reread her draft to get a sense of how she might open and close the essay. Then she drafted her introduction and conclusion; both appear here, together with the body of the essay. The commentary following the draft will give you an even clearer sense of how Harriet proceeded. (Note that the marginal annotations reflect Harriet's comments to herself about areas she needs to address when revising her first draft.)

Challenges for Today's Parents
by Harriet Davids

Thesis: Being a parent today is much more difficult than it was a generation ago.

Raising children used to be much simpler in the '50s and '60s. I remember TV images from that era showing that parenting involved simply teaching kids to clean their rooms, do their homework, and _____ . But being a parent today is much more difficult because nowadays parents have to shield/protect kids from lots of things, like distractions from schoolwork, from sexual material, and from dangerous situations.   — ADD SPECIFICS

Parents have to control all the new distractions/ temptations that turn kids away from schoolwork. These days many kids have MP3 players, computers, and televisions in their rooms. Certainly, my girls can't resist the urge to watch TV and go online, especially if it's time to do homework. Unfortunately, though, kids aren't assigned much homework and what is assigned is too often busywork. And there are even more distractions outside the home. Teens no longer hang out/congregate on the corner where Dad and Mom can yell to them to come home and do homework. Instead they hang out at the mall, in movie theaters, and at fast-food restaurants. Obviously, parents and school can't compete with all this.   — WEAK TRANS.

Also, parents have to help kids develop responsible sexual values even though sex is everywhere. It's too easy for kids to access chat rooms and Web sites dealing with adult, sometimes pornographic material. Kids see sex magazines in convenience stores where they used to get candy and comic books. And instead of the artsy nude shots of the past, kids see ronchey, explicit shots in *Playboy* and *Penthouse*. And movies have sexy stuff in them today. People treat sex casually/as a sport. Not exactly traditional values. TV is no better. Kids see soap-opera characters in bed, sexy music videos, and cable shows full of nudity by just flipping the channel. The situation has gotten so out of hand that maybe the government should establish guidelines on what's permissible.   — SP?

Worst of all are the life-threatening dangers that parents must help children fend off over the years. With older kids, drugs fall into place as a main concern. Peer pressure to try drugs is bigger to kids than their parents' warnings. Other kinds of warnings are common when children are small. Then parents fear violence since news shows constantly report stories of little children being abused. And when kids aren't much older, they have to resist the pressure to drink. (Alcohol has always attracted kids, but nowadays they are drinking more and this can be deadly, especially when drinking is combined with driving.)   — AWK — WRONG WORD — ADD SPECIFICS — REDO

SP?

Most adults love their children and want to be good parents. But it's difficult because the world seems stacked against young people. Even Holden Caufield had trouble dealing with society's confusing pressures. Parents must give their children some freedom but not so much that the kids lose sight of what's important.

Commentary

As you can see, Harriet's draft is rough. Because she knew she would revise later on (pages 87 and 112), she "zapped out" the draft in an informal, colloquial style. For example, she occasionally expressed her thoughts in fragments ("Not exactly traditional values"), relied heavily on "and" as a transition, and used slangy expressions such as "kids" and "lots of things." She also used slashes between alternative word choices and left a blank space when wording just wouldn't come. Then, as Harriet reviewed the printed copy of this rough draft, she made handwritten marginal notes to herself in capital letters: "AWK"or "REDO" to signal awkward sentences; "ADD SPECIFICS" to mark overly general statements; "WRONG WORD" after an imprecise word; "SP?" to remind herself to check spelling in the dictionary; "WEAK TRANS." to indicate where a stronger signaling device was needed. (Harriet's final draft appears on pages 120–121.)

Continues on page 87

Writing a first draft may seem like quite a challenge, but the tips offered in this chapter should help you proceed with confidence. Indeed, as you work on the draft, you may be surprised by how much you enjoy writing. After all, this is your chance to get down on paper something you want to say.

ACTIVITIES: WRITING THE PARAGRAPHS IN THE FIRST DRAFT

1. For each paragraph that follows, determine whether the topic sentence is stated or implied. If the topic sentence is explicit, indicate its location in the paragraph (beginning, end, middle, or both beginning and end). If the topic sentence is implied, state it in your own words.

   a. In 1902, a well-known mathematician wrote an article "proving" that no airplane could ever fly. Just a year later, the Wright brothers made their first flight. In the 1950s, a famed British astronomer said in an interview that the idea of space travel was "utter bilge." Similarly, noted scholars in this country and abroad claimed that automobiles would never replace the trolley car and that the electric light was an impractical gimmick. Clearly, being an expert doesn't guarantee a clear vision of the future.

   b. Many American companies have learned the hard way that they need to know the language of their foreign customers. When Chevrolet began selling its Nova cars in Latin America, hardly anyone would buy them. The company finally realized that Spanish speakers read the car's name as the Spanish phrase "no va," meaning "doesn't go." When Pepsi-Cola ran its "Pepsi gives you life" ads in China, consumers either laughed or were offended. The company hadn't translated its slogan quite right. In Chinese, the slogan came out "Pepsi brings your ancestors back from the dead."

2. Using the strategies described on pages 62–63, strengthen the following vague paragraphs. Elaborate each one with striking specifics that clarify meaning and add interest. As you provide specifics, you may need to break each paragraph into several.

   a. Other students can make studying in the college library difficult. For one thing, they take up so much space that they leave little room for anyone else. By being inconsiderate in other ways, they make it hard to concentrate on the task at hand. Worst of all, they do things that make it almost impossible to find needed books and magazines.

   b. Some people have dangerous driving habits. They act as though there's no one else on the road. They also seem unsure of where they're going. Changing their minds from second to second, they leave it up to others to figure out what they're going to do. Finally, too many people drive at speeds that are either too slow or too fast, creating dangerous situations for both drivers and pedestrians.

3. Using the designations indicated in parentheses, identify the flaw(s) in the development of each of the following paragraphs. The paragraphs may lack one or more of the following: unity (U), specific and sufficient support (S), coherence (C). The paragraphs may also needlessly repeat a point (R). Revise the paragraphs, deleting, combining, and rearranging material. Also, add supporting evidence and signal devices where needed.

   a. Despite widespread belief to the contrary, brain size within a species has little to do with how intelligent a particular individual is. A human brain can range from 900 cubic centimeters to as much as 2,500 cubic centimeters, but a large brain does not indicate an equally large degree of intelligence. If humans could see the size of other people's brains, they would probably judge each other accordingly, even though brain size has no real significance.

   b. For the 50 percent of adult Americans with high cholesterol, heart disease is a constant threat. Americans can reduce their cholesterol significantly by taking a number of easy steps. Because only foods derived from animals contain cholesterol, eating a strict vegetarian diet is the best way to beat the cholesterol problem. Also, losing weight is known to reduce cholesterol levels—even in those who were as little as ten pounds overweight. Physicians warn, though, that quick weight loss almost always leads to an equally rapid regaining of the lost pounds. For those unwilling to try a vegetarian diet, poultry, fish, and low-fat dairy products can substitute for such high-cholesterol foods as red meat, eggs, cream, and butter. Adding oat bran to the diet has been shown to lower cholesterol. The bran absorbs excess cholesterol in the blood and removes it from the body through waste matter.

4. Strengthen the coherence of the following paragraphs by providing a clear organizational structure and by adding appropriate signal devices. To improve the flow of ideas, you may also need to combine and resequence sentences.

> I was a camp counselor this past summer. I learned that leading young children is different from leading people your own age. I was president of my high school Ecology Club. I ran it democratically. We wanted to bring a speaker to the school. We decided to do a fund-raiser. I solicited ideas from everybody. We got together to figure out which was best. It became obvious which was the most profitable and workable fund-raiser. Everybody got behind the effort. The discussion showed that the idea of a raffle with prizes donated by local merchants was the most profitable.

> I learned that little kids operate differently. I had to be more of a boss rather than a democratic leader. I took suggestions from the group on the main activity of the day. Everyone voted for the best suggestion. Some kids got especially upset. There was a problem with kids whose ideas were voted down. I learned to make the suggestions myself. The children could vote on my suggestions. No one was overly attached to any of the suggestions. They felt that the outcome of the voting was fair. Basically, I got to be in charge.

5. For an essay with the thesis shown here, indicate the implied pattern(s) of development for each topic sentence that follows.

Thesis: The college should make community service a requirement for graduation.

Topic Sentences

a. "Mandatory community service" is a fairly new and often misunderstood concept.
b. Here's the story of one student's community involvement.
c. Indeed, a single program offers students numerous opportunities.
d. Such involvement can have a real impact on students' lives.
e. However, the college could adopt two very different approaches—one developed by a university, the other by a community college.
f. In any case, the college should begin exploring the possibility of making community service a graduation requirement.

6. Select one of the topic sentences listed in activity 5. Use individual or group brainstorming to generate support for it. After reviewing your raw material,

delete, add, and combine points as needed. Finally, with the thesis in mind, write a rough draft of the paragraph.

7. Imagine you plan to write a serious essay on one of the following thesis statements. The paper will be read by students in your composition class. After determining your point of view, use any prewriting techniques you want to identify the essay's major and supporting points. Arrange the points in order and determine where background or transitional paragraphs might be helpful.

   a. Society needs stricter laws against noise pollution.
   b. Public buildings in this town should be redesigned to accommodate the disabled.
   c. Long-standing discrimination against women in college athletics must stop.

8. Use any of the techniques described on pages 67–71 to revise the opening and closing paragraphs of two of your own papers. When rewriting, don't forget to keep your purpose, audience, tone, and point of view in mind.

9. Reread Harriet Davids's first draft on pages 73–74. Overall, does it support Harriet's thesis? Which topic sentences focus paragraphs effectively? Where is evidence specific, unified, and coherent? Where does Harriet run into some problems? Make a list of the draft's strengths and weaknesses. Save your list for later review. (In the next chapter, you'll be asked to revise Harriet's draft.)

10. Freewrite or write in your journal about a subject that's been on your mind lately. Reread your raw material to see what thesis seems to emerge. What might your purpose, audience, tone, and point of view be if you wrote an essay with this thesis? What primary and secondary points would you cover? Prepare an outline of your ideas. Then draft the essay's body, providing background and transitional paragraphs if appropriate. Finally, write a rough version of the essay's introduction, conclusion, and title. (Save your draft so you can revise it after reading the next chapter.)

11. If you prepared a first draft in response to activity 3 in Chapter 5 (page 54) work with at least one other person to strengthen that early draft by applying the ideas presented in this chapter. (Save this stronger version of your draft so you can refine it further after reading the next chapter.)

12. Referring to the outline you prepared in response to activity 5 or activity 6 in Chapter 5 (page 55), draft the body of an essay. After reviewing the draft, prepare background and transitional paragraphs as needed. Then draft a rough introduction, conclusion, and title. Ask several people to react to what you've prepared, and save your draft so you can work with it further after reading the next chapter.

7

Revising Overall Meaning, Structure, and Paragraph Development

In this chapter, you will learn:

7.1 To use five strategies to make revision easier
7.2 To revise for overall meaning and structure
7.3 To revise paragraph development

In a sense, revision occurs throughout the writing process: At some earlier stage, you may have dropped an idea, overhauled your thesis, or shifted paragraph order. What, then, is different about the rewriting that occurs in the revision stage? The answer has to do with the literal meaning of the word *revision*—reseeing, or seeing again. Genuine revision involves casting clear eyes on your work, viewing it as though you're a reader rather than the writer. Revision is not, as some believe, simply touch-up work—changing a sentence here, a word there, eliminating spelling errors, typing a neat final copy. Revision means that you go through your paper looking for trouble, ready to pick a fight with your own writing. And then you must be willing to sit down and make the changes needed for your writing to be as effective as possible.

Because revision is hard work, you may resist it. After putting the final period in your first draft, you may feel done and have trouble accepting that more work remains. Or, as you read the draft, you may see so many weak spots that you view revision as

punishment for not getting things right the first time. And, if you feel shaky about how to proceed, you may be tempted to skip revising altogether.

Five Strategies to Make Revision Easier

Keep in mind that the revision strategies discussed here should be adapted to each writing situation. Other considerations include your professor's requirements and expectations, the time available, and the assignment's bearing on your grade. The following strategies will help you approach revision more confidently. (See Figure 7.1.)

Set Your First Draft Aside for a While

When you pick up or open your draft after having set it aside for a time, you'll approach it with a fresh, more objective point of view. How much of an interval to leave depends on the time available to you. In general, though, the more time between finishing the draft and starting to revise, the better.

FIGURE 7.1

Process Diagram: Revising Paragraphs

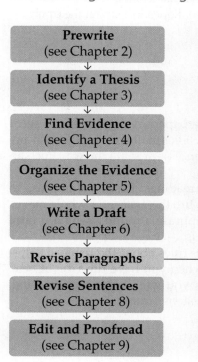

Prewrite
(see Chapter 2)
↓
Identify a Thesis
(see Chapter 3)
↓
Find Evidence
(see Chapter 4)
↓
Organize the Evidence
(see Chapter 5)
↓
Write a Draft
(see Chapter 6)
↓
Revise Paragraphs
↓
Revise Sentences
(see Chapter 8)
↓
Edit and Proofread
(see Chapter 9)

- Print a fresh copy of the essay and set it aside for a time.
- Read your draft aloud, noting any problems you hear.
- Write a brief outline of your draft, noting structural problems.
- Evaluate comments from your instructor and peers.
- Use a feedback chart or marginal annotations on your draft to list problems found by you, your instructor, and peer reviewers.
- Analyze your essay for overall meaning and structure using the checklist on page 85.
- Analyze paragraph development using the checklist on page 86.
- Revise the draft on your computer and print a clean copy.

Work from Printed Text

Working with an essay in printed form helps you see the paper impartially, as if someone else had written it. Each time you make major changes, print out your essay so that you can see it anew.

Read the Draft Aloud

Hearing how your writing sounds helps you pick up problems that might otherwise go undetected: places where sentences are awkward, meaning is ambiguous, and words are imprecise. Even better, have another person read your draft aloud to you. If a reader slows to a crawl over a murky paragraph or trips over a convoluted sentence, you know where you have to do some rewriting.

View Revision as a Series of Steps

Like many students, you may find the prospect of revising your draft to be a daunting one. You can overcome a bad case of revision jitters simply by viewing revision as a process. Instead of trying to tackle all of a draft's problems at once, proceed step by step. (The feedback chart and annotation system discussed on pages 84–85 will help you do just that.) If time allows, read your essay several times. Move from a broad overview (the *macro* level) to an up-close look at mechanics (the *micro* level). With each reading, focus on different issues and ask different questions about the draft.

Here is a recommended series of revision steps:

First step: Revise overall meaning and structure.

Second step: Revise paragraph development.

Third step: Revise sentences and words.

At first, the prospect of reading and rewriting a paper several times may seem to make revision more, not less, overwhelming. Eventually, though, you'll become accustomed to revision as a process, and you'll appreciate the way such an approach improves your writing.

Whenever possible, you should aim for three readings. Resist the impulse to tinker with, say, an unclear sentence until you're sure the essay as a whole makes its point clearly. After all, it can be difficult to rephrase a muddy sentence until you have the essay's overall meaning well in hand.

Remember, though: There are no hard-and-fast rules about the revision steps. For one thing, there are bound to be occasions when you have time for, at best, only one quick pass over a draft. Moreover, as you gain experience revising, you'll probably streamline the process or shift the steps around.

Evaluate and Respond to Instructor Feedback

Often, instructors collect and respond to students' first drafts. Like many students, you may be tempted to look only briefly at your instructor's comments.

Taking your instructor's comments into account when revising is often what's needed to turn a shaky first draft into a strong final draft.

When an instructor returns a final draft graded, you may think that the grade is all that counts. Remember, though: Grades are important, but comments are even more so. They can help you *improve* your writing—if not in this paper, then in the next one. If you don't understand or don't agree with the instructor's observations, you shouldn't hesitate to request a conference. Be sure to go to the conference prepared. You might, for example, put a check next to the instructor's comments you want to discuss. Your instructor will appreciate your thoughtful planning; getting together gives both you and the instructor a chance to clarify your respective points of view.

Peer Review: An Additional Revision Strategy

Many instructors include in-class or at-home peer review as a regular part of a composition course. Peer review—the critical reading of another person's writing with the intention of suggesting constructive changes—accomplishes several important goals. First, peer review helps you gain a more objective perspective on your work. When you write something, you're often too close to what you've prepared to evaluate it fairly; you may have trouble seeing where the writing is strong and where it needs to be strengthened. Peer review supplies the fresh, neutral perspective you need. Second, reviewing your classmates' work broadens your own composing options. You may be inspired to experiment with a technique you admired in a classmate's writing but wouldn't have thought of on your own. Finally, peer review trains you to be a better reader and critic of your *own* writing. When you get into the habit of critically reading other students' writing, you become more adept at critiquing your own.

The revision checklists on pages 85, 86, 102, and 111 of this book will help focus your revision—whether you're reworking your own paper or responding to a peer's. What follows is a peer review worksheet that Harriet Davids's instructor prepared to help students respond to first drafts based on the assignment on page 13. Wanting students to focus on four areas (thesis statement, support for thesis statement, overall organization, and signal devices), the instructor drew upon relevant sections from the revision checklists. With this customized worksheet in hand, Harriet's classmate Frank Tejada was able to give Harriet constructive feedback on her first draft (see page 82). (*Note:* Because Harriet didn't want to influence Frank's reaction, the draft she gave him didn't include her marginal notations to herself.) To see which of Frank's suggestions Harriet followed, take a look at her feedback chart on page 84, at her final draft on pages 120–121, and at the "Commentary" following the essay.

Becoming a Skilled Peer Reviewer

Effective peer review calls for rigor and care; you should give classmates the conscientious feedback that you hope for in return. Peer review also requires tact and kindness; feedback should always be constructive and include observations

Peer Review Worksheet

Essay Author's Name: Harriet Davids   Reviewer's Name: Frank Tejada

1. What is the essay's thesis? Is it explicit or implied? Does the thesis focus on a limited subject and express the writer's attitude toward that subject?

    Thesis: "Being a parent today is much more difficult [than it used to be]." The thesis is limited and expresses a clear attitude. But the sentence the thesis appears in (last sentence of para. 1) is too long because it also contains the plan of development. Maybe put thesis and plan of development in separate sentences.

2. What are the main points supporting the thesis? List the points. Is each supporting point developed sufficiently? If not, where is more support needed?

    (1) Parents have to control kids' distractions from school.
    (2) Parents have to help kids develop responsible sexual values despite sex being everywhere.
    (3) Parents have to protect kids from life threatening dangers.

    The supporting points are good and are explained pretty well, except for a few places. The "Unfortunately" sentence in para. 2 is irrelevant. Also, in para. 2, you use the example of your girls, but never again. Either include them throughout or not at all. In para. 3, the final sentence about the government guidelines opens a whole new topic; maybe steer away from this. The items in para. 4 seem vague and need specific examples. In the conclusion, omit Holden Caulfield; because he was from an earlier generation, this example undermines your thesis about parenting today.

3. What overall format (chronological, spatial, emphatic, simple-to-complex) is used to sequence the essay's main points? Does this format work? Why or why not? What organizational format is used in each supporting paragraph? Does the format work? Why or why not?

    The paper's overall emphatic organization seems good. Emphatic order also works in para. 3, and spatial order works well in para. 2. But the sentences in para. 4 need rearranging. Right now, the examples are in mixed-up chronological order, making it hard to follow. Maybe you should reorder the examples from young kids to older kids.

4. What signal devices are used to connect ideas within and between paragraphs? Are there too few signal devices or too many? Where?

    The topic sentence of para. 3 needs to be a stronger bridging sentence. Also, too many "and's" in para. 3. Try "in addition" or "another" in some places. I like the "worst of all" transition to para. 4.

about what works well in a piece of writing. People have difficulty mustering the energy to revise if they feel there's nothing worth revising.

To focus your readers' comments, you may adapt the revision checklists that appear throughout this book, or you may develop your own questions. If you prepare the questions yourself, be sure to solicit *specific* observations about what does and doesn't work in your writing. If you simply ask, "How's this?" you may receive a vague comment like "It's not very effective." What you want are concrete observations and suggestions: "I'm confused because what you say in the fifth sentence contradicts what you say in the second." To promote such specific responses, ask your readers targeted (preferably written) questions such as, "I'm having trouble moving from my second to my third point. How can I make the transition smoother?" Such questions require more than "yes" or "no" responses; they encourage readers to dig into your writing where you sense it needs work. (If it's feasible, encourage readers to *write* their responses to your questions.)

If you and your peer reviewer(s) can't meet in person, **e-mail** can provide a crucial means of contact. With a couple of clicks, you can simply send each other files of your work. Decide exactly how to exchange comments about your drafts. You might conclude, for example, that you'll use MS Word's "Track Changes" feature or type your responses, perhaps in bold capitals, into the file itself. Or you might decide to print out the drafts and reply to the comments in writing, later exchanging the annotated drafts in person. No matter what you and your peer(s) decide, you'll probably find e-mail an invaluable tool in the writing process.

Evaluate and Respond to Peer Review

Accepting criticism isn't easy (even if you asked for it), and not all peer reviewers will be tactful. Even so, try to listen with an open mind to those giving you feedback. Take notes on their oral observations or have them fill out the checklist described previously. Later, when you're ready to revise your draft, reread your notes. Which reviewer remarks seem valid? Which recommendations are workable? Which are not? In addition, try using a feedback chart or a system of marginal annotations to help you evaluate and remedy any perceived weaknesses in your draft.

Here's how to use a three-column **feedback chart.** In the first column, list the major problems you and your readers see in the draft. Next, rank the problems, designating the most critical as "1." Then in the second column, jot down possible solutions—your own as well as your readers'. Finally, in the third column, briefly describe what action you'll take to correct each problem. On page 84 is the chart that Harriet Davids composed following Frank Tejada's review of her first draft (the draft appears on pages 73–74; the peer review worksheet appears on page 82).

Whether or not you decide to use a feedback chart, be sure to enter **marginal annotations** on your draft (preferably a clean copy of it) before revising it. In the margins, jot down any major problems, numbered in order of importance, along with possible remedies. Marking your paper this way, much as an instructor might, helps you view your paper as though it were written by someone else. (To see how such marginal annotations work, turn to page 87 or look at the sample first drafts of student essays in Chapters 10–18.) Then, keeping the draft's problems in mind, start revising.

Problems	Suggestions	Decisions
① Thesis is too long	Break into two sentences.	Break after "difficult" and add "than it was a generation ago."
④ Irrelevant "Unfortunately" sentence in para. 2	Make sentence relevant or delete.	Delete sentence.
③ Abandoned example of my girls after para. 2	Either include throughout or delete everywhere.	Omit references to my girls.
② In para. 3, final sentence opens new topic	Steer away from new topic.	Delete sentence.
⑥ Vague items in para. 4	Give more specific examples.	Provide more specifics on violence against children and peer pressure.
⑤ Sentences in para. 4 need rearranging	Reorder examples from young kids to older kids.	Begin with small kids, then older kids, then teens.
⑦ Weak transitions in para. 3	Strengthen topic sentence; replace "and"s with other transitions.	Create stronger bridging sentence for para. 3. Substitute other transitions for "and"s.

Revising Overall Meaning and Structure

It's not uncommon when revising at this stage to find that the draft doesn't fully convey what you had in mind. Perhaps your intended thesis ends up being overshadowed by another idea. (If that happens, you have two options: you may pursue the new line of thought as your revised thesis, or you may bring the paper back into line with your original thesis by deleting extraneous material.) Another problem might be that readers miss a key point. Perhaps you initially believed the point could be implied, but you now realize it needs to be stated explicitly.

Preparing a *brief outline* of a draft can help evaluate the essay's overall structure. Either you or a reader can prepare the outline. In either case, your thesis, reflecting any changes made during the first draft, should be noted at the top of the outline page. Then you or your readers briefly outline the paper's basic structure. With the draft pared down to its essentials, you can see more easily how parts contribute to the whole and how points do or do not fit together.

> ## ☑ REVISING OVERALL MEANING AND STRUCTURE: A CHECKLIST
>
> ☐ What is your initial reaction to the draft? What do you like and dislike?
>
> ☐ What audience does the essay address? How suited to this audience are the essay's purpose, tone, and point of view?
>
> ☐ What is the essay's thesis? Is it explicit or implied? Does it focus on a limited subject and express the writer's attitude toward that subject? If not, what changes need to be made?
>
> ☐ What are the points supporting the thesis? List them. If any stray from or contradict the thesis, what changes need to be made?
>
> ☐ According to which organizing principle(s)—spatial, chronological, emphatic, simple to complex—are the main points arranged? Does this organizational scheme reinforce the thesis? Why or why not?
>
> ☐ Which patterns of development (narration, description, comparison-contrast, and so on) are used in the essay? How do these patterns reinforce the thesis?
>
> ☐ Where would background information, definition of terms, or additional material clarify meaning?

You are now ready to focus on the second step in the revising process.

Revising Paragraph Development

After you use feedback to refine the paper's fundamental meaning and structure, it's time to look closely at the essay's paragraphs. At this point, you and those giving you feedback should read the draft more slowly. How can the essay's paragraphs be made more unified (see page 61) and more specific (pages 61–63)? Which paragraphs seem to lack sufficient support (pages 63–64)? Which would profit from more attention to coherence (pages 64–66)?

At this stage, you may find that a paragraph needs more examples to make its point or that a paragraph should be deleted because it doesn't develop the thesis. Or perhaps you realize that a paragraph should come earlier in the essay because it defines a term readers need to understand from the outset.

Here's a strategy to help assess your paragraphs' effectiveness. In the margin next to each paragraph, make a brief notation that answers these two questions: (1) What is the paragraph's *purpose?* and (2) What is its *content?* Then skim the marginal notes to see if each paragraph does what you intended.

During this stage, you should also examine the *length of your paragraphs.* Paragraphs all the same length dull your readers' response, whereas variations encourage them to sit up and take notice.

If your paragraphs tend to run long, try breaking some of them into shorter, crisper chunks. Be sure, however, not to break paragraphs just anywhere. To preserve a paragraph's logic, you may need to reshape and add material, always keeping in mind that the paragraph should have a clear and distinctive focus.

☑ REVISING PARAGRAPH DEVELOPMENT: A CHECKLIST

☐ In what way does each supporting paragraph develop the essay's thesis? Which paragraphs fail to develop the thesis? Should they be deleted or revised?

☐ What is each paragraph's central idea? If this idea is expressed in a topic sentence, where is this sentence located? Where does something stray from or contradict the paragraph's main idea? How could the paragraph's focus be sharpened?

☐ Where in each paragraph does support seem irrelevant, vague, insufficient, inaccurate, nonrepresentative, or disorganized? What could be done to remedy these problems? Where would additional sensory details, examples, facts, statistics, expert authority, and personal observations be appropriate?

☐ By which organizational principle (spatial, chronological, or emphatic) are each paragraph's ideas arranged? Does this format reinforce the paragraph's main point? Why or why not?

☐ How could paragraph coherence be strengthened? Which signal devices are used to connect ideas within and between paragraphs? Where are there too few signals or too many?

☐ Where do too many paragraphs of the same length dull interest? Where would a short or a long paragraph be more effective?

☐ How could the introduction be strengthened? Which striking anecdote, fact, or statistic elsewhere in the essay might be moved to the introduction? How does the introduction establish the essay's purpose, audience, tone, and point of view? Which strategy links the introduction to the essay's body?

☐ How could the conclusion be strengthened? Which striking anecdote, fact, or statistic elsewhere in the essay might be moved to the conclusion? Would echoing something from the introduction help round off the essay more effectively? How has the conclusion been made an integral part of the essay?

However, don't go overboard and break up all your paragraphs. An abundance of brief paragraphs makes it difficult for readers to see how points are related. Furthermore, overreliance on short paragraphs may mean that you haven't provided sufficient evidence for your ideas. Finally, a succession of short paragraphs encourages readers to skim when, of course, you want them to consider carefully what you have to say. So use short paragraphs, but save them for places in the essay where you want to introduce variation or achieve emphasis. (The checklist at the top of this page is designed to help you and your readers evaluate a draft's paragraph development.)

Sample Student Revision of Overall Meaning, Structure, and Paragraph Development

The introduction to Harriet Davids's first draft that we saw in Chapter 6 (pages 73–74) is reprinted here with her revisions. In the margin, numbered in order of importance, are the problems with the introduction's meaning, structure, and paragraph development—as noted by Harriet's peer reviewer, Frank, and other classmates. (The group used the checklists on pages 85 and 86 to focus their critique.) The above-line changes show Harriet's first efforts to eliminate these problems through revision.

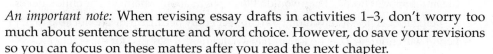

In the '50s and '60s, parents had it easy. TV comedies of that period show the
~~Raising children used to be much simpler in the 50s and 60s. I~~

Cleavers scolding Beaver about his dirty hands
~~remember TV images from that era showing that parenting involved~~

and the Nelsons telling Ricky to clean his room.
~~simply teaching kids to clean their rooms, do their homework,~~

                    B
~~and~~ _____. But ʌbeing a parent today is much more difficult₀

        N   must   their children   many
~~because~~ nowadays parents ~~have to shield~~/protect ~~kids~~ from ~~lots of~~
        ʌ

    —from a growing number of   ly explicit
things ʌlike distractions ~~from schoolwork~~, from sexual ʌmaterial, and

from dangerous situations.

② Take out personal reference

③ Give specific TV shows

① Thesis too long. Make plan of development separate sentence.

Continues on page 112

(If you'd like to see Harriet's final draft, turn to pages 120–121.)

ACTIVITIES: REVISING OVERALL MEANING, STRUCTURE, AND PARAGRAPH DEVELOPMENT

An important note: When revising essay drafts in activities 1–3, don't worry too much about sentence structure and word choice. However, do save your revisions so you can focus on these matters after you read the next chapter.

1. Look at the marginal notes and above-line changes that Harriet Davids added to her first draft introduction on this page, above. Now look at the draft's other paragraphs on pages 73–74 and identify problems in overall meaning, structure, and paragraph development. Working alone or in a group, start by asking questions like these: "Where does the essay stray from the thesis?" and "Where does a paragraph fail to present points in the most logical and

compelling order?" (The critique you prepared for activity 9 in Chapter 6, page 77, should help.) For further guidance, refer to the checklists on pages 85 and 86. Summarize and rank the perceived problems in marginal annotations or on a feedback chart. Then type your changes or handwrite them between the lines of the draft (work on a newly printed copy, a photocopy, or the text-book pages themselves). Don't forget to save your revision.

2. Retrieve the draft you prepared in response to activity 12 in Chapter 6 (page 77). Outline the draft. Does your outline reveal any problems in the draft's overall meaning and structure? If it does, make whatever changes are needed. The checklists on pages 85 and 86 will help focus your revising efforts. (Save your revised draft so you can work with it further after reading the next chapter.)

3. Following is the first draft of an essay advocating a longer elementary school day. Read it closely. Are tone and point of view consistent throughout? Is the thesis clear? Is the support in each body paragraph relevant, specific, and ad-equate? Are ideas arranged in the most effective order? Working alone or in a group, use the checklists on pages 85 and 86 to identify problems with the draft's overall meaning, structure, and paragraph development. Summarize and rank the perceived problems on a feedback chart or in marginal anno-tations. Then revise the draft by typing a new version or by entering your changes by hand (on a photocopy of the draft, a typed copy, or the textbook pages themselves). Don't forget to save your revision.

The Extended School Day

Imagine a seven-year-old whose parents work until five each night. When she arrives home after school, she is on her own. She's a good girl, but still a lot of things could happen. She could get into trouble just by being curious. Or something could hap-pen through no fault of her own. All over the country, there are many "latchkey" children like this little girl. Some way must be found to deal with the problem. One suggestion is to keep elementary schools open longer than they now are. There are many advantages to this idea.

Parents wouldn't have to be in a state of uneasiness about whether their child is safe and happy at home. They wouldn't get uptight about whether their child's needs are being met. They also wouldn't have to feel guilty because they are not able to help a child with homework. The longer day would make it possible for the teacher to provide such help. Extended school hours would also relieve families of the financial burden of hiring a home sitter. As my family learned, having a sitter can wipe out the budget. And having a sitter doesn't necessarily eliminate all problems. Parents still have the hassle of worrying whether the person will show up and be reliable.

It's a fact of life that many children dislike school, which is a sad commen-tary on the state of education in this country. Even so, the longer school day would benefit children as well. Obviously, the dangers of their being home alone after school would disappear because by the time the bus dropped them off after the longer school day, at least one parent would be home. The unnameable horrors feared by parents would not have a chance to happen. Instead, the children would be in school, under trained supervision. There, they would have a chance to work on subjects that give them trouble. In contrast, when my younger brother had difficulty with subtraction in second grade, he had to struggle along because there wasn't enough time to give him the help he needed. The longer day would also give children a chance to participate in extracurricular activities. They could join a science club, play on a softball team, sing in a school chorus, take an art class. Because school districts are trying to save money, they often cut back on such extracurricular activities. They don't realize how important such experiences are.

Finally, the longer school day would also benefit teachers. Having more hours in each day would relieve them of a lot of pressure. This longer workday would obviously require schools to increase teachers' pay. The added salary would be an incentive for teachers to stay in the profession.

Implementing an extended school day would be expensive, but I feel that many communities would willingly finance its costs because it provides benefits to parents, children, and even teachers. Young children, home alone, wondering whether to watch another TV show or to wander outside to see what's happening, need this longer school day now.

4. Look closely at your instructor's comments on an ungraded draft of one of your essays. Using a feedback chart, summarize and evaluate your instructor's comments. When that's done, rework the essay. Type your new version, or make your changes by hand. In either case, save the revision so you can work with it further after reading the next chapter.

5. Return to the draft you wrote in response to activity 10 or activity 11 in Chapter 6 (page 77). To identify any problems, meet with several people and request that one of them read the draft aloud. Then ask your listeners focused questions about the areas you sense need work. Alternatively, you may use the checklists on pages 85 and 86 to focus the group's feedback. In either case, summarize and rank the comments on a feedback chart or in marginal annotations. Then, using the comments as a guide, revise the draft. Either type a new version or do your revising by hand. (Save your revision so you can work with it further after reading the next chapter.)

8

Revising Sentences and Words

In this chapter, you will learn:

8.1 To revise your sentences for tone, length, and emphasis
8.2 To revise your words for appropriate tone and meaning

Revising Sentences

Having refined your essay's overall meaning, structure, and paragraph development, you can concentrate on sharpening individual sentences. Although polishing sentences inevitably involves decisions about individual words, for now focus on each sentence as a whole; you can evaluate individual words later (see Figure 8.1 on page 91).

Make Sentences Consistent with Your Tone

In Chapter 2, we saw how integral **tone** is to meaning (pages 20–21). As you revise, be sure each sentence's **content** (its images and ideas) and **style** (its structure and length) reinforce your intended tone: Both *what* you say and *how* you say it should support the essay's overall mood.

Consider the following excerpt from a piece by *Philadelphia Inquirer* columnist Melissa Dribben. Dribben supports legislation to limit handgun purchases to one per person per month. She writes:

> There are people who buy a new toothbrush every month. A new vacuum-cleaner bag. A fresh box of baking soda. A pair of $5 sunglasses. This you understand. You can never have too many.

FIGURE 8.1

Process Diagram: Revising Sentences

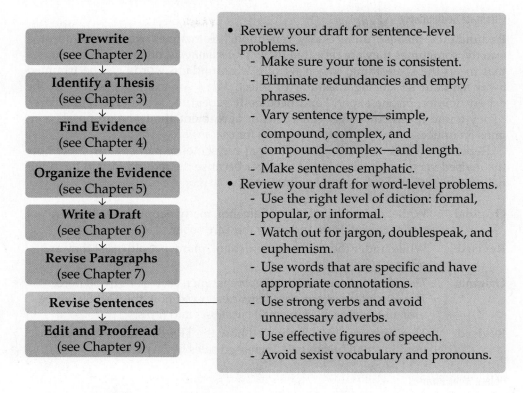

Prewrite
(see Chapter 2)

Identify a Thesis
(see Chapter 3)

Find Evidence
(see Chapter 4)

Organize the Evidence
(see Chapter 5)

Write a Draft
(see Chapter 6)

Revise Paragraphs
(see Chapter 7)

Revise Sentences

Edit and Proofread
(see Chapter 9)

- Review your draft for sentence-level problems.
    - Make sure your tone is consistent.
    - Eliminate redundancies and empty phrases.
    - Vary sentence type—simple, compound, complex, and compound–complex—and length.
    - Make sentences emphatic.
- Review your draft for word-level problems.
    - Use the right level of diction: formal, popular, or informal.
    - Watch out for jargon, doublespeak, and euphemism.
    - Use words that are specific and have appropriate connotations.
    - Use strong verbs and avoid unnecessary adverbs.
    - Use effective figures of speech.
    - Avoid sexist vocabulary and pronouns.

But when you reach the point where you have a stash of .38-caliber pistols bigger than your supply of clean underwear, you have a problem. And it isn't a shopping addiction.

Dribben's tone here is biting and sarcastic, her attitude exasperated and mocking. She establishes this tone partly through sentence content (what she says). For example, to her it is outrageous that people would want to buy guns more frequently than they purchase basic household and personal necessities. Dribben's style (how she says it) also contributes to her overall tone. The three fragments in the first paragraph convey an attitude of angry disbelief. These fragments, followed by two brief but complete sentences, build to the longer, climactic sentence at the beginning of the second paragraph. That sentence, especially when combined with the crisp last sentence, delivers a final, quick jab to those opposed to the proposed legislation. In short, content and style help express Dribben's impassioned attitude toward her subject.

Make Sentences Economical

Besides reinforcing your tone, your sentences should be **economical** rather than wordy. Use as few, not as many, words as possible. Your sentences won't be wordy if you (1) eliminate redundancy, (2) delete weak phrases, and (3) remove unnecessary *who, which,* and *that* clauses.

Eliminate Redundancy

Redundancy means "unnecessary repetition." Sometimes words are repeated exactly; sometimes they are repeated by way of *synonyms,* other words or phrases that mean the same thing. When writing is redundant, words can be trimmed away without sacrificing meaning or effect. Why, for example, write "In the expert opinion of one expert" and needlessly repeat the word *expert?* Similarly, "They found it difficult to get consensus or agreement about the proposal" contains an unnecessary synonym (*agreement*) for *consensus.*

Repetition weakens prose. Take a look at the sentence pairs below. Note how the revised versions are clearer and stronger because the redundancy in the original sentences (italicized) has been eliminated:

Original   While under the *influence* of alcohol, many people insist they are not under the *influence* and *swear* they are sober.

Revised   While under the influence of alcohol, many people insist they are sober.

Original   *They designed a computer program* that increased sales by 50 percent. The *computer program they designed* showed how the TRS-80 can be *used* and *implemented* in small *businesses* and *firms.*

Revised   Their program, which showed how the TRS-80 computer can be used in small businesses, increased sales by 50 percent.

Delete Weak Phrases

In addition to eliminating redundancy, you can make sentences more economical by **deleting the three types of weak phrases** described here.

1. **Empty Phrases.** In speaking, we frequently use empty phrases that give us time to think but don't add to our message ("Okay?" "You know what I mean?") In writing, though, we can eliminate such deadwood. Here are some expressions that are needlessly awkward and wordy, along with one-word alternatives:

Wordy Expressions	Revised
due to the fact that	because
in light of the fact that	since
regardless of the fact that	although
in the event that	if
in many cases	often
in that period	then
at this point in time	now
in the not-too-distant future	soon

for the purpose of	to
has the ability to	can
be aware of the fact that	know
is necessary that	must

Notice the improvement in the following sentences when wordy, often awkward phrases are replaced with one-word substitutes:

Original   *It is necessary that* the government outlaw the production of carcinogenic pesticides.

Revised   The government *must* outlaw the production of carcinogenic pesticides.

Original   Student leaders were upset by *the fact that* no one in the administration consulted them.

Revised   Student leaders were upset *because* no one in the administration consulted them.

Some phrases don't even call for concise substitutes. Because they add nothing at all to a sentence's meaning, they can simply be deleted.

Original   The hybrid azaleas were light blue *in color.*
Revised   The hybrid azaleas were light blue.

Other times, to avoid an empty phrase, you may need to recast a sentence slightly:

Original   The midterm assessment is *for the purpose of letting* students know if they are failing a course.

Revised   The midterm assessment *lets* students know if they are failing a course.

2. **Roundabout Openings with *There, It,* and Question Words Such as *How* and *What*.** The openings of sentences are especially vulnerable to unnecessary phrases. Common culprits include phrases beginning with *There* and *It* (when *It* does not refer to a specific noun) and words such as *How* and *What* (when they don't actually ask a question).

Original   It was their belief that the problem had been solved.
Revised   They believed the problem had been solved.

Original   There are now computer courses offered by many high schools.
Revised   Many high schools now offer computer courses.

Of course, feel free to open with *There* or *It* when some other construction would be less clear or effective. For example, don't write "Many reasons can be cited why students avoid art courses" when you can say "There are many reasons why students avoid art courses."

3. **Excessive Prepositional Phrases.** Strings of prepositional phrases (word groups beginning with *at, on,* and the like) tend to make writing choppy; they weigh sentences down and hide main ideas. Note how much smoother and clearer sentences become when prepositional phrases (italicized in the following examples) are eliminated:

Original	Growth *in the greenhouse effect* may result *in increases in the intensity of hurricanes.*
Revised	The growing greenhouse effect may intensify hurricanes.
Original	The reassurance *of a neighbor* who was the owner *of a pit bull* that his dog was incapable *of harm* would not be sufficient to prevent most parents *from calling* the authorities if the dog ran loose.
Revised	Despite a neighbor's reassurance that his pit bull was harmless, most parents would call the authorities if the dog ran loose.

These examples show that you can sometime eliminate prepositional phrases by substituting one strong verb (*intensify*) or by using the possessive form (*neighbor's reassurance, his pit bull*) rather than an *of* phrase.

Remove Unnecessary *Who, Which,* and *That* Clauses

Often *who, which,* or *that* clauses can be removed with no loss of meaning. Consider the tightening possible in these sentences:

Original	The townsfolk misunderstood the main point *that the developer made.*
Revised	The townsfolk misunderstood *the developer's main point.*
Original	The employees *who protested* the restrictions went on strike, *which was a real surprise to management.*
Revised	The employees *protesting* the restrictions *surprised management* by going on strike.

Vary Sentence Type

Another way to invigorate writing is to **vary sentence type**.

Simple Sentences

A **clause** is a group of words with both a subject and a verb. Clauses can be **independent** (able to stand alone) or **dependent** (unable to stand alone). A **simple sentence** consists of a single independent clause (whose subject and verb are italicized here):

Marie Curie investigated radioactivity and *died* from its effects.

Unlike most mammals, *birds* and *fish see* color.

A simple sentence can have more than one verb (sentence 1) or more than one subject (sentence 2). In addition, any number of modifying phrases (such as *Unlike most mammals*) can extend the sentence's length and add information. What distinguishes a simple sentence is its single *subject-verb combination.*

Simple sentences can convey dramatic urgency:

> Suddenly we heard the screech of brakes. Across the street, a small boy lay sprawled in front of a car. We started to run toward the child. The driver sped away.

Simple sentences are also excellent for singling out a climactic point, but in a series, they lose their impact and become boring. Also, because simple sentences highlight one idea at a time, they don't clarify the relationships among ideas:

Original

> Many first-year college students are apprehensive. They won't admit it to themselves. They hesitate to confide in their friends. They never find out that everyone else is anxious, too. They are nervous about being disliked and feeling lonely. They fear not "knowing the ropes."

Revised

> Many first-year college students are apprehensive, but they won't admit it to themselves. Because they hesitate to confide in their friends, they never find out that everyone else is anxious, too. Being disliked, feeling lonely, not "knowing the ropes"—these are what beginning college students fear.

The simple sentences in the original version fragment the passage into a series of disconnected ideas. The revised version includes a variety of sentence types and patterns, all of which are discussed on the pages ahead. This variety clarifies the relationships among ideas, so that the passage reads more easily.

Compound Sentences

Compound sentences consist of two or more independent clauses. There are four types of compound sentences. The most basic type consists of two simple sentences joined by a *coordinating conjunction* (*and, but, for, nor, or, so,* or *yet*):

> Chimpanzees and gorillas can learn sign language, *and* they have been seen teaching this language to others.

Another type of compound sentence has a semicolon (;), rather than a comma and coordinating conjunction, between the two simple sentences:

> Yesterday, editorials attacked the plan; a week ago, they praised it.

A third type of compound sentence links two simple sentences with a semicolon plus a *conjunctive adverb* such as *however, moreover, nevertheless, therefore,* or *thus:*

> Every year billions of U.S. dollars go to researching AIDS; *however,* recent studies show that a large percentage of the money has been mismanaged.

A final type of compound sentence consists of two simple sentences connected by a *correlative conjunction,* a word pair such as *either...or, neither...nor,* or *not only...but also:*

> *Either* the litigants will win the lawsuit, *or* they will end up in debt from court costs.

Compound sentences help clarify the relationship between ideas. Similarities are signaled by such words as *and* and *moreover,* contrasts by *but* and *however,* cause-effect by *so* and *therefore.* When only a semicolon separates the two parts of a compound sentence, the relationship between those two parts is often a contrast. ("Yesterday, editorials attacked the plan; a week ago, they praised it.")

Complex Sentences

In a **complex sentence**, a dependent (subordinate) clause is joined to an independent clause. Sometimes the dependent clause (italicized in the following example) is introduced by a subordinating conjunction such as *although, because, if, since,* or *when:*

> *Since they have relatively small circulations,* specialty magazines tend to be expensive.

Other dependent clauses are introduced by a relative pronoun such as *that, which,* or *who.*

> The USDA, *which controls food labeling,* sets the standards for organic food.

The order of the dependent and independent clause isn't fixed. The dependent clause may come first, last, or even in the middle of the independent clause:

> Nurses' uniforms, *although they are no longer the norm,* are still required by some hospitals.

Whether to use a comma between a dependent and an independent clause depends on a number of factors, including the location of the dependent clause and whether it's *restrictive* (essential for identifying whatever it modifies) or *nonrestrictive.*

Because a dependent clause is subordinate to an independent one, complex sentences can clarify the relationships among ideas. Consider the two paragraphs that follow. The first merely strings together a series of simple and compound sentences, all of them carrying roughly the same weight. In contrast, the complex sentences in the revised version use subordination to connect ideas and signal their relative importance.

Original

> Are you the "average American"? Then take heed. Here are the results of a time-management survey. You might want to budget your time differently. According to the survey, you spend six years of your life eating. Also, you're likely to spend two years trying to reach people by telephone, so you should think about texting instead of calling. Finally, you may be married and expect long conversations with your spouse to occur spontaneously, but you'll have to make a special effort. Ordinarily, your discussions will average only four minutes a day.

Revised

If you're the "average American," take heed. After you hear the results of a time-management survey, you might want to budget your time differently. According to the survey, you spend six years of your life eating. Also, unless you call less and text more, you're likely to spend two years trying to reach your friends by telephone. Finally, if you're married, you shouldn't expect long conversations with your spouse to occur spontaneously. Unless you make a special effort, your discussions will average only four minutes a day.

The following sentences illustrate how meaning shifts depending on what is placed in the main clause and what is subordinated:

Although most fraternities and sororities no longer allow hazing, pledging is still a big event on many campuses.

Although pledging is still a big event on many campuses, most fraternities and sororities no longer allow hazing.

In the first sentence, the focus is on *pledging;* in the second, it is on the *discontinuation of hazing.*

Compound-Complex Sentences

A **compound-complex sentence** connects one or more dependent clauses to two or more independent clauses. In the following example, the two independent clauses are underscored once and the two dependent clauses twice:

<u>The Procrastinators' Club</u>, <u><u>which is based in Philadelphia</u></u>, <u>issues a small magazine</u>, but <u>it appears infrequently</u>, only <u><u>when members get around to writing it</u></u>.

Go easy on the number of compound-complex sentences you use. They tend to be long, so a string of them is likely to overwhelm the reader.

Vary Sentence Length

Generally, by varying sentence type, a writer automatically **varies sentence length** as well. However, sentence type doesn't always determine length. In this example, the simple sentence is longer than the complex one:

Simple Sentence

Hot and thirsty, exhausted from the effort of carrying so many groceries, I desired nothing more than an ice-cold glass of lemonade.

Complex Sentence

Because I was hot and thirsty, I craved lemonade.

The difference lies in the number of **modifiers**—words or groups of words used to describe another word or group of words. So, besides considering sentence type, check sentence length when revising.

Short Sentences

Too many short sentences, like too many simple ones, can sound childish and create a choppy effect that muddies the relationship among ideas. Used wisely, though, a series of short sentences gives writing a staccato rhythm that carries more punch and conveys a faster pace than the same number of words gathered into longer sentences:

> Witches bring their faces close. Goblins glare with fiery eyes. Fiendish devils stealthily approach to claw a beloved stuffed bear. The toy recoils in horror. These are among the terrifying happenings in the world of children's nightmares.

> Witches bring their faces close as goblins glare, their eyes fiery. Approaching stealthily, fiendish devils come to claw a beloved stuffed bear that recoils in horror. These are among the terrifying happenings in the world of children's nightmares.

Brevity also highlights a sentence, especially when surrounding sentences are longer. Consider the dramatic effect of the final sentence in this paragraph:

> Starting in June, millions of Americans pour onto the highways, eager to begin vacation. At the same time, city, state, and federal agencies deploy hundreds, even thousands of workers to repair roads that have, until now, managed to escape bureaucratic attention. Chaos results.

The sentence "Chaos results" stands out because it's so much shorter than the other sentences. The emphasis is appropriate because, in the writer's view, chaos is the dramatic consequence of prolonged bureaucratic inertia.

Long Sentences

Long sentences often convey a leisurely pace and establish a calm tone:

> As I look across the lake, I see the steady light of a campfire at the water's edge, the flames tinting to copper an aluminum rowboat tied to the dock, the boat glimmering in the darkness.

Too many long sentences can be hard to follow. And remember: A sentence stands out most when it differs in length from surrounding sentences. Glance back at the first paragraph on children's nightmares above. The final long sentence stands in contrast to the preceding short ones. The resulting emphasis works because the final sentence is also the paragraph's topic sentence.

Make Sentences Emphatic

Within a single sentence, you can use a number of techniques to make parts of the sentence stand out from the rest. To achieve such **emphasis**, you can: (1) place key ideas at the beginning or end, (2) set them in parallel constructions, (3) express them as fragments, or (4) express them in inverted word order.

Place Key Points at the Beginning or End

A sentence's start and close are its most prominent positions. So, keeping your overall meaning in mind, use those two spots to highlight key ideas.

Let's look first at the **beginning** position. Here are two versions of a sentence; the meanings differ because the openers differ.

> The potentially life-saving drug, developed by junior researchers at the medical school, will be available next month.

> Developed by junior researchers at the medical school, the potentially life-saving drug will be available next month.

In the first version, the emphasis is on the life-saving potential of a drug. Reordering the sentence shifts attention to those responsible for discovering the drug.

An even more emphatic position than a sentence's beginning is its **end**. Place whatever you want to emphasize at the end of the sentence:

> Kindergarten is wasted on the young—especially the co-ed naptime.

Now look at two versions of another sentence, each with a slightly different meaning because of what's at the end:

> Increasingly, overt racism is showing up in—of all places—popular song lyrics.

> Popular song lyrics are showing—of all things—increasingly overt racism.

In the first version, the emphasis is on lyrics; in the second, it's on racism.

Be sure, though, that whatever you place in the climactic position merits the emphasis. The following sentence is so anticlimactic that it's unintentionally humorous:

> The family, waiting anxiously for the results of the medical tests, sat.

Similarly, don't build toward a strong climax only to defuse it with some less important material:

> On the narrow parts of the trail, where jagged cliffs drop steeply from the path, keep your eyes straight ahead and don't look down, toward the town of Belmont in the east.

In the preceding sentence, "toward the town of Belmont in the east" should be deleted. The important point surely isn't Belmont's location but how to avoid an accident.

Use Parallelism

Parallelism occurs when ideas of comparable weight are expressed in the same grammatical form, which underscores their equality. Parallel elements may be words, phrases, clauses, or full sentences. Here are some examples:

Parallel Nouns

We bought *pretzels*, *nachos*, and *candy bars* to feed our pre-exam jitters.

Parallel Adverbs

Smoothly, *steadily*, *quietly*, the sails tipped toward the sun.

Parallel Verbs

The guest lecturer *spoke* to the group, *showed* her slides, and then *invited* questions.

Parallel Adjective Phrases

Playful as a kitten but *wise as a street Tom*, the old cat toyed with the string while keeping a watchful eye on his surroundings.

Parallel Prepositional Phrases

Gloomy predictions came *from political analysts*, *from the candidate's staff*, and, surprisingly, *from the candidate herself*.

Parallel Dependent Clauses

Because our rivals were in top form, *because their top player would soon come up to bat*, we knew that all was lost.

As you can see, the repetition of grammatical forms creates a pleasing symmetry that emphasizes the sequenced ideas. Parallel structure also conveys meaning economically. Look at the way the following sentences can be tightened using parallelism:

Nonparallel

Studies show that most women today are different from those in the past. They want to have their own careers. They want to be successful. They also want to enjoy financial independence.

Parallel

Studies show that most women today are different from those in the past. They want to have careers, be successful, and enjoy financial independence.

Parallel constructions are often signaled by word pairs (correlative conjunctions) such as *either...or*, *neither...nor*, and *not only...but also*. To maintain parallelism, the same grammatical form must follow each half of the word pair.

Either professors are too rigorous, *or* they are too lax.

When my roommate argues, she tends to be *not only* totally stubborn *but also* totally wrong.

Parallelism can create elegant and dramatic writing. Too much, though, seems artificial, so use it sparingly. Save it for your most important points.

Use Fragments

A **fragment** is part of a sentence punctuated as if it were a whole sentence—that is, with a period at the end. A sentence fragment consists of words, phrases, and/or dependent clauses, *without an independent clause.* Here are some examples:

Resting quietly.   Because they admired her.
Except for the trees.   A demanding boss who accepted no excuses.

Ask your composition instructor whether an occasional fragment—used as a stylistic device—will be considered acceptable. Here's an example showing the way fragments (underlined) can be used effectively for emphasis:

One of my aunt's eccentricities is her belief that only personally made gifts show the proper amount of love. Her gifts are often strange. Hand-drawn calendars. Home-brewed cologne that smells like jam. Crocheted washcloths. Frankly, I'd rather receive a gift certificate from a department store.

Notice how the three fragments focus attention on the aunt's charmingly offbeat gifts. Remember, though: When overused, fragments lose their effect, so draw on them sparingly.

Use Inverted Word Order

In most English sentences, the subject comes before the verb. When you use **inverted word order**, at least part of the verb comes before the subject. The resulting sentence is so atypical that it automatically stands out.
Inverted statements, like those that follow, are used to emphasize an idea:

Normal   My Uncle Bill is a strange man.
Inverted   A strange man is my Uncle Bill.

Normal   Their lies about the test scores were especially brazen.
Inverted   Especially brazen were their lies about the test scores.

A note of caution: Inverted statements should be used infrequently and with special care. Bizarre can they easily sound.
Another form of inversion, the question, also acts as emphasis. A question may be a genuine inquiry, one that focuses attention on the issue at hand:

Since the 1960s, only about half of this country's eligible voters have gone to the polls during national elections. *Why are Americans so apathetic?* Let's look at some of the reasons.

Or a question may be *rhetorical*; that is, one that implies its own answer and encourages the reader to share the writer's view:

> Yesterday, there was yet another accident at the intersection of Fairview and Springdale. Given the disproportionately high number of collisions at that crossing, *can anyone question the need for a traffic light?*

The following checklist is designed to help you and your readers evaluate the sentences in a first draft. (Activities at the end of the chapter will refer you to this checklist when you revise several essays.) To see how one student, Harriet Davids, used the checklist when revising, turn to page 112.

✔ REVISING SENTENCES: A CHECKLIST

☐ Which sentences seem inconsistent with the essay's intended tone? How could the problem be fixed?

☐ Which sentences could be more economical? Where could unnecessary repetition, empty phrases, and weak openings be eliminated? Which prepositional phrases could be deleted? Where are there unnecessary *who, which*, and *that* clauses?

☐ Where should sentence type be more varied? Where would subordination clarify the connections among ideas? Where would simpler sentences make the writing less inflated and easier to understand?

☐ Where does sentence length become monotonous and predictable? Which short sentences should be connected to enhance flow and convey a more leisurely pace? Which long sentences would be more effective if broken into crisp, short ones?

☐ Where would a different sentence pattern add variety? Better highlight key sentence elements? Seem more natural?

☐ Which sentences could be more emphatic? Which strategy would be most effective— expressing the main point at the beginning or end, using parallelism, or rewriting the sentence as a fragment, question, or inverted-word-order statement?

Revising Words

After refining the sentences in your first draft, you're in a good position to look closely at individual words. (Refer back to Figure 8.1 on page 91.) During this stage, you should aim for:

- Words consistent with your intended tone
- An appropriate level of diction
- Words that neither overstate nor understate
- Words with appropriate connotations
- Specific rather than general words
- Strong verbs

- No unnecessary adverbs
- Original figures of speech
- Nonsexist language

Make Words Consistent with Your Tone

Like full sentences, individual words and phrases should also reinforce your intended tone. Reread the Melissa Dribben excerpt on gun control (see pages 90–92). Earlier we discussed how sentence structure and length contribute to the excerpt's biting tone. Word choice also plays an important role. The word *stash* mocks the impulse to hoard guns as if they were essential but depletable goods—like clean underwear. And the specific phrase *.38-caliber pistols* evokes the image of a weapon with frightening lethal power. Such word choices reinforce the overall tone Dribben wants to convey.

Use an Appropriate Level of Diction

Diction refers to the words a writer selects. Those words should be appropriate for the writer's purpose, audience, point of view, and tone. If, for example, you are writing a straightforward, serious piece about on-the-job incompetence, you would be better off saying that people "don't concentrate on their work" and they "make frequent errors," rather than saying they "screw up" or "goof off."

There are three broad levels of diction: *formal, popular,* and *informal.* Within each level of diction, there are degrees of formality and informality.

Formal Diction

Impersonal and distant in tone, **formal diction** is the type of language found in scholarly journals. Contractions are rare; long, specialized, technical words are common. Unfortunately, many people mistakenly equate word length with education: The longer the words, they think, the more impressed readers will be. So rather than using the familiar and natural words *improve* and *think,* they thumb through a thesaurus (literally or figuratively) for such fancy-sounding alternatives as *ameliorate* and *conceptualize.*

Similarly, when writing for a general audience, don't use **jargon**, which is insiders' terms from a particular area of expertise (say, a term such as *authorial omniscience* from literary theory). Such "shoptalk" should be used only when less specialized words would lack the necessary precision. If readers are apt to be unfamiliar with a term, provide a definition.

Some degree of formality is appropriate—when, for example, you write up survey results for a sociology class. In such a case, your instructor may expect you to avoid the pronoun *I* (see page 21). Other instructors may think it's pretentious for a student to refer to himself or herself in the third person ("The writer observed that..."). These instructors may be equally put off by the artificiality of the passive voice (page 107): "It was observed that..." To be safe, find out what your instructors expect. If possible, use *I* when you mean "I."

Popular Diction

Popular, or **mainstream**, **diction** is found in most magazines, newspapers, books, and texts (including this one). In such prose, the writer may use the first person and address the reader as "you." Contractions appear frequently; specialized vocabulary is kept to a minimum.

You should aim for popular diction in most of the writing you do—in and out of college. Also keep in mind that an abrupt downshift to slang (*freaked out* instead of *lost control*) or a sudden turn to highly formal language (*myocardial infarction* instead of *heart attack*) will disconcert readers and undermine your credibility.

Informal Diction

Informal diction, which conveys a sense of everyday speech, is friendly and casual. First-person and second-person pronouns are common, as are contractions and fragments. Colloquial expressions (*rub the wrong way*) and slang (*you wimp*) are used freely. Informal diction isn't appropriate for academic papers, except where it is used to indicate *someone else's* speech.

Avoid Words That Overstate or Understate

When revising, be on the lookout for **doublespeak**, language that deliberately overstates or understates reality. For example, in their correspondence, Public Works Departments often refer to "ground-mounted confirmatory route markers"—a grandiose way of saying "road signs."

Other organizations go to the other extreme and use **euphemisms**, words that minimize something's genuine gravity or importance. Hospital officials, for instance, sometimes call deaths resulting from staff negligence "unanticipated therapeutic misadventures." When revising, check that you haven't used words that exaggerate or downplay something's significance.

Select Words with Appropriate Connotations

The dictionary meaning of a word is its **denotation**. The word *motorcycle,* for example, is defined as "a two- or three-wheeled vehicle propelled by an internal-combustion engine that resembles a bicycle, but is usually larger and heavier, and often has two saddles." Yet how many of us think of a motorcycle in these terms? Certainly, there is more to a word than its denotation. A word also comes surrounded by **connotations**—associated sensations, emotions, images, and ideas. For some, the word *motorcycle* probably calls to mind danger and noise. For motorcyclists themselves, the word most likely summons pleasant memories of high-speed movement through the open air.

Given the wide range of responses that any one word can elicit, you need to be sensitive to each word's shades of meaning so you can judge when to use it rather than some other word. Examine the following word series to get a better feel for the subtle but often critical differences between similar words:

contribution, donation, handout

quiet, reserved, closemouthed

Notice the extent to which words' connotations create different impressions in these two examples:

The young woman emerged from the interview, her face *aglow*. Moving *briskly* to the coat rack, she *tossed* her raincoat over one arm. After a *carefree* "Thank you" to the receptionist, she *glided* from the room.

The young woman emerged from the interview, her face *aflame*. Moving *hurriedly* to the coat rack, she *flung* her raincoat over one arm. After a *perfunctory* "Thank you" to the receptionist, she *bolted* from the room.

In the first paragraph, the words *aglow, carefree,* and *glided* have positive connotations, so the reader surmises that the interview was a success. In contrast, the second paragraph contains words loaded with negative connotations: *aflame, perfunctory,* and *bolted*. Reading this paragraph, the reader assumes something went awry.

A print or online thesaurus can help you select words with the right connotations. Just look up any word with which you aren't satisfied, and you'll find a list of synonyms. To be safe, stay away from unfamiliar words. Choose only those words whose nuances you understand.

Use Specific Rather Than General Words

Besides carrying the right connotations, words should be **specific** rather than general. That is, they must avoid vagueness and ambiguity by referring to *particular* people, animals, events, objects, and phenomena. If they don't, readers may misinterpret what you mean.

Besides clarifying meaning, specific words enliven writing and make it more convincing. Compare these two paragraphs:

Original

Sponsored by a charitable organization, a group of children from a nearby town visited a theme park. The kids had a great time. They went on several rides and ate a variety of foods. Reporters and a TV crew shared in the fun.

Revised

Sponsored by the United Glendale Charities, twenty-five underprivileged Glendale grade-schoolers visited the Universe of Fun Themepark. The kids had a great time. They roller-coastered through a meteor shower on the Space Probe, encountered a giant squid on the Submarine Voyage, and screamed their way past coffins and ghosts in the House of Horrors. At the International Cuisine arcade, they sampled foods ranging from Hawaiian poi to German strudel. Reporters from *The Texas Herald* and a camera crew from WGLD, the Glendale cable station, shared in the fun.

You may have noticed that the specific words in the second paragraph provide answers to "which," "how," and similar questions. In contrast, when reading the first paragraph, you probably wondered, "*Which* charitable organization? *Which* theme park? *Which* rides?" Similarly, you may have asked, "*How* large a group? *How* young were the kids?" Specific language also answers "In what way?" The revised paragraph details *in what way* the children "had a great time." They didn't just eat "a variety of foods." Rather, they "sampled foods ranging from Hawaiian poi to German strudel." So, when you revise, check to make sure that your wording doesn't leave unanswered questions like "How?," "Why?," and "In what way?" (For more on making writing specific, see pages 43–44 and 61–63.)

Use Strong Verbs

Replacing weak verbs and nouns with **strong verbs** is another way to tighten and energize language. Consider the following strategies.

Replace *To Be* and Linking Verbs with Action Verbs

Overreliance on *to be* verbs (*is, were, has been,* and so on) tends to stretch sentences, making them flat and wordy. The same is true of motionless **linking verbs** such as *appear, become, sound, feel, look,* and *seem.* Because these verbs don't communicate any action, more words are required to complete their meaning and explain what is happening. Even *to be* verb forms combined with present participles (*is laughing, were running*) are weaker than bare **action verbs** (*laughs, ran*). Similarly, linking verbs combined with adjectives (*becomes shiny, seemed offensive*) aren't as vigorous as the action verb alone (*shines, offended*). Look how much more effective a paragraph becomes when weak verbs are replaced with dynamic ones:

Original

> The waves *were* so high that the boat *was* nearly *tipping* on end. The wind *felt* rough against our faces, and the salt spray *became* so strong that we *felt* our breath *would be* cut off. Suddenly, in the air *was* the sound I had dreaded most—the snap of the rigging. I *felt* panicky.

Revised

> The waves *towered* until the boat nearly *tipped* on end. The wind *lashed* our faces, while the salt spray *clogged* our throats and *cut* off our breath. Suddenly, the sound I had dreaded most *splintered* the air—the snap of the rigging. Panic *gripped* me.

The second paragraph is not only less wordy, it's also more vivid.

When you revise, look closely at your verbs. If you find too many *to be* and linking verb forms, ask yourself, "What's happening in the sentence?" Your response will help you substitute stronger verbs that will make your writing more compelling.

Change Passive Verbs to Active Ones

To be verb forms (*is, has been*, and so on) may also be combined with a past participle (*cooked, stung*); the result is a **passive verb**. A passive verb creates a sentence structure in which the subject is *acted on* and the doer of the action appears in a prepositional phrase—or not at all. In contrast, the subject of an **active verb** *performs* the action. Consider the following active and passive forms:

Passive	**Active**
A suggestion was made by the instructor that the project plan be revised by the students.	The instructor suggested that the students revise the project plan.

Although they're not grammatically incorrect, passive verbs generally weaken writing, making it wordy and stiffly formal. Sometimes, though, it makes sense to use the passive voice. Perhaps you don't know who performed an action. ("When I returned to my car, I noticed the door had been dented.") Or you may want to emphasize an event, not the agent responsible for the event. For example, in an article about academic dishonesty on your campus, you might deliberately use the passive voice: "Every semester, research papers are plagiarized and lab reports falsified."

Unfortunately, corporations, government agencies, and other institutions often use the passive voice to avoid taking responsibility for controversial actions. Notice how easily the passive conceals the agent: "The rabbits were injected with a cancer-causing chemical."

Because the passive voice *is* associated with "official" writing, you may think it sounds scholarly and impressive. It doesn't. Unless you have good reason for deemphasizing the agent, change passive verbs to active ones.

Replace Weak Verb-Noun Combinations

Just as *to be*, linking, and passive verbs tend to lengthen sentences needlessly, so do weak verb-noun combinations. Whenever possible, replace such combinations with their strong verb counterparts. Change "made an estimate" to "estimated," "gave approval" to "approved." Notice how revision tightens these sentences, making them livelier and less pretentious:

Original	They *were* of the *belief* that the report was due next week.
Revised	They *believed* the report was due next week.

Delete Unnecessary Adverbs

Strong verbs can further tighten your writing by ridding it of unnecessary adverbs. "She *strolled* down the path" conveys the same message as "She *walked slowly* and *leisurely* down the path"—but more economically.

Adverbs such as *extremely*, *really*, and *very* usually weaken writing. Although they are called "intensifiers," they make writing less, not more, intense. Notice that the following sentence reads more emphatically *without* the intensifier:

Original   Although the professor's lectures are controversial, no one denies that they are *really* brilliant.

Revised   Although the professor's lectures are controversial, no one denies that they are brilliant.

"Qualifiers" such as *quite*, *rather*, and *somewhat* also tend to weaken writing. When you spot one, try to delete it:

Original   When planning a summer trip to the mountains, remember to pack warm clothes; it turns *quite* cool at night.

Revised   When planning a summer trip to the mountains, remember to pack warm clothes; it turns cool at night.

Use Original Figures of Speech

Another strategy for adding vitality to your writing is to create imaginative, non-literal comparisons, called **figures of speech**. For example, you might describe midsummer humidity this way: "Going from an air-conditioned building to the street is like being hit in the face with peanut butter." Notice that the comparison yokes essentially dissimilar things (humidity and peanut butter). Such unexpected connections surprise readers and help keep their interest.

Figures of speech also tighten writing. Because they create sharp images in the reader's mind, you don't need many words to convey as much information. If someone writes, "My teenage years were like a perpetual root canal," the reader immediately knows how painful and never-ending the author found adolescence.

Similes, Metaphors, Personification

Figures of speech come in several varieties. A **simile** is a direct comparison of two unlike things using the words *like* or *as*: "The moon brightened the yard *like* a floodlight." In a **metaphor**, the comparison is implied rather than directly stated: "The girl's *barbed-wire hair* set off *electric shocks* in her parents." In **personification**, an inanimate object is given human characteristics: "The couple robbed the store without noticing a silent, hidden eyewitness who later would tell all—a video camera." (For more on figures of speech, see pages 130–131.)

Avoid Clichés

Trite and overused, some figures of speech signal a lack of imagination: *a tough nut to crack, cool as a cucumber, green with envy.* Such expressions, called **clichés**, are so predictable that you can hear the first few words (*Life is a bowl of…*) and fill in the rest (*cherries*). Clichés lull writer and reader alike into passivity because they encourage rote, habitual thinking.

When revising, either eliminate tired figures of speech or give them an unexpected twist. For example, seeking a humorous effect, you might write, "Beneath his rough exterior beat a heart of lead" (instead of "gold"); rather than, "Last but not least," you might write, "Last but also least."

Two Other Cautions

First, if you include figures of speech, *don't pile one on top of another,* as in the following sentence:

> Whenever the dorm residents prepared for the first party of the season, hairdryers howled like a windstorm, hairspray rained down in torrents, stereos vibrated like an earthquake, and shouts of excitement shook the walls like an avalanche.

Second, guard against *illogical* or *mixed* figures of speech. In the following example, note the ludicrous and contradictory comparisons:

> They rode the roller coaster of high finance, dodging bullets and avoiding ambushes from those trying to lasso their streak of good luck.

To detect outlandish comparisons, visualize each figure of speech. If it calls up some unintentionally humorous or impossible image, revise or eliminate it.

Avoid Sexist Language

Sexist language gives the impression that one gender is more important, powerful, or valuable than the other. **Gender-neutral** or **nonsexist** terms convey no sexual prejudice.

Sexist Vocabulary

Using nonsexist vocabulary means staying away from terms that demean or exclude one of the sexes. Such slang words as *stud, jock, chick,* and *fox* portray people as one-dimensional. Just as adult males should be called *men,* adult females should be referred to as *women,* not *girls.* In addition, consider replacing *Mrs.* and *Miss* with *Ms.;* like *Mr., Ms.* doesn't indicate marital status.

Be alert as well to the fact that words not inherently sexist can become so in certain contexts. Asking "What does the *man* in the street think of the teachers' strike?" excludes the possibility of asking women for their reactions.

Because language in our culture tends to exclude women rather than men, we list here a number of common words that exclude women. When you write (or speak), make an effort to use the more inclusive alternatives given.

Sexist	Nonsexist
the average guy	the average person
chairman	chairperson, chair
congressman	congressional representative
fireman	fire fighter
foreman	supervisor
layman	layperson
mailman	mail carrier, letter carrier
mankind, man	people, humans, human beings
policeman	police officer
salesman	salesperson

Also, be on the lookout for phrases that suggest a given profession or talent is unusual for someone of a particular sex: *woman judge, woman doctor, male secretary, male nurse.*

Sexist Pronoun Use

Indefinite singular nouns—representing one person in a general group of people consisting of both genders—can lead to **sexist pronoun use**: "On *his* first day of school, a young child often experiences separation anxiety," or " Each professor should be responsible for monitoring *her* own students' progress" are sexist because the language excludes one gender.

Indefinite pronouns such as *anyone, each,* and *everybody* may also pave the way to sexist language. Although such pronouns often refer to a number of individuals, they are considered singular. So, wanting to be grammatically correct, you may write a sentence like the following: "Everybody wants *his* favorite candidate to win." The sentence, however, is sexist because *everybody* is certainly not restricted to men. But writing "Everybody wants *her* candidate to win" is equally sexist because now males aren't included.

Here's one way to avoid these kinds of sexist constructions: Use *both* male and female pronouns, instead of just one or the other. For example, you could write "On *his or her* first day of school, a young child often experiences separation anxiety," or "Everybody wants *his or her* favorite candidate to win." If you use both pronouns, you might try to vary their order; that is, alternate *his or her* with *her or his,* and so on. Another approach is to use the gender-neutral pronouns *they, their,* or *themselves:* "Everybody wants *their* favorite candidate to win." Be warned, though. Some people object to using these plural pronouns with singular indefinite pronouns, even though the practice is common in everyday speech. To be on the safe side, ask your instructors if they object to any of the approaches described here. If not, feel free to choose whichever nonsexist construction seems most graceful and least obtrusive.

If you're still unhappy with the result, two alternative strategies enable you to eliminate the need for *any* gender-marked singular pronouns. First, you can change singular general nouns or indefinite pronouns to their plural equivalents and then use nonsexist plural pronouns:

Original   A *workaholic* feels anxious when *he* isn't involved in a task-related project.

Revised   *Workaholics* feel anxious when *they're* not involved in task-related projects.

Second, you can recast the sentence to omit the singular pronoun:

Original   A *manager* usually spends part of each day settling squabbles among *his* staff.

Revised   A manager usually spends part of each day settling *staff squabbles.*

The following checklist is designed to help you and your readers evaluate the words in a draft. (Activities at the end of the chapter will refer you to this checklist when you revise several essays.) To see how one student, Harriet Davids, used the checklist when revising, turn to page 112.

☑ REVISING WORDS: A CHECKLIST

☐ Which words seem inconsistent with the essay's tone? What words would be more appropriate?

☐ Which words seem vague and overly general? Where would more specific and concrete words add vitality and clarify meaning?

☐ Where is language overly formal? Which words are unnecessarily long or specialized? Where is language too informal? Where do unintended shifts in diction level create a jarring effect?

☐ Which words overstate? Which understate? What alternatives would be less misleading?

☐ Which words carry connotations unsuited to the essay's purpose and tone? What synonyms would be more appropriate?

☐ Where could weak verbs be replaced by vigorous ones? Which *to be* and linking verb forms should be changed to action verbs? Which passive verbs could be replaced by active ones? Where could a noun-verb combination be replaced by a strong verb?

☐ Which adverbs, especially intensifiers (*very*) and qualifiers (*quite*), could be eliminated?

☐ Where would original similes, metaphors, and personifications add power? Which figures of speech are hackneyed, illogical, or mixed? How could these problems be fixed?

☐ Where does sexist language appear? What terms could be used instead? How could sexist pronouns be eliminated?

Sample Student Revision of Sentences and Words

Reprinted here is the introduction to Harriet Davids's first draft—as it looked after she entered on a word processor the changes she made in overall meaning, structure, and paragraph development (see page 87). To help identify problems with words and sentences, Harriet asked someone in her editing group to read the revised version aloud. Then she asked the group to comment on her paper, using the checklists on pages 102 and 111. The marginal notes indicate her ranking of the group's comments in order of importance. The above-line changes show how Harriet revised in response to these suggestions for improving the paragraph's sentences and words.

Combine into one
sentence idea of
'50s/'60s parents
and TV shows

Make each family's
problems a sepa-
rate sentence

Use stronger verbs
(not "telling")

Make "dangerous
situations" more
specific

                                        Reruns of   *from the '50s and '60s dramatize*
~~In the 50s and 60s, parents had it easy,~~ TV comedies ~~of that period show~~ the Cleavers
the kinds of problems that parents used to have.   *dock*   *'s allowance because he*
scolding Beaver about his dirty hands, the Nelsons ~~telling~~ Ricky to clean his room. Being
forgets   *than it was a generation ago.*
a parent today is much more difficult. Nowadays parents must protect their children from

many things—from a growing number of distractions, from sexually explicit material, and from
life-threatening
~~dangerous~~ situations.

Once you, like Harriet, have carefully revised sentences and words, your essay needs only to be edited (for errors in grammar, punctuation, and spelling) and proofread. In the next chapter, you'll read about these final steps. You'll also see a student essay that has gone through all phases of the writing process.

Continues
on page 119

ACTIVITIES: REVISING SENTENCES AND WORDS

1. Revise the following sentences, making them economical and clear.

   a. What a person should do before subletting a rental apartment is make sure to have the sublet agreement written up in a formal contract.

   b. In high school, it often happens that young people deny liking poetry because of the fact that they fear running the risk of having people mock or make fun of them because they actually enjoy poetry.

   c. In light of the fact that college students are rare in my home neighborhood, being a college student gives me immediate and instant status.

    d. There were a number of people who have made the observation that the new wing of the library looks similar in appearance to several nearby buildings with considerable historical significance.

2. Using only simple or simple and compound sentences, write a paragraph based on one of the following topic sentences. Then rewrite the paragraph, making some of the sentences complex and others compound-complex. Examine your two versions of the paragraph. What differences do you see in meaning and emphasis?

    a. The campus parking lot is dangerous at night.

    b. Silent body language speaks loudly.

    c. Getting on a teacher's good side is an easily mastered skill.

3. The following sentences could be more emphatic. Examine each one to determine its focus; then revise the sentence, using one of the following strategies: placing the most important item first or last, parallelism, inverted word order, a fragment. Try to use a different strategy in each sentence.

    a. Most of us find rude salespeople difficult to deal with.

    b. The politician promises, "I'll solve all your problems."

    c. We meet female stereotypes such as the gold digger, the dangerous vixen, and the "girl next door" in the movies.

    d. It's a wise teacher who encourages discussion of controversial issues in the classroom.

4. The following paragraph is pretentious and murky. Revise to make it crisp and clear.

> Since its founding, the student senate on this campus has maintained essentially one goal: to upgrade the quality of its student-related services. Two years ago, the senate, supported by the opinions of three consultants provided by the National Council of Student Governing Boards, was confident it was operating from a base of quality but felt that, if given additional monetary support from the administration, a significant improvement in student services would be facilitated. This was a valid prediction, for that is exactly what transpired in the past fifteen months once additional monetary resources were, in fact, allocated by the administration to the senate and its activities.

5. Write a sentence for each word in the series that follows, making sure your details reinforce each word's connotations:

    a. chubby, voluptuous, portly

    b. stroll, trudge, loiter

    c. turmoil, anarchy, hubbub

6. Write three versions of a brief letter voicing a complaint to a store, a person, or an organization. One version should be charged with negative connotations;

another should "soft pedal" the problem. The final version should present your complaint using neutral, objective words. Which letter do you prefer? Why?

7. Describe each of the following in one or two sentences, using a creative figure of speech to convey each item's distinctive quality:

   a. a baby's hand
   b. a pile of dead leaves
   c. an empty room
   d. an old car

8. Enliven the following dull, vague sentences. Use your knowledge of sentence structure to dramatize key elements. Also, replace weak verbs with vigorous ones and make language more specific.

   a. I got sick on the holiday.
   b. He stopped the car at the crowded intersection.
   c. The class grew restless.
   d. The TV broadcaster put on a concerned air as she announced the tragedy.

9. The following paragraph contains too many linking verbs, passives, adverbs, and prepositions. In addition, noun forms are sometimes used where their verb counterparts would be more effective. Revise the paragraph by eliminating unnecessary prepositions and providing more vigorous verbs. Then add specific, concrete words that dramatize what is being described.

   The farmers in the area conducted a meeting during which they formulated a discussion of the vandalism problem in the county in which they live. They made the estimate that, on the average, each of them had at least an acre of crops destroyed the past few weekends by gangs of motorcyclists who have been driving maliciously over their land. The increase in such vandalism has been caused by the encroachment of the suburbs on rural areas.

10. Revise the following sentences to eliminate sexist language.

    a. The manager of a convenience store has to guard his cash register carefully.
    b. When I broke my arm in a car accident, a male nurse, aided by a physician's assistant, treated my injury.
    c. All of us should contact our congressman if we're not satisfied with his performance.
    d. The chemistry professors agree that nobody should have to buy her own Bunsen burner.

An important note: When revising essay drafts in activities 11 and 12, don't worry too much about grammar, punctuation, and spelling. However, do save your revisions, so you can focus on these matters after reading the next chapter.

11. In response to activity 1 in Chapter 7 (pages 87–88), you revised the overall meaning, structure, and paragraph development of Harriet Davids's first draft. Find that revision so that you can now focus on its sentences and words. Get together with at least one other person and ask yourselves questions like these: "Where should sentence type, length, or pattern be more varied?" and "Where would more specific and concrete words add vitality and clarify meaning?" For further guidance, refer to the checklists on pages 102 and 111. Summarize and rank any perceived problems in marginal annotations or a feedback chart. Then type your changes into a word processor or enter them between the lines of the draft. (Save your revision so you can edit and proofread it after reading the next chapter.)

12. Return to the draft you prepared in response to activity 2, 3, or activity 4 in Chapter 7 (pages 88–89). Get together with several people and request that one of them read the draft aloud. Then, using the checklists on pages 102 and 111, ask the group members focused questions about any sentences and words that you feel need sharpening. After evaluating the feedback, revise the draft. Either key your changes into a computer or do your revising by hand. (Save your revision so you can edit and proofread it after reading the next chapter.)

9

Editing and Proofreading

In this chapter, you will learn:

9.1 To edit your paper
9.2 To use the correct format for your paper
9.3 To proofread your paper

Wanting to finally finish a writing assignment is a normal human response. But if you don't edit and proofread—that is, closely check your writing for grammar, spelling, and typographical errors—you run the risk of sabotaging your previous efforts. Readers may assume that a piece of writing isn't worth their time if they're jolted by surface flaws that make it difficult to read. So, to make sure that your good ideas get a fair hearing (and as detailed in Figure 9.1 on page 117), you should do the following.

Edit Carefully

When revising the paper, you probably spotted some errors in grammar, punctuation, or spelling, perhaps flagging them for later correction. Now—after you're satisfied with the essay's organization, development, and style—it's time to return to these errors. It's also time to search for and correct errors that have slipped by you so far.

If you're working with pen and paper or on a printed draft with handwritten annotations, use a different color ink, so your new corrections will stand out. If you

FIGURE 9.1

Process Diagram: Editing and Proofreading

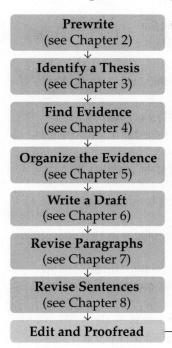

- Use the computer spell-check program to identify and correct misspelled words.
- Read the screen slowly, looking for wrong words, errors in proper names, and errors in grammar.
- Format the essay according to your instructor's guidelines.
- Print a clean copy of your essay.
- Proofread slowly to correct typos and other mistakes.
- Use proofreader's marks to make corrections.
- Correct the errors, print a clean copy, and hand it in.

use a computer, search for errors both on the screen and on a printout. Use spell check; your search for misspellings will be greatly simplified. Be aware, however, that such programs may not find errors in the spelling of proper nouns, and that they won't flag errors that constitute legitimate words (for example, *he* when you meant *the*, or *their* when you meant *there*).

To be a successful editor of your own work, you need two standard tools: a grammar handbook and a good dictionary. Use a handbook to correct any errors in grammar, style, and punctuation; use a dictionary to check your spelling.

Use the Appropriate Manuscript Format

After correcting all grammar and spelling problems, you're ready to produce the final copy. In doing so, you should follow accepted academic practice, adapted to your instructor's requirements. Most instructors will require that you type your papers. Even if this isn't the case, computer-printed papers look neater, are easier to grade, and show that you have made the transition to college-level format.

The checklist on manuscript format (see page 118) describes the basic rules for college essays. In addition, check for any specific format preferences your instructor may have.

✔ MANUSCRIPT FORMAT: A CHECKLIST

- ☐ Use standard-sized (8½; by 11 inches), white printer paper.
- ☐ Use a standard font, such as Times Roman or Courier, 12-point size.
- ☐ Use only black ink for text. Print illustrations in color if possible.
- ☐ Leave one-inch margins at the top, bottom, left, and right.
- ☐ Double-space all text, including extracts, notes, bibliographies, and Works Cited and References lists.
- ☐ Follow the citation style (for example, MLA or APA) required by your instructor.
- ☐ Use the computer's page-numbering feature to add a header, one-half inch from the top of the sheet.
- ☐ If you include a title page, place the title about one-third of the way down the page. Enter the title, and double-space between lines of the title and your name. Give the course and section, instructor's name, and date on separate lines, double-spaced and centered.
- ☐ If you don't include a title page, use a standard heading, as specified by your instructor, at the top of the first page.
- ☐ Center the title of your paper one double-space below the heading. Capitalize only the first letter of all main words. Don't use all caps, underlining, quotation marks, or bold type. Double-space a title having more than one line.
- ☐ Double-space between the title and the first paragraph of your essay.
- ☐ Indent the first line of each paragraph one-half inch, the default setting for most word-processing software.
- ☐ Place any illustrations as close as possible to their mention in the text. Position a caption below the illustration.
- ☐ Print on only one side of each sheet of paper.
- ☐ Paper-clip or staple the pages, placing the outline wherever your instructor requests.
- ☐ Don't use a report cover unless your instructor requests one.
- ☐ If you are sending the essay by e-mail, follow your instructor's directions for naming the file.
- ☐ Keep a backup copy of the essay on a disc or external hard drive.

Proofread Closely

Proofreading means checking your final copy carefully for "typos" or other mistakes. One trick is to read your material backward, sentence by sentence or word by word: If you read from the end of each paragraph to the beginning, you can focus on each word individually to make sure no letters have been left out or transposed. This technique prevents you from getting caught up in the flow of ideas and missing small defects, which is easy to do when you've read your own words many times.

What should you do when you find a typo? Working from a print copy of your essay, simply use a pen with dark ink to make an above-line correction. The following standard proofreader's marks will help you indicate some common types of corrections:

Proofreader's Mark	Meaning	Example
∧	insert missing letter or word	telev_ision
ℓ	delete	reports the the findings
∼	reverse order	the gang's here all
¶	start new paragraph	to dry. Next, put
#	add space	thegirls
⊂	close up space	boy cott

If you make so many corrections on a page that it begins to look like a draft, make the corrections and reprint the page for fresh review.

Student Essay: From Prewriting through Proofreading

In the last several chapters, we've taken you through the various stages in the writing process—from prewriting to proofreading. You've seen how Harriet Davids used prewriting (pages 15–28) and outlining (pages 29–31) to arrive at her thesis (page 38) and her first draft (pages 73–74). You also saw how Harriet's peer reviewer, Frank Tejada, critiqued her first draft (page 82). You then observed how Harriet revised, first, her draft's overall meaning and paragraph development (page 87) and, second, its sentences and words (page 112). In the following pages, you'll look at Harriet's final draft—the paper she submitted to her instructor after completing all the stages of the writing process.

This is the assignment that prompted Harriet's essay:

Goodman implies that, in some ways, today's world is hostile to children. Do you agree? Drawing upon but not limiting yourself to the material in your pre-reading journal, write an essay in which you support or reject this viewpoint.

Harriet's essay is annotated so you can see how it illustrates the essay format shown in Figure 6.2 on page 72. As you read the essay, try to determine how well it reflects the principles of effective writing. The commentary following the paper will help you look at the essay more closely and give you some sense of the way Harriet went about revising her first draft.

Harriet Davids

Professor Kinne

College Composition, Section 203

4 October 2013

Challenges for Today's Parents

Introduction   Reruns of situation comedies from the 1950s and early 1960s dramatize the kinds of 1

problems that parents used to have with their children. On classic television shows

such as *Leave It to Beaver*, the Cleavers scold their son Beaver for not washing his

hands before dinner; on *Ozzie* and *Harriet*, the Nelsons dock little Ricky's allowance

because he keeps forgetting to clean his room. But times have changed dramati-

Thesis — cally. Being a parent today is much more difficult than it was a generation ago.

Plan of — Parents nowadays must protect their children from a growing number of distrac-

Development tions, from sexually explicit material, and from life-threatening situations.

First supporting   Today's parents must try, first of all, to control all the new distractions that tempt 2

paragraph children away from schoolwork. At home, a child may have a room furnished with an

MP3 player, television, and computer. Not many young people can resist the urge to

Topic sentence — listen to music, watch TV, go online or play computer games and IM their friends—

especially if it's time to do schoolwork. Outside the home, the distractions are even

more alluring. Children no longer "hang out" on a neighborhood corner within earshot

of Mom or Dad's reminder to come in and do homework. Instead, they congregate in

vast shopping malls, movie theaters, and gleaming fast-food restaurants. Parents and

school assignments have obvious difficulty competing with such enticing alternatives.

Second   Besides dealing with these distractions, parents have to shield their children from 3

supporting a flood of sexually explicit materials. Today, children can find pornographic Web sites and

paragraph chat rooms on the Internet with relative ease. With the click of a mouse, they can be trans-

ported, intentionally or unintentionally, to a barrage of explicit images and conversations.

Topic sentence Easily obtainable copies of sex magazines can be found at most convenience stores, many

with link to times alongside the candy. Children will not see the fuzzily photographed nudes that a pre-

previous paragraph vious generation did but will encounter the hard-core raunchiness of *Playboy* or *Penthouse*.

Moreover, the movies young people view often focus on highly sexual situations. It is dif-

ficult to teach children traditional values when films show young people treating sex as a

casual sport. Unfortunately, television, with its often heavily sexual content, is no better.

With just a flick of the channel, children can see sexed-up music videos, watch reality-TV stars cavorting in bed, or watch cable programs where nudity is common.

4   Most disturbing to parents today, however, is the increase in life-threatening dangers that face young people. When children are small, parents fear that their youngsters may be victims of violence. Every news program seems to carry a report about a school shooting or child predator who has been released from prison, only to repeat an act of violence against a minor. When children are older, parents begin to worry about their kids' use of drugs. Peer pressure to experiment with drugs is often stronger than parents' warnings. This pressure to experiment can be fatal. Finally, even if young people escape the hazards associated with drugs, they must still resist the pressure to drink. Although alcohol has always held an attraction for teenagers, reports indicate that they are drinking more than ever before. As many parents know, the consequences of this attraction can be deadly—especially when drinking is combined with driving.

Third supporting paragraph

Topic sentence with emphasis signal

5   Within a generation, the world as a place to raise children has changed dramatically. One wonders how yesterday's parents would have dealt with today's problems. Could the Nelsons have shielded little Ricky from sexually explicit material on the Internet? Could the Cleavers have protected Beaver from drugs and alcohol? Parents must be aware of all these distractions and dangers yet be willing to give their children the freedom they need to become responsible adults. This is not an easy task.

Conclusion

References to TV shows recall introduction

Commentary

Introduction and Thesis

The opening paragraph attracts readers' interest by recalling some vintage television shows that have almost become part of our cultural heritage. Harriet begins with these examples from the past because they offer such a sharp contrast to the present, thus underscoring the idea expressed in her *thesis:* "Being a parent today is much more difficult than it was a generation ago." Opening in this way, with material that serves as a striking contrast to what follows, is a common and effective strategy. Note, too, that Harriet's thesis states the paper's subject (being a parent) as well as her attitude toward the subject (the job is more demanding than it was years ago).

Plan of Development

Harriet follows her thesis with a *plan of development* that anticipates the three major points to be covered in the essay's supporting paragraphs. When revising her first draft, Harriet followed peer reviewer Frank Tejada's recommendation (page 82) to put her thesis and plan of development in separate sentences. Unfortunately, though, her plan of development ends up being somewhat mechanical, with the major points being trotted past the reader in one long, awkward sentence. To deal with the problem, Harriet could have rewritten the sentence or eliminated the plan of development altogether, ending the introduction with her thesis.

Patterns of Development

Although Harriet develops her thesis primarily through *examples*, she also draws on two other patterns of development. The whole paper implies a *contrast* between the way life and parenting are now and the way they used to be. The essay also contains an element of *causal analysis* because all the factors that Harriet cites affect children and the way they are raised.

Purpose, Audience, Tone, and Point of View

Given the essay's *purpose* and *audience*, Harriet adopts a serious *tone*, providing no-nonsense evidence to support her thesis. Note, too, that she uses the *third-person point of view*. Although she writes from the perspective of a mother of two teenage daughters, she doesn't write in the first person or refer specifically to her own experiences and those of her daughters. You may recall that Frank flagged Harriet's unsustained reference to her children (page 82). In the final draft, Harriet follows his advice and omits mention of her kids. Instead, she adopts an objective stance because she wants to keep the focus on the issue rather than on her family.

Organization

Structuring the essay around a series of *relevant* and *specific examples*, Harriet uses *emphatic order* to sequence the paper's three main points: that a growing number of distractions, sexually explicit materials, and life-threatening situations make parenting difficult today. The third supporting paragraph begins with the words, "Most disturbing to parents today...," signaling that Harriet feels particular concern about the physical dangers children face. Moreover, she uses basic organizational strategies to sequence the supporting examples within each paragraph. The details in the first supporting paragraph are organized *spatially*, starting with distractions at home and moving to those outside the home. The second supporting paragraph arranges examples *emphatically*. Harriet starts with sexually explicit materials that can be found on the Internet and ends with the "heavily sexual content" on TV. Note that Harriet follows Frank's peer review advice (page 82) about omitting her first-draft observation that kids don't get enough homework—or that they get too much busy work. The third and final supporting paragraph is organized *chronologically*; it begins by discussing dangers to small children and concludes by talking about teenagers. Again, Frank's advice—to use a clearer time sequence in this paragraph (page 82)—was invaluable when Harriet was revising.

The essay also displays Harriet's familiarity with other kinds of organizational strategies. Each supporting paragraph opens with a *topic sentence*. Further, *signal devices* are used throughout the paper to show the relationship among ideas: *transitions* ("*Instead,* they congregate in vast shopping malls"; "*Moreover,* the movies young people attend often focus on highly sexual situations"); *repetition* ("*sexual* situations" and "*sexual* content"); *synonyms* ("distractions...enticing alternatives" and "life-threatening...fatal"); *pronouns* ("young people...*they*"); and *bridging sentences* ("Besides dealing with these distractions, parents have to shield their children from a flood of sexually explicit materials").

Two Minor Problems

Harriet's efforts to write a well-organized essay result in a somewhat predictable structure. It might have been better had she rewritten one of the paragraphs, perhaps embedding the topic sentence in the middle of the paragraph or saving it for the end. Similarly, Harriet's signal devices are a little heavy-handed. Even so, an essay with a sharp focus and clear signals is preferable to one with a confusing or inaccessible structure. As she gains more experience, Harriet can work on making the structure of her essays more subtle.

Conclusion

Harriet brings the essay to a satisfying *close* by reminding readers of the paper's central idea and three main points. The final paragraph also extends the essay's scope by introducing a new but related issue: that parents have to strike a balance between their need to provide limitations and their children's need for freedom.

Revising the First Draft

As you saw on pages 87 and 112, Harriet reworked her essay a number of times. For a clearer sense of her revision process, compare the final version of her conclusion (on page 121) with the original version reprinted here. Harriet wisely waited to rework her conclusion until after she had fine-tuned the rest of the essay. The marginal annotations, ranked in order of importance, indicate the problems that Harriet and her editing group detected in the conclusion.

Original Conclusion

Most adults love their children and want to be good parents. But it's difficult because the world seems stacked against young people. Even Holden Caulfield had trouble dealing with society's pressures. Parents must give their children some freedom but not so much that kids lose sight of what's important.

① Paragraph seems tacked on

③ Boring sentence—too vague

② Inappropriate reference to Holden

    As soon as Harriet heard her paper read aloud during a group session, she realized her conclusion didn't work at all. Rather than bringing the essay to a pleasing finish, the final paragraph seemed like a tired afterthought. Frank, her peer reviewer, also pointed out that her allusion to *The Catcher in the Rye* misrepresented the essay's focus because Harriet discusses children of all ages, not just teens.

    Keeping these points in mind, Harriet decided to scrap her original conclusion. Working at a computer, she prepared a new, much stronger concluding paragraph. Besides eliminating the distracting reference to Holden Caulfield, she replaced the shopworn opening sentence ("Most adults love their children...") with two interesting and rhythmical questions ("Could the Nelsons...? Could the Cleavers...?"). Because these questions recall the essay's main points and echo the introduction's reference to vintage television shows, they help unify Harriet's paper and bring it to a rounded close.

These are just a few of the changes Harriet made when reworking her essay. Realizing that writing is a process, she left herself enough time to revise—and to carefully consider Frank Tejada's comments. Early in her composition course, Harriet learned that attention to the various stages in the writing process yields satisfying results, for writer and reader alike.

 ## ACTIVITIES: EDITING AND PROOFREADING

1. Applying for a job, a student wrote the following letter. Edit and proofread it carefully, as if it were your own. If you have trouble spotting many grammar, spelling, and typing errors, that's a sign you need to review the appropriate sections of a grammar handbook.

Dear Mr. Eno:

I am a sophomore at Harper College who will be returning home to Brooktown this June, hopefully, to fine a job for the the summer. One that would give me further experience in the retail field. I have heard from my freind, Sarah Snyder, that your hiring college studnets as assistant mangers, I would be greatly intrested in such a postion.

I have quite a bit of experience in retail sales. Having worked after school in a "Dress Place" shop at Mason Mall, Pennsylvania. I started their as a sales clerk, by my second year I was serving as assistant manger.

I am reliable and responsible, and truely enjoy sales work. Mary Carver, the owner of the "Dress Place," can verify my qualifications, she was my supervisor for two years.

I will be visiting Brooktown from April 25 to 30. I hope to have an oppurtunity to speak to you about possible summer jobs at that time, and will be available for interview at your convience. Thank-you for you're consideration.

Sincerley,

Joan Ackerman

Joan Ackerman

2. Retrieve the revised essay you prepared in response to either activity 11 or activity 12 in Chapter 8 (page 115). Following the guidelines described on the preceding pages, edit and proofread your revision. After making the needed changes, prepare your final draft of the essay, using the appropriate manuscript format. Before submitting your paper to your instructor, ask someone to check it for grammar, spelling, and typographical errors that may have slipped by you.

Description

In this chapter, you will learn:

10.1 To use the pattern of description to develop your essays
10.2 To consider how description can fit your purpose and audience
10.3 To develop prewriting, writing, and revision strategies for using description in an essay
10.4 To analyze how description is used effectively in one student-written and three professionally authored selections
10.5 To write your own essays using description as a strategy

What Is Description?

All of us respond in a strong way to sensory stimulation. The sweet perfume of a candy shop takes us back to childhood, or the blank white walls of the campus infirmary remind us of long vigils at a hospital where a grandmother lay dying.

Because sensory impressions are so potent, descriptive writing has a unique power and appeal. **Description** can be defined as the expression, in vivid language, of what the five senses experience. A richly rendered description freezes a subject in time, evoking sights, smells, sounds, textures, and tastes in such a way that readers become one with the writer's world.

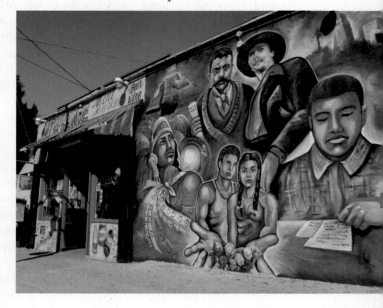

How Description Fits Your Purpose and Audience

Description can be a supportive technique that develops part of an essay, or it can be the dominant technique used throughout an essay. Here are some examples of the way description can help you meet the objective of an essay developed chiefly through another pattern of development:

- In a *causal analysis* showing the *consequences* of pet overpopulation, you might describe the desperate appearance of a pack of starving stray dogs.
- In an *argumentation-persuasion essay* urging more rigorous gun control, you might start with a description of a violent family confrontation that ended in murder.
- In a *process analysis* explaining the pleasure of making ice cream at home, you might describe the beauty of an old-fashioned, hand-cranked ice cream maker.

Each essay's overall purpose would affect the amount of description needed.

Your readers also influence how much description to include. As you write, ask yourself, "What do my particular readers need to know to understand and experience keenly what I'm describing? What descriptive details will they enjoy most?" Your answers to these and similar questions will help you tailor your description to specific readers.

Although your purpose and audience define *how much* to describe, you have great freedom deciding *what* to describe. Description is especially suited to objects (your car or desk, for example), but you can also describe a person, an animal, a place, a time, and a phenomenon or concept. You might write an effective description about a friend who runs marathons (person), the kitchen of a fast-food restaurant (place), or a period when you were unemployed (time).

Description can be divided into two types: objective and subjective. In an **objective description**, you describe the subject in a straightforward and literal way, without revealing your attitude or feelings. Reporters, as well as technical and scientific writers, specialize in objective description; their jobs depend on their ability to detail experiences without emotional bias. For example, a reporter may write an unemotional account of a township meeting that ended in a fistfight.

In contrast, when writing a **subjective description**, you convey a highly personal view of your subject and seek to elicit a strong emotional response from your readers. Such subjective descriptions often take the form of reflective pieces or character studies. For example, in an essay describing the rich plant life in an inner-city garden, you might reflect on people's longing to connect with the soil and express admiration for the gardeners' hard work—an admiration you'd like readers to share.

The *tone* of a subjective description is determined by your purpose, your attitude toward the subject, and the reader response you wish to evoke. Consider an essay about a dynamic woman who runs a center for disturbed children. If your goal is to make readers admire the woman, your tone will be serious and appreciative. But if you want to criticize the woman's high-pressure tactics and create distaste for her management style, your tone will be disapproving and severe.

The language of a descriptive piece also depends, to a great extent, on whether your purpose is primarily objective or subjective. If the description is objective, the language is straightforward, precise, and factual. Such *denotative* language consists of neutral dictionary meanings. If you want to describe as dispassionately as possible fans' violent behavior at a football game, you might write about the "large crowd" and its "mass movement onto the field." But if you are shocked by the fans' behavior and want to write a subjective piece that inspires similar outrage in readers, then you might write about the "swelling mob" and its "rowdy stampede onto the field." In the latter case, the language used would be *connotative* and emotionally charged so that readers would share your feelings. (For more on denotation and connotation, see pages 20–21 and 104–105.)

Subjective and objective descriptions often overlap. Sometimes a single sentence contains both objective and subjective elements: "Although his hands were large and misshapen by arthritis, they were gentle to the touch, inspiring confidence and trust." Other times, part of an essay may provide a factual description (the physical appearance of a summer cabin your family rented), whereas another part of the essay may be highly subjective (how you felt in the cabin, sitting in front of a fire on a rainy day).

Prewriting Strategies

The following checklist shows how you can apply to description some of the prewriting strategies discussed in Chapter 2.

☑ DESCRIPTION: A PREWRITING CHECKLIST

Choose a Subject to Describe

☐ Might a photograph, postcard, prized possession, or journal entry suggest a subject worth describing?

☐ Will you describe a person, animal, object, place, time period, or phenomenon? Is the subject readily observable, or will you have to reconstruct it from memory?

Determine Your Purpose, Audience, Tone, and Point of View

☐ Is your purpose to inform or to evoke an emotional response? If you want to do both, which is your predominant purpose?

☐ What audience are you writing for? How much does the audience already know about the subject you plan to describe?

☐ What tone and point of view will best serve your purpose and make readers receptive to your description?

Use Prewriting to Generate Details About the Subject

☐ How could freewriting, journal entries, or brainstorming help you gather sensory specifics about your subject?

☐ What relevant details about your subject come to mind when you apply the questioning technique to each of the five senses—sight, sound, taste, touch, and smell?

Strategies for Using Description in an Essay

After prewriting, you're ready to draft your essay. The suggestions in Figure 10.1 (on this page) and those that follow will be helpful whether you use description as a dominant or supportive pattern of development.

1. **Focus a descriptive essay around a dominant impression.** Like other kinds of writing, a descriptive essay must have a thesis, or main point. In a descriptive essay with a subjective slant, the thesis usually centers on the **dominant impression** you want to convey about your subject.

FIGURE 10.1
Development Diagram: Writing a Description Essay

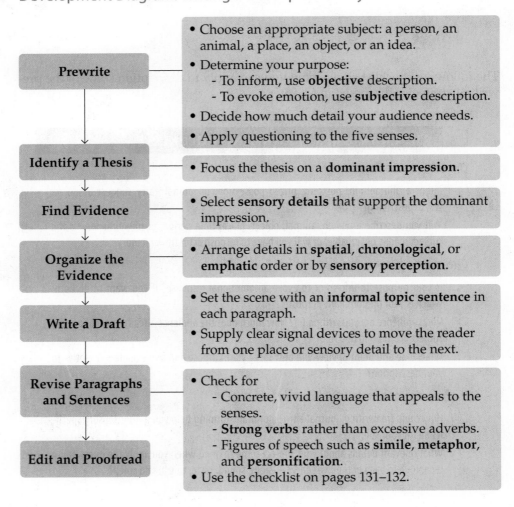

Prewrite	• Choose an appropriate subject: a person, an animal, a place, an object, or an idea.
	• Determine your purpose:
	  - To inform, use **objective** description.
	  - To evoke emotion, use **subjective** description.
	• Decide how much detail your audience needs.
	• Apply questioning to the five senses.

Identify a Thesis	• Focus the thesis on a **dominant impression**.
Find Evidence	• Select **sensory details** that support the dominant impression.
Organize the Evidence	• Arrange details in **spatial**, **chronological**, or **emphatic** order or by **sensory perception**.
Write a Draft	• Set the scene with an **informal topic sentence** in each paragraph. • Supply clear signal devices to move the reader from one place or sensory detail to the next.

Revise Paragraphs and Sentences	• Check for
	  - Concrete, vivid language that appeals to the senses.
	  - **Strong verbs** rather than excessive adverbs.
	  - Figures of speech such as **simile**, **metaphor**, and **personification**.

Edit and Proofread	• Use the checklist on pages 131–132.

2. **Select the details to include.** The prewriting techniques discussed on pages 22–28 can help you develop heightened powers of observation and recall. The power of description hinges on your ability to select from all possible details *only those that support the dominant impression*. All others—no matter how vivid or interesting—must be left out. If you were describing how flamboyant your ninth-grade teacher could be, the details in the following paragraph would be appropriate:

> A large-boned woman, Ms. Hazzard wore her bright red hair piled on top of her head, where it perched precariously. By the end of class, wayward strands of hair tumbled down and fell into eyes fringed by spiky false eyelashes. Ms. Hazzard's nails, filed into crisp points, were painted either bloody burgundy or neon pink. Plastic bangle bracelets, also either burgundy or pink, clattered up and down her ample arms as she scrawled on the board the historical dates that had, she claimed, "changed the world."

Such details—the heavy eye makeup, stiletto nails, gaudy bracelets—contribute to the impression of a flamboyant, unusual person. Even if you remembered times that Ms. Hazzard seemed perfectly conventional and understated, most likely you wouldn't describe those times because they would contradict the dominant impression.

You must also be selective in the *number of details* you include. Excessive detailing dilutes the essay's focus. You end up with a seemingly endless list of specifics, rather than with a carefully crafted word picture. Having a dominant impression helps you eliminate many details gathered during prewriting.

3. **Organize the descriptive details.** It's important to select the organizational pattern (or combination of patterns) that best supports your dominant impression. You might, for instance, use a *spatial* pattern to organize a description of a large city as you viewed it from the air, a taxi, or a subway car. A description of your first day on a new job might move *chronologically*, starting with how you felt the first hour on the job and proceeding through the rest of the day. In a paper describing a bout with the flu, you might arrange details *emphatically*, beginning with a description of your low-level aches and pains and concluding with an account of your raging fever. An essay about a neighborhood garbage dump could be organized by *sensory impressions:* the sights of the dump, its smells, its sounds. Regardless of the organizational pattern you use, provide enough *signal devices* (for example, *about, next, worst of all*) so that readers can follow the description easily.

Finally, although descriptive essays don't always have conventional topic sentences, each descriptive paragraph should have a clear focus. Often this focus is indicated by a sentence early in the paragraph that names the scene, object, or individual to be described. Such a sentence functions as a kind of *informal topic sentence;* the paragraph's descriptive details then develop that topic sentence.

4. **Use vivid sensory language and varied sentence structure.** The connotative language typical of subjective description should etch in readers' minds the same picture that you have in yours. Use language that involves readers' senses. Consider the difference between the following paired descriptions:

Vague	Vivid
The food was unappetizing.	The stew congealed into an oval pool of muddy brown fat.
The lemonade was refreshing.	As I gulped the icy lemonade, its sweet tartness tingled my tongue.

Although all good writing blends abstract and concrete language, descriptive writing demands an abundance of specific sensory language. (For more on specific language, see pages 105–106 in Chapter 8.)

Although you should aim for rich, sensory images, avoid overloading your sentences with *too many adjectives:* "A stark, smooth, blinding glass cylinder, the fifty-story skyscraper dominated the crowded city street." Delete unnecessary words, retaining only the most powerful: "A blinding glass cylinder, the skyscraper dominated the street."

Remember, too, that *verbs pack more of a wallop* than adverbs. The following sentence has to rely on adverbs (italicized) because its verbs are so weak: "She walked *casually* into the room and *deliberately* tried not to pay attention to their stares." Rewritten, so that verbs (italicized), not adverbs, do the bulk of the work, the sentence becomes more powerful: "She *strolled* into the room and *ignored* their stares." *Onomatopoetic* verbs, like *buzz, sizzle,* and *zoom,* can be especially effective because their sounds convey their meaning. (For more on vigorous verbs, see pages 106–107 in Chapter 8.)

Figures of speech—nonliteral, imaginative comparisons between two basically dissimilar things—are another way to enliven descriptive writing. *Similes* use the word *like* or *as* when comparing; *metaphors* state or imply that the two things being compared are alike; and *personification* attributes human characteristics to inanimate things. (For further discussion of figures of speech, refer to pages 108–109 in Chapter 8.)

The examples that follow show how effective figurative language can be in descriptive writing:

Simile

Moving as jerkily as a marionette on strings, the man picked himself up off the sidewalk and staggered down the street.

Metaphor

Stalking their prey, the hall monitors remained hidden in the corridors, motionless and ready to spring on any student who tried to sneak into class late.

Personification

> The scoop of vanilla ice cream, plain and unadorned, cried out for hot fudge sauce and a sprinkling of sliced pecans.

(For suggestions on avoiding clichéd figures of speech, see page 109 in Chapter 8.)

Finally, when writing descriptive passages, you need to *vary sentence structure.* Don't use the same subject-verb pattern in all sentences. The metaphor example above, for instance, could have been written as follows: "The hall monitors stalked their prey. They hid in the corridors. They remained motionless and ready to spring on any student who tried to sneak into class late." But the sentence is richer and more interesting when the descriptive elements are embedded, so that a clipped and predictable subject-verb pattern is avoided. (For more on sentence variety, see pages 94–98 in Chapter 8.)

Revision Strategies

Once you have a draft of the essay, you're ready to revise. The following checklist will help you and those giving you feedback apply to description some of the revision techniques discussed in Chapters 7 and 8.

✔ DESCRIPTION: A REVISION/PEER REVIEW CHECKLIST

Revise Overall Meaning and Structure

- ☐ What dominant impression does the essay convey? Is the dominant impression stated or implied? Where? Should it be made more obvious or more subtle?
- ☐ Is the essay primarily objective or subjective? Should the essay be more personal and emotionally charged or less so?
- ☐ Which descriptive details don't support the dominant impression? Should they be deleted, or should the dominant impression be adjusted to encompass the details?

Revise Paragraph Development

- ☐ How are the essay's descriptive paragraphs (or passages) organized—spatially, chronologically, emphatically, or by sensory impressions? Would another organizational pattern be more effective? Which one(s)?
- ☐ Which paragraphs lack a distinctive focus?
- ☐ Which descriptive paragraphs are mere lists of sensory impressions?
- ☐ Which descriptive paragraphs are too abstract or general? Which fail to engage the reader's senses? How could they be made more concrete and specific?

Revise Sentences and Words

- ☐ What signal devices (such as *above, next, worst of all*) guide readers through the description? Are there enough signals? Too many?

   ☐   Where should sentence structure be varied to make it less predictable?

   ☐   Which sentences should include sensory images?

   ☐   Where should flat verbs and adverbs be replaced with vigorous ones? Where would onomatopoeia enliven a sentence?

   ☐   Where should there be more or fewer adjectives?

   ☐   Do any figures of speech seem contrived or trite? Which ones?

Student Essay: From Prewriting Through Revision

The student essay that follows was written by Marie Martinez in response to this assignment:

> The essay "El Hoyo" is an evocative piece about a place that has special meaning for Mario Suárez. Write an essay about a place that holds rich significance for you, centering the description on a dominant impression.

After deciding to write about the salt marsh near her grandparents' home, Marie used the prewriting technique of *questioning* to gather sensory details about this special place. To enhance her power of recall, she focused, one at a time, on each of the five senses. Then, typing as quickly as she could, she listed the sensory specifics that came to mind.

When Marie later reviewed the details listed under each sensory heading, she concluded that her essay's dominant impression should be the marsh's peaceful beauty. With that dominant impression in mind, she added some details to her prewriting and deleted others. Below is Marie's original prewriting; the handwritten insertions indicate her later efforts to develop the material:

Questioning Technique

See: What do I see at the marsh?

- line of tall, waving reeds *bordering the creek*
- path—flattened grass
- spring—bright green *(brilliant green)*
- autumn—gold *(tawny)*
- winter—gray
- soil—spongy
- dark soil
- birds—little, brown
- low tide—steep bank of creek
- ~~an occasional beer can or potate chip bag~~

- grass under the water—green waves, shimmers _____ *(minnows)*
- fish—tiny, with silvery sides, dart water and vegetation *and underwater tangles*
- blue crabs
- creek—narrow, sinuous, can't see beginning or end *less than 15' wide*
- center of creek— everything water and sky

Hear: How does it sound there?

- chirping of birds ("tweep, tweep")
- splash of turtle or otter
- mainly silent

Feel: How does it feel?

- soil—spongy
- water—warmer than ocean; rub
- my face and neck; mucky and oily

Smell: Why can't I forget its smell?

- salt
- soil

- mud—slimy (through toes)
- crabs brush my legs
- feel buoyant, weightless

When Marie reviewed her annotated prewriting, she decided that, in the essay, she would order her brainstormed impressions by location rather than by sensory type. Using a spatial method of organization, she would present details as she moved from place to place—from her grandparents' home to the creek. The arrangement of details was now so clear to Marie that she felt comfortable moving to a first draft without further shaping her prewriting or preparing an outline. As she wrote, though, she frequently referred to her prewriting to retrieve sensory details about each location.

Now read Marie's paper, "Salt Marsh," noting the similarities and differences between her prewriting and final essay. You'll see that the essay's introduction and conclusion weren't drawn from the prewriting material, whereas most of the sensory details were. Notice, too, that when she wrote the essay, Marie expanded these details by adding more specifics and providing several powerful similes. Finally, consider how well the essay applies the principles of description discussed in this chapter. (The commentary that follows the paper will help you look at the essay more closely and will give you some sense of how Marie went about revising her first draft.)

Salt Marsh

by Marie Martinez

1   In one of his journals, Thoreau told of the difficulty he had escaping the obligations and cares of society: "It sometimes happens that I cannot easily shake off the village. The thought of some work will run in my head and I am not where my body is—I am out of my senses. In my walks I…return to my senses." All of us feel out of our senses at times. Overwhelmed by problems or everyday annoyances, we lose touch with sensory pleasures as we spend our days in noisy cities and stuffy classrooms. Just as Thoreau walked in the woods to return to his senses, I have a special place where I return to mine: the salt marsh behind my grandparents' house.

Introduction

Dominant impression (thesis)

2   My grandparents live on the East Coast, a mile or so inland from the sea. Between the ocean and the mainland is a wide fringe of salt marsh. A salt marsh is not a swamp, but an expanse of dark, spongy soil threaded with saltwater creeks and clothed in a kind of grass called salt meadow hay. All the water in the marsh rises and

Informal topic sentence: Definition paragraph

falls daily with the ocean tides, an endless cycle that changes the look of the marsh—partly flooded or mostly dry—as the day progresses.

ormal topic
ntence: First
ragraph in a
ır-part spatial
quence

3

Heading out to the marsh from my grandparents' house, I follow a short path through the woods. As I walk along, a sharp smell of salt mixed with the rich aroma of peaty soil fills my nostrils. I am always amazed by the way the path changes with the seasons. Sometimes I walk in the brilliant green of spring, sometimes in the tawny gold of autumn, sometimes in the grayish-tan of winter. No matter the season, the grass

nile

flanking the trail is often flattened into swirls, like thick Van Gogh brush strokes that curve and recurve in circular patterns. No people come here. The peacefulness heals me like a soothing drug.

ormal topic
ntence: Second
ragraph in the
atial sequence

4

After a few minutes, the trail suddenly opens up to a view that calms me no matter how upset or discouraged I might be: a line of tall waving reeds bordering and nearly hiding the salt marsh creek. To get to the creek, I part the reeds.

ormal topic
ntence: Third
ragraph in the
atial sequence

5

The creek is a narrow body of water no more than fifteen feet wide, and it ebbs and flows as the ocean currents sweep toward the land or rush back toward the sea. The creek winds in a sinuous pattern so that I cannot see its beginning or end, the places where it trickles into the marsh or spills into the open ocean. Little brown birds dip in and out of the reeds on the far shore of the creek, making a special "tweep-tweep" sound peculiar to the marsh. When I stand at low tide on the shore of the creek, I am on a miniature cliff, for the bank of the creek falls abruptly and steeply into the water. Below me, green grasses wave and shimmer under the water while tiny minnows flash their silvery sides as they dart through the underwater tangles.

ormal topic
ntence: Last
ragraph in the
atial sequence

6

The creek water is often much warmer than the ocean, so I can swim there in three seasons. Sitting on the edge of the creek, I scoop some water into my hand, rub my face and neck, then ease into the water. Where the creek is shallow, my feet sink into a foot of muck that feels like mashed potatoes mixed with motor oil. But

nile

once I become accustomed to it, I enjoy squishing the slimy mud through my toes. Sometimes I feel brushing past my legs the blue crabs that live in the creek. Other times, I hear the splash of a turtle or an otter as it slips from the shore into the water. Otherwise, it is silent. The salty water is buoyant and lifts my spirits as I stroke through it to reach the middle of the creek. There in the center, I float weightlessly, surrounded by tall reeds that reduce the world to water and sky. I am at peace.

Conclusion

7

The salt marsh is not the kind of dramatic landscape found on picture postcards. There are no soaring mountains, sandy beaches, or lush valleys. The marsh is a flat world that some consider dull and uninviting. I am glad most people do not respond to the marsh's subtle beauty because that means I can be alone there. Just as the rising tide sweeps over the marsh, floating debris out to the ocean, the marsh washes away my concerns and restores me to my senses.

Echo of idea in introduction

Commentary

The Dominant Impression

Marie responded to the assignment by writing a moving tribute to a place having special meaning for her—the salt marsh near her grandparents' home. Like most descriptive pieces, Marie's essay is organized around a *dominant impression:* the marsh's peaceful solitude and gentle, natural beauty. The essay's introduction provides a context for the dominant impression by comparing the pleasure Marie experiences in the marsh to the happiness Thoreau felt in his walks around Walden Pond.

Combining Patterns of Development

Before developing the essay's dominant impression, Marie uses the second paragraph to *define* a salt marsh. An *objective description,* the definition clarifies that a salt marsh—with its spongy soil, haylike grass, and ebbing tides—is not to be confused with a swamp. Because Marie offers such a factual definition, readers have the background needed to enjoy the personalized view that follows.

Besides the definition paragraph and the comparison in the opening paragraph, the essay contains a strong element of *causal analysis:* Throughout, Marie describes the marsh's effect on her.

Sensory Language

At times, Marie develops the essay's dominant impression explicitly, as when she writes "No people come here" (paragraph 3) and "I am at peace" (6). But Marie generally uses the more subtle techniques characteristic of *subjective description* to convey the dominant impression. First of all, she fills the essay with strong *connotative language,* rich with *sensory images.* The third paragraph describes what she smells (the "sharp smell of salt mixed with the rich aroma of peaty soil") and what she sees ("brilliant green," "tawny gold," and "grayish-tan"). In the fifth paragraph, she uses *onomatopoeia* ("tweep-tweep") to convey the birds' chirping sound. And the sixth paragraph includes vigorous descriptions of how the marsh feels to Marie's touch. She splashes water on her face and neck; she digs her toes into the mud at the bottom of the creek; she delights in the delicate brushing of crabs against her legs.

Figurative Language, Vigorous Verbs, and Varied Sentence Structure

You might also have noted that *figurative language, energetic verbs,* and *varied sentence patterns* contribute to the essay's descriptive power. Marie develops a simile in the third paragraph when she compares the flattened swirls of swamp grass to the brush strokes in a painting by Van Gogh. Later she uses another simile when she writes that the creek's thick mud feels "like mashed potatoes mixed with motor oil." Moreover, throughout the essay, she uses lively verbs ("shimmer," "flash") to capture the marsh's magical quality. Similarly, Marie enhances descriptive passages by vary-ing the length of her sentences. Long, fairly elaborate sentences are interspersed with short, dramatic statements. In the third paragraph, for example, the long sentence describing the circular swirls of swamp grass is followed by the brief statement "No people come here." And the sixth paragraph uses two short sentences ("Otherwise, it is silent" and "I am at peace") to punctuate the paragraph's longer sentences.

Organization

We can follow Marie's journey through the marsh because she uses an easy-to-follow combination of *spatial, chronological,* and *emphatic* patterns to sequence her experience. The essay relies primarily on a spatial arrangement because the four body paragraphs focus on the different spots that Marie reaches: first, the path behind her grandparents' house (paragraph 3); then the area bordering the creek (4); next, her view of the creek (5); last, the creek itself (6). Each stage of her walk is signaled by an *informal topic sentence* near the start of each para-graph. Furthermore, *signal devices* (marked by italics here) indicate not only her location but also the chronological passage of time: "*As* I walk along, a sharp smell...fills my nostrils" (3); "*After* a few minutes, the trail suddenly opens up..." (4); "*Below* me, green grasses wave..." (5). And to call attention to the creek's serene beauty, Marie saves for last the description of the peace she feels while floating in the creek.

An Inappropriate Figure of Speech

Although the four body paragraphs focus on the distinctive qualities of each loca-tion, Marie runs into a minor problem in the third paragraph. Take a moment to reread that paragraph's last sentence. Comparing the peace of the marsh to the effect of a "soothing drug" is jarring. The effectiveness of Marie's essay hinges on her ability to create a picture of a pure, natural world. A reference to drugs is inappropriate. Now, reread the paragraph aloud, stopping after "No people come here." Note how much more in keeping with the essay's dominant impression the paragraph is when the reference to drugs is omitted.

Conclusion

The concluding paragraph brings the essay to a graceful close. The powerful *simile* found in the last sentence contains an implied reference to Thoreau and to Marie's earlier statement about the joy to be found in special places having re-storative powers. Such an allusion echoes, with good effect, the paper's opening comments.

Revising the First Draft

When Marie met with some classmates during a peer review session, the students agreed that Marie's first draft was strong and moving. But they also said that they had difficulty following her route through the marsh; they found her third para-graph especially confusing. Marie reviewed her classmates' peer review work-sheets and then entered their comments, numbered in order of importance, in the margin of her first draft. Reprinted here is the original version of Marie's third paragraph, along with her annotations:

Original Version of Third Paragraph

As I head out to the marsh from the house, I follow a short trail through the woods. ① Chronology is confusing
A smell of salt and soil fills my nostrils. The end of the trail suddenly opens up to
a view that calms me no matter how upset or discouraged I might be: a line of tall,
waving reeds bordering the salt marsh creek. Civilization seems far away as I walk
the path of flattened grass and finally reach my goal, the salt marsh creek hidden
behind the tall, waving reeds. The path changes with the seasons; sometimes I walk ③ Make more specific
in the brilliant green of spring, sometimes in the tawny gold of autumn, sometimes
in the gray of winter. In some areas, the grass is flattened into swirls that make the
marsh resemble one of those paintings by Van Gogh. No people come here. The ② Develop more fully—maybe use simile
peacefulness heals me like a soothing drug. The path stops at the line of tall, waving
reeds standing upright at the border of the creek. I part the reeds to get to the creek.

When Marie looked more carefully at the paragraph, she agreed it was confusing. For one thing, the paragraph's third and fourth sentences indicated that she had come to the path's end and had reached the reeds bordering the creek. In the following sentences, however, she was on the path again. Then, at the end, she was back at the creek, as if she had just arrived there. Marie resolved this confusion by breaking the single paragraph into two separate ones—the first describing the walk along the path, the second describing her arrival at the creek. This restructuring, especially when combined with clearer transitions, eliminated the confusion.

While revising her essay, Marie also intensified the sensory images in her original paragraph. She changed the "smell of salt and soil" to the "sharp smell of salt mixed with the rich aroma of peaty soil." And when she added the phrase "thick Van Gogh brush strokes that curve and recurve in circular patterns," she made the comparison between the marsh grass and a Van Gogh painting more vivid.

These are just some of the changes Marie made while rewriting the paper. Her skillful revisions provided the polish needed to make an already strong essay even more evocative.

ACTIVITIES: DESCRIPTION

Prewriting Activities

1. Imagine you're writing two essays: One explains how students get "burned out"; the other contends that being a spendthrift is better (or worse) than being frugal. Jot down ways you might use description in each essay.

2. Go to a place on campus where students congregate. In preparation for an *objective* description of this place, make notes of various sights, sounds,

smells, and textures, as well as the overall "feel" of the place. Then, in preparation for a *subjective* description, observe and take notes on another sheet of paper. Compare the two sets of material. What differences do you see in word choice and selection of details?

3. Prepare to interview an interesting person by outlining several questions ahead of time. When you visit that person's home or workplace, bring a notebook in which to record his or her responses. During the interview, observe the person's surroundings, voice, body language, dress, and so on. As soon as the interview is over, make notes on these matters. Then review your notes and identify your dominant impression of the person. With that impression in mind, which details would you omit if you were writing an essay? Which would you elaborate? Which organizational pattern (spatial, emphatic, chronological, or sensory) would you select to organize your description? Why?

Revising Activities

4. Revise each of the following sentence sets twice. The first time, create an unmistakable mood; the second time, create a sharply contrasting mood. To convey atmosphere, vary sentence structure, use vigorous verbs, provide rich sensory details, and pay special attention to words' connotations.

   a. The card players sat around the table. The table was old. The players were, too.

   b. A long line formed outside the movie theater. People didn't want to miss the show. The movie had received a lot of attention recently.

   c. A girl walked down the street in her first pair of high heels. This was a new experience for her.

5. The following sentences contain clichés. Rewrite each sentence, supplying a fresh and imaginative figure of speech. Add whatever descriptive details are needed to provide a context for the figure of speech.

   a. They were as quiet as mice.

   b. My brother used to get green with envy if I had a date and he didn't.

   c. The little girl is proud as a peacock of her Girl Scout uniform.

6. The following descriptive paragraph is from the first draft of an essay showing that personal growth may result when romanticized notions and reality collide. How effective is the paragraph in illustrating the essay's thesis? Which details are powerful? Which could be more concrete? Which should be deleted? Where should sentence structure be more varied? How could the description be made more coherent? Revise the paragraph, correcting any problems you discover and adding whatever sensory details are needed to enliven the description. Feel free to break the paragraph into two or more separate ones.

   As a child, I was intrigued by stories about the farm in Harrison County, Maine, where my father spent his teens. Being raised on a farm seemed more interesting than growing up in the suburbs. So about a year ago, I decided to see for myself what the farm was like. I got there by driving on Route 334, a surprisingly easy-to-drive, four-lane highway that had recently been built with matching state and federal funds. I turned into the dirt road leading to the farm and got out of my car. It had been washed and waxed for the occasion. Then I headed for a dirt-colored barn. Its roof was full of huge, rotted holes. As I rounded the bushes, I saw the house. It too was dirt-colored. Its paint must have worn off decades ago. A couple of dead-looking old cars were sprawled in front of the barn. They were dented and windowless. Also by the barn was an ancient refrigerator, crushed like a discarded accordion. The porch steps to the house were slanted and wobbly. Through the open windows came a stale smell and the sound of television. Looking in the front door screen, I could see two chickens jumping around inside. Everything looked dirty both inside and out. Secretly grateful that no one answered my knock, I bolted down the stairs, got into my clean, shiny car, and drove away.

PROFESSIONAL SELECTIONS: DESCRIPTION

Mario Suárez

Mario Suárez (1923–1998), author of *Chicano Sketches,* a collection of short stories (2004), is considered by many to be the first contemporary Chicano writer. Suárez was one of five children born to Mexican immigrants who moved to Arizona. After serving in the U.S. Navy during World War II, he attended the University of Arizona, and while still an undergraduate, he wrote for the *Arizona Quarterly.* A journalist and college teacher, Suárez wrote primarily about the lives of immigrants and life in El Hoyo, the barrio where he grew up.

For ideas on how this description essay is organized, see Figure 10.2 on page 142.

Pre-Reading Journal Entry

Think of a place that is important to you from your childhood or adolescence—perhaps the place (or one of the places) where you grew up. Why was the place important to you? How would you describe it to someone who had never been there?

EL HOYO

1   From the center of downtown Tucson, the ground slopes gently away to Main Street, drops a few feet, and then rolls to the banks of the Santa Cruz River. Here lies the section of the city known as El Hoyo. Why it is called El Hoyo is not very clear.

In no sense is it a hole as its name would imply; it is simply the river's immediate valley. Its inhabitants are chicanos who raise hell on Saturday night and listen to Padre Estanislao on Sunday morning. While the term *chicano* is the short way of saying Mexicano, it is not restricted to the paisanos who came from old Mexico with the territory or the last famine to work for the railroad, labor, sing, and go on relief. Chicano is the easy way of referring to everybody. Pablo Gut'errez married the Chinese grocer's daughter and now runs a meat department; his sons are chicanos. So are the sons of Killer Jones who threw a fight in Harlem and fled to El Hoyo to marry Cristina Mendez. And so are all of them. However, it is doubtful that all these spiritual sons of Mexico live in El Hoyo because they love each other—many fight and bicker constantly. It is doubtful they live in El Hoyo because of its scenic beauty—it is everything but beautiful. Its houses are simple affairs of unplastered adobe, wood, and abandoned car parts. Its narrow streets are mostly clearings which have, in time, acquired names. Except for some tall trees which nobody has ever cared to identify, nurse, or destroy, the main things known to grow in the general area are weeds, garbage piles, dark-eyed chavalos, and dogs. And it is doubtful that the chicanos live in El Hoyo because it is safe—many times the Santa Cruz has risen and inundated the area.

In other respects, living in El Hoyo has its advantages. If one is born with a weakness   2
for acquiring bills, El Hoyo is where the collectors are less likely to find you. If one has acquired the habit of listening to Octavio Perea's Mexican Hour in the wee hours of the morning with the radio on at full blast, El Hoyo is where you are less likely to be reported to the authorities. Besides, Perea is very popular and sooner or later to everyone "Smoke in the Eyes" is dedicated between the pinto beans and white flour commercials. If one, for any reason whatever, comes on an extended period of hard times, where, if not in El Hoyo, are the neighbors more willing to offer solace? When Teofila Malacara's house burned to the ground with all her belongings and two children, a benevolent gentleman carried through the gesture that made tolerable her burden. He made a list of five hundred names and solicited from each a dollar. At the end of a month, he turned over to the tearful but grateful señora one hundred dollars in cold cash and then accompanied her on a short vacation. When the new manager of a local store decided that no more chicanas were to work behind the counters, it was the chicanos of El Hoyo who, on taking their individually small but collectively great buying power elsewhere, drove the manager out and the girls returned to their jobs. When the Mexican Army was en route to Baja, California, and the chicanos found out that the enlisted men ate only at infrequent intervals, it was El Hoyo's chicanos who crusaded across town with pots of beans and trays of tortillas to meet the train. When someone gets married, celebrating is not restricted to the immediate friends of the couple. Everybody is invited. Anything calls for a celebration, and a celebration calls for anything. On Memorial Day there are no less than half a dozen good fights at the Riverside Dance Hall. On Mexican Independence Day, more than one flag is sworn allegiance to amid cheers for the queen.

And El Hoyo is something more. It is this something more which brought Felipe   3
Sanchez back from the wars after having killed a score of Vietnamese with his body resembling a patchwork quilt to marry Julia Armijo. It brought Joe Zepeda, a gunner,...back to compose boleros. He has a metal plate for a skull. Perhaps El Hoyo is proof that those people exist, and perhaps exist best, who have as yet failed to observe the more popular modes of human conduct. Perhaps the humble appearance of El Hoyo justifies the indifferent shrug of those made aware of its existence. Perhaps El Hoyo's simplicity motivates an occasional chicano to move away from its

narrow streets, babbling comadres, and shrieking children to deny the bloodwell from which he springs and to claim the blood of a conquistador while his hair is straight and his face beardless. Yet El Hoyo is not an outpost of a few families against the world. It fights for no causes except those which soothe its immediate angers. It laughs and cries with the same amount of passion in times of plenty and of want.

4   Perhaps El Hoyo, its inhabitants, and its essence can best be explained by telling a bit about a dish called capirotada. Its origin is uncertain. But, according to the time and the circumstance, it is made of old, new, or hard bread. It is softened with water and then cooked with peanuts, raisins, onions, cheese, and panocha. It is fired with sherry wine. Then it is served hot, cold, or just "on the weather" as they say in El Hoyo. The Sermeños like it one way, the Garcias another, and the Ortegas still another. While it might differ greatly from one home to another; nevertheless, it is still capirotada. And so it is with El Hoyo's chicanos. While being divided from within and from without, like the capirotada, they remain chicanos.

FIGURE 10.2

Essay Structure Diagram: "El Hoyo" by Mario Suárez

Introductory paragraph **Background** **Sensory details** (paragraph 1)	Description of who lives in El Hoyo and how the place looks: "unplastered adobe, wood, and abandoned car parts"; "weeds, garbage piles, dark-eyed chavalos, and dogs." **Dominant impression:** El Hoyo isn't particularly a peaceful, beautiful, or safe place to live.
Narrative details (2)	Anecdotes to show the advantages of life in El Hoyo, especially unexpected generosity from people who have very little: collecting funds for a woman who lost her home and children; pressuring a store manager to rehire workers; giving food to passing Mexican soldiers.
Thesis Narrative details Sensory details (3)	Anecdotes of people returning to El Hoyo. Sensory details: "body resembling a patchwork quilt"; "metal plate for a skull." (Disdain for those who "deny" their origins.) Thesis: El Hoyo is "proof" people live meaningful lives regardless of their circumstances. El Hoyo "laughs and cries with the same amount of passion in times of plenty and of want."
Concluding paragraph (4)	Analogy reinforcing the humanness of El Hoyo's people: "divided from within and without, like the capirotada, they remain chicanos."

Questions for Close Reading

1. What is the selection's thesis (or dominant impression)? Locate the sentence(s) in which Suárez states his main idea. If he doesn't state the thesis explicitly, express it in your own words.

2. According to the author, what do the words *el hoyo* and *chicano* mean?

3. Why do people choose to live in El Hoyo?

4. Suárez tries to create an essay that describes for his readers the place where he grew up and why it is important in his life. Do you think his essay succeeds in communicating his ideas? Why or why not?

Questions About the Writer's Craft

1. **The pattern.** Focus on the first paragraph of "El Hoyo." Carefully re-read the paragraph and make notes regarding its organization. What does Suárez accomplish in his opening paragraph? What negative aspects of El Hoyo does he include, and why do you think he includes these in the opening paragraph? What might be his purpose?

2. How would you characterize the author's tone? Serious? Humorous? Down to earth? Give some examples to support your idea. Why do you think the author adopts the tone that he uses?

3. **Other patterns.** Although the primary focus of "El Hoyo" is on describing the barrio where Suárez grew up, the essay also *compares* and *contrasts* both positive and negative aspects of life in this Tucson neighborhood. First, list three negative aspects of the community, and then list three of the positive aspects he describes. How does the inclusion of both positive and negative characteristics of El Hoyo strengthen the overall impact of the essay?

4. In the closing paragraph of the essay Suárez creates an analogy between El Hoyo and *capirotada,* a Mexican dish made of leftovers. In what ways might *capirotada* represent life in the barrio? Make a list of three similarities you can draw between the neighborhood and the dish.

Writing Assignments Using Description as a Pattern of Development

1. Suárez describes the barrio where he grew up: where it is located, the people who live there, the positive and negative aspects of the neighborhood, and how it is different from other places. He brings his essay to closure with an analogy that captures the essence of El Hoyo. Write an essay in which you describe the neighborhood (or one of the neighborhoods) where you grew up. Do your best to present a multifaceted view of your neighborhood for your reader. Consider

including images of the neighborhood or its residents that enhance your essay and strengthen its visual impact. Be sure to integrate your images into your written text by referencing them in your essay.

2. In his essay Suárez mentions specific individuals who stood out for him from the community—among them Pablo Gut'errez, Killer Jones, Felipe Sanchez, Julia Amijo, and Joe Zepeda. Write a descriptive essay about particular people from your neighborhood, your elementary school, a team you were a part of, or another group that played a role in your life. Go beyond describing these individuals and reflect on why they stand out in your mind. Why did they create a lasting impression on you? Consider integrating images that enhance your essay and strengthen its visual impact. Be sure to integrate your images into your written text by referencing them in your essay.

Writing Assignment Combining Patterns of Development

3. Although El Hoyo is the barrio where Suárez grew up—a neighborhood he cherishes—it is clearly not the upscale, upper-class part of town. Write an essay in which you *compare* and *contrast* two neighborhoods—or two cities or countries—you are familiar with. Describe both areas, but also compare the ways they are alike and the ways they differ. Bring in outside sources as needed to strengthen your essay, and consider using images such as a pie chart showing income or education levels, or perhaps a map of the areas discussed in your essay.

Cherokee Paul McDonald

Cherokee Paul McDonald (1949–) is a fiction writer and journalist, a military veteran, and a former ten-year member of the Fort Lauderdale (Florida) Police Force. His publications include *Into the Green* (2001), in which he draws on his experiences as an Army lieutenant, and *Blue Truth* (1992), a graphic memoir of his day-to-day life as a police officer. He is also a fisherman and the father of three children. "A View from the Bridge" was first published February 12, 1989, in the Florida *Sun Sentinel*.

Pre-Reading Journal Entry

Think of a time when you did something to help someone—perhaps a friend, a family member, a classmate, or a stranger—and later realized that your actions had benefitted you just as much as, or perhaps even more than, they had helped the other person.

A VIEW FROM THE BRIDGE

1   I was coming up on the little bridge in the Rio Vista neighborhood of Fort Lauderdale, deepening my stride and my breathing to negotiate the slight incline without altering my pace. And then, as I neared the crest, I saw the kid.

He was a lumpy little guy with baggy shorts, a faded T-shirt, and heavy sweat socks   2
falling down over old sneakers.

Partially covering his shaggy blond hair was one of those blue baseball caps with   3
gold braid on the bill and a sailfish patch sewn onto the peak. Covering his eyes and
part of his face was a pair of those stupid-looking '50s-style wrap-around sunglasses.

He was fumbling with a beat-up rod and reel, and he had a little bait bucket by his   4
feet. I puffed on by, glancing down into the empty bucket as I passed.

"Hey, mister! Would you help me, please?"   5

The shrill voice penetrated my jogger's concentration, and I was determined to   6
ignore it. But for some reason, I stopped.

With my hands on my hips and the sweat dripping from my nose I asked, "What do   7
you want, kid?"

"Would you please help me find my shrimp? It's my last one and I've been getting   8
bites and I know I can catch a fish if I can just find that shrimp. He jumped outta my
hand as I was getting him from the bucket."

Exasperated, I walked slowly back to the kid, and pointed.   9

"There's the damn shrimp by your left foot. You stopped me for *that?"*   10

As I said it, the kid reached down and trapped the shrimp.   11

"Thanks a lot, mister," he said.   12

I watched as the kid dropped the baited hook down into the canal. Then I turned to   13
start back down the bridge.

That's when the kid let out a "Hey! Hey!" and the prettiest tarpon I'd ever seen   14
came almost six feet out of the water, twisting and turning as he fell through the air.

"I got one!" the kid yelled as the fish hit the water with a loud splash and took off   15
down the canal.

I watched the line being burned off the reel at an alarming rate. The kid's left hand   16
held the crank while the extended fingers felt for the drag setting.

"No, kid!" I shouted. "Leave the drag alone . . . just keep that damn rod tip up!"   17

Then I glanced at the reel and saw there were just a few loops of line left on the   18
spool.

"Why don't you get yourself some decent equipment?" I said, but before the kid   19
could answer I saw the line go slack.

"Ohhh, I lost him," the kid said. I saw the flash of silver as the fish turned.   20

"Crank, kid, crank! You didn't lose him. He's coming back toward you. Bring in the   21
slack!"

The kid cranked like mad, and a beautiful grin spread across his face.   22

"He's heading in for the pilings," I said. "Keep him out of those pilings!"   23

The kid played it perfectly. When the fish made its play for the pilings, he kept just   24
enough pressure on to force the fish out. When the water exploded and the silver mis-
sile hurled into the air, the kid kept the rod tip up and the line tight.

As the fish came to the surface and began a slow circle in the middle of the canal, I   25
said, "Whooee, is that a nice fish or what?"

The kid didn't say anything, so I said, "Okay, move to the edge of the bridge and I'll   26
climb down to the seawall and pull him out."

When I reached the seawall I pulled in the leader, leaving the fish lying on its side   27
in the water.

"How's that?" I said.   28

"Hey, mister, tell me what it looks like."   29

30   "Look down here and check him out," I said, "He's beautiful."

31   But then I looked up into those stupid-looking sunglasses and it hit me. The kid was blind.

32   "Could you tell me what he looks like, mister?" he said again.

33   "Well, he's just under three, uh, he's about as long as one of your arms," I said. "I'd guess he goes about 15, 20 pounds. He's mostly silver, but the silver is somehow made up of *all* the colors, if you know what I mean." I stopped. "Do you know what I mean by colors?"

34   The kid nodded.

35   "Okay. He has all these big scales, like armor all over his body. They're silver too, and when he moves they sparkle. He has a strong body and a large powerful tail. He has big round eyes, bigger than a quarter, and a lower jaw that sticks out past the upper one and is very tough. His belly is almost white and his back is a gunmetal gray. When he jumped he came out of the water about six feet, and his scales caught the sun and flashed it all over the place."

36   By now the fish had righted itself, and I could see the bright-red gills as the gill plates opened and closed. I explained this to the kid, and then said, more to myself, "He's a beauty."

37   "Can you get him off the hook?" the kid asked. "I don't want to kill him."

38   I watched as the tarpon began to slowly swim away, tired but still alive.

39   By the time I got back up to the top of the bridge the kid had his line secured and his bait bucket in one hand.

40   He grinned and said, "Just in time. My mom drops me off here, and she'll be back to pick me up any minute."

41   He used the back of one hand to wipe his nose.

42   "Thanks for helping me catch that tarpon," he said, "and for helping me to see it."

43   I looked at him, shook my head, and said, "No, my friend, thank you for letting *me* see that fish."

44   I took off, but before I got far the kid yelled again.

45   "Hey, mister!"

46   I stopped.

47   "Someday I'm gonna catch a sailfish and a blue marlin and a giant tuna and all those big sportfish!"

48   As I looked into those sunglasses I knew he probably would. I wished I could be there when it happened.

Questions for Close Reading

1. What is the selection's thesis (or dominant impression)? Locate the sentence(s) in which McDonald states his main idea. If he doesn't state the thesis explicitly, express it in your own words.

2. Why is McDonald initially determined to ignore the boy's request for help? Why does he hesitate to stop for the boy?

3. What details are provided to let the reader know that the boy is blind, and at what point does McDonald finally come to this realization?

4. Why do you think McDonald titled this "A View from the Bridge," and how does the view change—both literally and figuratively— as the essay progresses?

Questions About the Writer's Craft

1. **The pattern.** Choose a passage that you consider to be especially rich in detail and description, and make a list of the descriptors McDonald uses in the passage to draw a picture in words of the image. Then using those descriptors, take a few minutes to sketch out the image as you see it in your mind.

2. How does McDonald organize his essay? What transitional words and phrases does he use to keep the reader oriented as his essay progresses?

3. **Other patterns.** Because McDonald's descriptive essay has a strong *narrative* component, there is extensive dialogue in the selection. How does the use of dialogue enrich the essay? In what ways might the essay be less effective if the reader could not "hear" what McDonald and the boy said to each other?

4. Most of the description in this essay focuses on visual details, but McDonald also describes some other sensations. Find the passages in which McDonald presents other details that help the reader have a clearer understanding of the changing dynamic between the two characters as the essay moves along.

Writing Assignments Using Description as a Pattern of Development

1. In his essay, McDonald uses description to allow his readers to "see" the jogger-narrator (McDonald), the boy, the fish they caught, the view from the bridge, and more. Think of a scene that you came upon suddenly—a vista you encountered hiking, a street musician playing for spare change, a solitary animal at the zoo. Use vivid language to describe the scene and its impact on you.

2. While stories of incidents in our lives provide rich contexts for description, so do a host of other subjects. Write an essay in which you describe a place that is meaningful to you—perhaps the house where you grew up, the home of a friend or relative, the elementary school you attended, or a place where you and your friends spend time together. Be sure to convey a dominant impression: Did you feel safe in this place? comfortable? on edge? invisible? Select descriptive terms that enhance your feelings.

Writing Assignment Combining Patterns of Development

3. McDonald's essay describes the process of catching a fish. Write an essay in which you guide the reader through a familiar *process*, for example, baking cookies, planting flowers, or uploading a video to a social media site such as *YouTube. Describe* how each stage of the process would look, sound, smell, feel, or taste. You might want to research images online to *illustrate* your essay. If so, write a descriptive caption for each image.

Gordon Parks

The son of deeply religious tenant farmers, Gordon Parks (1912–2006) grew up in Kansas knowing both the comforts of familial love and the torments of poverty and racism. A series of odd jobs when he was a teenager gave Parks the means to buy his first camera. So evocative were his photographic studies that both *Life* and *Vogue* brought him on staff, the first black photographer to be hired by the two magazines. Parks's prodigious creativity found expression in filmmaking (*Shaft* in 1971), musical composition (both classical and jazz), fiction, nonfiction, and poetry. In the following essay, taken from his 1990 autobiography, *Voices in the Mirror*, Parks tells the story behind one of his most memorable photographic works—that of a twelve-year-old boy and his family, living in the slums of Rio de Janeiro.

Pre-Reading Journal Entry

The problem of poverty has provoked a wide array of proposed solutions. One controversial proposal argues that the government should pay poor women financial incentives to use birth control. What do you think of this proposal? Why is such a policy controversial? Use your journal to explore your thinking on this issue.

FLAVIO'S HOME

1   I've never lost my fierce grudge against poverty. It is the most savage of all human afflictions, claiming victims who can't mobilize their efforts against it, who often lack strength to digest what little food they scrounge up to survive. It keeps growing, multiplying, spreading like a cancer. In my wanderings I attack it wherever I can—in barrios, slums and favelas.

2   Catacumba was the name of the favela[1] where I found Flavio da Silva. It was wickedly hot. The noon sun baked the mud-rot of the wet mountainside. Garbage and human excrement clogged the open sewers snaking down the slopes. José Gallo, a *Life* reporter, and I rested in the shade of a jacaranda tree halfway up Rio de Janeiro's most infamous deathtrap. Below and above us were a maze of shacks, but in the distance alongside the beach stood the gleaming white homes of the rich.

3   Breathing hard, balancing a tin of water on his head, a small boy climbed toward us. He was miserably thin, naked but for filthy denim shorts. His legs resembled sticks covered with skin and screwed into his feet. Death was all over him, in his sunken eyes, cheeks and jaundiced coloring. He stopped for breath, coughing, his chest heaving as water slopped over his bony shoulders. Then jerking sideways like a mechanical toy, he smiled a smile I will never forget. Turning, he went on up the mountainside.

4   The detailed *Life* assignment in my back pocket was to find an impoverished father with a family, to examine his earnings, political leanings, religion, friends, dreams and

---

[1]Slums on the outskirts of Rio de Janeiro, Brazil, inhabited by seven hundred thousand people (editors' note).

frustrations. I had been sent to do an essay on poverty. This frail boy bent under his load said more to me about poverty than a dozen poor fathers. I touched Gallo, and we got up and followed the boy to where he entered a shack near the top of the mountainside. It was a leaning crumpled place of old plankings with a rusted tin roof. From inside we heard the babblings of several children. José knocked. The door opened and the boy stood smiling with a bawling naked baby in his arms.

Still smiling, he whacked the baby's rump, invited us in and offered us a box to sit   5
on. The only other recognizable furniture was a sagging bed and a broken baby's crib. Flavio was twelve, and with Gallo acting as interpreter, he introduced his younger brothers and sisters: "Mario, the bad one; Baptista, the good one; Albia, Isabel and the baby Zacarias." Two other girls burst into the shack, screaming and pounding on one another. Flavio jumped in and parted them. "Shut up, you two." He pointed at the older girl. "That's Maria, the nasty one." She spit in his face. He smacked her and pointed to the smaller sister. "That's Luzia. She thinks she's pretty."

Having finished the introductions, he went to build a fire under the stove—a   6
rusted, bent top of an old gas range resting on several bricks. Beneath it was a piece of tin that caught the hot coals. The shack was about six by ten feet. Its grimy walls were a patchwork of misshapen boards with large gaps between them, revealing other shacks below stilted against the slopes. The floor, rotting under layers of grease and dirt, caught shafts of light slanting down through spaces in the roof. A large hole in the far corner served as a toilet. Beneath that hole was the sloping mountainside. Pockets of poverty in New York's Harlem, on Chicago's south side, in Puerto Rico's infamous El Fungito seemed pale by comparison. None of them had prepared me for this one in the favela of Catacumba.

Flavio washed rice in a large dishpan, then washed Zacarias's feet in the same   7
water. But even that dirty water wasn't to be wasted. He tossed in a chunk of lye soap and ordered each child to wash up. When they were finished he splashed the water over the dirty floor, and, dropping to his knees, he scrubbed the planks until the black suds sank in. Just before sundown he put beans on the stove to warm, then left, saying he would be back shortly. "Don't let them burn," he cautioned Maria. "If they do and Poppa beats me, you'll get it later." Maria, happy to get at the licking spoon, switched over and began to stir the beans. Then slyly she dipped out a spoonful and swallowed them. Luzia eyed her. "I see you. I'm going to tell on you for stealing our supper."

Maria's eyes flashed anger. "You do and I'll beat you, you little bitch." Luzia threw a   8
stick at Maria and fled out the door. Zacarias dropped off to sleep. Mario, the bad one, slouched in a corner and sucked his thumb. Isabel and Albia sat on the floor clinging to each other with a strange tenderness. Isabel held onto Albia's hair and Albia clutched at Isabel's neck. They appeared frozen in an act of quiet violence.

Flavio returned with wood, dumped it beside the stove and sat down to rest for   9
a few minutes, then went down the mountain for more water. It was dark when he finally came back, his body sagging from exhaustion. No longer smiling, he suddenly had the look of an old man and by now we could see that he kept the family going. In the closed torment of that pitiful shack, he was waging a hopeless battle against starvation. The da Silva children were living in a coffin.

When at last the parents came in, Gallo and I seemed to be part of the family.   10
Flavio had already told them we were there. "Gordunn Americano!" Luzia said, pointing at me. José, the father, viewed us with skepticism. Nair, his pregnant wife,

seemed tired beyond speaking. Hardly acknowledging our presence, she picked up Zacarias, placed him on her shoulder and gently patted his behind. Flavio scurried about like a frightened rat, his silence plainly expressing the fear he held of his father. Impatiently, José da Silva waited for Flavio to serve dinner. He sat in the center of the bed with his legs crossed beneath him, frowning, waiting. There were only three tin plates. Flavio filled them with black beans and rice, then placed them before his father. José da Silva tasted them, chewed for several moments, then nodded his approval for the others to start. Only he and Nair had spoons; the children ate with their fingers. Flavio ate off the top of a coffee can. Afraid to offer us food, he edged his rice and beans toward us, gesturing for us to take some. We refused. He smiled, knowing we understood.

11   Later, when we got down to the difficult business of obtaining permission from José da Silva to photograph his family, he hemmed and hawed, wallowing in the pleasant authority of the decision maker. He finally gave in, but his manner told us that he expected something in return. As we were saying good night Flavio began to cough violently. For a few moments his lungs seemed to be tearing apart. I wanted to get away as quickly as possible. It was cowardly of me, but the bluish cast of his skin beneath the sweat, the choking and spitting were suddenly unbearable.

12   Gallo and I moved cautiously down through the darkness trying not to appear as strangers. The Catacumba was no place for strangers after sundown. Desperate criminals hid out there. To hunt them out, the police came in packs, but only in daylight. Gallo cautioned me. "If you get caught up here after dark it's best to stay at the da Silvas' until morning." As we drove toward the city the large white buildings of the rich loomed up. The world behind us seemed like a bad dream. I had already decided to get the boy Flavio to a doctor, and as quickly as possible.

13   The plush lobby of my hotel on the Copacabana waterfront was crammed with people in formal attire. With the stink of the favela in my clothes, I hurried to the elevator hoping no passengers would be aboard. But as the door was closing a beautiful girl in a white lace gown stepped in. I moved as far away as possible. Her escort entered behind her, swept her into his arms and they indulged in a kiss that lasted until they exited on the next floor. Neither of them seemed to realize that I was there. The room I returned to seemed to be oversized; the da Silva shack would have fitted into one corner of it. The steak dinner I had would have fed the da Silvas for three days.

14   Billowing clouds blanketed Mount Corcovado as we approached the favela the following morning. Suddenly the sun burst through, silhouetting Cristo Redentor, the towering sculpture of Christ with arms extended, its back turned against the slopes of Catacumba. The square at the entrance to the favela bustled with hundreds of favelados. Long lines waited at the sole water spigot. Others waited at the only toilet on the entire mountainside. Women, unable to pay for soap, beat dirt from their wash at laundry tubs. Men, burdened with lumber, picks and shovels and tools important to their existence threaded their way through the noisy throngs. Dogs snarled, barked and fought. Woodsmoke mixed with the stench of rotting things. In the mist curling over the higher paths, columns of favelados climbed like ants with wood and water cans on their heads.

We came upon Nair bent over her tub of wash. She wiped away sweat with her   15
apron and managed a smile. We asked for her husband and she pointed to a tiny shack
off to her right. This was José's store, where he sold kerosene and bleach. He was sitting on a box, dozing. Sensing our presence, he awoke and commenced complaining
about his back. "It kills me. The doctors don't help because I have no money. Always
talk and a little pink pill that does no good. Ah, what is to become of me?" A woman
came to buy bleach. He filled her bottle. She dropped a few coins and as she walked
away his eyes stayed on her backside until she was out of sight. Then he was complaining about his back again.

"How much do you earn a day?" Gallo asked.   16
"Seventy-five cents. On a good day maybe a dollar."   17
"Why aren't the kids in school?"   18
"I don't have money for the clothes they need to go to school."   19
"Has Flavio seen a doctor?"   20

He pointed to a one-story wooden building. "That's the clinic right there.   21
They're mad because I built my store in front of their place. I won't tear it down
so they won't help my kids. Talk, talk, talk and pink pills." We bid him good-bye
and started climbing, following mud trails, jutting rock, slime-filled holes and shack
after shack propped against the slopes on shaky pilings. We sidestepped a dead cat
covered with maggots. I held my breath for an instant, only to inhale the stench of
human excrement and garbage. Bare feet and legs with open sores climbed above
us—evils of the terrible soil they trod every day, and there were seven hundred
thousand or more afflicted people in favelas around Rio alone. Touching me, Gallo
pointed to Flavio climbing ahead of us carrying firewood. He stopped to glance at
a man descending with a small coffin on his shoulder. A woman and a small child
followed him. When I lifted my camera, grumbling erupted from a group of men
sharing beer beneath a tree.

"They're threatening," Gallo said. "Keep moving. They fear cameras. Think they're   22
evil eyes bringing bad luck." Turning to watch the funeral procession, Flavio caught
sight of us and waited. When we took the wood from him he protested, saying he was
used to carrying it. He gave in when I hung my camera around his neck. Then, beam-
ing, he climbed on ahead of us.

The fog had lifted and in the crisp morning light the shack looked more squalid.   23
Inside the kids seemed even noisier. Flavio smiled and spoke above their racket.
"Someday I want to live in a real house on a real street with good pots and pans
and a bed with sheets." He lit the fire to warm leftovers from the night before.
Stale rice and beans—for breakfast and supper. No lunch; midday eating was out
of the question. Smoke rose and curled up through the ceiling's cracks. An air
current forced it back, filling the place and Flavio's lungs with fumes. A coughing spasm doubled him up, turned his skin blue under viscous sweat. I handed
him a cup of water, but he waved it away. His stomach tightened as he dropped
to his knees. His veins throbbed as if they would burst. Frustrated, we could only
watch; there was nothing we could do to help. Strangely, none of his brothers or
sisters appeared to notice. None of them stopped doing whatever they were doing.
Perhaps they had seen it too often. After five interminable minutes it was over,

and he got to his feet, smiling as though it had all been a joke. "Maria, it's time for Zacarias to be washed!"

24   "But there's rice in the pan!"

25   "Dump it in another pan—and don't spill water!"

26   Maria picked up Zacarias, who screamed, not wanting to be washed. Irritated, Maria gave him a solid smack on his bare bottom. Flavio stepped over and gave her the same, then a free-for-all started with Flavio, Maria and Mario slinging fists at one another. Mario got one in the eye and fled the shack calling Flavio a dirty son-of-a-bitch. Zacarias wound up on the floor sucking his thumb and escaping his washing. The black bean and rice breakfast helped to get things back to normal. Now it was time to get Flavio to the doctor.

27   The clinic was crowded with patients—mothers and children covered with open sores, a paralytic teenager, a man with an ear in a state of decay, an aged blind couple holding hands in doubled darkness. Throughout the place came wailings of hunger and hurt. Flavio sat nervously between Gallo and me. "What will the doctor do to me?" he kept asking.

28   "We'll see. We'll wait and see."

29   In all, there were over fifty people. Finally, after two hours, it was Flavio's turn and he broke out in a sweat, though he smiled at the nurse as he passed through the door to the doctor's office. The nurse ignored it; in this place of misery, smiles were unexpected.

30   The doctor, a large, beady-eyed man with a crew cut, had an air of impatience. Hardly acknowledging our presence, he began to examine the frightened Flavio. "Open your mouth. Say 'Ah.' Jump up and down. Breathe out. Take off those pants. Bend over. Stand up. Cough. Cough louder. Louder." He did it all with such cold efficiency. Then he spoke to us in English so Flavio wouldn't understand. "This little chap has just about had it." My heart sank. Flavio was smiling, happy to be over with the examination. He was handed a bottle of cough medicine and a small box of pink pills, then asked to step outside and wait.

31   "This the da Silva kid?"

32   "Yes."

33   "What's your interest in him?"

34   "We want to help in some way."

35   "I'm afraid you're too late. He's wasted with bronchial asthma, malnutrition and, I suspect, tuberculosis. His heart, lungs and teeth are all bad." He paused and wearily rubbed his forehead. "All that at the ripe old age of twelve. And these hills are packed with other kids just as bad off. Last year ten thousand died from dysentery alone. But what can we do? You saw what's waiting outside. It's like this every day. There's hardly enough money to buy aspirin. A few wealthy people who care help keep us going." He was quiet for a moment. "Maybe the right climate, the right diet, and constant medical care might..." He stopped and shook his head. "Naw. That poor lad's finished. He might last another year—maybe not." We thanked him and left.

36   "What did he say?" Flavio asked as we scaled the hill.

37   "Everything's going to be all right, Flav. There's nothing to worry about."

38   It had clouded over again by the time we reached the top. The rain swept in, clearing the mountain of Corcovado. The huge Christ figure loomed up again with clouds swirling around it. And to it I said a quick prayer for the boy walking beside us. He

smiled as if he had read my thoughts. "Papa says 'El Cristo' has turned his back on the favela."

"You're going to be all right, Flavio."   39

"I'm not scared of death. It's my brothers and sisters I worry about. What would   40
they do?"

"You'll be all right, Flavio."[2]   41

---

[2]Park's photo-essay on Flavio generated an unprecedented response from *Life* readers. Indeed, they sent so much money to the da Silvas that the family was able to leave the *favela* for better living conditions. Parks brought Flavio to the United States for medical treatment, and the boy's health was restored. However, Flavio's story didn't have an unqualified happy ending. Although he overcame his illness and later married and had a family, Flavio continuously fantasized about returning to the United States, convinced that only by returning to America could he improve his life. His obsession eventually eroded the promise of his life in Brazil (editors' note).

Questions for Close Reading

1. What is the selection's thesis (or dominant impression)? Locate the sentence(s) in which Parks states his main idea. If he doesn't state the thesis explicitly, express it in your own words.

2. What is Flavio's family like? Why does Flavio have so much responsibility in the household?

3. What are some of the distinctive characteristics of Flavio's neighborhood and home?

4. What seems to be the basis of Flavio's fear of giving food to Parks and Gallo? What did Parks and Gallo understand that led them to refuse?

Questions About the Writer's Craft

1. **The pattern.** Without stating it explicitly, Parks conveys a dominant impression about Flavio. What is that impression? What details create it?

2. **Other patterns.** When relating how Flavio performs numerous household tasks, Parks describes several *processes*. How do these step-by-step explanations reinforce Parks's dominant impression of Flavio?

3. Parks provides numerous sensory specifics to depict Flavio's home. Look closely, for example, at the description in paragraph 6. Which words and phrases convey strong sensory images? How does Parks use transitions to help the reader move from one sensory image to another?

4. Paragraph 13 includes a scene that occurs in Parks's hotel. What's the effect of this scene? What does it contribute to the essay that the most detailed description of the *favela* could not?

Writing Assignments Using Description as a Pattern of Development

1. Parks paints a wrenching portrait of a person who remains vibrant and hopeful even though he is suffering greatly—from physical illness, poverty, overwork, and worry. Write a description about someone you know who has shown courage or other positive qualities during a time of personal trouble. Include, as Parks does, plentiful details about the person's appearance and behavior so that you don't have to state directly what you admire about the person.

2. Parks presents an unforgettable description of the *favela* and the living conditions there. Write an essay about a region, city, neighborhood, or building that also projects an overwhelming negative feeling. Include only those details that convey your dominant impression, and provide—as Parks does—vivid sensory language to convey your attitude toward your subject.

Writing Assignments Combining Patterns of Development

3. The doctor reports that a few wealthy people contribute to the clinic, but the reader can tell from the scene in Parks's hotel that most people are insensitive to those less fortunate. Write an essay *describing* a specific situation that you feel reflects people's tendency to ignore the difficulties of others. Analyze why people distance themselves from the problem; then present specific *steps* that could be taken to sensitize them to the situation.

ADDITIONAL WRITING TOPICS: DESCRIPTION

General Assignments

Using description, develop one of these topics into an essay.

1. A favorite item of clothing
2. A school as a young child might see it
3. A coffee shop, bus shelter, newsstand, or some other small place
4. A parade or victory celebration
5. One drawer in a desk or bureau
6. A TV, film, or music celebrity
7. The inside of something, such as a cave, boat, car, shed, or machine
8. A friend, roommate, or other person you know well
9. An essential or a useless gadget
10. A once-in-a-lifetime event

Assignments Using Visuals

Use the suggested visuals to help develop a descriptive essay on one of these topics:

1. Your best friend and the role that person has played in your life (photos)

2. Effective Super Bowl advertisements (links to ads on *YouTube*)

3. The best (or worst) gift you have received (photo or Web link)

4. Your vision of an ideal house (sketches or photos)

5. A place you love to visit and why (photos and/or Web links)

Assignments with a Specific Purpose, Audience, and Point of View

1. **Academic life.** For an audience of incoming first-year students, prepare a speech describing registration day at your college. Use specific details to help prepare students for the actual event. Choose an adjective that represents your dominant impression of the experience, and keep that word in mind as you write.

2. **Academic life.** Your college has decided to replace an old campus structure (for example, a dorm or dining hall) with a new version. Write a letter of protest to the administration, describing the place so vividly and appealingly that its value and need for preservation are unquestionable.

3. **Academic life.** As a staff member of the campus newspaper, you have been asked to write a weekly column of social news and gossip. For your first column, you plan to describe a recent campus event—a dance, party, concert, or other social activity. With a straightforward or tongue-in-cheek tone, describe where the event was held, the appearance of the people who attended, and so on.

4. **Civic activity.** As a subscriber to a community-wide dating service, you've been asked to submit a description of the kind of person you'd like to meet. Describe your ideal date. Focus on specifics about physical appearance, personal habits, character traits, and interests.

5. **Civic activity.** As a resident of a particular town, you're angered by the appearance of a certain spot and by the activities that take place there. Write a letter to the town council, describing in detail the undesirable nature of this place (an adult bookstore, a bar, a bus station, a neglected park or beach). End with some suggestions about ways to improve the situation.

6. **Workplace action.** You've noticed a recurring problem in your workplace and want to bring it to the attention of your boss, who typically is inattentive. Write a letter to your boss describing the problem. Your goal is not to provide solutions, but rather, to provide a vivid description—complete with sensory details—so that your boss can no longer deny the problem.

11

Narration

In this chapter, you will learn:

11.1 To use the pattern of narration to develop your essays
11.2 To consider how narration can fit your purpose and audience
11.3 To develop prewriting, writing, and revision strategies for using narration in an essay
11.4 To analyze how narration is used effectively in one student-written and three professionally authored selections
11.5 To write your own essays using narration as a strategy

What Is Narration?

Human beings are instinctively storytellers. Our hunger for telling and listening to stories is basic.

Narration means telling a single story or several related stories. The story can be a means to an end, a way to support a main idea or thesis. Every public speaker, from politician to classroom teacher, knows that stories capture the attention of listeners as nothing else can. We want to know what happened to others, not simply because we're curious, but also because their experiences shed light on our own lives. Narration lends force to opinion, triggers the flow of memory, and evokes places, times, and people in ways that are compelling and affecting.

How Narration Fits Your Purpose and Audience

Because narratives tell a story, you may think they're found only in novels or short stories. But narration can also appear in essays,

sometimes as a supplemental pattern of development. For example, if your purpose in a paper is to *persuade* apathetic readers that airport security regulations must be followed strictly, you might lead off with a brief account of armed terrorists who easily boarded planes on September 11. In a paper *defining* good teaching, you might keep readers engaged by including satirical anecdotes about one hapless instructor, the antithesis of an effective teacher. An essay on the *effects* of an overburdened judicial system might provide—in an attempt to involve readers—a dramatic account of the way one clearly guilty murderer plea-bargained his way to freedom.

In addition to providing effective support in one section of your paper, narration can also serve as an essay's dominant pattern of development. In fact, most of this chapter shows you how to use a single narrative to convey a central point and share with readers your view of what happened.

Although some narratives relate unusual experiences, most tread familiar ground, telling tales of joy, love, loss, frustration, fear—all common emotions experienced during life. Narratives can take the ordinary and transmute it into something significant, even extraordinary. The challenge lies in applying your own vision to a tale, thereby making it unique.

Prewriting Strategies

The following checklist shows how you can apply to narration some of the prewriting strategies discussed in Chapter 2.

☑ NARRATION: A PREWRITING CHECKLIST

Select Your Narrative Event(s)

☐ What event evokes strong emotion in you and is likely to have a powerful effect on your readers?

☐ Does a scrapbook souvenir, snapshot, old letter, or prized object (an athletic trophy, a political button) point to an event worth writing about?

☐ Will you focus on a personal experience, an incident in someone else's life, or a public event?

☐ Can you recount your story effectively, given the length of a typical college essay? If not, will relating one key incident from the fuller, more complete event enable you to convey the point and feeling of the entire experience?

☐ If you write about an event in someone else's life, will you have time to interview the person?

Focus on the Conflict in the Event

☐ What is the source of tension in the event: one person's internal dilemma, a conflict between characters, or a struggle between a character and a social institution or natural phenomenon?

☐   Will the conflict create enough tension to "hook" readers and keep them interested?

☐   What point does the conflict and its resolution convey to readers?

☐   What tone is appropriate for recounting the conflict?

Use Prewriting to Generate Specifics About the Conflict

☐   Would the questioning technique, brainstorming, freewriting, mapping, or interviewing help you generate details about the conflict?

Strategies for Using Narration in an Essay

After prewriting, you're ready to draft your essay. Figure 11.1 (on page 158) and the suggestions that follow will be helpful whether you use narration as a dominant or supportive pattern of development.

1. **Identify the point of the narrative conflict.** As you know, most narratives center on a conflict (see the checklist on pages 156–157). When you relate a story, it's up to you to convey the *significance* or *meaning* of the event's conflict. When recounting your narrative, be sure to begin with a clear sense of your *narrative point,* or *thesis.* Then either state that point directly or select details and a tone that imply the point you want readers to take away from your story.

2. **Develop only those details that advance the narrative point.** Nothing is more boring than a storyteller who gets sidetracked and drags out a story with nonessential details. Maintain an effective narrative pace by focusing on your point and eliminating any details that don't support it. A good narrative depends not only on what is included, but also on what has been left out.

   How do you determine which specific points to omit, which to treat briefly, and which to emphasize? Having a clear sense of your narrative point and knowing your audience are crucial.

   You also need to keep your audience in mind when selecting narrative details that support your specific points. As you write, keep asking yourself, "Is this detail or character or snippet of conversation essential? Does my audience need this detail to understand the conflict in the situation? Does this detail advance or intensify the narrative action?" Summarize details that have some importance but do not deserve lengthy treatment ("Two hours went by..."). And try to limit *narrative commentary*—statements that tell rather than show what happened—because such remarks interrupt the narrative flow. Focus instead on the specifics that propel action forward in a vigorous way.

   Sometimes, especially if the narrative re-creates an event from the past, you won't be able to remember what happened detail for detail. In such a case, you should take advantage of what is called **dramatic license**. Using your current perspective as a guide, feel free to add or reshape details to suit your narrative point.

FIGURE 11.1

Development Diagram: Writing a Narration Essay

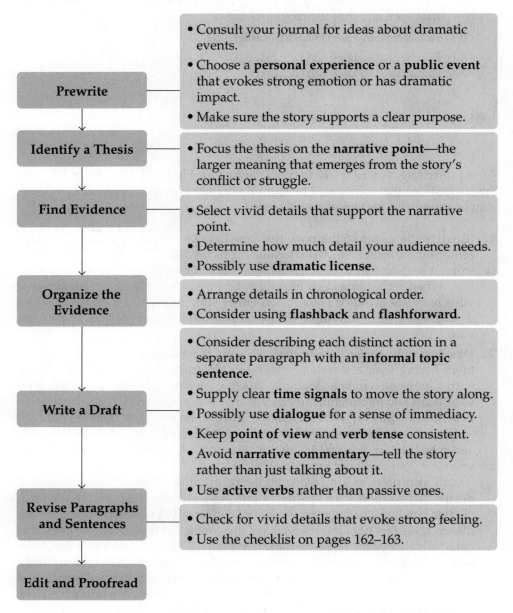

| Prewrite | • Consult your journal for ideas about dramatic events.
• Choose a **personal experience** or a **public event** that evokes strong emotion or has dramatic impact.
• Make sure the story supports a clear purpose. |

| Identify a Thesis | • Focus the thesis on the **narrative point**—the larger meaning that emerges from the story's conflict or struggle. |

| Find Evidence | • Select vivid details that support the narrative point.
• Determine how much detail your audience needs.
• Possibly use **dramatic license**. |

| Organize the Evidence | • Arrange details in chronological order.
• Consider using **flashback** and **flashforward**. |

| Write a Draft | • Consider describing each distinct action in a separate paragraph with an **informal topic sentence**.
• Supply clear **time signals** to move the story along.
• Possibly use **dialogue** for a sense of immediacy.
• Keep **point of view** and **verb tense** consistent.
• Avoid **narrative commentary**—tell the story rather than just talking about it.
• Use **active verbs** rather than passive ones. |

| Revise Paragraphs and Sentences | • Check for vivid details that evoke strong feeling.
• Use the checklist on pages 162–163. |

| Edit and Proofread | |

3. **Organize the narrative sequence.** All of us know the traditional beginning of fairy tales: "Once upon a time…" Every narrative begins somewhere, presents a span of time, and ends at a certain point. Frequently, you will want to use a straightforward time order, following the event *chronologically* from beginning to end: first this happened, next this happened, finally this happened.

But sometimes a strict chronological recounting may not be effective—especially if the high point of the narrative gets lost somewhere in the middle of the time sequence. To avoid that possibility, you may want to disrupt chronology, plunge the reader into the middle of the story, and then return in a **flashback** to the tale's beginning. Narratives can also use **flashforward**—you give readers a glimpse of the future (the main character being jailed) before the story continues in the present (the events leading to the arrest). These techniques shift the story onto several planes and keep it from becoming a step-by-step, predictable account. Reserve flashforwards and flashbacks, however, for crucial incidents only, because breaking out of chronological order acts as emphasis. Here are examples of how flashback and flashforward can be used in narrative writing:

Flashback

Standing behind the wooden counter, Greg wielded his knife expertly as he shucked clams—one every ten seconds—with practiced ease. The scene contrasted sharply with his first day on the job, when his hands broke out in blisters and when splitting each shell was like prying open a safe.

Flashforward

Rushing to move my car from the no-parking zone, I waved a quick good-bye to Karen as she climbed the steps to the bus. I didn't know then that by the time I picked her up at the bus station later that day, she had made a decision that would affect both our lives.

Whether or not you choose to include flashbacks or flashforwards in an essay, remember to limit the time span covered by the narrative. Otherwise, you'll have trouble generating the details needed to give the story depth and meaning. Also, regardless of the time sequence you select, organize the tale so it drives toward a strong finish. Be careful that your story doesn't trail off into minor, anticlimactic details.

4. **Make the narrative easy to follow.** Describing each distinct action in a separate paragraph helps readers grasp the flow of events. Although narrative essays don't always have conventional topic sentences, each narrative paragraph should have a clear focus. Often this focus is indicated by a sentence early in the paragraph that directs attention to the action taking place. Such a sentence functions as a kind of *informal topic sentence*; the rest of the paragraph then develops that topic sentence. You should also be sure to use time signals when narrating a story. Words like *now, then, next, after,* and *later* ensure that your reader won't get lost as the story progresses.

5. **Make the narrative vigorous and immediate.** A compelling narrative provides an abundance of specific details, making readers feel as if they're experiencing the story being told. Readers must be able to see, hear, touch, smell,

and taste the event you're narrating. *Vivid sensory description* is, therefore, an essential part of an effective narrative. (See pages 62–63 in Chapter 6 and pages 105–106 in Chapter 8 for more on concrete, sensory language.) Not only do specific sensory details make writing a pleasure to read—we all enjoy learning the particulars about people, places, and things—but they also give the narrative the stamp of reality. The specifics convince the reader that the event being described actually did, or could, occur.

Compare the following excerpts from a narrative essay. The first version is lifeless and dull; the revised version, packed with sensory images, grabs readers with its sense of foreboding:

Original Version

That eventful day started out like every other summer day. My sister, Tricia, and I made several elaborate mud pies that we decorated with care. A little later on, as we were spraying each other with the garden hose, we heard my father walk up the path.

Revised

That sad summer day started out uneventfully enough. My sister Tricia and I spent a few hours mixing and decorating mud pies. Our hands caked with dry mud, we sprinkled each lopsided pie with alternating rows of dandelion and clover petals. Later, when the sun got hotter, we tossed our white T-shirts over the red picket fence—forgetting my grandmother's frequent warnings to be more ladylike. Our sweaty backs bared to the sun, we doused each other with icy sprays from the garden hose. Caught up in the primitive pleasure of it all, we barely heard my father as he walked up the garden path, the gravel crunching under his heavy work boots.

A caution: Sensory language enlivens narration, but it also slows the pace. Be sure that the slower pace suits your purpose.

Another way to create an aura of narrative immediacy is to use **dialogue** while telling a story. Our sense of other people comes, in part, from what they say and the way they sound. Conversational exchanges allow the reader to experience characters directly. Compare the following fragments of a narrative, one with dialogue and one without, noting how much more energetic the second version is.

Original

As soon as I found my way back to the campsite, the trail guide commented on my disheveled appearance. I explained that I had heard some gunshots and had run back to camp as soon as I could.

Revised

As soon as I found my way back to the campsite, the trail guide took one look at me and drawled, "What on earth happened to you, Daniel Boone? You look as though you've been dragged through a haystack backwards."

"I'd look a lot worse if I hadn't run back here. When a bullet whizzes by me, I don't stick around to see who's doing the shooting."

Note that, when using dialogue, you generally begin a new paragraph to indicate a shift from one person's speech to another's (as in the second example). Dialogue can also be used to convey a person's inner thoughts. Like conversation between people, such interior dialogue is enclosed in quotation marks.

The challenge in writing dialogue, both exterior and interior, is to make each character's speech distinctive and convincing. Reading the dialogue aloud—even asking friends or family members to speak the lines—will help you develop an ear for authentic speech. What sounds most natural is often a compressed and reshaped version of what was actually said. As with other narrative details, include only those portions of dialogue that serve your purpose, fit the mood you want to create, and reveal character.

Another way to enliven narratives is to use *varied sentence structure*. Sentences that plod along with the same predictable pattern put readers to sleep. Experiment with your sentences by varying their length and type; mix long and short sentences, simple and complex. (For more on sentence structure, see pages 94–97 in Chapter 8.) Compare the following original and revised version to get an idea of how effective varied sentence structure can be in narrative writing:

Original

The store manager went to the walk-in refrigerator every day. The heavy metal door clanged shut behind her. I had visions of her freezing to death among the hanging carcasses. The shiny door finally swung open. She waddled out.

Revised

Each time the store manager went to the walk-in refrigerator, the heavy metal door clanged shut behind her. Visions of her freezing to death among the hanging carcasses crept into my mind until, finally, the shiny door swung open and out she waddled.

Finally, *vigorous verbs* lend energy to narratives. Use active verb forms ("The boss *yelled* at him") rather than passive ones ("He *was yelled at* by the boss"), and try to replace anemic *to be* verbs ("She *was* a good basketball player") with more dynamic constructions ("She *played* basketball well"). (For more on strong verbs, see pages 106–107 in Chapter 8.)

6. **Keep your point of view and verb tense consistent.** All stories have a *narrator,* the person who tells the story. If you, as narrator, tell a story as you experienced it, the story is written in the *first-person point of view* ("I saw the dog pull loose"). But if you want to tell how someone else experienced the incident, you use the *third-person point of view* ("Anne saw the dog pull loose"). Each point of view has advantages and limitations. First person allows you to express ordinarily private thoughts and to re-create an event as you actually experienced it. It is limited, though, in its ability to depict the inner thoughts of other people. By way of contrast, third person makes it easier to provide insight into the thoughts of all the participants. However, its objective, broad perspective may undercut some of the subjective immediacy of the "I was there" point of view. No matter which you select, stay with that vantage point throughout the entire narrative. Remember also that research reports and other academic papers are usually written from the third-person point of view. (For more on point of view, see pages 21–22 in Chapter 2.)

Knowing whether to use the ***past*** or ***present tense*** ("I *strolled* into the room" as opposed to "I *stroll* into the room") is important. In most narrations, the past tense predominates, enabling the writer to span a considerable period of time. Although more rarely used, the present tense can be powerful for events of short durations—a wrestling match or a medical emergency, for instance. A narrative in the present tense prolongs each moment, intensifying the reader's sense of participation. Be careful, though; unless the event is intense and fast-paced, the present tense can seem contrived. Whichever tense you choose, avoid shifting midstream—starting, let's say, in the past tense ("she skated") and switching to the present tense ("she runs").

Revision Strategies

Once you have a draft of the essay, you're ready to revise. The following checklist will help you and those giving you feedback apply to narration some of the revision techniques discussed in Chapters 7 and 8.

☑   **NARRATION: A REVISION/PEER REVIEW CHECKLIST**

Revise Overall Meaning and Structure

☐   What is the essay's main point? Is it stated explicitly or is it implied? Could the point be conveyed more clearly? How?

☐   What is the narrative's conflict? Is it stated explicitly or is it implied? Could the conflict be made more dramatic? How?

☐   From which point of view is the narrative told? Is it the most effective point of view for this essay? Why or why not?

Revise Paragraph Development

- ☐ Which paragraphs (or passages) fail to advance the action, reveal character, or contribute to the story's mood? Should these sections be condensed or eliminated?
- ☐ Where should the narrative pace be slowed down or quickened?
- ☐ Where is it difficult to follow the chronology of events? Should the order of paragraphs be changed? How? Where would additional time signals help?
- ☐ How could flashback or flashforward paragraphs be used to highlight key events?
- ☐ What can be done to make the essay's opening paragraph more compelling? Would dramatic dialogue or mood-setting description help?
- ☐ What could be done to make the essay's closing paragraph more effective? Should the essay end earlier? Should it close by echoing an idea or image from the opening?

Revise Sentences and Words

- ☐ Where is sentence structure monotonous? Where would combining sentences, mixing sentence type, and alternating sentence length help?
- ☐ Where could dialogue replace commentary to convey character and propel the story forward?
- ☐ Which sentences and words are inconsistent with the essay's tone?
- ☐ Which sentences would benefit from sensory details that heighten the narrative mood?
- ☐ Where do vigorous verbs convey action? Where could active verbs replace passive ones? Where could dull *to be* verbs be converted to more dynamic forms?
- ☐ Where are there inappropriate shifts in point of view or verb tense?

Student Essay: From Prewriting Through Revision

The student essay that follows was written by Paul Monahan in response to this assignment:

> In "The Fourth of July," Audre Lorde says her parents felt they should have anticipated and avoided an unpleasant situation. Write a narrative about a time you faced a disturbing conflict and ended up doing something you later regretted.

After deciding to write about an encounter he had with an elderly woman in the store where he worked, Paul did some *freewriting* on his computer to gather material on his subject. When he later reviewed this freewriting, he crossed out unnecessary commentary, wrote notes signaling where dialog and descriptive details were needed, and indicated where paragraph breaks might occur. After annotating his freewriting in this manner, Paul felt comfortable launching into his first draft, without further shaping his freewriting or preparing an outline. As he wrote, though, he frequently referred to his warm-up material to organize his narrative and retrieve details. Paul's original freewriting is shown here; the handwritten marks indicate Paul's later efforts to shape and develop this material:

Freewriting

An old woman entered the store. She pushed the door, hobbled in, coughed, and seemed to be in pain. She wore a faded dress and a sweater that was much too small for her. The night was cold, but she didn't wear any stockings. You could see her veins. She strolled around the store, sneezing and hacking. She picked up a can of corn and stared at it. She made me nervous. I walked over to see what was going on. Asked if she needed help.

I was the one to do this because I was on duty. Had worked at 7–11 for two years. Felt confident. Always tried to be friendly and polite. Hadn't had any trouble. But the old woman worried me.

"I need food," she said. I told her how much the corn cost and also that the bologna was on sale (what a stupid, insensitive thing to do!). She said she couldn't pay. I almost told her to take the can of corn, but all the rules stopped me. Be polite, stay in control. I told her I couldn't give anything away. Her face looked even more saggy. She kind of shook and put the can back. She left, I rushed out after her. Too late. Felt ashamed about acting like a robot. Mad at myself. If only I'd acted differently.

Now read Paul's paper, "If Only," noting the similarities and differences between his prewriting and final essay. You'll notice, for example, that Paul decided to move background information to the essay's opening, and that he ended up using as his title a shortened version of the final sentence in his prewriting. Finally, consider how well the essay applies the principles of narration discussed in this chapter. (The commentary that follows the paper will help you look at Paul's essay more closely and will give you some sense of how he went about revising his first draft.)

If Only
by Paul Monahan

Having worked at a 7-Eleven store for two years, I thought I had become successful at what our manager calls "customer relations." I firmly believed that a friendly smile and an automatic "sir," "ma'am," and "thank you" would see me through any situation that might arise, from soothing impatient or unpleasant people to apologizing for giving out the wrong change. But the other night an old woman shattered my belief that a glib response could smooth over the rough spots of dealing with other human beings.

2   The moment she entered, the woman presented a sharp contrast to our shiny *Informal topic sentence*
store with its bright lighting and neatly arranged shelves. Walking as if each step were
painful, she slowly pushed open the glass door and hobbled down the nearest aisle.
She coughed dryly, wheezing with each breath. On a forty-degree night, she was wear- *Sensory details*
ing only a faded print dress, a thin, light-beige sweater too small to button, and black
vinyl slippers with the backs cut out to expose calloused heels. There were no stockings or socks on her splotchy, blue-veined legs.

3   After strolling around the store for several minutes, the old woman stopped in
front of the rows of canned vegetables. She picked up some corn niblets and stared
with a strange intensity at the label. At that point, I decided to be a good, courteous *Informal topic sentence*
employee and asked her if she needed help. As I stood close to her, my smile became
harder to maintain; her red-rimmed eyes were partially closed by yellowish crusts; her *Sensory details*
hands were covered with layer upon layer of grime, and the stale smell of sweat rose in
a thick vaporous cloud from her clothes.

4   "I need some food," she muttered in reply to my bright "Can I help you?" *Start of dialogue*

5   "Are you looking for corn, ma'am?"

6   "I need some food," she repeated. "Any kind."

7   "Well, the corn is ninety-five cents," I said in my most helpful voice. "Or, if you like,
we have a special on bologna today."

8   "I can't pay," she said.

9   For a second, I was tempted to say, "Take the corn." But the employee rules *Conflict established*
flooded into my mind: Remain polite, but do not let customers get the best of you. Let
them know that you are in control. For a moment, I even entertained the idea that this
was some sort of test, and that this woman was someone from the head office, testing
my loyalty. I responded dutifully, "I'm sorry, ma'am, but I can't give away anything for
free." *Informal topic sentence*

10   The old woman's face collapsed a bit more, if that were possible, and her hands
trembled as she put the can back on the shelf. She shuffled past me toward the door,
her torn and dirty clothing barely covering her bent back.

11   Moments after she left, I rushed out the door with the can of corn, but she was *Conclusion*
nowhere in sight. For the rest of my shift, the image of the woman haunted me. I had
been young, healthy, and smug. She had been old, sick, and desperate. Wishing with *Echoing of narrative point in the introduction*
all my heart that I had acted like a human being rather than a robot, I was saddened to
realize how fragile a hold we have on our better instincts.

Commentary

Point of View, Tense, and Conflict

Paul chose to write "If Only" from the *first-person point of view,* a logical choice because he appears as a main character in his own story. Using the *past tense,* Paul recounts an incident filled with *conflict*—between him and the woman and between his fear of breaking the rules and his human instinct to help someone in need.

Narrative Point

It isn't always necessary to state the *narrative point* of an essay; it can be implied. But Paul decided to express the controlling idea of his narrative in two places—in the introduction ("But the other night an old woman shattered my belief that a glib response could smooth over the rough spots of dealing with other human beings") and again in the conclusion, where he expands his idea about rote responses overriding impulses of independent judgment and compassion. All of the essay's *narrative details* contribute to the point of the piece; Paul does not include any extraneous information that would detract from the central idea he wants to convey.

Organization

The narrative is *organized chronologically,* from the moment the woman enters the store to Paul's reaction after she leaves. Paul limits the narrative's time span. The entire incident probably occurs in under ten minutes, yet the introduction serves as a kind of *flashback* by providing some necessary background about Paul's past experiences. To help the reader follow the course of the narrative, Paul uses *time signals: "The moment* she entered, the woman presented a sharp contrast" (paragraph 2); *"At that point,* I decided to be a good, courteous employee" (3); *"For the rest of my shift,* the image of the woman haunted me" (11).

The paragraphs (except for those consisting solely of dialogue) also contain *informal topic sentences* that direct attention to the specific stage of action being narrated. Indeed, each paragraph focuses on a distinct event: the elderly woman's actions when she first enters the store, the encounter between Paul and the woman, Paul's resulting inner conflict, the woman's subsequent response, and Paul's delayed reaction.

Combining Patterns of Development

This chronological chain of events, with one action leading to another, illustrates that the *cause-effect* pattern underlies the basic structure of Paul's essay. And by means of another pattern—*description*—Paul gives dramatic immediacy to the events being recounted. Throughout, he provides rich sensory details to engage the reader's interest. For instance, the sentence "her red-rimmed eyes were partially closed by yellowish crusts" (3) vividly re-creates the woman's appearance while also suggesting Paul's inner reaction to the woman.

Dialogue and Sentence Structure

Paul uses other techniques to add energy and interest to his narrative. For one thing, he dramatizes his conflict with the woman through *dialogue* that crackles with tension. And he achieves a vigorous narrative pace by *varying the length and structure of his sentences.* In the second paragraph, a short sentence ("There were no stockings or socks on her splotchy, blue-veined legs") alternates with a longer one ("On a forty-degree night, she was wearing only a faded print dress, a thin, light-beige sweater too small to button, and black vinyl slippers with the backs cut out to expose calloused heels"). Some sentences in the essay open with a subject and verb ("She coughed dryly"), whereas others start with dependent clauses or participial phrases ("As I stood close to her, my smile became harder to maintain"; "Walking as if each step were painful, she slowly pushed open the glass door") or with a prepositional phrase ("For a second, I was tempted").

Revising the First Draft

To get a sense of how Paul went about revising his essay, take a moment to look at the original version of his third paragraph shown here. The handwritten annotations, numbered in order of importance, represent Paul's ideas for revision. Compare this preliminary version with the final version in the full essay:

Original Version of Third Paragraph

③ Inappropriate words—sound humorous

After (sneezing) and (hacking) her way around the store, the old woman stopped in front of the vegetable shelves. (She) picked up a can of corn and stared at the label. (She) stayed like this for several minutes. Then I walked over to her and asked if I could be of help.

① Boring—not enough details

② Choppy sentence

As you can see, Paul realized the paragraph lacked power, so he decided to add compelling descriptive details about the woman ("the stale smell of sweat," for example). When revising, he also worked to reduce the paragraph's choppiness. By expanding and combining sentences, he gave the paragraph an easier, more graceful rhythm. Much of the time, revision involves paring down excess material. In this case, though, Paul made the right decision to elaborate his sentences. Furthermore, he added the following comment to the third paragraph: "I decided to be a good, courteous employee." These few words introduce an appropriate note of irony and serve to echo the essay's controlling idea.

Finally, Paul decided to omit the words "sneezing and hacking" because he realized they were too comic or light for his subject. Still, the first sentence in the revised paragraph is somewhat jarring. The word *strolling* isn't quite appropriate because it implies a leisurely grace inconsistent with the impression he wants to convey. Replacing *strolling* with, say, *shuffling* would bring the image more into line with the essay's overall mood.

Despite this slight problem, Paul's revisions are right on the mark. The changes he made strengthened his essay, turning it into a more evocative, more polished piece of narrative writing.

ACTIVITIES: NARRATION

Prewriting Activities

1. Imagine you're writing two essays: One analyzes the effect of insensitive teachers on young children; the other argues the importance of family traditions. With the help of your freewriting, identify different narratives you could use to open each essay.

2. Use brainstorming or any other prewriting technique to generate narrative details about *one* of the following events. After examining your raw material, identify two or three narrative points (thesis statements) that might focus an essay. Then edit the prewriting material for each narrative point, noting which items would be appropriate, which would be inappropriate, and which would have to be developed more fully.

   a. An injury you received
   b. The loss of an important object
   c. An event that made you wish you had a certain skill

3. For each of the following situations, identify two different conflicts that would make a story worth relating:

   a. Going to the supermarket with a friend
   b. Telling your parents which college you've decided to attend
   c. Participating in a demonstration

4. Prepare six to ten lines of vivid and natural-sounding dialogue to convey the conflict in *two* of the following situations:

   a. One member of a couple trying to break up with the other
   b. An instructor talking to a student who plagiarized a paper
   c. A young person talking to his or her parents about dropping out of college for a semester

Revising Activities

5. Revise each of the following narrative sentence groups twice: once with words that carry negative connotations, and again with words that carry positive connotations. Use varied sentence structure, sensory details, and vigorous verbs to convey mood.

   a. The bell rang. It rang loudly. Students knew the last day of class was over.

b. Last weekend, our neighbors burned leaves in their yard. We went over to speak with them.

c. The sun shone in through my bedroom window. It made me sit up in bed. Daylight was finally here, I told myself.

6. The following paragraph is the introduction from the first draft of an essay proposing harsher penalties for drunk drivers. Revise this narrative paragraph to make it more effective. How can you make sentence structure less predictable? Which details should you delete? As you revise, provide language that conveys the event's sights, smells, and sounds. Also, clarify the chronological sequence.

> As I drove down the street in my bright blue sports car, I saw a car coming rapidly around the curve. The car didn't slow down as it headed toward the traffic light. The light turned yellow and then red. A young couple, dressed like models, started crossing the street. When the woman saw the car, she called out to her husband. He jumped onto the shoulder. The man wasn't hurt but, seconds later, it was clear the woman was. I ran to a nearby emergency phone and called the police. The ambulance arrived, but the woman was already dead. The driver, who looked terrible, failed the sobriety test, and the police found out that he had two previous offenses. It's apparent that better ways have to be found for getting drunk drivers off the road.

PROFESSIONAL SELECTIONS: NARRATION

Audre Lorde

Named poet laureate of the state of New York in 1991, Audre Lorde (1934–1992) was a New Yorker born of African-Caribbean parents. Lorde taught at Hunter College for many years and published numerous poems and nonfiction pieces in a variety of magazines and literary journals. Her books include *A Burst of Light* (1988), *Sister Outsider: Essays and Speeches* (1984), and *The Black Unicorn: Poems* (1978). "The Fourth of July" is an excerpt from her autobiography, *Zami: A New Spelling of My Name* (1982).

For ideas on how this narration essay is organized, see Figure 11.2 on page 173.

Pre-Reading Journal Entry

When you were a child, what beliefs about the United States did you have? List these beliefs. For each, indicate whether subsequent experience maintained or shattered your childhood understanding of these beliefs. Take a little time to explore these issues in your journal.

THE FOURTH OF JULY

The first time I went to Washington, D.C., was on the edge of the summer when I 1
was supposed to stop being a child. At least that's what they said to us all at graduation
from the eighth grade. My sister, Phyllis, graduated at the same time from high school.
I don't know what she was supposed to stop being. But as graduation presents for us
both, the whole family took a Fourth of July trip to Washington, D.C., the fabled and
famous capital of our country.

It was the first time I'd ever been on a railroad train during the day. When I was 2
little, and we used to go to the Connecticut shore, we always went at night on the
milk train, because it was cheaper.

Preparations were in the air around our house before school was even over. We 3
packed for a week. There were two very large suitcases that my father carried, and a
box filled with food. In fact, my first trip to Washington was a mobile feast; I started
eating as soon as we were comfortably ensconced in our seats, and did not stop until
somewhere after Philadelphia. I remember it was Philadelphia because I was disap-
pointed not to have passed by the Liberty Bell.

My mother had roasted two chickens and cut them up into dainty bite-size pieces. 4
She packed slices of brown bread and butter and green pepper and carrot sticks. There
were little violently yellow iced cakes with scalloped edges called "marigolds," that
came from Cushman's Bakery. There was a spice bun and rock-cakes from Newton's,
the West Indian bakery across Lenox Avenue from St. Mark's School, and iced tea in
a wrapped mayonnaise jar. There were sweet pickles for us and dill pickles for my
father, and peaches with the fuzz still on them, individually wrapped to keep them
from bruising. And, for neatness, there were piles of napkins and a little tin box with a
washcloth dampened with rosewater and glycerine for wiping sticky mouths.

I wanted to eat in the dining car because I had read all about them, but my mother 5
reminded me for the umpteenth time that dining car food always cost too much
money and besides, you never could tell whose hands had been playing all over that
food, nor where those same hands had been just before. My mother never mentioned
that Black people were not allowed into railroad dining cars headed south in 1947. As
usual, whatever my mother did not like and could not change, she ignored. Perhaps it
would go away, deprived of her attention.

I learned later that Phyllis's high school senior class trip had been to Washington, 6
but the nuns had given her back her deposit in private, explaining to her that the
class, all of whom were white, except Phyllis, would be staying in a hotel where
Phyllis "would not be happy," meaning, Daddy explained to her, also in private, that
they did not rent rooms to Negroes. "We will take you to Washington, ourselves," my
father had avowed, "and not just for an overnight in some measly fleabag hotel."

American racism was a new and crushing reality that my parents had to deal with 7
every day of their lives once they came to this country. They handled it as a private
woe. My mother and father believed that they could best protect their children from
the realities of race in america and the fact of american racism by never giving them
name, much less discussing their nature. We were told we must never trust white people, but *why* was never explained, nor the nature of their ill will. Like so many other
vital pieces of information in my childhood, I was supposed to know without being told.
It always seemed like a very strange injunction coming from my mother, who looked so
much like one of those people we were never supposed to trust. But something always

warned me not to ask my mother why she wasn't white, and why Auntie Lillah and Auntie Etta weren't, even though they were all that same problematic color so different from my father and me, even from my sisters, who were somewhere in-between.

8   In Washington, D.C., we had one large room with two double beds and an extra cot for me. It was a back-street hotel that belonged to a friend of my father's who was in real estate, and I spent the whole next day after Mass squinting up at the Lincoln Memorial where Marian Anderson[1] had sung after the D.A.R.[2] refused to allow her to sing in their auditorium because she was Black. Or because she was "Colored," my father said as he told us the story. Except that what he probably said was "Negro," because for his time, my father was quite progressive.

9   I was squinting because I was in that silent agony that characterized all of my childhood summers, from the time school let out in June to the end of July, brought about by my dilated and vulnerable eyes exposed to the summer brightness.

10   I viewed Julys through an agonizing corolla of dazzling whiteness and I always hated the Fourth of July, even before I came to realize the travesty such a celebration was for Black people in this country.

11   My parents did not approve of sunglasses, nor of their expense.

12   I spent the afternoon squinting up at monuments to freedom and past presidencies and democracy, and wondering why the light and heat were both so much stronger in Washington, D.C., than back home in New York City. Even the pavement on the streets was a shade lighter in color than back home.

13   Late that Washington afternoon my family and I walked back down Pennsylvania Avenue. We were a proper caravan, mother bright and father brown, the three of us girls step-standards in-between. Moved by our historical surroundings and the heat of the early evening, my father decreed yet another treat. He had a great sense of history, a flair for the quietly dramatic and the sense of specialness of an occasion and a trip.

14   "Shall we stop and have a little something to cool off, Lin?"

15   Two blocks away from our hotel, the family stopped for a dish of vanilla ice cream at a Breyer's ice cream and soda fountain. Indoors, the soda fountain was dim and fan-cooled, deliciously relieving to my scorched eyes.

16   Corded and crisp and pinafored, the five of us seated ourselves one by one at the counter. There was I between my mother and father, and my two sisters on the other side of my mother. We settled ourselves along the white mottled marble counter, and when the waitress spoke at first no one understood what she was saying, and so the five of us just sat there.

17   The waitress moved along the line of us closer to my father and spoke again. "I said I kin give you to take out, but you can't eat here. Sorry." Then she dropped her eyes looking very embarrassed, and suddenly we heard what it was she was saying all at the same time, loud and clear.

---

[1]An acclaimed African-American opera singer (1902–1993), famed for her renderings of Black spirituals.

[2]Daughters of the American Revolution. A society, founded in 1890, for women who can prove direct lineage to soldiers or others who aided in winning American independence from Great Britain during the Revolutionary War (1775–1783). The DAR has admitted non-white women as members since 1977.

Straight-backed and indignant, one by one, my family and I got down from the   18
counter stools and turned around and marched out of the store, quiet and outraged,
as if we had never been Black before. No one would answer my emphatic questions
with anything other than a guilty silence. "But we hadn't done anything!" This
wasn't right or fair! Hadn't I written poems about Bataan and freedom and democracy for all?

My parents wouldn't speak of this injustice, not because they had contributed to   19
it, but because they felt they should have anticipated it and avoided it. This made me
even angrier. My fury was not going to be acknowledged by a like fury. Even my two
sisters copied my parents' pretense that nothing unusual and anti-american had occurred. I was left to write my angry letter to the president of the united states all by
myself, although my father did promise I could type it out on the office typewriter next
week, after I showed it to him in my copybook diary.

The waitress was white, and the counter was white, and the ice cream I never ate   20
in Washington, D.C., that summer I left childhood was white, and the white heat and
the white pavement and the white stone monuments of my first Washington summer
made me sick to my stomach for the whole rest of that trip and it wasn't much of a
graduation present after all.

Questions for Close Reading

1. What is the selection's thesis (or narrative point)? Locate the sentence(s) in which
   Lorde states her main idea. If she doesn't state the thesis explicitly, express it in
   your own words.

2. In paragraph 4, Lorde describes the elaborate picnic her mother prepared for the
   trip to Washington, D.C. Why did Lorde's mother make such elaborate preparations? What do these preparations tell us about Lorde's mother?

3. Why does Lorde have trouble understanding her parents' dictate that she "never
   trust white people" (paragraph 7)?

4. In general, how do Lorde's parents handle racism? How does the family as a whole
   deal with the racism they encounter in the ice cream parlor? How does the family's
   reaction to the ice cream parlor incident make Lorde feel?

Questions About the Writer's Craft

1. **The pattern.** What techniques does Lorde use to help readers follow the unfolding
   of the story as it occurs in both time and space?

2. When telling a story, skilled writers limit narrative commentary—statements that
   tell rather than show what happened—because such commentary tends to interrupt the narrative flow. Lorde, however, provides narrative commentary in several
   spots. Find these instances. How is the information she provides in these places essential to her narrative?

3. In paragraphs 7 and 19, Lorde uses all lowercase letters when referring to America/
   American and to the President of the United States. Why do you suppose she

FIGURE 11.2

Essay Structure Diagram: "The Fourth of July" by Audre Lorde

Introductory paragraph: Narrative point (paragraph 1)	Going on a trip to Washington, D.C., as a graduation present. **Narrative point:** This experience marked the end of the narrator's childhood.
Narrative details (2-19) Also, descriptive and explanatory material (in parentheses at right)	Preparing for the train trip. (The food packed for the trip.) *Foreshadowing:* Not allowed in the dining car. *Flashforward:* Learning later that her sister had been denied a trip to Washington because of racist hotel policies. (How the author's parents and relatives dealt with the "crushing reality" of racism.) (The hotel room and its location.) Spending the day "squinting up at monuments." Deciding to stop for ice cream at a soda fountain and waiting to be served. Waitress refusing to serve the family. Leaving the soda fountain. (The parents' response and the author's anger.)
Concluding paragraph (20)	The incident at the soda fountain marked an end to the narrator's childhood.

doesn't follow the rules of capitalization? In what ways does her rejection of these rules reinforce what she is trying to convey through the essay's title?

4. What key word does Lorde repeat in paragraph 20? What effect do you think she hopes the repetition will have on readers?

Writing Assignments Using Narration as a Pattern of Development

1. Lorde recounts an incident during which she was treated unfairly. Write a narrative about a time when either you were treated unjustly or you treated someone else in an unfair manner. Like Lorde, use vivid details to make the incident come alive and to convey how it affected you.

2. Write a narrative about an experience that dramatically changed your view of the world. The experience might have been jarring and painful, or it may have been positive and uplifting. In either case, recount the incident with compelling narrative details. To illustrate the shift in your perspective, begin with a brief statement of the way you viewed the world before the experience.

Writing Assignment Combining Patterns of Development

3. In her essay, Lorde decries and by implication takes a strong stance against racial discrimination. Brainstorm with friends, family members, and classmates to identify other injustices in American society. Focusing on *one* such injustice, write an essay *arguing* that such an injustice indeed exists. To document the nature and extent of the injustice, use library and/or Internet research. You should also consider *recounting* your own and other people's experiences. Acknowledge and, when you can, dismantle the views of those who think there isn't a problem.

Lynda Barry

Cartoonist, novelist, and playwright, Lynda Barry (1956–) combines the genres of collage, memoir, novel, graphic novel, and workbook in her work. Her creations include the syndicated strip *Ernie Pook's Comeek* and the illustrated novels *Cruddy* (2001), *One Hundred Demons* (2002), *What It Is* (2008), and *Picture This: The Near-Sighted Monkey Book* (2010). Her 2002 novel *The Good Times Are Killing Me* was adapted into an off-Broadway play. The following essay was originally published in the *Baltimore Sun* on January 24, 1992.

Pre-Reading Journal Entry

In her essay, Lynda Barry writes about a time in her childhood when she was "filled with a panic . . . like the panic that strikes kids when they realize they are lost." Think of a time during your childhood when you were filled with panic. Why were you afraid? How did you feel? What did you do?

THE SANCTUARY OF SCHOOL

I was 7 years old the first time I snuck out of the house in the dark. It was winter 1 and my parents had been fighting all night. They were short on money and long on relatives who kept "temporarily" moving into our house because they had nowhere else to go.

My brother and I were used to giving up our bedroom. We slept on the couch, 2 something we actually liked because it put us that much closer to the light of our lives, our television.

3   At night when everyone was asleep, we lay on our pillows watching it with the sound off. We watched Steve Allen's mouth moving. We watched Johnny Carson's mouth moving. We watched movies filled with gangsters shooting machine guns into packed rooms, dying soldiers hurling a last grenade and beautiful women crying at windows. Then the sign-off finally came and we tried to sleep.

4   The morning I snuck out, I woke up filled with a panic about needing to get to school. The sun wasn't quite up yet but my anxiety was so fierce that I just got dressed, walked quietly across the kitchen and let myself out the back door.

5   It was quiet outside. Stars were still out. Nothing moved and no one was in the street. It was as if someone had turned the sound off on the world.

6   I walked the alley, breaking thin ice over the puddles with my shoes. I didn't know why I was walking to school in the dark. I didn't think about it. All I knew was a feeling of panic, like the panic that strikes kids when they realize they are lost.

7   That feeling eased the moment I turned the corner and saw the dark outline of my school at the top of the hill. My school was made up of about 15 nondescript portable classrooms set down on a fenced concrete lot in a rundown Seattle neighborhood, but it had the most beautiful view of the Cascade Mountains. You could see them from anywhere on the playfield and you could see them from the windows of my classroom—Room 2.

8   I walked over to the monkey bars and hooked my arms around the cold metal. I stood for a long time just looking across Rainier Valley. The sky was beginning to whiten and I could hear a few birds.

9   In a perfect world my absence at home would not have gone unnoticed. I would have had two parents in a panic to locate me, instead of two parents in a panic to locate an answer to the hard question of survival during a deep financial and emotional crisis.

10   But in an overcrowded and unhappy home, it's incredibly easy for any child to slip away. The high levels of frustration, depression and anger in my house made my brother and me invisible. We were children with the sound turned off. And for us, as for the steadily increasing number of neglected children in this country, the only place where we could count on being noticed was at school.

11   "Hey there, young lady. Did you forget to go home last night?" It was Mr. Gunderson, our janitor, whom we all loved. He was nice and he was funny and he was old with white hair, thick glasses and an unbelievable number of keys. I could hear them jingling as he walked across the playfield. I felt incredibly happy to see him.

12   He let me push his wheeled garbage can between the different portables as he unlocked each room. He let me turn on the lights and raise the window shades and I saw my school slowly come to life. I saw Mrs. Holman, our school secretary, walk into the office without her orange lipstick on yet. She waved.

13   I saw the fifth-grade teacher, Mr. Cunningham, walking under the breezeway eating a hard roll. He waved.

14   And I saw my teacher, Mrs. Claire LeSane, walking toward us in a red coat and calling my name in a very happy and surprised way, and suddenly my throat got tight and my eyes stung and I ran toward her crying. It was something that surprised us both.

15   It's only thinking about it now, 28 years later, that I realize I was crying from relief. I was with my teacher, and in a while I was going to sit at my desk, with my crayons and pencils and books and classmates all around me, and for the next six hours I was

going to enjoy a thoroughly secure, warm and stable world. It was a world I absolutely relied on. Without it, I don't know where I would have gone that morning.

Mrs. LeSane asked me what was wrong and when I said "Nothing," she seemingly   16
left it at that. But she asked me if I would carry her purse for her, an honor above all honors, and she asked if I wanted to come into Room 2 early and paint.

She believed in the natural healing power of painting and drawing for troubled children.   17
In the back of her room there was always a drawing table and an easel with plenty of supplies, and sometimes during the day she would come up to you for what seemed like no good reason and quietly ask if you wanted to go to the back table and "make some pictures for Mrs. LeSane." We all had a chance at it—to sit apart from the class for a while to paint, draw and silently work out impossible problems on 11×17 sheets of newsprint.

Drawing came to mean everything to me. At the back table in Room 2, I learned to   18
build myself a life preserver that I could carry into my home.

We all know that a good education system saves lives, but the people of this country   19
are still told that cutting the budget for public schools is necessary, that poor salaries for teachers are all we can manage and that art, music and all creative activities must be the first to go when times are lean.

Before- and after-school programs are cut and we are told that public schools are not   20
made for baby-sitting children. If parents are neglectful temporarily or permanently, fox whatever reason, it's certainly sad, but their unlucky children must fend for themselves. Or slip through the cracks. Or wander in a dark night alone.

We are told in a thousand ways that not only are public schools not important, but   21
that the children who attend them, the children who need them most, are not important either. We leave them to learn from the blind eye of a television, or to the mercy of "a thousand points of light"[1] that can be as far away as stars.

I was lucky. I had Mrs. LeSane. I had Mr. Gunderson. I had an abundance of art   22
supplies. And I had a particular brand of neglect in my home that allowed me to slip away and get to them. But what about the rest of the kids who weren't as lucky? What happened to them?

By the time the bell rang that morning I had finished my drawing and Mrs. LeSane   23
pinned it up on the special bulletin board she reserved for drawings from the back table. It was the same picture I always drew—a sun in the corner of a blue sky over a nice house with flowers all around it.

Mrs. LeSane asked us to please stand, face the flag, place our right hands over our   24
hearts and say the Pledge of Allegiance. Children across the country do it faithfully. I wonder now when the country will face its children and say a pledge right back.

------

[1]In his inaugural address, President George H. W. Bush used this phrase to encourage non-governmental community action (editors' note).

Questions for Close Reading

1. What is the selection's thesis? Locate the sentence(s) in which Barry states her main idea. If she doesn't state the thesis explicitly, express it in your own words.

2. Various details from Barry's narrative essay let the reader know that her childhood home life was far from perfect. Skim back over the essay and make a list of the details she includes to describe what she refers to as "a particular brand of neglect in [her] home" (paragraph 22).

3. Barry says that the first time she sneaked out of her house early that morning when she was seven, she did not know why she was leaving and she "did not think about it" (paragraph 6). She only knew that she was seized by panic and had to escape. From what was she escaping, and what was there about her school that made it a "sanctuary" for her? Why do you think she "did not want to think about" why she was sneaking away from home?

4. What details both for and against budget cuts in education are included in Barry's essay?

Questions About the Writer's Craft

1. **The pattern.** What kind of organizational pattern does Barry use in her narrative essay, and in what ways is this an appropriate choice for organizing the selection?

2. In her essay Barry uses repeated references to the absence of sound. Locate those references and reflect on how she uses them. In what ways do you think they add to or take away from the essay's effectiveness?

3. **Other patterns.** While the primary focus of Barry's essay is on narrating a story from her childhood and the important role school played as a safe refuge, her essay is also *persuasive*. She takes a stand and makes a strong *argument*. In what ways does the personal anecdote she tells in the first sixteen paragraphs of the essay make her political argument stronger than it would be had she not included her own story?

4. In the essay, Barry reflects on her childhood experience and comes to realizations about herself that she did not make when she was a small child. Read through the essay, listing the discoveries she makes about herself as she reflects. In what ways do Barry's reflections add to the effectiveness of her essay?

Writing Assignments Using Narration as a Pattern of Development

1. Barry's essay tells about a time when she was seized by panic and felt that she had to escape. Write an essay about a time in your life when you felt that you had to get away from a particular situation—a time when you had to make a change in your life. Go beyond telling your story and reflect on *why* you needed to get away and *why* you took the steps needed to make the change.

2. Barry writes about individuals in her life who were there when she desperately needed them. Write a narrative essay about a time when someone reached out to you and helped you when you especially needed help. Use vivid details and believable dialogue to enrich your essay.

3. In her essay Barry combines *narration* and *argumentation-persuasion*. Write an essay in which you *argue* for an educational or child-rearing issue that matters to you. Include a story that helps the reader understand why the issue is important to you. Take time to conduct any research needed to substantiate your claims, and include those findings in your essay. Consider using images—perhaps charts or graphs—that illustrate your findings for your readers.

Joan Murray

Joan Murray—a poet, writer, editor, and playwright—was born in New York City in 1945. She attended Hunter College and New York University, and published her first volume of poetry, which she also illustrated, in 1975. Her most recent volume of poetry is *Dancing on the Edge*, published in 2002. This essay appeared in the "Lives" section of the weekly *New York Times Magazine* on May 13, 2007.

Pre-Reading Journal Entry

We are used to having our mothers care for us, but sometimes we have to care for our mothers. Reflect on an occasion when you had to do something important for your mother or other caregiver. What was the situation? How did you help? How did you feel about helping someone who normally helped you? Use your journal to respond to these questions.

SOMEONE'S MOTHER

Hitchhiking is generally illegal where I live in upstate New York, but it's not unusual to see someone along Route 20 with an outstretched thumb or a handmade sign saying "Boston." This hitchhiker, though, was waving both arms in the air and grinning like a president boarding Air Force One. 1

I was doing 60—eager to get home after a dental appointment in Albany—and I was a mile past the hitchhiker before something made me turn back. I couldn't say if the hitchhiker was a man or a woman. All I knew was that the hitchhiker was old. 2

As I drove back up the hill, I eyed the hitchhiker in the distance: dark blue raincoat, jaunty black beret. Thin arms waving, spine a little bent. Wisps of white hair lilting as the trucks whizzed by. I made a U-turn and pulled up on the gravel, face to face with an eager old woman who kept waving till I stopped. I saw no broken-down vehicle. There was no vehicle at all. She wore the same broad grin I noticed when I passed her. 3

I rolled my window down. "Can I call someone for you?" 4
"No, I'm fine—I just need a ride." 5
"Where are you going?" 6
"Nassau." 7
That was three miles away. "Are you going there to shop?" 8
"No. I live there." 9
"What are you doing here?" I asked with a tone I hadn't used since my son was a teenager. 10

11   "I was out for a walk."

12   I glanced down the road: Jet's Autobody. Copeland Coating. Thoma Tire Company. And the half-mile hill outside Nassau—so steep that there's a second lane for trucks. She must have climbed the shoulder of that hill. And the next one. And the next. Until something made her stop and throw her hands in the air.

13   "Did you get lost?" I asked, trying to conceal my alarm.

14   "It was a nice day," she said with a little cry. "Can't an old lady go for a walk on a nice day and get lost?"

15   It wasn't a question meant to be answered. She came around to the passenger side, opened the door and sat down. On our way to Nassau, she admitted to being 92. Though she ducked my questions about her name, her address and her family. "Just leave me at the drugstore," she said.

16   "I'll take you home," I said. "Then you can call someone."

17   "Please," she said, "just leave me at the drugstore."

18   "I can't leave you there," I replied just as firmly. "I'm going to take you to your house. Or else to the police station."

19   "No, no," she begged. She was agitated now. "If my son finds out, he'll put me in a home."

20   Already I was seeing my own mother, who's 90. A few years ago, she was living in her house on Long Island, surrounded by her neighbors, her bird feeders, her azaleas. Then one morning she phoned my brother to say she didn't remember how to get dressed anymore. A few weeks later, with sorrow and worry, we arranged her move to a nursing home.

flashback

21   I noticed that the hitchhiker had a white dove pinned to her collar. "Do you belong to a church?" I tried. "Yes," she said. She was grinning. "I'd like to take you there," I said. "No, please," she said again. "My son will find out."

22
23   Things were getting clearer. "You've gotten lost before?"
    "A few times," she shrugged. "But I always find my way home. Just take me to the drugstore."

24   As we drove, I kept thinking about my mother, watched over and cared for in a bright, clean place. I also thought about her empty bird feeders, her azaleas blooming for no one, the way she whispers on the phone, "I don't know anyone here."

25   When I pulled into the parking strip beside the drugstore, the hitchhiker let herself out. "I just need to sit on the step for a while," she said before closing the door. I stepped out after her. "Can't I take you home?" I asked as gently as I could.

26   She looked into my eyes for a moment. "I don't know where I live," she said in the tiniest voice. "But someone will come along who knows me. They always do."

27   I watched as she sat herself down on the step. Already she had dismissed me from her service. She was staring ahead with her grin intact, waiting for the next person who would aid her.

28   I should call the police, I thought. But then surely her son would be told. I should speak with the pharmacists. Surely they might know her—though they might know her son as well. Yet who was I to keep this incident from him? And yet how could I help him put the hitchhiker in a home?

29   "Promise me you'll tell the druggist if no one comes soon," I said to her with great seriousness.

30   "I promise," she said with a cheerful little wave.

Questions for Close Reading

1. What is the selection's thesis? Locate the sentence(s) in which Murray states her main idea. If she doesn't state her thesis explicitly, express it in your own words.

2. What is the external conflict Murray experiences in this essay? What is the internal conflict?

3. In paragraph 22, the author says "Things were getting clearer." What does she mean by this?

4. Why does Murray finally go along with the hitchhiker's wishes?

Questions About the Writer's Craft

1. **The pattern.** How does Murray organize the events in this essay? How does she keep the reader oriented as her story progresses?

2. **Other patterns.** In some passages, Murray *describes* the hitchhiker's appearance. What do these descriptions contribute to the narrative?

3. In paragraphs 12, 20, 24 and 28, Murray tells us her thoughts. What effect do these sections have on the pace of the narrative? How do they affect our understanding of what is happening?

4. Murray uses a lot of dialogue in this essay. Explain why the use of dialogue is (or is not) effective. What function does the dialogue have?

Writing Assignments Using Narration as a Pattern of Development

1. Murray's encounter with the hitchhiker happens as she is driving home. Recall a time when you were traveling in a car, bus, or other vehicle and something surprising occurred. Were you frightened, puzzled, amused? Did you learn something about people or about yourself? Tell the story using first-person narration, being sure to include your thoughts as well as your actions and the actions of others.

2. Write a narrative about an incident in your life in which a stranger helped you, and explain how this made you feel. The experience might have made you grateful, resentful, or anxious like the hitchhiker. Use either flashback or flashforward to emphasize an event in your narrative.

Writing Assignment Combining Patterns of Development

3. Did Murray do the right thing when she left the elderly woman sitting in front of the drugstore? Write an essay in which you *argue* that Murray did or did not act properly. You can support your argument using *examples* from the essay showing the hitchhiker's state of mental and physical health. You can also support your argument by presenting the possible positive or negative effects of Murray's action, depending on your point of view.

ADDITIONAL WRITING TOPICS: NARRATION

General Assignments

Using narration, develop one of these topics into an essay.

1. An emergency that brought out the best or worst in you
2. The hazards of taking children out to eat
3. An incident that made you believe in fate
4. Your best or worst day at school or work
5. An important learning experience
6. A narrow escape
7. Your first date or first day on the job
8. A memorable childhood experience
9. An unpleasant confrontation
10. An imagined meeting with a historical figure

Assignments Using Visuals

Use the suggested visuals to help develop a narrative essay on one of these topics:

1. The best (or worst) vacation of your life (photos)
2. A school experience that had a positive impact on you (sketches or photos)
3. A family outing with an unexpected outcome (photos)
4. Something you did that you wish you could undo (diagram, photo)
5. A civic event you participated in (photos and/or Web links)

Assignments with a Specific Purpose, Audience, and Point of View

1. **Academic life.** Write an article for your old high school newspaper. The article will be read primarily by seniors who are planning to go away to college next year. In the article, narrate a story that points to some truth about the "breaking away" stage of life.

2. **Academic life**. A friend of yours has seen someone cheat on a test, plagiarize an entire paper, or seriously violate some other academic policy. In a letter, convince this friend to inform the instructor or a campus administrator by narrating an incident in which a witness did (or did not) speak up in such a situation. Tell what happened as a result.

3. **Civic activity.** You have had a disturbing encounter with one of the people who seems to have "fallen through the cracks" of society—a street person, an

unwanted child, or anyone else who is alone and abandoned. Write a letter to the local newspaper describing this encounter. Your purpose is to arouse people's indignation and compassion and to get help for such unfortunates.

4. **Civic activity.** Your younger brother, sister, relative, or neighborhood friend can't wait to be your age. Write a letter in which you narrate a dramatic story that shows the young person that your age isn't as wonderful as he or she thinks. Be sure to select a story that the person can understand and appreciate.

5. **Workplace action.** As fund-raiser for a particular organization (for example, Red Cross, SPCA, Big Brothers/Big Sisters), you're sending a newsletter to contributors. Support your cause by telling the story of a time when your organization made all the difference—the blood donation that saved a life, the animal that was rescued from abuse, and so on.

6. **Workplace action.** A customer has written a letter to you (or your boss) telling about a bad experience that he or she had with someone in your workplace. On the basis of that single experience, the customer now regards your company and its employees with great suspicion. It's your job to respond to this complaint. Write a letter to the customer balancing his or her negative picture by narrating a story that shows the "flip side" of your company and its employees.

12

Illustration

In this chapter, you will learn:

12.1 To use the pattern of illustration to develop your essays
12.2 To consider how illustration can fit your purpose and audience
12.3 To develop prewriting, writing, and revision strategies for using illustration in an essay
12.4 To analyze how illustration is used effectively in one student-written and three professionally authored selections
12.5 To write your own essays using illustration as a strategy

What Is Illustration?

If someone asked you, "Have you been to any good restaurants lately?" you probably wouldn't answer "Yes" and then immediately change the subject. Most likely, you would go on to **illustrate** with examples. Perhaps you'd give the names of restaurants you've enjoyed and talk briefly about the specific things you liked. Such examples and details are needed to convince others that your opinion—in this or any matter—is valid.

Examples are equally important when you write an essay. Facts, details, anecdotes, statistics, expert opinion, and personal observations are at the heart of effective writing; they give your work substance and solidity.

How Illustration Fits Your Purpose and Audience

The wording of assignments and essay exam questions may signal the need for illustration:

> Some observers claim that college students are less interested in learning than in getting ahead in their careers. Cite evidence to support or refute this claim.

☐ fat?
☐ fit?

Does true beauty only squee...

campaignforrealbeauty.c

A number of commentators claim that social media, such as *Facebook* and *Twitter*, have caused us to value personal privacy less than we did before. Basing your conclusion on your own experiences and observations, indicate whether you think this point of view is reasonable.

Such phrases as "Cite evidence" and "Basing your conclusion on your own experiences and observations" signal that each essay would be developed through illustration.

Usually, though, you won't be told so explicitly to provide examples. Instead, as you think about the best way to achieve your essay's purpose, you'll see the need for illustrative details—no matter which patterns of development you use. For instance, to *persuade* skeptical readers that the country needs a national health system, you might mention specific cases to dramatize the inadequacy of our current health-care system: a family bankrupted by medical bills; an uninsured accident victim turned away by a hospital; a chronically ill person rapidly deteriorating because he didn't have enough money to visit a doctor. Or imagine a lightly satiric piece that pokes fun at cat lovers. Insisting that "cat people" are pretty strange creatures, you might make your point—and make readers chuckle—with a series of examples *contrasting* cat lovers and dog lovers: the qualities admired by each group (loyalty in dogs versus independence in cats) and the different expectations each group has for its pets (dog lovers want Fido to be obedient and lovable, whereas cat lovers are satisfied with Felix's occasional spurts of docility and affection). Similarly, you would supply examples in a *causal analysis* speculating on the likely impact of a proposed tuition hike at your college. To convince the college administration of the probable negative effects of such a hike, you might cite the following examples: articles reporting a nationwide upswing in student transfers to less expensive schools; statistics indicating a significant drop in grades among already employed students forced to work more hours to pay increased tuition costs; interviews with students too financially strapped to continue their college education.

Whether you use illustration as a primary or supplemental method of development, it serves a number of important purposes. For one thing, illustrations make writing *interesting*. Assume you're writing an essay showing that television commercials are biased against women. Your essay would be lifeless and boring if all it did was repeat, in a general way, that commercials present stereotyped views of women:

Original

An anti-female bias is rampant in television commercials. It is very much alive, yet most viewers seem to take it all in stride. Few people protest the obviously sexist characters and statements on such commercials. Surely, these commercials misrepresent the way most of us live.

Without interesting particulars, readers may respond, "Who cares?" But if you provide specific examples, you'll attract your readers' attention:

Revised

An anti-female bias is rampant in television commercials. Although millions of women hold responsible jobs outside the home, commercials continue to portray women as simple creatures who spend much of their time thinking about wax buildup, cottony-soft bathroom tissue, and static-free clothes. Men, apparently, have better things to do than fret over such mundane household matters. How many commercials can you recall that depict men proclaiming the virtues of squeaky-clean dishes or sparkling bathrooms? Not many.

Illustrations also make writing *persuasive*. Most writing conveys a point, but many readers are reluctant to accept someone else's point of view unless evidence demonstrates its validity. Without specific examples your readers will question your position's validity.

Further, illustrations help *explain* difficult, abstract, or unusual ideas. As a writer, you have a responsibility to your readers to make difficult concepts concrete and understandable. Examples ground your discussion, making it immediate and concrete, preventing it from flying off into the vague and theoretical.

Finally, examples help *prevent unintended ambiguity*. All of us have experienced the frustration of having someone misinterpret what we say. In face-to-face communication, we can provide on-the-spot clarification. In writing, however, instantaneous feedback isn't available, so it's crucial that meaning be as unambiguous as possible. Illustrations will help.

Prewriting Strategies

The following checklist shows how you can apply to illustration some of the prewriting techniques discussed in Chapter 2.

☑ ILLUSTRATION: A PREWRITING CHECKLIST

Choose a Subject to Illustrate

- ☐ What general situation or phenomenon (for example, campus apathy, organic farming) can you depict through illustration?
- ☐ What difficult or misunderstood concept (nuclear winter, passive aggression) would examples help to explain and make concrete?

Determine Your Purpose, Audience, Tone, and Point of View

- ☐ What is your purpose in writing?
- ☐ What audience do you have in mind?
- ☐ What tone and point of view will best serve your purpose and lead readers to adopt the desired attitude toward the subject?

(continued)

Use Prewriting to Generate Examples

☐ How can brainstorming, freewriting, or mapping help you generate relevant examples from your own or others' experiences?

☐ How could library research help you gather pertinent examples (expert opinion, case studies, statistics)?

Strategies for Using Illustration in an Essay

After prewriting, you're ready to draft your essay. The following suggestions and Figure 12.1 (on page 187) will be helpful whether you use illustration as a dominant or supportive pattern of development.

1. **Select the examples to include.** Examples can take several forms, including specific names (of people, places, products, and so on), anecdotes, personal observations, and expert opinion, as well as facts, statistics, and case studies gathered through research. Once you've used prewriting to generate as many examples as possible, you're ready to limit your examples to the strongest. Keeping your thesis, audience, tone, and point of view in mind, ask yourself several key questions: "Which examples support my thesis? Which do not? Which are most convincing? Which are most likely to interest readers and clarify meaning?"

   You may include several brief examples within a single sentence:

   The French people's fascination with some American literary figures, such as Poe and Hawthorne, is understandable, but their great respect for "artists" like comedian Jerry Lewis is a mystery to many Americans.

   Or you may develop a paragraph with a number of "for instances":

   A uniquely American style of movie-acting reached its peak in the 1950s. Certain charismatic actors completely abandoned the stage techniques and tradition that had been the foundation of acting up to that time. Instead of articulating their lines clearly, the actors mumbled; instead of making firm eye contact with their colleagues, they hung their heads, shifted their eyes, even talked with their eyes closed. Marlon Brando, Montgomery Clift, and James Dean were three actors who exemplified this new trend.

   As the preceding paragraph shows, *several examples* are usually needed to achieve your purpose. An essay with the thesis, "Video games are dangerously violent" wouldn't be convincing if you gave only one example of a violent video game. Several strong examples would be needed for readers to feel you had illustrated your point sufficiently.

FIGURE 12.1

Development Diagram: Writing an Illustration Essay

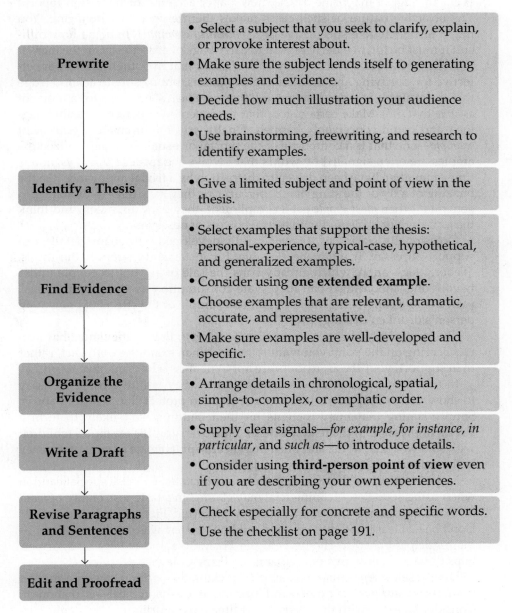

Prewrite	• Select a subject that you seek to clarify, explain, or provoke interest about. • Make sure the subject lends itself to generating examples and evidence. • Decide how much illustration your audience needs. • Use brainstorming, freewriting, and research to identify examples.
Identify a Thesis	• Give a limited subject and point of view in the thesis.
Find Evidence	• Select examples that support the thesis: personal-experience, typical-case, hypothetical, and generalized examples. • Consider using **one extended example**. • Choose examples that are relevant, dramatic, accurate, and representative. • Make sure examples are well-developed and specific.
Organize the Evidence	• Arrange details in chronological, spatial, simple-to-complex, or emphatic order.
Write a Draft	• Supply clear signals—*for example, for instance, in particular*, and *such as*—to introduce details. • Consider using **third-person point of view** even if you are describing your own experiences.
Revise Paragraphs and Sentences	• Check especially for concrete and specific words. • Use the checklist on page 191.
Edit and Proofread	

As a general rule, you should strive for variety in the kinds of examples you include. For instance, you might choose a *personal-experience example* drawn from your own life or from the life of someone you know. Such examples pack the wallop of personal authority and lend drama to writing. Or you might include a *typical-case example,* an actual event or situation that did occur—but not to you or to anyone you know. (Perhaps you learned about the event through a magazine article, newspaper account, or television report.) The objective nature of such cases makes them especially convincing. You might also include a speculative or *hypothetical example* ("Imagine how difficult it must be for an elderly person to carry bags of groceries from the market to a bus stop several blocks away"). You'll find that hypothetical cases are effective for clarifying and dramatizing key points, but be sure to acknowledge that the example is indeed invented ("*Suppose* that...." or "Let's for a moment *assume* that...."). Make certain, too, that the invented situation is easily imagined and could conceivably happen. Finally, you might create a *generalized example*—one that is a composite of the typical or usual. Such generalized examples are often signaled by words that involve the reader ("*All of us,* at one time or another, have been driven to distraction by a trivial annoyance like the buzzing of a fly or the sting of a papercut"), or they may refer to humanity in general ("When *most people* get a compliment, they perk up, preen, and think the praise-giver is blessed with astute powers of observation").

Occasionally, *one extended example,* fully developed with many details, can support an essay. It might be possible, for instance, to support the thesis, "Federal legislation, which already bans the sale of alcohol to people under twenty-one, should also ban its private consumption by those individuals" with a single compelling, highly detailed example of the effects of one young person's drunken-driving spree.

The examples you choose must also be *relevant;* that is, they must have direct bearing on the point you want to make. When examples *contradict,* rather than support, your thesis, readers are apt to dismiss what you have to say.

In addition, try to select *dramatic* examples. Say you're writing an essay to show that society needs to take more steps to protect children from abuse. Simply stating that many parents hit their children isn't likely to form a strong impression in the reader's mind. However, graphic examples (children with stab wounds, welts, and burn marks) are apt to create a sense of urgency in the reader.

 Make certain, too, that your examples are *accurate.* Exercise special caution when using statistics. A commercial may claim, "In a taste test, eighty percent of those questioned indicated that they preferred Fizzy Cola." Impressed? Don't be—at least, not until you find out how the test was conducted. Perhaps the participants had to choose between Fizzy Cola and battery acid, or perhaps there were only five participants, all Fizzy Cola vice presidents.

Finally, select *representative* examples. Picking the oddball, one-in-a-million example to support a point—and passing it off as typical—is dishonest. Consider an essay with the thesis, "Part-time jobs contribute to academic success." Citing only one example of a student who works at a job twenty-five hours a week while earning straight *A*'s isn't playing fair. Why not? You've made a *hasty generalization* based on only one case. To be convincing, you need to show how holding down a job affects *most* students' academic performance. (For more on hasty generalizations, see page 393.)

2. **Develop your examples sufficiently.** To ensure that you get your ideas across, you must make sure your examples are *specific*. An essay on the types of heroes in American movies wouldn't succeed if you simply strung together a series of undeveloped examples in paragraphs like this one:

Original

Heroes in American movies usually fall into types. One kind of hero is the tight-lipped loner, men like Clint Eastwood and Humphrey Bogart. Another movie hero is the quiet, shy, or fumbling type who has appeared in movies since the beginning. The main characteristic of this hero is lovableness, as seen in actors like Jimmy Stewart. Perhaps the most one-dimensional and predictable hero is the superman who battles tough odds. This kind of hero is best illustrated by Sylvester Stallone as Rocky and Rambo.

The examples in the preceding paragraph could be developed in paragraphs of their own. You could, for instance, develop the first example this way:

Revised

Heroes can be tight-lipped loners who appear out of nowhere, form no permanent attachments, and walk, drive, or ride off into the sunset. In most of his Westerns, from the low-budget "spaghetti Westerns" of the 1960s to *Unforgiven* in 1992, Clint Eastwood personifies this kind of hero. He is remote, mysterious, and untalkative. Yet he guns down an evil sheriff, runs other villains out of town, and helps a handicapped girl—acts that cement his heroic status. The loner might also be Sam Spade as played by Humphrey Bogart. Spade solves the crime and sends the guilty off to jail, yet he holds his emotions in check and has no permanent ties beyond his faithful secretary and shabby office. One gets the feeling that he could walk away from these, too, if necessary. Even in *The Right Stuff*, an account of America's early astronauts, the scriptwriters mold Chuck Yeager, the man who broke the sound barrier, into a classic loner. Yeager, portrayed by the aloof Sam Shepard, has a wife, but he is nevertheless insular. Taking mute pride in his ability to distance himself from politicians, bureaucrats, even colleagues, he soars into space, dignified and detached.

(For hints on making evidence specific, see pages 62–63 in Chapter 6.)

3. **Organize the examples.** If, as is usually the case, several examples support your point, be sure to present the examples in an *organized* manner. Often you'll find that other *patterns of development* (cause-effect, comparison-contrast, definition, and so on) suggest ways to sequence examples. Let's say you're writing an essay showing that stay-at-home vacations offer

numerous opportunities to relax. You might begin the essay with examples that *contrast* stay-at-home and get-away vacations. Then you might move to a *process analysis* that illustrates different techniques for unwinding at home. The essay might end with examples showing the *effect* of such leisurely at-home breaks.

Finally, you need to select an *organizational approach consistent* with your *purpose* and *thesis.* Imagine you're writing an essay about students' adjustment during the first months of college. The supporting examples could be arranged *chronologically.* You might start by illustrating the ambivalence many students feel the first day of college when their parents leave for home; you might then offer an anecdote or two about students' frequent calls to Mom and Dad during the opening weeks of the semester; the essay might close with an account of students' reluctance to leave campus at the midyear break.

Similarly, an essay demonstrating that a room often reflects the character of its occupant might be organized *spatially:* from the empty soda cans on the floor to the spitballs on the ceiling. In an essay illustrating the kinds of skills taught in a composition course, you might move from *simple* to *complex* examples: starting with relatively matter-of-fact skills such as spelling and punctuation and ending with more conceptually difficult skills like formulating a thesis and organizing an essay. Last, the *emphatic sequence*—in which you lead from your first example to your final, most significant one—is another effective way to organize an essay with many examples. A paper about Americans' characteristic impatience might progress from minor examples (dependence on fast food, obsession with texting and Instant Messaging) to more disturbing manifestations of impatience (using drugs as quick solutions to problems, advocating simple answers to complex international problems: "Bomb them!").

4. **Choose a point of view.** Many essays developed by illustration place the subject in the foreground and the writer in the background. Such an approach calls for the *third-person point of view.* For example, even if you draw examples from your own personal experience, you can present them without using the *first-person "I."* You might convert such personal material into generalized examples (see pages 90–91), or you might describe the personal experience as if it happened to someone else. Just because an event happened to you personally doesn't mean you have to use the first-person point of view. Remember also that many instructors discourage the use of "I" in an academic paper.

Revision Strategies

Once you have a draft of the essay, you're ready to revise. The following checklist will help you and those giving you feedback apply to illustration some of the revision techniques discussed in Chapters 7 and 8.

> ☑ **ILLUSTRATION: A REVISION/PEER REVIEW CHECKLIST**

Revise Overall Meaning and Structure

- ☐ What thesis is being advanced? Which examples don't support the thesis? Should these examples be deleted, or should the thesis be reshaped to fit the examples? Why?
- ☐ Which patterns of development and methods of organization (chronological, spatial, simple-to-complex, emphatic) provide the essay's framework? Would other ordering principles be more effective? If so, which ones?

Revise Paragraph Development

- ☐ Which paragraphs contain too many or too few examples? Which contain examples that are too brief or too extended? Which include insufficiently or overly detailed examples?
- ☐ Which paragraphs rely on predictable examples? How could the examples be made more compelling?
- ☐ Which paragraphs include examples that are atypical or inaccurate?

Revise Sentences and Words

- ☐ What signal devices (*for example, for instance, in particular, such as*) introduce examples and clarify the line of thought? Where are there too many or too few of these devices?
- ☐ Where would more varied sentence structure heighten the effect of the essay's illustrations?
- ☐ Where would more concrete and specific words make the examples more effective?

Student Essay: From Prewriting Through Revision

The student essay that follows was written by Michael Pagano in response to this assignment:

> One implication in Beth Johnson's "Bombs Bursting in Air" is that, given life's unanticipated tragedies, people need to focus on what's really important rather than on trivial complications and distractions. Observe closely the way you and others conduct your daily lives. Use your observations for an essay that supports or refutes Johnson's point of view.

After deciding to write an essay on the way possessions complicate life, Michael sat down at his computer and did some *freewriting* to generate material on the topic. His original freewriting follows; the handwritten comments indicate Michael's later efforts to develop and shape this material. Note that Michael deleted some points, added others, and made several items more specific; he also labeled and sequenced key ideas. These annotations paved the way for a sentence outline, which is presented after the freewriting.

Freewriting

① Buying

I shop too much. So do my parents—practically every weekend ~~and nearly every~~ ~~holiday except Christmas and Easter. All those Washington's Birthday sales.~~ Then they yell at us kids for watching so much TV, although they're not around to do much with us. In fact, Mom and Dad were the ones who thought our old ^{19-inch} TV wasn't good enough

④ Discarding items

anymore so they replaced it with a huge ^{35-inch} flat-screen set. I remember all those annoying phone calls when they put the ad in the paper to sell the old set. People coming and going. Then Mom and Dad only got $25 for it anyway. It wasn't worth paying for the ad. ~~They never seem to come out ahead.~~ No wonder Mom works part-time at the

⑤ Running into debt

library and Dad stays so late at the office. I'm getting into the same situation. Already up to my ears in debt, paying off the car. I spend hours washing it and

② Running out of room

waxing it, and it doesn't even fit into the garage, which is loaded with discarded junk. The whole house is cluttered. Maybe that's why people move so much—to escape the clutter. There was hardly room for my new computer in my room. I also have to shove my new clothes into the closets and drawers. My snazzy new pants get all wrinkled. They

③ Having maintenance problems

shrank when I washed them. Now they're too tight. I should have sent them to the dry cleaners. But I'd already paid enough for them. ~~Well, everything's shoddy nowadays.~~ Possessions don't hold up. So what lasts? Basic values—love, family, friends.

(margin annotations: *classified section*, *2nd job-*, *overtime*, *time payments*, *③ vacuuming car—maintenance*, *My computer's giving me trouble*, *conclusion?*)

Outline

Thesis: We clutter our lives with material goods.

    I.   We waste a lot of time deciding what to buy.
        A.   We window-shop for good-looking footwear.
        B.   We look through magazines for stereos and exercise equipment.
        C.   Family life suffers when everyone is out shopping.

    II.   Once we take our new purchases home, we find we don't have enough room for them.
        A.   We stack things in crowded closets, garages, and basements.
        B.   When things get too cluttered, we simply move.

    III.   Our possessions require continual maintenance.
        A.   Cars have to be washed and waxed.
        B.   New pants have to go to the cleaners.
        C.   Computers and other items break down and have to be replaced.

    IV.   Before we replace broken items, we try to get rid of them by placing ads in the classified section.
        A.   We have to deal with annoying phone calls.
        B.   We have to deal with people coming to the house to see the items.

V. Our mania for possessions puts us in debt.
   A. We accumulate enormous credit-card balances.
   B. We take second jobs or work overtime to make time payments.

Now read Michael's paper, "Pursuit of Possessions," noting the similarities and differences among his freewriting, outline, and final essay. You'll see, for example, that Michael changed the "I" of his freewriting to the more general "We" in the outline and essay. He made this change because he wanted readers to see themselves in the situations being illustrated. In addition, Michael's outline, while more detailed than his freewriting, doesn't include highly concrete examples, but the essay does. In the outline, for instance, he simply states, "Computers and other items break down…" In the essay, though, he spins out this point with vivid details: "The home computer starts to lose data, the microwave has to have its temperature controls adjusted, and the DVD player has to be serviced when a disc becomes jammed."

As you read Michael's essay, also consider how well it applies the principles of illustration. (The commentary that follows the paper will help you look at the essay more closely and will give you some sense of how Michael went about revising his first draft.)

Pursuit of Possessions
By Michael Pagano

1   In the essay "Bombs Bursting in Air," Beth Johnson develops the extended metaphor of bombs exploding unexpectedly to represent the tragedies that occur without warning in our daily lives. Herself a survivor of innumerable life bombs, Johnson suggests that in light of life's fragility, we need to remember and appreciate what's really important to us. But very often, we lose sight of what really matters in our lives, instead occupying ourselves with trivial distractions. In particular, many of us choose to spend our lives in pursuit of material possessions. Much of our time goes into buying new things, dealing with the complications they create, and working madly to buy more things or pay for the things we already have.

Introduction

Thesis

Plan of development

2   We devote a great deal of our lives to acquiring the material goods we imagine are essential to our well-being. Hours are spent planning and thinking about our future purchases. We window-shop for designer running shoes; we leaf through magazines looking at ads for elaborate sound equipment; we research back issues of *Consumer Reports* to find out about recent developments in exercise equipment. Moreover, once we find what we are looking for, more time is taken up when we decide to actually buy the items. How do we find this time? That's easy. We turn evenings, weekends, and holidays—times that used to be set aside for family and friends—into shopping

Topic sentence

The first of three paragraphs in a chronological sequence

expeditions. No wonder family life is deteriorating and children spend so much time in front of television sets. Their parents are seldom around.

Topic sentence ———→   As soon as we take our new purchases home, they begin to complicate our lives.   3

The second paragraph in the chronological sequence

A paragraph with many specific examples

A sleek new sports car has to be washed, waxed, and vacuumed. A fashionable pair of overpriced dress pants can't be thrown in the washing machine but has to be taken to the dry cleaner. New sound equipment has to be connected with a tangled network of cables to the TV, computer, and speakers. Eventually, of course, the inevitable happens. Our indispensable possessions break down and need to be repaired. The home computer starts to lose data, the microwave has to have its temperature controls adjusted, and the DVD player has to be serviced when a disc becomes jammed in the machine.

Topic sentence ———→   After more time has gone by, we sometimes discover that our purchases don't   4

The third paragraph in the chronological sequence

suit us anymore, and so we decide to replace them. Before making our replacement purchases, though, we have to find ways to get rid of the old items. If we want to replace our 19-inch television set with a 35-inch flat-screen, we have to find time to put an ad in the classified section of the paper. Then we have to handle phone calls and set up times people can come to look at the old TV. We could store the set in the basement—if we are lucky enough to find a spot that isn't already filled with other discarded purchases.

Topic sentence with emphasis signal

Worst of all, this mania for possessions often influences our approach to work. It   5 is not unusual for people to take a second or even a third job to pay off the debt they fall into because they have overbought. After paying for food, clothing, and shelter, many people see the rest of their paycheck go to Visa, MasterCard, department store charge accounts, and time payments. Panic sets in when they realize there simply is not enough money to cover all their expenses. Just to stay afloat, people may have to work overtime or take on additional jobs.

Conclusion

It is clear that many of us have allowed the pursuit of possessions to dominate   6 our lives. We are so busy buying, maintaining, and paying for our worldly goods that we do not have much time to think about what is really important. We should try to step back from our compulsive need for more of everything and get in touch with the basic values that are the real point of our lives.

Commentary

Thesis, Combining Patterns of Development, and Plan of Development

In "Pursuit of Possessions," Michael analyzes the mania for acquiring material goods that permeates our society. He begins by addressing an implication conveyed in Beth Johnson's "Bombs Bursting in Air"—that life's fragility dictates that we need to focus on what really matters in our lives. This reference to Johnson gives Michael a chance to contrast the reflective way she suggests we should live with the acquisitive and frenzied way many people lead their lives. This contrast leads to the essay's thesis: "[M]any of us choose to spend our lives in pursuit of material possessions."

Besides introducing the basic contrast at the heart of the essay, Michael's opening paragraph helps readers see that the essay contains an element of *causal analysis*. The final sentence of the introductory paragraph lays out the effects of our possession obsession. This sentence also serves as the essay's *plan of development* and reveals that Michael feels the pursuit of possessions negatively affects our lives in three key ways.

Essays of this length often don't need a plan of development. But because Michael's paper is filled with many *examples,* the plan of development helps readers see how all the details relate to the essay's central point.

Evidence

Support for the thesis consists of numerous examples presented in the *first-person plural point of view* ("*We* lose sight...," "*We* devote a great deal of our lives...," and so on). Many of these examples seem drawn from Michael's, his friends', or his family's experiences; however, to emphasize the events' universality, Michael converts these essentially personal examples into generalized ones that "we" all experience.

These examples, in turn, are organized around the three major points signaled by the plan of development. Michael uses one paragraph to develop his first and third points and two paragraphs to develop his second point. Each of the four supporting paragraphs is focused by a *topic sentence* that appears at the beginning of the paragraph. The transitional phrase, "Worst of all" (paragraph 5) signals that Michael has sequenced his major points *emphatically,* saving for last the issue he considers most significant: how the "mania for possessions...influences our approach to work."

Organizational Strategies

Emphatic order isn't Michael's only organizational technique. When reading the paper, you probably felt that there was an easy flow from one supporting paragraph to the next. How does Michael achieve such *coherence between paragraphs?* For one thing, he sequences paragraphs 2–4 *chronologically:* what happens before a purchase is made; what happens afterward. Secondly, topic sentences in paragraphs 3 and 4 include *signal devices* that indicate this passage of time. The topic sentences also strengthen coherence by *linking back* to the preceding paragraph: "*As soon as we take our new purchases home, they...complicate our lives*" and "*After more time has gone by, we...discover that our purchases don't suit us anymore.*"

The same organizing strategies are used *within paragraphs* to make the essay coherent. Details in paragraphs 2–4 are sequenced *chronologically,* and to help readers follow the chronology, Michael uses *signal devices:* "*Moreover, once* we find what we are looking for, more time is taken up..." (2); "*Eventually*, of course, the inevitable happens" (3); "*Then* we have to handle phone calls..." (4).

Problems with Paragraph Development

You probably recall that an essay developed primarily through illustration must include examples that are *relevant, interesting, convincing, representative, accurate*, and *specific*. On the whole, Michael's examples meet these requirements. The third and fourth paragraphs, especially, include vigorous details that show how our mania for buying things can govern our lives. We may even laugh with self-recognition when reading about "overpriced dress pants that can't be thrown in the washing machine" or a basement "filled...with discarded purchases."

The fifth paragraph, however, is underdeveloped. We know that this paragraph presents what Michael considers his most significant point, but the paragraph's examples are rather *flat* and *unconvincing*. To make this final section more compelling, Michael could mention specific people who overspend, revealing how much they are in debt and how much they have to work to become solvent again. Or he could cite a television documentary or magazine article dealing with the issue of consumer debt. Such specifics would give the paragraph the solidity it now lacks.

Shift in Tone

The fifth paragraph has a second, more subtle problem: a *shift in tone*. Although Michael has, up to this point, been critical of our possession-mad culture, he has poked fun at our obsession and kept his tone conversational and gently satiric. In this paragraph, though, he adopts a serious tone, and, in the next paragraph, his tone becomes even weightier, almost preachy. It is, of course, legitimate to have a serious message in a lightly satiric piece. In fact, most satiric writing has such an additional layer of meaning. But because Michael has trouble blending these two moods, there's a jarring shift in the essay.

Shift in Focus

The second paragraph shows another kind of shift—in *focus*. The paragraph's controlling idea is that too much time is spent acquiring possessions. However, starting with "No wonder family life is deteriorating," Michael includes two sentences that introduce a complex issue beyond the scope of the essay. Because the sentences disrupt the paragraph's unity, they should be deleted.

Revising the First Draft

Although the final version of the essay needs work in spots, it's much stronger than Michael's first draft. To see how Michael went about revising the draft, compare his paper's second and third supporting paragraphs with his draft version reprinted here. The annotations, numbered in order of importance, show the ideas Michael hit upon when he returned to his first draft and reworked this section.

Original Version of the Second Paragraph

Our lives are spent not only buying things but in dealing with the inevitable complications that are created by our newly acquired possessions. First, we have to find places to put all the objects we bring home. More clothes demand more closets; a second car demands more garage space; a home-entertainment center requires elaborate shelving. We shouldn't be surprised that the average American family moves once every three years. A good many families move simply because they need more space to store all the things they buy. In addition, our possessions demand maintenance time. A person who gets a new car will spend hours washing it, waxing it, and vacuuming it. A new pair of pants has to go to the dry cleaners. New sound systems have to be connected to already existing equipment. Eventually, of course, the inevitable happens. Our new items need to be repaired. Or we get sick of them and decide to replace them. Before making our replacement purchases, though, we have to get rid of the old items. That can be a real inconvenience.

② Awkward first sentence

① Paragraph goes in too many directions. Cut idea about moving because not enough space.

③ Make problem with pants more specific

④ Develop more fully

Referring to the revision checklist on page 191 helped Michael see that the paragraph rambled and lacked energy. He started to revise by tightening the first sentence, making it more focused and less awkward. Certainly, the revised sentence ("As soon as we take our new purchases home, they begin to complicate our lives") is crisper than the original. Next, he decided to omit the discussion about finding places to put new possessions; these sentences about inadequate closet, garage, and shelf space were so exaggerated that they undercut the valid point he wanted to make. He also chose to eliminate the sentences about the mobility of American families. This was, he felt, an interesting point, but it introduced an issue too complex to be included in the paragraph.

Michael strengthened the rest of the paragraph by making his examples more specific. A "new car" became a "sleek new sports car," and a "pair of pants" became a "fashionable pair of overpriced dress pants." Michael also realized he had to do more than merely write, "Eventually,...our new items need to be repaired." This point had to be dramatized by sharp, convincing details. Therefore, Michael added lively examples to describe how high-tech possessions—microwaves, home computers, DVD players—break down. Similarly, Michael realized it wasn't enough simply to say, as he had in the original, that we run into problems when we try to replace out-of-favor purchases. Vigorous details were again needed to illustrate the point. Michael thus used a typical "replaceable" (an old TV) as his key example and showed the annoyance involved in handling phone calls and setting up appointments so that people could see the TV.

After adding these specifics, Michael realized that he had enough material to devote a separate paragraph to the problems associated with replacing old purchases. By dividing his original paragraph, Michael ended up with two well-focused paragraphs, rather than a single rambling one.

In short, Michael strengthened his essay through substantial revision. Another round of rewriting would have made the essay stronger still. Even without this additional work, Michael's essay provides an interesting perspective on a current social preoccupation.

 ## ACTIVITIES: ILLUSTRATION

Prewriting Activities

1. Imagine you're writing two essays: One is a serious paper analyzing why large numbers of public school teachers leave the profession each year; the other is a light essay defining *preppie, thug,* or some other slang term used to describe a kind of person. Jot down ways you might use examples in each essay.

2. Use mapping or another prewriting technique to gather examples illustrating the truth of *one* of the following familiar sayings. Then, using the same or a different prewriting technique, accumulate examples that counter the saying. Weigh both sets of examples to determine the saying's validity. After developing an appropriate thesis, decide which examples you would elaborate in an essay.

   a. Haste makes waste.
   b. There's no use crying over spilled milk.
   c. A bird in the hand is worth two in the bush.

3. Turn back to activity 4 and activity 5 in Chapter 4, and select *one* thesis statement for which you didn't develop supporting evidence earlier. Identify a purpose, audience, tone, and point of view for an essay with this thesis. Then meet with at least one other person to generate as many examples as possible to support the thesis. Next, evaluate the material to determine which examples should be eliminated. Finally, from the remaining examples, take the strongest one and develop it as fully as you can.

4. Freewrite or use your journal to generate examples illustrating how widespread a recent fad or trend has become. After reviewing your prewriting to determine a possible thesis, narrow the examples to those you would retain for an essay. How might the patterns of development or a chronological, emphatic, spatial, or simple-to-complex approach help you sequence the examples?

Revising Activities

5. The following paragraph is from the first draft of an essay about the decline of small-town shopping districts. The paragraph is meant to show what small

towns can do to revitalize business. Revise the paragraph, strengthening it with specific and convincing examples.

A small town can compete with a large new mall for shoppers. But merchants must work together, modernizing the stores and making the town's main street pleasant, even fun to walk. They should also copy the malls' example by including attention-getting events as often as possible.

6. The paragraph that follows is from the first draft of an essay showing how knowledge of psychology can help us understand behavior that might otherwise seem baffling. The paragraph is intended to illustrate the meaning of the psychological term *superego*. Revise the paragraph, replacing its vague, unconvincing examples with one extended example that conveys the meaning of *superego* clearly and dramatically.

The superego is the part of us that makes us feel guilty when we do something that we know is wrong. When we act foolishly or wildly, we usually feel qualms about our actions later on. If we imagine ourselves getting revenge, we most likely discover that the thoughts make us feel bad. All of these are examples of the superego at work.

7. Reprinted here is a paragraph from the first draft of a light-spirited essay showing that Americans' pursuit of change for change's sake has drawbacks. The paragraph is meant to illustrate that infatuation with newness costs consumers money yet leads to no improvement in product quality. How effective is the paragraph? Which examples are specific and convincing? Which are not? Do any seem nonrepresentative, offensive, or sexist? How could the paragraph's organization be improved? Consider these questions as you rewrite the paragraph. Add specific examples where needed. Depending on the way you revise, you may want to break this one paragraph into several.

We end up paying for our passion for the new and improved. Trendy clothing styles convince us that last year's outfits are outdated, even though our old clothes are fine. Women are especially vulnerable in this regard. What, though, about items that have to be replaced periodically, like shampoo? Even slight changes lead to new formulations requiring retooling of the production process. That means increased manufacturing costs per item—all of which get passed on to us, the consumer. Then there are those items that tout new, trend-setting features that make earlier versions supposedly obsolete. Some manufacturers, for example, boast that their stereo sound systems transmit an expanded-frequency range. The problem is that humans can't even hear such frequencies, But the high-tech feature dazzles men who are too naive to realize they're being hoodwinked.

PROFESSIONAL SELECTIONS: ILLUSTRATION

Kay S. Hymowitz

A senior fellow at the Manhattan Institute and a contributing editor of the urban-policy magazine *City Journal*, Kay S. Hymowitz (1948–) writes on education and childhood in the United States. A native of Philadelphia, Hymowitz received an undergraduate English degree from Brandeis University and graduate degrees from Tufts University and Columbia University. She has taught English literature and composition at Brooklyn College and at Parsons School of Design. Her work has appeared in publications including *The New York Times, The Washington Post,* and *The New Republic.* The following essay appeared in the Autumn 1998 issue of *City Journal.*

For ideas on how this illustration essay is organized, see Figure 12.2 on page 204.

Pre-Reading Journal Entry

Think back on your childhood. What were some possessions and activities that you cherished and enjoyed? Freewrite for a few moments in your pre-reading journal about these beloved objects and/or pastimes. What exactly were they? Why did you enjoy them so much? Did your feelings about them change as you matured into adolescence?

TWEENS: TEN GOING ON SIXTEEN

During the past year my youngest morphed from child to teenager. Down came the   1
posters of adorable puppies and the drawings from art class; up went the airbrushed faces of Leonardo di Caprio and Kate Winslet. CDs of Le Ann Rimes and Paula Cole appeared mysteriously, along with teen fan magazines featuring glowering movie and rock-and-roll hunks....She started reading the newspaper—or at least the movie ads—with all the intensity of a Talmudic scholar, scanning for glimpses of her beloved Leo or, failing that, Matt Damon. As spring approached and younger children skipped past our house on their way to the park, she swigged from a designer water bottle, wearing the obligatory tank top and denim shorts as she whispered on the phone to friends about games of Truth or Dare. The last rites for her childhood came when, embarrassed at reminders of her foolish past, she pulled a sheet over her years-in-the-making American Girl doll collection, now dead to the world.

So what's new in this dog-bites-man story? Well, as all this was going on, my daugh-   2
ter was ten years old and in the fourth grade.

Those who remember their own teenybopper infatuation with Elvis or the Beatles   3
might be inclined to shrug their shoulders as if to say, "It was ever thus." But this is different. Across class lines and throughout the country, elementary and middle-school principals and teachers, child psychologists and psychiatrists, marketing and demographic researchers all confirm the pronouncement of Henry Trevor, middle-school director of the Berkeley Carroll School in Brooklyn, New York: "There is no such thing as preadolescence anymore. Kids are teenagers at ten."

Marketers have a term for this new social animal, kids between eight and 12: they   4
call them "tweens." The name captures the ambiguous reality: though chronologically

midway between early childhood and adolescence, this group is leaning more and more toward teen styles, teen attitudes, and, sadly, teen behavior at its most troubling.

5   The tween phenomenon grows out of a complicated mixture of biology, demography, and the predictable assortment of Bad Ideas. But putting aside its causes for a moment, the emergence of tweendom carries risks for both young people and society. Eight- to 12-year-olds have an even more wobbly sense of themselves than adolescents; they rely more heavily on others to tell them how to understand the world and how to place themselves in it. Now, for both pragmatic and ideological reasons, they are being increasingly "empowered" to do this on their own, which leaves them highly vulnerable both to a vulgar and sensation-driven marketplace and to the crass authority of their immature peers. In tweens, we can see the future of our society taking shape, and it's not at all clear how it's going to work.

6   Perhaps the most striking evidence for the tweening of children comes from market researchers. "There's no question there's a deep trend, not a passing fad, toward kids getting older younger," says research psychologist Michael Cohen of Arc Consulting, a public policy, education, and marketing research firm in New York. "This is not just on the coasts. There are no real differences geographically." It seems my daughter's last rites for her American Girl dolls were a perfect symbol not just for her own childhood but for childhood, period. The Toy Manufacturers of America Factbook states that, where once the industry could count on kids between birth and 14 as their target market, today it is only birth to ten. "In the last ten years we've seen a rapid development of upper-age children," says Bruce Friend, vice president of worldwide research and planning for Nickelodeon, a cable channel aimed at kids. "The 12- to 14-year-olds of yesterday are the ten to 12s of today." The rise of the preteen teen is "the biggest trend we've seen."

7   Scorning any symbols of their immaturity, tweens now cultivate a self-image that emphasizes sophistication. The Nickelodeon-Yankelovich Youth Monitor found that by the time they are 12, children describe themselves as "flirtatious, sexy, trendy, athletic, cool." Nickelodeon's Bruce Friend reports that by 11, children in focus groups say they no longer even think of themselves as children.

8   They're very concerned with their "look," Friend says, even more so than older teens. Sprouting up everywhere are clothing stores like the chain Limited Too and the catalog company Delia, geared toward tween girls who scorn old-fashioned, little-girl flowers, ruffles, white socks, and Mary Janes[1] in favor of the cool—black mini-dresses and platform shoes.... Teachers complain of ten- or 11-year-old girls arriving at school looking like madams, in full cosmetic regalia, with streaked hair, platform shoes, and midriff-revealing shirts. Barbara Kapetanakes, a psychologist at a conservative Jewish day school in New York, describes her students' skirts as being about "the size of a belt." Kapetanakes says she was told to dress respectfully on Fridays, the eve of the Jewish Sabbath, which she did by donning a long skirt and a modest blouse. Her students, on the other hand, showed their respect by looking "like they should be hanging around the West Side Highway," where prostitutes ply their trade.

9   Lottie Sims, a computer teacher in a Miami middle school, says that the hooker look for tweens is fanning strong support for uniforms in her district. But uniforms and tank-top

---

[1]Trademark name of patent-leather shoes for girls, usually having a low heel and a strap that fastens at the side (editors' note).

bans won't solve the problem of painted young ladies. "You can count on one hand the girls not wearing makeup," Sims says. "Their parents don't even know. They arrive at school with huge bags of lipstick and hair spray, and head straight to the girls' room."

Though the tweening of youth affects girls more visibly than boys, especially since   10
boys mature more slowly, boys are by no means immune to these obsessions. Once upon a time, about ten years ago, fifth- and sixth-grade boys were about as fashion-conscious as their pet hamsters. But a growing minority have begun trading in their baseball cards for hair mousse and baggy jeans. In some places, $200 jackets, embla-zoned with sports logos like the warm-up gear of professional athletes, are *de rigueur*[2]; in others, the preppy look is popular among the majority, while the more daring go for the hipper style of pierced ears, fade haircuts, or ponytails. Often these tween pea-cocks strut through their middle-school hallways taunting those who have yet to catch on to the cool look....

Those who seek comfort in the idea that the tweening of childhood is merely a   11
matter of fashion—who maybe even find their lip-synching, hip-swaying little boy or girl kind of cute—might want to think twice. There are disturbing signs that tweens are not only eschewing the goody-goody childhood image but its substance as well....

The clearest evidence of tweendom's darker side concerns crime. Although chil-   12
dren under 15 still represent a minority of juvenile arrests, their numbers grew dis-proportionately in the past 20 years. According to a report by the Office of Juvenile Justice and Delinquency Prevention, "offenders under age 15 represent the leading edge of the juvenile crime problem, and their numbers are growing." Moreover, the crimes committed by younger teens and preteens are growing in severity. "Person of-fenses,[3] which once constituted 16 percent of the total court cases for this age group," continues the report, "now constitute 25 percent." Headline grabbers—like Nathaniel Abraham of Pontiac, Michigan, an 11-year-old who stole a rifle from a neighbor's ga-rage and went on a shooting spree in October 1997, randomly killing a teenager com-ing out of a store; and 11-year-old Andrew Golden, who, with his 13-year-old partner, killed four children and one teacher at his middle school in Jonesboro, Arkansas—are extreme, exceptional cases, but alas, they are part of a growing trend toward preteen violent crime....

The evidence on tween sex presents a troubling picture, too. Despite a decrease   13
among older teens for the first time since records have been kept, sexual activity among tweens increased during that period. It seems that kids who are having sex are doing so at earlier ages. Between 1988 and 1995, the proportion of girls saying they began sex before 15 rose from 11 percent to 19 percent. (For boys, the number remained stable, at 21 percent.) This means that approximately one in five middle-school kids is sexually active. Christie Hogan, a middle-school counselor for 20 years in Louisville, Kentucky, says: "We're beginning to see a few pregnant sixth-graders." Many of the principals and counselors I spoke with reported a small but striking mi-nority of sexually active seventh-graders....

Certainly the days of the tentative and giggly preadolescent seem to be passing.   14
Middle-school principals report having to deal with miniskirted 12-year-olds "draping themselves over boys" or patting their behinds in the hallways, while 11-year-old boys

---

[2]French term referring to something that fashion or custom requires (editors' note).
[3]Crimes against a person. They include assault, robbery, rape, and homicide (editors' note).

taunt girls about their breasts and rumors about their own and even their parents' sexual proclivities. Tweens have even given new connotations to the word "playground": one fifth-grade teacher from southwestern Ohio told me of two youngsters discovered in the bushes during recess.

15 Drugs and alcohol are also seeping into tween culture. The past six years have seen more than a doubling of the number of eighth-graders who smoke marijuana (10 percent today) and those who no longer see it as dangerous. "The stigma isn't there the way it was ten years ago," says Dan Kindlon, assistant professor of psychiatry at Harvard Medical School and co-author with Michael Thompson of *Raising Cain*. "Then it was the fringe group smoking pot. You were looked at strangely. Now the fringe group is using LSD."

16 Aside from sex, drugs, and rock and roll, another teen problem—eating disorders— is also beginning to affect younger kids. This behavior grows out of premature fashion-consciousness, which has an even more pernicious effect on tweens than on teens, because, by definition, younger kids have a more vulnerable and insecure self-image. Therapists say they are seeing a growing number of anorexics and obsessive dieters even among late-elementary-school girls. "You go on Internet chat rooms and find ten- and 11-year-olds who know every [fashion] model and every statistic about them," says Nancy Kolodny, a Connecticut-based therapist and author of *When Food's a Foe: How You Can Confront and Conquer Your Eating Disorder*. "Kate Moss is their god. They can tell if she's lost a few pounds or gained a few. If a powerful kid is talking about this stuff at school, it has a big effect."

17 What change in our social ecology has led to the emergence of tweens? Many note that kids are reaching puberty at earlier ages, but while earlier physical maturation may play a small role in defining adolescence down, its importance tends to be overstated. True, the average age at which girls begin to menstruate has fallen from 13 to between 11 and 12½ today, but the very gradualness of this change means that 12-year-olds have been living inside near-adult bodies for many decades without feeling impelled to build up a cosmetics arsenal or head for the bushes at recess. In fact, some experts believe that the very years that have witnessed the rise of the tween have also seen the age of first menstruation stabilize. Further, teachers and principals on the front lines see no clear correlation between physical and social maturation. Plenty of budding girls and bulking boys have not put away childish things, while an abundance of girls with flat chests and boys with squeaky voices ape the body language and fashions of their older siblings....

18 Of course, the causes are complex, and most people working with tweens know it. In my conversations with educators and child psychologists who work primarily with middle-class kids nationwide, two major and fairly predictable themes emerged: a sexualized and glitzy media-driven marketplace and absentee parents. What has been less commonly recognized is that at this age, the two causes combine to augment the authority of the peer group, which in turn both weakens the influence of parents and reinforces the power of the media. Taken together, parental absence, the market, and the peer group form a vicious circle that works to distort the development of youngsters....

Questions for Close Reading

1. What is the selection's thesis? Locate the sentence(s) in which Hymowitz states her main idea. If she doesn't state the thesis explicitly, express it in your own words.

FIGURE 12.2

Essay Structure Diagram: "Tweens: Ten Going On Sixteen"
by Kay S. Hymowitz

Introductory paragraphs: Personal anecdote Thesis (paragraphs 1–3)	Author's ten-year-old daughter becoming a teenager: examples of changes in her room décor, music tastes, and dress styles. **Thesis:** These days children become teens without going through preadolescence.
Background: Quotations and statistics (4–7)	Definition of "tweens" as a new market: quotations from a research psychologist and a TV executive; statistics from a toy trade publication; market research on tweens' self-image as "sexy" and "cool."
Quotations, examples, and statistics (8–16)	Psychologist's and teacher's descriptions of girls' adult-style clothes, hairstyles, makeup. Examples of boys' new concern with fashion. Evidence of trend's "darker side": statistics on growth in juvenile crime and sexual activity; quotations about tweens' sexualized behavior in school; statistics on drug and alcohol use; therapists' comments on increase in eating disorders.
Concluding paragraphs (17–18)	Experts' ideas about children's earlier physical maturation. Author's view of the real causes of the tweens phenomenon.

2. According to Hymowitz, what self-image do tweens cultivate? How do they project this image to others?

3. What physically dangerous behavioral trends does Hymowitz link to the tween phenomenon?

4. According to Hymowitz, what are the primary causes of the tween phenomenon?

Questions About the Writer's Craft

1. **The pattern.** Hymowitz uses a range of examples, citing specific names, anecdotes, expert opinion, and studies. Find the places where Hymowitz uses statistics to

support her ideas about crime, sexuality, and drug use. What are the sources? Are the statistics reliable? How persuasive are they?

2. **The pattern.** What types of examples does Hymowitz provide in her essay? (See pages 200–203 for a discussion of the various forms that examples can take.) Cite at least one example of each type. How does each type of example contribute to her thesis?

3. How would you characterize Hymowitz's tone in the selection? Cite vocabulary that conveys this tone.

4. **Other patterns.** In paragraph 8, Hymowitz uses clothing as a means of presenting an important *contrast*. What does she contrast in these paragraphs? How does this contribute to her thesis?

Writing Assignments Using Illustration as a Pattern of Development

1. Hymowitz is troubled and perplexed by her daughter's behavior. Think about an older person, such as a parent or another relative, who finds *your* behavior troubling and perplexing. Write an essay in which you illustrate why your behavior distresses this person. (Or, conversely, think of an elder whose behavior *you* find problematic, and write an essay illustrating why that person evokes this response in you.) Be sure to provide abundant examples throughout.

2. The cultivation of a sophisticated self-image is, according to Hymowitz, a hallmark of tweenhood. Think back to when you were around that age. What was your self-image at that time? Did you think of yourself as worldly or inexperienced? Cool or awkward? Attractive or unappealing? Freewrite about the traits that you would have identified in yourself as either a tween or an adolescent. Write an essay in which you illustrate your self-image at that age, focusing on two to three dominant characteristics you associated with yourself. Conclude your essay by reflecting on whether the way you saw yourself at the time was accurate, and whether your feelings about yourself have changed since then.

Writing Assignment Combining Patterns of Development

3. Hymowitz advances a powerful argument about the alarming contemporary trend of tweenhood. But many would disagree with her entirely pessimistic analysis. Write an essay in which you *argue,* contrary to Hymowitz, that tweens today actually exhibit several *positive* characteristics. To develop your argument, you'll need to show how each characteristic you're discussing *contrasts* favorably with that characteristic in a previous generation of kids. Be sure, too, to acknowledge opposing arguments as you proceed. Research conducted in the library and/or on the Internet might help you develop your pro-tween argument.

Beth Johnson

Beth Johnson (1956–) is a writer, occasional college teacher, and freelance editor. A graduate of Goshen College and Syracuse University, Johnson is the author of numerous inspirational real-life accounts. Containing profiles of men and women who have triumphed over obstacles to achieve personal and academic success, her books have provided a motivational boost to college students nationwide. The following piece is one of several that Johnson has written about the complexities and wonders of life.

Pre-Reading Journal Entry

When you were young, did adults acknowledge the existence of life's tragedies, or did they deny such harsh truths? In your journal, list several difficult events that you observed or experienced firsthand as a child. How did the adults in your life explain these hardships? In each case, do you think the adults acted appropriately? If not, how should they have responded?

BOMBS BURSTING IN AIR

It's Friday night and we're at the Olympics, the Junior Olympics, that is. My son is on a relay-race team competing against fourth-graders from all over the school district. His little sister and I sit high in the stands, trying to pick Isaac out from the crowd of figures milling around on the field during these moments of pre-game confusion. The public address system sputters to life and summons our attention. "And now," the tinny voice rings out, "please join together in the singing of our national anthem." 1

"Oh saaay can you seeeeee," we begin. My arm rests around Maddie's shoulders. I am touching her a lot today, and she notices. "Mom, you're *squishing* me," she chides, wriggling from my grip. I content myself with stroking her hair. News that reached me today makes me need to feel her near. We pipe along, squeaking out the impossibly high note of "land of the freeeeeeeee." Maddie clowns, half-singing, half-shouting the lyrics, hitting the "b's" explosively on "bombs bursting in air." 2

Bombs indeed, I think, replaying the sound of my friend's voice over the phone that afternoon: "Bumped her head sledding. Took her in for an x-ray, just to make sure. There was something strange, so they did more tests…a brain tumor…Children's Hospital in Boston Tuesday…surgery, yes, right away…." Maddie's playmate Shannon, only five years old. We'd last seen her at Halloween, dressed in her blue princess costume, and we'd talked of Furby and Scooby-Doo and Tootsie Rolls. Now her parents were hurriedly learning a new vocabulary—CAT scans, glioma, pediatric neurosurgery, and frontal lobe.[1] A bomb had exploded in their midst, and, like troops under attack, they were rallying in response. 3

---

[1] A CT scan is a computerized cross-sectional image of an internal body structure; a glioma is a tumor in the brain or spinal cord; pediatric neurosurgery is surgery performed on the nerves, brain, or spinal cord of a child; the frontal lobe is the largest section of the brain (editors' note).

4   The games over, the children and I edge our way out of the school parking lot, bumper to bumper with other parents ferrying their families home. I tell the kids as casually as I can about Shannon. "She'll have to have an operation. It's lucky, really, that they found it by accident this way while it's small."

5   "I want to send her a present," Maddie announces. "That'd be nice," I say, glad to keep the conversation on a positive note.

6   But my older son is with us now. Sam, who is thirteen, says, "She'll be OK, though, right?" It's not a question, really; it's a statement that I must either agree with or contradict. I want to say yes. I want to say of course she'll be all right. I want them to inhabit a world where five-year-olds do not develop silent, mysterious growths in their brains, where "malignancy" and "seizure" are words for *New York Times* crossword puzzles, not for little girls. They would accept my assurance; they would believe me and sleep well tonight. But I can't; the bomb that exploded in Shannon's home has sent splinters of shrapnel into ours as well, and they cannot be ignored or lied away. "We hope she'll be just fine," I finally say. "She has very good doctors. She has wonderful parents who are doing everything they can. The tumor is small. Shannon's strong and healthy."

7   "*She'll* be OK," says Maddie matter-of-factly. "In school we read about a little boy who had something wrong with his leg and he had an operation and got better. Can we go to Dairy Queen?"

8   Bombs on the horizon don't faze Maddie. Not yet. I can just barely remember from my own childhood the sense that still surrounds her, that feeling of being cocooned within reassuring walls of security and order. Back then, Monday meant gym, Tuesday was pizza in the cafeteria, Wednesday brought clarinet lessons. Teachers stood in their familiar spots in the classrooms, telling us with reassuring simplicity that World War II happened because Hitler, a very bad man, invaded Poland. Midterms and report cards, summer vacations and new notebooks in September gave a steady rhythm to the world. It wasn't all necessarily happy—through the years there were poor grades, grouchy teachers, exclusion from the desired social group, dateless weekends when it seemed the rest of the world was paired off—but it was familiar territory where we felt walled off from the really bad things that happened to other people.

9   There were hints of them, though, even then. Looking back, I recall the tiny shock waves, the tremors from far-off explosions that occasionally rattled our shelter. There was the little girl who was absent for a week and when she returned wasn't living with her mother and stepfather anymore. There was a big girl who threw up in the bathroom every morning and then disappeared from school. A playful, friendly custodian was suddenly fired, and it had something to do with an angry parent. A teacher's husband had a heart attack and died. These were interesting tidbits to report to our families over dinner, mostly out of morbid interest in seeing our parents bite their lips and exchange glances.

10   As we got older, the bombs dropped closer. A friend's sister was arrested for selling drugs; we saw her mother in tears at church that Sunday. A boy I thought I knew, a school clown with a sweet crooked grin, shot himself in the woods behind his house. A car full of senior boys, going home from a dance where I'd been sent into ecstasy when the cutest of them all greeted me by name, rounded a curve too fast and crashed, killing them. We wept and hugged each other in the halls. Our teachers listened to us grieve and tried to comfort us, but their words came out impatient and almost angry. I realize now that what sounded like anger was a helplessness to teach us lessons we were still too young or too ignorant to learn. For although our sorrow

was real, we still had some sense of a protective curtain between us and the bombs. If only, we said. If only she hadn't used drugs. If only he'd told someone how depressed he was. If only they'd been more careful. *We* weren't like them; we were careful. Like magical incantations, we recited the things that we would or wouldn't do in order to protect ourselves from such sad, unnecessary fates.

And then my best friend, a beautiful girl of sixteen, went to sleep one January night 11 and never woke up. I found myself shaken to the core of my being. My grief at the loss of my vibrant, laughing friend was great. But what really tilted my universe was the nakedness of my realization that there was no "if only." There were no drugs, no careless action, no crime, no accident, nothing I could focus on to explain away what had happened. She had simply died. Which could only mean that there was no magic barrier separating me and my loved ones from the bombs. We were as vulnerable as everyone else. For months the shock stayed with me. I sat in class watching my teachers draw diagrams of Saturn, talk about Watergate,[2] multiply fractions, and wondered at their apparent cheer and normalcy. Didn't they *know* we were all doomed? Didn't they know it was only a matter of time until one of us took a direct hit? What was the point of anything?

But time moved on, and I moved with it. College came and went, graduate school, 12 adulthood, middle age. My heightened sense of vulnerability began to subside, though I could never again slip fully into the soothing security of my younger days. I became more aware of the intertwining threads of joy, pain, and occasional tragedy that weave through all our lives. College was stimulating, exciting, full of friendship and challenge. I fell in love for the first time, reveled in its sweetness, then learned the painful lesson that love comes with no guarantee. A beloved professor lost two children to leukemia, but continued with skill and passion to introduce students to the riches of literature. My father grew ill, but the last day of his life, when I sat by his bed holding his hand, remains one of my sweetest memories. The marriage I'd entered into with optimism ended in bitter divorce, but produced three children whose existence is my daily delight. At every step along the way, I've seen that the most rewarding chapters of my life have contained parts that I not only would not have chosen, but would have given much to avoid. But selecting just the good parts is not an option we are given.

The price of allowing ourselves to truly live, to love and be loved, is (and it's the 13 ultimate irony) the knowledge that the greater our investment in life, the larger the target we create. Of course, it is within our power to refuse friendship, shrink from love, live in isolation, and thus create for ourselves a nearly impenetrable bomb shelter. There are those among us who choose such an existence, the price of intimacy being too high. Looking about me, however, I see few such examples. Instead, I am moved by the courage with which most of us, ordinary folks, continue soldiering on. We fall in love, we bring our children into the world, we forge our friendships, we give our hearts, knowing with increasing certainty that we do so at our own risk. Still we move ahead with open arms, saying yes, yes to life.

Shannon's surgery is behind her; the prognosis is good. Her mother reports that 14 the family is returning to its normal routines, laughing again and talking of ordinary

---

[2]In June 1972, supporters of Republican President Richard Nixon were caught breaking into the Democratic campaign headquarters in the Watergate office complex in Washington, D.C. The resulting investigation of the White House connection to the break-in led to President Nixon's eventual resignation in August 1974 (editors' note).

things, even while they step more gently, speak more quietly, are more aware of the precious fragility of life and of the blessing of every day that passes without explosion.

15   Bombs bursting in air. They can blind us, like fireworks at the moment of explosion. If we close our eyes and turn away, all we see is their fiery image. But if we have the courage to keep our eyes open and welcoming, even bombs finally fade against the vastness of the starry sky.

Questions for Close Reading

1. What is the selection's thesis? Locate the sentence(s) in which Johnson states her main idea. If she doesn't state the thesis explicitly, express it in your own words.

2. In paragraph 2, Johnson describes her "need to feel her [daughter] near." What compels her to want to be physically close to her daughter? Why do you think Johnson responds this way?

3. In describing her family's responses to Shannon's illness, Johnson presents three reactions: Maddie's, Sam's, and her own. How do these responses differ? In what ways do Maddie's, Sam's, and Johnson's reactions typify the age groups to which they belong?

4. In paragraph 13, Johnson describes two basic ways people respond to life's inevitable "bombs." What are these ways? Which response does Johnson endorse?

Questions About the Writer's Craft

1. **The pattern.** Although Johnson provides many examples of life's "bombs," she gives more weight to some examples than to others. Which examples does she emphasize? Which ones receive less attention? Why?

2. **Other patterns.** What important *contrast* does Johnson develop in paragraph 6? How does this contrast reinforce the essay's main idea?

3. Writers generally vary sentence structure in an effort to add interest to their work. But in paragraphs 9 and 10, Johnson employs a repetitive sentence structure. Where is the repetition in these two paragraphs? Why do you think she uses this technique?

4. Johnson develops her essay by means of an extended metaphor (see pages 130–131), using bombs as her central image. Identify all the places where Johnson draws upon language and imagery related to bombs and battles. What do you think Johnson hopes to achieve with this sustained metaphor?

Writing Assignments Using Illustration as a Pattern of Development

1. In paragraphs 9 and 10, Johnson catalogues a number of events that made her increasingly aware of life's bombs. Write an essay of your own, illustrating how you came to recognize the inevitability of painful life events. Start by listing the difficult events you've encountered. Select the three most compelling occurrences, and do

some freewriting to generate details about each. Before writing, decide whether you will order your examples chronologically or emphatically; use whichever illustrates more effectively your dawning realization of life's complexity. End with some conclusions about your ability to cope with difficult times.

2. Johnson describes her evolving understanding of life. In an essay of your own, show the way several events combined to change your understanding of a specific aspect of your life. Cite only those events that illustrate your emerging understanding. Your decision to use either chronological or emphatic sequence depends on which illustrates more dramatically the change in your perception.

Writing Assignment Combining Patterns of Development

3. Johnson explores the lasting impact the death of her friend had on her life. Write an essay about the *effect* of a *single* "bomb" on your life. Your causal analysis should make clear how the event affected your life.

France Borel

Belgian author France Borel (1952–), who studies tattooing, piercing, plastic surgery, and other alterations to the human body from an anthropological context point of view, has published widely on the history of art, costume, and fashion. Her publications include *The Seduction of Venus* (1990), *The Splendor of Ethnic Jewelry* (1994), and *Le Peintre et son miroir* (The painter and his mirror) (2002). The following essay appeared in *Parabola* in 1994.

Pre-Reading Journal Entry

Before you read the following essay, which illustrates the various ways cultures from around the world alter the human body, think about what you have done to transform your own body. What do you do on a daily basis to alter your appearance? What steps have you taken that have permanently altered the way you look? What prompts you to make these alterations? Explore these ideas in your journal.

THE DECORATED BODY

Nothing goes as deep as dress nor as far as the skin; ornaments have the dimensions of the world.

—Michel Serres, *The Five Senses*

Human nakedness, according to social custom, is unacceptable, unbearable, and dangerous. From the moment of birth, society takes charge, managing, dressing, forming, and deforming the child—sometimes even with a certain degree of   1 violence. Aside from the most elementary caretaking concerns—the very diversity of which shows how subjective the motivation is—an unfathomably deep and universal tendency pushes families, clans, and tribes to rapidly modify a person's physical appearance.

2   One's genuine physical makeup, one's given anatomy, is always felt to be unacceptable. Flesh, in its raw state, seems both intolerable and threatening. In its naked state, body and skin have no possible existence. The organism is acceptable only when it is transformed, covered with signs. The body only speaks if it is dressed in artifice.

3   For millennia, in the four quarters of the globe, mothers have molded the shape of their newborn babies' skulls to give them silhouettes conforming to prevalent criteria of beauty. In the nineteenth century, western children were tightly swaddled to keep their limbs straight. In the so-called primitive world, children were scarred or tattooed at a very early age in rituals which were repeated at all the most important steps of their lives. At a very young age, children were fitted with belts, necklaces, or bracelets; their lips, ears, or noses were pierced or stretched.

4   Some cultures have designed sophisticated appliances to alter physical structure and appearance. American Indian cradleboards crushed the skull to flatten it; the Mangbetus of Africa wrapped knotted rope made of bark around the child's head to elongate it into a sugar-loaf shape, which was considered to be aesthetically pleasing. The feet of very young Chinese girls were bound and spliced, intentionally and irreversibly deforming them, because this was seen to guarantee the girls' eventual amorous and matrimonial success.

5   Claude Lévi-Strauss said about the Caduveo of Brazil: "In order to be a man, one had to be painted; whoever remained in a natural state was no different from the beasts" (Lévi-Strauss 214). In Polynesia, unless a girl was tattooed, she would not find a husband. An unornamented hand could not cook, nor dip into the communal food bowl. Pink lips were despicable and ugly. Anyone who refused the test of the tattoo was seen to be marginal and suspect.

6   Among the Tivs of Nigeria, women called attention to their legs by means of elaborate scarification and the use of pearl leg bands; the best decorated calves were known for miles around. Tribal incisions behind the ears of Chad men rendered the skin "as smooth and stretched as that of a drum." The women would laugh at any man lacking these incisions, and they would never accept him as a husband. Men would subject themselves willingly to this custom, hoping for scars deep enough to leave marks on their skulls after death.

7   At the beginning of the eighteenth century, Father Laurent de Lucques noted that any young girl of the Congo who was not able to bear the pain of scarification and who cried so loudly that the operation had to be stopped was considered "good for nothing" (Cuvelier 144). That is why, before marriage, men would check to see if the pattern traced on the belly of their intended bride was beautiful and well-detailed.

8   The fact that such motivations and pretexts depend on aesthetic, erotic, hygienic, or even medical considerations has no influence on the result, which is always in the direction of transforming the appearance of the body. Such a transformation is wished for, whether or not it is effective.

9   The body is a supple, malleable, and transformable prime material, a kind of modeling clay, easily molded by social will and wish. Human skin is an ideal subject for

inscription, a surface for all sorts of marks which make it possible to differentiate the human from the animal. The physical body offers itself willingly for tattooing or scarring so that, visibly and recognizably, it becomes a social entity.

The absolutely naked body is considered as brutish, reduced to the level of nature where no distinction is made between man and beast. The decorated body, on the other hand, dressed (if even only in a belt), tattooed, or mutilated, publicly exhibits humanity and membership in an established group. As Theophile Gautier said, "The ideal disturbs even the roughest nature, and the taste for ornamentation distinguishes the intelligent being from the beast more exactly than anything else. Indeed, dogs have never dreamed of putting on earrings."   10

So, it is by their categorical refusal of nakedness that human beings are distinguished from nature. The "mark makes unremarkable"—it creates an interval between what is biologically and brutally given in the animal realm and what is won in the cultural realm. The body is tamed continuously; social custom demands, at any price—including pain, constraint, or discomfort—that wildness be abandoned.   11

Each civilization chooses—through a network of elective relationships which are difficult to determine—which areas of the body deserve transformation. These areas are as difficult to define and as shifting as those of eroticism or modesty. An individual alone eludes bodily modifications; they are the expression of a homogeneous collectivity which, at a chosen moment, comes to a tacit agreement to attack one or another part of the anatomy.   12

Whatever the choices, options, or differences may be, that which remains constant is the transformation of appearance. In spite of our contemporary western belief that the body is perfect as it is, we are constantly changing it: clothing it in musculature, suntan, or makeup; dying its head hair or pulling out its bodily hair. The seemingly most innocent gestures for taking care of the body very often hide a persistent and disguised tendency to make it adhere to the strictest of norms, reclothing it in a veil of civilization. The total nudity offered at birth does not exist in any region of the world. Man puts his stamp on man. The body is not a product of nature, but of culture.   13

Note

1. Of course, there are also many different sexual mutilations, including excisions and circumcisions, which we will not go into at this time as they constitute a whole study in themselves.

Works Cited

Cuvelier, Jean. *Relations sur le Congo du Père Laurent de Lucques*. Brussels: Institut Royal Colonial Belge, 1953. Print.

Lévi-Strauss, Claude. *Tristes Tropiques*. Paris: Plon, 1955. Print.

Questions for Close Reading

1. **Thesis.** What is the selection's thesis? Locate the sentence(s) in which Borel states her main idea. If she doesn't state the thesis explicitly, express it in your own words.

2. The second paragraph of Borel's essay ends with the statement "The body only speaks if it is dressed in artifice." What point(s) is the author making in this sentence?

3. According to Borel, what distinguishes humans from nature?

4. Explore the meaning of the following statement from Borel: "The physical body offers itself willingly for tattooing or scarring so that, visibly and recognizably, it becomes a social entity" (paragraph 9). Rewrite the sentence in your own words. In what ways do you agree or disagree with the statement?

Questions About the Writer's Craft

1. **The pattern.** In her essay Borel illustrates her main point with examples. Make a list of ten examples she includes.

2. Of the ten examples you listed for question 1, which two stand out as the most effective at substantiating Borel's thesis? Why?

3. Borel begins her essay with a quote from Michel Serres. Why might she have chosen to use this strategy? Do you think beginning with the quote was an effective move? Why or why not?

4. **Other patterns.** Although Borel provides one example after another in her essay, she is also making an *argument*. State her *argument* in your own words. In what ways do her *illustrations* make her *argument* stronger?

Writing Assignments Using Illustration as a Pattern of Development

1. Borel provides illustrations of ways cultures from around the world have "an unfathomably deep and universal tendency" to push their members to alter their physical appearance (paragraph 1). Write an essay about how you or some other person or group of individuals have been encouraged to alter their appearance by some segment of society. For example, you might write about how peer pressure encourages individuals to wear particular brands and styles of clothing or shoes or to wear their hair a certain way. Or you might write about how the pressure to look perfect drives individuals to anorexia and other eating disorders. Choose examples that illustrate your main point and that would be most effective for the audience for which you are writing.

2. Choose one of the practices Borel mentions in her essay, and conduct research to find out more about that particular body-altering procedure. For example, you might research the practice of molding the shape of newborn babies' skulls that has been used in cultures around the world, or the nineteenth-century practice of swaddling children to keep their limbs straight. Or you might choose a particular group Borel refers to, such as the Caduveo of Brazil or the Tivs of Nigeria, and research the group's body-altering practices. Be sure to provide an adequate number of examples to substantiate your main point and to correctly reference your outside sources. If you decide to include images to strengthen your essay, be sure to reference the images in your written text.

Writing Assignment Combining Patterns of Development

3. Borel's essay *illustrates* the ways cultures encourage their members to alter their appearances. Write an essay in which you *compare* and *contrast* differences in the popularity of a particular body-altering practice between generations. For example, you might compare the popularity of tattoos today with their popularity in the 1940s and 1950s, when many World War II soldiers were coming home with tattoos. You might explore how the demographic of those getting tattoos has changed, along with how the designs and the placement of tattoos on the body have changed between then and now. Consider including one or more images and several outside sources to strengthen the effectiveness of your essay, and be sure to reference the images or sources in your essay.

ADDITIONAL WRITING TOPICS: ILLUSTRATION

General Assignments

Using illustration, develop one of these topics into an essay.

1. Today's drivers' dangerous habits

2. Taking care of our neighborhoods

3. The best things in life: definitely not free

4. The importance of part-time jobs for college students

5. How cell phones have changed communication

6. Learning about people from what they wear

7. Americans' obsession with or neglect of physical fitness

8. How to avoid bad eating habits

9. Eliminating obstacles faced by people with handicaps

10. _____ (someone you know) as a _____ (reliable, open-minded, dishonest, pushy, etc.) person

Assignments Using Visuals

Use the suggested visuals to help develop an illustration essay on one of these topics:

1. How cell phones have changed our lives (photos and/or charts)

2. The benefits of a college education (graphs and/or charts)

3. How the Internet has affected society (slide show)

4. Characteristics of college students with high GPAs (charts or cartoons)

5. How a hobby such as hiking or singing can expand our horizons (Web links)

Assignments with a Specific Purpose, Audience, and Point of View

1. **Academic life.** Lately, many people at your college have been experiencing stress. As a member of the Student Life Committee, you've been asked to prepare a pamphlet illustrating strategies for reducing different kinds of stress. Decide which stresses to discuss and explain coping strategies for each, providing helpful examples as you go.

2. **Academic life.** A friend of yours will be going away to college in an unfamiliar environment—in a bustling urban setting or in a quiet rural one. To help your friend prepare for this new environment, write a letter giving examples of what life on an urban or a rural campus is like. You might focus on the benefits and dangers with which your friend is unlikely to be familiar.

3. **Civic activity.** Shopping for a new car, you become annoyed at how many safety features are available only as expensive options. Write a letter of complaint to the auto manufacturer, citing at least three examples of such options. Avoid sounding hostile.

4. **Civic activity.** A pet food company is having an annual contest to choose a new animal to feature in its advertising. To win the contest, you must convince the company that your pet is personable, playful, and unique. Write an essay giving examples of your pet's special qualities.

5. **Workplace action.** Assume that you're an elementary school principal planning to give a speech in which you'll try to convince parents that television distorts children's perceptions of reality. Write the speech, illustrating your point with vivid examples.

6. **Workplace action.** The online publication you work for has asked you to write an article on what you consider to be the "three best consumer products of the past twenty-five years." Support your opinion with lively, engaging specifics that are consistent with the website's offbeat and slightly ironic tone.

13

Division-Classification

In this chapter, you will learn:

13.1 To use the pattern of division-classification to develop your essays
13.2 To consider how division-classification can fit your purpose and audience
13.3 To develop prewriting, writing, and revision strategies for using division-classification in an essay
13.4 To analyze how division-classification is used effectively in one student-written and three professionally authored selections
13.5 To write your own essays using division-classification as a strategy

What Is Division-Classification?

All of us instinctively look for ways to order our environment. Without systems, categories, or sorting mechanisms, we would be overwhelmed by life's complexity. An organization such as a college or university, for example, is made manageable by being divided into various schools (Liberal Arts, Performing Arts, Engineering, and so on). The schools are then separated into departments (English, History, Political Science), and each department's offerings are grouped into distinct categories—English, for instance, into Literature and Composition—before being further divided into specific courses.

The kind of ordering system we've been discussing is called **division-classification**, a way of thinking that allows us to make sense of a complex world. Division and classification, though separate processes, often complement each other. **Division** involves taking a single unit or concept, breaking it down into parts, and then analyzing the connections among the parts and between the parts and the whole. For instance, a **hospital** could be broken down into its components. We might come up with the following breakdown:

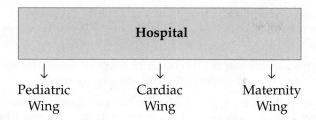

What we have just done involves division: We've taken a single entity (a hospital) and divided it into some of its component parts (wings), each with its own facilities and patients.

In contrast, **classification** brings two or more related items together and categorizes them according to type or kind. In a supermarket, clerks classify the items in the store:

How Division-Classification Fits Your Purpose and Audience

The hospital and supermarket examples show the way division and classification work in everyday life. But division and classification also come into play during the writing process. Because division involves breaking a subject into parts, it can be a helpful strategy during prewriting, especially if you're analyzing a broad, complex subject: the structure of a film; the motivation of a character in a novel; the problem your community has with vandalism; the controversy surrounding school prayer.

Classification can be useful for imposing order on the hodgepodge of ideas generated during prewriting. You examine that material to see which of your rough ideas are alike and which are dissimilar, so that you can cluster related items in the same category. Classification would, then, be a helpful strategy when analyzing topics such as these: techniques for impressing teachers; comic styles of talk-show hosts; views on abortion; reasons for the current rise in volunteerism.

Division-classification can be crucial when responding to college assignments like the following:

> Based on your observations, what kinds of appeals do television advertisers use when selling automobiles? In your view, are any of these appeals morally irresponsible?

> Analyze the components that go into being an effective parent. Indicate those you consider most vital for raising confident, well-adjusted children.

> Describe the hierarchy of the typical high school clique, identifying the various parts of the hierarchy. Use your analysis to support or refute the view that adolescence is a period of rigid conformity.

These assignments suggest division-classification through the use of such words as *kinds, components,* and *parts.* Generally, though, you won't receive such clear signals to use division-classification. Instead, the broad purpose of the essay—and the point you want to make—will lead you to the analytical thinking characteristic of division-classification.

Sometimes division-classification will be the dominant technique for structuring an essay; other times it will be used as a supplemental pattern in an essay organized primarily according to another pattern of development. Let's look at some examples. Say you want to write a paper *explaining a process,* such as using the Heimlich maneuver on people who are choking. You could *divide* the process into parts or stages, showing, for instance, that the Heimlich maneuver is an easily mastered skill that readers should acquire. Or imagine you plan to write a light-spirited essay analyzing the *effect* that increased awareness of sexual stereotypes has had on college students' social lives. In such a case, you might use *classification.* To show readers that shifting gender roles make young men and women comically self-conscious, you could categorize the places where students scope out each other in class, at the library, at parties, in dorms. You could then show how students—not wanting to be macho or coyly feminine—approach each other with laughable tentativeness in these four environments.

Now imagine that you're writing an *argumentation-persuasion* essay urging that the federal government prohibit the use of growth-inducing antibiotics in livestock feed. The paper could begin by *dividing* the antibiotics cycle into stages: the effects of antibiotics on livestock; the short-term effects on humans who consume the animals; the possible long-term effects of consuming antibiotic-tainted meat. To increase readers' understanding of the problem, you might also discuss the antibiotics controversy in terms of an even larger issue: the dangerous ways food is treated before being consumed. In this case, you would consider the various procedures (use of additives, preservatives, artificial colors, and so on), *classifying* these treatments into several types—from least harmful (some additives or artificial colors, perhaps) to most harmful (you might slot the antibiotics here). Such an essay would be developed using both division *and* classification: first, the division of the antibiotics cycle and then the classification of the various food treatments.

Frequently, this interdependence will be reversed, and classification will precede rather than follow division.

Prewriting Strategies

The following checklist shows how you can apply to division-classification some of the prewriting techniques discussed in Chapter 2.

☑ DIVISION-CLASSIFICATION: A PREWRITING CHECKLIST

Choose a Subject to Analyze

- ☐ What fairly complex subject (sibling rivalry, religious cults) can be made more understandable through division-classification?
- ☐ Will you divide a single entity or concept (domestic violence) into parts (toward spouse, parent, or child)? Will you classify a number of similar things (college courses) into categories (easy, of average difficulty, tough)? Or will you use both division and classification?

Determine Your Purpose, Audience, Tone, and Point of View

- ☐ What is the purpose of your analysis?
- ☐ Toward what audience will you direct your explanations?
- ☐ What tone and point of view will make readers receptive to your explanation?

Use Prewriting to Generate Material on Parts or Types

- ☐ How can brainstorming, mapping, or any other prewriting technique help you divide your subject into parts? What differences or similarities among parts will you emphasize?
- ☐ How can brainstorming, mapping, or any other prewriting technique help you categorize your subjects? What differences or similarities among categories will you emphasize?
- ☐ How can the patterns of development help you generate material about your subjects' parts or categories? How can you describe the parts or categories? What can you narrate about them? What examples illustrate them? What process do they help explain? How can they be compared or contrasted? What causes them? What are their effects? How can they be defined? What arguments do they support?

Strategies for Using Division-Classification in an Essay

After prewriting, you're ready to draft your essay. Figure 13.1 (on page 220) and the suggestions that follow will be helpful whether you use division-classification as a dominant or supportive pattern of development.

FIGURE 13.1

Development Diagram: Writing a Division-Classification Essay

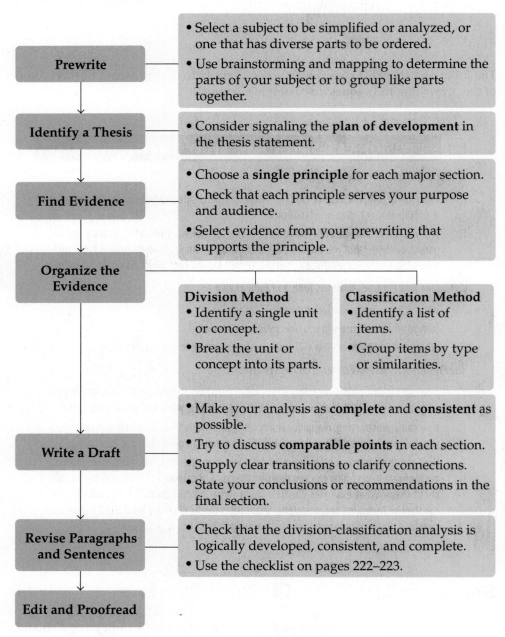

1. **Select a principle of division-classification consistent with your purpose.** Most subjects can be divided or classified according to *several different principles.* In all cases, though, the principle of division-classification you select must meet one stringent requirement: It must help you meet your overall purpose and reinforce your central point.

   Don't, however, take this to mean that essays can never use more than one principle of division-classification as they unfold. They can—as long as the *shift from one principle to another* occurs in *different parts* of the paper.

2. **Apply the principle of division-classification logically.** In an essay using division-classification, you need to demonstrate to readers that your analysis is the result of careful thought. First of all, your division-classification should be as *complete* as possible. Your analysis should include—within reason—all the parts into which you can divide your subject, or all the types into which you can categorize your subjects.

   Your division-classification should also be *consistent:* the parts into which you break your subject or the groups into which you place your subjects should be as mutually exclusive as possible. The parts or categories should not be mixed, nor should they overlap.

3. **Prepare an effective thesis.** If your essay uses division-classification as its dominant method of development, it might be helpful to prepare a thesis that does more than signal the paper's subject and suggest your attitude toward that subject. You might also want the thesis to state the principle of division-classification at the heart of the essay. Furthermore, you might want the thesis to reveal which part or category you regard as most important.

   Consider the two thesis statements that follow:

Thesis 1

As the observant beachcomber moves from the tidal area to the upper beach to the sandy dunes, rich variations in marine life become apparent.

Thesis 2

Although most people focus on the dangers associated with the disposal of toxic waste in the land and ocean, the incineration of toxic matter may pose an even more serious threat to human life.

The first thesis statement makes clear that the writer will organize the paper by classifying forms of marine life according to location. Because the purpose of the essay is to inform as objectively as possible, the thesis doesn't suggest the writer's opinion about which category is most significant.

The second thesis signals that the essay will evolve by dividing the issue of toxic waste according to methods of disposal. Moreover, because the paper takes a stance on a controversial subject, the thesis is worded to reveal which aspect of the topic the writer considers most important. Such a clear statement of the writer's position is an effective strategy in an essay of this kind.

You may have noted that each thesis statement also signals the paper's plan of development. The first essay, for example, will use specific facts, examples, and details to describe the kinds of marine life found in the tidal area, upper beach, and dunes. However, thesis statements in papers developed primarily through division-classification don't have to be so structured. If a paper is well written, your principle of division-classification, your opinion about which part or category is most important, and the essay's plan of development will become apparent as the essay unfolds.

4. **Organize the paper logically.** Whether your paper is developed wholly or in part by division-classification, it should have a logical structure. As much as possible, you should try to discuss *comparable points* in each section of the paper. You should also use *signal devices* to connect various parts of the paper: "*Another* characteristic of…"; "A *final* important trait of…"; "*Unlike* the…" Such signals clarify the connections among the essay's ideas.

5. **State any conclusions or recommendations in the paper's final section.** The analytic thinking that occurs during division-classification often leads to surprising insights. Such insights may be introduced early on, or they may be reserved for the end, where they are stated as conclusions or recommendations.

Revision Strategies

Once you have a draft of the essay, you're ready to revise. The following checklist will help you and those giving you feedback apply to division-classification some of the revision techniques discussed in Chapters 7 and 8.

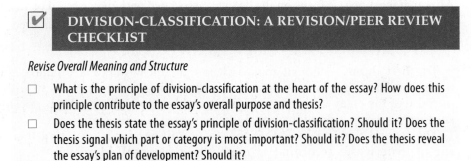

☑ DIVISION-CLASSIFICATION: A REVISION/PEER REVIEW CHECKLIST

Revise Overall Meaning and Structure

☐ What is the principle of division-classification at the heart of the essay? How does this principle contribute to the essay's overall purpose and thesis?

☐ Does the thesis state the essay's principle of division-classification? Should it? Does the thesis signal which part or category is most important? Should it? Does the thesis reveal the essay's plan of development? Should it?

☐ Is the essay organized primarily through division, classification, or a blend of both?

☐ If the essay is organized mainly through division, is the subject sufficiently broad and complex to be broken down into parts? What are the parts?

☐ If the essay is organized mainly through classification, what are the categories? How does this categorizing reveal similarities and/or differences that would otherwise not be apparent?

Revise Paragraph Development

☐ Are comparable points discussed in each of the paper's sections? What are these points?

☐ In which paragraphs does the division-classification seem illogical, incomplete, or inconsistent? In which paragraphs are parts or categories not clearly explained?

☐ Are the subject's different parts or categories discussed in separate paragraphs? Should they be?

Revise Sentences and Words

☐ What signal devices help integrate the paper? Are there enough signals? Too many?

☐ Where should sentences and words be made more specific in order to clarify the parts and categories being discussed?

Student Essay: From Prewriting Through Revision

The student essay that follows was written by Gail Oremland in response to this assignment:

> In "Propaganda Techniques in Today's Advertising," Ann McClintock describes the flaws in many of the persuasive strategies used by advertisers. Choose another group of people whose job is also to communicate—for example, parents, bosses, teachers. Then, in an essay of your own, divide the group into types according to the flaws they make when communicating.

Gail wanted to prepare a light-spirited paper about college professors' foibles. Right from the start, she decided to focus on three kinds of professors: the "Knowledgeable One," the "Leader of Intellectual Discussion," and the "Buddy." She used the *patterns of development* to generate prewriting material about each kind, typing whatever ideas came to mind as she focused on one pattern at a time. Reprinted here is Gail's prewriting for the Knowledgeable One. Note that not every pattern sparked ideas. When Gail later reviewed her prewriting, she added some details and deleted others. The handwritten marks on the prewriting indicate Gail's later efforts to refine her rough material.

After annotating her prewriting for all the categories, Gail prepared her first draft, without shaping her prewriting further or making an outline. As she wrote, though, she frequently referred to her warm-up material to retrieve specifics about each professorial type.

Prewriting Using the Patterns of Development

Knowledgeable One

Even in a blizzard or hurricane

Narration: Enters, walks to podium, puts notes on stand, begins lecture exactly on schedule. Talks on and on, stating facts. ~~Even when she had a cold, she kept on lecturing, although we could hardly hear her and her voice kept cracking.~~ Always ends lecture exactly on time. Packs her notes. Hurries away. Shoots out the back door. Back to the privacy of her office, away from students.

Description: Self-important air, yellowed notes, all weather, drones, students' glazed eyes, yawns

Doesn't stop, so students feel they can't interrupt

Cause-Effect: Thinks she's an expert and that students are ignorant, so students are intimidated. States one dry fact after another, so students get bored. Addresses students as "Mr." or "Miss," so she establishes distance.

Definition: A fact person

Illustration: History prof who knows death toll of every battle; biology prof who knows all the molecules; accounting prof who knows every clause of tax form

Comparison-Contrast: Interest in specialized academic area vs. no interest in students

Now read Gail's paper, "The Truth About College Teachers," noting the similarities and differences between her prewriting and final essay. As you may imagine, the patterns of development that yielded the most details during prewriting became especially prominent in the final essay. Note, too, that Gail's prewriting consisted of unconnected details within each pattern, whereas the essay flows easily. To achieve such coherence, Gail used commentary and transitional phrases to connect the prewriting details. As you read the essay, also consider how well it applies the principles of division-classification discussed in this chapter. (The commentary that follows the paper will help you look at the essay more closely and will give you some sense of how Gail went about revising her first draft.)

The Truth About College Teachers
by Gail Oremland

Introduction

A recent TV news story told about a group of college professors from a nearby university who were hired by a local school system to help upgrade the teaching in the community's public schools. The professors were to visit classrooms, analyze teachers' skills, and then conduct workshops to help the teachers become more effective at their jobs. But after the first round of workshops, the superintendent of schools decided to cancel the whole project. He fired the learned professors and sent them back

1

to their ivory tower. Why did the project fall apart? There was a simple reason. The college professors, who were supposedly going to show the public school teachers how to be more effective, were themselves poor teachers. Many college students could have predicted such a disastrous outcome. They know, firsthand, that college teachers are strange. They know that professors often exhibit bizarre behaviors, relating to students in ways that make it difficult for students to stay awake, or—if awake—to learn.

Thesis

2   One type of professor assumes, legitimately enough, that her function is to pass on to students the vast store of knowledge she has acquired. But because the "Knowledgeable One" regards herself as an expert and her students as the ignorant masses, she adopts an elitist approach that sabotages learning. The Knowledgeable One enters a lecture hall with a self-important air, walks to the podium, places her yellowed-with-age notes on the stand, and begins her lecture at the exact second the class is officially scheduled to begin. There can be a blizzard or hurricane raging outside the lecture hall; students can be running through freezing sleet and howling winds to get to class on time. Will the Knowledgeable One wait for them to arrive before beginning her lecture? Probably not. The Knowledgeable One's time is precious. She's there, set to begin, and that's what matters.

Topic sentence

The first of three paragraphs on the first category of teacher

The first paragraph in a three-part chronological sequence: What happens before class

3   Once the monologue begins, the Knowledgeable One drones on and on. The Knowledgeable One is a fact person. She may be the history prof who knows the death toll of every Civil War battle, the biology prof who can diagram all the common biological molecules, the accounting prof who enumerates every clause of the federal tax form. Oblivious to students' glazed eyes and stifled yawns, the Knowledgeable One delivers her monologue, dispensing one dry fact after another. The only advantage to being on the receiving end of this boring monologue is that students do not have to worry about being called on to question a point or provide an opinion; the Knowledgeable One is not willing to relinquish one minute of her time by giving students a voice. Assume for one improbable moment that a student actually manages to stay awake during the monologue and is brave enough to ask a question. In such a case, the Knowledgeable One will address the questioning student as "Mr." or "Miss." This formality does not, as some students mistakenly suppose, indicate respect for the student as a fledgling member of the academic community. Not at all. This impersonality represents the Knowledgeable One's desire to keep as wide a distance as possible between her and her students.

Topic sentence

The second paragraph on the first category of teacher

The second paragraph in the chronological sequence: What happens during class

4   The Knowledgeable One's monologue always comes to a close at the precise second the class is scheduled to end. No sooner has she delivered her last forgettable

Topic sentence

he third paragraph
n the first category
f teacher

he final paragraph
n the chronological
equence: What
appens *after* class

word than the Knowledgeable One packs up her notes and shoots out the door, heading back to the privacy of her office, where she can pursue her specialized academic
interests—free of any possible interruption from students. The Knowledgeable One's
hasty departure from the lecture hall makes it clear she has no desire to talk with
students. In her eyes, she has met her obligations; she has taken time away from her
research to transmit to students what she knows. Any closer contact might mean she
would risk contagion from students, that great unwashed mass. Such a danger is to be
avoided at all costs.

Unlike the Knowledgeable One, the "Leader of Intellectual Discussion" seems   5
to respect students. Emphasizing class discussion, the Leader encourages students
to confront ideas ("What is Twain's view of morality?" "Was our intervention in Iraq
justified?" "Should big business be given tax breaks?") and discover their own truths.
Then, about three weeks into the semester, it becomes clear that the Leader wants

opic sentence ─────▸

students to discover his version of the truth. Behind the Leader's democratic guise

Paragraph on the
econd category of
eacher

lurks a dictator. When a student voices an opinion that the Leader accepts, the student
is rewarded by hearty nods of approval and "Good point, good point." But if a student
is rash enough to advance a conflicting viewpoint, the Leader responds with killing
politeness: "Well, yes, that's an interesting perspective. But don't you think that…?"
Grade-conscious students soon learn not to chime in with their viewpoint. They know
that when the Leader, with seeming honesty, says, "I'd be interested in hearing what
you think. Let's open this up for discussion," they had better figure out what the Leader
wants to hear before advancing their own theories. "Me-tooism" rather than independent thinking, they discover, guarantees good grades in the Leader's class.

Then there is the professor who comes across as the students' "Buddy." This kind   6

opic sentence ─────▸

of professor does not see himself as an imparter of knowledge or a leader of discus-

Paragraph on the
hird category of
eacher

sion but as a pal, just one in a community of equals. The Buddy may start his course
this way: "All of us know that this college stuff—grades, degrees, exams, required
reading—is a game. So let's not play it, okay?" Dressed in jeans, sweatshirt, and scuffed
sneakers, the Buddy projects a relaxed, casual attitude. He arranges the class seats in
a circle (he would never take a position in front of the room) and insists that students
call him by his first name. He uses no syllabus and gives few tests, believing that such
constraints keep students from directing their own learning. A free spirit, the Buddy
often teaches courses like "The Psychology of Interpersonal Relations" or "The Social
Dynamics of the Family." If students choose to use class time to discuss the course

material, that's fine. If they want to discuss something else, that's fine, too. It's the self-expression, the honest dialogue, that counts. In fact, the Buddy seems especially fond of digressions from academic subjects. By talking about his political views, his marital problems, his tendency to drink one too many beers, the Buddy lets students see that he is a regular guy—just like them. At first, students look forward to classes with the Buddy. They enjoy the informality, the chitchat, the lack of pressure. But after a while, they wonder why they are paying for a course where they learn nothing. They might as well stay home and watch talk shows.

7   Obviously, some college professors are excellent. They are learned, hardworking, and imaginative; they enjoy their work and like being with students. On the whole, though, college professors are a strange lot. Despite their advanced degrees and their own exposure to many different kinds of teachers, they do not seem to understand how to relate to students. Rather than being hired as consultants to help others upgrade their teaching skills, college professors should themselves hire consultants to tell them what they are doing wrong and how they can improve. Who should these consultants be? That's easy: the people who know them best—their students.

Conclusion

Echoes opening anecdote

Commentary

Introduction and Thesis

After years of being graded by teachers, Gail took special pleasure in writing an essay that gave her a chance to evaluate her teachers—in this case, her college professors. Even the essay's title, "The Truth About College Teachers," implies that Gail is going to have fun knocking profs down from their ivory towers. To introduce her subject, she uses a timely news story. This brief anecdote leads directly to the essay's *thesis:* "Professors often exhibit bizarre behaviors, relating to students in ways that make it difficult for students to stay awake, or—if awake—to learn." Note that Gail's thesis isn't highly structured; it doesn't, for example, name the specific categories to be discussed. Still, her thesis suggests that the essay is going to *categorize* a range of teaching behaviors, using as a *principle of classification* the strange ways that college profs relate to students.

Purpose

As with all good papers developed through division-classification, Gail's essay doesn't use classification as an end in itself. Gail uses classification because it helps her achieve a broader *purpose.* She wants to *convince* readers—without moralizing or abandoning her humorous tone—that such teaching styles inhibit learning. In other words, there's a serious undertone to her essay. This additional layer of meaning is characteristic of satiric writing.

Categories and Topic Sentences

The essay's body, consisting of five paragraphs, presents the three categories that make up Gail's analysis. According to Gail, college teachers can be categorized as the Knowledgeable One (paragraphs 2–4), the Leader of Intellectual Discussion (5), or the Buddy (6). Obviously, there are other ways professors might be classified. But given Gail's purpose, audience, tone, and point of view, her categories are appropriate; they are reasonably *complete, consistent*, and *mutually exclusive*. Note, too, that Gail uses *topic sentences* near the beginning of each category to help readers see which professorial type she's discussing.

Overall Organization and Paragraph Structure

Gail is able to shift smoothly and easily from one category to the next. How does she achieve such graceful transitions? Take a moment to reread the sentences that introduce her second and third categories (paragraphs 5 and 6). Look at the way each sentence's beginning (in italics here) links back to the preceding category or categories: "*Unlike the Knowledgeable One*, the 'Leader of Intellectual Discussion' seems to respect students"; and the "Buddy...*does not see himself as an imparter of knowledge or a leader of discussion* but as a pal..."

Gail is equally careful about providing an easy-to-follow structure within each section. She uses a *chronological sequence* to organize her three-paragraph discussion of the Knowledgeable One. The first paragraph deals with the beginning of the Knowledgeable One's lecture; the second, with the lecture itself; the third, with the end of the lecture. And the paragraphs' *topic sentences* clearly indicate this passage of time. Similarly, *transitions* are used in the paragraphs on the Leader of Intellectual Discussion and the Buddy to ensure a logical progression of points: "*Then*, about three weeks into the semester, it becomes clear that the Leader wants students to discover *his* version of the truth" (5), and "*At first*, students look forward to classes with the Buddy...But *after a while*, they wonder why they are paying for a course where they learn nothing" (6).

Tone

The essay's unity can also be traced to Gail's skill in sustaining her satiric tone. Throughout the essay, Gail selects details that fit her gently mocking attitude. She depicts the Knowledgeable One lecturing from "yellowed-with-age notes..., oblivious to students' glazed eyes and stifled yawns," unwilling to wait for students who "run...through freezing sleet and howling winds to get to class on time." Then she presents another tongue-in-cheek description, this one focusing on the way the Leader of Intellectual Discussion conducts class: "Good point, good point...Well, yes, that's an interesting perspective. But don't you think that...?" Finally, with similar killing accuracy, Gail portrays the Buddy, democratically garbed in "jeans, sweatshirt, and scuffed sneakers."

Combining Patterns of Development

Gail's satiric depiction of her three professorial types employs a number of techniques associated with *narrative* and *descriptive writing*: vigorous images, highly connotative language, and dialogue. *Definition, illustration, causal analysis,* and *comparison-contrast* also come into play. Gail defines the characteristics of each type of professor; she provides numerous examples to support her categories; she explains the effects of the different teaching styles on students; and, in her description of the Leader of Intellectual Discussion, she contrasts the appearance of democracy with the dictatorial reality.

Unequal Development of Categories

Although Gail's essay is unified, organized, and well developed, you may have felt that the first category outweighs the other two. There is, of course, no need to balance the categories exactly. But Gail's extended treatment of the first category sets up an expectation that the others will be treated as fully. One way to remedy this problem would be to delete some material from the discussion of the Knowledgeable One. Gail might, for instance, omit the first five sentences in the third paragraph (about the professor's habit of addressing students as Mr. or Miss). Such a change could be made without taking the bite out of her portrayal. Even better, Gail could simply switch the order of her sections, putting the portrait of the Knowledgeable One at the essay's end. Here, the extended discussion wouldn't seem out of proportion. Instead, the sections would appear in *emphatic order*, with the most detailed category saved for last.

Revising the First Draft

It's apparent that an essay as engaging as Gail's must have undergone a good deal of revising. Along the way, Gail made many changes in her draft, but it's particularly interesting to see how she changed her original introduction (reprinted here). The annotation represents her peer reviewers' impressions of the paragraph's problems.

Original Version of the Introduction

Despite their high IQs, advanced degrees, and published papers, some college professors just don't know how to teach. Found almost in any department, in tenured and untenured positions, they prompt student apathy. They fail to convey ideas effectively and to challenge or inspire students. Students thus finish their courses having learned very little. Contrary to popular opinion, these professors' ineptitude is not simply a matter of delivering boring lectures or not caring about students. Many of them care a great deal. Their failure actually stems from their unrealistic perceptions of what a teacher should be. Specifically, they adopt teaching styles or roles that alienate students and undermine learning. Three of the most common ones are "The Knowledgeable One," "The Leader of Intellectual Discussion," and "The Buddy."

Too serious. Doesn't fit rest of essay.

When Gail showed the first draft of the essay to her composition instructor, he laughed—and occasionally squirmed—as he read what she had prepared. He was enthusiastic about the paper but felt there was a problem with the introduction's tone; it was too serious when compared to the playful, lightly satiric mood of the rest of the essay. When Gail reread the paragraph, she agreed, but she was uncertain about the best way to remedy the problem. After revising other sections of the essay, she decided to let the paper sit for a while before going back to rewrite the introduction.

In the meantime, Gail switched on the TV. The timing couldn't have been better; she tuned into a news story about several supposedly learned professors who had been fired from a consulting job because they had turned out to know so little about teaching. This was exactly the kind of item Gail needed to start her essay. Now she was able to prepare a completely new introduction, making it consistent in spirit with the rest of the paper.

With this stronger introduction and the rest of the essay well in hand, Gail was ready to write a conclusion. Now, as she worked on the concluding paragraph, she deliberately shaped it to recall the story about the fired consultants. By echoing the opening anecdote in her conclusion, Gail was able to end the paper with another poke at professors—a perfect way to close her clever and insightful essay.

 ACTIVITIES: DIVISION-CLASSIFICATION

Prewriting Activities

1. Imagine you're writing two essays: One is a humorous paper showing how to impress college instructors; the other is a serious essay explaining why volunteerism is on the rise. What about the topics might you divide and/or classify?

2. Use group brainstorming to identify at least three possible principles of division for *one* of the following topics. For each principle, determine what your thesis might be if you were writing an essay.

   a. Prejudice
   b. Hip-hop music
   c. A good horror movie

3. Through group brainstorming, identify three different principles of classification that might provide the structure for an essay about the possible effects of a controversial decision to expand your college's enrollment. Focusing on one of the principles, decide what your thesis might be. How would you sequence the categories?

Revising Activities

4. Following is a scratch outline for an essay developed through division-classification. On what principle of division-classification is the essay based? What problem do you see in the way the principle is applied? How could the problem be remedied?

Thesis: The same experience often teaches opposite things to different people.

- What working as a fast-food cook teaches: Some learn responsibility; others learn to take a "quick-and-dirty" approach.

- What a negative experience teaches optimists: Some learn from their mistakes; others continue to maintain a positive outlook.

- What a difficult course teaches: Some learn to study hard; others learn to avoid demanding courses.

- What the breakup of a close relationship teaches: Some learn how to negotiate differences; others learn to avoid intimacy.

5. Following is a paragraph from the first draft of an essay urging that daycare centers adopt play programs tailored to children's developmental needs. What principle of division-classification focuses the paragraph? Is the principle applied consistently and logically? Are parts or categories developed sufficiently? Revise the paragraph, eliminating any problems you discover and adding specific details where needed.

Within a few years, preschool children move from self-absorbed to interactive play. Babies and toddlers engage in solitary play. Although they sometimes prefer being near other children, they focus primarily on their own actions. This is very different from the highly interactive play of the elementary school years. Sometime in children's second year, solitary play is replaced by parallel play, during which children engage in similar activities near one another. However, they interact only occasionally. By age three, most children show at least some cooperative play, a form that involves interaction and cooperative role-taking. Such role-taking can be found in the "pretend" games that children play to explore adult relationships (games of "Mommy and Daddy") and anatomy (games of "Doctor"). Additional signs of youngsters' growing awareness of peers can be seen at about age four. At this age, many children begin showing a special devotion to one other child and may want to play only with that child. During this time, children also begin to take special delight in physical activities such as running and jumping, often going off by themselves to expend their abundant physical energy.

PROFESSIONAL SELECTIONS: DIVISION-CLASSIFICATION

Ann McClintock

Ann McClintock (1946–), formerly director of occupational therapy at Ancora State Hospital in New Jersey, has also worked as a freelance editor and writer. A frequent speaker before community groups, McClintock is especially interested in the effects of advertising on American life. The following selection, revised for this text, is part of a work on the way propaganda techniques are used to sell products and political candidates.

For ideas on how this division-classification essay is organized, see Figure 13.2 on page 237.

Pre-Reading Journal Entry

How susceptible are you to ads and commercials? Do you consider yourself an easy target, or are you a "hard sell"? Have you purchased any products simply because you were won over by effective advertising strategies? What products have you not purchased because you deliberately didn't let yourself be swayed by advertisers' tactics? In your journal, reflect on these questions.

PROPAGANDA TECHNIQUES IN TODAY'S ADVERTISING

Americans, adults and children alike, are being seduced. They are being brain- 1
washed. And few of us protest. Why? Because the seducers and the brainwashers are the advertisers we willingly invite into our homes. We are victims, content—even eager—to be victimized. We read advertisers' propaganda messages in news-papers and magazines; we watch their alluring images on television. We absorb their messages and images into our subconscious. We all do it—even those of us who claim to see through advertisers' tricks and therefore feel immune to advertis-ing's charm. Advertisers lean heavily on propaganda to sell products, whether the "products" are a brand of toothpaste, a candidate for office, or a particular political viewpoint.

Propaganda is a systematic effort to influence people's opinions, to win them over 2
to a certain view or side. Propaganda is not necessarily concerned with what is true or false, good or bad. Propagandists simply want people to believe the messages being sent. Often, propagandists will use outright lies or more subtle deceptions to sway people's opinions. In a propaganda war, any tactic is considered fair.

When we hear the word "propaganda," we usually think of a foreign menace: anti- 3
American radio programs broadcast by a totalitarian regime or brainwashing tactics practiced on hostages. Although propaganda may seem relevant only in the political arena, the concept can be applied fruitfully to the way products and ideas are sold in advertising. Indeed, the vast majority of us are targets in advertisers' propaganda war. Every day, we are bombarded with slogans, print and Internet pop-up ads, commer-cials, packaging claims, billboards, trademarks, logos, and designer brands—all forms of propaganda. One study reports that each of us, during an average day, is exposed to over *five hundred* advertising claims of various types. This saturation may even in-crease in the future since current trends include ads on movie screens, shopping carts, videocassettes, even public television.

4　　What kind of propaganda techniques do advertisers use? There are seven basic types:

5　**1.** *Name Calling* Name calling is a propaganda tactic in which negatively charged names are hurled against the opposing side or competitor. By using such names, propagandists try to arouse feelings of mistrust, fear, and hate in their audiences. For example, a political advertisement may label an opposing candidate a "loser," "fence-sitter," or "warmonger." Depending on the advertiser's target market, labels such as "a friend of big business" or "a dues-paying member of the party in power" can be the epithets that damage an opponent. Ads for products may also use name calling. An American manufacturer may refer, for instance, to a "foreign car" in its commercial—not an "imported" one. The label of foreignness will have unpleasant connotations in many people's minds. A childhood rhyme claims that "names can never hurt me," but name calling is an effective way to damage the opposition, whether it is another car maker or a congressional candidate.

6　**2.** *Glittering Generalities* Using glittering generalities is the opposite of name calling. In this case, advertisers surround their products with attractive—and slippery—words and phrases. They use vague terms that are difficult to define and that may have different meanings to different people: *freedom, democratic, all-American, progressive, Christian*, and *justice.* Many such words have strong, affirmative overtones. This kind of language stirs positive feelings in people, feelings that may spill over to the product or idea being pitched. As with name calling, the emotional response may overwhelm logic. Target audiences accept the product without thinking very much about what the glittering generalities mean—or whether they even apply to the product. After all, how can anyone oppose "truth, justice, and the American way"?

7　　　The ads for politicians and political causes often use glittering generalities because such "buzz words" can influence votes. Election slogans include high-sounding but basically empty phrases like the following:

"He cares about people." (That's nice, but is he a better candidate than his opponent?)

"Vote for progress." (Progress by *whose* standards?)

"They'll make this country great again." (What does "great" mean?

Does "great" mean the same thing to others as it does to me?)

"Vote for the future." (What kind of future?)

"If you love America, vote for Phyllis Smith." (If I don't vote for Smith, does that mean I don't love America?)

8　　　Ads for consumer goods are also sprinkled with glittering generalities. Product names, for instance, are supposed to evoke good feelings: *Luvs* diapers, *Stayfree* feminine hygiene products, *Joy* liquid detergent, *Loving Care* hair color, *Almost Home* cookies, *Yankee Doodle* pastries. Product slogans lean heavily on vague but comforting phrases: Sears is "Good life. Great price," General Electric "brings good things to life," and Dow Chemical "lets you do great things." Chevrolet, we are told, is the "heartbeat of America," and Chrysler boasts cars that are "imported from Detroit."

3. *Transfer* In transfer, advertisers try to improve the image of a product by associat- 9
ing it with a symbol most people respect, like the American flag or Uncle Sam.
The advertisers hope that the prestige attached to the symbol will carry over
to the product. Many companies use transfer devices to identify their products:
Lincoln Insurance shows a profile of the president; Continental Insurance portrays
a Revolutionary War minuteman; Amtrak's logo is red, white, and blue; Liberty
Mutual's corporate symbol is the Statue of Liberty; Allstate's name is cradled by a
pair of protective, fatherly hands.

Corporations also use the transfer technique when they sponsor prestigious 10
shows on radio and television. These shows function as symbols of dignity and
class. Kraft Corporation, for instance, sponsored a "Leonard Bernstein Conducts
Beethoven" concert, while Gulf Oil sponsored *National Geographic* specials and
Mobil supported public television's *Masterpiece Theater.* In this way, corporations
can reach an educated, influential audience and, perhaps, improve their public image by associating themselves with quality programming.

Political ads, of course, practically wrap themselves in the flag. Ads for a 11
political candidate often show either the Washington Monument, a Fourth of
July parade, the Stars and Stripes, a bald eagle soaring over the mountains, or a
white-steepled church on the village green. The national anthem or "America
the Beautiful" may play softly in the background. Such appeals to Americans'
love of country can surround the candidate with an aura of patriotism and
integrity.

4. *Testimonial* The testimonial is one of advertisers' most-loved and most-used propa- 12
ganda techniques. Similar to the transfer device, the testimonial capitalizes on the
admiration people have for a celebrity to make the product shine more brightly—
even though the celebrity is not an expert on the product being sold.

Print and television ads offer a nonstop parade of testimonials: here's William 13
Shatner for Priceline.com; here's basketball star Michael Jordan eating Wheaties;
a slew of well-known people (including pop star Madonna) advertise clothing
from the Gap; and Jerry Seinfeld assures us he never goes anywhere without his
American Express card. Testimonials can sell movies, too; newspaper ads for films
often feature favorable comments by wellknown reviewers. And, in recent years,
testimonials have played an important role in pitching books; the backs of paper-
backs frequently list complimentary blurbs by celebrities.

Political candidates, as well as their ad agencies, know the value of testi- 14
monials. Barbra Streisand lent her star appeal to the presidential campaign of
Bill Clinton, while Arnold Schwarzenegger endorsed George H. W. Bush. Even
controversial social issues are debated by celebrities. The nuclear-freeze debate, for instance, starred Paul Newman for the pro side and Charlton Heston
for the con.

As illogical as testimonials sometimes are (Pepsi's Michael Jackson, for in- 15
stance, was a health-food adherent who did not drink soft drinks), they are effective propaganda. We like the *person* so much that we like the *product* too.

5. *Plain Folks* The plain folks approach says, in effect, "Buy me or vote for me. I'm 16
just like you." Regular folks will surely like Bob Evans's Down on the Farm Country
Sausage or good old-fashioned Countrytime Lemonade. Some ads emphasize the

idea that "we're all in the same boat." We see people making long-distance calls for just the reasons we do—to put the baby on the phone to Grandma or to tell Mom we love her. And how do these folksy, warmhearted (usually saccharine) scenes affect us? They're supposed to make us feel that AT&T—the multinational corporate giant—has the same values we do. Similarly, we are introduced to the little people at Ford, the ordinary folks who work on the assembly line, not to bigwigs in their executive offices. What's the purpose of such an approach? To encourage us to buy a car built by these honest, hardworking "everyday Joes" who care about quality as much as we do.

17   Political advertisements make almost as much use of the "plain folks" appeal as they do of transfer devices. Candidates wear hard hats, farmers' caps, and assembly-line coveralls. They jog around the block and carry their own luggage through the airport. The idea is to convince voters that the candidates are average people, not the elite—not wealthy lawyers or executives but common citizens.

18   **6.** *Card Stacking* When people say that "the cards were stacked against me," they mean that they were never given a fair chance. Applied to propaganda, card stacking means that one side may suppress or distort evidence, tell half-truths, oversimplify the facts, or set up a "straw man"—a false target—to divert attention from the issue at hand. Card stacking is a difficult form of propaganda both to detect and to combat. When a candidate claims that an opponent has "changed his mind five times on this important issue," we tend to accept the claim without investigating whether the candidate had good reasons for changing his mind. Many people are simply swayed by the distorted claim that the candidate is "waffling" on the issue.

19   Advertisers often stack the cards in favor of the products they are pushing. They may, for instance, use what are called "weasel words." These are small words that usually slip right past us, but that make the difference between reality and illusion. The weasel words are underlined in the following claims:

"Helps control dandruff symptoms." (The audience usually interprets this as *stops* dandruff.)

"Most dentists surveyed recommend sugarless gum for their patients who chew gum." (We hear the "most dentists" and "for their patients," but we don't think about how many were surveyed or whether the dentists first recommended that the patients not chew gum at all.)

"Sticker price $1,000 lower than most comparable cars." (How many is "most"? What car does the advertiser consider "comparable"?)

20   Advertisers also use a card stacking trick when they make an unfinished claim. For example, they will say that their product has "twice as much pain reliever." We are left with a favorable impression. We don't usually ask, "Twice as much pain reliever as what?" Or advertisers may make extremely vague claims that sound alluring but have no substance: Toyota's "Oh, what a feeling!"; Vantage cigarettes' "The taste of success"; "The spirit of Marlboro"; Coke's "the real thing." Another way to stack the cards in favor of a certain product is to use scientific-sounding claims that are not supported by sound research. When Ford

claimed that its LTD model was "400% quieter," many people assumed that the LTD must be quieter than all other cars. When taken to court, however, Ford admitted that the phrase referred to the difference between the noise level inside and outside the LTD. Other scientific-sounding claims use mysterious ingredients that are never explained as selling points: "Retsyn," "special whitening agents," "the ingredient doctors recommend."

7. *Bandwagon* In the bandwagon technique, advertisers pressure, "Everyone's doing 21 it. Why don't you?" This kind of propaganda often succeeds because many people have a deep desire not to be different. Political ads tell us to vote for the "winning candidate." Advertisers know we tend to feel comfortable doing what others do; we want to be on the winning team. Or ads show a series of people proclaiming, "I'm voting for the Senator. I don't know why anyone wouldn't." Again, the audience feels under pressure to conform.

In the marketplace, the bandwagon approach lures buyers. Ads tell us that 22 "nobody doesn't like Sara Lee" (the message is that you must be weird if you don't). They tell us that "most people prefer Brand X two to one over other leading brands" (to be like the majority, we should buy Brand X). If we don't drink Pepsi, we're left out of "the Pepsi generation." To take part in "America's favorite health kick," the National Dairy Council asks us, "Got Milk?" And Honda motorcycle ads, praising the virtues of being a follower, tell us, "Follow the leader. He's on a Honda."

Why do these propaganda techniques work? Why do so many of us buy the 23 products, viewpoints, and candidates urged on us by propaganda messages? They work because they appeal to our emotions, not to our minds. Often, in fact, they capitalize on our prejudices and biases. For example, if we are convinced that environmentalists are radicals who want to destroy America's record of industrial growth and progress, then we will applaud the candidate who refers to them as "treehuggers." Clear thinking requires hard work: analyzing a claim, researching the facts, examining both sides of an issue, using logic to see the flaws in an argument. Many of us would rather let the propagandists do our thinking for us.

Because propaganda is so effective, it is important to detect it and understand 24 how it is used. We may conclude, after close examination, that some propaganda sends a truthful, worthwhile message. Some advertising, for instance, urges us not to drive drunk, to become volunteers, to contribute to charity. Even so, we must be aware that propaganda is being used. Otherwise, we have consented to handing over to others our independence of thought and action.

Questions for Close Reading

1. What is the selection's thesis? Locate the sentence(s) in which McClintock states her main idea. If she doesn't state the thesis explicitly, express it in your own words.

2. What is *propaganda?* What mistaken associations do we have with this term?

FIGURE 13.2

Essay Structure Diagram: "Propaganda Techniques in Today's Advertising" by Ann McClintock

Introductory paragraph: Thesis (paragraph 1)	Advertising messages as propaganda. **Thesis:** Advertisers lean heavily on propaganda to sell products, candidates, and viewpoints.
Background: Definition and statistics (2–3)	Propaganda as an "effort to influence people's opinions," not just about a "foreign menace." Exposure to over 500 advertising claims a day.
Details of classification with examples (4–22)	Kinds of propaganda techniques advertisers use: • Name calling–using negative labels, such as "fence-sitter" for competitors. • Glittering generalities–using vague, emotionally charged terms like "Vote for progress." • Transfer–associating someone or something with a positive symbol, such as the flag. • Testimonial–using well-known people to pitch a product, candidate, or position. • Plain folks–depicting everyday people that viewers can identify with. • Card stacking–making an unfair claim by distorting or suppressing evidence, over-simplifying, or using "weasel words." • Bandwagon–asserting "Everyone's doing it."
Concluding paragraphs (23–24)	Author's view that propaganda works by appealing to emotions rather than logic, so it's important to detect it and understand its use.

3. What are "weasel words"? How do they trick listeners?

4. Why does McClintock believe we should know about propaganda techniques?

Questions About the Writer's Craft

1. **The pattern and other patterns.** Before explaining the categories into which propaganda techniques can be grouped, McClintock provides a *definition* of propaganda. Is the definition purely informative, or does it have a larger objective? If you think the latter, what is the definition's broader purpose?

2. In her introduction, McClintock uses loaded words such as *seduced* and *brainwashed*. What effect do these words have on the reader?

3. Locate places in the essay where McClintock uses questions. Which are rhetorical and which are genuine queries?

4. What kind of conclusion does McClintock provide for the essay?

Writing Assignments Using Division-Classification as a Pattern of Development

1. McClintock cautions us to be sensitive to propaganda in advertising. Young children, however, aren't capable of this kind of awareness. With pen or pencil in hand, watch some commercials aimed at children, such as those for toys, cereals, and fast food. Then analyze the use of propaganda techniques in these commercials. Using division-classification, write an essay describing the main propaganda techniques you observed. Support your analysis with examples drawn from the commercials. Remember to provide a thesis that indicates your opinion of the advertising techniques.

2. Like advertising techniques, television shows can be classified. Avoiding the obvious system of classifying according to game shows, detective shows, and situation comedies, come up with your own original division-classification principle. Using one such principle, write an essay in which you categorize popular TV shows into three types. Refer to specific shows to support your classification system. Your attitude toward the shows being discussed should be made clear.

Writing Assignment Combining Patterns of Development

3. McClintock says that card stacking "distort[s] evidence, tell[s] half-truths, oversimpli[fies] the facts" (paragraph 18). Focusing on an extended *example* such as an editorial, a political campaign, a print ad, or a television commercial, analyze the extent to which card stacking is used as a *persuasive* strategy.

Scott Russell Sanders

Scott Russell Sanders was born in 1945 to a farming family in Tennessee. His work has been diverse, encompassing historical novels, children's stories, essays, and fiction. Two of Sanders's best-known works are the fictional *Fetching the Dead* (1984) and *The Engineer of Beasts* (1988). His more recent books include the novel *Bad Man Ballad* (2004) and the memoir *A Private History of Awe* (2007). The following essay is taken from *The Paradise of Bombs* (1987), an essay collection for which Sanders won the Associated Writing Programs Award for Creative Nonfiction.

Pre-Reading Journal Entry

Though one might argue that gender roles haven't evolved quickly or dramatically enough, they have changed considerably in recent decades. In your own lifetime, what are some changes that you've witnessed in the roles men and women play? Using your journal, brainstorm your ideas about gender transformations in areas such as education, athletics, employment, dating, marriage, and parenting. Then, for each category, go back and indicate whether the changes have been for the better. As you explore this issue, you might also benefit from discussing it with your friends and family, especially individuals from an older generation.

THE MEN WE CARRY IN OUR MINDS

1   The first men, besides my father, I remember seeing were black convicts and white guards, in the cotton field across the road from our farm on the outskirts of Memphis. I must have been three or four. The prisoners wore dingy gray-and-black zebra suits, heavy as canvas, sodden with sweat. Hatless, stooped, they chopped weeds in the fierce heat, row after row, breathing the acrid dust of boll-weevil poison. The overseers wore dazzling white shirts and broad shadowy hats. The oiled barrels of their shotguns flashed in the sunlight. Their faces in memory are utterly blank. Of course those men, white and black, have become for me an emblem of racial hatred. But they have also come to stand for the twin poles of my early vision of manhood—the brute toiling animal and the boss.

2   When I was a boy, the men I knew labored with their bodies. They were marginal farmers, just scraping by, or welders, steelworkers, carpenters; they swept floors, dug ditches, mined coal, or drove trucks, their forearms ropy with muscle; they trained horses, stoked furnaces, built fires, stood on assembly lines wrestling parts onto cars and refrigerators. They got up before light, worked all day long whatever the weather, and when they came home at night they looked as though somebody had been whipping them. In the evenings and on weekends they worked on their own places, tilling gardens that were lumpy with clay, fixing broken-down cars, hammering on houses that were always too drafty, too leaky, too small.

3   The bodies of the men I knew were twisted and maimed in ways visible and invisible. The nails of their hands were black and split, the hands tattooed with scars. Some had lost fingers. Heavy lifting had given many of them finicky backs and guts weak from hernias. Racing against conveyor belts had given them ulcers. Their ankles and knees ached from years of standing on concrete. Anyone who had worked for long around machines was hard of hearing. They squinted, and the skin of their faces was creased like the leather of old work gloves. There were times, studying them, when I dreaded growing up. Most of them coughed, from dust or cigarettes, and most of them drank cheap wine or whisky, so their eyes looked bloodshot and bruised. The fathers of my friends always seemed older than the mothers. Men wore out sooner. Only women lived into old age.

4   As a boy I also knew another sort of men, who did not sweat and break down like mules. They were soldiers, and so far as I could tell they scarcely worked at all. During my early school years we lived on a military base, an arsenal in Ohio, and every day I saw GIs in the guard shacks, on the stoops of barracks, at the wheels of olive drab Chevrolets. The chief fact of their lives was boredom. Long after I left the Arsenal I came to recognize the sour smell the soldiers gave off as that of souls in limbo. They

were all waiting—for wars, for transfers, for leaves, for promotions, for the end of their hitch—like so many braves waiting for the hunt to begin. Unlike the warriors of older tribes, however, they would have no say about when the battle would start or how it would be waged. Their waiting was broken only when they practiced for war. They fired guns at targets, drove tanks across the churned-up fields of the military reservation, set off bombs in the wrecks of old fighter planes. I knew this was all play. But I also felt certain that when the hour for killing arrived, they would kill. When the real shooting started, many of them would die. This was what soldiers were *for*, just as a hammer was for driving nails.

Warriors and toilers: those seemed, in my boyhood vision, to be the chief destinies for men. They weren't the only destinies, as I learned from having a few male teachers, from reading books, and from watching television. But the men on television—the politicians, the astronauts, the generals, the savvy lawyers, the philosophical doctors, the bosses who gave orders to both soldiers and laborers—seemed as removed and unreal to me as the figures in tapestries. I could no more imagine growing up to become one of these cool, potent creatures than I could imagine becoming a prince.

A nearer and more hopeful example was that of my father, who had escaped from a red-dirt farm to a tire factory, and from the assembly line to the front office. Eventually he dressed in a white shirt and tie. He carried himself as if he had been born to work with this mind. But his body, remembering the earlier years of slogging work, began to give out on him in his fifties, and it quit on him entirely before he turned sixty-five. Even such a partial escape from man's fate as he had accomplished did not seem possible for most of the boys I knew. They joined the Army, stood in line for jobs in the smoky plants, helped build highways. They were bound to work as their fathers had worked, killing themselves or preparing to kill others.

A scholarship enabled me not only to attend college, a rare enough feat in my circle, but even to study in a university meant for the children of the rich. Here I met for the first time young men who had assumed from birth that they would lead lives of comfort and power. And for the first time I met women who told me that men were guilty of having kept all the joys and privileges of the earth for themselves. I was baffled. What privileges? What joys? I thought about the maimed, dismal lives of most of the men back home. What had they stolen from their wives and daughters? The right to go five days a week, twelve months a year, for thirty or forty years to a steel mill or a coal mine? The right to drop bombs and die in war? The right to feel every leak in the roof, every gap in the fence, every cough in the engine, as a wound they must mend? The right to feel, when the lay-off comes or the plant shuts down, not only afraid but ashamed?

I was slow to understand the deep grievances of women. This was because, as a boy, I had envied them. Before college, the only people I had ever known who were interested in art or music or literature, the only ones who read books, the only ones who ever seemed to enjoy a sense of ease and grace were the mothers and daughters. Like the menfolk, they fretted about money, they scrimped and made do. But, when the pay stopped coming in, they were not the ones who had failed. Nor did they have to go to war, and that seemed to me a blessed fact. By comparison with the narrow, ironclad days of fathers, there was an expansiveness, I thought, in the days of mothers. They went to see neighbors, to shop in town, to run errands at school, at the library, at church. No doubt, had I looked harder at their lives, I would have envied them less. It was not my fate to become a woman, so it was easier for me to see the graces. Few of them held jobs outside the home, and those who did filled thankless roles as clerks and waitresses. I didn't see, then, what a prison a house could be, since houses seemed to me brighter, handsomer places than any factory. I did not realize—because such things were never spoken of—how often women suffered from men's bullying. I did learn about the wretchedness of abandoned wives, single mothers, widows; but I also learned about the wretchedness of lone men. Even then I could see how exhausting it was for a mother to cater all day to the needs of young children. But if I had been asked, as a boy, to choose between tending a baby and tending a machine, I think I would have chosen the baby. (Having now tended both, I know I would choose the baby.)

9   So I was baffled when the women at college accused me and my sex of having cornered the world's pleasures. I think something like my bafflement has been felt by other boys (and girls as well) who grew up in dirt-poor farm country, in mining country, in black ghettos, in Hispanic barrios, in the shadows of factories, in Third World nations—any place where the fate of men is as grim and bleak as the fate of women. Toilers and warriors. I realize now how ancient these identities are, how deep the tug they exert on men, the undertow of a thousand generations. The miseries I saw, as a boy, in the lives of nearly all men I continue to see in the lives of many—the body-breaking toil, the tedium, the call to be tough, the humiliating powerlessness, the battle for a living and for territory.

10   When the women I met at college thought about the joys and privileges of men, they did not carry in their minds the sort of men I had known in my childhood. They thought of their fathers, who were bankers, physicians, architects, stockbrokers, the big wheels of the big cities. These fathers rode the train to work or drove cars that cost more than any of my childhood houses. They were attended from morning to night by female helpers, wives and nurses and secretaries. They were never laid off, never short of cash at month's end, never lined up for welfare. These fathers made decisions that mattered. They ran the world.

11   The daughters of such men wanted to share in this power, this glory. So did I. They yearned for a say over their future, for jobs worthy of their abilities, for the right to live at peace, unmolested, whole. Yes, I thought, yes yes. The difference between me and these daughters was that they saw me, because of my sex, as destined from birth to become like their fathers, and therefore as an enemy to their desires. I was an ally. If I had known, then, how to tell them so, would they have believed me? Would they now?

Questions for Close Reading

1. What is the selection's thesis? Locate the sentence(s) in which Sanders states his main idea. If he doesn't state the thesis explicitly, express it in your own words.

2. Who were the men Sanders knew most about in his childhood? What does Sanders mean when he says that these men were damaged "in ways both visible and invisible" (paragraph 3)?

3. How did Sanders learn that some men don't toil with their bodies? How did he feel about such men?

4. Why, according to Sanders, was he "slow to understand the deep grievances of women" (8)? Why did the women Sanders met at college consider men to be privileged? Why does Sanders feel he is "an ally" rather than "an enemy" of these women? What prevented the women from understanding how he felt?

Questions About the Writer's Craft

1. **The pattern.** Sanders categorizes men into three types; toiling animals, warriors, and bosses. Of the three categories, which two does he describe most vividly? Why might he have chosen to describe these two in such detail?

2. In paragraphs 2 and 3, Sanders offers a vivid portrait of workingmen's lives. How does his word choice, as well as his use of parallel structure and repetition, lend power to this portrait?

3. **Other patterns.** In the second half of the essay, Sanders *contrasts* the lives of workingmen with those of women (paragraphs 7–8) and with those of professional men (10). What is the value of these contrasts?

4. From the middle of paragraph 7 to its end, Sanders frames his sentences as questions. Why might he have decided to pose all these questions? How do they help him achieve his purpose?

Writing Assignments Using Division-Classification as a Pattern of Development

1. "Warriors and toilers," Sanders writes, "those seemed, in my boyhood vision, to be the chief destinies for men." Identify several men *or* women who helped create your "vision" of what it means to be male *or* female. Group these individuals into types. Then write an essay describing these types and the people representing each type; your goal is to show whether these people enlarged or restricted your understanding of what it means to be male or female.

2. Sanders admits he was "slow to understand the deep grievances of women" against men. Consider another group that has grievances. Start by brainstorming with others to generate examples of the group's grievances; then write an essay in which you categorize the grievances by type, illustrating each with vivid examples. At the end, reach some conclusions about the validity of the group's complaints.

Writing Assignment Combining Patterns of Development

3. Sanders's father transformed his life when he "escaped from a red-dirt farm…to the front office." Think about someone else who also made a positive life change. Write an essay in which you *describe* the change that was made and explain the *steps* that

the person took to make effective and lasting alterations in his or her life. To high-light the change the person made, start by showing what the person's life was like before it was turned around.

Bianca Bosker

Princeton University graduate Bianca Bosker is Executive Tech Editor for *The Huffington Post*, an online news Web site and blog that covers U.S. politics, world news, entertainment, and style. Bosker's publications have appeared in *The Wall Street Journal*, *Condé Nast Traveler*, and *The Far Eastern Economic Review*. She is the co-author of *Bowled Over: A Roll Down Memory Lane*, a tribute to the tradition and culture of bowling. The following article was published on the *Huffington Post* Web site on May 21, 2013.

Pre-Reading Journal Entry

In what ways do you make use of social media sites such as *Facebook*, *Twitter*, *Instagram*, and *MySpace*? How have the ways you use these sites changed over the past several years? If you don't use any of these sites, why not? Why do you think they are a major part of the lives of millions? Explore these ideas in your journal.

HOW TEENS ARE REALLY USING FACEBOOK: IT'S A "SOCIAL BURDEN," PEW STUDY FINDS

1   The Facebook generation is fed up with Facebook.

2   That's according to a report released Tuesday by the Pew Research Center, which surveyed 802 teens between the ages of 12 and 17 [in September 2012] to produce a 107-page report on their online habits.

3   Pew's findings suggest teens' enthusiasm for Facebook is waning, lending cre-dence to concerns, raised by the company's investors and others, that the social network may be losing a crucial demographic that has long fueled its success ("Facebook's CEO").

4   Facebook has become a "social burden" for teens, write the authors of the Pew report. "While Facebook is still deeply integrated in teens' everyday lives, it is some-times seen as a utility and an obligation rather than an exciting new platform that teens can claim as their own" (Madden et al. 18).

5   Teens aren't abandoning Facebook—deactivating their accounts would mean miss-ing out on the crucial social intrigues that transpire online—and 94 percent of teen-age social media users still have profiles on the site, Pew's report notes. But they're simultaneously migrating to Twitter and Instagram, which teens say offer a parent-free place where they can better express themselves. Eleven percent of teens surveyed had Instagram accounts, while the number of teen Twitter users climbed from 16 per-cent in 2011 to 24 percent in 2012. Five percent of teens have accounts on Tumblr,

Where teens have social media profiles or accounts
% of teen social media users who use the following sites...

	2011	2012
Facebook	93%	94%
Twitter	12	26
Instagram	n/a	11
MySpace	24	7
YouTube	6	7
Tumblr	2	5
Google Plus	n/a	3
Yahoo (unspecified)	7	2
myYearbook	2	*
Pinterest	n/a	1
Gmail	n/a	1
Meet Me	n/a	1
Other	8	6
Don't know / Don't have own profile	2	1

Source: Madden et al., p. 24.

which was just purchased by Yahoo for $1.1 billion, while 7 percent have accounts on MySpace (Kleinman).

Facebook, teens say, has been overrun by parents, fuels unnecessary social "drama" and 6 gives a mouthpiece to annoying oversharers who drone on about inane events in their lives.

"Honestly, Facebook at this point, I'm on it constantly but I hate it so much," one 7 15 year-old girl told Pew during a focus group (Madden et al. 38).

"I got mine [Facebook account] around sixth grade. And I was really obsessed with 8 it for a while," another 14 year-old said. "Then towards eighth grade, I kind of just— once you get into Twitter, if you make a Twitter and an Instagram, then you'll just kind of forget about Facebook, is what I did" (Madden et al. 27).

On the whole, teens' usage of social media seems to have plateaued, and the frac- 9 tion of those who check social sites "several times a day" has stayed steady at around 40 percent since 2011 (Madden et al. 22).

Female (age 19): "Yeah, that's why we go on Twitter and Instagram [instead of Facebook]. My mom doesn't have that."

Female (age 15): "If you are on Facebook, you see a lot of drama."

Female (age 14): "OK, here's something I want to say. I think Facebook can be fun, but also it's drama central. On Facebook, people imply things and say things, even just by a like, that they wouldn't say in real life."

Male (age 18): "It's because [Facebook] it's where people post unnecessary pictures and they say unnecessary things, like saying he has a girlfriend, and a girl will go on and tag him in the picture like, me and him in the sun having fun. Why would you do that?" (Madden et al. 26)

10   Asked about teens' Facebook habits during a recent earnings call with investors, Facebook's chief financial officer answered that the company "remain[s] really pleased with the high level of engagement on Facebook by people of all ages around the world" and called younger users "among the most active and engaged users that we have on Facebook" ("Facebook's CEO").

11   Here's what that "high level of engagement" really looks like, according to Pew:

They're deleting, lying and blocking: Some three-quarters of Facebook users have purged friends on Facebook, 58 percent have edited or deleted content they've shared and 26 percent have tried to protect their privacy by sharing false information. Among all teens online (not just Facebook users), 39 percent have lied about their age. The report also notes, "Girls are more likely than boys to delete friends from their network (82 percent vs. 66 percent) and block people (67 percent vs. 48 percent)."

Superusers on Facebook are superusers on other social sites: Teens with large friend networks on Facebook are more likely than their peers to have profiles on other social media sites: 46 percent of teens with over 600 Facebook friends have a Twitter profile, and 12 percent of such users have an Instagram account. By comparison, just 21 percent and 11 percent of teens who have 150 to 300 friends have Twitter and Instagram accounts, respectively.

Teens have hundreds of friends, but they haven't met them all: The typical Facebook-using teen has 300 friends, though girls are more likely to have more friends (the median is 350) than boys (300). Seventy percent of teens are friends with their parents, 30 percent are friends with teachers or coaches, and 33 percent are friends with people they've never met in person.

It turns out parents actually do see what their kids are posting: Just 5 percent of teens tweak their privacy to limit what their parents see.

They're watching out for their privacy: Sixty percent of teens on Facebook say they've checked their privacy settings in the past month—a third of them within the past seven days. The majority (60 percent) of teens have their profiles set to private, while 14 percent have profiles that are completely public.

But yes, they are sharing personal details: Teens with more Facebook friends are more likely to share a greater variety of personal details about themselves online. Among all teens on Facebook, 21 percent share their cell phone number, 63 percent share their relationship status and 54 percent share their email address.

Seventeen percent of teens on Facebook will automatically share their location in their posts, and 18 percent say they've shared something they later regret posting.

They're enjoying themselves, but they've been contacted by creeps: Among all teens surveyed by Pew, 17 percent have been contacted by strangers in a way that made them "scared or uncomfortable." However, 57 percent of social media-using teens said they've had an experience online that "made them feel good about themselves," and 37 percent say social media has made them feel more connected to someone else.

Works Cited

"Facebook's CEO Discusses Q1 2013 Results—Earnings Call Transcript." *Seeking Alpha*. Seeking Alpha, 1 May 2013. Web. 20 May 2013.

Kleinman, Alexis. "Yahoo Tumblr Deal Is Officially Announced." *Huffington Post*. Huffington Post, 20 May 2013. Web. 20 May 2013.

Madden, Mary, et al. "Teens, Social Media, and Privacy." *Pew Internet & American Life Project*. Pew Research Center, 21 May 2013. Web. 21 May 2013.

Questions for Close Reading

1. **Thesis.** What is the selection's thesis? Locate the sentence(s) in which Bosker states her main idea. If she doesn't state the thesis explicitly, express it in your own words.

2. According to the Pew report by Madden et al. that Bosker references in her article, in what ways has *Facebook* become a "social burden" for many users?

3. The chart from the Pew report that is included in this reading shows the percentage of teens using various social media sites. According to the chart, which two sites have shown the largest increases in use and which two have shown the greatest decreases?

4. The phrase "high level of engagement" appears in paragraphs 10 and 11 of the article. How does *Facebook*'s chief financial officer's use of the term differ from the way, according to Bosker, the Pew report interprets "what that 'high level of engagement' really looks like"?

Questions About the Writer's Craft

1. **The pattern.** In what ways does Bosker's article classify teens' use of social media sites? Does the classification scheme seem reasonable to you? Why or why not?

2. **Other patterns.** In addition to classifying the ways teens use social media sites, Bosker provides examples that *illustrate* the points she is making. List three of the examples she uses that you think work especially well to support her thesis.

3. Bosker references three sources in her article. Which one does she rely most heavily on and why? In what ways does the use of the other two sources enrich her article?

4. Why do you think Bosker decided to include a chart from the Pew report in her article? In what ways does the chart add to the effectiveness of her article?

Writing Assignments Using Division-Classification as a Pattern of Development

1. The authors of the Pew report gathered information on the online habits of teens between the ages of 12 and 17. Conduct your own research by designing a questionnaire on the online habits of another group—perhaps the students in your composition class or the members of another group or community to which you belong. Write an essay in which you present the information you gathered, classifying the ways the members of your research group use online media sites. Consider designing a chart similar to the one in the Bosker article, and include it in your composition to illustrate the various sites where the members of your research group have social media profiles or accounts.

2. Write an essay in which you classify the types of music most popular today among a particular demographic. You might rely on secondary sources for the information you include in your essay—as Bosker did in hers—or you might conduct your own primary research using questionnaires or surveys that you design. Consider using visuals such as charts or graphs to clearly present your findings to your readers.

Writing Assignment Combining Patterns of Development

3. Write an essay in which you *compare* and *contrast* various social media sites. For example, you might compare *Facebook*, *Twitter*, and *Instagram* and explore what the sites have in common as well as how they differ from one another. You might also include quotes from individuals you interview to *illustrate* what these social media users consider to be advantages and disadvantages of the various sites.

ADDITIONAL WRITING TOPICS: DIVISION-CLASSIFICATION

General Assignments

Using division-classification, develop one of these topics into an essay.

Division	Classification
1. A shopping mall	1. Commercials
2. A video system	2. Holidays
3. A particular kind of team	3. Roommates
4. A school library	4. Summer movies
5. A college campus	5. Internet surfers

Assignments Using Visuals

Use the suggested visuals to help develop a division-classification essay on one of these topics:

1. Types of friends and the roles they play in our lives (slide show or cartoons)

2. Novels made into movies in the past two years (Web links to movie trailers)

3. Various parenting styles by period or region (charts)

4. This year's most popular TV shows (links to Web sites and/or *YouTube* videos)

5. Personality types identified by psychologists (charts and/or graphs)

Assignments with a Specific Purpose, Audience, and Point of View

1. **Academic life.** You're a dorm counselor. During orientation week, you'll be talking to students on your floor about the different kinds of problems they may have with roommates. Write your talk, describing each kind of problem and explaining how to cope.

2. **Academic life.** As your college newspaper's TV critic, you plan to write a review of the fall shows, most of which—in your opinion—lack originality. To show how stereotypical the programs are, select one type (for example, situation comedies or crime dramas). Then use a specific division-classification principle to illustrate that the same stale formulas are trotted out from show to show.

3. **Academic life.** Asked to write an editorial for the campus paper, you decide to do a half-serious piece on taking "mental health" days off from classes. Structure your essay around three kinds of occasions when "playing hooky" is essential for maintaining sanity.

4. **Civic activity.** Your favorite magazine runs an editorial asking readers to send in what they think are the main challenges facing their particular gender group. Write a letter to the editor in which you identify at least three categories of problems that your sex faces. Be sure to provide lively, specific examples to illustrate each category. In your letter, you may adopt a serious or lighthearted tone, depending on your overall subject matter.

5. **Workplace action.** As a driving instructor, you decide to prepare a lecture on the types of drivers that your students are likely to encounter on the road. In your lecture, categorize drivers according to a specific principle and show the behaviors of each type.

6. **Workplace action.** A seasoned camp counselor, you've been asked to prepare, for new counselors, an informational sheet on children's emotional needs. Categorizing those needs into types, explain what counselors can do to nurture youngsters emotionally.

14

Process Analysis

In this chapter, you will learn:

14.1 To use the pattern of process analysis to develop your essays
14.2 To consider how process analysis can fit your purpose and audience
14.3 To develop prewriting, writing, and revision strategies for using process analysis in an essay
14.4 To analyze how process analysis is used effectively in one student-written and three professionally authored selections
14.5 To write your own essays using process analysis as a strategy

What Is Process Analysis?

We spend a good deal of our lives learning—everything from speaking our first word to balancing our first bank statement. Indeed, the milestones in our lives are often linked to the processes we have mastered: how to cross the street alone; how to drive a car; how to make a speech without being paralyzed by fear.

Process analysis, a technique that explains the steps or sequence involved in doing something, satisfies our need to learn as well as our curiosity about how the world works. Process analysis can be more than merely interesting or entertaining, though; it can be of critical importance. Consider a waiter hurriedly skimming the "Choking Aid" instructions posted on a restaurant wall or an air-traffic controller following emergency procedures in an effort to prevent a midair collision. In these examples, the consequences could be fatal if the process analyses are slipshod, inaccurate, or confusing.

Undoubtedly, all of us have experienced less dramatic effects of poorly written process analyses. Perhaps you've tried to

249

assemble a bicycle and spent hours sorting through a stack of parts, only to end up with one or two extra pieces never mentioned in the instructions. No wonder many people stay clear of anything that actually admits "assembly required."

How Process Analysis Fits Your Purpose and Audience

You will use process analysis in two types of writing situations: (1) when you want to give step-by-step instructions to readers showing how they can do something, or (2) when you want readers to understand how something happens even though they won't actually follow the steps outlined. The first kind of process analysis is **directional**; the second is **informational**.

When you follow guidelines for completing a job application, you're reading directional process analysis. A serious essay explaining how to select a college is also an example of a directional process analysis. Using a variety of tones, informational process analyses can range over equally diverse subjects; they can describe mechanical, scientific, historical, sociological, artistic, or psychological processes: for example, how the core of a nuclear power plant melts down or how television became so important in political campaigns.

Process analysis, both directional and informational, is often appropriate in *problem-solving situations*. In such cases, you say, "Here's the problem and here's what should be done to solve the problem." Indeed, college assignments frequently take the form of problem-solving process analyses. Consider these examples:

> Because many colleges and universities have changed the eligibility requirements for financial aid, fewer students can depend on loans or scholarships. How can students cope with the increasing costs of obtaining a higher education?

> Community officials have been accused of mismanaging recent unrest over the public housing ordinance. Describe the steps the officials took, indicating why you think their strategy was unwise. Then explain how you think the situation should have been handled.

Note that the last assignment asks students to explain what's wrong with the current approach before they present their own step-by-step solution. Problem-solving process analyses are often organized in this way. You may also have noticed that neither assignment explicitly requires an essay response using process analysis. However, the wording of the assignments—*"Describe the steps," "How can students cope"*—indicates that process analysis would be an appropriate strategy for developing the responses.

Assignments don't always signal the use of process analysis so clearly. But during the prewriting stage, as you generate material to support your thesis, you'll often realize that you can best achieve your purpose by developing the essay—or part of it—using process analysis.

Sometimes process analysis will be the primary strategy for organizing an essay; other times it will be used to help make a point in an essay organized around another pattern of development. Let's take a look at process analysis as a supporting strategy.

   Assume that you're writing a *causal analysis* examining the impact of television commercials on people's buying behavior. To help readers see that commercials create a need where none existed before, you might describe the various stages in an advertising campaign to pitch a new, completely frivolous product. In an essay *defining* a good boss, you could convey the point that effective managers must be skilled at settling disputes by explaining the steps your boss took to resolve a heated disagreement between two employees. If you write an *argumentation-persuasion* paper urging the funding of programs to ease the plight of the homeless, you would have to dramatize for readers the tragedy of these people's lives. To achieve your purpose, you could devote part of the paper to an explanation of how the typical street person goes about finding a place to sleep and getting food to eat.

Prewriting Strategies

The following checklist shows how you can apply to process analysis some of the prewriting strategies discussed in Chapter 2.

> ☑ **PROCESS ANALYSIS: A PREWRITING CHECKLIST**
>
> *Choose a Process to Analyze*
>
> ☐ What processes do you know well and feel you can explain clearly?
>
> ☐ What processes have you wondered about?
>
> ☐ What process needs changing if a current problem is to be solved?
>
> *Determine Your Purpose, Audience, Tone, and Point of View*
>
> ☐ What is the central purpose of your process analysis? Do you want to inform readers so that they will acquire a new skill? Do you want readers to gain a better understanding of a complex process? Do you want to persuade readers to accept your point of view about a process, perhaps even urge them to adopt a particular course of action?
>
> ☐ What audience are you writing for? What will they need to know to understand the process? What will they not need to know?
>
> ☐ What point of view will you adopt when addressing the audience?
>
> ☐ What tone do you want to project? Do you want to come across as serious, humorous, sarcastic, ironic, objective, impassioned?
>
> *Use Prewriting to Generate the Stages of the Process*
>
> ☐ How could brainstorming or mapping help you identify primary and secondary steps in the process?
>
> ☐ How could brainstorming or mapping help you identify the ingredients or materials that the reader will need?

Strategies for Using Process Analysis in an Essay

After prewriting, you're ready to draft your essay. Figure 14.1 and the suggestions that follow will be helpful whether you use process analysis as a dominant or supportive pattern of development.

1. **Formulate a thesis that clarifies your attitude toward the process.** Like the thesis in any other paper, the thesis in a process analysis should do more than announce your subject. It should also state or imply your attitude toward the process.

2. **Keep your audience in mind when deciding what to cover.** Only after you gauge how much your readers already know (or don't know) about the process can you determine how much explanation to provide.

   The audience's level of knowledge determines whether or not you should define technical terms. To determine how much explanation is needed, put yourself in your readers' shoes. Don't assume readers will know something just because you do. Ask questions like these about your audience: "Will my readers need some background about the process before I describe it in depth?" and "If my essay is directional, should I specify near the beginning the ingredients, materials, and equipment needed to perform the process?" (For more help in analyzing your audience, see the checklist on page 251.)

3. **Focusing on your purpose, thesis, and audience, explain the process—one step at a time.** After using prewriting techniques to identify primary and secondary steps and needed equipment, you're ready to organize your raw material into an easy-to-follow sequence. At times your purpose will be to explain a process with a *fairly fixed chronological sequence:* how to make a pizza or how to pot a plant. In such cases, you should include all necessary steps in the correct chronological order. However, if a strict chronological ordering of steps means that a particularly important part of the sequence gets buried in the middle, the sequence probably should be juggled so that the crucial step receives the attention it deserves.

   Other times your goal will be to describe a process having *no commonly accepted sequence.* For example, in an essay explaining how to discipline a child or how to pull yourself out of a blue mood, you will have to come up with your own definition of the key steps and then arrange those steps in some logical order. You may also use process analysis to *reject* or *reformulate* a traditional sequence. In this case, you would propose a more logical series of steps: "Our system for electing congressional representatives is inefficient and undemocratic; it should be reformed in the following ways."

   Whether the essay describes a generally agreed-on process or one that is not commonly accepted, you must provide all the details needed to explain the process. Your readers should be able to understand, even visualize, the process. There should be no fuzzy patches or confusing cuts from one step to another. Don't, however, go into obsessive detail about minor stages or steps.

FIGURE 14.1

Development Diagram: Writing a Process Analysis Essay

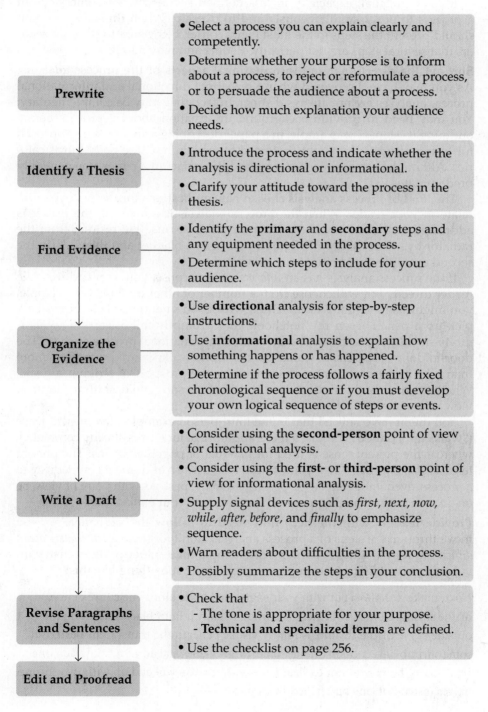

Prewrite
- Select a process you can explain clearly and competently.
- Determine whether your purpose is to inform about a process, to reject or reformulate a process, or to persuade the audience about a process.
- Decide how much explanation your audience needs.

Identify a Thesis
- Introduce the process and indicate whether the analysis is directional or informational.
- Clarify your attitude toward the process in the thesis.

Find Evidence
- Identify the **primary** and **secondary** steps and any equipment needed in the process.
- Determine which steps to include for your audience.

Organize the Evidence
- Use **directional** analysis for step-by-step instructions.
- Use **informational** analysis to explain how something happens or has happened.
- Determine if the process follows a fairly fixed chronological sequence or if you must develop your own logical sequence of steps or events.

Write a Draft
- Consider using the **second-person** point of view for directional analysis.
- Consider using the **first-** or **third-person** point of view for informational analysis.
- Supply signal devices such as *first, next, now, while, after, before,* and *finally* to emphasize sequence.
- Warn readers about difficulties in the process.
- Possibly summarize the steps in your conclusion.

Revise Paragraphs and Sentences
- Check that
  - The tone is appropriate for your purpose.
  - **Technical and specialized terms** are defined.
- Use the checklist on page 256.

Edit and Proofread

If you dwell for several hundred words on how to butter the pan, your readers will never stay with you long enough to learn how to make the omelet.

It's not unusual, especially in less defined sequences, for some steps in a process to occur simultaneously and to overlap. When this happens, you should present the steps in the most logical order, being sure to tell your readers that several steps are not perfectly distinct and may merge.

4. **Sort out the directional and informational aspects of the process analysis.** As you may have discovered when prewriting, directional and informational process analyses are not always distinct. In fact, they may be complementary: You may need to provide background information about a process before outlining its steps. For example, in a paper describing a step-by-step approach for losing weight, you might first need to explain how the body burns calories. Although both approaches may be appropriate in a paper, one generally predominates.

The kind of process analysis chosen has implications for the way you will relate to your reader. When the process analysis is *directional*, the reader is addressed in the *second person:* "You should first rinse the residue from the radiator by..." or "Wrap the injured person in a blanket and then..." (In the second example, the pronoun *you* is implied.)

If the process analysis has an *informational* purpose, you won't address the reader directly but will choose from a number of other options. For example, you might use the *first person:* "Filled with good intentions, I sit on my bed, pick up a pencil, open my notebook, and promptly fall asleep." The *third-person singular or plural* can also be used in informational process essays: "The door-to-door salesperson walks up the front walk, heart pounding, more than a bit nervous, but also challenged by the prospect of striking a deal." Whether you use the first, second, or third person, avoid shifting point of view midstream.

You might have noticed that in the third-person examples, the present tense ("walks up") is used. The past tense is appropriate for events already completed, whereas the present tense is used for habitual or ongoing actions. The present tense is also effective when you want to lend a sense of dramatic immediacy to a process, even if the steps were performed in the past. As with point of view, be on guard against changing tenses in the middle of your explanation.

5. **Provide readers with the help they need to follow the sequence.** As you move through the steps of a process analysis, don't forget to *warn readers about difficulties* they might encounter. For example, in a paper on the artistry involved in butterflying a shrimp, you might write something like this:

Next, make a shallow cut with your sharpened knife along the convex curve of the shrimp's intestinal tract. The tract, usually a faint black line along the outside curve of the shrimp, is faintly visible beneath the translucent flesh. But some shrimp have a thick orange, blue, or gray line instead of a thin black one. In all cases, be careful not to slice too deeply, or you will end up with two shrimp halves instead of one butterflied shrimp.

You have told readers what to look for, citing the exceptions, and have warned them against making too deep a cut. Anticipating spots where communication might break down is a key part of writing an effective process analysis.

Transitional words and phrases are also critical in helping readers understand the order of the steps being described. Time signals like *first, next, now, while, after, before,* and *finally* provide readers with a clear sense of the sequence. Entire sentences can also be used to link parts of the process, reminding your audience of what has already been discussed and indicating what will now be explained.

6. **Select and maintain an appropriate tone.** When writing a process analysis essay, be sure your tone is consistent with your purpose, your attitude toward your subject, and the effect you want to have on readers. Take into account readers' attitudes toward your subject. Does your audience have a financial or emotional investment in the process being described? Does your own interest in the process coincide or conflict with that of your audience? Awareness of your readers' stance can be crucial. You'd do well to be tactful in your criticisms. Offend your reader, and your cause is lost. Once you settle on the essay's tone, maintain it throughout.

7. **Open and close the process analysis effectively.** A paper developed primarily through process analysis should have a strong beginning. The introduction should state the process to be described and imply whether the essay has an informational or directional intent.

   If you suspect readers are indifferent to your subject, use the introduction to motivate them, telling them how important the subject is:

Do you enjoy the salad bars found in many restaurants? If you do, you probably have noticed that the vegetables are always crisp and fresh—no matter how many hours they have been exposed to the air. What are the restaurants doing to make the vegetables look so inviting? There's a simple answer. Many restaurants dip and spray the vegetables with potent chemicals to make them look appetizing.

   If you think your audience may be intimidated by your subject (perhaps because it's complex or relatively obscure), the introduction is the perfect spot to reassure them that the process being described is not beyond their grasp:

Studies show that many people prefer to accept a defective product rather than deal with the uncomfortable process of making a complaint. But once a few easy-to-learn basics are mastered, anyone can register a complaint that gets results.

   Most process analysis essays don't end as soon as the last step in the sequence is explained. Instead, they usually include some brief final comments that round out the piece and bring it to a satisfying close. This final section of the essay may summarize the main steps in the process—not by repeating the steps verbatim but by rephrasing and condensing them in several concise sentences. The conclusion can also be an effective spot to underscore the significance of the process, recalling what may have been said in the introduction about the subject's importance. Or the essay can end by echoing the note of reassurance that may have been included at the start.

Revision Strategies

Once you have a draft of the essay, you're ready to revise. The following checklist will help you and those giving you feedback apply to process analysis some of the revision techniques discussed in Chapters 7 and 8.

☑ **PROCESS ANALYSIS: A REVISION/PEER REVIEW CHECKLIST**

Revise Overall Meaning and Structure

☐ What purpose does the process analysis serve—to inform, to persuade, or to do both?

☐ Is the process analysis primarily *directional* or *informational*? How can you tell?

☐ Where does the process seem confusing? Where have steps been left out? Which steps need simplifying?

☐ What is the essay's tone? Is the tone appropriate for the essay's purpose and readers? Where are there distracting shifts in tone?

Revise Paragraph Development

☐ Does the introduction specify the process to be described? Does it provide an overview? Should it?

☐ Which paragraphs are difficult to follow? Have any steps or materials been omitted or explained in too much or too little detail? Which paragraphs should warn readers about potential trouble spots or overlapping steps?

☐ Where are additional time signals (*after, before, next*) needed to clarify the sequence within and between paragraphs? Where does overreliance on time signals make the sequence awkward and mechanical?

☐ Which paragraph describes the most crucial step in the sequence? How has the step been highlighted?

☐ How could the conclusion be more effective?

Revise Sentences and Words

☐ What technical or specialized terms appear in the essay? Have they been sufficiently explained? Where could simpler, less technical language be used?

☐ Are there any places where the essay's point of view awkwardly shifts? How could this problem be corrected?

☐ Does the essay use correct verb tenses—the past tense for completed events, the present tense for habitual or ongoing actions?

☐ Where does the essay use the passive voice ("The hole is dug")? Would the active voice ("You dig the hole") be more effective?

Student Essay: From Prewriting Through Revision

The student essay that follows was written by Robert Barry in response to this assignment:

> In "What Shamu Taught Me About a Happy Marriage," Amy Sutherland uses humor to show how she employed animal training techniques to "improve" her husband's behavior. Think of an element of our culture involving personal inter-action, entertainment, hobbies, or the like. Show, step-by-step, how our everyday behavior involving this element has changed. Your essay may be either serious or light in tone.

Before writing his essay, Robert used the prewriting strategy of *mapping* to generate material for the subject he decided to write on: DVR addiction. Then, with his map as a foundation, he prepared a topic outline that orga-nized and developed his thoughts more fully. Both the map and the outline are reprinted here.

Mapping

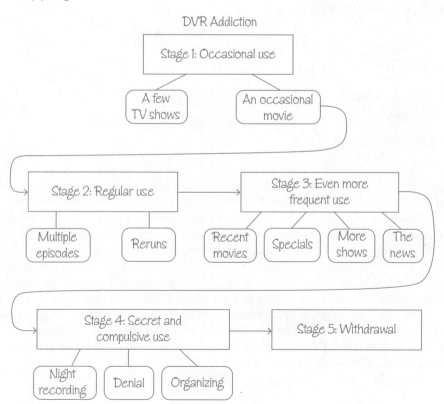

Outline

Thesis: Without realizing it, a person can turn into a compulsive recorder. This movement from innocent hobby to full-blown addiction occurs in several stages.

  I. Stage One: Occasional use
     A. TV show reruns
        1. *Seinfeld*
        2. *The Simpsons*
     B. An occasional movie

 II. Stage Two: More frequent use
     A. Many episodes of *Seinfeld* and *The Sopranos*
     B. Episodes of *Heroes*, *The Simpsons*, and *Grey's Anatomy*

III. Stage Three: Much more frequent use
     A. Recording of news shows
     B. Recording of recent movies—add examples
     C. Not enough time to watch recorded shows

 IV. Stage Four: Secret and compulsive use
     A. Reaction to family's concern
        1. Denial
        2. Sneaking downstairs to record at night
     B. Obsessive organization of recording schedule

  V. Stage Five: Withdrawal
     A. Forced withdrawal at college
     B. Success at last

After looking at Robert's map and outline, read his paper, "Becoming a Recordoholic," noting the similarities and differences among his map, outline, and final essay. You'll see that Robert dropped one idea (recording news shows), expanded other points (his obsessive organization by means of a secret calendar), and added some completely new details (his near backsliding during withdrawal). Note, too, that the analogy between DVR addiction and alcoholism doesn't appear in either the map or the outline. The analogy didn't occur to Robert until he began writing his first draft. Despite these differences, the map and outline depict essentially the same five stages in DVR addiction as the essay. Finally, as you read the essay, consider how well it applies the principles of process analysis discussed in this chapter. (The commentary that follows the paper will help you look at Robert's essay more closely and will give you some sense of how he went about revising.)

Becoming a Recordoholic
by Robert Barry

1   As a technological breakthrough, the DVR (Digital Video Recorder) has been an   *Introduction*

enormous success—almost as popular as television itself. Not only can you watch TV

while you record other programs but you can pause and rewind live TV. Better yet, you

can program the DVR to record a roster of programs—even entire seasons—with a

simple push of a button. No consumer warning labels are attached to this ingenious

invention, DVRs, but there should be. DVRs can be dangerous. Barely aware of what is   *Start of two-senten*

happening, a person can turn into a compulsive recorder. The descent from innocent   *thesis*

hobby to full-blown addiction takes place in several stages.

2   In the first innocent stage, the unsuspecting person buys a DVR for occasional

use. I was at this stage when I asked my parents if they would buy me a DVR as a   *Topic sentence*

birthday gift. With the DVR, I could record reruns of *Seinfeld* and new episodes of *The*   *First stage in proce*

Simpsons while watching *Grey's Anatomy*. The DVR was perfect. I hooked it up to the   *(DVR addiction)*

TV in my bedroom; recorded the antics of Jerry, Elaine, George, and Kramer and the

adventures of my favorite cartoon family, while watching the residents of Seattle Grace

save lives and make utter fools of themselves. Occasionally, I'd DVR a movie, which

my friends and I watched over the weekend. I recorded only a few shows, and once I

watched those shows, I'd delete them from the DVR. In these early days, my use of the   *Beginning of*

DVR was the equivalent of light social drinking.   *analogy to*
     alcoholism

3   In the second phase on the road to recordoholism, an individual uses the DVR

more frequently and begins to stockpile recordings rather than watch them. My trou-   *Topic sentence*

bles began in July when my family and I went to the shore for two weeks of vacation. I   *Second stage in*

set my DVR to record all five episodes of *Seinfeld* and *The Sopranos*, and two episodes   *process*

each of *Heroes*, *The Simpsons*, and *Grey's Anatomy*, while I was at the beach working

on my tan. Even I, an avid TV viewer, didn't have time to sit and watch all those shows.

The DVR continued to record these programs, but there weren't enough hours in the

day to watch everything and do my schoolwork, so the programs piled up in my DVR

queue. How did I resolve this problem? Very easily. I set my DVR to record episodes of

Seinfeld three days a week, rather then five. However, with this notion that I had such

control with my DVR, I began to realize that there were probably other shows out there

that I could record and watch whereever I desired. I could DVR classics like *Law &*

Order and *Buffy the Vampire Slayer*. Very quickly, I accumulated six *Seinfelds*, four

Law & Orders, and three *Buffys*. Then a friend—who shall go nameless—told me that only 144 episodes of *Buffy* were ever made. Excited by the thought that I could acquire as impressive a collection of episodes as a Hollywood executive, I continued recording Buffy, even recording shows while I watched them. Clearly, my once innocent hobby was getting out of control. I was now using the DVR on a regular basis—the equivalent of several stiff drinks a day.

In the third stage of recordoholism, the amount of recording increases significantly, leading to an even more irrational stockpiling of programs in the DVR queue. The catalyst that propelled me into this third stage was my parents' decision to get a premium movie package added to their cable. Selfless guy that I am, I volunteered to move my DVR in to the living room, where the connection was located. Now I could record all the most recent movies and specials. I began to record a couple of other shows every day. I also went movie-crazy and taped *Gangs of New York*, *Barbershop 2*, and *The Godfather I, II, and III*. I taped an HBO comedy special with Chris Rock and an MTV concert featuring Radiohead. Where did I get time to watch all these shows? I didn't. Using the DVR was more satisfying than watching. Reason and common sense were abandoned. Getting things on the DVR had become an obsession, and I was setting the DVR to record programs all the time.

In the fourth stage, recordoholism creeps into other parts of the addict's life, influencing behavior in strange ways. Secrecy becomes commonplace. One day, my mother came into my room and asked about a recent test I had taken. What she didn't know was that the night before the exam, I had checked my DVR recording list and found that I had run out of storage space. For three hours after everyone went to bed, I watched episodes of *The Sopranos* so I could delete them and record a movie on Showtime. I was so tired the next morning that I wound up getting a bad grade on my Biology exam. "Robert," my mother exclaimed, "isn't this getting a bit out of hand?" I assured her it was just a hobby, but I continued to sneak downstairs in the middle of the night to watch recorded shows, removing any trace of my presence from the living room when I was finished. Also, denial is not unusual during this stage of DVR addiction. At the dinner table, when my younger sister commented, "Robert records all the time," I laughingly told everyone—including myself—that the recording was no big deal. I was getting bored with it and was going to stop any day, I assured my family. Obsessive behavior also characterizes the fourth stage of recordoholism. Each week, I pulled out the TV magazine from the Sunday paper and went through it carefully,

(margin annotations:)
Continuation of analogy

Topic sentence

Third stage in process

Continuation of analogy

4

Topic sentence

Fourth stage in process

Continuation of analogy

5

circling in red all the shows I wanted to record. Another sign of addiction was the secret calender I kept in my desk drawer. With more diligence than I ever had for any term paper, I would log in each program I recorded and plan for the coming week's recording schedule.

6   In the final stage of an addiction, the individual either succumbs completely to   *Topic sentence*
the addiction or is able to break away from the habit. I broke my addiction, and I broke   *Continuation of*
it cold turkey. This total withdrawal occurred when I went off to college. There was   *analogy*
no point in taking my DVR to school because TVs were not allowed in the freshman
dorms. Even though there were many things to occupy my time during the school
week, cold sweats overcame me whenever I thought about everything on TV I was not   *Final stage in*
recording. I even considered calling home and asking members of my family to record   *process*
things for me, but I knew they would think I was crazy. At the beginning of the semester, I also had to resist the overwhelming desire to travel the three hours home every
weekend so I could get my fix. But after a while, the urgent need to record subsided.
Now, months later, as I write this, I feel detached and sober.

7   I have no illusions, though. I know that once a recordoholic, always a   *Conclusion*
recordoholic. Soon I will return home for the holidays, which, as everyone knows, can
be a time for excess eating—and recording. But I will cope with the pressure. I will take   *Final references to*
each day one at a time. I plan to watch what I'm able to, and no more. And if I feel my-   *analogy*
self succumbing to the temptations of recording, I will pick up the telephone and dial
the recordoholics' hot line: 1–800-DVR-STOP. I will win the battle.

Commentary

Purpose, Thesis, and Tone

Robert's essay is an example of *informational process analysis;* his purpose is to describe—rather than teach—the process of becoming a "recordoholic." The title, with its coined term *recordoholic,* tips us off that the essay is going to be entertaining. And the introductory paragraph clearly establishes the essay's playful, mock-serious tone. The tone established, Robert briefly defines the term *recordoholic* as a "compulsive recorder" and then moves to the essay's *thesis:* "Barely aware of what is happening, a person can turn into a compulsive recorder. The descent from innocent hobby to full-blown addiction takes place in several stages."

Throughout the essay, Robert sustains the introduction's humor by mocking his own motivations and poking fun at his quirks: "Selfless guy that I am, I volunteered to move my DVR" (paragraph 4), and "Working more diligently than I ever had for any term paper, I would log in each program I recorded and plan for the coming week's recording schedule" (5). Robert probably uses a bit of *dramatic license* when reporting some of his obsessive behavior, and we, as readers, understand that he's exaggerating for comic effect. Most likely he didn't break out in a cold sweat at the thought of the TV shows he was unable to record. Nevertheless, this tinkering with the truth is legitimate because it allows Robert to create material that fits the essay's lightly satiric tone.

Organization and Topic Sentences

To meet the requirements of the assignment, Robert needed to provide a *step-by-step* explanation of a process. And because he invented the term *recordoholism,* Robert also needed to invent the stages in the progression of his addiction. During his prewriting, Robert discovered five stages in his recordoholism. Presented *chronologically,* these stages provide the organizing focus for his paper. Specifically, each supporting paragraph is devoted to one stage, with the *topic sentence* for each paragraph indicating the stage's distinctive characteristics.

Transitions

Although Robert's essay is playful, it is nonetheless a process analysis and so must have an easy-to-follow structure. Keeping this in mind, Robert wisely includes *transitions* to signal what happened at each stage of his recordoholism: "*However* with this notion that I had such control" (paragraph 3); "*Now,* I could record all the most recent movies and specials." (4); "*One day,* my mother came into my room" (5); and "*But after a while,* the urgent need to record subsided" (6). In addition to such transitions, Robert uses crisp questions to move from idea to idea within a paragraph: "How did I resolve this problem? Very easily. I set my DVR to record episodes of *Seinfeld* three days a week, rather than five" (3), and "Where did I get time to watch all these shows? I didn't" (4).

Combining Patterns of Development

Even though Robert's essay is a process analysis, it contains elements of other patterns of development. For example, his paper is unified by an *analogy*—a sustained *comparison* between Robert's recording addiction and the obviously more serious addiction to alcohol. Handled incorrectly, the analogy could have been offensive, but Robert makes the comparison work to his advantage. The analogy is stated specifically in several spots: "In these early days, my use of the DVR was the equivalent of light social drinking" (2); "I was now using the DVR on a regular basis—the equivalent of several stiff drinks a day" (3). Finally, he generates numerous lively details or *examples* to illustrate the different stages in his addiction.

Two Unnecessary Sentences

Perhaps you noticed that Robert runs into a minor problem at the end of the fourth paragraph. Starting with the sentence, "Reason and common sense were abandoned," he begins to ramble and repeat himself. The paragraph's last two sentences fail to add anything substantial. Take a moment to read paragraph 4 aloud, omitting the last two sentences. Note how much sharper the new conclusion is: "Where did I get time to watch all these tapes? I didn't. Using the DVR was more satisfying than watching." This new ending says all that needs to be said.

Revising the First Draft

When it was time to revise, Robert—despite his apprehension—showed his paper to his roommate and asked him to read it out loud. Robert knew this strategy would provide a more objective point of view on his work. His roommate, at first an unwilling recruit, nonetheless laughed as he read the essay aloud. That was just the response Robert wanted. But when his roommate got to the conclusion, Robert heard that the closing paragraph was flat and anticlimactic. His roommate agreed, so the two of them brainstormed ways to make the conclusion livelier and more in spirit with the rest of the essay.

Reprinted here is Robert's original conclusion. The handwritten notes, numbered in order of importance, represent both Robert's ideas for revision and those of his roommate.

Original Version of the Conclusion

I have no illusions, though, that I am over my recordoholism. Soon I will be returning home for the holidays, which can be a time for excess recording. All I can do is watch what I'm able to and not use the DVR. After that, I will hope for the best.

[3] Shorten first sentence.

[1] Get back to analo

[2] Boring. Add humo

As you can see, Robert and his roommate decided that the best approach would be to reinforce the playful, mock-serious tone that characterized earlier parts of the essay. Robert thus made three major changes to his conclusion. First, he tightened the first sentence of the paragraph ("I have no illusions, though, that I am over my recordoholism"), making it crisper and more dramatic: "I have no illusions, though." Second, he added a few sentences to sustain the light, self-deprecating tone he had used earlier: "I know that once a recordoholic, always a recordoholic"; "But I will cope with the pressure"; "I will win the battle." Third, and perhaps most important, he returned to the alcoholism analogy: "I will take each day one at a time....And if I feel myself succumbing to the temptations of recording, I will pick up the telephone and dial the recordoholics' hotline..."

These weren't the only changes Robert made while reworking his paper, but they help illustrate how sensitive he was to the effect he wanted to achieve. Certainly, the recasting of the conclusion was critical to the overall success of this amusing essay.

ACTIVITIES: PROCESS ANALYSIS

Prewriting Activities

1. Imagine you're writing two essays: One defines the term *comparison shopping;* the other contrasts two different teaching styles. Jot down ways you might use process analysis in each essay.

2. Look at the essay topics that follow. Assuming that your readers will be students in your composition class, which topics would lend themselves to directional process analysis, informational process analysis, or a blend of both? Explain your responses.

   a. Going on a job interview   d. Negotiating personal conflicts
   b. Using a computer in the library   e. Curing a cold
   c. Cleaning up oil spills   f. Growing vegetables organically

3. For *one* of the following essay topics, decide—given the audience indicated in parentheses—what your purpose, tone, and point of view might be. Then use brainstorming, questioning, mapping, or another prewriting technique to identify the steps you'd include in a process analysis for that audience. After reviewing the material generated, delete, add, and combine points as needed. Then organize the material in the most logical sequence.

   a. How malls encourage spending sprees (*general public*)
   b. How to get along with parents (*high school students*)
   c. How the college administration handled a controversial campus issue (*alumni*)
   d. How to deal with a bully (*elementary school children*)

4. Select *one* of the essay topics that follow and determine what your purpose, tone, and point of view would be for each audience indicated in parentheses. Then use prewriting to identify the points you'd cover for each audience. Finally, organize the raw material, noting the differences in emphasis and sequence for each group of readers.

   a. How to buy a car (*young people who have just gotten a driver's license; established professionals*)
   b. How children acquire their values (*first-time parents; elementary school teachers*)
   c. How to manage money (*grade-school children; college students*)
   d. How arguments can strengthen relationships (*preteen children; young adults*)

5. For *one* of the following process topics, identify an appropriate audience, purpose, tone, and point of view. Then use prewriting to generate raw material showing that there's a problem with the way the process is performed. After organizing that material, use prewriting once again—this time to identify how the process *should* be performed. Sequence this new material in a logical order.

   a. How students select a college or a major
   b. How local television news covers national events
   c. How your campus or your community is handling a difficult situation

Revising Activities

6. The following paragraph is from an essay making the point that over-the-phone sales can be a challenging career. The paragraph, written as a process

analysis, describes the steps involved in making a sales call. Revise the paragraph, deleting any material that undermines the paragraph's unity, organizing the steps in a logical sequence, and supplying transitions where needed. Also be sure to correct any inappropriate shifts in person. Finally, do some brainstorming—individually or in a group—to generate details to bolster underdeveloped steps in the sequence.

Establishing rapport with potential customers is the most challenging part of phone sales. The longer you can keep customers on the phone, the more you can get a sense of their needs. And the more you know about customers, the more successful the salesperson is bound to be. Your opening comments are critical. After setting the right tone, you gently introduce your product. There are a number of ways you can move gracefully from your opening remarks to the actual selling phase of the call. Remember: Don't try to sell the customer at the beginning. Instead, try in a friendly way to keep the prospective customer on the phone. Maintaining such a connection is easier than you think because many people have an almost desperate need to talk. Their lives are isolated and lonely—a sad fact of contemporary life. Once you shift to the distinctly selling phase of the call, you should present the advantages of the product, especially the advantages of price and convenience. Mentioning installment payments is often effective. If the customer says that he or she isn't interested, the salesperson should try to determine—in a genial way—why the person is reluctant to buy. Don't, however, push aggressively for reasons or try to steamroll the person into thinking his or her reservations are invalid. Once the person agrees to buy, try to encourage credit card payment, rather than check or money order. The salesperson can explain that credit card payment means the customer will receive the product sooner. End the call as you began—in an easy, personable way.

7. Reprinted here is a paragraph from the first draft of a humorous essay advising shy college students how to get through a typical day. Written as a process analysis, the paragraph outlines techniques for surviving class. Revise the paragraph, deleting digressions that disrupt the paragraph's unity, eliminating unnecessary repetition, and sequencing the steps in the proper order. Also correct inappropriate shifts in person and add transitions where needed. Feel free to add any telling details.

Simply attending class can be stressful for shy people. Several strategies, though, can lessen the trauma. Shy students should time their arrival to coincide with that of most other class members—about two minutes before the class is scheduled to begin. If you arrive too early, you may be seen sitting alone or, even worse, may actually be forced to talk with another early arrival. If you arrive late, all eyes will be upon you. Before heading to class, the shy student should dress in the least conspicuous manner possible—say, in the blue jeans, sweatshirt, and sneakers that 99.9 percent of your classmates wear. That way you won't stand out from everyone else. Take a seat near the back of the room. Don't, however, sit at the very back since professors often take sadistic pleasure in calling on students back there, assuming they chose those seats because they didn't want to be called on. A friend of mine who is far from shy uses just the opposite ploy. In an attempt to get in good with her professors, she sits in the front row and, incredibly enough, volunteers to participate. However, since shy people don't want to call attention to themselves, they should stifle any urge to sneeze or cough. You run the risk of having people look at you or offer you a tissue or cough drop. And of course, never, ever volunteer to answer. Such a display of intelligence is sure to focus all eyes on you. In other words, make yourself as inconspicuous as possible. How, you might wonder, can you be inconspicuous if you're blessed (or cursed) with great looks? Well,...have you ever considered earning your degree through the mail?

PROFESSIONAL SELECTIONS: PROCESS ANALYSIS

Amy Sutherland

Amy Sutherland was born in 1959 and grew up in suburban Cincinnati, Ohio. Her book, *Kicked, Bitten, and Scratched: Life and Lessons at the Premier School for Exotic Animal Trainers* (2003), inspired the essay that follows, which appeared in *The New York Times*. In turn, the essay led to another book, *What Shamu Taught Me About Life, Love, and Marriage* (2008) as well as a movie.

For ideas on how this process analysis essay is organized, see Figure 14.2 on page 270.

Pre-Reading Journal Entry

All of us have habits—patterns of behavior that we repeat, sometimes even without being aware that we are performing them. Reflect on your own habits, good and bad, past and present. In your journal, list some of your habits, and describe the situations in which they arise and the patterns of behavior that characterize them.

WHAT SHAMU TAUGHT ME ABOUT A HAPPY MARRIAGE

As I wash dishes at the kitchen sink, my husband paces behind me, irritated. "Have   1
you seen my keys?" he snarls, then huffs out a loud sigh and stomps from the room with our dog, Dixie, at his heels, anxious over her favorite human's upset.

In the past I would have been right behind Dixie. I would have turned off the faucet   2
and joined the hunt while trying to soothe my husband with bromides like, "Don't worry, they'll turn up." But that only made him angrier, and a simple case of missing keys soon would become a full-blown angst-ridden drama starring the two of us and our poor nervous dog.

3   Now, I focus on the wet dish in my hands. I don't turn around. I don't say a word. I'm using a technique I learned from a dolphin trainer.

4   I love my husband. He's well read, adventurous and does a hysterical rendition of a northern Vermont accent that still cracks me up after 12 years of marriage.

5   But he also tends to be forgetful, and is often tardy and mercurial. He hovers around me in the kitchen asking if I read this or that piece in *The New Yorker* when I'm trying to concentrate on the simmering pans. He leaves wadded tissues in his wake. He suffers from serious bouts of spousal deafness but never fails to hear me when I mutter to myself on the other side of the house. "What did you say?" he'll shout.

6   These minor annoyances are not the stuff of separation and divorce, but in sum they began to dull my love for Scott. I wanted—needed—to nudge him a little closer to perfect, to make him into a mate who might annoy me a little less, who wouldn't keep me waiting at restaurants, a mate who would be easier to love.

7   So, like many wives before me, I ignored a library of advice books and set about improving him. By nagging, of course, which only made his behavior worse: he'd drive faster instead of slower; shave less frequently, not more; and leave his reeking bike garb on the bedroom floor longer than ever.

8   We went to a counselor to smooth the edges off our marriage. She didn't understand what we were doing there and complimented us repeatedly on how well we communicated. I gave up. I guessed she was right—our union was better than most—and resigned myself to stretches of slow-boil resentment and occasional sarcasm.

9   Then something magical happened. For a book I was writing about a school for exotic animal trainers, I started commuting from Maine to California, where I spent my days watching students do the seemingly impossible: teaching hyenas to pirouette on command, cougars to offer their paws for a nail clipping, and baboons to skateboard.

10   I listened, rapt, as professional trainers explained how they taught dolphins to flip and elephants to paint. Eventually it hit me that the same techniques might work on that stubborn but lovable species, the American husband.

11   The central lesson I learned from exotic animal trainers is that I should reward behavior I like and ignore behavior I don't. After all, you don't get a sea lion to balance a ball on the end of its nose by nagging. The same goes for the American husband.

12   Back in Maine, I began thanking Scott if he threw one dirty shirt into the hamper. If he threw in two, I'd kiss him. Meanwhile, I would step over any soiled clothes on the floor without one sharp word, though I did sometimes kick them under the bed. But as he basked in my appreciation, the piles became smaller.

13   I was using what trainers call "approximations," rewarding the small steps toward learning a whole new behavior. You can't expect a baboon to learn to flip on command in one session, just as you can't expect an American husband to begin regularly picking up his dirty socks by praising him once for picking up a single sock. With the baboon you first reward a hop, then a bigger hop, then an even bigger hop. With Scott the husband, I began to praise every small act every time: if he drove just a mile an hour slower, tossed one pair of shorts into the hamper, or was on time for anything.

14   I also began to analyze my husband the way a trainer considers an exotic animal. Enlightened trainers learn all they can about a species, from anatomy to social

structure, to understand how it thinks, what it likes and dislikes, what comes easily to it and what doesn't. For example, an elephant is a herd animal, so it responds to hierarchy. It cannot jump, but can stand on its head. It is a vegetarian.

The exotic animal known as Scott is a loner, but an alpha male. So hierarchy matters, but being in a group doesn't so much. He has the balance of a gymnast, but moves slowly, especially when getting dressed. Skiing comes naturally, but being on time does not. He's an omnivore, and what a trainer would call food-driven.   15

Once I started thinking this way, I couldn't stop. At the school in California, I'd be scribbling notes on how to walk an emu or have a wolf accept you as a pack member, but I'd be thinking, "I can't wait to try this on Scott."   16

On a field trip with the students, I listened to a professional trainer describe how he had taught African crested cranes to stop landing on his head and shoulders. He did this by training the leggy birds to land on mats on the ground. This, he explained, is what is called an "incompatible behavior," a simple but brilliant concept.   17

Rather than teach the cranes to stop landing on him, the trainer taught the birds something else, a behavior that would make the undesirable behavior impossible. The birds couldn't alight on the mats and his head simultaneously.   18

At home, I came up with incompatible behaviors for Scott to keep him from crowding me while I cooked. To lure him away from the stove, I piled up parsley for him to chop or cheese for him to grate at the other end of the kitchen island. Or I'd set out a bowl of chips and salsa across the room. Soon I'd done it: no more Scott hovering around me while I cooked.   19

I followed the students to SeaWorld San Diego, where a dolphin trainer introduced me to least reinforcing syndrome (L. R. S.). When a dolphin does something wrong, the trainer doesn't respond in any way. He stands still for a few beats, careful not to look at the dolphin, and then returns to work. The idea is that any response, positive or negative, fuels a behavior. If a behavior provokes no response, it typically dies away.   20

In the margins of my notes I wrote, "Try on Scott!"   21

It was only a matter of time before he was again tearing around the house searching for his keys, at which point I said nothing and kept at what I was doing. It took a lot of discipline to maintain my calm, but results were immediate and stunning. His temper fell far shy of its usual pitch and then waned like a fast-moving storm. I felt as if I should throw him a mackerel.   22

Now he's at it again; I hear him banging a closet door shut, rustling through papers on a chest in the front hall and thumping upstairs. At the sink, I hold steady. Then, sure enough, all goes quiet. A moment later, he walks into the kitchen, keys in hand, and says calmly, "Found them."   23

Without turning, I call out, "Great, see you later."   24

Off he goes with our much-calmed pup.   25

After two years of exotic animal training, my marriage is far smoother, my husband much easier to love. I used to take his faults personally; his dirty clothes on the floor were an affront, a symbol of how he didn't care enough about me. But thinking of my husband as an exotic species gave me the distance I needed to consider our differences more objectively.   26

I adopted the trainers' motto: "It's never the animal's fault." When my training attempts failed, I didn't blame Scott. Rather, I brainstormed new strategies, thought up more incompatible behaviors and used smaller approximations. I dissected my own behavior, considered how my actions might inadvertently fuel his. I also accepted that   27 some behaviors were too entrenched, too instinctive to train away. You can't stop a badger from digging, and you can't stop my husband from losing his wallet and keys.

28   Professionals talk of animals that understand training so well they eventually use it back on the trainer. My animal did the same. When the training techniques worked so beautifully, I couldn't resist telling my husband what I was up to. He wasn't offended, just amused. As I explained the techniques and terminology, he soaked it up. Far more than I realized.

29   Last fall, firmly in middle age, I learned that I needed braces. They were not only humiliating, but also excruciating. For weeks my gums, teeth, jaw and sinuses throbbed. I complained frequently and loudly. Scott assured me that I would become used to all the metal in my mouth. I did not.

30   One morning, as I launched into yet another tirade about how uncomfortable I was, Scott just looked at me blankly. He didn't say a word or acknowledge my rant in any way, not even with a nod.

31   I quickly ran out of steam and started to walk away. Then I realized what was happening, and I turned and asked, "Are you giving me an L.R.S.?" Silence. "You are, aren't you?"

32   He finally smiled, but his L.R.S. has already done the trick. He'd begun to train me, the American wife.

Questions for Close Reading

1. What is the selection's thesis? Locate the sentence(s) in which Sutherland states her main idea. If she doesn't state her thesis explicitly, express it in your own words.

2. Sutherland tries a couple of solutions to her problems with her husband before she starts using the behavioral techniques that are the main focus of the essay. What were these initial solutions, and why did they fail to improve her relationship with her husband?

3. What techniques for changing behavior did Sutherland learn from the animal trainers? How did she apply each of these techniques to her husband Scott's behavior?

4. Why did changing her husband's behavior improve Sutherland's marriage?

Questions About the Writer's Craft

1. **The pattern.** What type of process analysis does Sutherland use in this essay? How does the first-person point of view support the pattern of development?

2. What is the tone of Sutherland's essay? What contributes to the tone?

3. **Other patterns.** What pattern of development, besides process analysis, helps organize this essay? What does the other pattern contribute to the essay?

4. Is Sutherland's conclusion effective? How does her conclusion change your response to the essay?

FIGURE 14.2

Essay Structure Diagram: "What Shamu Taught Me About a Happy Marriage" by Amy Sutherland

Introductory paragraphs Background: descriptive examples (paragraphs 1–2)	Description of what the author loves about her husband, Scott, with a description of his annoying habits and how she used to react to them.
Informational process analysis: unsuccessful (7–8)	How the author first tried unsuccessfully to change her husband's behavior—by nagging and seeking help from a counselor.
Informational process analysis: successful examples (9–26)	How the author "trained" her husband, employing techniques used by exotic animal trainers. Ex.: Teaching incompatible behaviors. Ex.: L.R.S.—ignoring negative behavior and rewarding the positive.
Concluding paragraph (19)	How thinking about "training" helped her consider their differences more objectively. How her husband began using the same techniques to change her behavior when she complained about her braces. **Thesis:** Marriage is less about "training" your spouse than understanding and communicating with him or her.

Writing Assignments Using Process Analysis as a Pattern of Development

1. In this essay, Sutherland describes how animal trainers teach cranes, dolphins, and other animals to behave in certain ways. Imagine turning this scenario around, and thinking of animals teaching their human masters how to behave. Write an essay from an animal's point of view in which you explain how the animal trains its human "master" to meet its needs.

2. The animal-training techniques Sutherland describes in this essay are similar to behavioral therapies used by psychologists and other mental health professionals to treat people for phobias, anxiety, and other disorders, and to change specific behaviors, like smoking and other undesirable habits. Do some research in the

library and on the Internet about behavioral therapies. Select one type of behavioral therapy and write an essay explaining how it works. Give examples of its use in your essay.

Writing Assignment Combining Patterns of Development

3. Sutherland's essay shows how irritating even the people we love can sometimes be. Select one of your own close relationships, and write an essay in which you *describe* what you find annoying about the other person. Give *examples* of the person's behavior to illustrate your points. What *effects* do this person's annoying traits have on the relationship as a whole? How would you change this person if you could?

David Shipley

David Shipley, a journalist, is the deputy editor of *The New York Times*'s op-ed page, on which opinion pieces by *New York Times* columnists and other journalists, as well as private citizens, are published. Shipley joined *The New York Times* in 1998 and was deputy editor of the Sunday *New York Times Magazine*'s millennium issues, senior editor of the magazine, and enterprise editor of the national desk before moving to his present position as op-ed editor. This essay, originally entitled "What We Talk About When We Talk About Editing," appeared in *The New York Times* on July 31, 2005.

Pre-Reading Journal Entry

People often seek advice and help from others to help them do a job or improve their performance. For example, if you were writing your résumé, you might ask a friend to edit and proofread it. Or if you were trying out for a sports team, you might ask a coach for feedback and advice. Think of some occasions in the past when you asked others for help with your work or gave help to someone else when asked. What was the task? What was your goal in helping or being helped? Did the assistance actually improve the end product, or was it useless? Use your journal to answer these questions.

TALK ABOUT EDITING

1   ...Not surprisingly, readers have lots of questions about the editing that goes on [on the *New York Times* op-ed page]. What kind of changes do we suggest—and why? What kind of changes do we insist on—and why? When do we stay out of the way? And the hardy perennial: do we edit articles to make them adhere to a particular point of view? I thought I'd try to provide a few answers.

2   Just like *Times* news articles and editorials, Op-Ed essays are edited. Before something appears in our pages, you can bet that questions have been asked, arguments have been clarified, cuts have been suggested—as have additions—and factual, typographical and grammatical errors have been caught. (We hope.)

Our most important rule, however, is that nothing is published on the Op-Ed page   3
unless it has been approved by its author. Articles go to press only after the person
under whose name the article appears has explicitly O.K.'d the editing.

While it's important to know that we edit, it's also important to know how we edit.   4
The best way to explain this is to take a walk through the process.

Say you send us an article by regular mail, e-mail, fax or, this summer at least,   5
owl post[1]—and it's accepted. You'll be told that we'll contact you once your article is
scheduled for publication. That could be days, weeks or even months away.

When your article does move into the on-deck circle, you'll be sent a contract, and   6
one of the several editors here will get to work.

Here are the clear-cut things the editor will do: 7

- Correct grammatical and typographical errors.   8
- Make sure that the article conforms to *The New York Times Manual of Style and Us-*   9
  age. Courtesy titles, for example, will miraculously appear if they weren't there before; expletives will be deleted; some words will be capitalized, others lowercased.
- See to it that the article fits our allotted space. With staff columnists, advertise-   10
  ments and illustrations, there's a limit to the number of words we can squeeze
  onto the page.
- Fact-check the article. While it is the author's responsibility to ensure that ev-   11
  erything written for us is accurate, we still check facts—names, dates, places,
  quotations.

We also check assertions. If news articles—from *The Times* and other publica-   12
tions—are at odds with a point or an example in an essay, we need to resolve whatever discrepancy exists.

For instance, an Op-Ed article critical of newly aggressive police tactics in Town X   13
can't flatly say the police have no reason to change their strategy if there have been
news reports that violence in the town is rising. This doesn't mean the writer can't
still argue that there are other ways to deal with Town X's crime problem—he just
can't say that the force's decision to change came out of the blue.

How would we resolve the Town X issue? Well, we'd discuss it with the writer—   14
generally by telephone or e-mail—and we'd try to find a solution that preserves the
writer's argument while also adhering to the facts.

Now to some people, this may sound surprising, as if we're putting words in   15
people's mouths. But there's a crucial distinction to be made between changing a
writer's argument—and suggesting language that will help a writer make his point
more effectively.

Besides grammar and accuracy, we're also concerned about readability. Our editors try   16
to approach articles as average readers who know nothing about the subject. They may
ask if a point is clear, if a writer needs transitional language to bridge the gap between two
seemingly separate points, if a leap of logic has been made without sufficient explanation.

To make a piece as clear and accessible as possible, the editor may add a transi-   17
tion, cut a section that goes off point or move a paragraph. If a description is highly

---

[1]In J. K. Rowling's Harry Potter books, mail is delivered each morning to Hogwarts,
Harry's school, by owls (editors' note).

technical, the editor may suggest language that lay readers will understand. If it isn't clear what a writer is trying to say, the editor may take a guess, based on what he knows from the author, and suggest more precise language. (There are also times when we do precious little.)

18   The editor will then send the edited version of the article to the writer. The changes will often be highlighted to make it easy for the author to see what's been done. (I tend to mark edits I've made with an //ok?//.) If a proposed revision is significant, the editor will often write a few sentences to describe the reasoning behind the suggestion.

19   Every change is a suggestion, not a demand. If a solution offered by an editor doesn't work for a writer, the two work together to find an answer to the problem. Editing is not bullying.

20   Of course, it's not always warm and cuddly, either. The people who write for Op-Ed have a responsibility to be forthright and specific in their arguments. There's no room on the page for articles that are opaque or written in code.

21   What our editors expressly do not do is change a point of view. If you've written an article on why New York's street fairs should be abolished, we will not ask you to change your mind and endorse them. We're going to help you make the best case you can. If you followed this page carefully in the run-up to the Iraq war, for example, you saw arguments both for and against the invasion—all made with equal force.

22   Editing is a human enterprise. Like writing, it is by nature subjective. Sometimes an editor will think a writer is saying something that she isn't. But our editing process gives writer and editor plenty of time to sort out any misunderstandings before the article goes to press. And if a mistake gets through, we do our best to correct it as quickly as possible.

23   The Op-Ed page is a venue for people with a wide range of perspectives, experiences and talents. Some of the people who appear in this space have written a lot; others haven't. If we published only people who needed no editing, we'd wind up relying on only a very narrow range of professional writers, and the page would be much the worse for it.

24   So what's the agenda? A lively page of clashing opinions, one where as many people as possible have the opportunity to make the best arguments they can.

25   And just so you know, this article has been edited. Changes have been suggested— and gratefully accepted. Well, most of them.

Questions for Close Reading

1. What is the selection's thesis? Locate the sentence(s) in which Shipley states his main idea. If he doesn't state his thesis explicity, express it in your own words.

2. What tasks are involved in editing an op-ed piece for *The New York Times*? Of these, which does Shipley seem to think need the most explanation?

3. In paragraphs 18 through 22, Shipley describes the relationship between the editor and writer of an op-ed piece. What is the nature of this relationship?

4. In paragraph 22, Shipley says that "Editing is a human enterprise." What does he mean by this?

Questions About the Writer's Craft

1. **The pattern.** Who is the audience for Shipley's essay? Why would this audience be interested in this topic? What type of process analysis does Shipley use?

2. **Other patterns.** Shipley *divides* the editing process into three main types of tasks and covers each type in its own section. Identify the main editing tasks and the paragraph(s) that introduce each type. Why does he break down the process this way rather than deal with the editing process as a whole?

3. In paragraphs 13 and 14, Shipley uses an example to clarify what he means by checking "assertions." Why does he provide an example here? Is the example effective?

4. Shipley concludes this essay with some mild humor. What is the joke? What does this use of humor contribute to the point he has been making in his essay?

Writing Assignments Using Process Analysis as a Pattern of Development

1. Shipley describes the process involved in editing opinion pieces, or arguments, that appear in a newspaper with national circulation. However, many other types of works are edited. For example, news articles, news broadcasts, documentaries, movies, commercials, advertisements, novels, and comic strips are all edited. Select one of these media and do research on the tasks involved in editing it. Write an essay in which you *analyze* the editing *process* and explain why it is important.

2. Before a piece can be edited, it must be written. Examine the process involved in producing an essay from the writer's rather than the editor's point of view. What process do you use when you write an essay in your English course? Write an essay in which you analyze your own writing process. Your tone might be serious or humorous as you lay out your process. Consider concluding your essay by evaluating how effective your process is and what you might do differently in the future.

Writing Assignment Combining Patterns of Development

3. Op-ed pieces are usually arguments about current issues; in contrast, news articles are more objective, describing or narrating events. From *The New York Times* or your local newspaper, select one op-ed page essay and one news article on a related topic, if possible. *Compare* and *contrast* the two pieces, analyzing their purpose and content. What patterns of development are used in each piece? Give *examples* to support your analysis.

Alex Horton

Alex Horton (1985–) is known as "Army of Dude," the title of the blog that he has been keeping since 2006, when he was deployed to Iraq for a fifteen-month tour. He is currently the senior writer for *VAntage Point*, the official blog of the U.S. Department of Veterans Affairs, and is studying writing at Georgetown University in Washington, D.C. His work has appeared in *The Atlantic*, *The New York Times*, and the *St. Petersburg Times*. Horton was a finalist for Weblog Awards for Best Military Blog in 2007 and 2008. The selection that follows was posted on *Army of Dude* on January 13, 2010.

Pre-Reading Journal Entry

What do you know about blogs? Have you ever created one or posted to one? If so, what kind(s) of blog(s) did you post to? What is the purpose of a blog? Explore these questions in your journal and use the Internet to find out more about blogs if you are unfamiliar with them.

ON GETTING BY

1   In my previous post, I outlined some basic principles (Horton) needed to successfully navigate the murky waters of education under the GI Bill. The challenges in dealing with the VA for education benefits are considerable, yet veterans new to college face an unfamiliar, unpredictable and strange environment on campus. If taken all at once, these hurdles can quickly overwhelm a student veteran and distract from the overall goal: to finish a degree on time with benefits to spare. Next week I will be in class for my fifth semester of higher education, and in my time I have tinkered with a system of how to bring up my veteran status, discussing Iraq and Afghanistan in the classroom and dealing with the myriad reactions fellow students have had. The system cannot be expected to work for everyone, but as veterans file into classrooms for the first time this spring, these tips could help in the development of a coping system better tailored for you. These should simply help to get you started.

Modesty Is the Best Policy

2   There are only two kinds of veterans in school: those who prattle on about their time in the military and overseas, and those who do not. The former will find any opportunity to bring up their time in Afghanistan or Iraq, even if it is not relevant to class discussion. They forget one of the tenets of military experience—the role of the consummate professional. Joining the military and serving in a time of war are sacred acts and carry a certain degree of respect and modesty. We owe it to our injured buddies and fallen friends not to brag about our exploits overseas. We have done our fair share of things that set us apart from others in the classroom, and that is exactly why it is best to retain an understated presence among others.

3   This is a difficult situation as it applies to reintegration, as the chasm between veterans and civilians has never been wider. From World War II to Vietnam, it would

have been a difficult task to know someone that neither served overseas nor had a family member or friend who did. Now there are whole classrooms filled with those people. As Matthew McConaughey spoke prophetically in *Dazed and Confused*, "I get older, they stay the same age." An 18 year old in college this year would have been nine years old during the invasion of Afghanistan and eleven years old during the invasion of Iraq. They have grown up with war to the point of it becoming a mind numbingly prosaic concept. It would be a frustrating battle to try and close the rift with those who don't see a rift at all. The best thing to do is use your judgment when bringing up your veteran status in the classroom. I've done it just a few times and felt uncomfortable enough to think twice about the next time. Now I tend to mention it in private conversation, not when I have the floor in public, and even then it is a casual touch on the subject. When you are ready to talk...

...Prepare for a Question Salvo

No matter how much you try to keep it stashed away from students and cowork-   4
ers, your military experience will come out sooner or later. There are things you simply cannot hide forever, like going to prison or reading *Twilight*. Once you begin to move past casual conversation, it's only a matter of time before that period of your life is visited. It usually begins with a discussion of age. When I tell people I'm 24, the followup questions are almost always, "What have you done since high school?" or, "Why did you wait so long to go to school?" People tend to catch on if you mention extended vacations in the Middle East or recite monologues, so at that point it is best to come clean. However, be prepared for the questions they are more than willing to hurl your way. They might not know anyone who has deployed, but our hyperviolent culture has removed any restraint left in the world and enables them to ask any question that comes to mind. Here is what you can expect, in order of the most frequently asked:

1. What's it like?
2. Was it really hot?
3. Did you kill anyone?
4. Seriously, how hot was it?
5. Do you regret it?
6. Did you see any camel spiders?
7. Were you in Iran?

It's hard to get upset at some of those questions, as I find it difficult to think of what   5
I'd ask if the roles were switched. #3 can be blamed on ignorance and apathy, but #5 is the most troubling I've heard. It suggests that there is something shameful about service, duty and sacrifice. Both questions trivialize an important part of our lives. The best answer to #3 I've heard comes from the The Kitchen Dispatch comment section: "I will forgive you for asking that question if you forgive me for not answering it." Something that personal should never be asked, only told (Fong).

The flip side to some of those cavalier probes are questions that handle the   6
topic with kid gloves. Once a coworker found out I was in the Army, she asked,

"Did you go to...one of those places they send people?" It was uncomfortable for her just to utter those dirty "I" and "A" words, like we were speaking about some subversive topic. The kind of questions you will get will be all over the map, spanning from a place of genuine interest to the depths of sheer morbidity. Be prepared to answer anything, or politely let them know the subject isn't appropriate for casual banter.

Let the Right Ones In

7   Popular culture is replete with images of the maladjusted veteran, from Rambo to Travis Bickle to Red Forman. These characters are ingrained in our national conscious and typically become placeholders in the event someone doesn't personally know a veteran. When these sources are taken at face value, war veterans are invariably crazy, depressive, easily startled, quick to anger and alcoholics. We come from broken homes, trying to escape jail time and were too dumb or poor to go to college after high school. The best way to combat these silly notions is to let people get to know you, the person, before you, the veteran. Those stereotypes aren't going anywhere soon, so the best idea is to take the concept of guarding your veteran status in the classroom and carry it over to blossoming relationships. That way your service and overseas experience complement your personality and don't define it. Revealing too much at one time can damage a friendship before it takes off. Just like in the classroom, take it slow. If they are worth keeping around, they'll understand why. We have met our lifelong friends already; we can afford to be picky.

Try to Keep a Straight Face

8   There's a huge disparity between what you have been asked to do in the service and what you will be asked to do in school. At the very basic level you were asked to maintain a clean weapon and uniform. Many of you were tasked with watching the back of your fellow soldiers while in imminent danger or operate complex machinery and vehicles. At school, you'll be held responsible for showing up and turning in work before deadlines. That's it. Like I mentioned in the earlier post, college seems like an insurmountable gauntlet of crushed dreams when you're in the military. Once you transition to civilian life and take a few classes, you'll be astounded at the lack of discipline and drive in some of your classmates. It's a big joke, but try to maintain composure. I'm not saying it's easy the whole way through, but I guarantee you've done something harder than a five page essay. As they say, the rest is downhill.

Find Another Brother

9   If you were in active duty, the friends you met along the way are now scattered across the country. Perhaps I've always been an introvert, but I don't make friends as easy as some people. I've met just two people in fourteen classes that I consider friends, and one of them is an Afghanistan veteran. It's easy to understand why we get along. Do your best to find other veterans in your class and say hello. Talking to them will come easier than the 18 year old hipster next to you about his passion for ironic hats.

Find out if there is a veteran's organization on campus, but be wary of their motives. While some will join to find support and befriend fellow veterans, others will use it for recognition....

Enjoy the Ride

Besides getting a degree or learning new skills, people go to college to meet new 10 people and to experience a different life. If you've served since Sept. 12, 2001, you've already had a bit of each. But don't let that stop you from enjoying everything school has to offer. It's the last time very little will be expected of you, unless you get another government job. Then you're golden.

If you are recently out of the military and on your way to college, these tenets, 11 coupled with the GI Bill pointers, should help you get started in academia (*The Post 9/11*). Like most things, your experience may vary, and I would hope you don't safeguard your veteran status like it's a dark secret or the true location of Jimmy Hoffa's body. It's something to be proud of, but not flaunted. It's something to share with your friends who genuinely want to know about the world you lived in, but not with the people who have twisted notions of what you have done overseas. The last thing you want people to know you as is the guy who went to Iraq. You want them to say "Hey, that's Alex, he's good people," and not "I wonder how many ear necklaces he has. I'm betting two." Hopefully these tips will help even just a tiny bit in that regard.

Works Cited

Fong, Kanani. "Seven Things Never to Say to a Veteran." *The Kitchen Dispatch: A View from the Breakfast Table during War,* 3 Jan. 2010. Web. 13 Jan. 2010.

Horton, Alex. "Here to There: Tips and Tricks for the Student Veteran." *Army of Dude,* 29 Dec. 2009. Web. 13 Jan. 2010.

The Post-9/11 GI Bill. US Dept. of Veterans Affairs. Facebook, n.d. Web. 13 Jan. 2010.

Questions for Close Reading

1. What is the selection's thesis? Locate the sentence(s) in which Horton states his main idea. If he doesn't state the thesis explicitly, express it in your own words.

2. What reason does Horton give veterans for why they should generally avoid talking about their military experiences when they are at school?

3. Of the questions Horton lists as those other students are likely to ask when they discover one of their classmates is a veteran, which one does Horton find most troubling and why?

4. What does Horton have to say about what those in the military think college will be like, compared with what he thinks they are likely to discover when they actually go to college?

Questions About the Writer's Craft

1. **The pattern.** How does Horton organize his process analysis? What tool does he use, and how does his strategy make his blog more effective?

2. **The pattern.** Is Horton's process analysis primarily *directional* or *informational*? Explain. To what extent does Horton try to persuade readers that the process he describes should be followed?

3. **Other patterns.** Although Horton organizes his selection as a process analysis, he also weaves in his own experience—his own *narrative* about what he learned when he returned to civilian life and started taking college classes. How does this combination of patterns make Horton's writing stronger than it would be without the inclusion of his own story?

4. Horton's intended audience is those currently or formerly in the military—not students and their teachers. What parts of his essay might some students and instructors find offensive and why?

Writing Assignments Using Process Analysis as a Pattern of Development

1. In his essay Horton, a military veteran, provides other military veterans with a plan for how to "get by" in college. Write an essay in which you present a process analysis of ways a member of a group to which you belong or have belonged can adjust to a particular situation—perhaps an essay written to high school seniors on how to adjust to college life or an essay for new employees on how to adjust to working at your place of employment.

2. Horton is an expert on the subject he addresses. Write an essay in which you present a process analysis that provides both directions and information for an audience unfamiliar with or less experienced than you on a particular subject. For example, if you are an avid gamer, you might write an essay on how to successfully navigate a challenging game such as Call of Duty, Forza, or Portal. Or if you have learned how to survive as a student on a bare-bones budget, you might write an essay in which you offer tips to other college students in a similar economic situation.

Writing Assignment Combining Patterns of Development

3. In his *process analysis* Horton also tells a story—a *narrative*—about the common societal experience of adjusting to college life. Write an essay in which you examine another common process, for example, applying for a driver's license, or a larger societal process, such as electing a president. Give the process involved, but also include sufficient *description*—for example, of an exam room at the license bureau or the crowds at a political rally—to support your thesis. You might find it helpful to conduct some original research on the subject.

ADDITIONAL WRITING TOPICS: PROCESS ANALYSIS

General Assignments

Using process analysis, develop one of these topics into an essay.

Directional: How to Do Something

1. How to drive defensively
2. How to improve the place where you work or study
3. How to relax
4. How to show appreciation to others
5. How to get through school despite personal problems

Informational: How Something Happens

1. How a student becomes burned out
2. How a dead thing decays (or some other natural process)
3. How humans choose a mate
4. How a bad habit develops
5. How people fall into debt

Assignments Using Visuals

Use the suggested visuals to help develop a process analysis essay on one of these topics:

1. Making it through freshman year without gaining the "Freshman 15" (photos)
2. Juggling school, friends, relationships, and a job (pie chart)
3. Deciding on the right career path to your dream job (Web links)
4. The evolution of the national parks system (Web links)
5. Becoming a successful entrepreneur (diagrams and/or links to videos)

Assignments with a Specific Purpose, Audience, and Point of View

1. **Academic life.** As an experienced campus tour guide for prospective students, you've been asked by your school's Admissions Office to write a pamphlet explaining to new tour guides how to conduct a tour of your school's campus. When explaining the process, keep in mind that tour guides need to portray the school in its best light.

2. **Academic life.** You write an "advice to the lovelorn" column for the campus newspaper. A correspondent writes saying that he or she wants to break up with a steady girlfriend/boyfriend but doesn't know how to do it without hurting the person. Give the writer guidance on how to end a meaningful relationship with a minimal amount of pain.

3. **Civic activity.** To help a sixteen-year-old friend learn how to drive, explain a specific driving maneuver one step at a time. You might, for example, describe how to make a three-point turn, parallel park, or handle a skid. Remember, your friend lacks self-confidence and experience.

4. **Civic activity.** Your best friend plans to move into his or her own apartment but doesn't know the first thing about how to choose one. Explain the process of selecting an apartment—where to look, what to investigate, what questions to ask before signing a lease.

5. **Workplace action.** As a staff writer for a consumer magazine, you've been asked to write an article on how to shop for a certain product. Give specific steps explaining how to save money, buy a quality product, and the like.

6. **Workplace action.** An author of books for elementary school children, you want to show children how to do something—take care of a pet, get along with siblings, keep a room clean. Explain the process in terms a child would understand yet not find condescending.

15

Comparison-Contrast

In this chapter, you will learn:

15.1 To use the pattern of comparison-contrast to develop your essays

15.2 To consider how comparison-contrast can fit your purpose and audience

15.3 To develop prewriting, writing, and revision strategies for using comparison-contrast in an essay

15.4 To analyze how comparison-contrast is used effectively in one student-written and three professionally authored selections

15.5 To write your own essays using comparison-contrast as a strategy

What Is Comparison-Contrast?

We frequently try to make sense of the world by finding similarities and differences in our experiences. Seeing how things are alike (**comparing**) and seeing how they are different (**contrasting**) help us impose meaning on experiences that otherwise might remain fragmented and disconnected.

Comparing and contrasting also help us make choices. We compare and contrast everything—from two brands of soap we might buy to two colleges we might attend. When we have to make important decisions, we tend to think rigorously about how things are alike or different: Should I accept the higher-paying job or the lower-paying one that offers more challenges? Such a deliberate approach to comparison-contrast may also provide us with needed insight into complex contemporary issues: Is television's coverage of political candidates more or less objective than it used to be?

How Comparison-Contrast Fits Your Purpose and Audience

When is it appropriate in writing to use the comparison-contrast pattern of development? Comparison-contrast works well if you want to demonstrate any of the following: (1) that one thing is better than another (the first example below); (2) that things that seem different are actually alike (the second example below); (3) that things that seem alike are actually different (the third example below).

> Compare and contrast the way male and female relationships are depicted in *Cosmopolitan, Ms., Playboy,* and *Esquire.* Which publication has the most limited view of men and women? Which has the broadest perspective?

> Football, basketball, and baseball differ in the ways they appeal to fans. Describe the unique drawing power of each sport, but also reach some conclusions about the appeals the three sports have in common.

> Studies show that both college students and their parents feel that post-secondary education should equip young people to succeed in the marketplace. Yet the same studies report that the two groups have a very different understanding of what it means to succeed. What differences do you think the studies identify?

Other assignments will, in less obvious ways, lend themselves to comparison-contrast. For instance, although words like *compare, contrast, differ,* and *have in common* don't appear in the following assignments, essay responses to the assignments could be organized around the comparison-contrast format:

> The emergence of the two-career family is one of the major phenomena of our culture. Discuss the advantages and disadvantages of having both parents work, showing how you feel about such two-career households.

> There has been considerable criticism recently of the news coverage by the city's two leading newspapers, the *Herald* and the *Beacon.* Indicate whether you think the criticism is valid by discussing the similarities and differences in the two papers' news coverage.

Note: The second assignment shows that a comparison-contrast essay may cover similarities *and* differences, not just one or the other.

As you have seen, comparison-contrast can be the key strategy for achieving an essay's purpose. But comparison-contrast can also be a supplemental method used to help make a point in an essay organized chiefly around another pattern of development. A serious, informative essay intended for laypeople might *define* clinical depression by contrasting that state of mind with ordinary run-of-the-mill blues. Writing humorously about the exhausting *effects* of trying to get in shape, you might dramatize your plight for readers by contrasting the leisurely way you used to spend your day with your current rigidly compulsive exercise regimen. Or, in an urgent *argumentation-persuasion* essay on the need for stricter controls over drug abuse in the workplace, you might provide readers with background by comparing several companies' approaches to the problem.

Prewriting Strategies

The following checklist shows how you can apply to comparison-contrast some of the prewriting strategies discussed in Chapter 2.

☑ **COMPARISON-CONTRAST: A PREWRITING CHECKLIST**

Choose Subjects to Compare and Contrast

☐ What have you recently needed to compare and contrast (subjects to major in, events to attend, ways to resolve a disagreement) in order to make a choice? What would a comparison-contrast analysis disclose about the alternatives, your priorities, and the criteria by which you judge?

☐ Can you show a need for change by contrasting one way of doing something with a better way?

☐ Do any people you know show some striking similarities and differences? What would a comparison-contrast analysis reveal about their characters and the personal qualities you prize?

☐ How does your view on an issue differ from that of other people? What would a comparison-contrast analysis of these views indicate about your values?

Determine Your Purpose, Audience, Tone, and Point of View

☐ Is your purpose primarily to inform readers of similarities and differences? To evaluate your subjects' relative merits? To persuade readers to choose between alternative courses of action?

☐ What audience are you writing for? To what tone and point of view will they be most receptive?

Use Prewriting to Generate Points of Comparison-Contrast

☐ How could brainstorming, freewriting, mapping, or journal entries help you gather information about your subjects' most significant similarities and differences?

Strategies for Using Comparison-Contrast in an Essay

After prewriting, you're ready to draft your essay. The following suggestions and Figure 15.1 (on page 285) will be helpful whether you use comparison-contrast as a dominant or supportive pattern of development.

1. **Be sure your subjects are at least somewhat alike.** Unless you plan to develop an *analogy* (see the following numbered suggestion), the subjects you choose to compare or contrast should share some obvious characteristics or qualities. It makes sense to compare different parts of the country, but a reasonable paper wouldn't result from a comparison of a television game show with a soap opera. Your subjects must belong to the same general group so that your comparison-contrast stays within logical bounds and doesn't veer off into pointlessness.

FIGURE 15.1

Development Diagram: Writing a Comparison-Contrast Essay

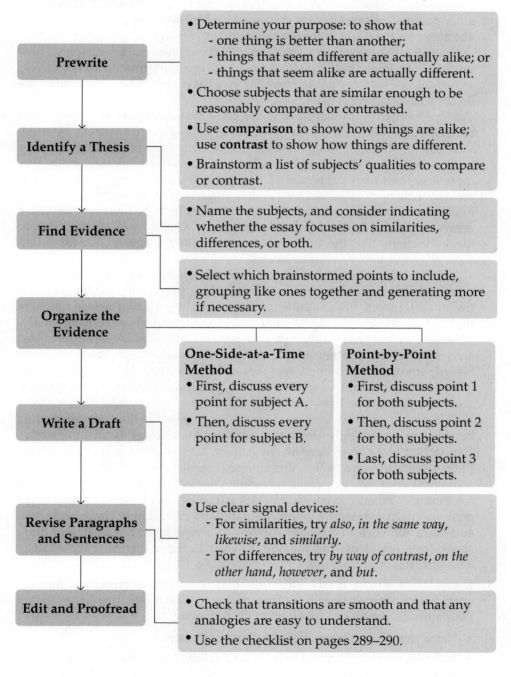

2. **Stay focused on your purpose.** When writing, remember that comparison-contrast isn't an end in itself. That is, your objective isn't to turn an essay into a mechanical list of "how *A* differs from *B*" or "how *A* is like *B*." As with the other patterns of development discussed in this book, comparison-contrast is a strategy for making a point or meeting a larger purpose.

   Consider the assignment on page 283 about the two newspapers. Your purpose here might be simply to *inform*, to present information as objectively as possible: "This is what the *Herald*'s news coverage is like. This is what the *Beacon*'s news coverage is like."

   More frequently, though, you'll use comparison-contrast to *evaluate* your subjects' pros and cons, your goal being to reach a conclusion or make a judgment: "Both the *Herald* and the *Beacon* spend too much time reporting local news," or "The *Herald*'s analysis of the recent hostage crisis was more insightful than the *Beacon*'s." Comparison-contrast can also be used to *persuade* readers to take action: "People interested in thorough coverage of international events should read the *Herald* rather than the *Beacon*." Persuasive essays may also propose a change, contrasting what now exists with a more ideal situation: "For the *Beacon* to compete with the *Herald*, it must assign more reporters to international stories."

   Yet another purpose you might have in writing a comparison-contrast essay is to *clear up misconceptions* by revealing previously hidden similarities or differences. For example, perhaps your town's two newspapers are thought to be sharply different. However, a comparison-contrast analysis might reveal that—although one paper specializes in sensationalized stories whereas the other adopts a more muted approach—both resort to biased, emotionally charged analyses of local politics. Or the essay might illustrate that the tabloid's treatment of the local arts scene is surprisingly more comprehensive than that of its competitor.

   Comparing and contrasting also make it possible to *draw an analogy* between two seemingly unrelated subjects. An **analogy** is an imaginative comparison that delves beneath the surface differences of subjects to expose their significant and often unsuspected similarities or differences. The analogical approach can make a complex subject easier to understand—as, for example, when the national deficit is compared to a household budget gone awry. Analogies are often dramatic and instructive, challenging you and your audience to consider subjects in a new light. But analogies don't speak for themselves. You must make clear to the reader how the analogy demonstrates your purpose.

3. **Formulate a strong thesis.** An essay that is developed primarily through comparison-contrast should be focused by a solid thesis. Besides revealing your attitude, the thesis will often do the following:

   - Name the subjects being compared and contrasted
   - Indicate whether the essay focuses on the subjects' similarities, differences, or both
   - State the essay's main point of comparison or contrast

Not all comparison-contrast essays need thesis statements as structured as those that follow. Even so, these examples can serve as models of clarity. Note that the first thesis statement signals similarities, the second differences, and the last both similarities and differences:

> Middle-aged parents are often in a good position to empathize with adolescent children because the emotional upheavals experienced by the two age groups are much the same.

> The priorities of most retired people are more conducive to health and happiness than the priorities of most young professionals.

> College students in their thirties and forties face many of the same pressures as younger students, but they are better equipped to withstand these pressures.

4. **Select the points to be discussed.** Once you have identified the essay's subject, purpose, and thesis, you need to decide which of the many points generated during prewriting you will discuss: You have to identify which aspects of the subjects to compare or contrast. College professors, for instance, could be compared and contrasted on the basis of their testing methods, ability to motivate students, confidence in front of a classroom, personalities, level of enthusiasm, and so forth.

   When selecting points to cover, be sure to consider your audience. Ask yourself: "Will my readers be familiar with this item? Will I need it to get my message across? Will my audience find this item interesting or convincing?" What your readers know, what they don't know, and what you can project about their reactions should influence your choices. And, of course, you need to select points that support your thesis.

5. **Organize the points to be discussed.** After deciding which points to include, you should use a systematic, logical plan for presenting those ideas. If the points aren't organized, your essay will be little more than a confusing jumble of ideas. There are two common ways to organize an essay developed wholly or in part by comparison-contrast. Although both strategies may be used in a paper, one method usually predominates.

   In the **one-side-at-a-time method** of organization, you discuss everything relevant about one subject before moving to another subject. For example, responding to the earlier assignment that asked you to analyze the news coverage in two local papers, you might first talk about the *Herald*'s coverage of international, national, and local news; then you would discuss the *Beacon*'s coverage of the same categories. Note that the areas discussed should be the same for both newspapers. It wouldn't be logical to review the *Herald*'s coverage of international, national, and local news and then to detail the *Beacon*'s magazine supplements, modern living section, and comics page. Moreover, the areas compared and contrasted should be presented in the same order.

This is how you would organize the essay using the one-side-at-a-time method:

Everything about subject *A*   *Herald*'s news coverage:

- International
- National
- Local

Everything about subject *B*   *Beacon*'s news coverage:

- International
- National
- Local

In the **point-by-point method** of organization, you alternate from one aspect of the first subject to the same aspect of your other subject(s). For example, to use this method when comparing or contrasting the *Herald* and the *Beacon*, you would first discuss the *Herald*'s international coverage, then the *Beacon*'s international coverage; next, the *Herald*'s national coverage, then the *Beacon*'s; and finally, the *Herald*'s local coverage, then the *Beacon*'s.

An essay using the point-by-point method would be organized like this:

First aspect of subjects *A* and *B*   *Herald:* International coverage
                                             Beacon: International coverage

Second aspect of subjects *A* and *B*   *Herald:* National coverage
                                             Beacon: National coverage

Third aspect of subjects *A* and *B*   *Herald:* Local coverage
                                             Beacon: Local coverage

Deciding which of these two methods of organization to use is largely a personal choice, though there are several factors to consider. The one-side-at-a-time method tends to convey a more unified feeling because it highlights broad similarities and differences. It is, therefore, an effective approach for subjects that are fairly uncomplicated. This strategy also works well when essays are brief; the reader won't find it difficult to remember what has been said about subject *A* when reading about subject *B*.

Because the point-by-point method permits more extensive coverage of similarities and differences, it is often a wise choice when subjects are complex. This pattern is also useful for lengthy essays because readers would probably find it difficult to remember, let's say, ten pages of information about subject *A* while reading the next ten pages about subject *B*. The point-by-point approach, however, may cause readers to lose sight of the broader picture, so remember to keep them focused on your central point.

6. **Supply the reader with clear transitions.** Although a well-organized comparison-contrast format is important, it doesn't guarantee that readers will be able to follow your line of thought easily. *Transitions*—especially those

signaling similarities or differences—are needed to show readers where they have been and where they are going. Such cues are essential in all writing, but they're especially crucial in a paper using comparison-contrast. By indicating clearly when subjects are being compared or contrasted, the transitions help weave the discussion into a coherent whole.

The transitions (in boldface) in the following examples could be used to *signal similarities* in an essay discussing the news coverage in the *Herald* and the *Beacon:*

- The *Beacon* **also** allots only a small portion of the front page to global news.
- **In the same way,** the *Herald* tries to include at least three local stories on the first page.
- **Likewise,** the *Beacon* emphasizes the importance of up-to-date reporting of town meetings.

The transitions (in boldface) in these examples could be used to *signal differences:*

- **By way of contrast,** the *Herald*'s editorial page deals with national matters on the average of three times a week.
- **On the other hand,** the *Beacon* does not share the *Herald*'s enthusiasm for interviews with national figures.
- **But** the *Herald*'s coverage of the Washington scene is much more comprehensive than its competitor's.

Revision Strategies

Once you have a draft of the essay, you're ready to revise. The following checklist will help you and those giving you feedback apply to comparison-contrast some of the revision techniques discussed in Chapters 7 and 8.

☑ **COMPARISON-CONTRAST: A REVISION/PEER REVIEW CHECKLIST**

Revise Overall Meaning and Structure

☐ Are the subjects sufficiently alike for the comparison-contrast to be logical and meaningful?

☐ What purpose does the essay serve—to inform, to evaluate, to persuade readers to accept a viewpoint, to eliminate misconceptions, or to draw a surprising analogy?

☐ What is the essay's thesis? How could the thesis be stated more effectively?

☐ Is the overall essay organized primarily by the one-side-at-a-time method or by the point-by-point method? What is the advantage of that strategy for this essay?

(continued)

☐ Are the same features discussed for each subject? Are they discussed in the same order?

☐ Which points of comparison and/or contrast need further development? Which points should be deleted? Where do significant points seem to be missing? How has the most important similarity or difference been emphasized?

Revise Paragraph Development

☐ If the essay uses the one-side-at-a-time method, which paragraph marks the switch from one subject to another?

☐ If the essay uses the point-by-point method, do paragraphs consistently alternate between subjects? If this alternation becomes too elaborate or predictable, what could be done to eliminate the problem?

☐ If the essay uses both the one-side-at-a-time and the point-by-point methods, which paragraph marks the switch from one method to the other? If the switch is confusing, how could it be made less so?

☐ Where would signal devices (*also, likewise, in contrast*) make it easier to see similarities and differences between the subjects being discussed?

Revise Sentences and Words

☐ Where do too many signal devices make sentences awkward and mechanical?

☐ Which sentences and words fail to convey the intended tone?

Student Essay: From Prewriting Through Revision

The student essay that follows was written by Carol Siskin in response to this assignment:

> In "Euromail and Amerimail," Eric Weiner contrasts European and American e-mail habits and customs, showing that one is more favorable than the other. In an essay of your own, contrast two peronality types, lifestyles, or stages of life, demonstrating that one is superior to the other.

Having recently turned forty, Carol decided to write an essay taking issue with the idea that being young is better than being old. From time to time, Carol had used her *journal* to explore what it means to grow older. Rather than writing a new journal entry on the subject, she decided to look at earlier entries to see if they contained any helpful material for the assignment. One rather free-ranging entry, composed on the evening of her birthday, proved especially valuable. The original entry starts below. The handwritten marks indicate Carol's later efforts to shape and develop this raw material. Note the way Carol added details, circled main ideas, and indicated a possible sequence. These annotations paved the way for her outline, which is presented after the journal entry.

Journal Entry

Forty years old today. At 20 I thought 40 would mean the end of everything, but that's   *Possible conclusion*
not the case at all. I'm much happier now.

     Mom and Dad made a dinner for the occasion. Talking of happy, they
look great. Mom said this is the best part of their lives. They love retirement—and
obviously each other. I hope Mitch and I will be that happy when we're in our sixties.
And Dave and Elaine seem as good as ever. They look right together. What a pleasure it
is to be a couple. I remember how lonely I was before Mitch and how lonely Dave was
after his divorce. I sure don't envy young singles.

     Dave seems content now. He looks handsome and robust, partly because he feels   *I (Appearance)*
good about his life, partly because he tries to run pretty regularly. I remember how   *My diets. Hated big*
desperately he used to work out with weights because he worried about his appearance.   *waist and legs.*
I'm glad I don't have to be obsessed with my appearance the way I used to be.
Mitch loves me the way I am. And I'm not obsessed anymore with being super stylish. Or   *overcoats vs. leather*
thin. In fact, tonight, with no qualms whatever, I ate two healthy slices of birthday cake.   *jackets*

     Dave says that Nancy (I can't believe she's 22) is thinking of going to graduate
school, but she's not sure what to study. I can remember all the confusion I felt about   *II (Decisions)*
schools and majors. I don't miss those days at all. Dave thinks Nancy is just plain
confused about who she is and what she wants. Her goals change from day to day,   *III (sense of self)*
especially because she's trying to please everyone. One day she feels confident;
the next she's frightened. And she blames her parents' unhappy marriage for her
confusion. No wonder she can't decide whether to marry and have kids. What chaos!   *II*

     Tonight, though, was anything but chaos and confusion. It was an evening of
quiet contentment. All of us enjoyed each other and got along. Quite different from the
way it used to be. How I used to fight with Mom and Dad. I remember slamming the
door and yelling, "It's your fault I was born." What unhappy times those were.

Outline

Thesis: Being young is good, but being older is better.

    I. Appearance
        A. Dave and I when young
           1. Dave's weight lifting to build himself up
           2. My constant dieting to change my body
           3. Both begging for "right" clothes
        B. Attitudes now
           1. My contentment with my rounded shape
           2. Dave's satisfaction with his thinness
           3. Our clothes fashionable but comfortable

   II. Decisions

     A. My major decisions mostly in the past

       1. About education

       2. About marriage and children

     B. Nancy's major decisions mostly in the future

       1. About education

       2. About marriage and children

  III. Sense of self

     A. Nancy's uncertainty

       1. Unclear values and goals

       2. Strong need to be liked

       3. Unresolved feelings about parents

     B. Older person's surer self-identity

       1. Have clearer values and goals

       2. Can stand being disliked

       3. Don't blame parents

Now read Carol's paper, "The Virtues of Growing Older," noting the similarities and differences among her journal entry, outline, and final essay. You'll see that the essay is more developed than either the journal entry or outline. In the essay, Carol added numerous specific details—like those about Dave gobbling vitamins and milkshakes when he was a teen. In contrast, she omitted from the essay some journal material because it would have required burdensome explanations. For instance, if she hadn't eliminated the reference to Nancy, it would have been necessary to explain that Nancy is the daughter of Dave's wife by his first marriage. Despite these differences, you'll note that the essay's basic plan is derived largely from the journal entry and outline. As you read the essay, also consider how well it applies the principles of comparison-contrast discussed in this chapter. (The commentary that follows the paper will help you look at Carol's essay more closely and will give you some sense of how she went about revising her first draft.)

The Virtues of Growing Older
by Carol Siskin

The first of a
two-paragraph
introduction

Our society worships youth. Advertisements convince us to buy Grecian Formula   1
and Oil of Olay so we can hide the gray in our hair and smooth the lines on our face.
Television shows feature attractive young stars with firm bodies, perfect complexions,
and thick manes of hair. Middle-aged folks work out in gyms and jog down the street,
trying to delay the effects of age.

2   Wouldn't any person over thirty gladly sign with the devil just to be young again? Isn't aging an experience to be dreaded? Perhaps it is un-American to say so, but I believe the answer is "No." Being young is often pleasant, but being older has distinct advantages.

3   When young, you are apt to be obsessed with your appearance. When my brother Dave and I were teens, we worked feverishly to perfect the bodies we had. Dave lifted weights, took megadoses of vitamins, and drank a half-dozen milkshakes a day in order to turn his wiry adolescent frame into some muscular ideal. And as a teenager, I dieted constantly. No matter what I weighed, though, I was never satisfied with the way I looked. My legs were too heavy, my shoulders too broad, my waist too big. When Dave and I were young, we begged and pleaded for the "right" clothes. If our parents didn't get them for us, we felt our world would fall apart. How could we go to school wearing loose-fitting overcoats when everyone else would be wearing fitted leather jackets? We could be considered freaks. I often wonder how my parents, and parents in general, manage to tolerate their children during the adolescent years. Now, however, Dave and I are beyond such adolescent agonies. My rounded figure seems fine, and I don't deny myself a slice of pecan pie if I feel in the mood. Dave still works out, but he has actually become fond of his tall, lanky frame. The two of us enjoy wearing fashionable clothes, but we are no longer slaves to style. And women, I'm embarrassed to admit, even more than men, have always seemed to be at the mercy of fashion. Now my clothes—and my brother's—are attractive yet easy to wear. We no longer feel anxious about what others will think. As long as we feel good about how we look, we are happy.

4   Being older is preferable to being younger in another way. Obviously, I still have important choices to make about my life, but I have already made many of the critical decisions that confront those just starting out. I chose the man I wanted to marry. I decided to have children. I elected to return to college to complete my education. But when you are young, major decisions await you at every turn. "What college should I attend? What career should I pursue? Should I get married? Should I have children?" These are just a few of the issues facing young people. It's no wonder that, despite their care-free facade, they are often confused, uncertain, and troubled by all the unknowns in their future.

5   But the greatest benefit of being forty is knowing who I am. The most unsettling aspect of youth is the uncertainty you feel about your values, goals, and dreams.

The second intro-
ductory paragraph

Thesis

First half of topic
sentence for point
Appearance

Start of what it's li[ke]
being young

Second half of topi[c]
sentence for point

Start of what it's li[ke]
being older

First half of topic
sentence for point
Life choices

Start of what it's li[ke]
being older

Second half of topi[c]
sentence for point

Start of what it's li[ke]
being younger

Topic sentence for
point 3: Self-conce[pt]

Start of what it's li[ke]
being younger

Being young means wondering what is worth working for. Being young means feeling happy with yourself one day and wishing you were never born the next. It means trying on new selves by taking up with different crowds. It means resenting your parents

Start of what it's like
being older

and their way of life one minute and then feeling you will never be as good or as accomplished as they are. By way of contrast, forty is sanity. I have a surer self-concept now. I don't laugh at jokes I don't think are funny. I can make a speech in front of a town meeting or complain in a store because I am no longer terrified that people will laugh at me; I am no longer anxious that everyone must like me. I no longer blame my parents for my every personality quirk or keep a running score of everything they did wrong raising me. Life has taught me that I, not they, am responsible for who I am. We are all human beings—neither saints nor devils.

Conclusion

Most Americans blindly accept the idea that newer is automatically better. But a human life contradicts this premise. There is a great deal of happiness to be found as we grow older. My own parents, now in their sixties, recently told me that they are happier now than they have ever been. They would not want to be my age. Did this surprise me? At first, yes. Then it gladdened me. Their contentment holds out great promise for me as I move into the next—perhaps even better—phase of my life.

6

Commentary

Purpose and Thesis

In her essay, Carol disproves the widespread belief that being young is preferable to being old. The *comparison-contrast* pattern allows her to analyze the drawbacks of one and the merits of the other, thus providing the essay with an *evaluative purpose.* Using the title to indicate her point of view, Carol places the *thesis* at the end of her two-paragraph introduction: "Being young is often pleasant, but being older has distinct advantages." Note that the thesis accomplishes several things. It names the two subjects to be discussed and clarifies Carol's point of view about her subjects. The thesis also implies that the essay will focus on the contrasts between these two periods of life.

Points of Support and Overall Organization

To support her assertion that older is better, Carol supplies examples from her own life and organizes the examples around three main points: attitudes about appearance, decisions about life choices, and questions of self-concept. Using the *point-by-point method* to organize the overall essay, she explores each of these key ideas in a separate paragraph. Each paragraph is further focused by one or two sentences that serve as a topic sentence.

Sequence of Points, Organizational Cues, and Paragraph Development

Let's look more closely at the way Carol presents her three central points in the essay. She obviously considers appearance the least important of a person's worries, life choices more important, and self-concept the most critical. So she uses *emphatic order* to sequence the supporting paragraphs, with the phrase "But the greatest benefit" signaling the special significance of the last issue. Carol is also careful to use *transitions* to help readers follow her line of thinking: "*Now, however,* Dave and I are beyond such adolescent agonies" (paragraph 3); "*But* when you are young, major decisions await you at every turn" (4); and "*By way of contrast,* forty is sanity" (5).

Although Carol has worked hard to write a well-organized paper—and has on the whole been successful—she doesn't feel compelled to make the paper fit a rigid format. As you've seen, the essay as a whole uses the point-by-point method, but each supporting paragraph uses the *one-side-at-a-time method*—that is, everything about one age group is discussed before there is a shift to the other age group. Notice too that the third and fifth paragraphs start with young people and then move to adults, whereas the fourth paragraph reverses the sequence by starting with older people.

Combining Patterns of Development

Carol uses the comparison-contrast format to organize her ideas, but other patterns of development also come into play. To illustrate her points, she makes extensive use of *illustration*, and her discussion also contains elements typical of *causal analysis*. Throughout the essay, for instance, she traces the effect of being a certain age on her brother, herself, and her parents.

A Problem with Unity

As you read the third paragraph, you might have noted that Carol's essay runs into a problem. Two sentences in the paragraph disrupt the *unity* of Carol's discussion: "I often wonder how my parents, and parents in general, manage to tolerate their children during the adolescent years," and "women, I'm embarrassed to admit…have always seemed to be at the mercy of fashion." These sentences should be deleted because they don't develop the idea that adolescents are overly concerned with appearance.

Conclusion

Carol's final paragraph brings the essay to a pleasing and interesting close. The conclusion recalls the point made in the introduction: Americans overvalue youth. Carol also uses the conclusion to broaden the scope of her discussion. Rather than continuing to focus on herself, she briefly mentions her parents and the pleasure they take in life. By bringing her parents into the essay, Carol is able to make a gently philosophical observation about the promise that awaits her as she grows older. The implication is that a similarly positive future awaits us, too.

Revising the First Draft

To help guide her revision, Carol asked her husband to read her first draft aloud. As he did, Carol took notes on what she sensed were the paper's strengths and weaknesses. She then jotted down her observations, as well as her husband's, onto the draft. Because Carol wasn't certain which observations were most valid, she didn't rank them. Carol made a number of changes when revising the essay. You'll get a good sense of how she proceeded if you compare the annotated original introduction reprinted here with the final version in the full essay.

Original Version of the Introduction

ing paragraph
t sentence dull
?

ke point about TV
e specific

ke questions more
rous

ybe cut plan of
elopment

America is a land filled with people who worship youth. We admire dynamic young achievers; our middle-aged citizens work out in gyms; all of us wear tight tops and colorful sneakers—clothes that look fine on the young but ridiculous on aging bodies. Television shows revolve around perfect-looking young stars, while commercials entice us with products that will keep us young.

Wouldn't every older person want to be young again? Isn't aging to be avoided? It may be slightly unpatriotic to say so, but I believe the answer is "No." Being young may be pleasant at times, but I would rather be my forty-year-old self. I no longer have to agonize about my physical appearance, I have already made many of my crucial life decisions, and I am much less confused about who I am.

After hearing her original two-paragraph introduction read aloud, Carol was dissatisfied with what she had written. Although she wasn't quite sure how to proceed, she knew that the paragraphs were flat and that they failed to open the essay on a strong note. She decided to start by whittling down the opening sentence, making it crisper and more powerful: "Our society worships youth." That done, she eliminated two bland statements ("We admire dynamic young achievers" and "all of us wear tight tops and colorful sneakers") and made several vague references more concrete and interesting. For example, "commercials entice us with products that will keep us young" became "Grecian Formula and Oil of Olay...hide the gray in our hair and smooth the lines on our face"; "perfect-looking young stars" became "attractive young stars with firm bodies, perfect complexions, and thick manes of hair." With the addition of these specifics, the first paragraph became more vigorous and interesting.

Carol next made some subtle changes in the two questions that opened the second paragraph of the original introduction. She replaced "Wouldn't every older person want to be young again?" and "Isn't aging to be avoided?" with two more emphatic questions: "Wouldn't any person over thirty gladly sign with the devil just to be young again?" and "Isn't aging an experience to be dreaded?" Carol also made some changes at the end of the original second paragraph. Because the paper is relatively short and the subject matter easy to understand, she decided to omit her somewhat awkward *plan of development* ("I no longer have to agonize about my physical appearance, I have already made many of my crucial life decisions, and I am much less confused about who I am"). This deletion made it possible to end the introduction with a clear statement of the essay's thesis.

Once these revisions were made, Carol was confident that her essay got off to a stronger start. Feeling reassured, she moved ahead and made changes in other sections of her paper. Such work enabled her to prepare a solid piece of writing that offers food for thought.

ACTIVITIES: COMPARISON-CONTRAST

Prewriting Activities

1. Imagine you're writing two essays: One explores the effects of holding a job while in college; the other explains how to budget money wisely. Jot down ways you might use comparison-contrast in each essay.

2. Suppose you plan to write a series of articles for your college newspaper. What purpose might you have for comparing and/or contrasting each of the following subject pairs?

   a. Live concert and a recording of the concert
   b. Paper or plastic bags at the supermarket
   c. Two courses—one taught by an inexperienced newcomer, the other by an old pro
   d. Cutting class and not showing up at work

3. Use the patterns of development or another prewriting technique to compare or contrast a current situation with the way you would like it to be. After reviewing your prewriting material, decide what your purpose, audience, tone, and point of view might be if you were to write an essay. Finally, write out your thesis and main supporting points.

4. Using your journal or freewriting, jot down the advantages and disadvantages of two ways of doing something. Reread your prewriting and determine what your thesis, purpose, audience, tone, and point of view might be if you were to write an essay. Make a scratch list of the main ideas you would cover. Would a point-by-point or a one-side-at-a-time method of organization work more effectively?

Revising Activities

5. Of the statements that follow, which would *not* make effective thesis statements for comparison-contrast essays? Identify the problem(s) in the faulty statements and revise them accordingly.

   a. Although their classroom duties often overlap, teacher aides are not as equipped as teachers to handle disciplinary problems.
   b. This college provides more assistance to its students than most schools.
   c. There are many differences between American and foreign cars.

6. The following paragraph is from the draft of an essay detailing the qualities of a skillful manager. How effective is this comparison-contrast paragraph? What revisions would help focus the paragraph on the point made in the topic sentence? Where should details be added or deleted? Rewrite the paragraph, providing necessary transitions and details.

A manager encourages creativity and treats employees courteously, while a boss discourages staff resourcefulness and views it as a threat. At the hardware store where I work, I got my boss's approval to develop a system for organizing excess stock in the storeroom. I shelved items in roughly the same order as they were displayed in the store. The system was helpful to all the salespeople, not just to me, since everyone was stymied by the boss's helter-skelter system. What he did was store overstocked items according to each wholesaler, even though most of us weren't there long enough to know which items came from which wholesaler. His supposed system created chaos. When he saw what I had done, he was furious and insisted that we continue to follow the old slap-dash system. I had assumed he would welcome my ideas the way my manager did last summer when I worked in a drugstore. But he didn't and I had to scrap my work and go back to his eccentric system. He certainly could learn something about employee relations from the drugstore manager.

PROFESSIONAL SELECTIONS: COMPARISON–CONTRAST

Eric Weiner

Eric Weiner (1963–) is a national correspondent for NPR.org, part of National Public Radio. He began his journalism career by reporting on business issues for *The New York Times* and NPR's Washington, D.C., bureau and then spent most of the 1990s reporting on wars and world events from South Asia and the Middle East. A licensed pilot who loves to eat sushi, Weiner occasionally writes lighter pieces drawing on his experience with other cultures. He is the author of *The Geography of Bliss: One Grump's Search for the Happiest Places in the World* (2008) and *Man Seeks God: My Flirtations with the Divine* (2011). A short version of this piece about e-mail was broadcast on *Day to Day*, a National Public Radio magazine show, on March 24, 2005; the full version, which appears here, was posted on Slate.com the next day.

For ideas on how this comparison-contrast essay is organized, see Figure 15.2 on page 301.

Pre-Reading Journal Entry

Just one hundred years ago, people communicated only by speaking face to face or by writing a letter—with an occasional brief telegram in emergencies. Today, technology has given us many ways to communicate. Think over all the different ways you communicate with your family, friends, classmates, instructors, coworkers, and others. What methods of communication do you use with each of these groups? Which forms do you prefer, and why? Use your journal to answer these questions.

EUROMAIL AND AMERIMAIL

1   North America and Europe are two continents divided by a common technology: e-mail. Techno-optimists assure us that e-mail—along with the Internet and satellite TV—make the world smaller. That may be true in a technical sense. I can send a message from my home in Miami to a German friend in Berlin and it will arrive almost instantly. But somewhere over the Atlantic, the messages get garbled. In fact, two distinct forms of e-mail have emerged: Euromail and Amerimail.

2   Amerimail is informal and chatty. It's likely to begin with a breezy "Hi" and end with a "Bye." The chances of Amerimail containing a smiley face or an "xoxo" are disturbingly high. We Americans are reluctant to dive into the meat of an e-mail; we feel compelled to first inform hapless recipients about our vacation on the Cape which was really excellent except the jellyfish were biting and the kids caught this nasty bug so we had to skip the whale watching trip but about that investors' meeting in New York...Amerimail is a bundle of contradictions: rambling and yet direct; deferential, yet arrogant. In other words, Amerimail is America.

3   Euromail is stiff and cold, often beginning with a formal "Dear Mr. X" and ending with a brusque "Sincerely." You won't find any mention of kids or the weather or jellyfish in Euromail. It's also business. It's also slow. Your correspondent might take days, even weeks, to answer a message. Euromail is also less confrontational in tone, rarely filled with the overt nastiness that characterizes American e-mail disagreements. In other words, Euromail is exactly like the Europeans themselves. (I am, of course, generalizing. German e-mail style is not exactly the same as Italian or Greek, but they have more in common with each other than they do with American mail.)

4   These are more than mere stylistic differences. Communication matters. Which model should the rest of the world adopt: Euromail or Amerimail?

5   A California-based e-mail consulting firm called People-onthego sheds some light on the e-mail divide. It recently asked about 100 executives on both sides of the Atlantic whether they noticed differences in e-mail styles. Most said yes. Here are a few of their observations:

"Americans tend to write (e-mails) exactly as they speak."
"Europeans are less obsessive about checking e-mail."
"In general, Americans are much more responsive to email—they respond faster and provide more information."

6   One respondent noted that Europeans tend to segregate their e-mail accounts. Rarely do they send personal messages on their business accounts, or vice versa. These differences can't be explained merely by differing comfort levels with technology.

Other forms of electronic communication, such as SMS text messaging, are more popular in Europe than in the United States.

The fact is, Europeans and Americans approach e-mail in a fundamentally different way. Here is the key point: For Europeans, e-mail has replaced the business letter. For Americans, it has replaced the telephone. That's why we tend to unleash what e-mail consultant Tim Burress calls a "brain dump": unloading the content of our cerebral cortex onto the screen and hitting the send button. "It makes Europeans go ballistic," he says.

Susanne Khawand, a German high-tech executive, has been on the receiving end of American brain dumps, and she says it's not pretty. "I feel like saying, 'Why don't you just call me instead of writing five e-mails back and forth,'" she says. Americans are so overwhelmed by their bulging inboxes that "you can't rely on getting an answer. You don't even know if they read it." In Germany, she says, it might take a few days, or even weeks, for an answer, but one always arrives.

Maybe that's because, on average, Europeans receive fewer e-mails and spend less time tending their inboxes. An international survey of business owners in 24 countries (conducted by the accounting firm Grant Thornton) found that people in Greece and Russia spend the least amount of time dealing with e-mail every day: 48 minutes on average. Americans, by comparison, spend two hours per day, among the highest in the world. (Only Filipinos spend more time on e-mail, 2.1 hours.) The survey also found that European executives are skeptical of e-mail's ability to boost their bottom line.

It's not clear why European and American e-mail styles have evolved separately, but I suspect the reasons lie within deep cultural differences. Americans tend to be impulsive and crave instant gratification. So we send e-mails rapid-fire and get antsy if we don't receive a reply quickly. Europeans tend to be more methodical and plodding. They send (and reply to) e-mails only after great deliberation.

For all their Continental fastidiousness, Europeans can be remarkably lax about e-mail security, says Bill Young, an executive vice president with the Strickland Group. Europeans are more likely to include trade secrets and business strategies in e-mails, he says, much to the frustration of their American colleagues. This is probably because identity theft—and other types of hacking—are much less of a problem in Europe than in the United States. Privacy laws are much stricter in Europe.

So, which is better: Euromail or Amerimail? Personally, I'm a convert—or a defector, if you prefer—to the former. I realize it's not popular these days to suggest we have anything to learn from Europeans, but I'm fed up with an inbox cluttered with rambling, barely cogent missives from friends and colleagues. If the alternative is a few stiffly written, politely worded bits of Euromail, then I say...bring it on.

Questions for Close Reading

1. What is the selection's thesis? Locate the sentence(s) in which Weiner states his main idea. If he doesn't state his thesis explicitly, express it in your own words.

2. According to Weiner, what are the main characteristics of American e-mail? What are the main characteristics of European e-mail?

FIGURE 15.2

Essay Structure Diagram: "Euromail and Amerimail" by Eric Weiner

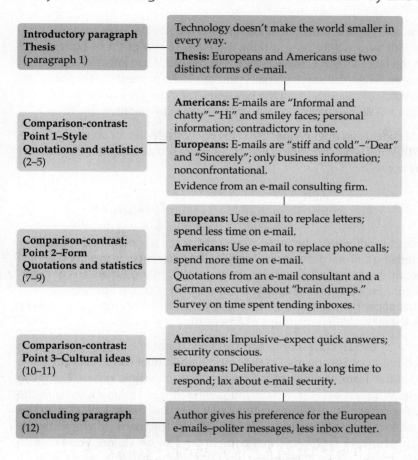

Introductory paragraph Thesis (paragraph 1)	Technology doesn't make the world smaller in every way. **Thesis:** Europeans and Americans use two distinct forms of e-mail.
Comparison-contrast: Point 1–Style Quotations and statistics (2–5)	**Americans:** E-mails are "Informal and chatty"–"Hi" and smiley faces; personal information; contradictory in tone. **Europeans:** E-mails are "stiff and cold"–"Dear" and "Sincerely"; only business information; nonconfrontational. Evidence from an e-mail consulting firm.
Comparison-contrast: Point 2–Form Quotations and statistics (7–9)	**Europeans:** Use e-mail to replace letters; spend less time on e-mail. **Americans:** Use e-mail to replace phone calls; spend more time on e-mail. Quotations from an e-mail consultant and a German executive about "brain dumps." Survey on time spent tending inboxes.
Comparison-contrast: Point 3–Cultural ideas (10–11)	**Americans:** Impulsive–expect quick answers; security conscious. **Europeans:** Deliberative–take a long time to respond; lax about e-mail security.
Concluding paragraph (12)	Author gives his preference for the European e-mails–politer messages, less inbox clutter.

3. When Americans and Europeans e-mail one another for business reasons, frustration often ensues. Why, according to Weiner, is this so? What are some examples of e-mail differences that cause frustration?

4. Which type of e-mail does Weiner favor? Why?

Questions About the Writer's Craft

1. The opening paragraph of this essay is full of technology-related words: *technology, e-mail, techno-optimists, Internet, Satellite TV, technical sense, Euromail,* and *Amerimail.* What is the effect of using all these "techno-terms"? How does the remainder of the essay contrast with the dominant impression of the first paragraph?

2. **The Pattern.** What type of organization does Weiner use for the essay? How else could he have organized the points he makes? Which method of organization do you think is more effective for this essay?

3. **The Pattern.** Identify the transitional expressions that Weiner uses to signal similarities and differences. Why do you think there are so few of these expressions? How might the fact that this essay was meant to be read aloud affect Weiner's transitions between Amerimail and Euromail? (You can listen to the short version of the essay at www.npr.org; search using the key term *Euromail.*) Do you think the essay would be better if Weiner had used more transitional expressions? Explain.

4. What type of conclusion does Weiner use? (To review strategies for conclusions, see pages 69–70). What is his concluding point? Were you surprised by this conclusion? Why or why not?

Writing Assignments Using Comparison-Contrast as a Pattern of Development

1. Weiner attributes differences between Americans and Europeans in the use of e-mail to underlying cultural differences. Consider the differences in the use of e-mail among specific subgroups of Americans, for example, among Americans of different generations, or different occupations. Drawing on your own personal experience and that of people you know, write an essay comparing and contrasting some of the ways these two different groups of Americans use e-mail.

2. The etiquette of e-mail correspondence certainly is not the only way in which Americans differ from Europeans. Consider some additional ways that Americans as a whole differ from another specific nationality or ethnic group, European or otherwise. Write an essay in which you *contrast* the way Americans and the other group approach at least three cultural practices. You might look at attitudes toward gender roles, child-rearing, personal fitness, treatment of the ill or the elderly, leisure to work ratios, the environment, and so on. Before you begin to write, consider what sort of tone might best suit your essay. You might adopt a straightforward tone (like Weiner's), or you might find a humorous approach better suits your material.

Writing Assignment Combining Patterns of Development

3. Weiner's preference for Euromail indicates that he longs for a more formal approach to communication. Over time, several other types of behaviors have evolved to be less formal than they once were. Select another aspect of behavior that has acquired a more casual mode; examples include dining etiquette, forms of address, dress codes, classroom protocol or student-teacher dynamics, and so on. Write an essay in which you explore at least two to three *causes* for the shift from more formal to more casual expressions of this behavior. As you examine the causes, you'll probably find yourself *contrasting* former and current practices. And your conclusion should *argue* for the superiority of either the casual or the formal approach.

Patricia Cohen

The journalist Patricia Cohen, currently the theater editor at *The New York Times*, previously created and edited the Arts & Ideas section for the same publication. Cohen also wrote for *The Washington Post, Rolling Stone* magazine, and *New York Newsday* and is the author of *In Our Prime: The Invention of Middle Age* (2012). The following essay (originally titled *"Cupid*: Spawn of Austen?") appeared in the Culturebox section of *Slate* online magazine on September 16, 2003.

Pre-Reading Journal Entry

The genre of reality-television shows has flourished in recent years, with the numbers and types of shows multiplying at a head-spinning pace. Consider various types of reality-TV shows: matchmaking and dating, athletic-challenge, housemate, secret-camera, personal makeover, home improvement, and so on. What are your feelings about each type of "real-life" show? Collectively, what is your opinion about the reality-TV genre as a whole? Spend some time recording your thoughts on these questions in your pre-reading journal.

REALITY TV: SURPRISING THROWBACK TO THE PAST?

1   Will Lisa Shannon find love and fortune? On tonight's finale of *Cupid*, CBS's latest reality dating show, fans will find out which suitor has been chosen to propose to the series's lovely 25-year-old heroine from among the remaining would-be romantics. If Shannon accepts the proposal, the couple will be married right then and there. And if they stay married for a year, they will receive a $1 million check.

2   To many critics, *Cupid* and other matchmaking shows that mix money and real-life marital machinations represent a cynical and tasteless new genre that is yet another sign of America's moral decline. But there's something familiar about the fortune hunters, the status seekers, the thwarted loves, the meddling friends, the public displays, the comic manners, and the sharp competitiveness—all find their counterparts in Jane Austen and Edith Wharton.[1] Only now, three-minute get-to-know-you tryouts in a TV studio substitute for three-minute waltzes at a ball. Traditional family values, it turns out, are back on television after all.

3   Lisa Shannon may lack the wit, depth, and cleverness of an Austen heroine, but like many of Austen's women, she has put herself in the hands of others (in this case her friends and the TV audience), trusting that they will choose the right match. Even the idea that Shannon, at 25, feels the need to go to such lengths to find a husband

---

[1]Jane Austen (1775–1817) and Edith Wharton (1862–1937) are renowned for their novels exploring the intricate social workings—particularly as they relate to courtship and marriage—of the upper classes. Austen wrote of England's country elite in the late 1700s and early 1800s, whereas Wharton most famously examined New York's high society in the late 1800s and early 1900s (editors' note).

suggests a troubling 19th-century ethos: A woman who is not married by her late 20s is doomed to be an Old Maid.

Undoubtedly, the hundreds of suitors who joined the pursuit are as attracted to   4
the $1 million dowry as to Shannon. But money played a large (and openly discussed) role in the Victorian and Edwardian[2] contract as well. In *Pride and Prejudice*,[3] for example, we learn that "Mr. Darcy soon drew the attention of the room by his fine, tall person, handsome features, noble mien—and the report which was in general circulation within five minutes after his entrance of his having ten thousand a year." And in *Emma*,[4] Mr. Knightly scolds the novel's eponymous heroine for imagining a match between Mr. Elton and her friend Harriet, without understanding he is more interested in money than in love: "I have heard him speak with great animation of a large family of young ladies that his sisters are intimate with, who have all twenty thousand pounds apiece."

On *Cupid*, Lisa's friends Laura and Kimberly are there to protect her from such   5
gold diggers. They helped Lisa screen the men who answered a coast-to-coast open call (which produced more candidates than did the California primary). After the three whittled down the list of hopefuls to 10, the final selection was turned over to TV viewers, who called in every week to vote for their favorite.

Like the secondary characters in Austen and Wharton, Shannon's companions are   6
clearly there to provide piquant social commentary, deliciously wicked judgments, and intrigue, sabotaging some suitors and championing others. "Freak," "boring," "awful," shrieks Laura, Lisa's confidante, as she ridicules suitors' looks, accents, clothing, schooling, and pronunciation.

Of course, nothing but superficial snap judgments can be made in the few min-   7
utes that each man is initially given to impress the three women. But the snap judgments aren't necessarily unanimous, and Laura and Kimberly's debating of the various virtues and flaws (is he "an arrogant jerk" or a dependable lawyer?) are a prosaic version of Mr. Knightly's and Emma's spirited sparring over the lovesick Robert Martin:

"A respectable, intelligent gentleman-farmer," says Mr. Knightly.   8

"His appearance is so much against him, and his manner so bad," Emma responds.   9

Likewise, the hopeful bachelors on *Cupid* understand what goes into a suitable   10
match. Corey, a rocket scientist with the Air Force, acknowledged up front, "I know you have your friends here because I have to fit in." One contestant, Rob, went so far as to boast, "I come from good stock, too. I have good hair and teeth," as if he were a racehorse, waiting for her to check his gums.

Even Richard Kaye, an English professor and the author of *The Flirt's Tragedy:*   11
Desire Without End in Victorian and Edwardian Fiction, confesses to being a "guilty watcher" of the new matchmaking shows, finding the parallels spookily similar. But inevitably, these series—*The Bachelorette*, *Meet My Folks*, *Married by America*, and *For Love or Money* (where a woman can keep the man or the million but not both)—have

---

[2]The Victorian period refers to the time of Queen Victoria's reign in England (1837–1901), and the Edwardian period refers to the reign of England's King Edward VII (1901–1910) (editors' note).

[3]Novel written by Jane Austen and published in 1813 (editors' note).

[4]Novel written by Austen and published in 1815 (editors' note).

all been scorned for debasing the sanctity of marriage and for their shallow, indecorous exhibitionism.

12   But the shows also betray dissatisfaction with the individualistic, go-it-alone ethic of modern courtship. The Victorians and Edwardians organized balls, dinners, afternoon teas, country walks, and the like to help their younger members find mates. Today, without such formal social arrangements, singles are pretty much left to their own devices to suss out partners. And while the elaborate courtship rituals and codes may now seem curiously antique, they did serve to cushion the brutally competitive marriage market. "I've been looking for Mr. Right and I've just not been able to find him," Lisa confesses. "Based on my track record, I obviously need help." She has discovered what Lily Bart in Wharton's *The House of Mirth*[5] learned after losing a sought-after bachelor. Upon hearing of the wealthy match that Grace Van Osburgh expertly concocted for her daughter, Bart concludes: "The cleverest girl may miscalculate where her own interests are concerned, may yield too much at one moment and withdraw too far at the next."

13   In the end, the American public will choose Lisa's potential spouse in what could be seen simply as a more democratic version of those literary heroes and heroines who gave themselves wholly over to society and allowed their extended family to pick an appropriate mate. And why not? The idea that a good husband is hard to find has become a cultural watchword. Meanwhile, the high divorce rate is evidence that love, American style, hasn't necessarily produced happier unions. Nor should anyone forget that Lisa, too, stands to gain the million only through an advantageous marriage. And if it doesn't work out after a year, she at least has one of the modern conveniences not available to Austen's or Wharton's protagonists: a no-fault divorce.[6]

Questions for Close Reading

1. What is the selection's thesis? Locate the sentence(s) in which Cohen states her main idea. If she doesn't state the thesis explicitly, express it in your own words.

2. What does Cohen assert is the common perception of reality-TV dating shows among critics? Does she agree or disagree with this evaluation?

3. What are three similarities between the dating shows and the plots of classic novels?

4. Though her essay is principally a comparison of reality dating shows and classic novels, Cohen also acknowledges some important contrasts between them. What are these differences?

---

[5]Novel published in 1905 (editors' note).

[6]Lisa Shannon and Hank Stapleton, the man selected for her, continued to date in the year following *Cupid's* conclusion, though they rejected the option of marrying during the final episode—along with the possibility of winning one million dollars on their first anniversary (editors' note).

Questions About the Writer's Craft

1. **The pattern.** Which comparison-contrast method of organization (point-by-point or one-side-at-a-time) does Cohen use to develop her essay? Why might she have chosen this pattern?

2. What kind of audience do you think Cohen is writing for—one that already agrees with her, disagrees, or is indifferent? How can you tell?

3. Throughout her essay, Cohen uses direct quotes from various sources. What kinds of sources does she quote? Why do you think she chose to quote rather than to paraphrase or summarize them?

4. **Other patterns.** In paragraphs 12 and 13, Cohen presents a *causal analysis* of modern-day dating. How does this examination of *causes* and *effects* help reinforce her thesis?

Writing Assignments Using Comparison-Contrast as a Pattern of Development

1. Cohen draws a surprisingly apt comparison between today's reality dating shows and classic novels of the 1800s and early 1900s. Think of another area, device, or activity in modern life that you think compares to one from a previous time. Write an essay in which you compare the two things you've selected, presenting two or three ways in which they are similar. Along the way, you should acknowledge obvious differences as a way of accounting for a skeptical audience.

2. One need not look as far back as the classic novels Cohen cites to observe that courtship rituals have changed—even a single generation is enough for such differences to surface. Spend some time interviewing a parent, grandparent, or other member of an older generation. Then write an essay comparing and/or contrasting the dating practices of that generation with those of your own. Either along the way or in your conclusion, offer some analysis of why things have changed so much, and indicate whether you think this change is for the better.

Writing Assignment Combining Patterns of Development

3. With the "marriage market" as "brutally competitive" as Cohen asserts, many average people are turning to how-to books for advice on dating and romance. Write your own instructional guide, but one with a twist: a how *not*-to dating guide for today's singles. Adopt whatever tone you'd like, though a humorous one might be especially appropriate. No matter what areas you address, clearly present the *steps* that would ensure romantic failure. Along the way, provide vivid *examples* of what to avoid, indicating the possible *effects* of not following your advice.

Alex Wright

As director of User Experience and Product Research at *The New York Times*, Alex Wright (1966–) worked on creating the *Times*'s iPod app as well as on other interactive projects. He is the author of *Glut: Mastering Information Through the Ages* (2007) and of articles appearing in numerous publications, including Salon. com, *The Christian Science Monitor,* and *Utne Reader.* The following article appeared in the "Week in Review" section of *The New York Times* on December 2, 2007.

Pre-Reading Journal Entry

Most of us would say that making and keeping friends is an essential part of life. Think about your friends and others with whom you have relationships. How did you meet them? When and how did you realize that these specific relationships were important to you? How do you keep those relationships meaningful? Use your journal to answer these questions.

FRIENDING, ANCIENT OR OTHERWISE

1   The growing popularity of social networking sites like Facebook, MySpace and Second Life has thrust many of us into a new world where we make "friends" with people we barely know, scrawl messages on each other's walls and project our identities using totem-like visual symbols.

2   We're making up the rules as we go. But is this world as new as it seems?

3   Academic researchers are starting to examine that question by taking an unusual tack: exploring the parallels between online social networks and tribal societies. In the collective patter of profile-surfing, messaging and "friending," they see the resurgence of ancient patterns of oral communication.

4   "Orality is the base of all human experience," says Lance Strate, a communications professor at Fordham University and devoted MySpace user. He says he is convinced that the popularity of social networks stems from their appeal to deep-seated, prehistoric patterns of human communication. "We evolved with speech," he says. "We didn't evolve with writing."

5   The growth of social networks—and the Internet as a whole—stems largely from an outpouring of expression that often feels more like "talking" than writing: blog posts, comments, homemade videos and, lately, an outpouring of epigrammatic one-liners broadcast using services like Twitter and Facebook status updates (usually proving Gertrude Stein's[1] maxim that "literature is not remarks").

6   "If you examine the Web through the lens of orality, you can't help but see it everywhere," says Irwin Chen, a design instructor at Parsons who is developing a new course to explore the emergence of oral culture online. "Orality is participatory, interactive, communal and focused on the present. The Web is all of these things."

---

[1]Gertrude Stein (1874–1946), an American author who lived primarily in Paris, was known for her interest in Modernist art and writing (editors' note).

An early student of electronic orality was the Rev. Walter J. Ong, a professor at St. 7
Louis University and student of Marshall McLuhan[2] who coined the term "secondary
orality" in 1982 to describe the tendency of electronic media to echo the cadences
of earlier oral cultures. The work of Father Ong, who died in 2003, seems especially
prescient in light of the social-networking phenomenon. "Oral communication," as he
put it, "unites people in groups."

In other words, oral culture means more than just talking. There are subtler—and 8
perhaps more important—social dynamics at work.

Michael Wesch, who teaches cultural anthropology at Kansas State University, 9
spent two years living with a tribe in Papua New Guinea, studying how people forge
social relationships in a purely oral culture. Now he applies the same ethnographic
research methods to the rites and rituals of Facebook users.

"In tribal cultures, your identity is completely wrapped up in the question of how 10
people know you," he says. "When you look at Facebook, you can see the same pattern at work: people projecting their identities by demonstrating their relationships to
each other. You define yourself in terms of who your friends are."

In tribal societies, people routinely give each other jewelry, weapons and ritual 11
objects to cement their social ties. On Facebook, people accomplish the same thing by
trading symbolic sock monkeys, disco balls and hula girls.

"It's reminiscent of how people exchange gifts in tribal cultures," says Dr. Strate, 12
whose MySpace page lists his 1,335 "friends" along with his academic credentials and
his predilection for "Battlestar Galactica."

As intriguing as these parallels may be, they only stretch so far. There are big 13
differences between real oral cultures and the virtual kind. In tribal societies, forging
social bonds is a matter of survival; on the Internet, far less so. There is presumably no
tribal antecedent for popular Facebook rituals like "poking," virtual sheep-tossing or
drunk-dialing your friends.

Then there's the question of who really counts as a "friend." In tribal societies, 14
people develop bonds through direct, ongoing face-to-face contact. The Web eliminates
that need for physical proximity, enabling people to declare friendships on the basis of
otherwise flimsy connections.

"With social networks, there's a fascination with intimacy because it simulates face- 15
to-face communication," Dr. Wesch says. "But there's also this fundamental distance.
That distance makes it safe for people to connect through weak ties where they can
have the appearance of a connection because it's safe."

And while tribal cultures typically engage in highly formalized rituals, social net- 16
works seem to encourage a level of casualness and familiarity that would be unthink-
able in traditional oral cultures. "Secondary orality has a leveling effect," Dr. Strate
says. "In a primary oral culture, you would probably refer to me as 'Dr. Strate,' but on
MySpace, everyone calls me 'Lance.' "

As more of us shepherd our social relationships online, will this leveling effect be- 17
gin to shape the way we relate to each other in the offline world as well? Dr. Wesch,
for one, says he worries that the rise of secondary orality may have a paradoxical consequence: "It may be gobbling up what's left of our real oral culture."

---

[2]The Canadian philosopher Herbert Marshall McLuhan (1911–1980), a pioneer in
the field of communication theory, coined the phrase "The medium is the message"
(editors' note).

18   The more time we spend "talking" online, the less time we spend, well, talking. And as we stretch the definition of a friend to encompass people we may never actually meet, will the strength of our real-world friendships grow diluted as we immerse ourselves in a lattice of hyperlinked "friends"?

19   Still, the sheer popularity of social networking seems to suggest that for many, these environments strike a deep, perhaps even primal chord. "They fulfill our need to be recognized as human beings, and as members of a community," Dr. Strate says. "We all want to be told: You exist."

Questions for Close Reading

1. What is the selection's thesis? Locate the sentence(s) in which Wright states his main idea. If he doesn't state his thesis explicitly, express it in your own words.

2. What fundamental need, in Wright's view, do social networks seem designed to satisfy? How successful are they in meeting this need?

3. To what other type of human community are academics comparing online social networks, according to Wright? Why? According to researchers, what is the importance of oral communication in any human group?

4. Why should we be concerned about the "growing popularity" of social networking sites, according to Wright's article?

Questions About the Writer's Craft

1. **The pattern.** Does Wright use the one-side-at-a-time or the point-by-point method to compare and contrast the two communities he is discussing? What specific points does he discuss in his analysis? How does he say the groups are similar? How does he say they are different?

2. Throughout his article, Wright relies on outside sources for evidence. What is the primary type of outside evidence that he uses? Give at least two examples. How effective is this evidence in supporting his thesis?

3. **Other patterns.** Wright uses the term *friend* seven times in the article. How does he *define* this term? How important is the use of definition in the essay? Why? Wright also uses *cause-effect* (17 and 18). What key term signals this pattern of development? What cause(s) and effect(s) does he discuss?

4. What strategy does Wright use to conclude his article? (To review strategies for conclusions, see pages 69–70.) How does the conclusion relate to his thesis?

Writing Assignments Using Comparison-Contrast as a Pattern of Development

1. Wright sees social networking sites as ways to communicate. Think of some other ways in which people communicate and the different kinds of communications for

which these methods might be suited. For example, how would you suggest vacation plans to a friend? Make an appointment to see an instructor? End a romantic relationship? Choose three communication methods, and write an essay comparing and contrasting how effective they are for conveying information, ideas, and feelings to other people. Your essay can be serious or light in tone.

2. Online social networks, such as *Facebook,* have made it possible for us to have "friendships" with people we never, or hardly ever, see. In the same way, the Internet has made it easy for us to engage in other kinds of long-distance activities—buying items from stores we never enter, taking classes with instructors we never meet, even consulting with attorneys we never see in person. Write an essay in which you compare and contrast the advantages and disadvantages of engaging in a specific online activity with those of pursuing the same activity in a more traditional way.

Writing Assignment Combining Patterns of Development

3. Wright's essay focuses on the purely social functions of networks such as *Facebook* and *Twitter.* Social network sites collect a lot of personal information about their subscribers, however, and some companies have sought ways to use that information for commercial purposes—to sell products and services. Some social network subscribers welcome the opportunity to learn about specific products matched to their tastes. Others argue that a network's commercial use of subscribers' personal data amounts to an unacceptable invasion of privacy. Do some online research on this subject. Then write an essay in which you *argue* one side of the issue, giving *examples* from personal experience or evidence from experts to support your arguments.

ADDITIONAL WRITING TOPICS: COMPARISON-CONTRAST

General Assignments

Using comparison-contrast, develop one of these topics into an essay.

1. Living at home versus living in an apartment or dorm

2. Two-career family versus one-career family

3. Children's pastimes today and yesterday

4. Neighborhood stores versus shopping malls

5. A sports team then and now

6. Watching a movie on television versus viewing it in a theater

7. Two approaches to parenting

8. Two approaches to studying

9. Marriage versus living together

10. Talking on the phone versus texting

Assignments Using Visuals

Use the suggested visuals to help develop a comparison-contrast essay on one of these topics:

1. Divorce rates of those who marry in their twenties and in their thirties (charts)

2. Owning and maintaining a small versus a large vehicle (photos or Web links)

3. Making choices about diet and/or exercise (graphs and/or cartoons)

4. Advantages and disadvantages of a career in health care (slide show)

5. Working in a fast-food versus a fine dining restaurant (charts)

Assignments with a Specific Purpose, Audience, and Point of View

1. **Academic life.** You would like to change your campus living arrangements. Perhaps you want to move from a dormitory to an off-campus apartment or from home to a dorm. Before you do, though, you'll have to convince your parents (who are paying most of your college costs) that the move will be beneficial. Write out what you would say to your parents. Contrast your current situation with your proposed one, explaining why the new arrangement would be better.

2. **Academic life.** Write a guide on "Passing Exams" for first-year college students, contrasting the right and wrong ways to prepare for and take exams. Although your purpose is basically serious, write the section on how *not* to approach exams with some humor.

3. **Civic activity.** As president of your local neighbors' association, you're concerned about the way your local government is dealing with a particular situation (for example, an increase in robberies, muggings, graffiti, and so on). Write a letter to your mayor contrasting the way your local government handles the situation with another city or town's approach. In your conclusion, point out the advantages of adopting the other neighborhood's strategy.

4. **Civic activity.** Your old high school has invited you back to make a speech before an audience of seniors. The topic will be "how to choose the college that is right for you." Write your speech in the form of a comparison-contrast analysis. Focus on the choices available (two-year versus four-year schools, large versus small, local versus faraway, and so on), showing the advantages and/or disadvantages of each.

5. **Workplace action.** As a store manager, you decide to write a memo to all sales personnel explaining how to keep customers happy. Compare and/or contrast

the needs and shopping habits of several different consumer groups (by age, spending ability, or sex), and show how to make each group comfortable in your store.

6. **Workplace action.** You work as a volunteer for a mental health hot line. Many people call simply because they feel "stressed out." Do some research on the subject of stress management, and prepare a brochure for these people, recommending a "Type B" approach to stressful situations. Focus the brochure on the contrast between "Type A" and "Type B" personalities: the former is nervous, hard-driving, competitive; the latter is relaxed and noncompetitive. Give specific examples of how each "type" tends to act in stressful situations.

Cause-Effect

In this chapter, you will learn:

16.1 To use the pattern of cause-effect to develop your essays
16.2 To consider how cause-effect can fit your purpose and audience
16.3 To develop prewriting, writing, and revision strategies for using cause-effect in an essay
16.4 To analyze how cause-effect is used effectively in one student-written and three professionally authored selections
16.5 To write your own essays using cause-effect as a strategy

What Is Cause-Effect?

Science, technology, history, and much of our literature, as well as our fascination with the past and the future, all spring from our determination to know "Why" and "What if." All of us think in terms of cause and effect, sometimes consciously, sometimes unconsciously: "Why did they give me such an odd look?" we wonder. This exploration of reasons and results is also at the heart of most professions: "What might these symptoms indicate?" physicians ask; "Will these methods yield the desired result?" educators ask.

Cause-effect writing, often called **causal analysis,** is rooted in this elemental need to make connections. Because the drive to understand reasons and results is so fundamental, causal analysis is a common kind of writing. An article analyzing the unexpected outcome of an election and an editorial analyzing the impact of a proposed tax cut are both examples of cause-effect writing.

Done well, cause-effect pieces uncover the subtle and often surprising connections between events or phenomena. By rooting out causes and projecting

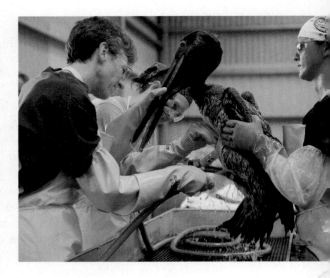

effects, causal analysis enables us to make sense of our experiences, revealing a world that is somewhat less arbitrary and chaotic.

How Cause-Effect Fits Your Purpose and Audience

Many assignments and exam questions in college involve writing essays that analyze causes, effects, or both. Sometimes, as in the following examples, you'll be asked to write an essay developed primarily through the cause-effect pattern:

> Although divorces have leveled off in the past few years, the number of marriages ending in divorce is still greater than it was a generation ago. What do you think are the causes of this phenomenon?

> Americans never seem to tire of gossip about the rich and famous. What effect has this fascination with celebrities had on American culture?

Other assignments and exam questions may not explicitly ask you to address causes and effects, but they may use words that suggest causal analysis would be appropriate. Consider these examples, paying special attention to the italicized words:

Cause

> In contrast to the socially involved youth of the 1960s, many young people today tend to remove themselves from political issues. What do you think are the *sources* of the political apathy found among 18- to 25-year-olds?

Effect

> A number of experts forecast that drug abuse will be the most significant factor affecting American productivity in the coming decade. Evaluate the validity of this observation by discussing the *impact* of drugs on the workplace.

Cause and Effect

> According to school officials, a predictable percentage of entering students drop out of college at some point during their first year. What *motivates* students to drop out? What *happens* to them once they leave?

In addition to serving as the primary strategy for achieving an essay's purpose, causal analysis can also be a supplemental method used to help make a point in an essay developed chiefly through another pattern of development. Assume, for example, that you want to write an essay *defining* the term *the homeless*. To help readers see that unfavorable circumstances can result in nearly anyone becoming homeless, you might discuss some of the unavoidable, everyday factors causing people to live on streets and in subway stations. Similarly, in a *persuasive* proposal urging your college administration to institute an honors program, you would probably spend some time analyzing the positive effects of such a program on students and faculty.

Prewriting Strategies

The following checklist shows how you can apply cause-effect to some of the prewriting techniques discussed in Chapter 2.

☑ **CAUSE-EFFECT: A PREWRITING CHECKLIST**

Choose a Topic

☐ Do your journal entries reflect an ongoing interest in the causes of and/or effects of something?

☐ Will you analyze a personal phenomenon, a change at your college, a nationwide trend, or a historical event?

☐ Does your subject intrigue, anger, puzzle you? Is it likely to interest your readers as well?

Make Sure the Topic Is Manageable

☐ Can you tackle your subject—especially if it's a social trend or historical event—in the number of pages allotted?

☐ Can you gather enough information for your analysis? Does the topic require library research? Do you have time for such research?

☐ Will you examine causes, effects, or both? Will your topic still be manageable if you discuss both causes and effects?

Identify Your Purpose, Audience, Tone, and Point of View

☐ Is the purpose of your causal analysis to inform? To persuade? To speculate about possibilities? Do you want to combine purposes?

☐ Given your purpose and audience, what tone and point of view should you adopt?

Use Individual and Group Brainstorming, Mapping, and/or Freewriting to Explore Causes and Effects

☐ *Causes:* What happened? What are the possible reasons? Which are most likely? Who was involved? Why?

☐ *Effects:* What happened? Who was involved? What were the observable results? What are some possible future consequences? Which consequences are negative? Which are positive?

Strategies for Using Cause-Effect in an Essay

After prewriting, you're ready to draft your essay. The following suggestions and Figure 16.1 will be helpful whether you use causal analysis as a dominant or supportive pattern of development.

FIGURE 16.1

Development Diagram: Writing a Cause-Effect Essay

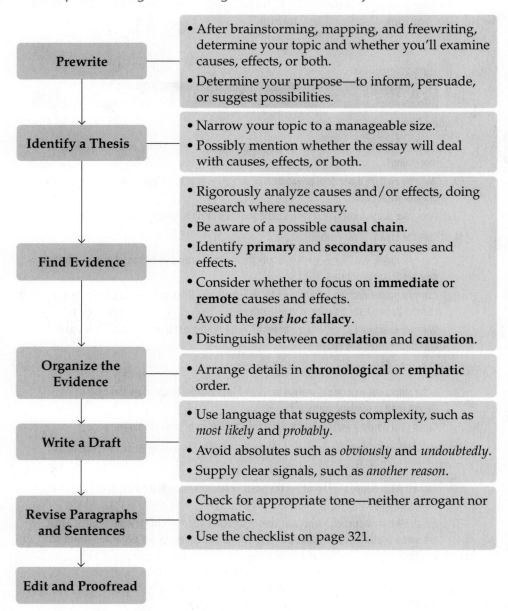

Prewrite
- After brainstorming, mapping, and freewriting, determine your topic and whether you'll examine causes, effects, or both.
- Determine your purpose—to inform, persuade, or suggest possibilities.

Identify a Thesis
- Narrow your topic to a manageable size.
- Possibly mention whether the essay will deal with causes, effects, or both.

Find Evidence
- Rigorously analyze causes and/or effects, doing research where necessary.
- Be aware of a possible **causal chain**.
- Identify **primary** and **secondary** causes and effects.
- Consider whether to focus on **immediate** or **remote** causes and effects.
- Avoid the *post hoc* **fallacy**.
- Distinguish between **correlation** and **causation**.

Organize the Evidence
- Arrange details in **chronological** or **emphatic** order.

Write a Draft
- Use language that suggests complexity, such as *most likely* and *probably*.
- Avoid absolutes such as *obviously* and *undoubtedly*.
- Supply clear signals, such as *another reason*.

Revise Paragraphs and Sentences
- Check for appropriate tone—neither arrogant nor dogmatic.
- Use the checklist on page 321.

Edit and Proofread

1. **Stay focused on the purpose of your analysis.** When writing a causal analysis, don't lose sight of your overall purpose. Consider, for example, an essay on the causes of widespread child abuse. If you're concerned primarily with explaining the problem of child abuse to your readers, you might take a purely *informative* approach:

   Although parental stress is the immediate cause of child abuse, the more compelling reason for such behavior lies in the way parents were themselves mistreated as children.

   Or you might want to *persuade* your audience about some point or idea concerning child abuse:

   The tragic consequences of child abuse provide strong support for more aggressive handling of such cases by social workers and judges.

   Then again, you could choose a *speculative* approach, your main purpose being to suggest possibilities:

   Psychologists disagree about the potential effect on youngsters of all the media attention given to child abuse. Will children exposed to this media coverage grow up assertive, self-confident, and able to protect themselves? Or will they become fearful and distrustful?

   These examples illustrate that an essay's causal analysis may have more than one purpose. For instance, although the last example points to a paper with a primarily speculative purpose, the essay would probably start by informing readers of experts' conflicting views. The paper would also have a persuasive slant if it ended by urging readers to complain to the media about their sensationalized treatment of the child-abuse issue.

2. **Adapt content and tone to your purpose and readers.** Your purpose and audience determine what supporting material and what tone will be most effective in a cause-effect essay. Assume you want to direct your essay on child abuse to general readers who know little about the subject. To *inform* readers, you might use facts, statistics, and expert opinion to provide an objective discussion of the causes of child abuse. Your analysis might show the following: (1) adults who were themselves mistreated as children tend to abuse their own offspring; (2) marital stress contributes to the mistreatment of children; and (3) certain personality disorders increase the likelihood of child abuse. Sensitive to what your readers would and wouldn't understand, you would stay away from a technical or formal tone.

   Now imagine that your purpose is to *convince* future social workers that the failure of social service agencies to act authoritatively in child-abuse cases often has tragic consequences. Hoping to encourage more responsible behavior in the prospective social workers, you would adopt a more emotional tone in the essay, perhaps citing wrenching case histories that dramatize what happens when child abuse isn't taken seriously.

3. **Think rigorously about causes and effects.** Cause-effect relationships are usually complex. To write a meaningful analysis, you should do some careful thinking about your subject. (The two sets of questions at the end of this chapter's Prewriting Checklist [page 315] will help you think creatively about causes and effects.)

If you look beyond the obvious, you'll discover that a cause may have many effects. In the same way, an effect may have multiple causes.

Your analysis may also uncover a **causal chain** in which one cause (or effect) brings about another, that, in turn, brings about another, and so on. Don't grapple with so complex a chain, however, that you become hopelessly entangled. If your subject involves multiple causes and effects, limit what you'll discuss. Identify which causes and effects are *primary* and which are *secondary*. How extensively you cover secondary factors will depend on your purpose and audience.

Similarly, decide whether to focus on *immediate,* more obvious causes and effects, or on less obvious, more *remote* ones. Or perhaps you need to focus on both. It may be more difficult to explore more remote causes and effects, but it can also lead to more original and revealing essays. Thoughtful analyses take these less obvious considerations into account.

When developing a causal analysis, be careful to avoid the **post hoc fallacy.** Named after the Latin phrase *post hoc, ergo propter hoc,* meaning "after this, therefore because of this," this kind of faulty thinking occurs when you assume that simply because one event *followed* another, the first event *caused* the second. For example, if the Republicans win a majority of seats in Congress and, several months later, the economy collapses, can you conclude that the Republicans caused the collapse? A quick assumption of "Yes" fails the test of logic, for the timing of events could be coincidental and not indicative of any cause-effect relationship. The collapse may have been triggered by uncontrolled inflation that began well before the congressional elections. (For more on *post hoc* thinking, see page 398 in Chapter 18.)

Also, be careful not to mistake *correlation* for *causation.* Two events correlate when they occur at about the same time. Such co-occurrence, however, doesn't guarantee a cause-effect relationship. For instance, while the number of ice cream cones eaten and the instances of heat prostration both increase during the summer months, this doesn't mean that eating ice cream causes heat prostration! A third factor—in this case, summer heat—is the actual cause. When writing causal analyses, then, use with caution words that imply a causal link (such as *therefore* and *because*). Words that express simply time of occurrence (*following* and *previously*) are safer and more objective.

Finally, keep in mind that a rigorous causal analysis involves more than loose generalizations about causes and effects. Creating plausible connections may require library research, interviewing, or both. Often you'll need to provide facts, statistics, details, personal observations, or other corroborative material if readers are going to accept the reasoning behind your analysis.

4. **Write a thesis that focuses the paper on causes, effects, or both.** The thesis in an essay developed through causal analysis often indicates whether the essay will deal mostly with causes, effects, or both. Here, for example, are three thesis statements for causal analyses dealing with the public school system. You'll see that each thesis signals that essay's particular emphasis:

Causes

Our school system has been weakened by an overemphasis on trendy electives.

Effects

An ineffectual school system has led to crippling teachers' strikes and widespread disrespect for the teaching profession.

Causes and Effects

Bureaucratic inefficiency has created a school system unresponsive to children's emotional, physical, and intellectual needs.

Note that the thesis statement—in addition to signaling whether the paper will discuss causes or effects or both—may also point to the essay's plan of development. Consider the last thesis statement; it makes clear that the paper will discuss children's emotional needs first, their physical needs second, and their intellectual needs last.

The thesis statement in a causal analysis doesn't have to specify whether the essay will discuss causes, effects, or both. Nor does the thesis have to be worded in such a way that the essay's plan of development is apparent. But when first writing cause-effect essays, you may find that a highly focused thesis will help keep your analysis on track.

5. **Choose an organizational pattern.** There are two basic ways to organize the points in a cause-effect essay: you may use a chronological or an emphatic sequence. If you select *chronological order,* you discuss causes and effects in the order in which they occur or will occur.

Chronology might also be used to organize a discussion about effects. Imagine you want to write an essay about the need to guard against disrupting delicate balances in the country's wildlife. You might start the essay by discussing what happened when the starling, a non-native bird, was introduced into the American environment. Because the starling had few natural predators, the starling population soared out of control; the starlings took over food sources and habitats of native species; the bluebird, a native species, declined and is now threatened with extinction.

Although a chronological pattern can be an effective way to organize material, a strict time sequence can present a problem if your primary cause or effect ends up buried in the middle of the sequence. In such a case, you might use *emphatic order,* saving the most important point for last.

Emphatic order is an especially effective way to sequence cause-effect points when readers hold what, in your opinion, are mistaken or narrow views about a subject. To encourage readers to look more closely at the issues, you present what you consider the erroneous or obvious views first, show why they are unsound or limited, then present what you feel to be the actual causes and effects. Such a sequence nudges the audience into giving further thought to the causes and effects you have discovered. Here is an informal outline for a causal analysis using this approach:

Subject: The effects of campus crime

1. Immediate problems
   a. Students feel insecure and fearful.
   b. Many nighttime campus activities have been curtailed.
2. More significant long-term problems
   a. Unfavorable publicity about campus crime will affect future student enrollment.
   b. Unfavorable publicity about campus crime will make it difficult to recruit top-notch faculty.

When using emphatic order, you might want to word the thesis in such a way that it signals which point your essay will stress. Look at the following thesis statements:

Although many immigrants arrive in this country without marketable skills, their most pressing problem is learning how to make their way in a society whose language they don't know.

The space program has led to dramatic advances in computer technology and medical science. Even more importantly, though, the program has helped change many people's attitudes toward the planet we live on.

These thesis statements reflect an awareness of the complex nature of cause-effect relationships. Although not dismissing secondary issues, the statements establish which points the writer considers most noteworthy. The second thesis, for instance, indicates that the paper will touch on the technological and medical advances made possible by the space program but will emphasize the way the program has changed people's attitudes toward the earth.

Whether you use a chronological or emphatic pattern to organize your essay, you'll need to provide clear *signals* to identify when you're discussing causes and when you're discussing effects. Expressions such as "Another reason" and "A final outcome" help readers follow your line of thought.

6. **Use language that hints at the complexity of cause-effect relationships.** Because it's difficult—if not impossible—to identify causes and effects with certainty, you

should avoid such absolutes as, "It must be obvious" and "There is no doubt." Instead, try phrases such as, "Most likely" or "It is probable." Such language isn't indecisive; it's reasonable and reflects your understanding of the often tangled nature of causes and effects. Don't, however, go to the other extreme and be reluctant to take a stand on the issues. If you have thought carefully about causes and effects, you have a right to state your analysis with conviction.

Revision Strategies

Once you have a draft of the essay, you're ready to revise. The following checklist will help you and those giving you feedback apply to cause-effect writing some of the revision techniques discussed in Chapters 7 and 8.

✔ CAUSE-EFFECT: A REVISION/PEER REVIEW CHECKLIST

Revise Overall Meaning and Structure

- ☐ Is the essay's purpose informative, persuasive, speculative, or a combination of these?
- ☐ What is the essay's thesis? Is it stated specifically or implied? Where? Could it be made any clearer? How?
- ☐ Does the essay focus on causes, effects, or both? How do you know?
- ☐ Where has correlation been mistaken for causation? Where is the essay weakened by *post hoc* thinking?
- ☐ Where does the essay distinguish between primary and secondary causes and effects? How do the most critical causes and effects receive special attention?
- ☐ Where does the essay dwell on the obvious?

Revise Paragraph Development

- ☐ Are the essay's paragraphs sequenced chronologically or emphatically? Could they be sequenced more effectively? How?
- ☐ Where would signal devices (such as *afterward, before, then*, and *next*) make it easier to follow the progression of thought within and between paragraphs?
- ☐ Which paragraphs would be strengthened by vivid examples (such as statistics, facts, anecdotes, or personal observations) that support the causal analysis?

Revise Sentences and Words

- ☐ Where do expressions like *as a result, because*, and *therefore* mislead the reader by implying a cause-effect relationship? Would words such as *following* and *previously* eliminate the problem?
- ☐ Do any words or phrases convey an arrogant or dogmatic tone (*there is no question, undoubtedly, always, never*)? What other expressions (*most likely, probably*) would improve credibility?

Student Essay: From Prewriting Through Revision

The student essay that follows was written by Carl Novack in response to this assignment:

> In "The Body Piercing Project," Josie Appleton explores the popularity of piercings and tattoos—an area in which many people's attitudes have dramatically changed over the years. Identify a significant shift in an activity, practice, or institution. Then write an essay in which you discuss the factors that you believe are responsible for the attitudinal change.

After deciding to write about Americans' changing food habits, Carl used the *mapping technique* to generate material on his subject. His map is shown on the next page. The marks in color indicate Carl's later efforts to organize and elaborate the original map. Note that he added some branches, eliminated others, drew arrows indicating that some topics should be moved, and changed the wording of some key ideas. These annotations paved the way for Carl's topic outline, which is presented below.

Outline

Thesis: America has changed and so has what we Americans eat and how we eat.

   I. We used to eat "All-American" meals.
      A. Heavy
      B. Meat-based

  II. Now our tastes are more international.
      A. Lighter—yogurt
      B. Less meat—pita sandwiches, quiches, tacos

 III. There are several reasons for our tastes becoming more international.
      A. Television
      B. Travel abroad
      C. Immigrants in this country

 IV. Two social trends have also changed how and what we eat.
      A. Health consciousness
          1. Concern about weight
          2. Concern about salt, fat, fiber, additives
             a. Changes in packaged foods (lunch meat, canned vegetables, soups)
             b. Changes in restaurants (salad bars)
      B. More women working outside the home because of the economy and the women's movement
          1. Increase in fast-food restaurants
          2. More frozen foods, some even gourmet

Mapping

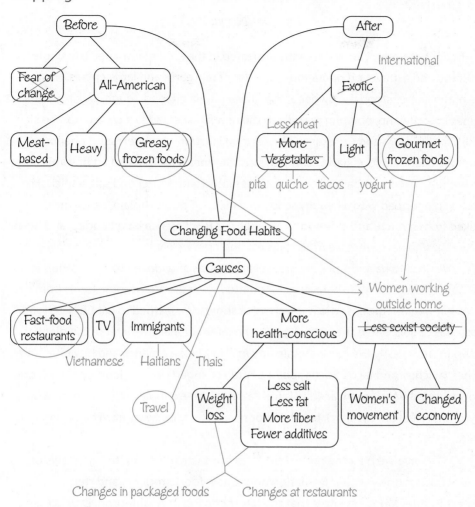

Now read Carl's paper, "Americans and Food," noting the similarities and differences among his map, outline, and final essay. See, for example, how the diagram suggests a "before" and "after" contrast—a contrast the essay develops. Also note Carl's decision to move "frozen foods" and "fast-food restaurants" to the "women working outside home" section of the diagram. This decision is reflected in the outline and in the final essay, where frozen foods and fast-food restaurants are discussed in the same paragraph. As you read the essay, also consider how well it applies the principles of causal analysis discussed in this chapter. (The commentary that follows the paper will help you look at Carl's essay more closely and will give you some sense of how he went about revising his first draft.)

Americans and Food
by Carl Novack

Introduction

An offbeat but timely cartoon recently appeared in the local newspaper. The single   1
panel showed a gravel-pit operation with piles of raw earth and large cranes. Next to
one of the cranes stood the owner of the gravel pit—a grizzled, tough-looking character, hammer in hand, pointing proudly to the new sign he had just tacked up. The sign
read, "Fred's Fill Dirt and Croissants." The cartoon illustrates an interesting phenomenon: the changing food habits of Americans. Our meals used to consist of something
like home-cooked pot roast, mashed potatoes laced with butter and salt, a thick slice
of apple pie topped with a healthy scoop of vanilla ice cream—plain, heavy meals,

Thesis

cooked from scratch, and eaten leisurely at home. But America has changed, and because it has, so have what we Americans eat and how we eat it.

We used to have simple, unsophisticated tastes and looked with suspicion at   2
anything more exotic than hamburger. Admittedly, we did adopt some foods from the

Topic sentence:
Background
paragraph

various immigrant groups who flocked to our shores. We learned to eat Chinese food,
pizza, and bagels. But in the last few years, the international character of our diet has
grown tremendously. We can walk into any mall in Middle America and buy pita sand-
wiches, quiches, and tacos. Such foods are often changed on their journey from exotic
imports to ordinary "American" meals (no Pakistani, for example, eats frozen-on-a-stick
boysenberry-flavored yogurt), but the imports are still a long way from hamburger on
a bun.

Topic sentence:
Three causes answer
the question

Why have we become more worldly in our tastes? For one thing, television   3
blankets the country with information about new food products and trends.

First cause

Viewers in rural Montana know that the latest craving in Washington, D.C., is Cajun
cooking or that something called tofu is now available in the local supermarket.
Another reason for the growing international flavor of our food is that many young

Second cause

Americans have traveled abroad and gotten hooked on new tastes and flavors.
Backpacking students and young professionals vacationing in Europe come home
with cravings for authentic French bread or German beer. Finally, continuing waves

Third cause

of immigrants settle in the cities where many of us live, causing significant changes
in what we eat. Vietnamese, Haitians, and Thais, for instance, bring their native
foods and cooking styles with them and eventually open small markets or restaurants. In time, the new food will become Americanized enough to take its place in
our national diet.

4   Our growing concern with health has also affected the way we eat. For the last *Topic sentence: Another cause*
few years, the media have warned us about the dangers of our traditional diet, high
in salt and fat, low in fiber. The media also began to educate us about the dangers of
processed foods pumped full of chemical additives. As a result, consumers began to *Start of a causal chain*
demand healthier foods, and manufacturers started to change some of their products.
Many foods, such as lunch meat, canned vegetables, and soups, were made available
in low-fat, low-sodium versions. Whole-grain cereals and high-fiber breads also began
to appear on the grocery shelves. Moreover, the food industry started to produce all-
natural products—everything from potato chips to ice cream—without additives and
preservatives. Not surprisingly, the restaurant industry responded to this switch to
healthier foods, luring customers with salad bars, broiled fish, and steamed vegetables.

5   Our food habits are being affected, too, by the rapid increase in the number of *Topic sentence: Another cause*
women working outside the home. Sociologists and other experts believe that two
important factors triggered this phenomenon: the women's movement and a changing economic climate. Women were assured that it was acceptable, even rewarding,
to work outside the home; many women also discovered that they had to work just
to keep up with the cost of living. As the traditional role of homemaker changed, so
did the way families ate. With Mom working, there wasn't time for her to prepare the
traditional three square meals a day. Instead, families began looking for alternatives to
provide quick meals. What was the result? For one thing, there was a boom in fast-food *Start of a causal chain*
restaurants. The suburban or downtown strip that once contained a lone McDonald's
now features Wendy's, Taco Bell, Burger King, and Pizza Hut. Families also began to depend on frozen foods as another time-saving alternative. Once again, though, demand
changed the kind of frozen food available. Frozen foods no longer consist of foil trays
divided into greasy fried chicken, watery corn niblets, and lumpy mashed potatoes.
Supermarkets now stock a range of supposedly gourmet frozen dinners—from fettu-
cini in cream sauce to braised beef en brochette.

6   It may not be possible to pick up a ton of fill dirt and a half-dozen croissants at *Conclusion*
the same place, but America's food habits are definitely changing. If it is true that "you
are what you eat," then America's identity is evolving along with its diet.

Commentary

Title and Introduction

Asked to prepare a paper analyzing the reasons behind a change in our lives, Carl
decided to write about a shift he had noticed in Americans' eating habits. The title

of the essay, "Americans and Food," identifies Carl's subject but could be livelier and more interesting.

Despite his rather uninspired title, Carl starts his *causal analysis* in an engaging way—with the vivid description of a cartoon. He then connects the cartoon to his subject with the following sentence: "The cartoon illustrates an interesting phenomenon: the changing food habits of Americans." To back up his belief that there has been a revolution in our eating habits, Carl uses the first paragraph to summarize the kind of meal that people used to eat. He then moves to his *thesis:* "But America has changed, and because it has, so have what we Americans eat and how we eat it." The thesis implies that Carl's paper will focus on both causes and effects.

Purpose

Carl's purpose was to write an *informative* causal analysis. But before he could present the causes of the change in eating habits, he needed to show that such a change had, in fact, taken place. He therefore uses the second paragraph to document one aspect of this change—the internationalization of our eating habits.

Topic Sentences

At the start of the third paragraph, Carl uses a question—"Why have we become more worldly in our tastes?"—to signal that his discussion of causes is about to begin. This question also serves as the paragraph's *topic sentence,* indicating that the paragraph will focus on reasons for the increasingly international flavor of our food. The next two paragraphs, also focused by topic sentences, identify two other major reasons for the change in eating habits: "Our growing concern with health has also affected the way we eat" (paragraph 4), and "Our food habits are being affected, too, by the rapid increase in the number of women working outside the home" (5).

Combining Patterns of Development

Carl draws on two patterns of development—*comparison-contrast* and *illustration*—to develop his causal analysis. At the heart of the essay is a basic *contrast* between the way we used to eat and the way we eat now. And throughout his essay, Carl provides convincing *examples* to demonstrate the validity of his points. Consider for a moment the third paragraph. Here Carl asserts that one reason for our new eating habits is our growing exposure to international foods. He then presents concrete evidence to show that we have indeed become more familiar with international cuisine: Television exposes rural Montana to Cajun cooking; students traveling abroad take a liking to French bread; urban dwellers enjoy the exotic fare served by numerous immigrant groups. The fourth and fifth paragraphs use similarly specific evidence (for example, "low-fat, low-sodium versions" of "lunch meat, canned vegetables, and soups") to illustrate the soundness of key ideas.

Causal Chains

Let's look more closely at the evidence in the essay. Not satisfied with obvious explanations, Carl thought through his ideas carefully and even brainstormed with friends to arrive at as comprehensive an analysis as possible. Not surprisingly, much of the evidence Carl uncovered took the form of *causal chains*. In the fourth paragraph, Carl writes, "The media also began to educate us about the dangers of processed foods pumped full of chemical additives. As a result, consumers began to demand healthier foods, and manufacturers started to change some of their products." And the next paragraph shows how the changing role of American women caused families to look for alternative ways of eating. This shift, in turn, caused the restaurant and food industries to respond with a wide range of food alternatives.

Making the Paper Easy to Follow

Although Carl's analysis digs beneath the surface and reveals complex cause-effect relationships, he wisely limits his pursuit of causal chains to *primary* causes and effects. He doesn't let the complexities distract him from his main purpose: to show why and how the American diet is changing. Carl is also careful to provide his essay with abundant *connecting devices*, making it easy for readers to see the links between points. Consider the use of *transitions* (signaled by italics) in the following sentences: "*Another* reason for the growing international flavor of our food is that many young Americans have traveled abroad" (paragraph 3); "*As a result,* consumers began to demand healthier foods" (4); and "*As* the traditional role of homemaker changed, so did the way families ate" (5).

A Problem with the Essay's Close

As you read the essay, you probably noticed that Carl's conclusion is a bit weak. Although his reference to the cartoon works well, the rest of the paragraph limps to a tired close. Ending an otherwise vigorous essay with such a slight conclusion undercuts the effectiveness of the whole paper. Carl spent so much energy developing the body of his essay that he ran out of the stamina needed to conclude the piece more forcefully. Careful budgeting of his time would have allowed him to prepare a stronger concluding paragraph.

Revising the First Draft

When Carl was ready to revise, during a peer review session he showed the first draft of his essay to several classmates who used a peer review worksheet customized by their instructor to focus their feedback. Carl jotted down their most helpful comments, numbered in order of importance, on his draft. Comparing Carl's original version of his fourth paragraph (shown below) with his final version in the essay will show you how he went about revising.

Original Version of the Fourth Paragraph

) First sentence
  cluttered, too long

(A growing concern with health has also affected the way we eat, especially because the media has sent us warnings the last few years about the dangers of salt, sugar, food additives, and high-fat and low-fiber diets.) We have started to worry that our traditional meals may have been shortening our lives. As a result, consumers demanded healthier foods and manufacturers started taking some of the salt and sugar out of canned foods. "All-natural" became an effective selling point, leading to many preservative-free products. Restaurants, too, adapted their menus, luring customers with light meals. Because we now know about the link between overweight and a variety of health problems, including heart attacks, we are counting calories. In turn, food companies made fortunes on diet beer and diet cola. Sometimes, though, we seem a bit confused about the health issue; we drink soda that is sugar-free but loaded with chemical sweeteners. Still, we believe we are lengthening our lives through changing our diets.

) Add specifics

) Doesn't fit point
  being made

On the advice of his peer reviewers, Carl decided to omit all references to the way our concern with weight has affected our eating habits. It's true, of course, that calorie-counting has changed how we eat. But as soon as Carl started to discuss this point, he got involved in a causal chain that undercut the paragraph's unity. He ended up describing the paradoxical situation in which we find ourselves: In an attempt to eat healthy, we stay away from sugar and turn to possibly harmful artificial sweeteners. This is an interesting issue, but it detracts from Carl's main point—that our concern with health has affected our eating habits in a *positive* way.

Carl's peer reviewers also pointed out that the fourth paragraph's first sentence contained too much material to be an effective topic sentence. Carl corrected the problem by breaking the overlong sentence into two short ones: "Our growing concern with health has also affected the way we eat. For the last few years, the media have warned us about the dangers of our traditional diet, high in salt and fat, low in fiber." The first of these sentences serves as a crisp topic sentence that focuses the rest of the paragraph.

Finally, when Carl heard the essay read aloud, he realized the fourth paragraph lacked convincing specifics. When revising, he changed "manufacturers started taking some of the salt and sugar out of canned foods" to the more specific "Many foods, such as lunch meat, canned vegetables, and soups, were made available in low-fat, low-sodium versions." Similarly, generalizations about "light meals" and "all-natural" products gained life through the addition of concrete examples: restaurants lured "customers with salad bars, broiled fish, and steamed vegetables," and the food industry produced "everything from potato chips to ice cream—without additives and preservatives."

Carl did an equally good job revising other sections of his paper. With the exception of the weak spots already discussed, he made the changes needed to craft a well-reasoned essay, one that demonstrates his ability to analyze a complex phenomenon.

ACTIVITIES: CAUSE-EFFECT

Prewriting Activities

1. Imagine you're writing two essays: One proposes the need for high school courses in personal finance (how to budget money, balance a checkbook, and the like); the other explains how to show appreciation. Jot down ways you might use cause-effect in each essay.

2. Use mapping, collaborative brainstorming, or another prewriting technique to generate possible causes or effects for *one* of the following topics. Then organize your raw material into a brief outline, with related causes and effects grouped in the same section.

   a. Pressure on students to do well

   b. Being physically fit

   c. Spiraling costs of a college education

3. For the topic you selected in activity 2, note the two potential audiences indicated below in parentheses. For each audience, devise a thesis and decide whether your essay's purpose would be informative, persuasive, speculative, or some combination of these. Then, with your thesis statements and purposes in mind, review the outline you prepared for the preceding activity. How would you change it to fit each audience? What points should be added? What points would be primary causes and effects for one audience but secondary for the other? Which organizational pattern—chronological, spatial, or emphatic—would be most effective for each audience?

   a. Pressure on students to do well (*college students, parents of elementary school children*)

   b. Being physically fit (*those who show a reasonable degree of concern, those who are obsessed with being fit*)

   c. Spiraling costs of a college education (*college officials, high school students planning to attend college*)

Revising Activities

4. Explain how the following statements demonstrate *post hoc* thinking and confuse correlation and cause-effect.

   a. Our city now has many immigrants from Latin American countries. The crime rate in our city has increased. Latin American immigrants are the cause of the crime wave.

   b. The divorce rate has skyrocketed. More women are working outside the home than ever before. Working outside the home destroys marriages.

   c. A high percentage of people in Dixville have developed cancer. The landfill, used by XYZ Industries, has been located in Dixville for twenty years. The XYZ landfill has caused cancer in Dixville residents.

5. The following paragraph is from the first draft of an essay arguing that technological advances can diminish the quality of life. How solid is the paragraph's causal analysis? Which causes or effects should be eliminated? Where is the analysis simplistic? Where does the writer make absolute claims even though cause-effect relationships are no more than a possibility? Keeping these questions in mind, revise the paragraph.

> How did the banking industry respond to inflation? It simply introduced a new technology—the automated teller machine (ATM). By making money more available to the average person, the ATM gives people the cash to buy inflated goods—whether or not they can afford them. Not surprisingly, automated teller machines have had a number of negative consequences for the average individual. Since people know they can get cash at any time, they use their lunch hours for something other than going to the bank. How do they spend this newfound time? They go shopping, and machine-vended money means more impulse buying, even more than with a credit card. Also, because people don't need their checkbooks to withdraw money, they can't keep track of their accounts and therefore develop a casual attitude toward financial matters. It's no wonder children don't appreciate the value of money. Another problem is that people who would never dream of robbing a bank try to trick the machine into dispensing money "for free." There's no doubt that this kind of fraud contributes to the immoral climate in the country.

PROFESSIONAL SELECTIONS: CAUSE-EFFECT

Stephen King

Probably the best-known living horror writer, Stephen King (1947–) is the author of more than thirty books. Much of King's prolific output has been adapted for the screen. In *On Writing: A Memoir of the Craft* (2000), King offers insight into the writing process and examines the role that writing has played in his own life—especially following a near-fatal accident in 1999. King lives with his family in Bangor, Maine. The following essay first appeared in *Playboy* in 1982.

For ideas on how this cause-effect essay is organized, see Figure 16.2 on page 333.

Pre-Reading Journal Entry

Several forms of entertainment, besides horror movies, are highly popular despite what many consider a low level of quality. In your journal, list as many "lowbrow" forms of entertainment as you can. Possibilities include professional wrestling, aggressive video games, Internet chat rooms, and so on. Review your list, and respond to the following question in your journal: What is it about each form of entertainment that attracts such popularity—and inspires such criticism?

WHY WE CRAVE HORROR MOVIES

1   I think that we're all mentally ill: those of us outside the asylums only hide it a little better—and maybe not all that much better, after all. We've all known people who talk to themselves, people who sometimes squinch their faces into horrible grimaces when they believe no one is watching, people who have some hysterical fear—of snakes, the dark, the tight place, the long drop...and, of course, those final worms and grubs that are waiting so patiently underground.

2   When we pay our four or five bucks and seat ourselves at tenth-row center in a theater showing a horror movie, we are daring the nightmare.

3   Why? Some of the reasons are simple and obvious. To show that we can, that we are not afraid, that we can ride this roller coaster. Which is not to say that a really good horror movie may not surprise a scream out of us at some point, the way we may scream when the roller coaster twists through a complete 360 or plows through a lake at the bottom of the drop. And horror movies, like roller coasters, have always been the special province of the young; by the time one turns 40 or 50, one's appetite for double twists or 360-degree loops may be considerably depleted.

4   We also go to re-establish our feelings of essential normality; the horror movie is innately conservative, even reactionary. Freda Jackson as the horrible melting woman in *Die, Monster, Die!* confirms for us that no matter how far we may be removed from the beauty of a Robert Redford or a Diana Ross, we are still light-years from true ugliness.

5   And we go to have fun.

6   Ah, but this is where the ground starts to slope away, isn't it? Because this is a very peculiar sort of fun indeed. The fun comes from seeing others menaced—sometimes killed. One critic has suggested that if pro football has become the voyeur's version of combat, then the horror film has become the modern version of the public lynching.

7   It is true that the mythic, "fairytale" horror film intends to take away the shades of gray....It urges us to put away our more civilized and adult penchant for analysis and to become children again, seeing things in pure blacks and whites. It may be that horror movies provide psychic relief on this level because this invitation to lapse into simplicity, irrationality and even outright madness is extended so rarely. We are told we may allow our emotions a free rein...or no rein at all.

8   If we are all insane, then sanity becomes a matter of degree. If your insanity leads you to carve up women like Jack the Ripper or the Cleveland Torso Murderer, we clap you away in the funny farm (but neither of those two amateur-night surgeons was ever caught, heh-heh-heh); if, on the other hand your insanity leads you only to talk to yourself when you're under stress or to pick your nose on the morning bus, then you are left alone to go about your business...though it is doubtful that you will ever be invited to the best parties.

9   The potential lyncher is in almost all of us (excluding saints, past and present; but then, most saints have been crazy in their own ways), and every now and then, he has to be let loose to scream and roll around in the grass. Our emotions and our fears form their own body, and we recognize that it demands its own exercise to maintain proper muscle tone. Certain of these emotional muscles are accepted—even exalted—in civilized society; they are, of course, the emotions that tend to maintain the status quo of civilization itself. Love, friendship, loyalty, kindness—these are all

the emotions that we applaud, emotions that have been immortalized in the couplets of Hallmark cards....

When we exhibit these emotions, society showers us with positive reinforcement; we learn this even before we get out of diapers. When, as children, we hug our rotten little puke of a sister and give her a kiss, all the aunts and uncles smile and twit and cry, "Isn't he the sweetest little thing?" Such coveted treats as chocolate-covered graham crackers often follow. But if we deliberately slam the rotten little puke of a sister's fingers in the door, sanctions follow—angry remonstrance from parents, aunts and uncles; instead of a chocolate-covered graham cracker, a spanking. 10

But anticivilization emotions don't go away, and they demand periodic exercise. We have such "sick" jokes as, "What's the difference between a truckload of bowling balls and a truckload of dead babies?" (You can't unload a truckload of bowling balls with a pitchfork...a joke, by the way, that I heard originally from a ten-year-old.) Such a joke may surprise a laugh or a grin out of us even as we recoil, a possibility that confirms the thesis: If we share a brotherhood of man, then we also share an insanity of man. None of which is intended as a defense of either the sick joke or insanity but merely as an explanation of why the best horror films, like the best fairy tales, manage to be reactionary, anarchistic, and revolutionary all at the same time. 11

The mythic horror movie, like the sick joke, has a dirty job to do. It deliberately appeals to all that is worst in us. It is morbidity unchained, our most base instincts let free, our nastiest fantasies realized...and it all happens, fittingly enough, in the dark. For those reasons, good liberals often shy away from horror films. For myself, I like to see the most aggressive of them—*Dawn of the Dead*, for instance—as lifting a trap door in the civilized forebrain and throwing a basket of raw meat to the hungry alligators swimming around in that subterranean river beneath. 12

Why bother? Because it keeps them from getting out, man. It keeps them down there and me up here. It was Lennon and McCartney who said that all you need is love, and I would agree with that. 13

As long as you keep the gators fed. 14

Questions for Close Reading

1. What is the selection's thesis? Locate the sentence(s) in which King states his main idea. If he doesn't state the thesis explicitly, express it in your own words.

2. In what ways do King's references to "Jack the Ripper" and the "Cleveland Torso Murderer" (paragraph 8) support his thesis?

3. What does King mean in paragraph 4 when he says that horror movies are "innately conservative, even reactionary"? What does he mean in paragraph 11 when he calls them "anarchistic, and revolutionary"?

4. In paragraphs 12 and 14, King refers to "alligators" and "gators." What does the alligator represent? What does King mean when he says that all the world needs is love—"[a]s long as you keep the gators fed"?

FIGURE 16.2

Essay Structure Diagram: "Why We Crave Horror Movies"
by Stephen King

Introductory paragraphs Thesis (paragraphs 1–2)	Examples of how we are "all mentally ill." **Implied Thesis:** Watching horror movies helps us control the anti-social instincts we all have.
Background: Obvious causes (3–5)	Why watch horror movies? To prove we're not afraid; to feel essentially "normal"; to have fun.
Causal chain Also, examples (in parentheses at right) (6–11)	Why is watching horror movies fun? (Analogy: Horror movies are the modern-day equivalent of public lynchings.) **First causal link:** Society rewards us for positive emotions but punishes us for negative ones. (Example of harming a little sister.) **Second causal link:** But negative emotions don't simply go away. (Example of "sick jokes.) **Third causal link:** Watching horror movies, we get to experience "anticivilization" feelings without harming anyone or enduring negative consequences.
Concluding paragraph (12–14)	(Analogy: Base instincts are like alligators needing to be fed.) Clearer statement of thesis.

Questions About the Writer's Craft

1. **The pattern.** Does King's causal analysis have an essentially informative, speculative, or persuasive (see page 317) purpose? What makes you think so? How might King's profession as a horror writer have influenced his purpose?

2. **Other patterns.** King *compares* and *contrasts* horror movies to roller coasters (3), public lynchings (6), and sick jokes (11–12). How do these comparisons and contrasts reinforce King's thesis about horror movies?

3. **Other patterns.** Throughout the essay, King uses several *examples* involving children. Identify these instances. How do these examples help King develop his thesis?

4. What is unusual about paragraphs 2, 5, and 14? Why do you think King might have designed these paragraphs in this way?

Writing Assignments Using Cause-Effect as a Pattern of Development

1. King argues that horror movies have "a dirty job to do": they feed the hungry monsters in our psyche. Write an essay in which you put King's thesis to the test. Briefly describe the first horror movie you ever saw; then explain its effect on you. Like King, speculate about the nature of your response—your feelings and fantasies—while watching the movie.

2. Many movie critics claim that horror movies nowadays are more violent and bloody than they used to be. Write an essay about *one* other medium of popular culture that you think has changed for the worse. Briefly describe key differences between the medium's past and present forms. Analyze the reasons for the change, and, at the end of the essay, examine the effects of the change.

Writing Assignment Combining Patterns of Development

3. King advocates the horror movie precisely because "It deliberately appeals to all that is worst in us." Write an essay in which you rebut King. *Argue* instead that horror movies should be avoided precisely *because* they satisfy monstrous feelings in us. To refute King, provide strong *examples* drawn from your own and other people's experience. Consider supplementing your informal research with material gathered in the library and/or on the Internet.

Belinda Luscombe with Kate Stinchfield

The Australian-born journalist Belinda Luscombe began her career at the *Daily Telegraph* in Sydney, Australia, before moving to the United States in 1995, where she became an editor for *Time.* Her articles, many of which focus on social issues, have appeared in several publications including *Vogue,* the *New York Times, Sports Illustrated, Travel and Leisure, Mademoiselle,* and *Fortune.* The following essay was published in *Time* on January 17, 2008. Kate Stinchfield, who has served as a reporter for *Time* magazine, contributed to this article.

Pre-Reading Journal Entry

Think of someone—perhaps yourself, perhaps a friend or acquaintance—you would describe as "a flirt." What is there about the person that makes you think of him or her this way? What kind of flirting behaviors does the individual exhibit? Why do you think the individual acts this way? Explore these ideas in your journal.

THE SCIENCE OF ROMANCE: WHY WE FLIRT

1   Contrary to widespread belief, only two very specific types of people flirt: those who are single and those who are married. Single people flirt because, well, they're single and therefore nobody is really contractually obliged to talk to them, sleep with them or scratch that difficult-to-reach part of the back. But married people, they're a tougher puzzle. They've found themselves a suitable—maybe even superior—mate, had a bit of productive fun with the old gametes and ensured that at least some of their genes are carried into the next generation. They've done their duty, evolutionarily speaking. Their genome will survive. Yay them. So for Pete's sake, why do they persist with the game?

2   And before you claim, whether single or married, that you never flirt, bear in mind that it's not just talk we're dealing with here. It's gestures, stance, eye movement. Notice how you lean forward to the person you're talking to and tip up your heels? Notice the quick little eyebrow raise you make, the sidelong glance coupled with the weak smile you give, the slightly sustained gaze you offer? If you're a woman, do you feel your head tilting to the side a bit, exposing either your soft, sensuous neck or, looking at it another way, your jugular? If you're a guy, are you keeping your body in an open, come-on-attack-me position, arms positioned to draw the eye to your impressive lower abdomen?

3   Scientists call all these little acts "contact-readiness" cues, because they indicate, nonverbally, that you're prepared for physical engagement. (More general body language is known as "nonverbal leakage." Deep in their souls, all scientists are poets.) These cues are a crucial part of what's known in human-ethology circles as the "heterosexual relationship initiation process" and elsewhere, often on the selfsame college campuses, as "coming on to someone." In primal terms, they're physical signals that you don't intend to dominate, nor do you intend to flee—both useful messages potential mates need to send before they can proceed to that awkward talking phase. They're the opening line, so to speak, for the opening line.

4   One of the reasons we flirt in this way is that we can't help it. We're programmed to do it, whether by biology or culture. The biology part has been investigated by any number of researchers. Ethologist Irenäus Eibl Eibesfeldt, then of the Max Planck Institute in Germany, filmed African tribes in the 1960s and found that the women there did the exact same prolonged stare followed by a head tilt away with a little smile that he saw in America. (The technical name for the head movement is a "cant." Except in this case it's more like "can.")

5   Evolutionary biologists would suggest that those individuals who executed flirting maneuvers most adeptly were more successful in swiftly finding a mate and reproducing and that the behavior therefore became widespread in all humans. "A lot of people feel flirting is part of the universal language of how we communicate, especially nonverbally," says Jeffry Simpson, director of the social psychology program at the University of Minnesota.

6   Simpson is currently studying the roles that attraction and flirting play during different times of a woman's ovulation cycle. His research suggests that women who are ovulating are more attracted to flirty men. "The guys they find appealing tend to have characteristics that are attractive in the short term, which include some flirtatious behaviors," he says. He's not sure why women behave this way, but it follows that men who bed ovulating women have a greater chance

Head cant: Women frequently tilt their head to one side, exposing their neck, and sometimes flick their hair at the same time.

of procreating and passing on those flirty genes, which means those babies will have more babies, and so on. Of course, none of this is a conscious choice, just as flirting is not always intentional. "With a lot of it, especially the nonverbal stuff, people may not be fully aware that they're doing it," says Simpson. "You don't see what you look like. People may emit flirtatious cues and not be fully aware of how powerful they are."

Flirting with Intent

Well, some people anyway. But then there are the rest of you. You know who you   7
are. You're the gentleman who delivered my groceries the other day and said we had a problem because I had to be 21 to receive alcohol. You're me when I told that same man that I liked a guy who knew his way around a dolly. (Lame, I know. I was caught off guard.) You're the fiftysomething guy behind me on the plane before Christmas telling his fortysomething seatmate how sensual her eyes were—actually, I hope you're not, because if so, you're really skeevy. My point is, once you move into the verbal phase of flirtation, it's pretty much all intentional.

And there are some schools of thought that teach there's nothing wrong with   8
that. Flirtation is a game we play, a dance for which everyone knows the moves. "People can flirt outrageously without intending anything," says independent sex researcher Timothy Perper, who has been researching flirting for 30 years.

"Flirting captures the interest of the other person and says 'Would you like to play?'" And one of the most exhilarating things about the game is that the normal rules of social interaction are rubberized. Clarity is not the point. "Flirting opens a window of potential. Not yes, not no," says Perper. "So we engage ourselves in this complex game of maybe." The game is not new. The first published guide for how to flirt was written about 2,000 years ago, Perper points out, by a bloke named Ovid. As dating books go, *The Art of Love* leaves more recent publications like *The Layguide: How to Seduce Women More Beautiful Than You Ever Dreamed Possible No Matter What You Look Like or How Much You Make* in its dust. And yes, that's a real book.

9   Once we've learned the game of maybe, it becomes second nature to us. Long after we need to play it, we're still in there swinging (so to speak) because we're better at it than at other games. Flirting sometimes becomes a social fallback position. "We all learn rules for how to behave in certain situations, and this makes it easier for people to know how to act, even when nervous," says Antonia Abbey, a psychology professor at Wayne State University. Just as we learn a kind of script for how to behave in a restaurant or at a business meeting, she suggests, we learn a script for talking to the opposite sex. "We often enact these scripts without even thinking," she says. "For some women and men, the script may be so well learned that flirting is a comfortable strategy for interacting with others." In other words, when in doubt, we flirt.

10   The thing that propels many already committed people to ply the art of woo, however, is often not doubt. It's curiosity. Flirting "is a way of testing one's mate-value and the possibility of alternatives—actually trying to see if someone might be available as an alternative," says Arthur Aron, professor of psychology at the State University of New York at Stony Brook. To evolutionary biologists, the advantages of this are clear: mates die, offspring die. Flirting is a little like taking out mating insurance.

11   If worst comes to worst and you don't still have it (and yes, I'm sure you do), the very act of flirting with someone else may bring about renewed attention from your mate, which has advantages all its own. So it's a win-win.

12   Flirting is also emotional capital to be expended in return for something else. Not usually for money, but for the intangibles—a better table, a juicier cut of meat, the ability to return an unwanted purchase without too many questions. It's a handy social lubricant, reducing the friction of everyday transactions, and closer to a strategically timed tip than a romantic overture. Have you ever met a male hairdresser who wasn't a flirt? Women go to him to look better. So the better they feel when they walk out of his salon, the happier they'll be to go back for a frequent blowout. Flirting's almost mandatory. And if the hairdresser is gay, so much the better, since the attention is much less likely to be taken as an untoward advance.

It's Dangerous Out There

13   But outside the hairdresser's chair, things are not so simple. Flirt the wrong way with the wrong person, and you run the risk of everything from a slap to a sexual-harassment lawsuit. And of course, the American virtue of plainspokenness is not an asset in an

activity that is ambiguous by design. Wayne State's Abbey, whose research has focused on the dark side of flirting—when it transmogrifies into harassment, stalking or acquaintance rape—warns that flirting can be treacherous. "Most of the time flirtation desists when one partner doesn't respond positively," she says. "But some people just don't get the message that is being sent, and some ignore it because it isn't what they want to hear."

One of the most fascinating flirting laboratories is the digital world. Here's a venue   14
that is all words and no body language; whether online or in text messages, nuance is almost impossible. And since text and e-mail flirting can be done without having to look people in the eye, and is often done with speed, it is bolder, racier and unimpeded by moments of reflection on whether the message could be misconstrued or is wise to send at all. "Flirt texting is a topic everyone finds fascinating, although not much research is out there yet," says Abbey. But one thing is clear: "People are often more willing to disclose intimate details via the Internet, so the process may escalate more quickly."

That's certainly the case on sites like Yahoo!'s Married and Flirting e-mail group,   15
as well as on Marriedbutplaying.com and Married-but-flirting.com. "Flirting" in this sense appears to be a euphemism for talking dirty. A University of Florida study of 86 participants in a chat room published in *Psychology Today* in 2003 found that while nearly all those surveyed felt they were initially simply flirting with a computer, not a real person, almost a third of them eventually had a face-to-face meeting with someone they chatted with. And all but two of the couples who met went on to have an affair. Whether the people who eventually cheated went to the site with the intention of doing so or got drawn in by the fantasy of it all is unclear. Whichever, the sites sure seem like a profitable place for people like the guy behind me on the pre-Christmas flight to hang out.

Most people who flirt—off-line at least—are not looking for an affair. But one   16
of the things that sets married flirting apart from single flirting is that it has a much greater degree of danger and fantasy to it. The stakes are higher and the risk is greater, even if the likelihood of anything happening is slim. But the cocktail is in some cases much headier. It is most commonly the case with affairs, therapists say, that people who cheat are not so much dissatisfied with their spouse as with themselves and the way their lives have turned out. There is little that feels more affirming and revitalizing than having someone fall in love with you. (It follows, then, that there's little that feels less affirming than being cheated on.) Flirting is a decaf affair, a way of feeling more alive, more vital, more desirable without actually endangering the happiness of anyone you love—or the balance of your bank account. So go ahead and flirt, if you can do it responsibly. You might even try it with your spouse.

A Field Guide to Flirting

Humans observed in a natural mating habitat…exhibit nearly all the major flirting behaviors, whether or not they're flirting at all!

1. **Open body position.** This come-and-get-me stance suggests the man is about to neither flee nor fight.

2. **Raised eyebrows.** Upon first seeing a potential mate, both men and women often briefly raise their eyebrows.

3. **Head cant.** Women frequently tilt their head to one side, exposing their neck, and sometimes flick their hair at the same time.

4. **Sustained eye contact.** Men and women both hold the gaze of someone they're interested in for longer than feels quite comfortable.

5. **Leaning forward.** Both genders tend to lean in toward people they're attracted to. Sometimes they'll unconsciously point to them too, even if they're across the room.

6. **Leading questions.** A man will often ask a woman questions that allow her to show off her most attractive features.

7. **Sideways glances.** Often followed by a glance away or down and a shy smile, these coy looks are a classic flirting behavior for both sexes.

Questions for Close Reading

1. What is the selection's thesis? Locate the sentence(s) in which Luscombe states her main idea. If she doesn't state the thesis explicitly, express it in your own words.

2. According to Luscombe, what does the act of flirting involve?

3. In her essay, Luscombe distinguishes between intentional and unintentional flirting. How does she describe the difference between the two?

4. What does Luscombe say about the difference between digital and face-to-face flirting? Do you agree with her assertions? Why or why not?

Questions About the Writer's Craft

1. **The pattern.** To what extent does Luscombe focus on causes of flirting and to what extent on effects? Does she balance references to causes and effects?

2. How would you describe Luscombe's tone in her essay? Point to several examples in her essay that illustrate her tone. Why do you think she chose to use this tone?

3. Luscombe includes parenthetical statements here and there throughout her essay. Locate these statements and comment on their effect.

4. **Other patterns.** In her cause-effect essay, Luscombe *illustrates* what she calls "flirting with intent" by providing examples. Make a list of these examples and comment on how they add to the overall effect of the essay. A captioned photo also appears with the essay. How effective is the photo in illustrating Luscombe's ideas? Why?

Writing Assignments Using Cause-Effect as a Pattern of Development

1. Choose a common behavior other than flirting, for example, exhibiting road rage or volunteering at a shelter. Write an essay in which you explain its possible causes or effects. Use examples from your own experience to support your thesis.

2. Luscombe makes reference to "the dark side" of flirting and to the potential dangers of what many consider a harmless act. Write a cause-effect essay in which you focus on the dangerous side of flirting or another seemingly harmless activity, using several outside sources to substantiate your claims. In addition to published sources, consider using material from personal interviews or surveys you conduct.

Writing Assignment Combining Patterns of Development

3. In her essay Luscombe humorously refers to Ovid's *The Art of Love* and briefly compares this ancient Latin poem to a more recent publication. Write an essay in which you *compare* and *contrast* people's expectations about love and romance today with the views held a generation or two ago. Comment either on what you think has *caused* attitudes to change or on what you think the *effects* of these changes have been. Include examples that *illustrate* your main points.

Josie Appleton

Josie Appleton is the director and spokesperson for the Manifesto Club, a British civil liberties campaign group that speaks out against excessive state regulation. As a journalist, Appleton frequently writes for *Spiked* (or *sp!ked*), an online publication based in London. The following article appeared in *Spiked* on July 9, 2003.

Pre-Reading Journal Entry

There's no denying the growing popularity of tattoos and piercings. What responses—both positive and negative—might people with tattoos or piercings expect or hope to experience at school, at work, or in other societal situations? Explore these ideas in your journal.

THE BODY PIERCING PROJECT

1   The opening of a tattoo and piercing section in the up-market London store Selfridges shows that body modification has lost its last trace of taboo.

2   "Metal Morphosis," nestled in the thick of the ladies clothing section, is a world away from the backstreets of Soho—where the company has its other branch. Teenagers, middle-aged women, men in suits and young guys in jeans flock to peer at the rows of tastefully displayed rings and leaf through the tattoo brochures.

3   Tattooist Greg said that he had seen a "broad variety" of people: "everything from the girl who turned 18 to the two Philippino cousins who just turned 40." The piercer, Barry, said that a number of "Sloanies" come for piercings (the most expensive navel bar retails at £3000 [$4,550], and there is a broad selection that would set you back several hundred pounds). A handful of women have even asked to be tattooed with the label of their favorite bottle of wine (Rumbelow).

4   This is not just affecting London high-streets. According to current estimates, between 10 and 25 percent of American adolescents have some kind of piercing or tattoo (Carroll 627). And their mothers are taking it up, too—in the late 1990s, the fastest growing demographic group seeking tattoo services in America was middle-class suburban women (Levins).

5   But while tattoos have been taken up by university students and ladies who lunch, more traditional wearers of tattoos—sailors, soldiers, bikers, gangs—find themselves increasingly censured.

6   In June 2003, the police rejected an applicant because his tattoos were deemed to have an "implication of racism, sexism or religious prejudice" ("Police"). The US Navy has banned "tattoos/body art/brands that are excessive, obscene, sexually explicit or advocate or symbolize sex, gender, racial, religious, ethnic or national origin discrimination" and "symbols denoting any gang affiliation, supremacist or extremist groups, or drug use" (Jontz). New-style tattoos are a very different ball-game to their frowned-upon forebears. While the tattoos of football supporters, sailors and gang-members tend to be symbols of camaraderie or group affiliation, the Selfridges brigade are seeking something much more individual.

7   For some, tattoos and piercing are a matter of personal taste or fashion. "It's purely aesthetic decoration," said 37-year-old Sarah, waiting to get her navel pierced at Metal Morphosis. The erosion of moral censure on tattooing, and the increasing hygiene of tattoo parlors, has meant that body modification has become a fashion option for a much wider group of people.

8   For others, tattooing seems to go more than skin-deep. Tattoo artist Greg thinks that many of those getting tattoos today are looking for "self-empowerment"—tattoos, he says, are about establishing an "identity for the self." As a permanent mark on your body that you choose for yourself, a tattoo is "something no one will ever be able to take away from you," that allows you to say *this is mine*."

9   Seventeen-year-old Laura said that she got her piercings done because she "wanted to make a statement." When she turned 18, she planned to have "XXX" tattooed on the base of her spine, symbolizing her pledge not to drink, smoke or take drugs. "It's not to prove anything to anyone else," she said: "it's a pact with myself completely."

Sue said that she had her navel pierced on her fortieth birthday to mark a turning   10
point in her life. Another young man planned to have his girlfriend's name, and the
dates when they met, tattooed on his arm "to show her that I love her"—and to remind himself of this moment. "The tattoo will be there forever. Whether or not I feel
that in the future, I will remember that I felt it at the time, that I felt strong enough to
have the tattoo."

The tattoos of bikers, sailors and gang-members would be a kind of social symbol,   11
that would establish them as having a particular occupation or belonging to a particular cultural subgroup. By contrast, Laura's "XXX" symbol is a sign to herself of how she
has chosen to live her life; Sue pierced her navel to mark her transition to middle-age.
These are not symbols that could be interpreted by anyone else. Even the man who
wanted to get tattooed with his girlfriend's name had a modern, personal twist to his
tale: the tattoo was less a pact to stay with her forever, than to remind himself of his
feelings at this point.

Much new-style body modification is just another way to look good. But the trend also 12
presents a more profound, and worrying, shift: the growing crisis in personal identity.

In his book, *Modernity and Self-Identity* (1991), sociologist Anthony Giddens ar-   13
gues that it is the erosion of important sources of identity that helps to explain the
growing focus on the body. Body modification began to really take off and move into
the mainstream in the late 1980s and early 1990s. At around this time, personal and
community relationships that previously helped to provide people with an enduring
sense of self could no longer be depended upon. The main ideological frameworks that
provided a system to understand the world and the individual's place in it, such as
class, religion, or the work ethic, began to erode.

These changes have left individuals at sea, trying to establish their own sense of   14
who they are. In their piercing or tattooing, people are trying to construct a "narrative
of self" on the last thing that remains solid and tangible: their physical bodies. While
much about social experience is uncertain and insecure, the body at least retains a
permanence and reliability. Making marks upon their bodies is an attempt by people to
build a lasting story of who they are.

Many—including, to an extent, Giddens—celebrate modification as a liberating   15
and creative act. "If you want to and it makes you feel good, you should do it,"
Greg tells me. Websites such as the *Body Modification Ezine* (*BMEzine*) are full
of readers' stories about how their piercing has completely changed their life.
One piercer said that getting a piercing "helped me know who I am." Another
said that they felt "more complete...a better, more rounded and fuller person"
(qtd. in Featherstone 68). Others even talk about unlocking their soul, or finally
discovering that "I AM."

But what these stories actually show is less the virtues of body piercing, than the   16
desperation of individuals' attempts to find a foothold for themselves. There is a no-
table contrast between the superlatives about discovering identity and Being, and the
ultimately banal act of sticking a piece of metal through your flesh.

Piercings and tattoos are used to plot out significant life moments, helping to   17
lend a sense of continuity to experience. A first date, the birth of a child, moving
house: each event can be marked out on the body, like the notches of time on a
stick. One woman said that her piercings helped to give her memory, to "stop me

forgetting who I am." They work as a "diary" that "no one can take off you" (qtd. in Featherstone 69).

18 This springs from the fact that there is a great deal of confusion about the stages of life today. Old turning points that marked adulthood—job, marriage, house, kids—have both stopped being compulsory and lost much of their significance. It is more difficult to see life in terms of a narrative, as a plot with key moments of transition and an overall aim. Piercings and tattoos are used to highlight formative experiences and link them together.

19 Some also claim that body modification helps them to feel "comfortable in my own skin," or proud of parts of their body of which they were previously ashamed. The whole process of piercing—which involves caring for the wound, and paying special attention to bodily processes—is given great significance. By modifying a body part, some argue that you are taking possession of it, making it truly yours. "The nipple piercings have really changed my relationship to my breasts," one woman said (qtd. in Siebers 175).

20 This is trying to resolve a sense of self-estrangement—the feeling of detachment from experiences, the feeling that your life doesn't really belong to you. One young woman says how she uses piercing: "[It's been] done at time when I felt like I needed to ground myself. Sometimes I feel like I'm not in my body—then its time" (Holtham).

21 But piercing is trying to deal with the problem at the most primitive and brutal level—in the manner of "I hurt therefore I am." The experience of pain becomes one of the few authentic experiences. It also tries to resolve the crisis in individual identity in relation to my breasts or my navel, rather than in relation to other people or anything more meaningful in the world.

22 Many claims are made as to the transformative and creative potential of body modification. One girl, who had just had her tongue pierced, writes: "I've always been kind of quiet in school and very predictable....I wanted to think of myself as original and creative, so I decided I wanted something pierced....Now people don't think of me as shy and predictable, they respect me and the person I've become and call me crazily spontaneous" ("My").

23 Others say they use modification to help master traumatic events. Transforming the body is seen as helping to re-establish a sense of self-control in the face of disrupting or degrading experiences. One woman carved out a Sagittarius symbol on her thigh to commemorate a lover who died. "It was my way of coming to terms with the grief I felt," she said. "It enabled me to always have him with me and to let him go" (Polhemus 79).

24 Here the body is being modified as a way of trying to effect change in people's lives. It is the way to express creativity, find a challenge, or put themselves through the hoops. "I was ecstatic. I did it!" writes one contributor to *BMEZine*. Instead of a life project, this is a "body project." In the absence of obvious social outlets for creativity, the individual turns back on himself and to the transformation of his own flesh.

25 Body piercing expresses the crisis of social identity—but it actually also makes it worse, too. Focusing on claiming control over my body amounts to making a declaration of independence from everybody else.

People with hidden piercings comment on how pleased they were they had some- 26
thing private. One says: "I get so happy just walking along and knowing that I have a
secret that no one else could ever guess!" Another said that they now had "something
that people could not judge me for, and something that I could hide." Another said
that her piercing made her realize that "what other people say or think doesn't matter.
The only thing that mattered at that moment was that I was happy with this piercing;
I felt beautiful and comfortable in my own skin....They remind me that I'm beautiful
to who it matters...*me*" ("My").

Body modification encourages a turn away from trying to build personal identity 27
through relationships with others, and instead tries to resolve problems in relation to
one's own body. When things are getting rough, or when somebody wants to change
their lives, the answer could be a new piercing or a new tattoo. There is even an underlying element of self-hatred here, as individuals try to deal with their problems by
doing violence to themselves. As 17-year-old Laura told me: "You push yourself to do
more and more....You want it to hurt."

This means that the biggest questions—of existence, self-identity, life progression, 28
creativity—are being tackled with the flimsiest of solutions. A mark on the skin or a
piercing through the tongue cannot genuinely resolve grief, increase creativity, or give
a solid grounding to self-identity. For this reason, body modification can become an
endless, unfulfilling quest, as one piercing only fuels a desire for another. All the contributions to *BMEZine* start by saying how much their life has been changed—but then
promptly go on to plan their next series of piercings. "Piercing can be addictive!" they
warn cheerily.

Body modification should be put back in the fashion box. As a way of improving 29
personal appearance, piercing and tattooing are no better or worse than clothes,
makeup or hair gel. It is when body modification is loaded with existential significance
that the problems start.

Works Cited

Carroll, Lynne, and Roxanne Anderson. "Body Piercing, Tattooing, Self-Esteem, and Body Invest-
    ment in Adolescent Girls." *Adolescence* 37.147 (2002): 627–37. Print.

Featherstone, Mike, ed. *Body Modification*. London: Sage, 2000. Print.

Giddens, Anthony. *Modernity and Self-Identity: Self and Society in the Late Modern Age*. Cambridge,
    UK: Polity, 1991. Print.

Holtham, Susan. "Body Piercing in the West: A Sociological Inquiry." *Ambient Inc: Body Art Resources*.
    Ambient, n. d. Web. 8 July 2003.

Jontz, Sandra. "Navy Draws a Line on Some Forms of Body Piercing, Ornamentation, Tattoos." *Stars
    and Stripes*. Stars and Stripes, 29 Jan. 2003. Web. 8 July 2003.

Levins, Hoag. "The Changing Cultural Status of the Tattoo Arts in America." *Tattoo Arts in America*.
    Tattoo Artist, 1997. Web. 8 July 2003.

"My Beautiful Piercing." *BMEZine: Body Modification Ezine*. BME, n. d. Web. 8 July 2003.

Polhemus, Ted, and Housk Randall. *The Customized Body*. 2nd ed. London: Serpent's Tail, 2000. Print.

"Police Reject Tattooed Applicant." *BBC News*. BBC News, 16 June 2003. Web. 8 July 2003.

Rumbelow, Helen. "Ladies Who Lunch Get a Tattoo for Starters." *Times* (London), Times Newspapers, 18 June 2003. Web. 8 July 2003.

Siebers, Tobin, ed. *The Body Aesthetic: From Fine Art to Body Modification*. Ann Arbor: U of Michigan P, 2000. Print.

Questions for Close Reading

1. What is the selection's thesis? Locate the sentence(s) in which Appleton states her main idea. If she doesn't state the thesis explicitly, express it in your own words.

2. According to Appleton, what are the two main factors that have made body modifications a fashion option for a growing number of individuals?

3. To what cause does the sociologist Anthony Giddens attribute what Appleton calls "the growing focus on the body"? Do you agree with Giddens's assertion? Explain your response.

4. Think of individuals you know—perhaps yourself, your friends, your family members—who have tattoos or piercings and those individuals' reasons for making these body modifications. In what ways does Appleton's thesis ring true or false when you consider her ideas in relation to those reasons?

Questions About the Writer's Craft

1. **The pattern.** Appleton reveals both causes and effects of body modifications. Do the two next-to-the last paragraphs of the essay (28 and 29) discuss causes, effects, or both? Why do you suppose Appleton organizes the paragraphs this way?

2. **The pattern.** Although most essays state their thesis near the beginning, Appleton saves hers for later in the selection. Why do you think she chose to organize her essay in this manner? Do you think her essay would have been more effective had she stated her thesis in the first or second paragraph? Why or why not?

3. **Other patterns.** Appleton *compares* and *contrasts* the types of tattoos typical of various demographic groups. She distinguishes "tattoos of football supporters,

sailors and gang-members" whose tattoos "tend to be symbols of camaraderie or group affiliation," from those of "the Selfridges brigade" who "are seeking something much more individual" (paragraph 6). Does this distinction make sense to you? Does it apply when you think of individuals you know with tattoos? Why or why not?

4. Appleton includes a number of sources in her essay. List the various types of sources she includes. Of those, which ones do you consider most effective in helping her convince readers of her thesis? Why?

Writing Assignments Using Cause-Effect as a Pattern of Development

1. Appleton's essay attempts to explain the increasing popularity and acceptance of body modifications such as tattooing and piercings. Write a cause-effect essay in which you focus on another growing trend or current fad such as the increase in popularity and acceptance of revealing clothing, the growing use of *Twitter*, or the explosion in popularity of 3D movies. Consider including one or more images and several outside sources to add to the effectiveness of your essay.

2. Write a cause-effect essay in which you focus on an individual who chose to modify his or her body—perhaps with tattoos or piercing, or perhaps through a surgical procedure. Explore the reasons the person decided to make these changes and the effect of the body modifications. Include information as to whether the modifications brought about the desired results.

Writing Assignment Combining Patterns of Development

3. Write an essay in which you *compare* and *contrast* the most popular types of tattoos—or alternatively, the types of clothing—favored by various demographic groups in the United States today. You might include some of the groups Appleton mentions in her essay: teenagers, middle-aged women, men in suits, football supporters, sailors, and gang members. Conduct research to gather information for your essay, and also consider including a chart to *illustrate* your findings.

ADDITIONAL WRITING TOPICS: CAUSE-EFFECT

General Assignments

Using cause-effect, develop one of these topics into an essay.

1. Sleep deprivation
2. Having the parents you have
3. Lack of communication in a relationship
4. Overexercising or not exercising
5. Traveling or living in a foreign country
6. Skill or ineptitude in sports
7. A major life decision
8. Changing attitudes toward the environment
9. Voter apathy
10. An act of violence or cruelty

Assignments Using Visuals

Use the suggested visuals to help develop a cause-effect essay on one of these topics:

1. Sleep deprivation and its effects (slide show)
2. Giving children responsibilities and holding them accountable (Web links)
3. Stress and its impact on the human body (charts and/or graphs)
4. The consequences of texting while driving (graphs)
5. The effects of stereotyping by gender, race, or disability (Web links)

Assignments with a Specific Purpose, Audience, and Point of View

1. **Academic life.** A debate about the prominence of athletics at colleges and universities is going to be broadcast on the local cable station. For this debate, prepare a speech pointing out either the harmful or the beneficial effects of "big-time" college athletic programs.

2. **Academic life.** Why do students "flunk out" of college? Write an article for the campus newspaper outlining the main causes of failure. Your goal is to steer students away from dangerous habits and situations that lead to poor grades or dropping out.

3. **Civic activity.** Write a letter to the editor of your favorite newspaper analyzing the causes of the country's current "trash crisis." Be sure to mention the

nationwide love affair with disposable items and the general disregard of the idea of thrift. Conclude by offering brief suggestions for how people in your community can begin to remedy this problem.

4. **Civic activity.** Write a letter to the mayor of your town or city suggesting a "Turn Off the TV" public relations effort, convincing residents to stop watching television for a month. Cite the positive effects that "no TV" would have on parents, children, and the community in general.

5. **Workplace action.** As the manager of a store or office, you've noticed that a number of employees have negative workplace habits and/or attitudes. Write a memo for your employees in which you identify these negative behaviors and show how they affect the workplace environment. Be sure to adopt a tone that will sound neither patronizing nor overly harsh.

6. **Workplace action.** Why do you think teenage suicide is on the rise? You're a respected psychologist. After performing some research, write a fact sheet for parents of teenagers and for high school guidance counselors describing the factors that could make a young person desperate enough to attempt suicide. At the end, suggest what parents and counselors can do to help confused, unhappy young people.

17

Definition

In this chapter, you will learn:

17.1 To use the pattern of definition to develop your essays
17.2 To consider how definition can fit your purpose and audience
17.3 To develop prewriting, writing, and revision strategies for using definition in an essay
17.4 To analyze how definition is used effectively in one student-written and three professionally authored selections
17.5 To write your own essays using definition as a strategy

What Is Definition?

For language to communicate, words must have accepted definitions. Dictionaries, the source texts for definitions, are compilations of current word meanings that enable speakers of a language to understand one another. But as you might suspect, things are not as simple as they first appear.

Words can be slippery. Each of us has unique experiences, attitudes, and values that influence the way we use words and the way we interpret the words of others.

In addition to the idiosyncratic interpretations we may attach to words, some words shift in meaning over time. The word *pedagogue,* for instance, originally meant "a teacher or leader of children." However, with the passage of time, *pedagogue* has come to mean "a dogmatic, pedantic teacher." And, of course, we invent new words as the need arises. For example, *modem* and *byte* are just two of many new words created in response to recent breakthroughs in computer technology.

Writing a **definition**, then, is no simple task. Primarily, the writer tries to answer basic questions: "What does this word mean?" and "What is the special or true nature of this word?" The word to be defined may refer to an object, a concept, a type of person, a place, or a phenomenon. As you will see, there are various strategies for expanding definitions far beyond the single-word synonyms or brief phrases that dictionaries provide.

How Definition Fits Your Purpose and Audience

Many times, short-answer exam questions call for definitions. Consider the following examples:

> Define the term *mob psychology.*
>
> What is the difference between a *metaphor* and a *simile?*
>
> How would you explain what a religious cult is?

In such cases, a good response might involve a definition of several sentences or several paragraphs.

Other times, definition may be used in an essay organized mainly around another pattern of development. In this situation, all that's needed is a brief formal definition or a short definition given in your own words. For instance, a *process analysis* showing readers how computers have revolutionized the typical business office might start with a textbook definition of the term *artificial intelligence.* In an *argumentation-persuasion* paper urging students to support recent efforts to abolish fraternities and sororities, you could refer to the definitions of *blackballing* and *hazing* found in the university handbook. Or your personal definition of *hero* could be the starting point for a *causal analysis* that explains to readers why there are few real heroes in today's world.

But the most complex use of definition, and the one we focus on in this chapter, involves exploring a subject through an **extended definition.** Extended definition allows you to apply a personal interpretation to a word, to propose a revisionist view of a commonly accepted meaning, to analyze words representing complex or controversial issues. *Pornography, gun control, secular humanism,* and *right to privacy* would be good subjects for extended definition; each is multifaceted, often misunderstood, and fraught with emotion. *Junk food, anger, leadership,* and *anxiety* could also make interesting subjects, especially if the extended definition helped readers develop a new understanding of the word. You might, for example, define *anxiety* not as a negative state but as a positive force that propels us to take action.

An extended definition may run several paragraphs or a few pages. Keep in mind, however, that some definitions require a chapter or even an entire book to develop. Theologians, philosophers, and pop psychologists have devoted entire texts to concepts like *evil* and *love.*

Prewriting Strategies

The following checklist shows how you can apply to definition some of the prewriting techniques discussed in Chapter 2.

☑ DEFINITION: A PREWRITING CHECKLIST

Choose Something to Define

☐ Is there something you're especially qualified to define? What about that thing do you hope to convey?

☐ Do any of your journal entries reflect an attempt to pinpoint something's essence: courage, pornography, a well-rounded education?

☐ Will you define a concept, an object, a type of person, a place, a phenomenon, a complex or controversial issue?

☐ Can your topic be meaningfully defined within the space and time allotted?

Identify Your Purpose, Audience, Tone, and Point of View

☐ Do you want simply to inform and explain—that is, to make the meaning clear? Or do you want to persuade readers to accept your understanding of a term? Do you want to do both?

☐ Will you offer a personal interpretation? Propose a revised meaning? Explain an obscure or technical term? Discuss shifts in meaning over time? Distinguish one term from another, closely related term? Show conflicts in definition?

☐ Are your readers apt to be open to your interpretation of a term? What information will they need to understand your definition and to feel that it is correct and insightful?

☐ What tone and point of view will make your readers receptive to your definition?

Use Prewriting to Develop the Definition

☐ How might mapping, brainstorming, freewriting, and speaking with others generate material that develops your definition?

☐ Which of the prewriting questions below would generate the most details and, therefore, suggest patterns for developing your definition?

Question	*Pattern*
How does *X* look, taste, smell, feel, and sound?	Description
What does *X* do? When? Where?	Narration
What are some typical instances of *X*?	Illustration
What are *X*'s component parts? What different forms can *X* take?	Division-classification
How does *X* work?	Process analysis
What is *X* like or unlike?	Comparison-contrast
What leads to *X*? What are *X*'s consequences?	Cause-effect

Strategies for Using Definition in an Essay

After prewriting, you're ready to draft your essay. Figure 17.1 and the suggestions that follow the figure will be helpful whether you use definition as a dominant or supportive pattern of development.

1. **Stay focused on the essay's purpose, audience, and tone.** Because your purpose for writing an extended definition shapes the entire paper, you

FIGURE 17.1
Development Diagram: Writing a Definition Essay

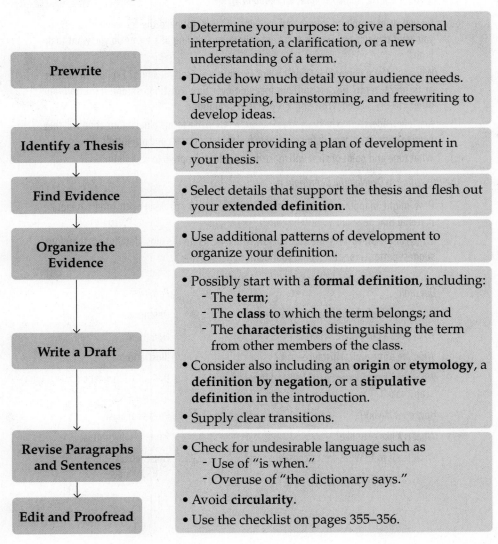

Prewrite
- Determine your purpose: to give a personal interpretation, a clarification, or a new understanding of a term.
- Decide how much detail your audience needs.
- Use mapping, brainstorming, and freewriting to develop ideas.

Identify a Thesis
- Consider providing a plan of development in your thesis.

Find Evidence
- Select details that support the thesis and flesh out your **extended definition**.

Organize the Evidence
- Use additional patterns of development to organize your definition.

Write a Draft
- Possibly start with a **formal definition**, including:
  - The **term**;
  - The **class** to which the term belongs; and
  - The **characteristics** distinguishing the term from other members of the class.
- Consider also including an **origin** or **etymology**, a **definition by negation**, or a **stipulative definition** in the introduction.
- Supply clear transitions.

Revise Paragraphs and Sentences
- Check for undesirable language such as
  - Use of "is when."
  - Overuse of "the dictionary says."
- Avoid **circularity**.

Edit and Proofread
- Use the checklist on pages 355–356.

need to keep that objective in mind when developing your definition. Suppose you decide to write an essay defining *jazz*. The essay could be purely *informative* and discuss the origins of jazz, its characteristic tonal patterns, and some of the great jazz musicians of the past. Or the essay could move beyond pure information and take on a *persuasive* edge. It might, for example, argue that jazz is the only contemporary form of music worthy of serious consideration.

Just as your purpose in writing will vary, so will your tone. A strictly informative definition will generally assume a detached, objective tone. By way of contrast, a definition essay with a persuasive slant might be urgent in tone, or it might take a satiric approach.

As you write, keep thinking about your audience as well. Not only do your readers determine the terms that need to be defined (and in how much detail), but they also keep you focused on the essay's purpose and tone.

2. **Formulate an effective definition.** A definition essay sometimes begins with a brief **formal definition**—the dictionary's, a textbook's, or the writer's—and then expands that initial definition with supporting details. Formal definitions are traditionally worded as three-part statements, including (1) the **term,** (2) the **class** to which the term belongs, and (3) the **characteristics** that distinguish the term from other members of its class. Consider these examples of formal definition:

Term	Class	Characteristics
The peregrine falcon,	an endangered bird,	is the world's fastest flyer.
Back to basics	is a trend in education	that emphasizes skill mastery through rote learning.

A definition that meets these three guidelines—term, class, and characteristics—will clarify what your subject *is* and what it *is not*. These guidelines also establish the boundaries or scope of your definition. For example, defining *back to basics* as "a trend that emphasizes rote...learning" signals a certain boundary; it lets readers know that other educational trends (such as those that emphasize children's social or emotional development) won't be part of the essay's definition.

Because they are formulaic, formal definitions tend to be dull. For this reason, it's best to reserve them for clarifying potentially confusing words—perhaps words with multiple meanings. For example, the term *the West* can refer to the western section of the United States, historically to the United States and its non-Communist allies (as in the "Western world"), or to the entire Western Hemisphere. Before discussing the West, then, you would need to provide a formal definition that clarifies your use of the term. Highly specialized or technical terms may also require clarification. Few readers are likely to feel confident about their understanding of the term *cognitive dissonance* unless you supply them with a formal definition: "a conflict of thoughts arising when two or more ideas do not go together."

If you decide to include a formal definition in your essay, avoid tired openings such as "the dictionary says" or "according to *Webster's.*" Such weak starts lack imagination. You should also keep in mind that a strict dictionary definition may actually confuse readers. *Remember:* The purpose of a definition is to clarify meaning, not obscure it.

You should also stay clear of ungrammatical "is when" definitions: "Blind ambition is when you want to get ahead, no matter how much other people are hurt." Instead, write "Blind ambition is wanting to get ahead, no matter how much other people are hurt." A final pitfall to avoid in writing formal definitions is **circularity,** saying the same thing twice and therefore defining nothing: "A campus tribunal is a tribunal composed of various members of the university community." Circular definitions such as this often repeat the term being defined (*tribunal*) or use words having the same meaning (*campus; university community*). In this case, we learn nothing about what a campus tribunal is; the writer says only that "*X* is *X.*"

3. **Develop the extended definition.** You can use the patterns of development when formulating an extended definition. Description, narration, process analysis, comparison-contrast, or any of the other patterns discussed in this book may be drawn upon—alone or in combination. Imagine you're planning to write an extended definition of *robotics.* You might develop the term by providing *examples* of the way robots are currently being used in scientific research; by *comparing* and *contrasting* human and robot capabilities; or by *classifying* robots, starting with the most basic and moving to the most advanced or futuristic models. (To deepen your understanding of which patterns to use when developing a particular extended definition, take a moment to review the last item in this chapter's Prewriting Checklist on page 351.)

4. **Organize the material that develops the definition.** If you use a single pattern to develop the extended definition, apply the principles of organization suited to that pattern, as described in the appropriate chapter of this book. Assume that you're defining *fad* by means of *process analysis.* You might organize your paragraphs according to the steps in the process: a fad's slow start as something avant-garde or eccentric; its wildfire acceptance by the general public; the fad's demise as it becomes familiar or tiresome. If you want to define *character* by means of a single *narration,* you would probably organize paragraphs chronologically. In a definition essay using several methods of development, you should devote separate paragraphs to each pattern. A definition of *relaxation,* for instance, might start with a paragraph that *narrates* a particularly relaxing day; then it might move to a paragraph that presents several *examples* of people who find it difficult to unwind; finally, it might end with a paragraph that explains a *process* for relaxing the mind and body.

5. **Write an effective introduction.** It can be helpful to provide—near the beginning of a definition essay—a brief formal definition of the term you're going to develop in the rest of the paper. Beyond this basic element, the introduction might include a number of other features. You may explain the *origin* of the term being defined: "*Acid* rock is a term first coined in the 1960s to describe

music that was written or listened to under the influence of the drug LSD."
Similarly, you could explain the *etymology*, or linguistic origin, of the key
word that focuses the paper: "The term *vigilantism* is derived from a Latin
word meaning 'to watch and be awake.'"

You may also use the introduction to clarify what your subject is *not*. Such
definition by negation can be an effective strategy at a paper's beginning,
especially if readers don't share your view of the subject. In such a case, you
might write something like this: "The gorilla, far from being the vicious killer of
jungle movies and popular imagination, is a sedentary, gentle creature living in a
closely knit family group." Such a statement provides the special focus for your
essay and signals some of the misconceptions or fallacies soon to be discussed.

In addition, you may include in the introduction a **stipulative definition,**
one that puts special restrictions on a term: "Strictly defined, a mall refers to a
one- or two-story enclosed building containing a variety of retail shops and at
least two large anchor stores. Highway-strip shopping centers or downtown
centers cannot be considered true malls." When a term has multiple meanings, or when its meaning has become fuzzy through misuse, a stipulative
definition sets the record straight right at the start, so that readers know exactly what is, and is not, being defined.

Finally, the introduction may end with a *plan of development* that indicates
how the essay will unfold. A student who returned to school after having
raised a family decided to write a paper defining the mid-life crisis that had
led to her enrollment in college. After providing a brief formal definition of
mid-life crisis, the student rounded off her introduction with this sentence:
"Such a mid-life crisis often starts with vague misgivings, turns into depression, and ends with a significant change in lifestyle."

Revision Strategies

Once you have a draft of the essay, you're ready to revise. The following checklist
will help you and those giving you feedback apply to definition some of the
revision techniques discussed in Chapters 7 and 8 .

> ### ✓ DEFINITION: A REVISION/PEER REVIEW CHECKLIST
>
> *Revise Overall Meaning and Structure*
>
> ☐ Is the essay's purpose informative, persuasive, or both?
>
> ☐ Is the term being defined clearly distinguished from similar terms?
>
> ☐ Where does a circular definition cloud meaning? Where are technical, nonstandard, or
> ambiguous terms a source of confusion?
>
> ☐ Where would a word's historical or linguistic origin clarify meaning? Where would a
> formal definition, stipulative definition, or definition by negation help?

(continued)

☐   Which patterns of development are used to develop the definition? How do these help the essay achieve its purpose?

☐   If the essay uses only one pattern, is the essay's method of organization suited to that pattern (step-by-step for process analysis, chronological for narration, and so on)?

☐   Where could a dry formal definition be deleted without sacrificing overall clarity?

Revise Paragraph Development

☐   If the essay uses several patterns of development, where would separate paragraphs for different patterns be appropriate?

☐   Which paragraphs are flat or unconvincing? How could they be made more compelling?

Revise Sentences and Words

☐   Which sentences and words are inconsistent with the essay's tone?

☐   Where should overused phrases, such as "the dictionary says" and "according to Webster's," be replaced by more original wording?

☐   Have "is when" definitions been avoided?

Student Essay: From Prewriting Through Revision

The student essay that follows was written by Laura Chen in response to this assignment:

> In "The Inner Corset," Laura Fraser writes about the changing definition of beauty, the factors that brought about the change, and the effects of this new ideal on the way we live our lives. Choose another term, one that is multifaceted, and define it in such a way that you reveal something significant about contemporary life.

Before writing her essay, Laura sat down at a computer and *brainstormed* material on the subject she decided to write about: inertia in everyday life. Later on, when she started shaping this material, she jotted down notes in the margin, starred important ideas, crossed out an item, added other ideas, drew connecting arrows, and used numbers and letters to sequence points. In the process, the essay's underlying structure began to emerge so clearly that an outline seemed unnecessary; Laura felt she could move directly from her brainstormed material to a first draft. Laura's original brainstormed list is reprinted on page 357. The handwritten marks indicate her later efforts to organize the preliminary material.

Now read Laura's paper, "Physics in Everyday Life," noting the similarities and differences between her prewriting and final essay. You'll see, for example, that Laura's decision to discuss national inertia *after* individual inertia makes the essay's sequence of points more emphatic. Similarly, by moving the mention of gravity to the essay's end, Laura creates a satisfying symmetry: The paper now opens and closes with principles of physics. As you read the essay, also consider how well it applies the principles of definition discussed in this chapter. (The commentary that follows the paper will help you look at Laura's essay more closely and will give you some sense of how she went about revising her first draft.)

Brainstorming

Entropy—an imp. term in physics. (Put in conclusion?) Just like gravity.

Formal definition
—Boulder sitting or rolling
*③ National inertia   (save broadest for last)

3b We accept pollution

3a Accept shoddy products

~~Accept growing homelessness~~
3c Go ahead with genetic engineering even though uncomfortable
3d Keep producing nuclear arms

3e Watch too much TV, despite all the reports

1c Racial discrimination remains a problem   Move to section on
                                                the individual

① Individual inertia, too

We resist change

1a Vote the same way all the time

1b Need jolts to change (a perfect teenage daughter
becomes pregnant) Add example here

② But on TV—no inertia

2a Soap operas, commercials—everyone changes easily   give
                                                         specifics

2b In real life—wear same hairstyle, use same products, wars and national problems
drag on

Physics in Everyday Life
by Laura Chen

1 A boulder sits on a mountainside for a thousand years. The boulder will remain there   Introduction
forever unless an outside force intervenes. Suppose a force does affect the boulder—an
earthquake, for instance. Once the boulder begins to thunder down the mountain, it will
remain in motion and head in one direction only—downhill—until another force interrupts its progress. If the boulder tumbles into a gorge, it will finally come to rest as gravity

ormal
efinition

anchors it to the earth once more. In both cases, the boulder is exhibiting the physical principle of inertia: the tendency of matter to remain at rest or, if moving, to keep moving in one direction unless affected by an outside force. Inertia, an important factor in the

hesis

world of physics, also plays a crucial role in the human world. Inertia affects our individual

lan of
evelopment

lives as well as the direction taken by society as a whole.

opic sentence

Inertia often influences our value systems and personal growth. Inertia is at   2
work, for example, when people cling to certain behaviors and views. Like the boulder firmly fixed to the mountain, most people are set in their ways. Without thinking, they vote Republican or Democratic because they have always voted that way. They regard with suspicion a couple having no children, simply because everyone else in

tart of a
eries of causes
nd effects

the neighborhood has a large family. It is only when an outside force—a jolt of some sort—occurs that people change their views. A white American couple may think little about racial discrimination, for instance, until they adopt an Asian child and must comfort her when classmates tease her because she looks different. Parents may consider promiscuous any unmarried girl who has a baby until their 17-year-old honors student confesses that she is pregnant. Personal jolts like these force people to think, perhaps for the first time, about issues that now affect them directly.

opic sentence

To illustrate how inertia governs our lives, it is helpful to compare the world of   3

tart of a series
f contrasts

television with real life. On TV, inertia does not exist. Television shows and commercials show people making all kinds of drastic changes. They switch brands of coffee or try a new hair color with no hesitation. In one car commercial, an ambitious young accountant abandons her career with a flourish and is seen driving off into the sunset as she heads for a small cabin by the sea to write poetry. In a soap opera, a character may progress from homemaker to hooker to nun in a single year. But in real life, inertia rules. People tend to stay where they are, to keep their jobs, to be loyal to products. A second major difference between television and real life is that, on television, everyone takes prompt and dramatic action to solve problems. The construction worker with a thudding headache is pain-free at the end of the sixty-second commercial; the police catch the murderer within an hour; the family learns to cope with their son's life-threatening drug addiction by the time the made-for-TV movie ends at eleven. But in the real world, inertia persists, so that few problems are solved neatly or quickly. Illnesses drag on, few crimes are solved, and family conflicts last for years.

opic sentence

Inertia is, most importantly, a force at work in the life of our nation. Again, in-   4
ertia is two-sided. It keeps us from moving and, once we move, it keeps us pointed in one direction. We find ourselves mired in a certain path, accepting the inferior,

even the dangerous. We settle for toys that break, winter coats with no warmth, and rivers clogged with pollution. Inertia also compels our nation to keep moving in one direction—despite the uncomfortable suspicion that it is the wrong direction. We are not sure if manipulating genes is a good idea, yet we continue to fund scientific projects in genetic engineering. More than fifty years ago, we were shaken when we saw the devastation caused by an atomic bomb. But we went on to develop weapons hundreds of times more destructive. Although warned that excessive television viewing may be harmful, we continue to watch hours of television each day.

Start of a series of examples

5   We have learned to defy gravity, one of the basic laws of physics; we fly high above the earth, even float in outer space. But most of us have not learned to defy inertia. Those special individuals who are able to act when everyone else seems paralyzed are rare. But the fact that such people do exist means that inertia is not all-powerful. If we use our reasoning ability and our creativity, we can conquer inertia, just as we have conquered gravity.

Conclusion

Commentary

Introduction

As the title of her essay suggests, Laura has taken a scientific term (*inertia*) from a specialized field and drawn on the term to help explain some everyday phenomena. Using the *simple-to-complex* approach to structure the introduction, she opens with a vivid *descriptive* example of inertia. This description is then followed by a *formal definition* of inertia: "the tendency of matter to remain at rest or, if moving, to keep moving in one direction unless affected by an outside force." Laura wisely begins the paper with the easy-to-understand description rather than with the more-difficult-to-grasp scientific definition. Had the order been reversed, the essay would not have gotten off to nearly as effective a start. She then ends her introductory paragraph with a *thesis*, "Inertia, an important factor in the world of physics, also plays a crucial role in the human world," and with a *plan of development*, "Inertia affects our individual lives as well as the direction taken by society as a whole."

Organization

To support her definition of inertia and her belief that it can rule our lives, Laura generates a number of compelling examples. She organizes these examples by grouping them into three major points, each point signaled by a *topic sentence* that opens each of the essay's three supporting paragraphs (2–4).

A definite organizational strategy determines the sequence of Laura's three central points. The essay moves from the way inertia affects the individual to the way it affects the nation. The phrase "most importantly" at the beginning of the fourth paragraph indicates that Laura has arranged her points emphatically, believing that inertia's impact on society is most critical.

A Problem with Organization and a Weak Example

When reading the fourth paragraph, you might have noticed that Laura's examples aren't sequenced as effectively as they could be. To show that we, as a nation, tend to keep moving in the same direction, Laura discusses our ongoing uneasiness about genetic engineering, nuclear arms, and excessive television viewing. The point about nuclear weapons is most significant, yet it gets lost in the middle. The paragraph would be stronger if it ended with the point about nuclear arms. Moreover, the example about excessive television viewing doesn't belong in this paragraph because, at best, it has limited bearing on the issue being discussed.

Combining Patterns of Development

In addition to using numerous *examples* to illustrate her points, Laura draws on several other patterns of development to show that inertia can be a powerful force. In the second and fourth paragraphs, she uses *causal analysis* to explain how inertia can paralyze people and nations. The second paragraph indicates that only "an outside force—a jolt of some sort—" can motivate inert people to change. To support this view, Laura provides two examples of parents who experience such jolts. Similarly, in the fourth paragraph, she contends that inertia causes the persistence of specific national problems: shoddy consumer goods and environmental pollution.

Another pattern, *comparison-contrast*, is used in the third paragraph to highlight the differences between television and real life: on television, people zoom into action, but in everyday life, people tend to stay put and muddle through. The essay also contains a distinct element of *argumentation-persuasion* because Laura clearly wants readers to accept her definition of inertia and her view that it often governs human behavior.

Conclusion

Laura's *conclusion* rounds off the essay nicely and brings it to a satisfying close. Laura refers to another law of physics, one with which we are all familiar—gravity. By creating an *analogy* between gravity and inertia, she suggests that our ability to defy gravity should encourage us to defy inertia. The analogy enlarges the scope of the essay; it allows Laura to reach out to her readers by challenging them to action. Such a challenge is, of course, appropriate in a definition essay having a persuasive bent.

Revising the First Draft

When it was time to rework her essay, Laura began by reading her paper out loud. Then, referring to the revision checklist on pages 355–356, she noted in the margin of her draft the problems she detected, numbering them in order of importance. After reviewing her notes, she started to revise in earnest, paying special attention to her third paragraph. The first draft of that paragraph, together with her annotations, is reprinted here:

Original Version of the Third Paragraph

The ordinary actions of daily life are, in part, determined by inertia. To understand this, it is helpful to compare the world of television with real life, for, in the TV-land of ads and entertainment, inertia does not exist. For example, on television, people are often shown making all kinds of drastic changes. They switch brands of coffee or try a new hair color with no hesitation. In one car commercial, <u>a young accountant leaves her career</u> and sets off for a cabin by the sea to write poetry. In a soap opera, a character may progress from homemaker to hooker to nun in a single year. In contrast, inertia rules in real life. People tend to stay where they are, to keep their jobs, to be loyal to products (wives get annoyed if a husband brings home the wrong brand or color of bathroom tissue from the market). Middle-aged people wear the hairstyles or makeup that suited them in high school. A second major difference between television and real life is that, on TV, everyone takes prompt and dramatic action to solve problems. A woman finds the solution to dull clothes at the end of a commercial; the police catch the murderer within an hour; the family learns to cope with a son's disturbing lifestyle by the time the movie is over. In contrast, the law of real-life inertia means that few problems are solved neatly or quickly. Things, once started, tend to stay as they are. Few crimes are actually solved. Medical problems are not easily diagnosed. Messy wars in foreign countries seem endless. National problems are identified, but Congress does not pass legislation to solve them.

① Paragraph rambles

④ First two sentences awkward

⑦ Make more specific

③ Delete part about annoyed wives and hairstyles

⑤ Trite—replace

⑥ Point about life-style not clea[r]

② Last two sentences don't belong

After rereading her draft, Laura realized that her third paragraph rambled. To give it more focus, she removed the last two sentences ("Messy wars in foreign countries seem endless," and "National problems are identified, but Congress does not pass legislation...") because they referred to national affairs but were located in a section focusing on the individual. Further, she eliminated two flat, unconvincing examples: wives who get annoyed when their husbands bring home the wrong brand of bathroom tissue and middle-aged people whose hairstyles and makeup are outdated. Condensing the two disjointed sentences that originally opened the paragraph also helped tighten this section of the essay. Note how much crisper the revised sentences are: "To illustrate how inertia governs our lives, it is helpful to compare the world of television with real life. On TV, inertia does not exist."

Laura also worked to make the details and the language in the paragraph more specific and vigorous. The vague sentence, "A woman finds the solution to dull clothes at the end of the commercial," is replaced by the more dramatic, "The construction worker with a thudding headache is pain-free at the end of the sixty-second commercial." Similarly, Laura changed a "son's disturbing lifestyle" to a "son's life-threatening drug addiction"; "by the time the movie is over" became "by the time the made-for-TV movie ends at eleven"; and "a young accountant leaves her career and sets off for a cabin by the sea to write poetry" was changed to "an ambitious young accountant abandons her career with a flourish and is seen driving off into the sunset as she heads for a small cabin by the sea to write poetry."

After making these changes, Laura decided to round off the paragraph with a powerful summary statement highlighting how real life differs from television: "Illnesses drag on, few crimes are solved, and family conflicts last for years."

These third-paragraph revisions are similar to those that Laura made elsewhere in her first draft. Her astute changes enabled her to turn an already effective paper into an especially thoughtful analysis of human behavior.

 ## ACTIVITIES: DEFINITION

Prewriting Activities

1. Imagine you're writing two essays: One explains an effective strategy for registering a complaint; the other contrasts the styles of two stand-up comics. Jot down ways you might use definition in each essay.

2. Use the prewriting questions for the patterns of development on page 351 to generate material for an extended definition of *one* of the terms that follow. Then answer these questions about your prewriting material: What thesis does the prewriting suggest? Which pattern(s) yielded the most supporting material? In what order would you present this support when writing an essay?

    a. popularity   d. self-esteem
    b. cruelty   e. "wimp"
    c. "dork"   f. loneliness

3. Select a term whose meaning varies from person to person or one for which you have a personal definition. Some possibilities include:

success	femininity	a liberal
patriotism	affirmative action	a housewife
individuality	pornography	intelligence

    Brainstorm with others to identify variations in the term's meaning. Then examine your prewriting material. What thesis comes to mind? If you were writing an essay, would your purpose be informative, persuasive, or both? Finally, prepare a scratch list of the points you might cover.

Revising Activities

4. Explain why each of the following is an effective or ineffective definition. Rewrite those you consider ineffective.

    a. *Passive aggression* is when people show their aggression passively.

   b. A *terrorist* tries to terrorize people.

   c. Being *assertive* means knowing how to express your wishes and goals in a positive, noncombative way.

   d. *Loyalty* is when someone stays by another person during difficult times.

5. The following introductory paragraph is from the first draft of an essay contrasting walking and running as techniques for reducing tension. Although intended to be a definition paragraph, it actually doesn't tell us anything we don't already know. It also relies on the tired formula of referring to a dictionary. Rewrite the paragraph so it is more imaginative. You might use a series of anecdotes or one extended example to define *tension* and introduce the essay's thesis more gracefully.

> A dictionary will define *tension* as a kind of stress or strain, either mental or physical. Everyone feels tense at one time or another. It may occur when there's a deadline to meet. Or it could be caused by the stress of trying to fulfill academic, athletic, or social goals. Sometimes it comes from criticism by family, bosses, or teachers. Such tension puts wear and tear on our bodies and on our emotional well-being. Although some people run to relieve tension, research has found that walking is a more effective tension reducer.

PROFESSIONAL SELECTIONS: DEFINITION

Ann Hulbert

Writer Ann Hulbert was born in 1956 and attended Harvard College and Cambridge University. Hulbert is the author of *The Interior Castle: The Art and Life of Jean Stafford* (1993) and *Raising America: Experts, Parents, and a Century of Advice About Children* (2003). This article was published on March 11, 2007, in *The New York Times Magazine*.

For ideas on how this definition essay is organized, see Figure 17.2 on page 366.

Pre-Reading Journal Entry

One of the benefits of family life is getting to know people of other generations. What generations are represented by the people in your extended family? What generation do you belong to? What generation do your parents and your children, if any, belong to? How do the generations in your family differ? Use your journal to answer these questions.

BEYOND THE PLEASURE PRINCIPLE

It is a point of pride among baby boomers that after our kids leave home, we enjoy   1
a continuing closeness with them that our parents rarely had with us. We certainly do
keep in touch: 80 percent of 18- to 25-year-olds had talked to their parents in the past
day, according to "A Portrait of Generation Next," a recent study conducted by the
Pew Research Center in tandem with MacNeil/Lehrer Productions. Yet if the survey
is any guide, Gen Nexters aren't getting the credit they deserve for being—as many of
them told pollsters they felt they were—"unique and distinct." It is not easy carving
out your niche in the shadow of parents who still can't get over what an exceptional
generation they belong to.

So what is special about Gen Nexters? Don't count on them to capture their own   2
quintessence. "The words and phrases they used varied widely," the Pew researchers
noted, "ranging from 'lazy' to 'crazy' to 'fun.' " But if you look closely, what makes
Gen Nexters *sui generis*—and perhaps more mysterious than their elders appreciate—are their views on two divisive social topics, abortion and gay marriage. On the
by-now-familiar red-and-blue map of the culture wars, positions on those issues are
presumed to go hand in hand: those on the right oppose both as evidence of a promiscuous society and those on the left embrace them as rights that guarantee privacy and
dignity. Yet as a group, Gen Nexters seem to challenge the package deals.

Young Americans, it turns out, are unexpectedly conservative on abortion but no-   3
tably liberal on gay marriage. Given that 18- to 25-year-olds are the least Republican
generation (35 percent) and less religious than their elders (with 20 percent of them
professing no religion or atheism or agnosticism), it is curious that on abortion they
are slightly to the right of the general public. Roughly a third of Gen Nexters endorse
making abortion generally available, half support limits and 15 percent favor an outright ban. By contrast, 35 percent of 50- to 64-year-olds support readily available abor-
tions. On gay marriage, there was not much of a generation gap in the 1980s, but now
Gen Nexters stand out as more favorably disposed than the rest of the country. Almost
half of them approve, compared with under a third of those over 25.

It could simply be, of course, that some young people are pro-gay marriage and oth-   4
ers are pro-life and that we can expect more of the same old polarized culture warfare
ahead of us. But what if Gen Nexters, rather than being so, well, lazy, are forging their
own new crossover path? When I contacted John Green, an expert on religious voters
who is currently working at the Pew Forum on Religion and Public Life, he said that
pollsters hadn't tackled that question. But after crunching some numbers, he suggested that there might indeed be a middle way in the making. Many individual Gen
Nexters hold what seem like divergent views on homosexuality and government involvement with morality—either liberal on one while being conservative on the other
or else confirmed in their views on one question while ambivalent on the other.

Oh, how these young people can confound us! All this could amount to no more   5
than what the experts call a "life-cycle effect": Gen Nexters may hold heterogeneous views now because they are exploring diverse values that may congeal in
more conventional ways as they get older. But a more intriguing possibility is that
it is a "cohort effect," a distinctive orientation that will stick with them. Liberals
could take heart that perhaps homosexual marriage has replaced abortion as the
new "equality issue" for Gen Nexters, suggested John Russonello, a Washington
pollster whose firm is especially interested in social values; Gen Nexters may have

grown up after the backalley abortion era, but they haven't become complacent about sexual rights. Conservatives might take comfort from a different hypothesis that Green tried out: maybe Gen Nexters have been listening to their parents' lectures about responsibility. Don't do things that make you have an abortion, young people may have concluded, and do welcome everyone into the social bulwark of family responsibility.

6 Put the two perspectives together, and an ethos emerges that looks at once refreshingly pragmatic and yet still idealistic. On one level, Gen Nexters sound impatient with a strident stalemate between entrenched judgments of behavior; after all, experience tells them that in the case of both abortion and gay rights, life is complicated and intransigence has only impeded useful social and political compromises. At the same time, Gen Nexters give every indication of being attentive to the moral issues at stake: they aren't willing to ignore what is troubling about abortion and what is equally troubling about intolerant exclusion. A hardheadedness, but also a high-mindedness and softheartedness, seems to be at work.

7 And to risk what might be truly wishful thinking, maybe there are signs here that Gen Nexters are primed to do in the years ahead what their elders have so signally failed to manage: actually think beyond their own welfare to worry about—of all things—the next generation. For when you stop to consider it, at the core of Gen Nexters' seemingly discordant views on these hot-button issues could be an insistence on giving priority to children's interests. Take seriously the lives you could be creating: the Gen Next wariness of abortion sends that message. Don't rule out for any kid who is born the advantage of being reared by two legally wedded parents: that is at least one way to read the endorsement of gay marriage. However you end up sorting out the data, fun or crazy wouldn't be how I would describe the Gen Next mix. Judged against the boomers' own past or present, though, the outlook definitely looks unique.

Questions for Close Reading

1. What is the selection's thesis? Locate the sentence(s) in which Hulbert states her main idea. If she doesn't state her thesis explicitly, express it in your own words.

2. What statistics about Gen Nexters are the basis for much of the extended definition in this article?

3. What is the difference between a "life-cycle effect" and a "cohort effect"? Which type of effect does Hulbert claim her essay is about?

4. According to Hulbert, what has the elder generation—the baby boomers—failed to do?

Questions About the Writer's Craft

1. What is Hulbert's underlying purpose in defining the characteristics of Gen Nexters? Is her purpose mainly informative, speculative, or persuasive? How can you tell?

2. **The pattern.** Hulbert uses the "definition by negation" strategy throughout this essay. Identify examples of this strategy in the article and evaluate how well it works.

FIGURE 17.2

Essay Structure: "Beyond the Pleasure Principle" by Ann Hulbert

Introductory paragraphs
Narrowed topic
Definition by negation
(paragraphs 1–2)

Statistical evidence: Pew study points to distinctiveness of next generation.

Narrowed topic: Gen Nexters' uniqueness is their ideas on abortion and gay marriage.

Tentative definition: Their views are not like their parents' "culture wars" views.

Definitions through comparison-contrast and expert opinion
(3–6)

Comparison: More conservative than elders on abortion, but more liberal on gay marriage.

Expert opinion: A "middle way in the making."

Tentative definition: Gen Nexters are "forging their own … crossover path.

Comparison: Either they are "exploring diverse values" (life-cycle effect) or they are developing a "distinctive orientation" emphasizing "family responsibility."

Expert opinion: Gay marriage replacing abortion as the new "equality issue."

Tentative definition: Gen Nexters are merging persepectives to create their own "ethos" that's "pragmatic" yet "idealistic."

Concluding paragraph
Thesis
(7)

Maybe Gen Nexters will do what their parents failed to—"worry … about the next generation."

Thesis: "At the core of Gen Nexters' seemingly discordant views on these hot-button issues could be an insistence on giving priority to children's interests."

3. **Other patterns.** Hulbert also uses the compare-contrast strategy at many points in her article. What signal devices does she use to signal when she is comparing and contrasting?

4. What is the effect of the delayed thesis on the reader's experience of this article? Is the delayed thesis effective? Do you think Hulbert should have stated her thesis at the beginning of the essay?

Writing Assignments Using Definition as a Pattern of Development

1. In her essay, Hulbert presents an extended definition of Gen Nexters, Americans born in the 1980s. Write an essay in which you define the key characteristics of another generation. You might, for example, write an essay defining the characteristics of baby boomers (born from 1946 through the early 1960s), Generation Xers (born from 1965 to 1980), or the as-yet-unnamed youngest generation of those under 18 (born in the 1990s or later). If you choose to define the youngest generation, be sure to give it an "official" name. Before you write, decide whether your tone will be serious or humorous.

2. In her article, Hulbert mentions the current polarization of Americans—liberals versus conservatives and blue states versus red states. The meanings of these four terms can vary widely, however, often depending on the viewpoint of the writer. Write an essay in which you define what you think it means to be a liberal or a conservative, or to live in a red state or a blue state. What are the key characteristics of the term you chose? What are the values and attitudes associated with the term? Discussing these issues with friends and family might help you clarify your ideas before you write.

Writing Assignment Combining Patterns of Development

3. In paragraph 5, Hulbert mentions the "life-cycle effect," which refers to the way people's values and behaviors change as they pass from one stage of life to the next—from adolescence to adulthood, for example. Some of these life-cycle effects are marked by ritual. For example, there are many coming-of-age rites of passage, such as graduation, bar or bat mitzvah, confirmation, the debutante's ball, the *quinceañera,* and getting a driver's license. Choose one of your own life's rites of passage and write an essay about it. Narrate what happened, describe the *process* you went through, and give *examples* of how your life changed as a result.

Laura Fraser

Laura Fraser, born in 1961, is a San Francisco-based journalist and novelist whose work has appeared in a wide variety of publications including *Food and Wine,* the *New York Times, Salon, Health,* the *Oprah Magazine,* and *Mother Jones.* She is the author of the *New York Times* bestseller *An Italian Affair* (2001) and, more recently, of *All Over the Map* (2010), a travel memoir and sequel to her bestseller. Much of her writing focuses on women's health issues, travel, and cultural aspects of food. The essay that follows, adapted from Fraser's first book, *Losing It: America's Obsession with Weight and the Industry That Feeds on It* (1997), appeared in the 2009 book *The Fat Studies Reader,* edited by Esther Rothblum and Sondra Solovay.

Pre-Reading Journal Entry

Our ideas of what we think beautiful people should look like are influenced to a large extent by the culture in which we live. How similar or dissimilar is your concept of beauty from what you see in movies, fashion, and advertisements? What factors have contributed to your sense of what the word *beauty* means? Explore these ideas in your journal.

THE INNER CORSET

Once upon a time, a man with a thick gold watch swaying from a big, round   1
paunch was the very picture of American prosperity and vigor. Accordingly, a hundred years ago, a beautiful woman had plump cheeks and arms, and she wore a
corset and even a bustle to emphasize her full, substantial hips. Women were *sexy*
if they were heavy. In those days, Americans knew that a layer of fat was a sign that
you could afford to eat well and that you stood a better chance of fighting off infectious diseases than most people. If you were a woman, having that extra adipose
blanket also meant that you were probably fertile, and warm to cuddle up next to on
chilly nights.

Between the 1880s and 1920s, that pleasant image of fat thoroughly changed in the   2
United States. Some began early on to hint that fat was a health risk. In 1894, Woods
Hutchinson, a medical professor who wrote for women's magazines, defended fat
against this new point of view. "Adipose," he wrote, "while often pictured as a veri-
table Frankenstein, born of and breeding disease, sure to ride its possessor to death
sooner or later, is really a most harmless, healthful, innocent tissue" ("Fat and Its
Follies"). Hutchinson reassured his *Cosmopolitan* readers that fat was not only be-
nign, but also attractive, and that if a poll of beautiful women were taken in any city,
there would be at least three times as many plump ones as slender ones. He advised
them that no amount of starving or exercise—which were just becoming popular as
means of weight control—would change more than 10 percent of a person's body size
anyway. "The fat man tends to remain fat, the thin woman to stay thin—and both in
perfect health—in spite of everything they can do," he said in that article.

But by 1926, Hutchinson, who was by then a past president of the American   3
Academy of Medicine, had to defend fat against fashion, too, and he was showing
signs of strain. "In this present onslaught upon one of the most peaceable, useful and
law-abiding of all our tissues," he told readers of the *Saturday Evening Post,* "fashion
has apparently the backing of grave physicians, of food reformers and physical trainers,
and even of great insurance companies, all chanting in unison the new commandment
of fashion: 'Thou shalt be thin!'" ("Fat and Fashion").

Hutchinson mourned this trend, and was dismayed that young girls were ridding   4
themselves of their roundness and plumpness of figure. He tried to understand the
new view that people took toward fat: "It is an outward and visible sign of an inward
and spiritual disgrace, of laziness, of self-indulgence," he explained in that article, but
he remained unconvinced. Instead, he longed for a more cheerful period in the not-
so-distant past when a little fat never hurt anyone, and he darkly warned that some
physicians were deliberately underfeeding girls and young women solely for the purpose of giving them a more svelte figure. "The longed-for slender and boyish figure is
becoming a menace," Hutchinson wrote, "not only to the present, but also the future
generations" ("Fat and Fashion").

The thin ideal that developed in the United States from the 1880s to 1920s can be traced through the evolution of three ideal types: the plump Victorian woman (*top left*), the athletic but curvaceous Gibson Girl (*top right*), and the boyishly straight-bodied flapper (*bottom*).

5   And so it would. But why did the fashion for plumpness change so dramatically during those years? What happened that caused Americans to alter their tastes, not only to admire thinner figures for a time, but for the next century, culminating in fin de siècle extremes of thinness, where women's magazines in the 1990s would print ads featuring gaunt models side-by-side with photo essays on anorexia?

Many things were happening at once, and with dizzying speed. Foremost was   6
a changing economy: In the late 1800s, for the first time, ample amounts of food
were available to more and more people who had to do less and less work to eat.
The agricultural economy, based on family farms and home workshops, shifted to an
industrial one. A huge influx of immigrants—many of them genetically shorter and
rounder than the earlier American settlers—fueled the industrial machine. People
moved to cities to do factory work and service jobs, stopped growing their own food,
and relied more on store-bought goods. Large companies began to process food products, distribute them via railroads, and use refrigeration to keep perishables fresh.
Food became more accessible and convenient to all but the poorest families. People
who once had too little to eat now had plenty, and those who had a tendency to put
on weight began to do so. When it became possible for people of modest means to
become plump, being fat no longer was a sign of prestige. Well-to-do Americans of
northern European extraction wanted to be able to distinguish themselves, physically and racially, from stockier immigrants. As anthropologist Margaret Mackenzie
notes, the status symbols flipped: it became chic to be thin and all too ordinary to be
overweight.

In this new environment, older cultural undercurrents suspicious of fat began   7
to surface. Europeans had long considered slenderness a sign of class distinction
and finer sensibilities, and Americans began to follow suit. In Europe, during the
late 18th and early 19th centuries, many artists and writers—the poets John Keats
and Percy Bysshe Shelley, and authors Emily Brontë, Edgar Allan Poe, and Anton
Chekhov—had tuberculosis, which made them sickly thin. Members of the upper
classes believed that having tuberculosis, and being slender itself, were signs that
one possessed a delicate, intellectual, and superior nature. "For snobs and parvenus
and social climbers, TB was the one index of being genteel, delicate, [and] sensitive," writes essayist Susan Sontag in *Illness as Metaphor* (28). "It was glamorous to
look sickly." So interested was the poet Lord Byron in looking as fashionably ill as
the other Romantic poets that he embarked on a series of obsessive diets, consuming
only biscuits and water, or vinegar and potatoes, and succeeded in becoming quite
thin. Byron—who, at five feet six inches tall, with a clubfoot that prevented him
from walking much, weighed over two hundred pounds in his youth—disdained fat
in others. "A woman," he wrote, "should never be seen eating or drinking, unless
it be *lobster salad* and *champagne*, the only truly feminine and becoming viands"
(qtd. in Schwartz 38). Aristocratic European women, thrilled with the romantic figure that Byron cut, took his diet advice and despaired of appearing fat. Aristocratic
Americans, trying to imitate Europeans, adopted their enthusiasm for champagne
and slenderness.

Americans believed that it was not only a sign of class to be thin, but also a sign of   8
morality. There was a long tradition in American culture that suggested that indulging
the body and its appetites was immoral, and that denying the flesh was a sure way to
become closer to God. Puritans such as the minister Cotton Mather frequently fasted
to prove their worthiness and to cleanse themselves of their sins. Benjamin Franklin,
in his *Poor Richard's Almanack*, chided his readers to eat lightly to please not only
God, but also a new divinity, Reason: "Wouldst thou enjoy a long life, a healthy Body,
and a Vigorous Mind, and be acquainted also with the wonderful works of God?
Labour in the first place to bring thy Appetite into Subjection to Reason" (238).
Franklin's attitude toward food not only reveals a puritanical distrust of appetite as

overly sensual, but also presaged diets that would attempt to bring eating in line with rational, scientific calculations. "The Difficulty lies, in finding out an exact Measure;" he wrote, "but eat for Necessity, not Pleasure, for Lust knows not where Necessity ends" (238).

9 At the end of the 19th century, as Hutchinson observed, science was also help-ing to shape the new slender ideal. Physicians came to believe that they were able to arrive at an exact measure of human beings; they could count calories, weigh people on scales, calculate "ideal" weights, and advise those who deviated from that ideal that they could change themselves. Physicians were both following and encouraging the trend for thinness. In the 1870s, after all, when plumpness was in vogue, physicians had encouraged people to *gain* weight. Two of the most distinguished doctors of the age, George Beard and S. Weir Mitchell, believed that excessive thinness caused American women to succumb to a wide variety of nervous disorders, and that a large number of fat cells was absolutely necessary to achieve a balanced personality (Banner 113). But when the plump figure fell from favor, physicians found new theories to support the new fashion. They hastily developed treatments—such as thyroid, arsenic, and strychnine—to prescribe to their increasing numbers of weight loss patients, many of whom were not exactly corpulent, but who were more than willing to part with their pennies along with their pounds.

10 As the 20th century got underway, other cultural changes made slenderness seem desirable. When many women ventured out of their homes and away from their strict roles as mothers, they left behind the plump and reproductive physique, which began to seem old-fashioned next to a thinner, freer, more modern body. The new consumer culture encouraged the trend toward thinness with fashion illustra-tions and ads featuring slim models; advertisers learned early to offer women an unattainable dream of thinness and beauty to sell more products. In short, a cultural obsession with weight became firmly established in the United States when sev-eral disparate factors that favored a desire for thinness—economic status symbols, morality, medicine, modernity, changing women's roles, and consumerism—all col-lided at once.

11 Thinness is, at its heart, a peculiarly American preoccupation. Europeans admire slenderness, but without our Puritanism they have more relaxed and moderate at-titudes about food, eating, and body size (the British are most like us in both being heavy and fixating on weight loss schemes). In countries where people do not have quite enough to eat, and where women remain in traditional roles, plumpness is still widely admired. Other westernized countries have developed a slender ideal, but for the most part they have imported it from the United States. No other culture suffers from the same wild anxieties about weight, dieting, and exercise as we do because they do not share our history.

12 The thin ideal that developed in the United States from the 1880s to 1920s was not just a momentary shift in fashion; it was a monumental turning point in the way that women's bodies were appraised by men and experienced by women. The change can be traced through the evolution of three ideal types: the plump Victorian woman, the athletic but curvaceous Gibson Girl, and the boyishly straight-bodied flapper. By 1930, American women knew how very important it was for them to be thin. From then on, despite moments when voluptuousness was admired again (e.g., Marilyn Monroe), American women could never be too thin.

Works Cited

Banner, Lois. *American Beauty*. Chicago: U of Chicago P, 1983. Print.

Franklin, Benjamin. *The Complete Poor Richard Almanacks*. Vol. 1: 1733–47. Barre: Imprint Society, 1970. Print.

Hutchinson, Woods. "Fat and Fashion." *Saturday Evening Post* 21 Aug. 1926: 60. Print.

Hutchinson, Woods. "Fat and Its Follies." *Cosmopolitan* June 1894: 395. Print.

Mackenzie, Margaret. Letter to the author. 12 June 1996.

Schwartz, Hillel. *Never Satisfied: A Cultural History of Diets, Fantasies, and Fat*. New York: Free Press, 1986. Print.

Sontag, Susan. *Illness as Metaphor*. New York: Farrar, 1978. Print.

Questions for Close Reading

1. **Thesis.** What is the selection's thesis? Locate the sentence(s) in which Fraser states her main idea. If she doesn't state the thesis explicitly, express it in your own words.

2. What information does Fraser include in her essay to explain the influence of tuberculosis on Americans' fixation on being thin?

3. How does Fraser explain the change in America's definition of what it means to be beautiful? What six factors does she consider responsible for America's switch from a preference for plumpness to a desire to look almost anorexic?

4. According to Fraser, how is America's attitude toward thinness different from the attitude in most of Europe? In what parts of the world is plumpness still admired?

Questions About the Writer's Craft

1. **The pattern.** Why do you think Fraser chose to begin her essay by focusing on what many would consider to be overweight individuals? What might have been her purpose?

2. **The pattern.** Look closely at the manner in which Fraser structures her essay. How would you describe the order in which she presents the factors she believes are responsible for America's current definition of beauty? Why might she have organized her essay this way?

3. **Other patterns.** Although Fraser's essay focuses on the change in America's *definition* of what it means to be beautiful, she also incorporates other organizational patterns. What other patterns does she make use of and how?

☐ Who is your audience? How much do your readers already know about the issue? Are they best characterized as supportive, wavering, or hostile? What values and needs may motivate readers to be responsive to your position?

☐ What tone is most likely to increase readers' commitment to your point of view? Should you convey strong emotion or cool objectivity?

☐ What point of view is most likely to enhance your credibility?

Use Prewriting to Generate Supporting Evidence

☐ How might brainstorming, journal entries, freewriting, or mapping help you identify personal experiences, observations, and examples to support your viewpoint?

☐ How might the various patterns of development help you generate supporting material? What about the issue can you describe? Narrate? Illustrate? Compare and contrast? Analyze in terms of process or cause-effect? Define or categorize in some especially revealing way?

☐ How might interviews or other sources help you uncover relevant examples, facts, statistics, expert opinion?

Strategies for Using Argumentation-Persuasion in an Essay

After prewriting, you're ready to draft your essay. Figure 18.1 (on page 386) and the suggestions that follow will help you prepare a convincing and logical argument.

1. **At the beginning of the paper, identify the controversy surrounding the issue and state your position.** Your introduction should clarify the controversy about the issue. In addition, it should provide as much background information as your readers are likely to need.

   The thesis of an argumentation-persuasion paper is often called the **assertion** or **proposition**. Occasionally, the proposition appears at the paper's end, but it is usually stated at the beginning. If you state the thesis right away, your audience knows where you stand and is better able to evaluate the evidence presented.

   Remember: Argumentation-persuasion assumes conflicting viewpoints. Be sure your proposition focuses on a controversial issue and indicates your view. Avoid a proposition that is merely factual; what is demonstrably true allows little room for debate. To see the difference between a factual statement and an effective thesis, examine the two statements that follow.

Fact

In the past few years, the nation's small farmers have suffered financial hardships.

Thesis

Inefficient management, rather than competition from agricultural conglomerates, is responsible for the financial plight of the nation's small farmers.

4. How would you describe Fraser's tone in this essay? Why do you think she chose to address readers in this way? Do the photos add to our understanding of Fraser's thesis, or are they unnecessary?

Writing Assignments Using Definition as a Pattern of Development

1. Fraser's essay explores the changing definition of what it means to be beautiful. Think of another term that is used to describe or label individuals—a term whose definition has changed over the last century. Write an essay in which you explore how the changing definition has affected the way individuals think about themselves and others, as well as how they live their lives. For example, you might consider the changing definition of terms such as *educated, successful, middle-class,* or *well-traveled.*

2. In her essay, Fraser mentions that ideas about what it means to be healthy have changed since the early 1900s. Write an essay in which you focus on the differences between what it meant to be healthy a century ago, and what the term *healthy* means today. Consider using a variety of sources, ranging from personal interviews to published sources on the subject, along with charts or graphs that reference and support ideas and statistics in your essay.

Writing Assignment Combining Patterns of Development

3. Fraser's essay focuses on how and why the definition of beauty has changed. Write an essay in which you focus on the *effects* of the new definition. As you plan your essay about the *effects* of the pressure to be thin, consider *narrating* the stories of particular individuals and the lengths they have gone to in an effort to lose weight.

Keith Johnson

"Keith Johnson (1972–), a staff reporter for *The Wall Street Journal* for more than a decade, has been based in both Europe and Washington, D.C. Although he covers topics ranging from terrorism and homeland security to telecommunications, foreign affairs, and energy and the environment, his specialization is the geopolitics of energy. The following article was published in *The Wall Street Journal* on August 20, 2010.

Pre-Reading Journal Entry

Pirates have been romanticized in movies such as *Pirates of the Caribbean* and *The Sea Hawk* and in novels such as *Treasure Island.* Why do you think pirates are such glamorous figures? What other kinds of villains have been treated similarly? Do some freewriting in your journal on this subject.

WHO'S A PIRATE? IN COURT, A DUEL OVER DEFINITIONS

Not since Lt. Robert Maynard of the Royal Navy sailed back triumphantly to nearby   1
Hampton Roads in 1718 with the severed head of Blackbeard[1] swinging from his bow-
sprit has this Navy town been so embroiled in the fight against piracy.

Prosecuting pirates, rather than hanging them from the yardarm, is the modern   2
world's approach to the scourge of Somali piracy that has turned huge swathes of the
Indian Ocean into a no-go zone for commercial vessels.

But there's a problem: Some 2,000 years after Cicero[2] defined pirates as the "com-   3
mon enemy of all," nobody seems able to say, legally, exactly what a pirate is.

U.S. law long ago made piracy a crime but didn't define it. International law con-   4
tains differing, even contradictory, definitions. The confusion threatens to hamstring
U.S. efforts to crack down on modern-day Blackbeards.

The central issue in Norfolk: If you try to waylay and rob a ship at sea—but you   5
don't succeed—are you still a pirate?

It may seem strange there should be doubt about an offense as old as this one.   6
Piracy was the world's first crime with universal jurisdiction, meaning that any country had the right to apprehend pirates on the high seas.

The Romans took piracy so seriously they overrode a cautious Senate and gave   7
near-dictatorial powers to an up-and-coming general named Pompey,[3] who soon swept
away piracy in the Mediterranean.

In more recent centuries, European countries such as Britain cracked down on   8
pirates—except when busy enlisting certain ones, dubbed "privateers," to help them
fight their wars by raiding enemy ships.

Pirates even spurred the creation of the U.S. Navy, after Thomas Jefferson erupted   9
over the cost of paying tribute to the Barbary Corsairs[4] for safe passage of U.S. merchant ships. At the time, the U.S. was paying about one-tenth of the federal budget
to the pirates. Supplied with warships, President Jefferson waged war on the Barbary
pirates (whence the line "to the shores of Tripoli" in the Marines' Hymn). By 1815,
the North African pirate kingdoms had been subdued.

When Congress dealt with piracy in a statute four years later, the crime was so   10
easy to recognize that legislators didn't bother to describe it, just the punishment.
The 1819 statute that made piracy a capital offense (since changed to mandatory life
in prison) simply deferred to "the law of nations." That legal punt has kept American
jurists scrambling ever since.

The stage was set for the Norfolk trial on April 10 of this year [2010] when the USS   11
Ashland, cruising in the Gulf of Aden about 330 miles off Djibouti, was fired upon at
5 a.m. by Somali men in a small skiff. The Navy vessel, an amphibious dock landing

---

[1]Blackbeard is the pseudonym of an infamous British pirate who operated off the Eastern
Coast of the United States (editors' note).

[2]Cicero (106–43 B.C.E) was a philosopher and statesman in ancient Rome (editors' note).

[3]Pompey (106–48 B.C.E) was a statesman and great military leader in ancient Rome (editors'
note).

[4]The Barbary Corsairs were Muslim pirates or privateers who operated out of North Africa
(editors' note).

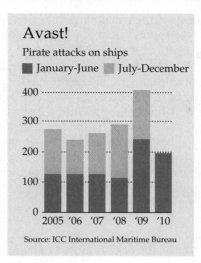

Avast!

Pirate attacks on ships
■ January–June ■ July–December

Source: ICC International Maritime Bureau

ship, returned fire with 25-mm cannon, wrecking the 18-foot skiff and sending its six occupants overboard.

12   The Ashland sent a search boat to recover the Somalis and photograph the smoking hulk of the skiff, which contained at least one weapon and what looked like a grappling hook or anchor. Though that boat was blasted to pieces, even when pirate skiffs survive, the ships they target are often loath to bring the skiffs aboard. One captured by a Navy force in 2006, according to the judge advocate's testimony in a subsequent trial in Kenya, was crawling with "roaches the size of leopards."

13   In Norfolk, the prosecution has begun its effort to convince the U.S. District Court for the Eastern District of Virginia that the quickly foiled Somalis are guilty not just of lesser charges they face but of the main charge of piracy.

14   "Violent attacks on the high seas without lawful authority have always been piracy under the law of nations, in 1819 and today," said the lead prosecutor, Benjamin Hatch, at a pretrial hearing last month [July 2010].

15   "So if one ship fires a bow-and-arrow," asked Judge Raymond Jackson, rubbing his brow, "or a slingshot, or a rock, those are all acts of violence, and thus piracy?" The prosecutor nodded.

16   The public defender, Geremy Kamens, weighed in. "That a slingshot fired upon another ship would expose the defendant to a mandatory life sentence shows the absurd result of this reading," he said. The defense added that under this broad definition, Greenpeace[5] activists could be considered pirates for their anti-whaling antics on the seas.

17   The defense lawyers trawled through history books, coming to rest upon an obscure 1820 Supreme Court ruling.

18   "We have, therefore, no hesitation in declaring that piracy, by the law of nations, is robbery upon the sea," Justice Joseph Story wrote for the majority in the case of United States v. Smith.

---

[5]Greenpeace, an activist environmental organization, is known for putting its ships between "whales and harpoons," as its website notes, on the high seas to deter whaling (editors' note).

That gave the defense lawyers their main argument: Piracy is robbery on the high   19
seas; it isn't merely attempted robbery at sea, which is covered by a separate statute
that the Somalis are charged with as well.

Since the attack on the Ashland clearly failed, it wasn't piracy, the defense argues,   20
and therefore, the most serious charge should be dropped.

But the prosecutors, too, have probed early sources—17th-century Dutch jurists,   21
18th-century British writers, 19th-century maritime cases, an 1800 speech by then-
congressman John Marshall, and a slew of international treaties.

The prosecution has leaned heavily on a 1934 ruling by Britain's Privy Council,[6]   22
which pondered the case of a similarly failed attack at sea, near Hong Kong. In that
case, the jury found the defendants guilty, but said its verdict was subject to the question of whether it's really piracy if no actual robbery occurs. The court in Hong Kong
said it isn't, and acquitted the attackers.

The Privy Council members, however, after hacking through thickets of legal tech-   23
nicalities, ultimately reached a different conclusion. "Actual robbery is not an essential
element in the crime of piracy," they said; "A frustrated attempt to commit piratical
robbery is equally piracy."

Troubled Waters

Attacks on ships in the first   Boarding or hijacking
half of 2010, by region   Failed attack

AFRICA: 114

EAST: Gulf of Aden,
Red Sea, Somalia,
Tanzania

WEST: Cameroon,
Congo, Republic of
Congo, Guinea, Ivory
Coast, Liberia, Nigeria

SOUTHEAST ASIA: 30

Indonesia, Malacca
Straits, Malaysia,
Philippines, Singapore
Straits, Thailand

FAR EAST: 23

China, Vietnam

AMERICAS: 15

Colombia, Ecuador,
Guyana, Haiti, Peru,
Venezuela

**INDIAN
SUB-CONTINENT: 12**

Bangladesh, India

ARABIAN SEA: 2   Source: ICC International
                             Maritime Bureau

---

[6]The Privy Council, formerly very powerful, is a group of advisors to the British sovereign
(editors' note).

24   They added, with more than a hint of exasperation: "Their Lordships are almost tempted to say that a little common sense is a valuable quality in the interpretation of international law."

25   Beyond the legal wrangling and obscure historical references, the implications of the case in Norfolk are serious. Piracy's golden age may have passed two centuries ago, but it remains a scourge in places like the Strait of Malacca in Indonesia and Malaysia, off the coast of Nigeria, and above all off the east coast of Africa, where the disintegration of Somalia has led to a major resurgence.

26   The first half of 2010 saw about 200 raids and unsuccessful attacks on ships at sea worldwide, the bulk of them off Somalia. In early August, two cargo ships were hijacked. In all, an estimated 18 ships and their crews are currently [as of August 2010] being held for ransom.

27   To fight the problem, the U.S. and the United Nations are counting on prosecuting pirates. Some U.N. officials dream of establishing an international piracy tribunal, similar to the one for war crimes in The Hague.

28   In the meantime, the U.S. and other countries have helped Kenya, the closest stable country to the source, to put scores of pirates on trial. But Kenyan law is cumbersome, requiring witnesses to testify on three separate occasions, a tough order logistically for merchant sailors. The European Union is now trying to jump–start Kenya's pirate prosecutions—the first sentence will come later this month—but progress is slow.

29   As a result, attackers captured by European warships in the Indian Ocean often are let go for lack of any real legal recourse. A Spanish warship caught seven Somali pirates red-handed in early August, men who had been trying to waylay a Norwegian chemical tanker. The Spanish frigate immediately released them because it would have been difficult to prosecute them, the EU naval force off Somalia said.

30   That leaves courtrooms like the one in Norfolk as among the best hopes for bringing pirates to justice and deterring future ones. But even seemingly clear-cut cases don't necessarily pass muster in court.

31   After a celebrated incident in April 2009, when U.S. Navy Seals snipers killed three Somali men holding an American captain hostage on a small boat after a raid, rescuing him, the lone Somali survivor of that attack on the Maersk Alabama pleaded guilty to lesser charges in New York, not to piracy.

32   Indeed, the last U.S. piracy conviction was in 1861, of a Confederate blockade runner.

33   Now the court in Norfolk must contend with the defense motion to dismiss the piracy charge, which would leaving only such lesser charges as attempted plunder.

34   The prosecution argues that U.S. courts should defer to international law, especially an 1982 U.N. Law of the Sea treaty the U.S. never ratified. Aping the 1958 Geneva Convention,[7] it offers an expansive definition of piracy as any illegal acts of violence, detention or depredation committed for private ends on the high seas.

35   Defense lawyers balk at that suggestion. "We do not interpret U.S. law based on U.N. resolutions, but rather what Congress meant at the time," says the public defender, Mr. Kamens.

36   Judge Jackson is expected to rule soon.[8]

---

[7]The Geneva Convention of April 29, 1958, sets forth internationally agreed-upon rules for conduct on the high seas, for example, fishing rights (editors' note).

[8]The Norfolk court ultimately ruled against trying the men on the charge of piracy.

Questions for Close Reading

1. What is the selection's thesis? Locate the sentence(s) in which Johnson states his main idea. If he doesn't state his thesis explicitly, express it in your own words.

2. What, according to the author, is the essential issue with defining *piracy*? What does the author have to say about the history of piracy before this century?

3. What were the prosecution's arguments in favor of trying the defendants for piracy? What arguments did the defense put forth?

4. Two graphs accompany the article. What information do the graphs supply? How do they support Johnson's point that it is important to resolve the definition of piracy at this time?

Questions About the Writer's Craft

1. **The pattern.** What are the term, class, and characteristics involved in the definition of *piracy*? In what way does the selection focus on definition by negation?

2. Does the author intend to inform, entertain, or persuade the reader? What is the selection's tone? Is it suitable to his purpose? How are the two graphs relevant, or not relevant, to the author's purpose?

3. What historical anecdote does Johnson use to open his article? What is the effect of this opening? Describe the two current-day piracy anecdotes, besides that of the Norfolk trial, that the author relates.

4. The author refers to a number of legal rulings and often gives technical terms for parts of ships. What language techniques does he use to keep the selection interesting and accessible to the average reader? Give some examples.

Writing Assignments Using Definition as a Pattern of Development

1. The Geneva Convention sets forth rules for treating noncombatants during wartime. One major controversy today concerns how to treat captured terrorists. Do some research, and write an essay in which you define *terrorism*. In your definition include your view of whether a non-U.S. citizen on trial for terrorism should be treated as a civilian or an enemy combatant. Consider including graphs or charts that support your main points.

2. *Piracy* has come to mean acts such as downloading music from the Internet without permission, knocking off designer handbags, or bootlegging copies of movies. Write an essay in which you establish a definition of *piracy* that focuses on these kinds of acts. Decide whether these acts should be considered theft.

Writing Assignment Combining Patterns of Development

3. Should crimes against humanity have universal jurisdiction, as piracy does? For example, in 1998 the Chilean dictator Augusto Pinochet was indicted by a magistrate in Spain for human rights violations committed in Chile. He was arrested in London, but then ultimately released and allowed to return to Chile. Do some research on how human rights crimes are prosecuted internationally. Write an essay in which you *describe* and *compare* the possibilities for prosecution of human rights violations.

ADDITIONAL WRITING TOPICS: DEFINITION

General Assignments

Using definition, develop one of these topics into an essay.

1. Fads	**6.** Inner peace	**11.** Exploitation
2. Helplessness	**7.** Obsession	**12.** A double bind
3. An epiphany	**8.** Generosity	**13.** A conflict of interest
4. A workaholic	**9.** Depression	**14.** An ethical quandary
5. A Pollyanna	**10.** Greed	**15.** A win-win situation

Assignments Using Visuals

Use the suggested visuals to help develop a definition essay on one of these topics:

1. Masculinity and how it is presented in ads (photos or Web links to ads)

2. Discrimination in the United States today (charts or graphs)

3. Various definitions of *success* and which one most resonates with you (photos)

4. What it means to be middle class (graphs or charts)

5. New technologies over the past 500 years (photos and Web links)

Assignments with a Specific Purpose, Audience, and Point of View

1. Academic life. You've been asked to write part of a pamphlet for students who come to the college health clinic. For this pamphlet, define *one* of the following conditions and its symptoms: *depression, stress, burnout, test anxiety,* *addiction* (to alcohol, drugs, or TV), *workaholism.* Part of the pamphlet should describe ways to cope with the condition described.

2. **Academic life.** One of your responsibilities as a peer counselor in the student counseling center involves helping students communicate more effectively. To assist students, write a definition of some term that you think represents an essential component of a strong interpersonal relationship. You might, for example, define *respect, sharing, equality,* or *trust.* Part of the definition should employ definition by negation, a discussion of what the term is *not.*

3. **Civic activity.** *Newsweek* magazine runs a popular column called "My Turn," consisting of readers' opinions on subjects of general interest. Write a piece for this column defining *today's college students.* Use the piece to dispel some negative stereotypes (for example, that college students are apathetic, ill-informed, self-centered, and materialistic).

4. **Civic activity.** In your apartment building, several residents have complained about their neighbors' inconsiderate and rude behavior. You're president of the residents' association, and it's your responsibility to address this problem at your next meeting. Prepare a talk in which you define *courtesy,* the quality you consider most essential to neighborly relations. Use specific examples of what courtesy is and isn't to illustrate your definition.

5. **Workplace action.** You're an attorney arguing a case of sexual harassment—a charge your client has leveled against an employer. To win the case, you must present to the jury a clear definition of exactly what *sexual harassment* is and isn't. Write such a definition for your opening remarks in court.

6. **Workplace action.** A new position has opened in your company. Write a job description to be sent to employment agencies that will screen candidates. Your description should define the job's purpose, state the duties involved, and outline essential qualifications.

Argumentation-Persuasion

In this chapter, you will learn:

18.1 To use the pattern of argumentation-persuasion to develop your essays

18.2 To consider how argumentation-persuasion can fit your purpose and audience

18.3 To develop prewriting, writing, and revision strategies for using argumentation-persuasion in an essay

18.4 To analyze how argumentation-persuasion is used effectively in one student-written and six professionally authored selections

18.5 To write your own essays using argumentation-persuasion as a strategy

What Is Argumentation-Persuasion?

"You can't possibly believe what you're saying."

"Look, I know what I'm talking about, and that's that."

Does this heated exchange sound familiar? Probably. When we hear the word *argument*, most of us think of a verbal battle propelled by stubbornness and irrational thought, with one person pitted against the other.

Argumentation in writing, though, is a different matter. Using clear thinking and logic, the writer tries to convince readers of the soundness of a particular opinion on a controversial issue. If, while trying to convince, the writer uses emotional language and dramatic appeals to readers' concerns, beliefs, and values, then the piece is called **persuasion.** Besides encouraging acceptance of an opinion, persuasion often urges readers (or another group) to commit themselves to a course of action.

Because people respond rationally *and* emotionally to situations, argumentation and persuasion are usually *combined*. When argumentation and persuasion blend in this way, emotion *supports*

FDA *Consumer Health Information*
www.fda.gov/consumer

Regulation of Genetica
Engineered Animals

The Food and Dr
Administration
has issued fina
guidance on its appo
to regulating genet
engineered (GE) ani

The guidance, issued Jan
is aimed at industry; ho
believes the guidance ma
the public gain a better un
of this important and deve
    FDA invited public co
60 days after the release
guidance on regulating GN
September 2008. The age
comments from groups a
uals ranging from cons
animal advocates, to foo
and trade associations, te
and researchers. FDA con
approximately 28,000 p
ments in producing the fir

Genetic Engineering
Genetic engineering is a
which scientists use re
DNA (rDNA) techn
introduce desirable tra
organism. DNA is the
inside the nucleus of
carries the genetic instr
making living organisms
use rDNA techniques to
DNA molecules.

rather than *replaces* logic and sound reasoning. Although some writers resort to emotional appeals to the exclusion of rational thought, when you prepare argumentation-persuasion essays, you should advance your position through a balanced appeal to reason and emotion.

How Argumentation-Persuasion Fits Your Purpose and Audience

You probably realize that argumentation, persuasion, or a combination of the two is everywhere: an editorial urging the overhaul of an ill-managed literacy program; a commercial for a new shampoo; a scientific report advocating increased funding for AIDS research. Your own writing involves argumentation-persuasion as well. When you prepare a *causal analysis, descriptive piece, narrative,* or *definition essay,* you advance a specific point of view: MTV has a negative influence on teens' view of sex; Cape Cod in winter is imbued with a special kind of magic; a disillusioning experience can teach people much about themselves; *character* can be defined as the willingness to take unpopular positions on difficult issues. Indeed, an essay organized around any of the patterns of development described in this book may have a persuasive intent. You might, for example, encourage readers to try out a *process* you've explained, or to see one of the two movies you've *compared.*

Argumentation-persuasion, however, involves more than presenting a point of view and providing evidence. Unlike other forms of writing, it assumes controversy and addresses opposing viewpoints. Consider the following assignments, which require the writer to take a position on a controversial issue:

> Citing the fact that the highest percentage of automobile accidents involve young men, insurance companies consistently charge their highest rates to young males. Is this practice fair? Why or why not?

> Some colleges and universities have instituted a "no pass, no play" policy for athletes. Explain why this policy is or is not appropriate.

It's impossible to predict with absolute certainty what will make readers accept the view you advance or take the action you propose. But the ancient Greeks, who formulated our basic concepts of logic, isolated three factors crucial to the effectiveness of argumentation-persuasion: *logos, pathos,* and *ethos.*

Your main concern in an argumentation-persuasion essay should be with the *logos*, or **soundness**, of your argument: the facts, statistics, examples, and authoritative statements you gather to support your viewpoint. This supporting evidence must be unified, specific, sufficient, accurate, and representative (see pages 43–46 and 61–63). Imagine, for instance, you want to convince people that a popular charity misappropriates the money it receives from that public. Your readers, inclined to believe in the good works of the charity, will probably dismiss your argument unless you can substantiate your claim with valid, well-documented evidence that enhances the *logos* of your position.

Sensitivity to the *pathos*, or the **emotional power of language**, is another key consideration for writers of argumentation-persuasion essays. *Pathos* appeals to readers' needs, values, and attitudes, encouraging them to commit themselves to a viewpoint or course of action. The *pathos* of a piece derives partly from the writer's language. *Connotative* language—words with strong emotional overtones—can move readers to accept a point of view and may even spur them to act.

Advertising and propaganda generally rely on *pathos* to the exclusion of logic, using emotion to influence and manipulate. Consider the following pitches for a man's cologne and a woman's perfume. The language—and the attitudes to which it appeals—are different in each case:

> Brawn: Experience the power. Bold. Yet subtle. Clean. Masculine. The scent for the man who's in charge.

> Black Lace is for you—the woman who dresses for success but who dares to be provocative, slightly naughty. Black Lace. Perfect with pearls by day and with diamonds by night.

The appeal to men plays on the impact that the words *Brawn, bold, power*, and *in charge* may have for some males. Similarly, the charged words *Black Lace, provocative, naughty*, and *diamonds* are intended to appeal to business women who—in the advertiser's mind, at least—may be looking for ways to reconcile sensuality and professionalism.

Like an advertising copywriter, you must select language that reinforces your message. In a paper supporting an expanded immigration policy, you might use evocative phrases such as "land of liberty," "a nation of immigrants," and "America's open-door policy." However, if you were arguing for strict immigration quotas, you might use language such as "save jobs for unemployed Americans," "flood of unskilled labor," and "illegal aliens." Remember, though: Such language should *support, not supplant,* clear thinking. (See page 389 for additional information on persuasive language.)

Finally, whenever you write an argumentation-persuasion essay, you should establish your *ethos*, or **credibility** and **reliability.** You cannot expect readers to accept or act on your viewpoint unless you convince them that you know what you're talking about and that you're worth listening to. You will come across as knowledgeable and trustworthy if you present a logical, reasoned argument that takes opposing views into account. Make sure, too, that your appeals to emotion aren't excessive. Overwrought emotionalism undercuts credibility. (For more on general ethical considerations in writing, see "Characteristics of Evidence" on pages 43–46.)

Writing an effective argumentation-persuasion essay involves an interplay of *logos, pathos*, and *ethos*. The exact balance among these factors is determined by your audience and purpose (that is, whether you want the audience simply to agree with your view or whether you also want them to take action). More than any other kind of writing, argumentation-persuasion requires that you *analyze your readers* and tailor your approach to them. You need to determine how much they know about the issue, how they feel about you and your position, what their values and attitudes are, what motivates them.

In general, most readers will fall into one of three broad categories: supportive, wavering, or hostile. Each type of audience requires a different blend of *logos, pathos*, and *ethos* in an argumentation-persuasion essay.

1. **A supportive audience.** If your audience agrees with your position and trusts your credibility, you don't need a highly reasoned argument dense with facts, examples, and statistics. Although you may want to solidify support by providing additional information (*logos*), you can rely primarily on *pathos*—a strong emotional appeal—to reinforce readers' commitment to your shared viewpoint.

2. **A wavering audience.** At times, readers may be interested in what you have to say but may not be committed fully to your viewpoint. Or perhaps they're not as informed about the subject as they should be. In either case, because your readers need to be encouraged to give their complete support, you don't want to risk alienating them with a heavy-handed emotional appeal. Concentrate instead on *ethos* and *logos*, bolstering your image as a reliable source and providing the evidence needed to advance your position.

3. **A hostile audience.** An apathetic, skeptical, or hostile audience is obviously most difficult to convince. With such an audience you should avoid emotional appeals because they might seem irrational, sentimental, or even comical. Instead, weigh the essay heavily in favor of logical reasoning and hard-to-dispute facts (*logos*). Readers may not be won over to your side, but your sound, logical argument may encourage them to be more tolerant of your viewpoint. Indeed, such increased receptivity may be all you can reasonably expect from a hostile audience. (*Note:* The checklists below and on pages 400–401 provide additional guidelines for analyzing your audience.)

Prewriting Strategies

The following checklist shows how you can apply to argumentation-persuasion some of the prewriting techniques discussed in Chapter 2.

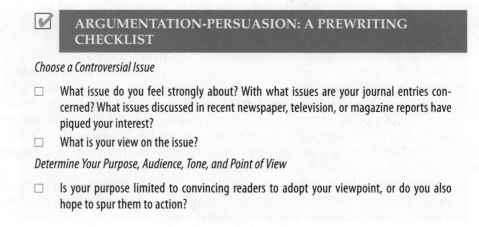

☑ **ARGUMENTATION-PERSUASION: A PREWRITING CHECKLIST**

Choose a Controversial Issue

☐ What issue do you feel strongly about? With what issues are your journal entries concerned? What issues discussed in recent newspaper, television, or magazine reports have piqued your interest?

☐ What is your view on the issue?

Determine Your Purpose, Audience, Tone, and Point of View

☐ Is your purpose limited to convincing readers to adopt your viewpoint, or do you also hope to spur them to action?

FIGURE 18.1

Development Diagram: Writing an Argumentation-Persuasion Essay

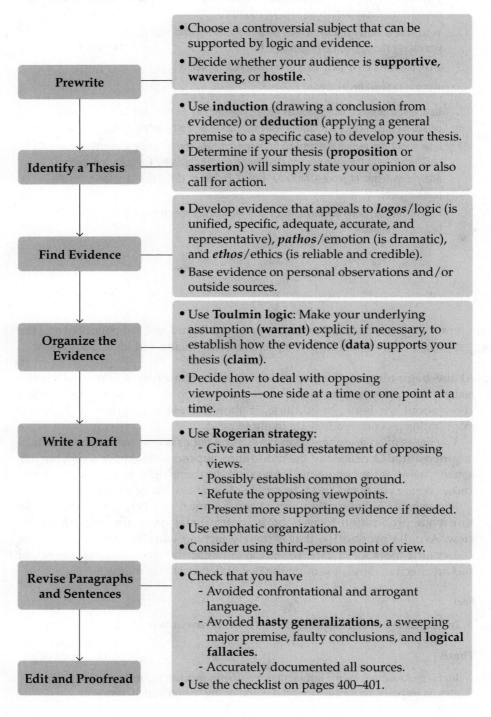

Prewrite
- Choose a controversial subject that can be supported by logic and evidence.
- Decide whether your audience is **supportive**, **wavering**, or **hostile**.

Identify a Thesis
- Use **induction** (drawing a conclusion from evidence) or **deduction** (applying a general premise to a specific case) to develop your thesis.
- Determine if your thesis (**proposition** or **assertion**) will simply state your opinion or also call for action.

Find Evidence
- Develop evidence that appeals to *logos*/logic (is unified, specific, adequate, accurate, and representative), *pathos*/emotion (is dramatic), and *ethos*/ethics (is reliable and credible).
- Base evidence on personal observations and/or outside sources.

Organize the Evidence
- Use **Toulmin logic**: Make your underlying assumption (**warrant**) explicit, if necessary, to establish how the evidence (**data**) supports your thesis (**claim**).
- Decide how to deal with opposing viewpoints—one side at a time or one point at a time.

Write a Draft
- Use **Rogerian strategy**:
  - Give an unbiased restatement of opposing views.
  - Possibly establish common ground.
  - Refute the opposing viewpoints.
  - Present more supporting evidence if needed.
- Use emphatic organization.
- Consider using third-person point of view.

Revise Paragraphs and Sentences
- Check that you have
  - Avoided confrontational and arrogant language.
  - Avoided **hasty generalizations**, a sweeping major premise, faulty conclusions, and **logical fallacies**.
  - Accurately documented all sources.

Edit and Proofread
- Use the checklist on pages 400–401.

The first statement is certainly true. It would be difficult to find anyone who believes that these are easy times for small farmers. Because the statement invites little opposition, it can't serve as the focus of an argumentation-persuasion essay. The second statement, though, takes a controversial stance on a complex issue. Such a proposition is a valid starting point for a paper intended to argue and persuade. However, don't assume that this advice means that you should take a highly opinionated position in your thesis. A dogmatic, overstated proposition ("Campus security is staffed by overpaid, badge-flashing incompetents") is bound to alienate some readers.

Remember also to keep the proposition narrow and specific, so you can focus your thoughts in a purposeful way. Consider the following statements:

Broad Thesis

The welfare system has been abused over the years.

Narrowed Thesis

Welfare payments should be denied to unmarried mothers under the age of eighteen.

If you tried to write a paper based on the first statement, you would face an unmanageable task—showing all the ways that welfare has been abused. Your readers would also be confused about what to expect in the paper: Will it discuss unscrupulous bureaucrats, fraudulent bookkeeping, dishonest recipients? In contrast, the revised thesis is limited and specific. It signals that the paper will propose severe restrictions. Such a proposal will surely have opponents and is thus appropriate for argumentation-persuasion.

The thesis in an argumentation-persuasion essay can simply state your opinion about an issue, or it can go a step further and call for some action:

Opinion

The lack of affordable day-care centers discriminates against low-income families.

Call for Action

The federal government should support the creation of more day-care centers in low-income neighborhoods.

In either case, your stand on the issue must be clear to your readers.

2. **Offer readers strong support for your thesis.** Finding evidence that relates to your readers' needs, values, and experience (see page 402) is a crucial part of writing an argumentation-persuasion essay. Readers will be responsive to evidence that is *unified, adequate, specific, accurate, dramatic,* and *representative* (see pages 43–46 and 61–63). The evidence might consist of personal experiences or observations. Or it could be gathered from outside sources—statistics; facts; examples; or expert opinion taken from books, articles, reports, interviews, and documentaries. A paper arguing that elderly

Americans are better off than they used to be might incorporate the following kinds of evidence:

- *Personal observation or experience:* A description of the writer's grandparents who are living comfortably on Social Security and pensions.
- *Statistics from a report:* A statement that the per-capita after-tax income of older Americans is $335 greater than the national average.
- *Fact from a newspaper article:* The point that the majority of elderly Americans do not live in nursing homes or on the streets; rather, they have their own houses or apartments.
- *Examples from interviews:* Accounts of several elderly couples living comfortably in well-managed retirement villages in Florida.
- *Expert opinion cited in a documentary:* A statement by Dr. Marie Sanchez, a specialist in geriatrics: "An over-sixty-five American today is likely to be healthier, and have a longer life expectancy, than a fifty-year-old living only a decade ago."

You may wonder whether to use the *first-person (I)* or *third-person (he, she, they)* point of view when presenting evidence based on personal observation, experience, or interviews. The subjective immediacy typical of the first person often delivers a jolt of persuasive power; however, many writers arguing a point prefer to present personal evidence in an objective way, using the third person to keep the focus on the issue rather than on themselves. When you write an argumentation-persuasion essay, your purpose, audience, and tone will help you decide which point of view will be most effective. If you're not sure which point of view to use, check with your instructor. Some encourage a first-person approach; others expect a more objective stance.

As you seek outside evidence, you may—perhaps to your dismay—come across information that undercuts your argument. Resist the temptation to ignore such material; instead, use the evidence to arrive at a more balanced, perhaps somewhat qualified viewpoint. Conversely, don't blindly accept or disregard flaws in the arguments made by sources agreeing with you. Retain a healthy skepticism, analyzing the material as rigorously as if it were advanced by the opposing side.

Also, keep in mind that outside sources aren't infallible. They may have biases that cause them to skew evidence. So be sure to evaluate your sources. Remember, too, that there are more than two sides to a complex issue. To get as broad a perspective as possible, you should track down sources that have no axe to grind—that is, sources that make a deliberate effort to examine all sides of the issue.

Whatever sources you use, be sure to *document* (give credit to) that material. Otherwise, readers may dismiss your evidence as nothing more than your subjective opinion, or they may conclude that you have *plagiarized*— tried to pass off someone else's ideas as your own. (Documentation isn't necessary when material is commonly known or is a matter of historical or scientific record.) For information about documenting sources in longer, more formal papers, see Chapters 19 and 20.

3. **Seek to create goodwill.** Because your goal is to convince others of your position's soundness, you need to be careful about alienating readers—especially those who don't agree with you. Be careful, then, about using close-minded, morally superior language ("*Anyone* can see that..."). Exaggerated, overly emotional language can also antagonize readers. Last, guard against using confrontational language: "*My opponents* find the existing laws more effective than the proposed legislation" sounds adversarial, whereas" *Opponents* of the proposed legislation...," "*Those opposed* to the proposed legislation...," and "*Supporters* of the existing laws...," seem more evenhanded and respectful. The last three statements also focus—as they should—on the issue, not on the people involved in the debate.

   Goodwill can also be established by finding a *common ground*—some points on which all sides can agree, despite their differences.

4. **Organize the supporting evidence.** The support for an argumentation-persuasion paper can be organized in a variety of ways. Any of the patterns of development described in this book (description, narration, definition, cause-effect, and so on) may be used—singly or in combination—to develop the essay's proposition. Imagine you're writing a paper arguing that car racing should be banned from television. Your essay might contain a *description* of a horrifying accident that was televised in graphic detail; you might devote part of the paper to a *causal analysis* showing that the broadcast of such races encourages teens to drive carelessly; you could include a *process analysis* to explain how young drivers soup up their cars in a dangerous attempt to imitate the racers seen on television. If your essay includes several patterns, you may need a separate paragraph for each.

   When presenting evidence, arrange it so you create the strongest possible effect. In general, you should end with your most compelling point, leaving readers with dramatic evidence that underscores your proposition's validity.

5. **Use Rogerian strategy to acknowledge differing viewpoints.** If your essay has a clear thesis and strong, logical support, you've taken important steps toward winning readers over. However, because argumentation-persuasion focuses on controversial issues, you should also take opposing views into account. As you think about and perhaps research your subject, seek out conflicting viewpoints. A good argument seeks out contrary viewpoints, acknowledges them, perhaps even admits they have some merit. Such a strategy strengthens your argument in several ways. It helps you anticipate objections, alerts you to flaws in your own position, and makes you more aware of the other sides' weaknesses. Further, by acknowledging the dissenting views, you come across as reasonable and thorough—qualities that may disarm readers and leave them more receptive to your argument. You may not convince them to surrender their views, but you can enlarge their perspectives and encourage them to think about your position.

Psychologist Carl Rogers took the idea of acknowledging contrary viewpoints a step further. He believed that argumentation's goal should be to *reduce conflict*, rather than to produce a "winner" and a "loser." But he recognized that people identify so strongly with their opinions that they experience any challenge to those opinions as highly threatening. Such a challenge feels like an attack on their identity. And what's the characteristic response to such a perceived attack? People become defensive; they dig in their heels and become more adamant than ever about their position. Indeed, when confronted with solid information that calls their opinion into question, they devalue that evidence rather than allow themselves to be persuaded. Experiments show that after people form a first impression of another person, they are unlikely to let future conflicting information affect that impression. If, for example, they initially perceive someone to be unpleasant and disagreeable, they tend to reject subsequent evidence that casts the person in a more favorable light.

For these reasons, Rogerian strategy rejects any adversarial approach and adopts, instead, a respectful, conciliatory posture that demonstrates a real understanding of opposing views and emphasizes shared interests and values. The ideal is to negotiate differences and arrive at a synthesis: a new position that both parties find at least as acceptable as their original positions. What follows are three basic Rogerian strategies to keep in mind as you write.

First, you may acknowledge the opposing viewpoint in a two-part proposition consisting of a subordinate clause followed by a main clause. The *first part of the proposition* (the subordinate clause) *acknowledges opposing opinions*; the *second part* (the main clause) *states your opinion* and implies that your view stands on more solid ground. (When using this kind of proposition, you may, but don't have to, discuss opposing opinions.) The following thesis illustrates this strategy (the opposing viewpoint is underlined once; the writer's position is underlined twice):

Although some instructors think that standardized finals restrict academic freedom, such exams are preferable to those prepared by individual professors.

Second, *in the introduction*, you may provide—separate from the proposition—a *one-* or *two-sentence summary of the opposing viewpoint*. Suppose you're writing an essay advocating a ten-day waiting period before an individual can purchase a handgun. Before presenting your proposition at the end of the introductory paragraph, you might include sentences like these: "Opponents of the waiting period argue that the ten-day delay is worthless without a nationwide computer network that can perform background checks. Those opposed also point out that only a percentage of states with a waiting period have seen a reduction in gun-related crime."

Third, you can take *one or two body paragraphs* near the beginning of the essay to *present in greater detail arguments raised by opposing viewpoints*. After that, you grant (when appropriate) the validity of some of those points ("It may be true that…," "Granted,…"). Then you go on to present evidence for your position ("Even so…," "Nevertheless…"). Because you prepared readers to listen to your opinion, they will tend to be more open to your argument.

☑   **USING ROGERIAN STRATEGY: A CHECKLIST**

☐   Begin by making a conscientious effort to *understand* the viewpoints of those with whom you disagree. As you listen to or read about their opinions, try to put yourself in their shoes; focus on *what they believe* and *why they believe it*, rather than on how you will challenge their beliefs.

☐   Open your essay with an unbiased, even-handed *restatement of opposing points of view*. Such an objective summary shows that you're fair and open-minded—and not so blinded by the righteousness of your own position that you can't consider any other. Typically, people respond to such a respectful approach by lowering their defenses. Because they appreciate your ability to understand what they have to say, they become more open to your point of view.

☐   When appropriate, *acknowledge the validity* of some of the arguments raised by those with differing views. What should you do if they make a well-founded point? You'll enhance your credibility if you concede that point while continuing to maintain that, overall, your position is stronger.

☐   Point out areas of *common ground* (see page 389) by focusing on interests, values, and beliefs that you and those with opposing views share. When you say to them, "Look at the beliefs we share. Look at our common concerns," you communicate that you're not as unlike them as they first believed.

☐   Finally, *present evidence* for your position. Because those not agreeing with you have been "softened up" by your noncombative stance and disarmed by the realization that you and they share some values and beliefs, they're more ready to consider your point of view.

6. **Refute differing viewpoint.** There will be times, though, when acknowledging opposing viewpoints and presenting your own case won't be enough. Particularly when an issue is complex and when readers strongly disagree with your position, you may have to *refute* all or part of the *dissenting view*. Refutation means pointing out the problems with opposing viewpoints, thereby highlighting your own position's superiority. You may focus on the opposing sides' inaccurate or inadequate evidence; or you may point to their faulty logic. (Some common types of illogical thinking are discussed on pages 393–396 and 398–400.)

There are various ways to develop a paper's refutation section. The best method to use depends on the paper's length and the complexity of the issue. Two possible sequences are outlined here:

First Strategy

• State your proposition.

• Cite opposing viewpoints and the evidence for those views.

• Refute opposing viewpoints by presenting counterarguments.

Second Strategy

• State your proposition.

• Cite opposing viewpoints and the evidence for those views.

• Refute opposing viewpoints by presenting counterarguments.

• Present additional evidence for your proposition.

In the first strategy, you simply refute all or part of the opposing positions' arguments. The second strategy takes the first one a step further by presenting *additional evidence* to support your proposition. In such a case, the additional evidence *must be different* from the points made in the refutation. The additional evidence may appear at the essay's end (as in the preceding outline), or it may be given near the beginning (after the proposition); it may also be divided between the beginning and end.

No matter which strategy you select, you may refute opposing views *one side at a time* or *one point at a time*. When using the one-side-at-a-time approach, you cite all the points raised by the opposing side and then present your counterargument to each point. When using the one-point-at-a-time strategy, you mention the first point made by the opposing side, refute that point, then move on to the second point and refute that, and so on. (For more on comparing and contrasting the sides of an issue, see pages 284–289.) No matter which strategy you use, be sure to provide clear signals so that readers can distinguish your arguments from the other side's: "Despite the claims of those opposed to the plan, many think that…" and "Those not in agreement think that…."

7. **Use induction or deduction to think logically about your argument.** The line of reasoning used to develop an argument is the surest indicator of how rigorously you have thought through your position. There are two basic ways to think about a subject: inductively and deductively. Though the following discussion treats induction and deduction as separate processes, the two often overlap and complement each other.

Inductive reasoning involves examination of specific cases, facts, or examples. Based on these specifics, you then draw a conclusion or make a generalization. This is the kind of thinking scientists use when they examine evidence (the results of experiments, for example) and then draw a *conclusion*: "Smoking increases the risk of cancer."

With inductive reasoning, the conclusion reached can serve as the proposition for an argumentation-persuasion essay. If the paper advances a course of action, the proposition often mentions the action, signaling an essay with a distinctly persuasive purpose.

Let's suppose that you're writing a paper about a crime wave in the small town where you live. You might use inductive thinking to structure the essay's argument:

Several people were mugged last month while shopping in the center of town. (*Evidence*)

Several homes and apartments were burglarized in the past few weeks. (*Evidence*)

Several cars were stolen from people's driveways over the weekend. (*Evidence*)

The police force hasn't adequately protected town residents. (*Conclusion, or proposition, for an argumentation essay with probable elements of persuasion*)

The police force should take steps to upgrade its protection of town residents. (*Conclusion, or proposition, for an argumentation essay with a clearly persuasive intent*)

This inductive sequence highlights a possible structure for the essay. After providing a clear statement of your proposition, you might detail recent muggings, burglaries, and car thefts. Then you could move to the opposing viewpoint: a description of the steps the police say they have taken to protect town residents. At that point, you would refute the police's claim, citing additional evidence that shows the measures taken have not been sufficient. Finally, if you wanted your essay to have a decidedly persuasive purpose, you could end by recommending specific action the police should take to improve its protection of the community.

As in all essays, your evidence should be *unified, specific, accurate, dramatic, sufficient,* and *representative* (see pages 43–46 and 61–63). These last two characteristics are critical when you think inductively; they guarantee that your conclusion would be equally valid even if other evidence were presented. Insufficient or atypical evidence often leads to **hasty generalizations** that mar the essay's logic. For example, you might think the following: "Some elderly people are wealthy and do not need Social Security checks" (Evidence), and "Some Social Security recipients illegally collect several checks" (Evidence). If you then conclude, "Social Security is a waste of taxpayers' money," your conclusion is invalid and hasty because it's based on only a few atypical examples. Millions of Social Security recipients aren't wealthy and don't abuse the system. If you've failed to consider the full range of evidence, any action you propose ("The Social Security system should be disbanded") will probably be considered suspect by thoughtful readers. It's possible, of course, that Social Security should be disbanded, but the evidence leading to such a conclusion must be sufficient and representative.

When reasoning inductively, you should also be careful that the evidence you collect is *recent* and *accurate*. No valid conclusion can result from dated or erroneous evidence. To ensure that your evidence is sound, you also need to evaluate the reliability of your sources. When a person who is legally drunk claims to have seen a flying saucer, the evidence is shaky, to say the least. But if two respected scientists, both with 20–20 vision, saw the saucer, their evidence is worth considering.

Finally, it's important to realize that there's always an element of uncertainty in inductive reasoning. The conclusion can never be more than an *inference*, involving what logicians call an **inductive leap.** There could be other explanations for the evidence cited and thus other positions to take and actions to advocate. For example, given a small town's crime wave, you might conclude not that the police force has been remiss but that residents are careless about protecting themselves and their property. In turn, you might call for a different kind of action—perhaps that the police conduct public workshops in self-defense and home security. In an inductive argument, your task is to weigh the evidence, consider alternative explanations, then choose the conclusion and course of action that seem most valid.

Unlike inductive reasoning, which starts with a specific case and moves toward a generalization or conclusion, **deductive reasoning** begins with a generalization that is then applied to a specific case. This movement from general to specific involves a three-step form of reasoning called a **syllogism**. The first part of a syllogism is called the **major premise**, a general statement about an entire group. The second part is the **minor premise**, a statement about an individual within that group. The syllogism ends with a **conclusion** about that individual.

Just as you use inductive thinking in everyday life, you use deductive thinking—often without being aware of it—to sort out your experiences. When trying to decide which car to buy, you might think as follows:

Major Premise	In an accident, large cars are safer than small cars.
Minor Premise	The Turbo Titan is a large car.
Conclusion	In an accident, the Turbo Titan will be safer than a small car.

Based on your conclusion, you might decide to take a specific action, buying the Turbo Titan rather than the smaller car you had first considered.

To create a valid syllogism and thus arrive at a sound conclusion, you need to avoid two major pitfalls of deductive reasoning. First, be sure not to start with a *sweeping* or *hasty generalization* (see page 188 in Chapter 12) as your *major premise*. Second, don't accept as truth a *faulty conclusion*. Let's look at each problem.

Sweeping major premise. Perhaps you're concerned about a trash-to-steam incinerator scheduled to open near your home. Your thinking about the situation might follow these lines:

Major Premise	Trash-to-steam incinerators have had serious problems and posed significant threats to the well-being of people living near the plants.
Minor Premise	The proposed incinerator in my neighborhood will be a trash-to-steam plant.
Conclusion	The proposed trash-to-steam incinerator in my neighborhood will have serious problems and pose significant threats to the well-being of people living near the plant.

Having arrived at this conclusion, you might decide to join organized protests against the opening of the incinerator. But your thinking is somewhat illogical. Your *major premise* is a *sweeping* one because it indiscriminately groups all trash-to-steam plants into a single category. It's unlikely that you're familiar with all the trash-to-steam incinerators in this country and abroad; it's probably not true that *all* such plants have had serious difficulties that endangered the public. For your argument to reach a valid conclusion, the major premise must be based on repeated observations or verifiable facts. You would have a better argument, and thus reach a more valid conclusion, if you restricted or qualified the major premise, applying it to some, not all, of the group:

Major Premise	A *number* of trash-to-steam incinerators have had serious problems and posed significant threats to the well-being of people living near the plants.
Minor Premise	The proposed incinerator in my neighborhood will be a trash-to-steam plant.
Conclusion	*It's possible* that the proposed trash-to-steam incinerator in my neighborhood will run into serious problems and pose significant threats to the well-being of people living near the plant.

This new conclusion, the result of more careful reasoning, would probably encourage you to learn more about trash-to-steam incinerators in general and about the proposed plant in particular. If further research still left you feeling uncomfortable about the plant, you would probably decide to join the protest. On the other hand, your research might convince you that the plant has incorporated into its design a number of safeguards that have been successful at other plants. This added information could reassure you that your original fears were unfounded. In either case, the revised deductive process would lead to a more informed conclusion and course of action.

Faulty conclusion. Your syllogism—and thus your reasoning—would also be invalid if your *conclusion reverses the "if...then" relationship implied in the major premise.* Assume you plan to write a letter to the college newspaper urging the resignation of the student government president. Perhaps you pursue a line of reasoning that goes like this:

Major Premise	Students who plagiarize papers must appear before the Faculty Committee on Academic Policies and Procedures.
Minor Premise	Yesterday Jennifer Kramer, president of the student government, appeared before the Faculty Committee on Academic Policies and Procedures.
Conclusion	Jennifer must have plagiarized a paper.
Action	Jennifer should resign her position as student government president.

Such a chain of reasoning is illogical and unfair. Here's why. *If* students plagiarize their term papers and are caught, *then* they must appear before the committee. However, the converse isn't necessarily true—that *if* students appear before the committee, *then* they must have plagiarized. In other words, not *all* students appearing before the Faculty Committee have been called up on plagiarism charges. For instance, Jennifer could have been speaking on behalf of another student; she could have been protesting some action taken by the committee; she could have been seeking the committee's help on an article she plans to write about academic honesty. The conclusion doesn't allow for these other possible explanations.

Now that you're aware of the problems associated with deductive reasoning, let's look at the way you can use a syllogism to structure an argumentation-persuasion essay. Suppose you decide to write a paper advocating support for a projected space mission. You know that controversy surrounds the space program, especially because seven astronauts died in a 1986 launch. Confident that the tragedy has led to more rigorous controls, you want to argue that the benefits of an upcoming mission outweigh its risks. A deductive pattern could be used to develop your argument. In fact, outlining your thinking as a syllogism might help you formulate a proposition, organize your evidence, deal with the opposing viewpoint, and—if appropriate—propose a course of action:

Major Premise	Space programs in the past have led to important developments in technology, especially in medical science.
Minor Premise	The *Cosmos* Mission is the newest space program.
Proposition *(essay might be persuasive)*	The *Cosmos* Mission will most likely lead to important developments in technology, especially in medical science.
Proposition *(essay is clearly persuasive)*	Congress should continue its funding of the *Cosmos* Mission.

Having outlined the deductive pattern of your thinking, you might begin by stating your proposition and then discuss some new procedures developed to protect the astronauts and the rocket system's structural integrity. With that background established, you could detail the opposing claim that little of value has been produced by the space program so far. You could then move to your refutation, citing significant medical advances derived from former space missions. Finally, the paper might conclude on a persuasive note, with a plea to Congress to continue funding the latest space mission.

8. **Use Toulmin logic to establish a strong connection between your evidence and thesis.** Whether you use an essentially inductive or deductive approach, your argument depends on strong evidence. In *The Uses of Argument*, Stephen Toulmin describes a useful approach for strengthening the connection between evidence and thesis. Toulmin divides a typical argument into three parts:

- **Claim**—the thesis, proposition, or conclusion
- **Data**—the evidence (facts, statistics, examples, observations, expert opinion) used to convince readers of the claim's validity
- **Warrant**—the underlying assumption that justifies moving from evidence to claim.

Here's a sample argument using Toulmin's terminology:

The train engineer was under the influence of drugs when the train crashed.	Transportation employees entrusted with the public's safety should be tested for drug use.
(Data)	**(Claim)**

Transportation employees entrusted with the public's safety should not be allowed on the job if they use drugs.

(Warrant)

As Toulmin explains in his book, readers are more apt to consider your argument valid if they know what your warrant is. Sometimes your warrant will be so obvious that you won't need to state it explicitly; an *implicit warrant* will be sufficient. Assume you want to argue that the use of live animals to test product toxicity should be outlawed. To support your claim, you cite the following evidence: first, current animal tests are painful and usually result in the animal's death; second, human cell cultures frequently offer more reliable information on how harmful a product may be to human tissue; and third, computer simulations often can more accurately rate a substance's toxicity. Your warrant, although not explicit, is nonetheless clear: "It is wrong to continue product testing on animals when more humane and valid test methods are available."

Other times, you'll do best to make your *warrant explicit*. Suppose you plan to argue that students should be involved in deciding which faculty members are granted tenure. To develop your claim, you present some evidence. You begin by noting that, currently, only faculty members and administrators review candidates for tenure. Next, you call attention to the controversy surrounding two professors, widely known by students to be poor teachers, who were nonetheless granted tenure. Finally, you cite a decision, made several years ago, to discontinue using student evaluations as part of the tenure process; you emphasize that since that time complaints about teachers' incompetence have risen dramatically. Some readers, though, still might wonder how you got from your evidence to your claim. In this case, your argument could be made stronger by stating your warrant explicitly: "Because students are as knowledgeable as the faculty and administrators about which professors are competent, they should be involved in the tenure process."

The more widely accepted your warrant, Toulmin explains, the more likely it is that readers will accept your argument. If there's no consensus about the warrant, you'll probably need to *back it up*. For the preceding example, you might mention several reports that found students evaluate faculty fairly (most students don't, for example, use the ratings to get back at professors against whom they have a personal grudge); further, students' ratings correlate strongly with those given by administrators and other faculty.

Toulmin describes another way to increase receptivity to an argument: *qualify the claim*—that is, explain under what circumstances it might be invalid or restricted. For instance, you might grant that most students know little about their instructors' research activities, scholarly publications, or participation in professional committees. You could, then, qualify your claim this way: "Because students don't have a comprehensive view of their instructors' professional activities, they should be involved in the tenure process but play a less prominent role than faculty and administrators."

As you can see, Toulmin's approach provides strategies for strengthening an argument. So, when prewriting or revising, take a few minutes to ask yourself the questions listed here.

☑️ **QUESTIONS FOR USING TOULMIN LOGIC: A CHECKLIST**

- ☐ What data (*evidence*) should I provide to support my claim (*thesis*)?
- ☐ Is my warrant clear? Should I state it explicitly? What backup can I provide to justify my warrant?
- ☐ Would qualifying my claim make my argument more convincing?

Your responses to these questions will help you structure a convincing and logical argument.

9. **Recognize logical fallacies.** When writing an argumentation-persuasion essay, you need to recognize **logical fallacies** both in your own argument and in points raised by the opposing side. Work to eliminate such gaps in logic from your own writing and, when they appear in the opposing argument, try to expose them in your refutation. Logicians have identified many logical fallacies—including the sweeping or hasty generalization and the faulty conclusion discussed earlier in this chapter. Other logical fallacies are described in the paragraphs that follow.

The *post hoc* **fallacy** (short for a Latin phrase meaning "after this, therefore because of this") occurs when you conclude that a cause-effect relationship exists simply because one event preceded another. Let's say you note the growing number of immigrants settling in a nearby city, observe the city's economic decline, and conclude that the immigrants' arrival caused the decline. Such a chain of thinking is faulty because it assumes a cause-effect relationship based purely on co-occurrence. Perhaps the immigrants' arrival was a factor in the economic slump, but there could also be other reasons: the lack of financial incentives to attract business to the city, restrictions on the size of the city's manufacturing facilities, citywide labor disputes that make companies leery of settling in the area. Your argument should also consider these possibilities. (For more on the *post hoc* fallacy, see page 318 in Chapter 16.)

The *non sequitur* **fallacy** (Latin for "it does not follow") is an even more blatant muddying of cause-effect relationships. In this case, a conclusion is drawn that has no logical connection to the evidence cited: "Millions of Americans own cars, so there is no need to fund public transportation." The faulty conclusion disregards the millions of Americans who don't own cars; it also ignores pollution and road congestion, both of which could be reduced if people had access to safe, reliable public transportation.

An *ad hominem* **argument** (from the Latin meaning "to the man") occurs when someone attacks a person rather than a point of view. Suppose your college plans to sponsor a physicians' symposium on the abortion controversy. You decide to write a letter to the school paper opposing the symposium. Taking swipes at two of the invited doctors who disapprove of abortion, you mention that one was recently involved in a messy divorce and that the other is alleged to have a drinking problem. By hurling personal invective, you avoid discussing the issue. Mudslinging is a poor substitute for reasoned argument. And as politician Adlai Stevenson once said, "He who slings mud generally loses ground."

Appeals to questionable or faulty authority also weaken an argument. Most of us have developed a healthy suspicion of phrases like *sources close to, an unidentified spokesperson states, experts claim,* and *studies show.* If these people and reports are so reliable, they should be clearly identified.

Begging the question involves failure to establish proof for a debatable point. The writer expects readers to accept as given a premise that's actually controversial. For instance, you would have trouble convincing readers that prayer should be banned from public schools if you based your argument on the premise that school prayer violates the U.S. Constitution. If the Constitution does, either explicitly or implicitly, prohibit prayer in public education, your essay must demonstrate that fact. You can't build a strong argument if you pretend there's no controversy surrounding your premise.

A **false analogy** disregards significant dissimilarities and wrongly implies that because two things share *some* characteristics, they are therefore *alike in all respects.* You might, for example, compare nicotine and marijuana. Both, you could mention, involve health risks and have addictive properties. If, however, you go on to conclude, "Driving while smoking a cigarette isn't illegal, so driving while smoking marijuana shouldn't be illegal either," you're employing a false analogy. You've overlooked a major difference between tobacco and marijuana: Marijuana impairs perception and coordination—important aspects of driving—whereas there's no evidence that tobacco does the same.

The *either/or* **fallacy** occurs when you assume that a particular viewpoint or course of action can have only one of two diametrically opposed outcomes—either totally this or totally that. Say you argue as follows: "Unless colleges continue to offer scholarships based solely on financial need, no one who is underprivileged will be able to attend college." Such a statement ignores the fact that bright, underprivileged students could receive scholarships based on their potential or their demonstrated academic excellence.

Finally, a **red herring** argument is an intentional digression from the issue—a ploy to deflect attention from the matter being discussed. Imagine you're arguing that condoms shouldn't be dispensed to high school students. You would introduce a red herring if you began to rail against parents who fail to provide their children with any information about sex. Most people would agree that parents *should* provide such information. However, the issue being discussed is not parents' irresponsibility but the pros and cons of schools' distributing condoms to students.

Revision Strategies

Once you have a draft of the essay, you're ready to revise. The following checklist will help you and those giving you feedback apply to argumentation-persuasion some of the revision techniques discussed in Chapters 7 and 8.

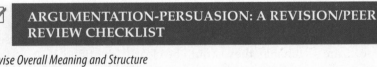

ARGUMENTATION-PERSUASION: A REVISION/PEER REVIEW CHECKLIST

Revise Overall Meaning and Structure

☐ What issue is being discussed? What is controversial about it?

☐ What is the essay's thesis? How does it differ from a generalization or mere statement of fact?

☐ What is the essay's purpose—to win readers over to a point of view, to spur readers to some type of action?

☐ For what audience is the essay written? What strategies are used to make readers receptive to the essay's thesis?

☐ What tone does the essay project? Is the tone likely to win readers over?

☐ If the essay's argument is essentially deductive, is the major premise sufficiently restricted? What evidence is the premise based on? Are the minor premise and conclusion valid? If not, how could these problems be corrected?

☐ Where is the essay weakened by hasty generalizations, a failure to weigh evidence honestly, or a failure to draw the most valid conclusion?

☐ Where does the essay commit any of the following logical fallacies: Concluding that a cause-effect relationship exists simply because one event preceded another? Attacking a person rather than an issue? Drawing a conclusion that isn't logically related to the evidence? Failing to establish proof for a debatable point? Relying on questionable or vaguely specified authority? Drawing a false analogy? Resorting to *either/or* thinking? Using a red herring argument?

Revise Paragraph Development

☐ How apparent is the link between the evidence (data) and the thesis (claim)? How could an explicit warrant clarify the connection?

☐ How would supporting the warrant or qualifying the claim strengthen the argument?

☐   Which paragraphs lack sufficient evidence (facts, examples, statistics, and expert opinion)?

☐   Which paragraphs lack unity? How could they be made more focused? In which paragraphs(s) does evidence seem bland, overly general, unrepresentative, or inaccurate?

☐   Which paragraphs take opposing views into account? Are these views refuted? How? Which counterarguments are ineffective?

☐   Where do outside sources require documentation?

Revise Sentences and Words

☐   What words and phrases help readers distinguish the essay's arguments from those advanced by the opposing side?

☐   Which words carry strong emotional overtones? Is this connotative language excessive? Where does emotional language replace rather than reinforce clear thinking?

☐   Where might dogmatic language ("Anyone can see that . . ." and "Obviously, . . .") alienate readers?

Student Essay: From Prewriting Through Revision

The student essay that follows was written by Mark Simmons in response to this assignment:

> In "How the Schools Shortchange Boys," Gerry Garibaldi invites controversy by claiming that the "newly feminized classroom" is responsible for boys' poor performance in school. Select another controversial issue, one that you feel strongly about. Using logic and solid evidence, convince readers that your viewpoint is valid.

Before writing his essay, Mark used the prewriting strategy of *group brainstorming* to generate material on the subject he decided to write about: compulsory national service. In a lively give-and-take with friends, Mark jotted down, as they occurred, ideas that seemed especially promising. Later on, he typed up his jottings so he could review them more easily. At that point, he began to organize the material.

Mark's typed version of the brainstormed list is on the next page . The handwritten marks indicate his later efforts to organize the material. As you can see, he started organizing the list by crossing out one item (the possibility of low morale) and adding several others (for example, that compulsory national service would be a relatively inexpensive way to repair bridges and roads). Then he labeled points raised by the opposing side and his counterarguments. In the process, the essay's underlying structure began to emerge so clearly that he had no trouble preparing an outline, which is presented on page 403.

Brainstorming

Definition

> Compulsory service—ages 17–25
>
> Two years—military or public service
> Serve after high school or college

Example, where to use?

Israel has it, and it works well

Opposing position: Point 3 (potentially fascist)

> Nazi Germany had it, too
>
> Too authoritarian
>
> Start of a dictatorship

Refutation of point 3 (not fascist)

> Can choose what kind of service
>
> No uniforms
>
> U.S. not a fascist country

Introduction

> Americans very lucky—economic opportunity, right to vote, etc.
>
> Take without giving
>
> Should have to give—program provides that chance

Opposing position: Point 1 (too expensive)

> Program too expensive
>
> Pay—at least minimum wage
>
> Have to provide housing, too

Less costly way to repair bridges and roads and help elderly and homeless

> Can live at home
> Payments from participating towns, cities, states
>
> Could be like AmeriCorps's small budget

Refutation of point 1 (not expensive)

~~Low morale because forced? (Unlike Volunteer peace corps)~~

Opposing position: Point 2 (demoralizing)

> Demoralizing
>
> Interfere with careers

Refutation of point 2 (not demoralizing)

> Learn skills
>
> Time to think about goals
>
> Make real contribution to society
>   Feel good and worthwhile

Outline

Thesis: Compulsory national service would be good for both young people and the country.

    I. Definition of compulsory national service

   II. Cost of compulsory national service

      A. Would be expensive

         1. Would have high administrative costs

         2. Would have high salary and housing costs

      B. Wouldn't be expensive

         1. Could follow AmeriCorps model

         2. Would require the towns, cities, and states using the corps to pay salary and housing costs

         3. Would cut costs by having young people live at home

         4. Would provide a cost-efficient way to repair deteriorating bridges, roads, and neighborhoods

         5. Would provide a cost-efficient way to help the elderly and homeless

  III. Effect of compulsory national service on young people

      A. Would be demoralizing

         1. Would interrupt career plans

         2. Would waste young people's time by making them do work that isn't personally meaningful

      B. Wouldn't be demoralizing

         1. Would give young people time to evaluate life and career goals

         2. Would equip young people with marketable skills

         3. Would make young people from different backgrounds feel good about coming together to contribute to society

  IV. Effect of compulsory national service on American democracy

      A. Could encourage fascism, as it did in Germany

      B. Wouldn't encourage fascism

         1. Wouldn't undermine our present system of checks and balances

         2. Would offer young people choices about when they would serve and in which branch they would serve

         3. Wouldn't require uniforms or confinement in a barracks

         4. Wouldn't be that different from a regular nine-to-five job

Now read Mark's paper, "Compulsory National Service," noting the similarities and differences between his prewriting, outline, and final essay. One difference is especially striking: During prewriting, Mark and his friends tended to identify an objection to compulsory service, brainstorm an appropriate counter-argument, then move to the next objection and its counterargument. Mark used the same *point-by-point* format in his outline. When drafting his paper, though, Mark decided to use the *one-side-at-a-time* format. He summarized all reservations first, then devoted the rest of the essay to a detailed refutation. This change in organization strengthened Mark's argument because his rebuttals acquired greater force when gathered together, instead of remaining scattered throughout the paper. As you read the essay, also consider how well it applies the principles of argumentation-persuasion discussed in this chapter. (The commentary that follows the paper will help you look at Mark's essay more closely and will give you some sense of how he went about revising his first draft.)

Simmons 1

Mark Simmons

Professor Chen

English 102

17 November 2013

Compulsory National Service

enter title and
oublespace all text.

Our high school history class spent several weeks studying the events of   1

the 1960s. The most interesting thing about that decade was the spirit of service

and social commitment among young people. In the '60s, young people thought

eginning of
vo-paragraph
ntroduction

about issues beyond themselves; they joined the Peace Corps, worked in poverty-

stricken Appalachian communities, and participated in freedom marches against

segregation. Most young people today, despite their concern with careers and get-

ting ahead, would also like an opportunity to make a worthwhile contribution to

society.

Convinced that many young adults are indeed eager for such an opportunity,   2

ommon
nowledge: No
eed to document

President Bill Clinton implemented in 1994 a pilot program of voluntary national ser-

vice. The following year, the program was formalized, placed under the management

of the Corporation for National Service (CNS), and given the name AmeriCorps. In

the years 1994–2007, approximately 400,000 AmeriCorps volunteers provided varied

arenthetical
itation of unpaged
nonymous
aterial. Use
bbreviated title.

assistance in communities across the country ("About AmeriCorps"). Such voluntary

national service was also endorsed by President George W. Bush. Following the dev-

astating terrorist attacks on September 11, 2001, President Bush urged Americans to

volunteer as a way of assisting in the nation's recovery and of demonstrating a spirit of national unity. He issued an executive order in early 2002 establishing USA Freedom Corps, an organization seeking to persuade Americans to perform 4,000 hours of volunteer service over a lifetime (Hutcheson). In general, programs such as USA Freedom Corps and the more established AmeriCorps hold out so much promise that it seems only natural to go one step further and make young people's participation in these programs or some kind of national service mandatory. By instituting a program of compulsory national service, the country could tap youth's idealistic desire to make a difference. Such a system would yield significant benefits.

Start of two-sentence thesis

3   What exactly is meant by compulsory national service? Traditionally, it has tended to mean that everyone between the ages of seventeen and twenty-five would serve the country for two years. These young people could choose between two major options: military service or a public-service corps. They could serve their time at any point within an eight-year span. The unemployed or the uncertain could join immediately after high school; collegebound students could complete their education before joining the national service. Years ago, Senator Sam Nunn and Representative Dave McCurdy gave a new twist to the definition of compulsory national service. They proposed a plan that would require all high school graduates applying for federal aid for college tuition to serve either in the military or in a Citizens Corps. Anyone in the Citizens Corps would be required to work full-time at public-service duties for one or two years. During that time, participants would receive a weekly stipend and, at the end, be given a voucher worth $10,000 for each year of civilian service. The voucher could then be applied toward college credit, employment training, or a down payment on a house (Sudo).

Definition paragraph

Beginning of summary of a source's ideas

No page number needed for a one-page source.

4   The traditional plan for compulsory national service and the one proposed by Nunn and McCurdy are just two of many variations that have been discussed over the years. While this country debates the concept, some nations such as France have gone ahead and accepted it enthusiastically. The idea could be workable in this country too. Unfortunately, opponents are doing all they can to prevent the idea from taking hold. They contend, first of all, that the program would cost too much. A great deal of money, they argue, would be spent administering the program, paying young people's wages, and providing housing for participants. Another argument against compulsory national service is that it would demoralize young people; supposedly, the plan would prevent the young from moving ahead with their careers and would make them feel

Topic sentence

Beginning of summary of three points made by the opposing viewpoint

as though they were engaged in work that offered no personal satisfaction. A third argument is that compulsory service would lay the groundwork for a dictatorship. The picture is painted of an army of young people, controlled by the government, much like the Hitler Youth of World War II.

Topic sentence: refutation of first point → Despite opponents' claims that compulsory national service would involve exorbitant costs, the program would not have to be that expensive to run. AmeriCorps has already provided an excellent model for achieving substantial benefits at reasonable cost. For example, a study conducted by universities in Iowa and Michigan showed that each dollar spent on AmeriCorps programs yielded $2.60 in reduced welfare costs, increased earnings, and other benefits **Parenthetical citation of a specific page of a source** (Garland 120). Also, the sums required for wages and housing could be reduced considerably through payments made by the towns, cities, and states using the corps's services. And the economic benefits of the program could be significant. AmeriCorps's official website gives an idea of the current scope of the program's activities. Volunteers provide crucial services including building affordable homes for families, improving health services, responding to natural disasters, **Information from two sources. Sources, separated by a semicolon, are given in the order in which they appear in the Works Cited list.** and tutoring children. A compulsory national corps could also clean up litter, provide day care services, staff libraries, immunize children, and care for the country's growing elderly population ("About AmeriCorps"; Clinton). All these projects would help solve many of the problems that plague our nation, and they would probably cost less than if they were handled by often inefficient government bureaucracies.

Topic sentence: refutation of second point Also, rather than undermining the spirit of young people, as opponents contend, the program would probably boost their morale. Many young people feel enormous pressure and uncertainty; they are not sure whether they want to find a job or further their education. Compulsory national service could give these young **Attribution giving author's full name and area of expertise** people much-needed breathing space. As Edward Lewis, president of St. Mary's College, says, "Many students are not ready for college at seventeen or eighteen. **Full-sentence quotation is preceded by a comma and begins with a capital letter.** This kind of program responds to that need" (qtd. in Fowler). Robert Coles, psychiatrist and social activist, argues that a public service stint enriches participants' lives **Where secondary source was quoted** in yet another way. Coles points out that young people often have little sense of the

5

6

job market. When they get involved in community service, though, they frequently "discover an area of interest…that launches them on a career" (93). Equally important, compulsory national service can provide an emotional boost for the young; all of them would experience the pride that comes from working hard, reaching goals, acquiring skills, and handling responsibilities (Wofford and Waldman). A positive mind-set would also result from the sense of community that would be created by serving in the national service. All young people—rich or poor, educated or not, regardless of sex and social class—would come together and perceive not their differences but their common interests and similarities (Wofford and Waldman). As President Clinton proclaimed at the Year 2000 swearing-in of AmeriCorps's recruits in Philadelphia, AmeriCorps gives volunteers a chance "to tear down barriers of distrust and misunderstanding and old-fashioned ignorance, and build a genuine American community" (Clinton).

7   Finally, in contrast to what opponents claim, compulsory national service would not signal the start of a dictatorship. Although the service would be required, young people would have complete freedom to choose any two years between the ages of seventeen and twenty-five. They would also have complete freedom to choose the branch of the military or public service corps that suits them best. And the corps would not need to be outfitted in military uniforms or to live in barrack-like camps. It could be set up like a regular job, with young people living at home as much as possible, following a nine-to-five schedule, enjoying all the personal freedoms that would ordinarily be theirs. Also, a dictatorship would no more likely emerge from compulsory national service than it has from our present military system. We would still have a series of checks and balances to prohibit the taking of power by one group or individual. We should also keep in mind that our system is different from that of fascist regimes; our long tradition of personal liberty makes improbable the seizing of absolute power by one person or faction. A related but even more important point to remember is that freedom does not mean people are guaranteed the right to pursue only their individual needs. That is mistaking selfishness for freedom. And, as everyone knows, selfishness leads only to misery. The national service would not take away freedom. On the contrary,

---

Marginal notes:

Quotation is blended into the sentence (no comma and the quotation begins with a lowercased word).

Just the page number is provided because the author name is cited in the preceding sentence.

Quotation with ellipsis

Parenthetical citation for source having two authors. No page given because electronic text is unpaged.

Topic sentence: Refutation of third point

serving in the corps would help young people grasp this larger concept of free-dom, a concept that is badly needed to counteract the deadly "look out for num-ber one" attitude that is spreading like a poison across the nation. "We think that there's an inherent idealism in every person, especially young people, that if we give them the right structure and opportunity, we can call it out," says John Sarvey, who trains AmeriCorps participants for work in City Year San Jose, the program he directs ("Helping").

arenthetical citation
ses abbreviated
tle.

Perhaps there will never be a time like the 1960s when so many young people   8
were concerned with remaking the world. Still, a good many of today's young people want meaningful work. They want to feel that what they do makes a difference. A program of compulsory national service would harness this idealism and help young people realize the best in themselves. Such a program would also help resolve some of the country's most critical social problems.

eginning of
wo-paragraph
onclusion

ttribution leading
o a long quotation.
ttribution is fol-
owed by a colon
ecause the lead-in
s a full sentence.
f the lead-in isn't
full sentence, use
comma after the
ttribution.

Almost two decades ago, political commentator Donald Eberly expressed his   9
belief in the power of national service. Urging the inauguration of such a program, Eberly wrote:

> The promise of national service can be manifested in many ways: in
> cleaner air and fewer forest fires; in well-cared-for infants and old folks;
> in a better-educated citizenry and better-satisfied work force; perhaps
> in a more peaceful world. National service has a lot of promise. It's a
> promise well worth keeping. (561)

ong quotation is
ndented one inch.
)on't leave any
xtra space within,
bove, or below the
uotation.

or an indented
uotation, the period
s placed before
ne parenthetical
itation.

Several years later, President Clinton took office, gave his support to the concept, and   10
AmeriCorps was born. This advocacy of public service was then championed, at least in word, by President Bush. During his administration, however, AmeriCorps was threat-ened by deep budget cuts advocated by opponents of the program and its Clintonian legacy. Fortunately, despite these measures, Congress voted in 2003 with overwhelm-ing bipartisan support to save AmeriCorps and salvage a portion of its budget ("Timely Help"). In the words of a *Philadelphia Inquirer* editorial, "The civic yield from that invest-ment is incalculable" ("Ill Served"). An efficient and successful program of voluntary service, AmeriCorps has paved the way. Now seems to be the perfect time to expand the concept and make compulsory national service a reality.

Simmons 6

Works Cited

"About AmeriCorps: What Is AmeriCorps?" *AmeriCorps*. Corp. for Natl. and Community Service, 3 Nov. 2008. Web. 3 Nov. 2013.

Clinton, William J. "Remarks by the President to AmeriCorps." Memorial Hall, Philadelphia. 11 Oct. 2000. Transcript. *Clinton Presidential Materials Project*. Natl. Archives and Records Admin. Web. 6 Nov. 2013.

Coles, Robert. *The Call of Service*. Boston: Houghton 1993. Print.

Eberly, Donald. "What the President Should Do about National Service." *Vital Speeches of the Day*. 15 Aug. 1989: 561-63. Print.

Fowler, Margaret. "New Interest in National Youth Corps." *New York Times* 16 May 1989, natl. ed.: A25. Print.

Garland, Susan B. "A Social Program CEOs Want to Save." *Business Week* 19 June 1996: 120-21. Print.

"Helping Hands." *Online NewsHour*. Transcript. Public Broadcasting Service, 19 July 2000. Web. 11 Nov. 2013.

Hutcheson, Ron. "Bush Moves to Establish His New Volunteer Program." *Philadelphia Inquirer* 31 Jan. 2002: A2. Print.

"Ill Served." Editorial. *Philadelphia Inquirer Online*. Philly.com, 27 June 2003. Web. 8 Nov. 2013.

Sudo, Phil. "Mandatory National Service?" *Scholastic Update* 23 Feb. 1990. Print.

"Timely Help for AmeriCorps." Editorial. *New York Times*. New York Times, 17 July 2003. Web. 11 Nov. 2013.

Wofford, Harris, and Steven Waldman. "AmeriCorps the Beautiful? Habitat for Conservative Values." *Policy Review* 79 (1996): n. pag. *EBSCOhost*. Web. 11 Nov. 2013.

Start Works Cited list on a new page, doublespaced, no extra space after heading or between entries. Each entry begins flush left; Indent successive lines half an inch.

For anonymous Internet material, start with title, give website (italicized) and sponsoring organization, followed by publication date. Give page number if available. State medium consulted ("Web") and date of access.

Transcript of a speech found online. Give URL only for hard-to-retrieve sources.

Book by a single author. Give medium ("Print") at the end of the citation.

Newspaper article whose text appears on only one page

Article from weekly magazine

TV show's transcript found online

Newspaper editorial found online

Scholarly journal article, by two authors, found in a database ("*EBSCOhost*"). Give issue number (or volume and issue number, if available) and year followed by pages or "n. pag." if no page numbers are given in the source.

Commentary

Blend of Argumentation and Persuasion

In his essay, Mark tackles a controversial issue. He takes the position that compulsory national service would benefit both the country as a whole and its young people in particular. Mark's essay is a good example of the way argumentation and persuasion often mix: Although the paper presents Mark's position in a logical, well-reasoned manner (argumentation), it also appeals to readers' personal values and suggests a course of action (persuasion).

Audience Analysis

When planning the essay, Mark realized that his audience—his composition class—would consist largely of two kinds of readers. Some, not sure of their views, would be inclined to agree with him if he presented his case well. Others would probably be reluctant to accept his view. Because of this mixed audience, Mark knew he couldn't depend on *pathos* (an appeal to emotion) to convince readers. Rather, his argument had to rely mainly on *logos* (reason) and *ethos* (credibility). So Mark organized his essay around a series of logical arguments—many of them backed by expert opinion—and he evoked his own authority by drawing on his knowledge of history and his "inside" knowledge of young people.

Introduction and Thesis

Mark introduces his subject by discussing an earlier decade when large numbers of young people worked for social change. Mark's references to the Peace Corps, community work, and freedom marches reinforce his image as a knowledgeable source and establish a context for his position. These historical references, combined with the comments about AmeriCorps, the program of voluntary national service, lead into the two-sentence thesis at the end of the two-paragraph introduction: "By instituting a program of compulsory national service, the country could tap youth's idealistic desire to make a difference. Such a system would yield significant benefits."

The second paragraph in the introduction also illustrates Mark's first use of outside sources. Because the assignment called for research in support of an argument, Mark went to the library and online and identified sources that helped him defend his position. If Mark's instructor had required extensive investigation of an issue, Mark would have been obligated both to dig more deeply into his subject and to use more scholarly and specialized sources. But given the instructor's requirements, Mark proceeded just as he should have: He searched out expert opinion that supported his viewpoint; he presented that evidence clearly; he documented his sources carefully.

Background Paragraph and Use of Outside Sources

The third paragraph provides a working *definition* of compulsory national service by presenting two common interpretations of the concept. Such background information guarantees that Mark's readers will share his understanding of the essay's central concept.

Acknowledging the Opposing Viewpoint

Having explained the meaning of compulsory national service, Mark is now in a good position to launch his argument. Even though he wasn't required to research the opposing viewpoint, Mark wisely decided to get together with some friends to brainstorm some issues that might be raised by the dissenting view. He acknowledges this position in the *topic sentence* of the essay's fourth paragraph: "Unfortunately, opponents are doing all they can to prevent the idea from taking hold." Next he summarizes the main points the dissenting opinion might advance: compulsory national service would be expensive, demoralizing to young people, and dangerously authoritarian. Mark uses the rest of the essay to counter these criticisms.

Refutation

The next three paragraphs (5–7) refute the opposing stance and present Mark's evidence for his position. Mark structures the essay so that against readers can follow his *counterargument* with ease. Each paragraph argues against one opposing point and begins with a *topic sentence* that serves as Mark's response to the dissenting view. Note the way the italicized portion of each topic sentence recalls a dissenting point cited earlier: "Despite opponents' claims that *compulsory national service would involve exorbitant costs*, the program would not have to be that expensive to run" (paragraph 5); "Also, rather than *undermining the spirit of young people*, as opponents contend, the program would probably boost their morale" (6); "Finally, in contrast to what opponents claim, *compulsory national service would not signal the start of a dictatorship*" (7). Mark also guides the reader through the various points in the refutation by using *transitions* within paragraphs: "*And* the economic benefits...could be significant" (5); "*Equally important*, compulsory national service could provide an emotional boost..." (6); "*Also*, a dictatorship would no more likely emerge..." (7).

Throughout the three-paragraph refutation, Mark uses outside sources to lend power to his argument. If the assignment had called for in-depth research, he would have cited facts, statistics, and case studies to develop this section of his essay. Given the nature of the assignment, though, Mark's reliance on expert opinion is perfectly acceptable.

Mark successfully incorporates material from these outside sources into his refutation. He doesn't, for example, string one quotation numbingly after another; instead, he usually develops his refutation by *summarizing* expert opinion and saves *direct quotations* for points that deserve emphasis. Moreover, whenever Mark quotes or summarizes a source, he provides clear signals to indicate that the material is indeed borrowed. (For suggestions for citing outside sources in an essay of your own, see Chapter 19.)

Some Problems with the Refutation

Overall, Mark's three-paragraph refutation is strong, but it would have been even more effective if the paragraph had been resequenced. As it now stands, the last paragraph in the refutation (7) seems anticlimactic. Unlike the preceding two paragraphs, which are developed through fairly extensive reference to outside sources, paragraph 7 depends entirely on Mark's personal feelings and interpretations for its support. Of course, Mark was under no obligation to provide research in all sections of the paper. Even so, the refutation would have been more persuasive if Mark had placed the final paragraph in the refutation in a less emphatic position. He could, for example, have put it first or second in the sequence, saving for last either of the other two more convincing paragraphs.

You may also have felt that there's another problem with the third paragraph in the refutation. Here, Mark seems to lose control of his counterargument. Beginning with "And, as everyone knows,..." Mark falls into the *logical fallacy* called *begging the question*. He shouldn't assume that everyone agrees that a selfish life inevitably brings misery. He also indulges in charged emotionalism when he refs—somewhat melodramatically—to the "deadly 'look out for number one' attitude that is spreading like a poison across the nation."

Inductive Reasoning

In part, Mark arrived at his position *inductively*, through a series of *inferences* or *inductive leaps*. He started with some personal *observations* about the nation and its young people. Then, to support those observations, he added his friends' insights as well as information gathered through research. Combined, all this material led him to the general *conclusion* that compulsory national service would be both workable and beneficial.

Combining Patterns of Development

To develop his argument, Mark draws on several patterns of development. The third paragraph relies on *definition* to clarify what is meant by compulsory national service. The first paragraph of both the introduction and conclusion *compares* and *contrasts* young people of the 1960s with those of today. And, to support his position, Mark uses a kind of *causal analysis*; he both speculates on the likely consequences of compulsory national service and cites expert opinion to illustrate the validity of some of those speculations.

Conclusion

Despite some problems in the final section of his refutation, Mark comes up with an effective two-paragraph conclusion for his essay. In the first closing paragraph, he echoes the point made in the introduction about the 1960s and restates his thesis. That done, he moves to the second paragraph of his conclusion. There, he quotes a dramatic statement from a knowledgeable source, cites efforts to undermine AmeriCorps, and ends by pointing out that AmeriCorps has earned the respect of some unlikely supporters. All that Mark does in this final paragraph lends credibility to the crisp assertion and suggested course of action at the very end of his essay.

Revising the First Draft

Given the complex nature of his argument, Mark found that he had to revise his essay several times. One way to illustrate some of the changes he made is to compare his final introduction with the original draft reprinted here:

Original Version of the Introduction

") Choppy

• Focus right from start on young people—maybe mention youth of 1960s

") Need stronger link between early part of paragraph and thesis

"There's no free lunch." "You can't get something for nothing." "You have to earn your way." In America, these sayings are not really true. In America, we gladly take but give back little. In America, we receive economic opportunity, legal protection, the right to vote, and, most of all, a personal freedom unequaled throughout the world. How do we repay our country for such gifts? In most cases, we don't. This unfair relationship must be changed. The best way to make a start is to institute a system of national compulsory service for young people. This system would be of real benefit to the country and its citizens.

When Mark met with a classmate for a peer review session, he found that his partner had a number of helpful suggestions for revising various sections of the essay. But Mark's partner focused most of her comments on the essay's introduction because she felt it needed special attention. Following his classmate's suggestion, Mark deleted the original introduction's references to Americans in general. He made this change because he wanted readers to know—from the very start of the essay—that the paper would focus not on all Americans but on American youth. To reinforce this emphasis, he also added the point about the social commitment characteristic of young people in the 1960s. This reference to an earlier period gave the discussion an important historical perspective and lent a note of authority to Mark's argument. The decision to mention the '60s also helped Mark realize that his introduction should point out more recent developments—specifically, the promise of AmeriCorps. Mark was pleased to see that adding this new material not only gave the introduction a sharper focus, but it also provided a smoother lead-in to his thesis.

These are just a few of the many changes Mark made while reworking his essay. Because he budgeted his time carefully, he was able to revise thoroughly. With the exception of some weak spots in the refutation, Mark's essay is well reasoned and convincing.

ACTIVITIES: ARGUMENTATION-PERSUASION

Prewriting Activities

1. Imagine you're writing two essays: One defines hypocrisy; the other contrasts license and freedom. Identify an audience for each essay. Then jot down how each essay might argue the merits of certain ways of behaving.

2. Following are several thesis statements for argumentation-persuasion essays. For each thesis, determine whether the three audiences indicated in parentheses are apt to be supportive, wavering, or hostile. Then select *one* thesis and use group brainstorming to identify, for each audience, general concerns on which you might successfully base your persuasive appeal (for example, the concern for approval, for financial well-being, for self-respect, for the welfare of others).

   a. The minimum wage should be raised every two years (*low-income employees, employers, congressional representatives*).

   b. Students should not graduate from college until they have passed a comprehensive exam in their majors (*college students, their parents, college officials*).

   c. The town should pass a law prohibiting residents near the reservoir from using pesticides on their lawns (*environmentalists, homeowners, members of the town council*).

3. Using the thesis you selected in activity 2, focus—for each group indicated in parentheses—on one or two of the general concerns you identified. Then brainstorm with others to determine the specific points you'd make to persuade each group. How would Rogerian argument (pages 389–391) and other techniques (page 384) help you disarm the most hostile audience?

4. Clip an effective advertisement from a magazine or newspaper. Through brainstorming, determine to what extent the ad depends on *logos, ethos,* and *pathos.* Consider the logical fallacies discussed in this chapter. After reviewing your brainstorming, devise a thesis that expresses your feelings about the ad's persuasive strategies. Are they responsible? Why or why not?

5. In a campus, local, or major newspaper, find an editorial with which you disagree. Using the patterns of development, freewriting, or another prewriting technique, generate points that refute the editorial. You may, for example, identify any logical fallacies in the editorial. Then, following one of the refutation strategies discussed in this chapter, organize your rebuttal, keeping in mind the power of Rogerian argument.

Revising Activities

6. Examine the following sets, each containing *data* (evidence) and a *claim* (thesis). For each set, identify the implied *warrant.* Which sets would benefit from an explicit warrant? Why? How might the warrant be expressed? In which sets would it be helpful to support the warrant or qualify the claim? Why? How might the warrant be supported or the claim qualified?

   a. *Data:* An increasing number of Americans are buying Japanese cars. The reason, they report, is that Japanese cars tend to have superior fuel efficiency and longevity. Japanese cars are currently manufactured under stricter quality control than American models.

      Claim: Implementing stricter quality controls is one way for the American auto industry to compete with Japanese imports.

   b. *Data:* Although laws guarantee learning-impaired children an education suitable to their needs, no laws safeguard the special needs of intellectually gifted children. There are, proportionately, far more programs that assist the slow learner than there are those that challenge the fast learner.

      Claim: Our educational system is unfair to gifted children.

   c. *Data:* In 2008, Barack Obama was elected the first nonwhite president of the United States.

      Claim: Obama's election shows that race prejudice no longer plays a major role in U. S. society.

7. Examine the faulty chains of reasoning that follow. Which use essentially inductive logic? Which use essentially deductive logic? In each set, determine, in general terms, why the conclusion is invalid. (The next activity offers practice in identifying specific logical fallacies that render conclusions invalid.)

a. Whenever I work in the college's computer lab, something goes wrong. The program crashes, the cursor freezes, the margins unset themselves.

Conclusion: The college needs to allocate additional funds to repair and upgrade the computers in the lab.

b. Many cars in the student parking lot are dented and look as though they have been in accidents.

Conclusion: Students are careless drivers.

c. Many researchers believe that children in families where both parents work develop confidence and independence. In a nearby community, the number of two-career families increased 15 percent over a two-year period.

Conclusion: Children in the nearby community will develop confidence and independence.

8. Each set of statements that follows contains at least one of the logical fallacies described earlier in the chapter. Identify the fallacy or fallacies in each set and explain why the statements are invalid.

a. Grades are irrelevant to learning. Students are in college to get an education, not good grades. The university should eliminate grading altogether.

b. The best policy is to put juvenile offenders in jail so that they can get a taste of reality. Otherwise, they will repeat their crimes again and again.

c. So-called sex education programs do nothing to decrease the rate of teenage pregnancy. Further expenditures on these programs should be curtailed.

d. This country should research environmentally sound ways to use coal as an energy source. If we don't, we will become enslaved to the oil-rich Middle East nations.

e. If we allow abortion, people will think it's acceptable to kill the homeless or pull the plug on sick people—two groups that are also weak and frail.

f. Two members of the state legislature have introduced gun-control legislation. Both have led sheltered, pampered lives that prevent them from seeing how ordinary people need guns to protect themselves.

9. Following is the introduction from the first draft of an essay advocating the elimination of mandatory dress codes in public schools. Revise the paragraph, being sure to consider these questions: How effectively does the writer deal with the opposing viewpoint? Does the paragraph encourage those who might disagree with the writer to read on? Why or why not? Do you see any logical fallacies in the writer's thinking? Where? Does the writer introduce anything that veers away from the point being discussed? Where? Before revising, you may find it helpful to do some brainstorming—individually or in a group—to find ways to strengthen the paragraph.

After reworking the paragraph, take a few minutes to consider how the rest of the essay might unfold. What persuasive strategies could be used? How could Rogerian argument win over readers? What points could be made? What action could be urged in the effort to build a convincing argument?

In three nearby towns recently, high school administrators joined forces to take an outrageously strong stand against students' constitutional rights. Acting like Fascists, they issued an edict in the form of a preposterous dress code that prohibits students from wearing expensive jewelry, name–brand jeans, leather jackets—anything that the administrators, in their supposed wisdom, consider ostentatious. Perhaps the next thing they'll want to do is forbid students to play hip hop music at school dances. What prompted the administrators' dictatorial prohibition against certain kinds of clothing? Somehow or other, they got it into their heads that having no restrictions on the way students dress creates an unhealthy environment, where students vie with each other for the flashiest attire. Students and parents alike should protest this and any other dress code. If such codes go into effect, we might as well throw out the Constitution.

PROFESSIONAL SELECTIONS: ARGUMENTATION-PERSUASION

Anna Quindlen

Writer Anna Quindlen was born in Philadelphia, Pennsylvania, in 1952, and now lives in New York City. At *The New York Times* she became a regular op-ed columnist, winning the Pulitzer Prize for Commentary in 1992. In 1995, Quindlen left newspaper work and devoted herself primarily to fiction. She has written novels, nonfiction, self-help books, and children's books. Quindlen also writes regularly for *Newsweek,* where this article appeared on June 11, 2007.

Please note the essay structure diagram that appears following this selection (Figure 18.2 on page 419).

Pre-Reading Journal Entry

Getting a driver's license is an important rite of passage for young people in the United States. It's often preceded by a highly stressful process of learning to drive. Recall your own driving lessons and licensing tests. Who taught you to drive? What were the lessons like? What emotions did you experience while learning to drive and taking your driving test? If you do not know how to drive, why not? How do you feel about not having a driver's license? Use your journal to answer these questions.

DRIVING TO THE FUNERAL

1   The four years of high school grind inexorably to a close, the milestones passed. The sports contests, the SATs, the exams, the elections, the dances, the proms. And too often, the funerals. It's become a sad rite of passage in many American communities, the services held for teenagers killed in auto accidents before they've even scored a tassel to hang from the rearview mirror. The hearse moves in procession followed by the late-model compact cars of young people, boys trying to control trembling lower lips and girls sobbing into one another's shoulders. The yearbook has a picture or two with a black border. A mom and dad rise from their seats on the athletic field or in the gym to accept a diploma posthumously.

2   It's simple and inarguable: car crashes are the No. 1 cause of death among 15- to 20-year-olds in this country. What's so peculiar about that fact is that so few adults focus on it until they are planning an untimely funeral. Put it this way: if someone told you that there was one single behavior that would be most likely to lead to the premature death of your kid, wouldn't you try to do something about that? Yet parents seem to treat the right of a 16-year-old to drive as an inalienable one, something to be neither questioned nor abridged.

3   This makes no sense unless the argument is convenience, and often it is. In a nation that developed mass-transit amnesia and traded the exurb for the small town, a licensed son or daughter relieves parents of a relentless roundelay of driving. Soccer field, Mickey Ds, mall, movies. Of course, if that's the rationale, why not let 13-year-olds drive? Any reasonable person would respond that a 13-year-old is too young. But statistics suggest that that's true of 16-year-olds as well. The National Highway Traffic Safety Administration has found that neophyte drivers of 17 have about a third as many accidents as their counterparts only a year younger.

4   In 1984 a solution was devised for the problem of teenage auto accidents that lulled many parents into a false sense of security. The drinking age was raised from 18 to 21. It's become gospel that this has saved thousands of lives, although no one actually knows if that's the case; fatalities fell, but the use of seat belts and airbags may have as much to do with that as penalties for alcohol use. And there has been a pronounced negative effect on college campuses, where administrators describe a forbidden-fruit climate that encourages binge drinking. The pitchers of sangria and kegs of beer that offered legal refreshment for 18-year-olds at sanctioned campus events 30 years ago have given way to a new tradition called "pre-gaming," in which dry college activities are preceded by manic alcohol consumption at frats, dorms and bars.

5   Given the incidence of auto-accident deaths among teenagers despite the higher drinking age, you have to ask whether the powerful lobby Mothers Against Drunk Driving simply targeted the wrong D. In a survey of young drivers, only half said they had seen a peer drive after drinking. Nearly all, however, said they had witnessed speeding, which is the leading factor in fatal crashes by teenagers today. In Europe, governments are relaxed about the drinking age but tough on driving regulations and licensing provisions; in most countries, the driving age is 18.

6   In America some states have taken a tough-love position and bumped up the requirements for young drivers: longer permit periods, restrictions or bans on night driving. Since the greatest danger to a teenage driver is another teenager in the car—the chance of having an accident doubles with two teenage passengers and

skyrockets with three or more—some new rules forbid novice drivers from transporting their peers.

In theory this sounds like a good idea; in fact it's toothless. New Jersey has some 7
of the most demanding regulations for new drivers in the nation, including a provision that until they are 18 they cannot have more than one nonfamily member in the car. Yet in early January three students leaving school in Freehold Township died in a horrific accident in which the car's 17-year-old driver was violating that regulation by carrying two friends. No wonder he took the chance: between July 2004 and November 2006, only 12 provisional drivers were ticketed for carrying too many passengers. Good law, bad enforcement.

States might make it easier on themselves, on police officers and on teenagers, 8
too, if instead of chipping away at the right to drive they merely raised the legal driving age wholesale. There are dozens of statistics to back up such a change: in Massachusetts alone, one third of 16-year-old drivers have been involved in serious accidents. Lots and lots of parents will tell you that raising the driving age is untenable, that the kids need their freedom and their mobility. Perhaps the only ones who wouldn't make a fuss are those parents who have accepted diplomas at graduation because their children were no longer alive to do so themselves, whose children traded freedom and mobility for their lives. They might think it was worth the wait.

Questions for Close Reading

1. What is the selection's thesis? Locate the sentence(s) in which Quindlen states her main idea. If she doesn't state her thesis explicitly, express it in your own words.

2. According to Quindlen, what solutions to the problem of teenage auto accidents have not worked over the last 25 years?

3. What approach to young adults' drinking and driving do European nations take?

4. According to Quindlen, what would be a more effective solution to the problem of teen auto accidents?

Questions About the Writer's Craft

1. **The pattern.** What type of audience—supportive, wavering, or hostile (see page 384)—does Quindlen seem to be addressing? How can you tell?

2. Quindlen bases much of her argument on the statistics she presents. Where do those statistics appear? How effective are they? Use the criteria for sound evidence on pages 382–384 to evaluate Quindlen's use of statistics.

3. **Other patterns.** What other patterns does Quindlen use in this essay? Where? What purpose do these passages serve?

4. **The pattern.** What appeals to *pathos* (see pages 382–383) does Quindlen use? How effective are they?

FIGURE 18.2

Essay Structure Diagram: "Driving to the Funeral" by Anna Quindlen

Introductory paragraphs (paragraph 1)

A "sad rite of passage" for American communities is funeral services held for high school students killed in auto accidents.

Background: Statistic and statement foreshadowing the thesis (2)

Statistic: "Car crashes are the No. 1 cause of death among 15- to 20-year-olds."

Statement: Communities aren't doing enough to change this situation.

Opposing and supporting arguments illustrated by examples, anecdotes, and statistics (3–7)

Opposing argument: A higher driving age is inconvenient for parents and teens, and most 16-year-olds are mature enough to drive safely.

Supporting argument with statistic: New 17-year-old drivers have one-third the accidents that new 16-year-old drivers do, according to the National Highway Safety Administration.

Opposing argument: Raising the drinking age from 18 to 21 has saved lives from accidents.

Supporting argument with examples and statistics: (1) No proof exists that raising the drinking age *alone* is responsible for fewer deaths. Use of seat belts and airbags may play a role. (2) Outlawing drinking doesn't stop students from "pre-gaming" on alcohol. (3) Outlawing alcohol doesn't stop teens from speeding, the leading factor in fatal crashes. (4) In Europe, teens can drink at 16 but cannot drive until 18.

Opposing argument: States have started restricting teen driving: longer permit periods; restrictions on night driving; a ban on teen drivers having more than one nonfamily member in the car.

Supporting argument with anecdote: New requirements are not rigourously reinforced. Despite New Jersey's strict laws, between July 2004 and November 2006, only 12 provisional drivers were ticketed for illegally driving with other teens in their car.

Thesis Concluding paragraph (8)

Thesis: Instead of "chipping away" at the right to drive, just raise the legal driving age.

Conclusion: The increased safety is worth the inconvenience for parents and teens, as parents of teens who have died in crashes will attest.

Writing Assignments Using Argumentation-Persuasion as a Pattern of Development

1. In paragraph 4 of her essay, Quindlen claims that raising the drinking age from 18 to 21 has had an unintended negative effect on college campuses, where binge drinking has become commonplace. Many college administrators agree with her. In fact, a hundred college and university presidents launched the Amethyst Initiative in 2008, calling for "an informed and dispassionate public debate over the effects of the 21-year-old drinking age." Although the college presidents did not actually call for lowering the drinking age, they argued that the current drinking age simply drives drinking underground, where it is more tempting for students and harder to control. Do you agree with the college presidents that the current drinking age of 21 should be reexamined and possibly lowered? Or do you disagree? Do some research on the Amethyst Initiative and the drinking age issue, and then write an essay in which you argue that the current drinking age should be lowered or should remain the same. Be sure to support your position with sound evidence (see pages 382–384).

2. Quindlen supports raising the legal driving age in order to decrease teen auto accidents, indicating that the main arguments for a low legal driving age are that it "relieves parents of an endless roundelay of driving" (paragraph 3) and that "the kids need their freedom and their mobility" (paragraph 8). Are there any other reasons that might support a low legal driving age? Write an essay opposing Quindlen's argument for a higher driving age and supporting a legal driving age of 16, with or without restrictions, depending on your view. Be sure to support your argument with reasons and examples.

Writing Assignment Combining Patterns of Development

3. Provisional driver's licenses vary from state to state, but all are designed to decrease teen auto accidents by restricting driving privileges among the youngest drivers and gradually allowing them more freedom as they get older and remain accident-free. Develop your own rules for a fair and effective provisional driver's license, and write a *process analysis* essay explaining your system. Indicate what drivers are allowed to do at various ages until they are granted full driving privileges as well as the penalties you would impose for infractions and accidents, and give *examples* to illustrate the provisions. In support of your plan, explain the beneficial *effects* that your provisional license would have on teen driving.

Mary Sherry

Following her graduation from Dominican University in 1962 with a degree in English, Mary Sherry (1940–) wrote freelance articles and advertising copy while raising her family. Founder and owner of a small research and publishing firm in Minnesota, she has taught creative and remedial writing to adults for more than sixteen years. The following selection first appeared as a 1991 "My Turn" column in *Newsweek*.

Pre-Reading Journal Entry

Imagine you had a son or daughter who didn't take school seriously. How would you go about motivating the child to value academic success? Would your strategies differ depending on the age and gender of the child? If so, how and why? What other factors might influence your approach? Use your journal to respond to these questions.

IN PRAISE OF THE "F" WORD

1   Tens of thousands of 18-year-olds will graduate this year and be handed meaningless diplomas. These diplomas won't look any different from those awarded their luckier classmates. Their validity will be questioned only when their employers discover that these graduates are semiliterate.

2   Eventually a fortunate few will find their way into educational repair shops—adult-literacy programs, such as the one where I teach basic grammar and writing. There, high-school graduates and high-school dropouts pursuing graduate-equivalency certificates will learn the skills they should have learned in school. They will also discover they have been cheated by our educational system.

3   As I teach, I learn a lot about our schools. Early in each session I ask my students to write about an unpleasant experience they had in school. No writers' block here! "I wish someone would have made me stop doing drugs and made me study." "I liked to party and no one seemed to care." "I was a good kid and didn't cause any trouble, so they just passed me along even though I didn't read well and couldn't write." And so on.

4   I am your basic do-gooder, and prior to teaching this class I blamed the poor academic skills our kids have today on drugs, divorce and other impediments to concentration necessary for doing well in school. But, as I rediscover each time I walk into the classroom, before a teacher can expect students to concentrate, he has to get their attention, no matter what distractions may be at hand. There are many ways to do this, and they have much to do with teaching style. However, if style alone won't do it, there is another way to show who holds the winning hand in the classroom. That is to reveal the trump card[1] of failure.

5   I will never forget a teacher who played that card to get the attention of one of my children. Our youngest, a world-class charmer, did little to develop his intellectual talents but always got by. Until Mrs. Stifter.

6   Our son was a high-school senior when he had her for English. "He sits in the back of the room talking to his friends," she told me. "Why don't you move him to the front row?" I urged, believing the embarrassment would get him to settle down. Mrs. Stifter looked at me steely-eyed over her glasses. "I don't move seniors," she said. "I flunk them." I was flustered. Our son's academic life flashed before my eyes. No teacher had ever threatened him with that before. I regained my composure and managed to say that I thought she was right. By the time I got home I was feeling pretty good about this. It was a radical approach for these times, but, well, why not? "She's going to flunk you," I told my son. I did not discuss it any further. Suddenly English became a priority in his life. He finished out the semester with an A.

---

[1]In cards, an advantage held in reserve until it's needed (editors' note).

I know one example doesn't make a case, but at night I see a parade of students   7
who are angry and resentful for having been passed along until they could no longer
even pretend to keep up. Of average intelligence or better, they eventually quit school,
concluding they were too dumb to finish. "I should have been held back" is a comment I hear frequently. Even sadder are those students who are high-school graduates
who say to me after a few weeks of class, "I don't know how I even got a high-school
diploma."

Passing students who have not mastered the work cheats them and the employers   8
who expect graduates to have basic skills. We excuse this dishonest behavior by saying kids can't learn if they come from terrible environments. No one seems to stop
to think that—no matter what environments they come from—most kids don't put
school first on their list unless they perceive something is at stake. They'd rather be
sailing.

Many students I see at night could give expert testimony on unemployment,   9
chemical dependency, abusive relationships. In spite of these difficulties, they have
decided to make education a priority. They are motivated by the desire for a better job or the need to hang on to the one they've got. They have a healthy fear of
failure.

People of all ages can rise above their problems, but they need to have a reason to   10
do so. Young people generally don't have the maturity to value education in the same
way my adult students value it. But fear of failure, whether economic or academic, can
motivate both.

Flunking as a regular policy has just as much merit today as it did two genera-   11
tions ago. We must review the threat of flunking and see it as it really is—a positive
teaching tool. It is an expression of confidence by both teachers and parents that
the students have the ability to learn the material presented to them. However,
making it work again would take a dedicated, caring conspiracy between teachers
and parents. It would mean facing the tough reality that passing kids who haven't
learned the material—while it might save them grief for the short term—dooms
them to long-term illiteracy. It would mean that teachers would have to follow
through on their threats, and parents would have to stand behind them, knowing
their children's best interests are indeed at stake. This means no more doing Scott's
assignments for him because he might fail. No more passing Jodi because she's such
a nice kid.

This is a policy that worked in the past and can work today. A wise teacher, with   12
the support of his parents, gave our son the opportunity to succeed—or fail. It's time
we return this choice to all students.

Questions for Close Reading

1. What is the selection's thesis? Locate the sentence(s) in which Sherry states
   her main idea. If she doesn't state the thesis explicitly, express it in your own
   words.

2. Sherry opens her essay with these words: "Tens of thousands of 18-year-olds will
   graduate this year and be handed meaningless diplomas." Why does Sherry consider these diplomas meaningless?

3. According to Sherry, what justification do many teachers give for "passing students who have not mastered the work" (paragraph 8)? Why does Sherry think that it is wrong to pass such students?

4. What does Sherry think teachers should do to motivate students to focus on school despite the many "distractions...at hand" (4)?

Questions About the Writer's Craft

1. **The pattern.** To write an effective argumentation-persuasion essay, writers need to establish their credibility. How does Sherry convince readers that she is qualified to write about her subject? What does this attempt to establish credibility say about Sherry's perception of her audience's point of view?

2. Sherry's title is deliberately misleading. What does her title lead you to believe the essay will be about? Why do you think Sherry chose this title?

3. Why do you suppose Sherry quotes her students rather than summarizing what they had to say? What effect do you think Sherry hopes the quotations will have on readers?

4. **Other patterns.** What *example* does Sherry provide to show that the threat of failure can work? How does this example reinforce her case?

Writing Assignments Using Argumentation-Persuasion as a Pattern of Development

1. Like Sherry, write an essay arguing your position on a controversial school-related issue. Once you select a topic, brainstorm with others to gather insight into varying points of view. When you write, restrict your argument to one level of education, and refute as many opposing arguments as you can.

2. Sherry acknowledges that she used to blame students' poor academic skills on "drugs, divorce and other impediments." To what extent should teachers take these and similar "impediments" into account when grading students? Are there certain situations that call for leniency, or should out-of-school forces affecting students not be considered? To gain perspective on this issue, interview several friends, classmates, and instructors. Then write an essay in which you argue your position. Provide specific examples to support your argument, being sure to acknowledge and—when possible—to refute opposing viewpoints.

Writing Assignment Combining Patterns of Development

3. Where else, besides in the classroom, do you see people acting irresponsibly, expending little effort, and taking the easy way out? Select *one* area and write an essay *illustrating the effects* of this behavior on everyone concerned.

DEBATING THE ISSUES: GENDER-BASED EDUCATION

Gerry Garibaldi

Writer and teacher Gerry Garibaldi was born in 1951, grew up in San Francisco, and attended San Francisco State University. Following college, he worked for Paramount Pictures, first as a reader and eventually as a vice president of production. He was also a freelance writer for film studios and a journalist. Then Garibaldi changed careers, to teach high school English. This article was published in *City Journal*, an urban policy quarterly, in summer 2006.

Pre-Reading Journal Entry

Think back to your own high school days. Recall how boys and girls were treated in school and how they behaved. Did you notice any differences in the way boys and girls were treated by teachers? In the way they behaved in class? In your journal, record some of the differences between the sexes that you noted. To what extent was your own behavior as a high school student influenced by your gender?

HOW THE SCHOOLS SHORTCHANGE BOYS

In the newly feminized classroom, boys tune out.   1

Since I started teaching several years ago, after 25 years in the movie business, I've   2
come to learn firsthand that everything I'd heard about the feminization of our schools is real—and far more pernicious to boys than I had imagined. Christina Hoff Sommers was absolutely accurate in describing, in her 2000 bestseller, *The War Against Boys*, how feminist complaints that girls were "losing their voice" in a male-oriented classroom have prompted the educational establishment to turn the schools upside down to make them more girl-friendly, to the detriment of males.

As a result, boys have become increasingly disengaged. Only 65 percent earned   3
high school diplomas in the class of 2003, compared with 72 percent of girls, education researcher Jay Greene recently documented. Girls now so outnumber boys on most university campuses across the country that some schools, like Kenyon College, have even begun to practice affirmative action for boys in admissions. And as in high school, girls are getting better grades and graduating at a higher rate.

As Sommers understood, it is boys' aggressive and rationalist nature—redefined by   4
educators as a behavioral disorder—that's getting so many of them in trouble in the feminized schools. Their problem: they don't want to be girls.

Take my tenth-grade student Brandon. I noted that he was on the no-pass list again,   5
after three consecutive days in detention for being disruptive. "Who gave it to you this time?" I asked, passing him on my way out.

"Waverly," he muttered into the long folding table.   6

"What for?"   7

"Just asking a question," he replied.   8

9   "No," I corrected him. "You said"—and here I mimicked his voice—" 'Why do we have to do this crap anyway?' Right?"

10   Brandon recalls one of those sweet, ruby-cheeked boys you often see depicted on English porcelain.

11   He's smart, precocious, and—according to his special-education profile—has been "behaviorally challenged" since fifth grade. The special-ed classification is the bane of the modern boy. To teachers, it's a yellow flag that snaps out at you the moment you open a student's folder. More than any other factor, it has determined Brandon's and legions of other boys' troubled tenures as students.

12   Brandon's current problem began because Ms. Waverly, his social studies teacher, failed to answer one critical question: What was the point of the lesson she was teaching? One of the first observations I made as a teacher was that boys invariably ask this question, while girls seldom do. When a teacher assigns a paper or a project, girls will obediently flip their notebooks open and jot down the due date. Teachers love them. God loves them. Girls are calm and pleasant. They succeed through cooperation.

13   Boys will pin you to the wall like a moth. They want a rational explanation for everything. If unconvinced by your reasons—or if you don't bother to offer any—they slouch contemptuously in their chairs, beat their pencils, or watch the squirrels outside the window. Two days before the paper is due, girls are handing in the finished product in neat vinyl folders with colorful clip-art title pages. It isn't until the boys notice this that the alarm sounds. "Hey, you never told us 'bout a paper! What paper?! I want to see my fucking counselor!"

14   A female teacher, especially if she has no male children of her own, I've noticed, will tend to view boys' penchant for challenging classroom assignments as disruptive, disrespectful—rude. In my experience, notes home and parent-teacher conferences almost always concern a boy's behavior in class, usually centering on this kind of conflict. In today's feminized classroom, with its "cooperative learning" and "inclusiveness," a student's demand for assurance of a worthwhile outcome for his effort isn't met with a reasonable explanation but is considered inimical to the educational process. Yet it's this very trait, innate to boys and men, that helps explain male success in the hard sciences, math, and business.

15   The difference between the male and female predilection for hard proof shows up among the teachers, too. In my second year of teaching, I attended a required seminar on "differentiated instruction," a teaching model that is the current rage in the fickle world of pop education theory. The method addresses the need to teach all students in a classroom where academic abilities vary greatly—where there is "heterogeneous grouping," to use the ed-school jargon—meaning kids with IQs of 55 sit side by side with the gifted. The theory goes that the "least restrictive environment" is best for helping the intellectually challenged. The teacher's job is to figure out how to dice up his daily lessons to address every perceived shortcoming and disability in the classroom.

16   After the lecture, we broke into groups of five, with instructions to work cooperatively to come up with a model lesson plan for just such a classroom situation. My group had two men and three women. The women immediately set to work; my seasoned male cohort and I reclined sullenly in our chairs.

17   "Are the women going to do all the work?" one of the women inquired brightly after about ten minutes.

"This is baloney," my friend declared, yawning, as he chucked the seminar handout into a row of empty plastic juice bottles. "We wouldn't have this problem if we grouped kids by ability, like we used to." 18

The women, all dedicated teachers, understood this, too. But that wasn't the point. Treating people as equals was a social goal well worth pursuing. And we contentious boys were just too dumb to get it. 19

Female approval has a powerful effect on the male psyche. Kindness, consideration, and elevated moral purpose have nothing to do with an irreducible proof, of course. Yet we male teachers squirm when women point out our moral failings—and our boy students do, too. This is the virtue that has helped women redefine the mission of education. 20

The notion of male ethical inferiority first arises in grammar school, where women make up the overwhelming majority of teachers. It's here that the alphabet soup of supposed male dysfunctions begins. And make no mistake: while girls occasionally exhibit symptoms of male-related disorders in this world, females diagnosed with learning disabilities simply don't exist. 21

For a generation now, many well-meaning parents, worn down by their boy's failure to flourish in school, his poor self-esteem and unhappiness, his discipline problems, decide to accept administration recommendations to have him tested for disabilities. The pitch sounds reasonable: admission into special ed qualifies him for tutoring, modified lessons, extra time on tests (including the SAT), and other supposed benefits. It's all a hustle, Mom and Dad privately advise their boy. Don't worry about it. We know there's nothing wrong with you. 22

To get into special ed, however, administrators must find something wrong. In my four years of teaching, I've never seen them fail. In the first IEP (Individualized Educational Program) meeting, the boy and his parents learn the results of disability testing. When the boy hears from three smiling adults that he does indeed have a learning disability, his young face quivers like Jell-O. For him, it was never a hustle. From then on, however, his expectations of himself—and those of his teachers—plummet. 23

Special ed is the great spangled elephant in the education parade. Each year, it grows larger and more lumbering, drawing more and more boys into the procession. Since the publication of Sommers's book, it has grown tenfold. Special ed now is the single largest budget item, outside of basic operations, in most school districts across the country. 24

Special-ed boosters like to point to the success that boys enjoy after they begin the program. Their grades rise, and the phone calls home cease. Anxious parents feel reassured that progress is happening. In truth, I have rarely seen any real improvement in a student's performance after he's become a special-ed kid. On my first day of teaching, I received manila folders for all five of my special-ed students—boys all—with a score of modifications that I had to make in each day's lesson plan. 25

I noticed early on that my special-ed boys often sat at their desks with their heads down or casually staring off into space, as if tracking motes in their eyes, while I proceeded with my lesson. A special-ed caseworker would arrive, take their assignments, and disappear with the boys into the resource room. The students would return the next day with completed assignments. 26

"Did you do this yourself?" I'd ask, dubious. 27

They assured me that they did. I became suspicious, however, when I noticed that they couldn't perform the same work on their own, away from the resource room. 28

A special-ed caseworker's job is to keep her charges from failing. A failure invites scrutiny and reams of paperwork. The caseworkers do their jobs.

29   Brandon has been on the special-ed track since he was nine. He knows his legal rights as well as his caseworkers do. And he plays them ruthlessly. In every debate I have with him about his low performance, Brandon delicately threads his response with the very sinews that bind him. After a particularly easy midterm, I made him stay after class to explain his failure.

30   "An 'F'?!" I said, holding the test under his nose.

31   "You were supposed to modify that test," he countered coolly. "I only had to answer nine of the 27 questions. The nine I did are all right."

32   His argument is like a piece of fine crystal that he rolls admiringly in his hand. He demands that I appreciate the elegance of his position. I do, particularly because my own is so weak.

33   Yet while the process of education may be deeply absorbing to Brandon, he long ago came to dismiss the content entirely. For several decades, white Anglo-Saxon males—Brandon's ancestors—have faced withering assault from feminism- and multiculturalism-inspired education specialists. Armed with a spiteful moral rectitude, their goal is to sever his historical reach, to defame, cover over, dilute...and then reconstruct.

34   In today's politically correct textbooks, Nikki Giovanni and Toni Morrison stand shoulder-to-shoulder with Mark Twain, William Faulkner, and Charles Dickens, even though both women are second-raters at best. But even in their superficial aspects, the textbooks advertise publishers' intent to pander to the prevailing PC[1] attitudes. The books feature page after page of healthy, exuberant young girls in winning portraits. Boys (white boys in particular) will more often than not be shunted to the background in photos or be absent entirely or appear sitting in wheelchairs.

35   The underlying message isn't lost on Brandon. His keen young mind reads between the lines and perceives the folly of all that he's told to accept. Because he lacks an adult perspective, however, what he cannot grasp is the ruthlessness of the war that the education reformers have waged. Often when he provokes, it's simple boyish tit for tat.

36   A week ago, I dispatched Brandon to the library with directions to choose a book for his novel assignment. He returned minutes later with his choice and a twinkling smile.

37   "I got a grreat book, Mr. Garibaldi!" he said, holding up an old, bleary, clothbound item. "Can I read the first page aloud, pahlease?"

38   My mind buzzed like a fly, trying to discover some hint of mischief.

39   "Who's the author?"

40   "Ah, Joseph Conrad," he replied, consulting the frontispiece. "Can I? Huh, huh, huh?"

41   "I guess so."

42   Brandon eagerly stood up before the now-alert class of mostly black and Puerto Rican faces, adjusted his shoulders as if straightening a prep-school blazer, then intoned solemnly: *"The Nigger of the 'Narcissus'"*—twinkle, twinkle, twinkle. "Chapter one...."

43   Merry mayhem ensued. Brandon had one of his best days of the year.

---

[1]Short for "politically correct," usually used pejoratively (editors' note).

Boys today feel isolated and outgunned, but many, like Brandon, don't lack pluck   44
and courage. They often seem to have more of it than their parents, who writhe
uncomfortably before a system steeled in the armor of "social conscience." The
game, parents whisper to themselves, is to play along, to maneuver, to outdistance
your rival. Brandon's struggle is an honest one: to preserve truth and his own
integrity.

Boys who get a compartment on the special-ed train take the ride to its end   45
without looking out the window. They wait for the moment when they can step
out and scorn the rattletrap that took them nowhere. At the end of the line, some,
like Brandon, may have forged the resiliency of survival. But that's not what school
is for.

Questions for Close Reading

1. What is the selection's thesis? Locate the sentence(s) in which Garibaldi states his
main idea. If he doesn't state his thesis explicitly, express it in your own words.

2. According to Garibaldi, how do boys and girls—and men and women—react to being given an assignment?

3. Why are so many boys tested for disabilities, according to Garibaldi?

4. How does Garibaldi's student Brandon take advantage of his special education
designation?

Questions About the Writer's Craft

1. The pattern. Garibaldi uses expert testimony, statistics, examples from his personal
experience, and anecdotes as evidence for his thesis. List the specific evidence he
uses. Which kinds of evidence does Garibaldi use most often? How does his use of
evidence make the essay more or less persuasive?

2. Other patterns. Garibaldi uses cause-effect, comparison-contrast, and process
analysis in this essay. Identify passages in which these patterns are used.

3. The first sentence in the essay is a strongly worded declaration: "In the newly
feminized classroom, boys tune out." Where else does Garibaldi use such strongly
worded statements? What is the effect of this style?

4. Where does Garibaldi use vulgar or offensive language? What effect, if any, does
this have on his argument?

Writing Assignments Using Argumentation-Persuasion as a Pattern of Development

1. Read Michael Kimmel's "A War Against Boys?" (page 429), an essay that takes exception to Garibaldi's view of boys' education. Decide which writer presents

his case more convincingly. Then write an essay arguing that the *other writer* has trouble making a strong case for his position. Consider the merits and flaws (including any logical fallacies) in the argument, plus such issues as the writer's credibility, strategies for dealing with the opposing view, and use of emotional appeals. Throughout, support your opinion with specific examples drawn from the selection. Keep in mind that you are critiquing the effectiveness of the writer's argument. It's not appropriate, then, simply to explain why you agree or disagree with the writer's position or merely to summarize what the writer says.

2. Although Garibaldi argues forcefully that boys are shortchanged by the "feminization" of education and the special education system, he does not propose any changes to improve the way boys are educated. How might public elementary, middle, and high school education be changed so that boys flourish? What activities or subjects would help boys in school? Using Garibaldi's essay as a take-off point, write an essay in which you argue for changes in education that would benefit boys.

Writing Assignment Combining Patterns of Development

3. As Garibaldi puts it, "Special ed is the great spangled elephant in the education parade." He is correct in asserting that the number of children in special education, and the amount spent to educate them, have increased dramatically in recent years. Brainstorm with others to identify *factors* that might be contributing to this growth; then do some research on the history of special education and current trends. Focusing on several related factors, write an essay showing how these factors contribute to the problem. Possible factors include the following: increases in the number of diagnoses of learning disabilities and autism; lack of standards for determining who needs special education; assigning all low-achieving students to special education whether or not they have a disability; racism; financial incentives for school districts to increase special education enrollment. At the end of the essay, offer some recommendations about *steps* that can be taken to ensure that only children who need it are assigned to special education.

Michael Kimmel

Michael Kimmel is a professor of sociology at State University of New York at Stonybrook and one of the world's leading researchers in gender studies. He is the author or editor of more than twenty volumes on men and masculinity, including *Manhood in America: A Cultural History* (1996) and his latest work, *Guyland: The Perilous World Where Boys Become Men* (2008). His articles appear in dozens of magazines, news-papers, and scholarly journals, and he lectures extensively. The following piece was excerpted from an article published in the Fall 2006 issue of *Dissent Magazine.*

Pre-Reading Journal Entry

The phrase "boys will be boys" is often cited to explain certain types of male behavior. What kinds of actions typically fall in this category? List a few of them in your journal. Which behaviors are positive? Why? Which are negative? Why?

A WAR AGAINST BOYS?

Doug Anglin isn't likely to flash across the radar screen at an Ivy League admissions office. A seventeen-year-old senior at Milton High School, a suburb outside Boston, Anglin has a B-minus average and plays soccer and baseball. But he's done something that millions of other teenagers haven't: he's sued his school district for sex discrimination.

Anglin's lawsuit, brought with the aid of his father, a Boston lawyer, claims that schools routinely discriminate against males. "From the elementary level, they establish a philosophy that if you sit down, follow orders, and listen to what they say, you'll do well and get good grades," he told a journalist. "Men naturally rebel against this." He may have a point: overworked teachers might well look more kindly on classroom docility and decorum. But his proposed remedies—such as raising boy's grades retroactively—are laughable.

And though it's tempting to parse the statements of a mediocre high school senior—what's so "natural" about rebelling against blindly following orders, a military tactician might ask—Anglin's apparent admissions angle is but the latest skirmish of a much bigger battle in the culture wars. The current salvos concern boys. The "trouble with boys" has become a staple on talk-radio, the cover story in *Newsweek*, and the subject of dozens of columns in newspapers and magazines. And when the First Lady offers a helping hand to boys, you know something political is in the works. "Rescuing" boys actually translates into bashing feminism.

There is no doubt that boys are not faring well in school. From elementary schools to high schools they have lower grades, lower class rank, and fewer honors than girls. They're 50 percent more likely to repeat a grade in elementary school, one-third more likely to drop out of high school, and about six times more likely to be diagnosed with attention deficit and hyperactivity disorder (ADHD).

College statistics are similar—if the boys get there at all. Women now constitute the majority of students on college campuses, having passed men in 1982, so that in eight years women will earn 58 percent of bachelor's degrees in U.S. colleges. One expert, Tom Mortensen, warns that if current trends continue, "the graduation line in 2068 will be all females." Mortensen may be a competent higher education policy analyst, but he's a lousy statistician. His dire prediction is analogous to predicting forty years ago that, if the enrollment of black students at Ol' Miss was one in 1964, and, say, two hundred in 1968 and one thousand in 1976, then "if present trends continue" there would be no white students on campus by 1982.

Doomsayers lament that women now outnumber men in the social and behavioral sciences by about three to one, and that they've invaded such traditionally male bastions as engineering (where they now make up 20 percent) and biology and business (virtually par).

6   These three issues—declining numbers, declining achievement, and increasingly problematic behavior—form the empirical basis of the current debate. But its political origins are significantly older and ominously more familiar. Peeking underneath the empirical façade helps explain much of the current lineup.

7   Why now?

8   If boys are doing worse, whose fault is it? To many of the current critics, it's women's fault, either as feminists, as mothers, or as both. Feminists, we read, have been so successful that the earlier "chilly classroom climate" has now become overheated to the detriment of boys. Feminist-inspired programs have enabled a whole generation of girls to enter the sciences, medicine, law, and the professions; to continue their education; to imagine careers outside the home. But in so doing, these same feminists have pathologized boyhood. Elementary schools are, we read, "anti-boy"—emphasizing reading and restricting the movements of young boys. They "feminize" boys, forcing active, healthy, and naturally exuberant boys to conform to a regime of obedience, "pathologizing what is simply normal for boys," as one psychologist puts it. Schools are an "inhospitable" environment for boys, writes Christina Hoff Sommers, where their natural propensities for rough-and-tumble play, competition, aggression, and rambunctious violence are cast as social problems in the making. Michael Gurian argues in *The Wonder of Boys,* that, with testosterone surging through their little limbs, we demand that they sit still, raise their hands, and take naps. We're giving them the message, he says, that "boyhood is defective." By the time they get to college, they've been steeped in anti-male propaganda. "Why would any self-respecting boy want to attend one of America's increasingly feminized universities?" asks George Gilder in *National Review.* The American university is now a "fluffy pink playpen of feminist studies and agitprop 'herstory,' taught amid a green goo of eco-motherism..." [author's ellipsis].

9   Such claims sound tinnily familiar. At the turn of the last century, cultural critics were concerned that the rise of white-collar businesses meant increasing indolence for men, whose sons were being feminized by mothers and female teachers. Then, as now, the solutions were to find arenas in which boys could simply be boys, and where men could be men as well. So fraternal lodges offered men a homo-social sanctuary, and dude ranches and sports provided a place where these sedentary men could experience what Theodore Roosevelt called the strenuous life. Boys could troop off with the Boy Scouts, designed as a fin-de-sie`cle "boys' liberation movement." Modern society was turning hardy, robust boys, as Boy Scouts' founder Ernest Thompson Seton put it, into "a lot of flat chested cigarette smokers with shaky nerves and doubtful vitality." Today, women teachers are once again to blame for boys' feminization. "It's the teacher's job to create a classroom environment that accommodates both male and female energy, not just mainly female energy," explains Gurian.

10   What's wrong with this picture? Well, for one thing, it creates a false opposition between girls and boys, assuming that educational reforms undertaken to enable girls to perform better hinder boys' educational development. But these reforms—new classroom arrangements, teacher training, increased attentiveness

to individual learning styles—actually enable larger numbers of boys to get a better education. Though the current boy advocates claim that schools used to be more "boy friendly" before all these "feminist" reforms, they obviously didn't go to school in those halcyon days, the 1950s, say, when the classroom was far more regimented, corporal punishment common, and teachers far more authoritarian; they even gave grades for "deportment." Rambunctious boys were simply not tolerated; they dropped out.

Gender stereotyping hurts both boys and girls. If there is a zero-sum game, it's not because of some putative feminization of the classroom. The net effect of the No Child Left Behind Act has been zero-sum competition, as school districts scramble to stretch inadequate funding, leaving them little choice but to cut noncurricular programs so as to ensure that curricular mandates are followed. This disadvantages "rambunctious" boys, because many of these programs are after-school athletics, gym, and recess. And cutting "unnecessary" school counselors and other remedial programs also disadvantages boys, who compose the majority of children in behavioral and remedial educational programs. The problem of inadequate school funding lies not at feminists' door, but in the halls of Congress. This is further compounded by changes in the insurance industry, which often pressure therapists to put children on medication for ADHD rather than pay for expensive therapy. 11

Another problem is that the frequently cited numbers are misleading. More people—that is, males and females—are going to college than ever before. In 1960, 54 percent of boys and 38 percent of girls went directly to college; today the numbers are 64 percent of boys and 70 percent of girls. It is true that the rate of increase among girls is higher than the rate of increase among boys, but the numbers are increasing for both. 12

The gender imbalance does not obtain at the nation's most elite colleges and universities, where percentages for men and women are, and have remained, similar. Of the top colleges and universities in the nation, only Stanford sports a fifty-fifty gender balance. Harvard[1] and Amherst enroll 56 percent men, Princeton and Chicago 54 percent men, Duke and Berkeley 52 percent, and Yale 51 percent. In science and engineering, the gender imbalance still tilts decidedly toward men: Cal Tech is 65 percent male and 35 percent female; MIT is 62 percent male, 38 percent female. 13

And the imbalance is not uniform across class and race. It remains the case that far more working-class women—of all races—go to college than do working-class men. Part of this is a seemingly rational individual decision: a college-educated woman still earns about the same as a high-school educated man, $35,000 to $31,000. By race, the disparities are more starkly drawn. Among middle-class, white, high school graduates going to college this year, half are male and half are female. But only 37 percent of black college students and 45 percent of Hispanic students are male. The numerical imbalance turns out to be more a problem of race and class than gender. It is what Cynthia Fuchs Epstein calls a "deceptive distinction"—a difference that appears to be about gender, but is actually about something else. 14

---

[1]Harvard University now enrolls more women than men (author's note).

15   Why don't the critics acknowledge these race and class differences? To many who now propose to "rescue" boys, such differences are incidental because, in their eyes, all boys are the same aggressive, competitive, rambunctious little devils. They operate from a facile, and inaccurate, essentialist dichotomy between males and females. Boys must be allowed to be boys—so that they grow up to be men.

16   This facile biologism leads the critics to propose some distasteful remedies to allow these testosterone-juiced boys to express themselves. Gurian, for example, celebrates all masculine rites of passage, "like military boot camp, fraternity hazings, graduation day, and bar mitzvah" as "essential parts of every boy's life." He also suggests reviving corporal punishment, both at home and at school—but only when administered privately with cool indifference and never in the heat of adult anger. He calls it "spanking responsibly," though I suspect school boards and child welfare agencies might have another term for it.

17   But what boys need turns out to be pretty much what girls need. In their best-selling *Raising Cain,* Michael Thompson and Dan Kindlon describe boys' needs: to be loved, get sex, and not be hurt. Parents are counseled to allow boys their emotions; accept a high level of activity; speak their language; and treat them with respect. They are to teach the many ways a boy can be a man, use discipline to guide and build, and model manhood as emotionally attached. Aside from the obvious tautologies, what they advocate is exactly what feminists have been advocating for girls for some time....

18   How does a focus on the ideology of masculinity explain what is happening to boys in school? Consider the parallel for girls. Carol Gilligan's work on adolescent girls describes how these assertive, confident, and proud young girls "lose their voices" when they hit adolescence. At that same moment, Pollack[2] notes, boys become more confident, even beyond their abilities. You might even say that boys find their voices, but it is the inauthentic voice of bravado, posturing, foolish risk-taking, and gratuitous violence. He calls it "the boy code." The boy code teaches them that they are supposed to be in power, and so they begin to act as if they are. They "ruffle in a manly pose," as William Butler Yeats[3] once put it, "for all their timid heart."

19   In adolescence, both boys and girls get their first real dose of gender inequality: girls suppress ambition, boys inflate it. Recent research on the gender gap in school achievement bears this out. Girls are more likely to undervalue their abilities, especially in the more traditionally "masculine" educational arenas such as math and science. Only the most able and most secure girls take courses in those fields. Thus, their numbers tend to be few, and their mean test scores high. Boys, however, possessed of this false voice of bravado (and facing strong family pressure) are likely to overvalue their abilities, to remain in programs though they are less capable of succeeding.

20   This difference, and not some putative discrimination against boys, is the reason that girls' mean test scores in math and science are now, on average, approaching that of boys. Too many boys remain in difficult math and science courses longer than they

---

[2]William Pollack, author of *Real Boys* (editors' note).

[3]Yeats (1865–1939) was a major Irish poet and playwright, (editors' note)

should; they pull the boys' mean scores down. By contrast, the smaller number of girls, whose abilities and self-esteem are sufficient to enable them to "trespass" into a male domain, skew female data upward.

A parallel process is at work in the humanities and social sciences. Girls' mean test scores in English and foreign languages, for example, outpace those of boys. But this is not the result of "reverse discrimination"; it is because the boys bump up against the norms of masculinity. Boys regard English as a "feminine" subject. Pioneering research by Wayne Martino in Australia and Britain found that boys avoid English because of what it might say about their (inauthentic) masculine pose. "Reading is lame, sitting down and looking at words is pathetic," commented one boy. "Most guys who like English are faggots." The traditional liberal arts curriculum, as it was before feminism, is seen as feminizing. As Catharine Stimpson[4] recently put it, "Real men don't speak French." 21

Boys tend to hate English and foreign languages for the same reasons that girls love them. In English, they observe, there are no hard-and-fast rules, one expresses one's opinion about the topic and everyone's opinion is equally valued. "The answer can be a variety of things, you're never really wrong," observed one boy. "It's not like maths and science where there is one set answer to everything." Another boy noted: 22

> I find English hard. It's because there are no set rules for reading texts... [author's ellipsis]. English isn't like maths where you have rules on how to do things and where there are right and wrong answers. In English you have to write down how you feel and that's what I don't like. 23

Compare this to the comments of girls in the same study: 24

> I feel motivated to study English because... [author's ellipsis] you have freedom in English—unlike subjects such as maths and science—and your view isn't necessarily wrong. There is no definite right or wrong answer, and you have the freedom to say what you feel is right without it being rejected as a wrong answer. 25

It is not the school experience that "feminizes" boys, but rather the ideology of traditional masculinity that keeps boys from wanting to succeed. "The work you do here is girls' work," one boy commented to a researcher. "It's not real work." 26

"Real work" involves a confrontation—not with feminist women, whose sensible educational reforms have opened countless doors to women while closing off none to men—but with an anachronistic definition of masculinity that stresses many of its vices (anti-intellectualism, entitlement, arrogance, and aggression) but few of its virtues. When the self-appointed rescuers demand that we accept boys' "hardwiring," could they possibly have such a monochromatic and relentlessly negative view of male biology? Maybe they do. But simply shrugging our collective shoulders in resignation and saying "boys will be boys" sets the bar much too low. Boys can do better than that. They can be men. 27

---

[4]Stimpson, a professor of English at New York University, has written about women in culture and society (editors' note).

Perhaps the real "male bashers" are those who promise to rescue boys from the   28
clutches of feminists. Are males not also "hardwired" toward compassion, nurtur-
ing, and love? If not, would we allow males to be parents? It is never a biological
question of whether we are "hardwired" for some behavior; it is, rather, a political question of which "hardwiring" we choose to respect and which we choose to
challenge. . . .

Questions for Close Reading

1. What is the selection's thesis? Locate the sentence(s) in which Kimmel states
   his main idea. If he doesn't state his thesis explicitly, express it in your own
   words.

2. Kimmel cites statistics showing that more girls than boys go to college. Where
   does he discuss these statistics? How does he interpret the statistics to support his idea that the imbalance in college attendance does not have to do with
   gender?

3. According to Kimmel, how do girls and boys change when they reach
   adolescence?

4. What does Kimmel mean by the phrase "'the boy code'" (paragraph 18)?

Questions About the Writer's Craft

1. **The pattern.** Kimmel cites a number of experts on both sides of the question he is
   arguing. Which experts oppose his main points? Which ones support them? What
   is the effect of citing so many experts?

2. **The pattern.** What is the purpose of paragraphs 4–6? Paragraphs 7–9? Where
   does Kimmel start presenting his own view of the causes of boys' difficulty in
   school?

3. **Other patterns.** What is the main pattern, other than argumentation-persuasion,
   that is used in this essay? Give specific examples.

4. Reread the biographical sketch of Kimmel on pages 429–430. How does Kimmel's
   background contribute to the *ethos* of this argument? Does it influence your response to his claims?

Writing Assignments Using Argumentation-Persuasion as a Pattern of Development

1. Kimmel focuses primarily on how gender inequality affects boys, but gender inequality affects girls as well (see Kimmel, paragraphs 19 and following). Write an
   essay in which you argue that gender roles and norms limit (or do not limit) what
   women can accomplish in school and in their careers.

2. Kimmel criticizes those who claim that biology, or inborn traits, are primarily responsible for shaping gender differences. He believes that biological differences may exist, but that the environment, including political and cultural forces, has a strong influence. Write an essay arguing your own position about the role that biology and environment play in determining sex-role attitudes and behaviors. Remember to acknowledge opposing views and to defend your own position with examples based on your experiences and observations.

Writing Assignment Combining Patterns of Development

3. Feminism is mentioned throughout Garibaldi's and Kimmel's essays, but neither of them defines the term. Do some research about the history of feminism. Brainstorm with others—both men and women—about the topic, and write an essay in which you *define* feminism. Be sure to give *examples* of what you mean by feminism, either from your own experience or from history.

DEBATING THE ISSUES: GOVERNMENT REGULATION TO HELP CONTROL OBESITY AND RELATED DISEASES

Robert Lustig, Laura Schmidt, and Claire Brindis

Dr. Robert H. Lustig is a professor of pediatrics at the Medical School of the University of California–San Francisco (UC–SF). He has authored or co-authored numerous articles in medical journals, as well as the book *Fat Chance: Beating the Odds Against Sugar, Processed Food, Obesity, and Disease*. His colleagues at UC–SF Medical School, Laura A. Schmidt and Claire Brindis, are professors of health policy, researchers, and authors of numerous professional articles. They are all adamant in their belief that sugar is toxic and that its use should be regulated. Their essay, excerpted here, was first published in *Nature* in 2012.

Pre-Reading Journal Entry

Various local governments have done their best to limit the intake of sugar through partial bans on selling sugary drinks containing more than 16 fluid ounces. What is your opinion regarding government regulation of sugar? Is it time for the government to step in and place regulations on sugar? Is this a necessary step, considering the fact that sugar consumption has tripled over the past fifty years? In what ways might this be a good idea? In what ways might it not be such a good idea? Use your journal to explore these questions.

THE TOXIC TRUTH ABOUT SUGAR

1   Last September, the United Nations declared that, for the first time in human history, chronic non-communicable diseases such as heart disease, cancer and diabetes pose a greater health burden worldwide than do infectious diseases, contributing to 35 million deaths annually.

2   This is not just a problem of the developed world. Every country that has adopted the Western diet—one dominated by low-cost, highly processed food—has witnessed rising rates of obesity and related diseases. There are now 30% more people who are obese than who are undernourished. Economic development means that the populations of low- and middle-income countries are living longer, and therefore are more susceptible to noncommunicable diseases; 80% of deaths attributable to them occur in these countries. Many people think that obesity is the root cause of these diseases. But 20% of obese people have normal metabolism and will have a normal lifespan. Conversely, up to 40% of normal-weight people manifest the diseases that constitute the metabolic syndrome: diabetes, hypertension, lipid problems, cardiovascular disease, non-alcoholic fatty liver disease, cancer and dementia. Obesity is not the cause; rather, it is a marker for metabolic dysfunction, which is even more prevalent.

3   The UN announcement targets tobacco, alcohol and diet as the central risk factors in non-communicable disease. Two of these three—tobacco and alcohol—are regulated by governments to protect public health, leaving one of the primary culprits behind this worldwide health crisis unchecked. Of course, regulating food is more complicated—food is required, whereas tobacco and alcohol are non-essential consumables. The key question is: what aspects of the Western diet should be the focus of intervention?

4   Denmark first chose, in October 2011, to tax foods high in saturated fat, despite the fact that most medical professionals no longer believe that fat is the primary culprit. But now, the country is considering taxing sugar as well—a more plausible and defensible step. Indeed, rather than focusing on fat and salt—the current dietary "bogeymen" of the US Department of Agriculture (USDA) and the European Food Safety Authority—we believe that attention should be turned to "added sugar," defined as any sweetener containing the molecule fructose that is added to food in processing.

5   Over the past 50 years, consumption of sugar has tripled worldwide. In the United States, there is fierce controversy over the pervasive use of one particular added sugar—high-fructose corn syrup (HFCS). It is manufactured from corn syrup (glucose), processed to yield a roughly equal mixture of glucose and fructose. Most other developed countries eschew HFCS, relying on naturally occurring sucrose as an added sugar, which also consists of equal parts glucose and fructose.

6   Authorities consider sugar as "empty calories"—but there is nothing empty about these calories. A growing body of scientific evidence shows that fructose can trigger processes that lead to liver toxicity and a host of other chronic diseases (Lustig). A little is not a problem, but a lot kills—slowly.... If international bodies are truly concerned about public health, they must consider limiting fructose—and its main delivery vehicles, the added sugars HFCS and sucrose—which pose dangers to individuals and to society as a whole.

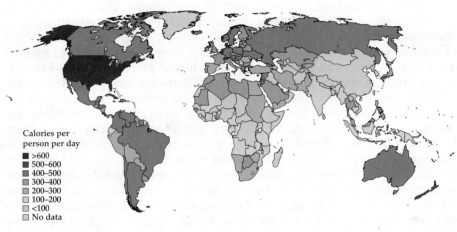

THE GLOBAL SUGAR GLUT

Global sugar supply (in the form of sugar and sugar crops, excluding fruit and wine) expressed as calories per person per day, for the year 2007.

Calories per
person per day

■ >600
■ 500–600
■ 400–500
□ 300–400
□ 200–300
□ 100–200
□ <100
□ No data

Source: Joint WHO/FAO.

No Ordinary Commodity

In 2003, social psychologist Thomas Babor and his colleagues published a landmark book called *Alcohol: No Ordinary Commodity*, in which they established four criteria, now largely accepted by the public-health community, that justify the regulation of alcohol—unavoidability (or pervasiveness throughout society), toxicity, potential for abuse and negative impact on society. Sugar meets the same criteria, and we believe that it similarly warrants some form of societal intervention.

First, consider unavoidability. Evolutionarily, sugar as fruit was available to our ancestors for only a few months a year (at harvest time), or as honey, which was guarded by bees. But in recent years, sugar has been added to virtually every processed food, limiting consumer choice (Vio and Uauy). Nature made sugar hard to get; man made it easy. In many parts of the world, people are consuming an average of more than 500 calories per day from added sugar alone (see "The Global Sugar Glut" map above).

Now, let's consider toxicity. A growing body of epidemiological and mechanistic evidence argues that excessive sugar consumption affects human health beyond simply adding calories (Joint WHO/FAO). Importantly, sugar induces all of the diseases associated with metabolic syndrome (Joint WHO/FAO; Tappy et al.). This includes: hypertension (fructose increases uric acid, which raises blood pressure); high triglycerides and insulin resistance through synthesis of fat in the liver; diabetes from increased liver glucose production combined with insulin resistance; and the aging process, caused by damage to lipids, proteins and DNA through nonenzymatic binding of fructose to these molecules. It can also be argued that fructose exerts toxic effects on the liver similar to those of alcohol (Lustig). This is no surprise, because alcohol is derived from the fermentation of sugar. Some early studies have also linked sugar consumption to human cancer and cognitive decline.

10   Sugar also has a clear potential for abuse. Like tobacco and alcohol, it acts on the brain to encourage subsequent intake. There are now numerous studies examining the dependence-producing properties of sugar in humans (Garber and Lustig). Specifically, sugar dampens the suppression of the hormone ghrelin, which signals hunger to the brain. It also interferes with the normal transport and signaling of the hormone leptin, which helps to produce the feeling of satiety. And it reduces dopamine signaling in the brain's reward center, thereby decreasing the pleasure derived from food and compelling the individual to consume more (Garber and Lustig; Lustig).

11   Finally, consider the negative effects of sugar on society. Passive smoking and drunk-driving fatalities provided strong arguments for tobacco and alcohol control, respectively. The long-term economic, health-care and human costs of metabolic syndrome place sugar overconsumption in the same category (Finkelstein, Fiebelkorn, and Wang). The United States spends $65 billion in lost productivity and $150 billion on health-care resources annually for co-morbidities associated with metabolic syndrome. Seventy-five percent of all US health-care dollars are now spent on treating these diseases and resultant disabilities. Because 75% of military applicants are now rejected for obesity-related reasons, the past three US surgeons general and the chairman of the US Joint Chiefs of Staff have declared obesity a "threat to national security." ...

The Possible Dream

12   Government-imposed regulations on the marketing of alcohol to young people have been quite effective, but there is no such approach to sugar-laden products. Even so, the city of San Francisco, California, recently instituted a ban on including toys with unhealthy meals such as some types of fast food. A limit—or, ideally, ban—on television commercials for products with added sugars could further protect children's health.

13   Reduced fructose consumption could also be fostered through changes in subsidization. Promotion of healthy foods in US low-income programs, such as the Special Supplemental Nutrition Program for Women, Infants and Children and the Supplemental Nutrition Assistance Program (also known as the food-stamps program) is an obvious place to start. Unfortunately, the petition by New York City to remove soft drinks from the food-stamp program was denied by the USDA.

14   Ultimately, food producers and distributors must reduce the amount of sugar added to foods. But sugar is cheap, sugar tastes good, and sugar sells, so companies have little incentive to change. Although one institution alone can't turn this juggernaut around, the US Food and Drug Administration could "set the table" for change (Engelhard, Garson, and Dorn). To start, it should consider removing fructose from the Generally Regarded as Safe (GRAS) list, which allows food manufacturers to add unlimited amounts to any food. Opponents will argue that other nutrients on the GRAS list, such as iron and vitamins A and D, can also be toxic when over-consumed. However,

unlike sugar, these substances have no abuse potential. Removal from the GRAS list would send a powerful signal to the European Food Safety Authority and the rest of the world.

Regulating sugar will not be easy—particularly in the "emerging markets" of devel-   15
oping countries where soft drinks are often cheaper than potable water or milk. We recognize that societal intervention to reduce the supply and demand for sugar faces an uphill political battle against a powerful sugar lobby, and will require active engagement from all stakeholders. Still, the food industry knows that it has a problem—even vigorous lobbying by fast-food companies couldn't defeat the toy ban in San Francisco. With enough clamor for change, tectonic shifts in policy become possible. Take, for instance, bans on smoking in public places and the use of designated drivers, not to mention airbags in cars and condom dispensers in public bathrooms. These simple measures—which have all been on the battleground of American politics—are now taken for granted as essential tools for our public health and wellbeing. It's time to turn our attention to sugar.

Works Cited

Babor, Thomas, et al. *Alcohol: No Ordinary Commodity: Research and Public Policy*. New York: Oxford UP, 2003. Print.

Engelhard, Carolyn L., Arthur Garson, Jr., and Stan Dorn. "Reducing Obesity: Policy Strategies from the Tobacco Wars." *Urban Institute*. Urban Institute, July 2009. Web. 12 Oct. 2011.

Finkelstein, Eric A., Ian C. Fiebelkorn, and Guijing Wang. "National Medical Spending Attributable to Overweight and Obesity: How Much, and Who's Paying?" *Health Affairs* 22.W3 (suppl., 2003): 219–26. Print.

Garber, Andrea K., and Robert H. Lustig. "Is Fast Food Addictive?" *Current Drug Abuse Reviews* 4.3 (2011): 146–62. Print.

Joint WHO/FAO Expert Consultation. *Diet, Nutrition and the Prevention of Chronic Diseases*. Geneva: WHO, 2003. WHO Technical Report Ser. 916. Print.

Lustig, Robert H. "Fructose: Metabolic, Hedonic, and Societal Parallels with Ethanol." *Journal of the American Dietary Association* 110 (2010): 1307–21. Print.

Tappy, Luc, et al. "Fructose and Metabolic Diseases: New Findings, New Questions." *Nutrition* 26.11 (2010): 1044–49. Print.

Vio, Fernando, and Ricardo Uauy. "The Sugar Controversy." *Food Policy for Developing Countries: Case Studies*. Ed. Per Pinstrup-Andersen and Fuzhi Cheng. No. 9-5. Ithaca: Cornell U, 2007. Web. 12 Oct. 2011.

Questions for Close Reading

1. What is the selection's thesis? Locate the sentence(s) in which Lustig, Schmidt, and Brindis state their main idea. If they don't state the thesis explicitly, express it in your own words.

2. The authors state that obesity is not the "root cause" of noncommunicable diseases such as diabetes and hypertension. What do they claim is the real cause of these diseases?

3. What similarities do the authors present between passive smoking, drunk driving, and the effects of sugar on society?

4. The authors include many interesting statistics to convince their readers that sugar is toxic and that its use should be regulated. Identify what you consider to be four of the most alarming statistics they cite, and comment on why these particular statistics stand out to you.

Questions About the Writer's Craft

1. **The pattern.** Which of the two possible strategies for organizing a refutation (focusing on the opposing side's inaccurate or inadequate evidence or pointing to your opponent's faulty logic) do the authors use in their essay? What role does evidence based on research play in their refutation? Do you consider the points they make in their refutation sufficiently persuasive? Explain.

2. **Other patterns.** What *divisions* do Lustig, Schmidt, and Brindis make in their essay? In other words, what categories do they break down into various components?

3. **Other patterns.** The authors use *division* and *classification* to make an *argument* for regulating the use of sugar. How would their argument be less convincing without the material that they divide and classify?

4. The authors include a visual component in their essay—a map titled "The Global Sugar Glut." What does the map add to the essay? How does it make their argument more convincing?

Writing Assignments Using Argument-Persuasion as a Pattern of Development

1. In their essay Lusting, Schmidt, and Brindis attempt to persuade their readers that sugar is a toxic substance whose use needs to be regulated. Think of something else in our society that some individuals feel poses a threat and needs to be regulated—perhaps texting or talking on cell phones while driving, testing for drugs in the workplace, or lowering the drinking age. Write an essay in which you take a stand on the issue, either for or against government regulation, and attempt to persuade your readers of the soundness of your stance on the issue. Consider including one or more images and several sources to add to the effectiveness of your essay.

2. Write an essay in which you take a stand on an issue that is in direct opposition to the stance taken in a published essay you have identified. For example, you might write an essay that references the Lustig, Schmidt, and Brindis essay on the need

for government regulation of sugar, and attempt to persuade your readers that such regulation is an abuse of government power and a threat to individual freedom. Or you might identify an essay that endorses government decriminalization of marijuana, and write an essay that references that essay and attempts to persuade readers of the negative impact that decriminalization could have on society. Consider including images such as charts or diagrams and other outside sources to add to the effectiveness of your essay.

Writing Assignment Combining Patterns of Development

1. In their argumentation-persuasion essay, Lustig, Schmidt, and Brindis *divide*, among other things, the list of various diseases associated with excessive intake of sugar, and they *classify* sugar as a substance that needs to be regulated. Write an essay in which you divide and classify some category of objects you find interesting—for example, motorcycles, weight-loss regimens, cell phones, household pets, types of music, or soft drinks. Consider including one or more images and several outside sources to add to the effectiveness of your essay.

Michael Marlow and Sherzod Abdukadirov

Michael Marlow and Sherzod Abdukadirov are researchers at the Mercatus Center at George Mason University, a nonprofit research center and think tank. Marlow, also a professor of economics at California Polytechnic State University, earned his Ph.D. in economics from Virginia Polytechnic Institute in 1978 and is widely published in scholarly journals. Abdukadirov holds a Ph.D. from George Mason. The essay that follows was originally published in *U.S. News and World Report* on June 5, 2012.

Pre-Reading Journal

There is no denying the fact that obesity has become a serious problem in the United States. Think of people you know who are dangerously obese. How does their size affect their lifestyle? Why do you think they are unable to control their weight? What kinds of programs, if any, do you think might actually help them lose weight and keep it off? Explore these ideas in your journal.

GOVERNMENT INTERVENTION WILL NOT SOLVE OUR OBESITY PROBLEM

It is clear the United States is facing a rising obesity problem. But the challenge remains: We have yet to determine a successful way to tackle it. According to the National Center for Health Statistics, the prevalence of obesity among adults more than doubled from 13.4 percent in 1960 to 34.3 percent in 2008 (Ogden

Trends in overweight, obesity, and extreme obesity among adults aged 20–74 years: United States, 1960–2008

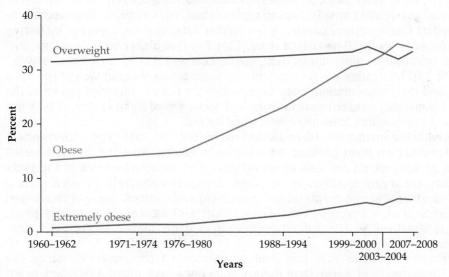

Notes: Age adjusted by the direct method to the 2000 U.S. Census population using age groups 20–39, 40–59, and 60–74. Pregnant females were excluded. Overweight is a body mass index (BMI) of 25 kg/m^2 or greater but less than 30 kg/m^2; obesity is a BMI greater than or equal to 30 kg/m^2; and extreme obesity is a BMI greater than or equal to 40 kg/m^2.

Sources: CDC/NCHS, National Health Examination Survey I 1960–1962; National Health and Nutrition Examination Survey (NHANES) I 1971–1974; NHANES II 1976–1980; NHANES III 1988–1994; NHANES 1999–2000, 2001–2002, 2003–2004, 2005–2006, 2007–2008, and 2009–2010. In Cynthia L. Ogden and Margaret D. Carroll, "Prevalence of Overweight, Obesity, and Extreme Obesity Among Adults: United States, Trends 1960–1962 Through 2007–2008," *Health E-Stats*, National Center for Health Statistics, Dept. of Health and Human Resources, June 2010.

and Carroll). A new report...by the *American Journal of Preventive Medicine* predicts that by 2030, 42 percent of Americans will be obese and 11 percent will be severely obese, or 100 pounds overweight (Finkelstein, Khavjou, Thompson, Trogdon, Pan, Sherry, and Dietz 563).

Despite the myriad of studies showing American obesity is increasing, research 2 does not clearly support that government can solve this complex problem. And yet, government solutions that provide information the public already knows—weight gain occurs when we eat too much and exercise too little—have been the focus to eliminate this epidemic.

Not only is this method not solving the problem, we may actually be increasing the 3 social stigma associated with weight gain. Rather than pursuing a one-size-fits-all solution, we need to push back against government intervention, and allow people to find the solution that best meets their needs.

One popular government solution requires restaurant chains to post calorie counts 4 on their menus to prevent citizens from underestimating their caloric intakes. A recent study examined the impact of New York City's 2008 law requiring restaurant chains to post calorie counts. While 28 percent of patrons said the information influenced their choices, researchers could not detect a change in calories purchased after the law (Elbel, Kersh, Brescoll, and Dixon 1110). A different study in Seattle found similar evidence that their mandatory menu labeling did little to change fast food purchasing behavior (Finkelstein, Strombotne, Chan, and Krieger 122).

Another government favorite, taxing sugary drinks, does more to shore up govern-   5
ment coffers than to reduce obesity. A few studies examined the impact of increasing sugary drinks taxes by 20 percent or more. They find that higher taxes do reduce obesity, but the effect is rather limited (Lin, Smith, Lee, and Hall 329; Fletcher, Frisvold, and Tefft 23). Interestingly, soda taxes mostly cause people without weight problems to cut back their consumption, even though they are not the intended targets of the policy. Meanwhile, frequent soda drinkers buy lower-priced soda, engage in bulk discounted purchases, and brew more sweetened ice tea.

Beyond being ineffective, there are serious harms from these state intervention-   6
ist polices. Government policies are subject to intense lobbying by well-heeled interest groups, which can lead to results that are counterproductive to the problems they are trying to solve. In one case, Congress effectively declared pizza a vegetable under the intense pressure from agricultural business lobby. This allowed Congress to block attempts by the U.S. Department of Agriculture to replace pizza, which is classified as a vegetable because it contains tomato paste, with more vegetables.

Government policies may also lead to unintended consequences. Since the   7
1970s, Department of Agriculture dietary guidelines have urged Americans to eat low fat diets to reduce their risk of coronary heart disease and obesity. Americans heeded the government's advice to switch to foods with less fat content. But because they were eating healthier foods, they ate more. Thus, while the share of calories coming from fat decreased between 1970 and 2000, the actual amount of fat calories in their diet increased, because of an increase in overall calories (Marantz, Bird, and Alderman 234).

The solutions that seem to work the best—the ones that allow individuals to tailor a   8
plan that meets their unique needs—are given short shrift by advocates of government intervention. The growing market for diet books, health foods, weight loss centers, exercise equipment, and athletic clubs is clear evidence that people are concerned about their weight. Unlike government policies, weight loss products and ideas are tested by consumers and failures are replaced by products that really help people control their weight. Consumers will not continue to buy products that don't work.

Unfortunately, citizens have little choice but to pay higher taxes and obey bans   9
when laws are passed. One can expect further tax hikes and bans as policymakers conclude that their well-intentioned policies failed simply because they were not harsh enough, but pushing more stringent, failed policies will not improve public health. Instead of wasting resources on inadequate solutions, consumers should return to the market for the innovative solutions, like healthy foods, gyms, and nutrition centers.

Works Cited

Elbel, Brian, Rogan Kersh, Victoria Brescoll, and L. Beth Dixon. "Calorie Labeling and Food Choices: A First Look at the Effects on Low-income People in New York City." *Health Affairs* 28: 1110–21. Print.

Finkelstein, Eric, Kiersten Strombotne, Nadine Chan, and James Krieger. "Mandatory Menu Labeling in One Fast-Food Chain in King County, Washington." *American Journal of Preventive Medicine* Feb. 2011: 122–27. Print.

Finkelstein, Eric, Olga Khavjou, Hope Thompson, Justin Trogdon, Liping Pan, Bettylou Sherry, and William Dietz. "Obesity and Severe Obesity Forecasts through 2030."*American Journal of Preventive Medicine* June 2012: 563–570. Print.

Fletcher, Jason, David Frisvold, and Nathan Tefft. "Can Soft Drink Taxes Reduce Population Weight?" *Contemporary Economic Policy* Jan. 2010: 23–35. Print.

Lin, B. H., T. A. Smith, J. Y. Lee, and K. D. Hall. "Measuring Weight Outcomes for Obesity Intervention Strategies: The Case of a Sugar-sweetened Beverage Tax." *Economics and Human Biology* Dec. 2011: 329–41. Print.

Marantz, Paul, Elizabeth Bird, and Michael Alderman. "A Call for Higher Standards of Evidence for Dietary Guidelines." *American Journal of Preventive Medicine* Mar. 2008: 234–40.

Ogden, Cynthia, and Margaret Carroll. "Prevalence of Overweight, Obesity, and Extreme Obesity among Adults: United States, Trends 1960–1962 through 2007–2008." *Health E-Stat.* Natl. Center for Health Statistics. Dept. of Health and Human Resources, June 2010. Web. 5 June 2012.

Questions for Close Reading

1. What is the selection's thesis? Locate the sentence(s) in which Marlow and Abdukadirov state their main idea. If they don't state the thesis explicitly, express it in your own words.

2. According to evidence cited by Marlow and Abdukadirov, what has been the effect of posting calorie counts on restaurant menus and taxing sugary drinks in an effort to change purchasing behavior and help control obesity?

3. According to the reading, what harmful and unintended consequences have resulted from government interventionist policies?

4. What solution does the reading offer, instead of government regulation, to help combat our nation's obesity problem?

Questions About the Writer's Craft

1. **The pattern.** Do Marlow and Abdukadirov use *inductive* or *deductive* reasoning (pages 392–395) to develop their argument and persuade their readers? Provide evidence from the reading to support your answer.

2. What does the argument put forth by Marlow and Abdukadirov have in common with the argument put forth by Lustig, Schmidt, and Brindis in the previous reading (pages 437–440)? In what ways do the arguments differ? In your opinion, which argument is more convincing and why?

3. **The pattern.** To what extent do Marlow and Abdukadirov employ the Rogerian strategy outlined earlier in this chapter (page 389–391)? In your opinion, is the strategy effective? Does it help them establish a strong argument that is likely to convince their readers? Do you think their essay would have been more effective if they had adhered more strictly to the Rogerian strategy? Why or why not?

4. The essay by Marlow and Abdukadirov is accompanied by a visual component—a graph that illustrates trends in overweight, obese, and extremely obese adults in the United States. What does the graph add to the essay? Does it make the argument more convincing?

Writing Assignments Using Argument-Persuasion as a Pattern of Development

1. In their essay, Marlow and Abdukadirov attempt to persuade their readers that government intervention is not the answer to our nation's obesity problem, and they employ a modified Rogerian strategy. Write an essay about an issue that is important to you, and use the Rogerian strategy to acknowledge differing viewpoints, point out areas of common ground, and finally, present evidence for your position. You might address an issue such as requiring all students at your school to live on campus during their first year, or banning freshmen and sophomores from having cars on campus. Or you might address a more widespread issue such as providing birth control without parental consent to people aged eleven to seventeen, or requiring all public school students to wear uniforms.

2. Marlow and Abdukadirov take a stand against government intervention to help control obesity. Many others, however, including Lusting, Schmidt, and Brindis, maintain an opposing view. Write an essay in which you argue that in light of the seriousness of the obesity problem in the United States, government intervention is both appropriate and necessary. Research specific evidence to support your position, and include at least one image to strengthen your argument.

Writing Assignment Combining Patterns of Development

3. In their argumentation-persuasion essay, Marlow and Abdukadirov state in the opening paragraph that although "it is clear the United States is facing a rising obesity problem...we have yet to determine a successful way to tackle it." Write an essay in which you *define* obesity and then *illustrate* possible solutions to this problem. You might interview one or more individuals who were once obese but managed to get their weight under control to find out how they accomplished the feat. You might also conduct research to find out more about programs such as Weight Watchers, Medifast, and Nutrisystem that claim to help individuals lose weight and keep it off. You could also explore how operations such as gastric bypass and gastric banding help some individuals control their weight.

ADDITIONAL WRITING TOPICS: ARGUMENTATION-PERSUASION

General Assignments

Using argumentation-persuasion, develop one of these topics into an essay.

1. Hiring or college admissions quotas
2. Giving birth control to teenagers
3. Prayer in the schools
4. Same-sex marriage
5. Reinstating the military draft
6. Penalties for plagiarism
7. Increasing the retirement age
8. Spouses sharing housework equally
9. Smoking in public places
10. Big-time sports in college

Assignments Using Visuals

Use the suggested visuals to help develop an argumentation-persuasion essay on one of these topics:

1. AIDS-prevention education and a decline in AIDS cases (graphs)
2. The influences of ethnic cultures on American culture (photos)
3. Societally beneficial uses of public lands (graphs and photos)
4. Bicycle-riding campaigns and the quality of life in cities (photos)
5. The financial expectations of college and high school graduates (graphs).

Assignments with a Specific Purpose, Audience, and Point of View

1. **Academic.** Your college's financial aid department has decided not to renew your scholarship, citing a drop in your grades and an unenthusiastic recommendation from an instructor. Write a letter to the Director of Financial Aid arguing for the renewal of your scholarship.

2. **Academic.** You strongly believe that a particular policy or regulation on campus is unreasonable or unjust. Write a letter to the Dean of Students (or other appropriate administrator) arguing that the policy needs to be, if not completely revoked, amended in some way. Support your contention with specific examples showing how the regulation has gone wrong. End by providing constructive suggestions for how the policy problem can be solved.

3. **Civic activity.** You and your family don't agree on some aspect of your romantic life (you want to live with your boyfriend/girlfriend and they don't

approve; you want to get married and they want you to wait). Write a letter explaining why your preference is reasonable. Try hard to win your family over to your side.

4. **Civic activity.** Assume you're a member of a racial, ethnic, religious, or social minority. You might, for example, be a Native American, an elderly person, a female executive. On a recent television show or in a TV commercial, you saw something that depicts your group in an offensive way. Write a letter (to the network or the advertiser) expressing your feelings and explaining why you feel the material should be taken off the air.

5. **Workplace action.** As a staff writer for an online pop-culture magazine, you've been asked to nominate the "Most Memorable TV Moment of the Last 50 Years" to be featured as the magazine's lead article. Write a letter to your supervising editor in support of your nominee.

6. **Workplace action.** As a high school teacher, you support some additional restriction on students. The restriction might be "no cell phones in school," "no T-shirts," "no food in class," "no smoking on school grounds." Write an article for the school newspaper justifying this new rule to the student body.

19

Locating, Evaluating, Analyzing, and Synthesizing Research Sources

In this chapter, you will learn:

19.1 To plan your research and develop a thesis
19.2 To conduct primary research—interviews and surveys
19.3 To conduct secondary research
19.4 To prepare a working bibliography and take notes
19.5 To evaluate your sources and analyze information
19.6 To use quotation, paraphrase, and summary to synthesize your research while avoiding plagiarism

Writing a research essay enlarges your perspective and enables you to move beyond off-the-top-of-your-head opinions to those that are firmly supported by evidence. You learn how to evaluate conflicting opinions and detect other people's biases; you acquire analytic skills that will benefit you during your college career, as well as throughout life.

The process of writing a research essay essentially expands what you already know about writing essays; many steps are the same. The two major differences are the greater length of the research essay—usually five or more pages—and the kind of support you offer for your thesis. Rather than relying on personal experiences, you use published information and expert opinion to support your thesis.

It's helpful to view the process as consisting of two major phases: (1) the research stage, when you find out all you can about your subject and identify a tentative, or working, thesis, and (2) the writing stage, when you present in an accepted format what you've discovered. This chapter focuses on the first stage, as shown in Figure 19.1; Chapter 20 examines the second stage. Although

FIGURE 19.1

The Research Essay: Locating, Evaluating, Analyzing, and Synthesizing Research Sources

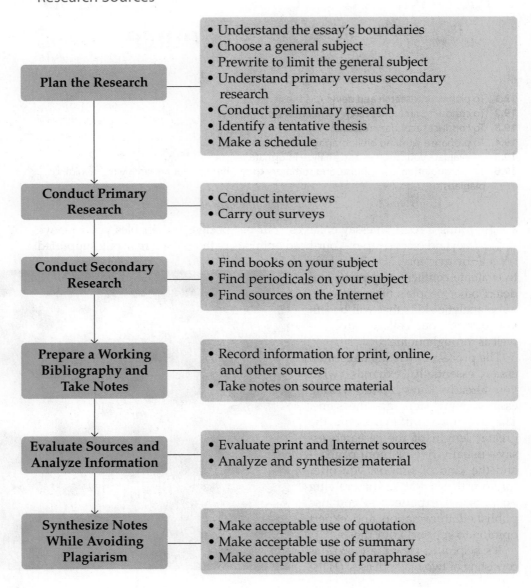

Plan the Research
- Understand the essay's boundaries
- Choose a general subject
- Prewrite to limit the general subject
- Understand primary versus secondary research
- Conduct preliminary research
- Identify a tentative thesis
- Make a schedule

Conduct Primary Research
- Conduct interviews
- Carry out surveys

Conduct Secondary Research
- Find books on your subject
- Find periodicals on your subject
- Find sources on the Internet

Prepare a Working Bibliography and Take Notes
- Record information for print, online, and other sources
- Take notes on source material

Evaluate Sources and Analyze Information
- Evaluate print and Internet sources
- Analyze and synthesize material

Synthesize Notes While Avoiding Plagiarism
- Make acceptable use of quotation
- Make acceptable use of summary
- Make acceptable use of paraphrase

we discuss the research process as a series of steps, we encourage you to modify the sequence to suit your subject, your personal approach to writing, and the requirements of a particular assignment. Remember to turn to relevant sections in Chapters 2 to 9 for in-depth help with the various steps.

Plan the Research

Understand the Essay's Boundaries

Your first step is to clarify the project's requirements. How long should the essay be? How extensively should you deal with opposing viewpoints? Are popular magazines, books, and Web sites acceptable as sources, or should you use only scholarly sources? Has the instructor limited your subject choices?

Also, be sure you understand the essay's overall purpose and audience. Unless you've been assigned a purely informative report ("Explain several psychologists' theories of hostility"), your research essay shouldn't merely patch together ideas from a variety of sources. You should develop your own position, using outside sources to arrive at a balanced but definitive conclusion. Determine also whether your essay will have any other audience in addition to your instructor. If so, you need to make sure to address the needs of that audience.

One more point: Most instructors expect students to use the third-person point of view in research papers. If you plan to include any personal experiences, observations, or interviews along with your outside research, ask your instructor whether the use of the first-person point of view would be appropriate.

Choose a General Subject

Your next step is to choose a general subject. If you have an area of interest—say, early childhood education—the subject might be suitable for a research essay. If you don't immediately know what you'd like to research, consider current events, journal entries, the courses you're taking, the reading you've done on your own, or some of the selections in this book.

You might also do some background reading on several possible general subjects or try using one or more prewriting techniques to identify areas that interest or puzzle you. Brainstorming, questioning, freewriting, and mapping should help you generate ideas worth exploring. When you have a list of possible topics, use the following checklist to help you determine which would be appropriate for a research essay.

Once you have a general topic in mind, you may want to clear it with your instructor. Or you can wait until the next stage to do so—after you've narrowed the topic further.

> ☑ **SELECTING AN APPROPRIATE SUBJECT TO RESEARCH: A CHECKLIST**
>
> ☐ Will you enjoy learning about the subject? Can you obtain enough information on the subject? Recent developments can be investigated through mass-circulation sources, both print and online, including newspapers , magazines, and blogs. Books and specialized or scholarly journal articles on recent events may not be available for some time.
>
> ☐ Has the topic been researched so often that there's nothing new or interesting left to say about it?
>
> ☐ Is the topic surrounded by unreliable testimony, which would make it unsuitable for a research paper?
>
> ☐ Is the topic too trivial for an academic project?
>
> ☐ Does the subject lend itself to or call for research? For example, the dangers of smoking, now almost universally acknowledged, wouldn't make an appropriate topic for a research paper.
>
> ☐ Has the topic been written about by only one major source? If so, your research will be one-sided.
>
> ☐ Can you be objective about your topic?

Prewrite to Limit the General Subject

Once you have a general subject, you'll need to limit or narrow it. "Pollution" is too broad a topic, but "The Effect of Acid Rain on Urban Structures" poses a realistic challenge. Similarly, "Cable Television" is too general, but "Trends in Cable Comedy" is manageable. Remember, you aren't writing a book but an essay of probably five to fifteen pages.

Sometimes you'll know the particular aspect of a subject you want to explore. Usually, though, you'll have to do some work to restrict your subject. In such cases, try using the prewriting techniques of questioning, mapping, freewriting, and brainstorming described in Chapter 2. Discussing the topic with other people and doing some background reading can also help focus your thinking.

Understand Primary versus Secondary Research

Most college research essays involve library or secondary research— information gathered from published print sources or from the Internet—including statistics, facts, case studies, expert opinion, critical interpretations, and experimental results. Occasionally, though, you may want or be asked to conduct primary research. You may, for example, run an experiment, visit an organization, observe a situation, do an interview, or conduct a survey. Pages 454–456 give guidance on doing primary research. If you decide to conduct primary research, you'll need to prepare carefully and establish a strict schedule for yourself.

Conduct Preliminary Research

Frequently, you won't be able to narrow your topic until you learn more about it through background reading of secondary sources, often called *preliminary research*. Just as prewriting precedes a first draft, preliminary research precedes the in-depth research you conduct further along in the process.

At this point, you don't have to track down highly specialized material. Instead, you simply browse the Internet and skim books and general magazine or newspaper articles on your topic to get an overview and to identify possible slants on your subject. If your broad subject is inspired by a class, you can check out the topic in your textbook. And, of course, you can consult library sources including the computerized catalog, various online databases, the reference section, and periodical indexes such as the *Readers' Guide to Periodical Literature*. All of these sources break broad subjects into subtopics, which will help you focus your research.

After you locate several promising books or articles on your general subject, glance through the material rapidly to get a sense of issues and themes. Do the sources suggest a particular angle of inquiry? If you don't find much material on your subject, think about selecting another about which more has been written. While conducting preliminary research, keep a record of the books and articles you skim in a working bibliography (see page 459). Recording basic information as you go along will help you relocate material later on, when you'll need to look at your sources more closely.

Once you arrive at your limited topic—or several possibilities—ask your instructor for feedback, listening carefully to any reservations he or she may have about your idea. Even after you've identified a limited subject, don't be surprised if it continues to shift and narrow as you go along. Such reshaping is part of the research process.

Identify a Tentative (Working) Thesis

After limiting your topic, start to form a working thesis—an idea of your own that is in some way original. Having a tentative thesis guides your research and helps you determine which sources will be appropriate. The thesis should take a stand by expressing your point of view, or attitude, about the subject. In the thesis statements that follow, the limited subjects are underlined once, the attitudes twice:

> The Congressional decision to reduce funding of school lunch programs has had unfortunate consequences for disadvantaged children.

> A moment of silence in public schools does not violate the constitutional separation of church and state.

It's important for you to view your working thesis as tentative; you probably won't have a final thesis until your research is almost complete. Indeed, if your thesis doesn't shift as you investigate your topic, you may not be tapping a wide enough range of sources, or you may be resisting challenges to your original point of view.

Make a Schedule

Before you begin the research stage, make a schedule. First, list what you need to do. Then, working back from your essay's due date, set rough time limits for the different phases of the project. For an essay due December 4, you might create the following four-week schedule.

November 13	Locate relevant sources
November 23	Read materials and take notes
November 25	Locate additional information—interviews, and so on
November 29	Write a first draft
December 1	Revise the draft
December 3	Edit, print, and proofread the essay
December 4	Submit the essay

Conduct Primary Research

Conduct Interviews

You may decide to conduct an information-gathering interview. Before you send your request for a personal interview, get feedback from your instructor on the effectiveness of your letter or e-mail message. Schedule enough interview time (30–60 minutes) to discuss your topic in depth. To record the interview, you must obtain permission from the interviewee beforehand. Also, ask in advance if you may quote the person directly.

Plan the interview carefully. First, determine what you want to accomplish: Do you want to get the interviewee's view on a controversial issue, or do you want to clear up confusion about a specific point? Then, well in advance, prepare a list of questions geared toward that goal. During the interview, though, remain flexible—follow up on interesting remarks even if they diverge somewhat from your original plan. (If you discover that your interviewee isn't as informed as you had hoped, graciously request the names of other people who might help you further.) Take accurate and complete notes (even if you're recording—equipment sometimes fails!). If certain comments seem especially quotable, make sure you get the statements down correctly. Finally, right after the interview ends, be sure to fill in any gaps in your notes. And of course, remember to thank the interviewee.

If a face-to-face interview isn't feasible, a phone interview often will provide the information you need. Contact the interviewee, explain the kind of help you would like, and see if the person is willing to schedule time to talk on the phone at a later date.

Another way to conduct an interview is by e-mail. You should describe the topic you're researching, explain your reasons for establishing contact, and list clearly and concisely the information you would like the interviewee to provide. It's also a good idea to give the date by which you hope he or she can get back to you.

Carry Out Surveys

A survey helps you gather a good deal of information from a large number of people (respondents). However, designing, administering, and interpreting a survey questionnaire are time-consuming tasks that demand considerable skill. So be sure to have someone knowledgeable about surveys evaluate both your questionnaire and its responses.

Develop Questions

Make your survey questions as clear and precise as possible. For example, if your goal is to determine the frequency of an occurrence, do not ask for vague responses such as "seldom," "often," and "occasionally." Instead, ask respondents to identify specific time periods: "weekly," "1–3 times a week," "4–6 times a week," and "daily."

Also, steer away from questions that favor one side of an issue or that restrict the range of responses. Consider the following survey questions:

Should already overburdened college students be required to participate in a community service activity before they can graduate?

Yes _____ No_____ Maybe_____

In your opinion, how knowledgeable are college students about jobs in their majors?

Knowledgeable_____ Not knowledgeable_____

Both of these questions need to be revised. The first, by assuming that students are "already overburdened," biases respondents to reply negatively. To make the question more neutral, you would have to eliminate the prejudicial words. The second question asks respondents to answer in terms of a simple contrast: "Knowledgeable" or "Not knowledgeable." It ignores the likelihood that some respondents may wish to reply "Very knowledgeable," "Somewhat knowledgeable," and so on.

Choose Respondents

Unless you can survey every member of your target group, you must poll a representative subgroup. By representative, we mean "having characteristics similar to the group as a whole." Imagine you're writing a research paper on unfair employment practices and you decide to poll students on campus about their job experiences. To gauge students' attitudes with accuracy, you'll have to hand out your survey in numerous places and on varied occasions on the campus. That way, your responses will be drawn from the whole spectrum of undergraduate backgrounds, majors, ages, and so forth.

To achieve a random sample, you must choose respondents by a scientific method. For example, to survey undergraduates on your campus, you would need a list of all enrolled students. From this list, you would pick names at a regular interval, perhaps every tenth, and you would poll only those selected students. With this method, every enrolled student would have the potential of being chosen as a respondent.

For your survey you'll most likely use an informal method of collecting responses, such as handing your survey to passersby on campus or to people seated in classes, in student lounges, and so on. Or, if you're collecting information about the service at a particular facility, you might (with permission) place a short questionnaire where respondents can pick it up, quickly fill it out, and return it. Also keep in mind that online survey software such as *SurveyMonkey* makes it relatively easy to distribute a survey via e-mail and then to analyze the results.

Conduct Secondary Research

Even if your essay contains some primary research, you are likely to get most of your information from secondary sources, such as books and periodicals, most of which you will find in your college library or through the library's online sources. See Figure 19.2 for information on the types of sources available.

You will probably find most of the print books you need to consult in your college or another library. Most college libraries contain several floors of bookshelves (called stacks), with fiction and nonfiction cataloged and arranged systematically. Sections are set aside for periodicals, microfilm and microfiche files, reference works, reserved books, government documents, rare books, and the like. Special collections may include, for example, an extensive music library or a rare book collection.

Don't wait until a paper is due to become familiar with your college library. It can be overwhelming to learn about the library and conduct research at the same time. Instead, early in the year, spend an hour or so at the library. Take an orientation tour, read any handouts that are provided, speak to the librarian, and experiment with the system. And when you are ready to begin your search for secondary sources, talk with a librarian who can explain to you the various types of sources available through your school's library and how to access them.

Find Books on Your Subject

In most college libraries, you will use a computerized catalog, available on a library computer or from your own computer, to locate books. A typical online catalog search is by author, title, or subject. If you're searching by author or title,

FIGURE 19.2

Research Sources

Source Material	Description	How to Locate It
Books	Background information and lengthy in-depth treatment of subjects	Library catalog, Web searches for e-books
Scholarly journals	Articles containing the latest research results by experts in a field	Online library databases
Serious magazines	Articles with less depth than scholarly articles but with a broader perspective	Online library databases, library catalog
General magazines	Easy-to-read overviews of subjects with some background information	Online library databases, Web searches, library catalog
Newspapers	Easy-to-read summaries and coverage of current developments in a field	Online library databases, Web searches, library catalog
Government publications	Statistical and research studies conducted by governments and others	Library catalog and government Web sites
Multimedia	Videos, reproductions of art, and so on	Library catalog, online library databases, Internet searches

you type into the search box the author's first and last names or the title. If you're searching by subject, you type in a key word or phrase describing your topic. You may have to try several key terms to discover where the catalog lists sources on your topic. Also be aware that many classic texts are available as free e-books online. Just make sure you access copies from a reliable source.

Find Periodicals on Your Subject

Periodicals are publications issued at regular or intermittent intervals throughout the year. There are three broad types of periodicals: general, scholarly, and serious (see Figure 19.2). You may be able to use all three types as sources, or your instructor may limit you to one or two types of periodicals. More than books, periodicals tend to contain information on the most recent discoveries, ideas, and trends in most fields. For many academic subjects, especially in the sciences, periodicals will be the main source of material for a research essay.

Libraries subscribe to a wide range of periodicals. Many periodicals come in print form and most have, in addition, an electronic or online version; other periodicals appear only online. You will find print and sometimes electronic (for example, CD-ROM) versions of some publications in your library. Other publications can be accessed online through your library's system, either with the library's computers or with your own computer.

To identify specific articles on your subject, you'll first need to consult periodical indexes, abstracts, bibliographies, or full-text databases. This may seem like a daunting task, but it doesn't have to be. Ask a librarian to assist you in finding and accessing the various databases and other sources you need to conduct your research. In fact, you might consider making an appointment with a librarian to ensure having enough time to explain your project and get the necessary help.

Find Sources on the Internet

The Web consists of uncounted millions of Web sites. Some feature text only; others contain illustrations and graphics; still others contain audio and video components. Although there's great variation in the content and design of Web sites, nearly all have a home page that provides the site's title, introductory descriptive material about the site, and a menu consisting of links to other pages on the site or to related Web sites.

Know the Advantages and Limitations of the Library and the Web

Because it's not subject to a central system of organization, and because anyone can post material on it at any time, the Web is in a state of constant flux. Also, the quality of information found online ranges from authoritative to speculative to fraudulent.

Both the library and the Web are good starting points for research. Depending on your topic and its focus, one may serve this function better than the other. Here are some issues to consider:

- The library is consistently organized. With some guidance from the catalog and the reference librarian, you can quickly locate materials that are relevant to your topic.

- Because the Web doesn't have a centralized organizational structure, you are automatically—and somewhat haphazardly—exposed to a staggering array of material. If you're not sure how to focus your topic, browsing the Web may help you narrow your topic by identifying directions you wouldn't have thought of on your own. Conversely, the sheer volume of material on your subject may leave you confused about how to proceed.

- Some sources in the library may be dated or even no longer accurate. By contrast, online material is usually up-to-date because it can be posted on the Web as soon as it's created. (See page 462 for hints on evaluating the currency of electronic data.)

- The instantaneous nature of Web postings can create problems, though. Library materials certainly aren't infallible, but most have gone through a process of editorial review before being published. They also have been chosen by knowledgeable librarians. This is often not the case with material on the Web. It's a good idea not to rely solely on the Web when you research your topic. (For more about evaluating the validity of material on the Web, see the checklist on page 462.)

Prepare a Working Bibliography and Take Notes

As you look up promising books, reference volumes, articles, and online material about your subject, prepare a working bibliography—a master list of potential sources. You will have the basis of such a list from the preliminary research you did at the beginning of the project. Keeping track of sources in a working bibliography means you won't have to waste time later tracking down a source whose title you remember only vaguely.

Record Information About the Source

As you consult sources, make note of at least the following information in your working bibliography. If you are in doubt about additional bibliographic information given by a source, record it.

- For each book, record the author, title, and library call number or Web address.
- For each article, record the author, title, publication name, date, and page numbers, as well as how it can be located in the library or electronically.
- For each Web site, record any author named, the title of the page, the name of the site, the Web address, and the date you consulted the site.

Because you want to read as much as you can about your subject, the working bibliography will contain more sources than you will eventually use in your essay. You might find it easiest to use a computer file for your working bibliography, because you can often e-mail library catalog information and journal articles to yourself and copy and paste Web addresses right into the bibliography. Both of these options can help you avoid transcription errors. A computer document can also be sorted and resorted alphabetically as you develop your list. (Check the Help feature on your word-processing program for instructions on sorting.) You also can add comments and notes to the individual items as you work.

Take Notes on the Source

You may also find it convenient to use your working bibliography for note-taking. Quotations can be copied and pasted into the bibliography, but be sure to identify completely the source of the quotation. Here's an example of a bibliography entry with a direct quotation added as a note:

Cazzuffi, Alessandra, Emilia Manzato, Malvina Gualandi, Fabio Fabbian, and Giovanni Scanelli. "Case Study: Young Man with Anorexia Nervosa." *JRSM Short Reports* 1.5 (2010): 39. Web. 15 May 2013.

Perfectionism:

"His parents underlined 'perfectionism' as a core feature of his personality: he wants to be the best in everything he does and he always organizes and plans his life and his future" (39).

If one source calls for extensive notes, you may need to open a separate file keyed to the working bibliography. Put the bibliographic entry at the beginning of the file and insert an identifier (for example, "p. 10") before each separate note. Make sure to use a filename that identifies the source. If quoted material covers several pages, indicate clearly where the page breaks occur in the source. That way, if you use only a portion of the material later, you will know its exact page number. You may also find it helpful to write a key word or phrase before the note. For example, in a paper on erosion, you might have notes labeled "Beach erosion" and "Mountain erosion." In the preceding working bibliography example, the direct quote is labeled "Perfectionism." If you print your working bibliography and notes to work with them, print on only one side of the sheet to avoid confusion and number the printed sheets to keep them in order.

Evaluate Sources and Analyze Information

At this point you've formed a tentative thesis, identified promising sources, and started compiling a working bibliography. Your goal now is to find support for your thesis—and to pay close attention to material suggesting alternative viewpoints. Sifting through this conflicting information will enable you to refine your working thesis with more precision.

Keep your working thesis firmly in mind as you assess and react to what others have to say about your subject. Some authors will support your working thesis; others will prod you to consider opposing viewpoints. In either case, evaluating, synthesizing, and reacting to your sources helps you refine your position and develop a sound basis for your conclusions.

Evaluate Sources

The success of your essay will depend in large part on the evidence you provide. Evidence from sources, whether print or electronic, needs to be evaluated for relevance, timeliness, seriousness of approach, and objectivity.

Relevance

For a book, read the preface or introduction, skim the table of contents, and check the index to see whether the book is likely to contain valuable information. If the source is an influential text in the field, you may want to read the entire book for background and specific ideas. For an article, read the abstract of the article or read the first few paragraphs and skim the rest to determine if it might be useful.

Timeliness

Often, the topic and the kind of research you're doing determine whether a work is outdated. If you're researching a historical topic such as the internment of Japanese Americans during World War II, you will most likely consult sources published in the 1940s and 1950s, as well as more up-to-date sources. In contrast, if you're investigating a recent scientific development—cloning, for example—it would make sense to restrict your search to current material. For most college research, a source older than ten years is considered outdated unless it was the first to present key concepts in a field.

Seriousness of Approach

Articles from general periodicals (newspapers and widely read magazines such as *The Economist*) and serious publications (such as *National Geographic*) may be sufficient to provide support in a personal essay. However, an in-depth research essay in your major field of study will require material from scholarly journals and texts.

Objectivity

Keep in mind that a strong conclusion or opinion is not in itself a sign of bias. As long as a writer doesn't ignore opposing positions or distort evidence, a source can't be considered biased. A biased source presents only those facts that fit the writer's predetermined conclusions. Such a source is often marked by emotionally charged language. Publications sponsored by special interest groups—a particular industry, religious association, advocacy group, or political party—are usually biased. Reading such materials familiarizes you with a specific point of view, but remember that contrary evidence has probably been ignored or skewed.

☑ EVALUATING ARTICLES AND BOOKS: A CHECKLIST

☐ If the work is scholarly, is the author well known in his or her field? Is the author affiliated with an accredited college or university? A nonscholarly author, such as a journalist, should have a reputation for objectivity and thoroughness.

☐ Is the publication reputable? If a scholarly publication is peer-reviewed, experts in the field have a chance to comment on the author's work before it is published. Nonscholarly publications such as newspapers and magazines should be well established and widely respected.

☐ Is the source recently published and up to date? Alternatively, is it a classic in its field? In the sciences and social sciences, recent publication is particularly critical.

☐ Is the material at an appropriate level—neither too scholarly nor too general—for your purpose and audience? Make sure you can understand and present the material for your readers.

☐ Does the information appear to be accurate, objectively presented, and complete? Statistics and other evidence should not be distorted or manipulated to make a point.

Special care must be taken to evaluate the worth of material found on the Web. Electronic documents often seem to appear out of nowhere and can disappear without a trace. And anyone—from scholar to con artist—can create a Web page. How, then, do you know if an Internet source is credible? As you evaluate online sources, ask yourself the questions in the following checklist.

☑ EVALUATING INTERNET MATERIALS: A CHECKLIST

☐ Who is the author of the material? Does the author provide a résumé or biographical note? Do these credentials qualify the author to provide reliable information on the topic? Is there an e-mail address so you can request more information? The less you know about an author, the more suspicious you should be about using the data.

☐ Can you verify the information's accuracy? Does the author refer to studies or to other authors you can investigate? If the author doesn't cite other works or other points of view, this may suggest the document is opinionated and one-sided. In such a case, it's important to track down material addressing alternative points of view.

☐ Who's sponsoring the Web site? Check for an "About Us" link on the home page, which may tell you the site's sponsorship and goals. Many sites are established by organizations—businesses, agencies, lobby groups—as well as by individuals. If a sponsor pushes a single point of view, you should use the material with great caution.

☐ Is the information up to date? Being on the Internet doesn't guarantee that information is current. Check at the top or bottom of the document for copyright date, publication date, or revision date. Those dates will help you determine whether the material is recent enough for your purposes.

☐ Is the information original or taken from another source? Is quoted material accurate? Nonoriginal material should be accurately quoted and acknowledged on the site.

Analyze Information

As you read your sources and begin keeping track of what you find, you may not be able to judge immediately how helpful a source will be. At that time, you probably should take fairly detailed notes. After a while, you'll become more selective. You'll find that you are thinking more critically about the material you read, isolating information and ideas that are important to your thesis, and formulating questions about your topic.

To begin with, you should spend some time analyzing each source for its central ideas, main supporting points, and key details. As you read, keep asking yourself how the source's content meshes with your working thesis and with what you know about your subject. Does the source repeat only what you already know, or does it supply new information? If a source provides detailed support for important ideas or suggests a new angle on your subject, read carefully and take full notes. If the source refers to other sources, you might decide to consult them.

Your notes might include any of the following: facts, statistics, anecdotal accounts, expert opinion, case studies, surveys, reports, and results of experiments. When you are recording data, check that you have copied the figures accurately. Also note how and by whom the statistics were gathered, as well as where and when they were first reported. As you take down your source's interpretation of the statistics, be sure to scrutinize the interpretation for any "spin" that distorts them. For example, if 80 percent of Americans think violent crime is our number-one national problem, that doesn't mean that violent crime is our main problem; it simply means that 80 percent of the people polled think it is. Make sure, also, that the statistics are based on a representative sample. For instance, assume the claim is made that 90 percent of the people sampled wouldn't vote for a candidate who had an extramarital affair. However, if only ten people were polled one Sunday as they left church, then the 90-percent statistic is misleading. If you have any reason to suspect distortion, corroborate such figures elsewhere.

As you go along, you may come across material that challenges your working thesis and forces you to think differently about your subject. Conflicting material indicates you've identified a pivotal issue within your topic.

To decide which position is more valid, first evaluate the sources for bias. On this basis alone, you might discover serious flaws in one or several sources. Then you need to compare the key points and supporting evidence in the sources. Where do they agree? Where do they disagree? Does one source argue against another 's position, perhaps even discrediting some of the opposing view's evidence? The answers to these questions may well cause you to question the quality, completeness, or fairness of one or more sources. Finally, you can also research your subject more fully. For example, if your conflicting sources are at the general or serious level, you should probably turn to more scholarly and authoritative sources to help determine which of the conflicting sources is more valid.

When you attempt to resolve discrepancies among sources, be sure not to let your own bias come into play. Remember, your goal is to arrive at the most well-founded position you can. In fact, researching a topic may lead you to change your original viewpoint. In this case, you shouldn't hesitate to revise your working thesis to accord with the evidence you gather.

Use Quotation, Summary, and Paraphrase to Synthesize Research While Avoiding Plagiarism

There are basically four ways to use source information in your essay as evidence in support of your ideas—in direct quotations, summaries, or paraphrases, or in a combination of these. Knowing how and when to use each type is an important part of the research process.

Plagiarism

Plagiarism occurs when a writer borrows someone else's ideas, facts, or language but doesn't properly credit that source. Summarizing and paraphrasing, in particular, can lead to plagiarism, but improper use of quotation can also constitute plagiarism.

Copyright law and the ethics of research require that you:

- Accurately present the words and ideas you borrow, including enclosing exact words in quotation marks, and
- Provide full documentation for all sources (see Chapter 20 for more on documentation).

The correct use of direct quotation, summary, and paraphrase will support your thesis with credible evidence; their incorrect use will compromise the effectiveness of your paper and can result in inadvertent plagiarism. To make sure you avoid plagiarism resulting from less-than-careful note-taking, follow these guidelines. (See Chapter 20 for guidelines on blending direct quotation, summary, and paraphrase into your paper and avoiding plagiarism in documentation.)

> ☑ **AVOIDING PLAGIARISM IN NOTE-TAKING: A CHECKLIST**
>
> ☐ Make sure to record all bibliographic information for a source in your working bibliography.
> ☐ Identify each note by source, including relevant page numbers.
> ☐ Always use quotation marks for the exact words that you copy from a source.
> ☐ Bracket or otherwise identify material in a note that paraphrases a source.
> ☐ Clearly indicate your own words, thoughts, and conclusions in the note.

Direct Quotation

A direct quotation reproduces, word for word, that which is stated in a source. Although quoting can demonstrate the thoroughness with which you reviewed relevant sources, don't simply use one quotation after another without any intervening commentary or analysis. To do so would mean you hadn't evaluated and synthesized your sources sufficiently. Aim for one to three quotations from each major source; more than that can create a problem in your essay. Consider using quotations in the following situations:

- If a source's ideas are unusual or controversial, include a representative quotation in your paper to show you have accurately conveyed the source's viewpoint.

- Record a quotation if a source's wording is so eloquent or convincing that it would lose its power if you restated the material in your own words.

- Use a quotation if a source's ideas reinforce your own conclusions. If the source is a respected authority, such a quotation will lend authority to your own ideas.

- In an analysis of a literary work, use quotations from the work to support your interpretations.

Remember to clearly identify quotes in your notes so that you don't confuse the quotation with your own comments when you begin drafting your paper. Record the author's statement exactly as it appears in the original work, right down to the punctuation. In addition, make sure to properly document the quotation. See "Creating In-Text References: MLA Format" and "Prepare the Works Cited List: MLA Format" on pages 482–497.

Original Passage 1. The following is the entire text of Amendment I of the Constitution of the United States.

> Congress shall make no law respecting an establishment of religion, or prohibiting the free exercise thereof; or abridging the freedom of speech, or of the press; or the right of the people peaceably to assemble, and to petition the Government for a redress of grievances.

Original Passage 2. In this excerpt from *The Canon: A Whirligig Tour of the Beautiful Basics of Science*, by Natalie Angier, page 22, the author is discussing the subject of scientific reasoning.

> Much of the reason for its success is founded on another fundamental of the scientific bent. Scientists accept, quite staunchly, that there is a reality capable of being understood, and understood in a way that can be shared with and agreed upon by others. We can call this "objective" reality if we like, as opposed to subjective reality, or opinion, or "whimsical set of predilections." The concept is deceptive, however, because it implies that the two are discrete entities with remarkably little in common.

Acceptable Use of Quotation. The following examples are acceptable uses of the preceding quotations. For a paper on society's perception of important freedoms, a student writer included a quotation (highlighted) from the Constitution.

> The First Amendment of the Constitution of the United States delineates what were thought to be society's most cherished freedoms: "Congress shall make no law respecting an establishment of religion, or prohibiting the free exercise thereof; or abridging the freedom of speech, or of the press; or the right of the people peaceably to assemble, and to petition the Government for a redress of grievances."

In a paper on science education in schools, one student writer used a direct quotation (highlighted) from Angier's book:

In explaining scientific reasoning, Angier says, "Scientists accept, quite staunchly, that there is a reality capable of being understood, and understood in a way that can be shared with and agreed upon by others" (22).

Notice that both quotations are reproduced exactly as they appear in the source and are enclosed in quotation marks. The parenthetical reference to the page number in the second example is a necessary part of documenting the quotation. (See page 482 for more on in-text references.) The first example requires no page number because quotations from well-known sources such as the Constitution and the Bible are sufficiently identified by their own numbering systems, in this case, the text's use of "First Amendment of the Constitution."

Incorrect Use of Quotation. Another student writer, attempting to provide some background on the scientific method, used the source material *incorrectly*.

To understand the scientific method, it is important to understand that scientists believe there is a reality capable of being understood (Angier 22).

The highlighted phrase "a reality capable of being understood," which consists of the source's exact words, should have quotations around it. Even though the source is identified correctly in the parenthetical reference, the lack of quotation marks constitutes plagiarism, the use of someone's words or ideas without proper acknowledgement.

Summary

A summary is a condensation of a larger work. You extract the essence of someone's ideas and restate it in your own words. The length of a summary depends on your topic and purpose, but generally a summary is much shorter than the item you are summarizing. For example, you may summarize the plot of a novel in a few short paragraphs, or you might summarize a reading from this book in a few sentences. You might choose to use a summary for the following reasons:

- To give a capsule presentation of the main ideas of a book or an article, use a summary.
- If the relevant information is too long to be quoted in full, use a summary.
- Use a summary to give abbreviated information about elements such as plot, background, or history.
- To present an idea from a source without including all the supporting details, use a summary.

To summarize a source, read the material; jot down or underline the main idea, main supporting points, and key details; and then restate the information in shortened form in your own words.

Your summary should follow the order of information in the original. Also be sure to treat any original wording as quotations in your summary. A caution: When summarizing, don't use the ellipsis to signal that you have omitted some ideas. The ellipsis is used only when quoting.

Original Passage 3. This excerpt is from *The Homeless and History*, by Julian Stamp, page 8.

> The key to any successful homeless policy requires a clear understanding of just who are the homeless. Since fifty percent of shelter residents have drug and alcohol addictions, programs need to provide not only a place to sleep but also comprehensive treatment for addicts and their families. Since roughly one-third of the homeless population is mentally ill, programs need to offer psychiatric care, perhaps even institutionalization, and not just housing subsidies. Since the typical head of a homeless family (a young woman with fewer than six months' working experience) usually lacks the know-how needed to maintain a job and a home, programs need to supply employment and life skills training; low-cost housing alone will not ensure the family's stability.
>
> However, if we switch our focus from the single person to the larger economic issues, we begin to see that homelessness cannot be resolved solely at the level of individual treatment. Beginning in the 1980s and through the 1990s, the gap between the rich and the poor has widened, buying power has stagnated, industrial jobs have fled overseas, and federal funding for low-cost housing has been almost eliminated. Given these developments, homelessness begins to look like a product of history, our recent history, and only by addressing shifts in the American economy can we begin to find effective solutions for people lacking homes. Moreover, these solutions—ranging from renewed federal spending to tax laws favoring job-creating companies—will require a sustained national commitment that transcends partisan politics.

Acceptable Use of Summary. The following summary was written by a student working on a paper related to the causes of homelessness.

> In his *The Homeless and History*, Stamp asserts that society must not only provide programs to help the homeless with their personal problems, it must also develop government programs to deal with the economic causes of homelessness (8).

The writer gives the gist of Stamp's argument in his own words. The parenthetical reference at the end tells the reader that the material being summarized appears on page 8 of the source (see pages 482–487 for more on in-text references).

Incorrect Use of Summary. The student who wrote the following has *incorrectly* summarized ideas from the Stamp passage.

> Who are the homeless? According to Stamp, the homeless are people with big problems like addiction, mental illness, and poor job skills. Because they haven't been provided with proper treatment and training, the homeless haven't been able to adapt to a changing economy. So their numbers soared in the 1990s (8).

The writer was so determined to put things her way that she added her own ideas and ended up distorting Stamp's meaning. For instance, note the way she emphasizes personal problems over economic issues, making the former the cause of the latter. Stamp does just the opposite and highlights economic solutions rather than individual treatment.

Paraphrase

Unlike a summary, which condenses the original, a paraphrase recasts material by using roughly the same number of words and retaining the same level of detail as the original. The challenge with paraphrasing is to capture the information without using the original language of the material. Paraphrasing is useful in these situations:

- If you want to include specific details from a source but you want to avoid using a long quotation or string of quotations, paraphrase the material.
- To interpret or explain material as you include it, try using a paraphrase.
- Paraphrase to avoid injecting another person's style into your own writing.

One way to compose a paraphrase is to read the original passage and then set it aside while you draft your restatement. As you write, make sure to use appropriate synonyms and to vary the sentence structure from that of the original. Then compare the passages to make sure you have not used any of the original language, unless you have enclosed it in quotation marks.

Acceptable Use of Paraphrase. In the following example, the student writer paraphrases the second paragraph of Stamp's original, fitting the restatement into her argument.

> Can we work together as a society to eliminate homelessness? <u>One historian</u> urges us to look at larger economic issues, claiming that the problem cannot be solved simply by the treatment of personal problems such as substance abuse. Economic conditions for the poor have worsened in the last few decades, with fewer jobs and substantially diminished federal support for low-cost housing. To find a solution to homelessness, society must deal with these economic causes. A "sustained national commitment," regardless of political ideology, to stepped-up federal spending and tax laws that promote the creation of jobs, as well as to other initiatives, is needed (Stamp 8).

Note that the paraphrase—beginning with "One historian" (underlined) and ending with the parenthetical reference—is nearly as long as the original. Apart from the single (highlighted) instance of original language, enclosed in quotation marks, the writer has not used phrases or even sentence structures from the original. Notice also that it is easy to see where the paraphrase starts and ends. Because the text does not identify the source by name, the source's name is included in the parenthetical reference.

Incorrect Use of Paraphrase. When preparing the paraphrase given here, the student stayed too close to the source and borrowed much of Stamp's language word for word (highlighted). Because the student did not enclose the original phrases in quotation marks, this paraphrase constitutes plagiarism, even though the student acknowledged Stamp in the paper. The lack of quotation marks implies that the language is the student's when, in fact, it is Stamp's.

> Only by addressing changes in the American economy—from the gap between the wealthy and the poor to the loss of industrial jobs to overseas markets—can we begin to find solutions for the homeless. And these solutions, ranging from renewed federal spending to tax law favoring job-creating companies, will not be easy to find or implement (Stamp 8).

The following example shows another student believed, erroneously, that if he changed a word here and omitted a word there, he'd be preparing an effective paraphrase. Note that the language is all Stamp's except for the words *not* highlighted, which are the student's.

> Only by addressing shifts in the economy can we find solutions for the homeless. These solutions will require a sustained federal commitment that avoids partisan politics (Stamp 8).

This student occasionally deleted a word from Stamp's original, thinking that such changes would result in a legitimate paraphrase. For example, in "Only by addressing shifts in the [American] economy can we [begin to] find [effective] solutions," the brackets show where the student omitted Stamp's words. The student couldn't place quotation marks around these near-quotes because his wording isn't identical to that of the source, yet the near-quotes are deceptive. The lack of quotation marks suggests that the language is the student's when actually it's substantially (but not exactly) Stamp's. Such near-quotes are also considered plagiarism, even if the student supplies a parenthetical reference citing the source.

ACTIVITIES: LOCATING, EVALUATING, AND INTEGRATING RESEARCH SOURCES

1. Use the computer catalog to answer the following questions:
   a. What are three books dealing with the subject of adoption? of the Internet? of urban violence? of genetic research?
   b. What is the title of a book by Betty Friedan? by John Kenneth Galbraith?
   c. Who is the author of *The Invisible Man?* of *A Swiftly Tilting Planet?*

2. Prepare a bibliography entry for each of the following books. Gather all the information necessary at the library so that you can write an accurate and complete bibliography entry:

   a. Barbara Tuchman, *Practicing History*
   b. L. Jacobs, *The Documentary Tradition*

    c. Margaret Mead, *Coming of Age in Samoa*

    d. Stephen Bank, *The Sibling Bond*

    e. Ronald Gross, *The New Old*

    f. Matthew Arnold, *Culture and Anarchy*

3. Using reference works available in your library, find the answers to the following questions:

    a. When was the Persian Gulf War fought?

    b. Who invented Kodachrome film, and when?

    c. What is the medical condition rosacea?

    d. What television show won the Emmy in 2003 for Outstanding Comedy Series?

    e. What was artist John Sartain known for?

    f. When was an African American first elected to Congress?

    g. In economics, what is Pareto's Law?

    h. In art, what is *écorché*?

    i. Give two other names for a mbira, a musical instrument.

    j. In the religion of the Hopi Tribe, what are Kachinas?

4. Select one of the following limited topics. Then, using the appropriate periodical indexes and bibliographies locate three periodicals that would be helpful in researching the topic. Examine each periodical to determine whether it is aimed at a general, serious, or scholarly audience.

    a. Drug abuse among health-care professionals

    b. Ethical considerations in organ-transplant surgery

    c. Women in prison

    d. Deforestation of the Amazon rain forest

    e. The difference between *Cold Mountain* as a novel and as a film

5. Select one of the following limited topics. Then, using the Internet, locate at least three relevant articles on the topic: one from a general-interest magazine, one from a newspaper, and one from a serious or scholarly journal. Make a bibliography entry for each article.

    a. Ordaining women in American churches

    b. Attempts to regulate Internet pornography

    c. The popularity of novelist and essayist Isak Dinesen

    d. The growing interest in painter David Hockney

    e. AIDS education programs

    f. The global economy

20

Writing the Research Essay

In this chapter, you will learn:

20.1 To create a refined thesis and an outline for your writing
20.2 To write a first draft of your essay
20.3 To integrate sources into your writing and document them properly using MLA or APA style to avoid plagiarism
20.4 To create in-text references to your sources
20.5 To revise, edit, and proofread your writing
20.6 To prepare a works cited or references list, depending on the documentation style used in your essay
20.7 To examine how research is used effectively in one student-authored selection

After you finish recording information from your sources, you're ready to begin the writing phase of the research project. This stage is shown in Figure 20.1 on page 472.

Refine Your Working Thesis

Your working thesis undoubtedly has evolved since you first started your research. Indeed, now that you're more informed about the topic, you may feel that your original thesis oversimplifies the issue. To refine your working thesis, begin by sifting through your notes, using your research to adjust your ideas. Then, revise your working thesis, keeping in mind the evidence in your notes. This new thesis

FIGURE 20.1

The Research Essay: Writing Stage

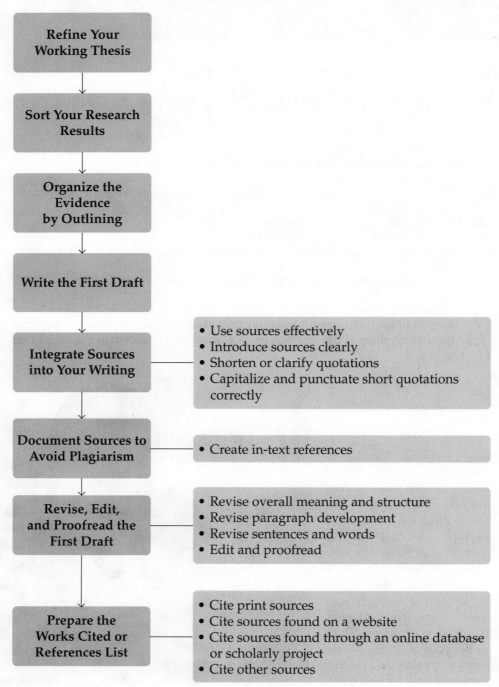

statement will serve as the starting point for your first draft. Remember, though—as you write the essay, new thoughts may emerge that will cause you to modify your thesis even further. (For more on thesis statements, see Chapter 3 and the writing process diagrams in Chapters 10–18.)

Sort Your Research Results

With your refined thesis in mind, sort your information by topic. If you have been taking notes on the computer, you may have a separate file for each source. During the research process, you may have identified each note by topic and collated the notes into separate subtopic files. You can now create one file out of these subtopic files to use for your draft.

If you have not yet collated your computer notes by topic, you can do so now. Print each source file on one side of a sheet. Read through the notes and label them by topic. Using the printed sheets as guide, copy and paste a note from a source file into your draft file. Make sure to circle or cross out the note on your printout so that you don't use the same notes more than once. One caution: For every note you copy into your draft, also copy the note's source information. You now have all your notes roughly sorted by topic in a file that will become your first draft.

At this point, you should consider which organizational approach (see pages 49–51) will help you sequence your material. Also, the writing process diagrams in Chapters 10–18 highlight tips for using specific patterns of development. Arrange your topics to reflect the organizational pattern you have chosen.

Once you've arranged your notes according to the topic headings, arrange the information by subtopic. For example, notes about types of state programs might be copied and pasted under three subtopics: programs for the elderly, programs for preschool children, programs for the physically disabled. Next, using the patterns of development and organizational approaches discussed, respectively, on pages 49–51, order each set of subtopics to match the sequence in which you think you'll discuss those subtopics in your essay. This sorting will make your next step—preparing an outline—much easier.

Organize the Evidence by Outlining

Whether or not your instructor requires an outline, it's a good idea to prepare one before you begin writing the essay. Because an outline groups and sequences points, it provides a blueprint you can follow when writing. Outlining clarifies what your main ideas are, what your supporting evidence is, and how everything fits together. It reveals where your argument is well supported and where it is weak.

To design your outline, focus first on the essay 's body. How can you best explain and support your thesis? For now, don't worry about your introduction or conclusion. General guidelines on outlining are discussed in Chapter 5. To apply those guidelines to a research essay, keep in mind the points listed in the checklist that follows.

☑ **OUTLINING RESEARCH EVIDENCE: A CHECKLIST**

☐ Base your outline on your organized notes.

☐ Ask yourself, "What are the main ideas that support my thesis?" These ideas are your main topic headings. Label them with roman numerals (I, II, III, and so on) to indicate the order in which you plan to discuss each in the essay.

☐ Next, for each main idea, ask yourself, "What subtopics do I want to discuss?" Label these with capital letters (A, B, C) and group them under the main topic headings. Indent the subtopic entries under their respective main topics, listing them in the order you plan to discuss them.

☐ Now, for each subtopic, ask, "What are the supporting points for this item?" Label supporting points with Arabic numerals (1, 2, 3) and indent them under the appropriate subtopics. Finally, for each supporting point, ask yourself, "What specific details support this item?" Label specific details (facts, quotations, statistics, examples, expert opinion) with lowercase letters (a, b, c) and indent them under the appropriate supporting points. Use shorthand for details. For example, write "Bitner quote here" instead of copying the entire quotation into your outline.

☐ Where appropriate, map out sections of the essay that will provide background information or define key terms.

Your first outline probably won't be a formal full-sentence one; it's more likely to be a topic (or phrase) outline, like those on pages 258, 291–292, and 403. A topic outline helps you clarify a essay's overall structure. A full-sentence outline (see pages 192–193) or a combined topic and sentence outline (see page 322) is better suited to mapping out in detail the development of an essay's ideas. If you're preparing an outline that will be submitted with the essay, find out in advance which kind your instructor prefers.

Before you go any further, it's a good idea to get some feedback on your outline—from an instructor or a critical friend—to make sure others agree that your meaning and organization are logical and clear. Then, using your readers' reactions, make whatever changes seem necessary.

Write the First Draft

Once you've refined your working thesis, sorted your notes, and constructed an outline, you're ready to write your first draft. As with the early versions of an essay, don't worry at this stage about grammar, spelling, or style. Just try to get down as much of the essay's basic content and structure as you can.

Chapter 6 offers general guidelines for writing a first draft. See also the writing process diagrams for the different patterns of development in Chapters 10–18. When applying those guidelines to a research essay, keep in mind the points discussed in the following checklist.

> ✅ **WRITING THE FIRST DRAFT OF A RESEARCH ESSAY: A CHECKLIST**
>
> ☐ As you write, use your notes, source files, and outline. Don't rely on your memory for the information you've gathered.
>
> ☐ Feel free to deviate from your outline if, as you write, you discover a more effective sequence, realize some material doesn't fit, or see new merit in previously discarded information.
>
> ☐ Include any quotations and summaries in the draft by copying and pasting material from your computer files or typing in material from your notes.
>
> ☐ Identify the sources for all borrowed material in your draft (see Chapter 19).
>
> ☐ Use the third-person point of view throughout, unless your instructor has indicated that you may use the first person when presenting primary research.
>
> ☐ Give your first draft and subsequent drafts different filenames: "Lotteries_draft1," "Lotteries_draft2," etc.

If your instructor requires you to conduct primary research, remember that your primary purpose is to provide evidence for your thesis. Include only that material that furthers your goal. To preserve the draft's overall unity, you should also avoid the temptation to mass, without commentary, all your primary research in one section of the essay. Instead, insert the material at those places where it supports the points you want to make. Sometimes instructors will ask you to devote one part of the essay to a detailed discussion of the process you used to conduct primary research—everything from your methodology to a detailed interpretation of your results. In such a case, before writing your draft, ask your instructor where you should cover that information. Perhaps it should be placed in a separate introductory section or in an appendix.

Integrate Sources into Your Writing

On the whole, your essay should be written in your own words. As you draft your essay, however, you will add evidence from sources to support your ideas. Depending on the source and the support you need, you may choose to use quotations, paraphrases, or summaries to present this evidence (see pages 464–469). Be mindful, however, that you must also correctly document the sources you use.

For specific guidelines on documentation, see pages 482–487 on MLA parenthetical references, pages 488–497 on MLA Works Cited lists, and pages 497–507 on APA documentation style.

Using Sources Effectively

As you write individual paragraphs, take care to use *introductions, transitions, and conclusions* to tie each paragraph to those that precede and follow it. At a minimum, every paragraph should have a topic sentence. Use quotations sparingly, drawing upon them only when they dramatically illustrate key points you want to make or when they lend authority to your own conclusions. Remember that a quotation, by itself, won't make your case for you. A string of quotations signals that you haven't sufficiently evaluated and distilled your sources.

Quotations, paraphrases, and summaries need to be seamlessly blended into your own writing to be effective. Successfully blending source material into your essay involves:

- Identifying the source with an appropriate introduction (known as an *attribution*).
- Quoting, paraphrasing, or summarizing the source material accurately.
- Providing a parenthetical reference to a Works Cited or References list. (For an explanation of the parenthetical reference at the end of the quotation, see pages 482–487.)
- Interpreting the material to show why it is important and explain how it supports your main points. Interpretive statements can come before or after the source material.

Your interpretive commentary is often precisely what's needed to blend the source material gracefully into your discussion. (For more on specific reasons to choose quotations, paraphrases, and summaries, see pages 464–469.)

Awkward Use of a Quotation

In the example paragraph that follows, the writer starts with a topic sentence. Note, though, that the quotation is dropped awkwardly into the text, without any transition or commentary.

> Studies of parenting styles are designed to control researcher bias. "Recent studies screen out researchers whose strongly held attitudes make objectivity difficult" (Layden 10).

Effective Use of a Source

In the following example, the first sentence provides a transition into the paragraph. The second sentence—the topic sentence—expresses the writer's idea. The third sentence gives the evidence (source material) to support that idea: the attribution (underlined), a paraphrase of the the source's words (**boldfaced**), the direct quotation (highlighted), and the parenthetical reference at the end. Notice how the source material (paraphrase and quotation) merge easily with the surrounding material:

One problem with research into parenting styles has been the preconceived notions of researchers. The latest studies of parenting styles, however, are designed to control researcher bias. The psychologist Marsha Layden, a harsh critic of earlier studies, acknowledges that **nowadays most investigations** "screen out researchers whose strongly held beliefs make objectivity difficult" (10).

In the next example, two plot summaries (highlighted) are used as evidence for the writer's main idea, expressed in the first sentence. Since the attributions (underlined) contain enough information for the source to be located in the Works Cited list, no parenthetical reference is needed.

Literature has many examples of lovers who must overcome the societal obstacles that separate them. Some stories, for example, Shakespeare's *Romeo and Juliet*, end tragically. In that play, a feud between Romeo's family, the Montagues, and Juliet's, the Capulets, forces the young lovers to meet in secret. They eventually devise a way to be together, but the plan goes wrong and ends in their deaths. Many stories, however, end happily. In Jane Austen's novel *Pride and Prejudice*, class differences and mistaken beliefs are successfully worked out so that Elizabeth Bennet and her sister Jane can end up marrying the men they love.

Introducing a Source

Avoid such awkward constructions as these attributions: "According to Julian Stamp, he says that…" and "In the book by Julian Stamp, he argues that…" Instead, follow these hints for writing smooth, graceful introductions.

Identifying the Source

An introduction to a source may specify the author's name, inform readers of an author's expertise, or refer to a source more generally. To call attention to an author who is prominent in the field, important to your argument, or referred to many times in your essay, you may give the author's full name and identifier at the first mention in the text. On subsequent mentions, give only the last name. Don't use personal titles such as *Mr.* or *Ms.* In the following two examples, language that identifies or explains the source is highlighted.

Natalie Angier, a Pulitzer Prize-winning journalist who writes about science, says that…. Angier goes on to explain….

The historian Julian Stamp argues that…. As Stamp explains….

For other sources, use a more general attribution and include the source's name (highlighted below), along with any page number, in the *parenthetical citation*.

One writer points out...(Angier 22).

According to statistics, fifty percent...(Stamp 8).

As part of an introduction, you may mention the title of the book, article, or other source.

In *The Homeless and History,* Stamp maintains that....

According to the National Aeronautics and Space Administration (NASA),...

When the author's name is provided in the text, don't repeat the name in the parenthetical reference.

One psychologist who is a harsh critic of earlier studies acknowledges that nowadays most investigations "screen out researchers whose strongly held beliefs make objectivity difficult" (Layden 10).

The psychologist Marsha Layden acknowledges that...(10).

Using Variety in Attributions

Don't always place attributions at the beginning of the sentence; experiment by placing them in the middle or at the end:

The key to any successful homeless policy, Stamp explains, "requires a clear understanding of just who are the homeless" (8).

Half of homeless individuals living in shelters are substance abusers, according to statistics (Stamp 8).

Try not to use a predictable subject-verb sequence ("Stamp argues that..."; "Stamp explains that...") in all your attributions. Aim for variations like the following:

The information compiled by Stamp shows....

In Stamp's opinion,...

Stamp's study reveals that....

Rather than repeatedly using the verbs *says* or *writes* in your introductions, seek out more vigorous verbs, making sure the verbs you select are appropriate to the tone and content of the work from which you're quoting. Also, take care to use the verbs in present tense when quoting or summarizing a source

("Stamp reports that..." rather than "Stamp reported that..."). The list that follows offers a variety of effective verbs for attributions.

acknowledges	compares	grants	questions	shows
adds	confirms	implies	reasons	speculates
admits	contends	insists	reports	states
argues	declares	maintains	responds	suggests
asserts	demonstrates	notes	reveals	wonders
believes	endorses	points out	says	writes

Shortening or Clarifying Quotations

To make the best use of quotations, you will often need to shorten or excerpt them. It is acceptable to omit parts of quotations as long as you do not change the wording or distort the meaning of the original.

Quoting a Single Word, a Phrase, or Part of a Sentence

Put double quotation marks around a quoted element you are integrating into your own sentence. In the following examples, the quotations are highlighted.

Angier says that to speak of "objective" and "subjective" realities is to imply that these are "discrete entities" (22).

Making these changes will necessitate "a sustained national commitment that transcends partisan politics," according to Stamp (8).

Omitting Material in the Middle of the Original Sentence

Insert three spaced periods, called an *ellipsis* (...), in place of the deleted words. Leave a space before the first period of the ellipsis and leave a space after the third period of the ellipsis before continuing with the quoted matter.

"However, if we switch our focus ... to the larger economic issues, we begin to see that homelessness cannot be resolved solely at the level of individual treatment" (Stamp 8).

Omitting Material at the End of the Original Sentence

If no parenthetical reference is needed, insert a period before the first ellipsis period and provide the closing quotation mark, as in the first example below. If a parenthetical reference is needed, use only the ellipsis and add the period after the parentheses.

The First Amendment of the Constitution of the United States lays the foundation for the doctrine of free speech: "Congress shall make no law respecting an establishment of religion, or prohibiting the free exercise thereof; or abridging the freedom of speech, or of the press. ..."

In discussing scientific reasoning, Angier states, "We can call this 'objective' reality if we like, as opposed to subjective reality..." (22).

Omitting Material at the Start of a Quotation

No ellipses are required. Simply place the quotation marks where you begin quoting directly. Capitalize the first word if the resulting quotation forms a complete sentence.

Simply providing housing for the homeless will not suffice: "Programs need to supply employment and life skills training" (Stamp 8) .

Adding Material to a Quotation

If, for the sake of clarity or grammar, you need to add a word or short phrase to a quotation (for example, by changing a verb tense or replacing a vague pronoun with a noun), enclose your insertion in brackets:

Moreover, Angier discredits the concept that "the two [objective and subjective reality] are discrete entities with remarkably little in common" (22).

Capitalizing and Punctuating Short Quotations

The way a short quotation is used in a sentence determines whether it begins or doesn't begin with a capital letter and whether it is or isn't preceded by a comma.

Introducing a Quotation That Can Stand Alone as a Sentence

If a quotation can stand alone as a grammatical sentence, capitalize the quotation's first word. Also, precede the quotation with a comma:

Stamp observes, "Beginning in the 1980s and through the 1990s, the gap between the rich and the poor has widened..." (8).

According to Stamp, "Federal funding for low-cost housing has been almost eliminated" (8).

Using *That, Which,* or *Who* (Stated or Implied)

If you use *that, which,* or *who* to blend a quotation into the structure of your own sentence, don't capitalize the quotation's first word and don't precede it with a comma.

Stamp observes that "beginning in the 1980s and through the 1990s, the gap between the rich and the poor has widened, buying power has stagnated, industrial jobs have fled overseas, and federal funding for low-cost housing has been almost eliminated" (8).

Angier describes scientists as firmly believing there is "a reality capable of being understood" (22).

Even if, as in the first example above, the material being quoted originally started with a capital letter, you still use lowercase when incorporating the quotation into your own sentence. Note that in the second example, the word *that* is implied (before the word *there*).

Interrupting a Full-Sentence Quotation With an Attribution

Place commas on both sides of the attribution, and resume the quotation with a lowercase letter.

"The key to any successful homeless policy," Stamp comments, "requires a clear understanding of just who are the homeless" (8).

Using a Quotation With a Quoted Word or Phrase

When a source you're quoting contains a quoted word or phrase, place single quotation marks around the quoted words.

"We can call this 'objective' reality if we like, as opposed to subjective reality, or opinion, or 'whimsical set of predilections,'" Angier posits (22).

Note that the comma after *predilections* goes inside the single quotation mark.

Punctuating With a Question Mark or an Exclamation Point

If the question mark or exclamation point is part of the quotation, place it inside the quotation marks. If the mark is part of the structure of the framing sentence, as in the second example below, place it outside the quotation marks and after any parenthetical reference.

Discussing a child's epileptic attack, the psychoanalyst Erik Erikson asks, in *Childhood and Society,* "What was the 'psychic stimulus'?" (26).

But what does Stamp see as the "key to any successful homeless policy" (8)?

Document Sources to Avoid Plagiarism

Copyright law and the ethics of research require that you give credit to those whose words and ideas you borrow; that is, you must provide full and accurate *documentation.* Missing documentation results in *plagiarism*—using someone's material without properly crediting the source. Faulty documentation undermines your credibility. The best way to guard against plagiarism is to take very careful notes and thoroughly check your essay and Works Cited list for errors.

What Needs to Be Documented?

In general, any material—written or visual—that you take from outside sources (such as books, periodicals, websites, any type of performance, speeches, etc.) must be documented. To avoid plagiarizing, you must provide documentation for the following:

- A direct (word-for-word) quotation from a source.
- A paraphrase or summary of ideas, facts, opinions, or information from a source.
- A reproduction of an image, such as a photograph, or a graphic from a source.
- Any combination of quotation, paraphrase, summary, and visuals.

What Does Not Need to Be Documented

Academic writers must provide full documentation for all borrowed information. However, an exception is made for *common knowledge*—information that is widely known and accepted (whether or not you yourself were previously aware of it) as a matter of record. Well-known historical, scientific, and geographical facts, in particular, are often common knowledge. To determine whether information is common knowledge, ask yourself:

- *Are people likely to know this information without looking it up?* For example, that the United States shares international borders with Canada and Mexico is common knowledge.
- *Is the information easily found in many sources?* For example, that Japan attacked Pearl Harbor on December 7, 1941, is common knowledge.
- *Can a general dictionary supply the information?* For example, that dogs belong to the same family of mammals as wolves is common knowledge.
- *Is it a commonly accepted view?* For example, that the separation of church and state is an important principle in American politics is common knowledge.

Remember, though, that your instructor might ask you to document *all* the information you acquire during your research, regardless of whether it is common knowledge.

Creating In-Text References: MLA Format

The following discussion focuses on the MLA—Modern Language Association—format for documenting borrowed material. The MLA format, based on the *MLA Handbook for Writers of Research Papers*, is used widely in the liberal arts. For a sample paper that uses MLA documentation, turn to the student essay on pages 508–516.

Whenever you quote or summarize material in the body of your essay, you must: (1) identify the source as it appears in the Works Cited list, and (2) specify the page(s) in your source on which the material appears. For this information, the MLA documentation system uses the *parenthetical reference,* a brief note in parentheses inserted after a quotation, paraphrase, or summary. The parenthetical reference presents enough information so that readers can turn to the Works Cited list (see pages 515–516) at the end of the essay for complete documentation.

What to Provide Within the Parentheses

- Give the author's last name only, even when you cite the author for the first time. If there is no author, use a shortened version of the title or whatever element is given first in the Works Cited entry for the item.
- If you give the author's name in the text ("Stamp says that..."), do not repeat it in the parenthetical reference.
- Write the page number after the author's last name, with no punctuation between. (If the source is only one page, only the author's name is needed.) If the material quoted, paraphrased, or summarized spans more than one page, give the full range of pages, if it is available. Don't use the designation *p.* or *page.*

Where to Place the Parentheses

- Place the parenthetical reference at the end of the sentence, or immediately after the borrowed material if necessary for clarity.
- Put any period after the parenthetical reference—unless that reference follows a long quotation that is set off from the text, in which case the reference comes after any final punctuation.
- Make sure the parenthetical reference appears after an ellipsis and bracket at the end of a quotation, but before the final period.

In the examples below, the two parts of the reference—author's name or identifier and page number—are highlighted.

Single Source: Parentheses Only

In the following example, the parenthetical reference following the summary contains the author's name and the page number of the material summarized.

According to statistics, half of the homeless individuals living in shelters are substance abusers (Stamp 8).

A complete parenthetical reference follows the quotations in the next example. Note that the comma in the quotation is not part of the original quotation. It has been added because the sentence grammar requires a comma.

If we look beyond the problems of homelessness, to "larger economic issues," it is clear that "homelessness cannot be resolved solely at the level of the individual" (Stamp 8).

Single Source: Parentheses and Attributions

When the attribution gives the author's name, only the page number appears in the parenthetical reference. The attribution should make it clear where the quotation, summary, or paraphrase begins.

Julian Stamp argues that homelessness must be addressed in terms of economics, not simply in terms of individual counseling, addiction therapy, or job training (8).

In *The Homeless and History,* Stamp maintains that economic issues, rather than difficulties in people's personal lives, are at the core of the homeless problem (8).

Stamp points out that "homelessness cannot be resolved solely at the level of the individual" (8), although other experts disagree.

Note that in the immediately preceding example, the parenthetical reference follows the quotation in the middle of the sentence; placing the reference at the end of the sentence would erroneously imply that the idea expressed by "although other experts disagree" is Stamp's.

More Than One Source by the Same Author

When your essay includes references to more than one work by the same author, you must specify—either in the parenthetical reference or in the attribution—the particular work being cited. You do this by providing the title, as well as the author's name and the page(s). Here are examples from an essay in which two works by Jean Piaget were used.

In *The Language and Thought of the Child,* Jean Piaget states that "discussion forms the basis for a logical point of view" (240).

Piaget considers dialogue essential to the development of logical thinking (*Language* 240).

Notice that when you name a work in your text, the full title appears; when you give a title in the parenthetic citation, though, only the first few significant words appear. (However, don't use an ellipsis to indicate that words have been omitted from the title; the ellipsis is used only within quotations.) When name, title, and page number all appear in the parenthetical reference, a comma follows the author's name.

Two or Three Authors

Supply all the authors' last names either in the attribution or in parentheses.

A classic book on writing, *The Elements of Style* is an "attempt to cut the vast tangle of English rhetoric down to size" (Strunk and White xi).

More Than Three Authors

Either in the attribution or in parentheses, give the last name of the first author followed by *et al.* (which means "and others").

Researchers have found that the relationship between childhood obesity rates and family income level differs somewhat by race (Freedman et al. 26).

Two or More Authors With the Same Last Name

When you use two or more sources written by authors with the same last name, you must include (either in the attribution or in parentheses) each author's first name or initial(s). The following example is from a paper that cites sources for both Bill Clinton and Hillary Clinton.

Discussing the fears young people have today, Hillary Clinton asserts that children are more "aware" than adults of "the threats posed by global climate change, catastrophic environmental events, and the spread of deadly diseases that know no national boundaries" (xvi).

A Source With No Author

For a source without a named author, use a shortened version of the title of the work or the name of the issuing organization, whichever you used to alphabetize the source on the Works Cited list. In the following example, the full title of the source is "Supreme Court of the United States." Because the source is an entry in an alphabetically arranged reference book, the parenthetical reference has no page number.

The U.S. Supreme Court is fundamentally an appeals court, responsible for "cases arising under the Constitution, laws, or treaties of the United States" among others ("Supreme Court").

Information Found in Two or More Sources

When you come across several sources who cite the same highly specialized information or who share the same controversial opinion, that material does need to be documented. In such a case, state the material in your own words. In the parenthetical reference list the sources, separated by semicolons, as they appear in the Works Cited list.

A number of educators agree that an overall feeling of competence—rather than innate intelligence—is a key factor in determining which students do well the first year in college (Greene 208; Jones 72; Smith 465).

If you use a quotation to express an idea that occurs in several sources, provide an attribution for the quoted source and, in the parentheses, give the source's page number followed by a note that other sources make the same point:

The educator Henry Schneider argues that "students with low self-esteem tend to disregard the academic success they achieve" (23; also pointed out in Rabb 401).

Source Within a Source

If you quote or summarize a *secondary source* (a source whose ideas come to you only through another source), you need to make this clear. The parenthetic documentation should indicate "as quoted in" with the abbreviation *qtd. in*:

According to Sherman, "Recycling has, in several communities, created unanticipated expenses" (qtd. in Pratt 3).

Sherman explains that recycling can be surprisingly costly (qtd. in Pratt 3).

If the material you're quoting includes a quotation, place single quotation marks around the secondary quotation:

Pratt believes that "recycling efforts will be successful if, as Sherman argues, 'communities launch effective public-education campaigns'" (3).

Note: Your Works Cited list should include the source you actually read ("Pratt"), rather than the source you refer to secondhand ("Sherman").

A Source With No Page Numbers, Such as a Website

The parenthetic reference does not give a page number when no page number is available or when the item is an entry in an alphabetically arranged reference book, such as an encyclopedia. See "A Source With No Author" for an example.

Each Volume of a Multivolume Source Paged Separately

Indicate the volume number—"3" in the following example—then the page number, with a colon between the two. Do not use *vol.* or *v.*

(Kahn 3: 246)

A Nonprint Source (Television Show, Lecture, Interview)

In a parenthetic citation, give only the item (title, speaker, person interviewed) you used to alphabetize the source on your Works Cited list. Or provide the identifying information in the attribution, thus eliminating the need for parenthetic information:

The world that director James Cameron creates in the movie *Avatar* can be seen, in some ways, as an idealized version of Earth.

Long (Block) Quotations

A quotation longer than four lines starts on a new line and is indented, throughout, one inch from the left margin and typed without quotation marks. Double-space the block quotation. Don't leave extra space above or below the quotation. Long quotations, always used sparingly, require a lead-in. A lead-in that isn't a full sentence is followed by a comma; a lead-in that is a full sentence (highlighted) is followed by a colon:

Stamp cites changing economic conditions as the key to a national homeless policy:

> Beginning in the 1980s and through the 1990s, the gap between the rich and the poor has widened, buying power has stagnated, industrial jobs have fled overseas, and federal funding for low-cost housing has been almost eliminated. Given these developments, homelessness begins to look like a product of history, our recent history, and only by addressing shifts in the American economy can we begin to find effective solutions for people lacking homes. (8)

Notice that the page number in parentheses appears *after* the period, not before as it would with a short quotation.

Revise, Edit, and Proofread the First Draft

After completing your first draft, set the essay aside for a while. When you pick it up later, you'll have a fresh, more objective view of it. Then, reread your entire draft to evaluate the essay's overall meaning and structure. Outlining the draft—without referring to the outline that guided the draft's preparation—is a helpful analytical tool.

Despite all your work, you may find that a main support point seems weak. Sometimes a review of your notes—including those you didn't use for your draft—will uncover material that you can add to the essay. Other times, though, you may need to do additional research. Once you're confident that the essay's overall meaning and structure are strong, write your introduction and conclusion—if you haven't already done so.

Evaluate your essay's paragraph development, consulting the writing process diagrams for each pattern of development (Chapters 10–18) for more tips on revising each pattern. As you work, pay special attention to the way you present evidence in the paragraphs.

Look closely at how you integrate borrowed material. Does your evidence consist of one quotation after another, or do you express borrowed ideas in your own words? Do you simply insert borrowed material without commentary, or do you interpret the material and show its relevance to the points you want to make? If you prepared the draft without providing many attributions, now is the time to supply them. Then, refine your draft's words and sentences.

Finally, when you start editing and proofreading, allow enough time to verify the accuracy of quoted material. Check such material against your notes, and check your documentation against both your working bibliography and your Works Cited list (pages 488–489), making sure everything matches. When preparing the final copy of your essay, follow the sample research paper (pages 508–516) as a model.

Prepare the Works Cited List: MLA Format

At this point, you need to assemble your essay's Works Cited list. This list will provide readers with full bibliographic information about the sources you cite in the essay. As a first step, pull out the working bibliography. Remove the sources you did not use in your essay, and alphabetize the remaining entries by the authors' last names. For now, put any anonymous works at the end.

General Instructions for the MLA Works Cited List

The instructions below and the sample entries that follow are for MLA style. If you don't spot an entry for the type of source you need to document, consult the *MLA Handbook* for more comprehensive examples. (See also the sample Works Cited list on pages 515–516.)

- Include only those works you actually quote, paraphrase, summarize, or otherwise directly refer to in your essay.
- Start a new page, with the heading *Works Cited* centered, at the top, and place the list at the end of your essay.
- Double-space the entries in the list, and don't add extra space between entries.
- Start the first line of each new entry at the left margin; indent all subsequent lines in an entry five spaces (half an inch).
- Alphabetize by author's last name. Give the last name, then a comma, and then the first name and any initial. End with a period. For an entry with two or three authors, give all the authors' names but reverse only the first name. List the names in the order given in the source. For a work with four or more authors, give only the first author's name followed by a comma and *et al.* (Latin for "and others"), not italicized.
- If an entry doesn't have an author, alphabetize it by the title. Disregard an initial "A," "An" or "The" in alphabetizing.
- Separate the major items in a bibliographic entry (the author's full name, the complete title, all the information on publication) with periods. Leave just one space after the period.
- Use italics as noted below, unless your instructor prefers underlining.
- For dates in entries, use the following: *Jan., Feb., Mar., Apr., May, June, July, Aug., Sept., Oct., Nov., Dec.*

Nine categories of information can be found in a Works Cited entry. An entry will contain most, but usually not all, of these categories, generally in this order.

- **Author or other creative individual**
- **Title of a shorter work**
- **Larger work or source of a shorter work**

- **Place of publication**
- **Publisher or distributor**
- **Relevant identifying numbers or letters**
- **Relevant dates**
- **Medium (format)**
- **Descriptive information**

Citing Print Sources—Periodicals

For a periodical in print form, you'll need to consult (1) the page with the journal title and copyright information and (2) all the pages on which the article appears.

Basic MLA Format for a Printed Periodical

Author's last name, Author's first name. "Article Title: Article Subtitle." *Journal Title* vol. issue (year): pages. Print.

- **Author.** Follow the guidelines for authors' names in the "General Instructions for the MLA Works Cited List" on page 488. If the article is unsigned, begin with its title.
- **Article title.** Give the article's complete title, with main words capitalized, followed by a period, all enclosed in quotation marks.
- **Periodical title.** Supply the periodical's name, with main words capitalized, in italics, without any initial *A, An* or *The.* Don't place any punctuation after the title.
- **Volume and issue numbers.** For scholarly journals, give the volume number, then a period, and then the issue number (if available), right after the period. Use arabic, not roman, numerals, without either *volume* or *vol.* Generally, a yearly *volume* consists of a number of *issues.* Most periodicals are paginated continuously; that is, the first issue of each yearly volume starts with page 1 and each subsequent issue picks up where the previous one left off. Some journals do not paginate continuously; they start each new issue in a volume with page 1.
- **Date of publication.** For scholarly publications, include the year, in parentheses, followed by a colon. For newspapers and weekly magazines, include the day, month, and year—in that order—followed by a colon.
- **Page numbers.** Do not use *p., pp., page,* or *pages* before the numbers. If the pages in an article are continuous, give the page range (for example, 67–72, 321–25, or 497–502). If the pages in an article aren't continuous (for example, 67–68, 70, 72), write the first page number and a plus sign (67+). End with a period.
- **Medium.** Include *Print* at the end of the citation, followed by period.

Article in a Weekly or Biweekly Magazine

Leo, John. "Campus Censors in Retreat." *US News and World Report* 16 Feb. 2004: 64-65. Print.

Article in a Monthly or Bimonthly Magazine

Wheeler, Jacob. "Outsourcing the Public Good." *Utne* Sept.-Oct. 2004: 13-14. Print.

Article in a Daily Newspaper

Omit the initial *The* from newspaper names.

Doolin, Joseph. "Immigrants Deserve a Fair Deal." *Boston Globe* 19 Aug. 2003: A19+.
       Print.

Editorial, Letter to the Editor, or Reply to a Letter

Baldwin, William. "Sidelines: Defend Yourself against Tax Torture." Editorial. *Forbes*
       10 May 2010: 10. Print.

"Playing Fair with Nuclear Cleanup." Editorial. *Seattle Times* 5 Oct. 2003: D2. Print.

Article in a Scholarly Journal

Regardless of how a journal is paginated, include *both* the volume number and
the issue number (if available).

Chew, Cassie. "Achieving Unity through Diversity." *Black Issues in Higher Education* 21.5
       (2004): 8-11. Print.

Manning, Wendy D. "Children and the Stability of Cohabiting Couples." *Journal of
       Marriage and Family* 66.3 (2004): 674-89. Print.

Article With More Than One Author

For a citation with up to four authors, see the first example. For one with more
than four authors, see the second example.

Juhila, Kirsi, Christopher Hall, and Suvi Raitakari. "Accounting for the Clients'
       Troublesome Behaviour in a Supported Housing Unit: Blames, Excuses and
       Responsibility in Professionals' Talk." *Journal of Social Work* 10.1 (2010): 59-79.
       Print.

Troubleyn, Liesbeth, et al. "Consumption Patterns and Living Conditions inside Het Steen,
       the Late Medieval Prison of Malines (Mechelen, Belgium)." *Journal of Archaeology
       in the Low Countries* 1.2 (2009): 5-47. Print.

Review of a Book

Chiasson, Don. "Forms of attention." Rev. of *Rain*, by Don Paterson. *New Yorker* 19 Apr.
       2010. 116-18. Print.

Citing Print Sources—Books

For a book, you'll need to consult (1) the title page and (2) the copyright notice on
the back of the title page. You will also need to know the specific page numbers of
any material you are citing.

Basic MLA Format for a Printed Book

Author's last name, Author's first name. *Book Title: Book Subtitle.* City of pubication:
Publisher, year of publication. Print.

- **Author.** Follow the guidelines for authors' names in the "General Instructions
  for the MLA Works Cited List" on page 488. If the article is unsigned, begin
  with its title.
- **Book title.** Give the complete book title in italics, capitalizing the major words.
  If the book has a subtitle, separate it from the title with a colon and a single
  space. End the title with a period.
- **City of publication.** Give the city of publication, followed by a colon and a
  space. Use the city listed first on the title page.
- **Publisher.** Supply the publisher's name, giving only key words and omitting
  the words *Company, Press, Publishers, Inc.,* and the like. (For example, write
  Rodale for *Rodale Press* and *Norton* for *W. W. Norton and Company.*) In addition,
  use *UP* to abbreviate the names of university presses (as in *Columbia UP* and *U
  of California P*). Place a comma and a space after the publisher's name.
- **Year of publication.** Supply the most recent year of copyright. Don't use the
  year of the most recent printing.
- **Medium.** Include *Print* at the end of the citation, followed by a period.

Book by One Author

McDonnell, Lorraine M. *Politics, Persuasion, and Educational Testing.* Cambridge: Harvard
UP, 2004. Print.

Book by Two or Three Authors

Douglas, Susan, and Meredith Michaels. *The Mommy Myth: The Idealization of Motherhood
and How It Has Undermined Women.* New York: Free, 2004. Print.

Gunningham, Neil A., Robert Kagan, and Dorothy Thornton. *Shades of Green: Business,
Regulation, and Environment.* Palo Alto: Stanford UP, 2003. Print.

Book by Four or More Authors

Brown, Michael K., et al. *Whitewashing Race: The Myth of a Color-Blind Society.* Berkeley:
U of California P, 2003. Print.

Two or More Works by the Same Author

List each book separately. Give the author's name in the first entry only; begin the
subsequent entries with three hyphens followed by a period. Arrange the works
alphabetically by title.

McChesney, Robert W. *The Problem of the Media: U.S. Communication Politics in the Twenty-
first Century.* New York: Monthly Rev., 2004. Print.

---. *Rich Media, Poor Democracy: Communication Politics in Dubious Times.* Champaign: U of
Illinios P, 1999. Print.

Revised Edition

Indicate the edition (*Rev. ed., 2nd ed., 3rd ed., 4th ed.,* and so on) after the title.

Weiss, Thomas G., David P. Forsythe, and Roger A. Coate. *The United Nations and Changing World Politics.* 3rd ed. Boulder: Westview, 2001. Print.

Zinn, Howard. *A People's History of the United States: 1492–Present.* Rev. ed. New York: Perennial, 2003. Print.

Book With an Author and Editor or Translator

Use *Ed.* (for "Edited by") or *Trans.* (for "Translated by") and then the name of the editor or translator.

Douglass, Frederick. *My Bondage and My Freedom.* Ed. John David Smith. New York: Penguin, 2003. Print.

Anthology or Compilation of Works by Different Authors

Use *ed.* or *eds.* (for "editor" or "editors").

Kasser, Tim, and Allen D. Kanner, eds. *Psychology and Consumer Culture: The Struggle for a Good Life in a Materialistic World.* Washington: Amer. Psychological Assn., 2004. Print.

Section of an Anthology or Compilation

Use *Ed.* (for "Edited by") and the editors' names. Note that the entry gives the page numbers on which the selection appears.

Levin, Diane E., and Susan Linn. "The Commercialization of Childhood: Understanding the Problem and Finding Solutions." *Psychology and Consumer Culture: The Struggle for a Good Life in a Materialistic World.* Ed. Tim Kasser and Allen D. Kanner. Washington: Amer. Psychological Assn., 2004. 212-28. Print.

Section, Poem, or Chapter in a Book by One Author

Wolfson, Evan. "Is Marriage Equality a Question of Civil Rights?" *Why Marriage Matters: America, Equality, and Gay People's Right to Marry.* New York: Simon, 2004. 242-69. Print.

Reference Work

"Temperance Movements." *Columbia Encyclopedia.* 6th ed. New York: Columbia UP, 2000. Print.

Book by an Institution (Corporate Author)

United Nations. Dept. of Economic and Social Affairs. *Human Development, Health, and Education: Dialogues at the Economic and Social Council.* New York: United Nations, 2004.

Citing Sources Found on a Website

Citations for sources found on the Internet require much of the same information used in citations for print sources. Do not give the URL (Internet address) in the citation unless the source would be very hard to locate without it. (See "Personal and Professional Website" for an example using a URL.) For a website, you will need information from (1) the entire screen of the Web page you are citing, including the address bar, and (2) the home page of the website, if that is different from the page you are citing.

Basic MLA Format for a Website

Author's last name, Author's first name. "Article or Item Title." *Website Title.* Version or edition, if any. Website Sponsor or Publisher, day month year of publication. Web. day month year of access.

- **Author's name.** Follow the guidelines for authors' names in the "General Instructions for the MLA Works Cited List" on page 488. If the article is unsigned, begin with its title.
- **Title of the selection.** To cite a selection on the website, give the title of the selection, followed by a period, all enclosed in quotation marks. To cite the entire website, see "Source," below.
- **Source.** Give the title of the website, italicized, and followed by a period.
- **Version or edition.** List any version or edition number (for example, for an online book), if relevant.
- **Publisher or sponsor.** Cite the publisher, owner, or sponsor of the website, followed by a comma. This information is often found at the bottom of the Web page. If none is available, use *N.p.* (for "no publisher").
- **Date of publication.** Give the date of publication as day, month, year, followed by a period. If the information is not available, use *n.d.* (for "no date").
- **Medium.** Include *Web* followed by a period.
- **Access date.** End with the date you retrieved the information (day, month, year) followed by a period.

Newspaper or Magazine Article

The second citation is to an online-only magazine.

Orecklin, Michele. "Stress and the Superdad." *Time.* Time.com, 16 Aug. 2004. Web. 2 Dec. 2013.

Nachtigal, Jeff. "We Own What You Think." *Salon.com.* Salon Media Group, 18 Aug. 2004. Web. 17 Mar. 2013.

"Restoring the Wetlands." Editorial. *Los Angeles Times.* Los Angeles Times, 26 July 2008. Web. 6 Jan. 2013.

Online Reference Work

"Salem Witch Trials." *Encyclopaedia Britannica Online.* Encyclopaedia Britannica, 2008. Web. 3 Jan. 2009.

Scholarly Journal Found on the Internet

For articles accessed from a website, follow the citation format for print articles (see "Article in a Scholarly Journal"), but specify *Web* as the medium and give the date of access. A journal published only online may paginate articles individually, starting each article with 1, instead of sequentially throughout the issue. In that case, as in the second example below, use *n. pag.* (for "no pages"). See also the entry for "Scholarly Journal Found in an Online Database."

Ensor, Rosie, and Claire Hughes. "With a Little Help from My Friends: Maternal Social
  Support, via Parenting, Promotes Willingness to Share in Preschoolers Born to
  Young Mothers." *Infant and Child Development* 19.2 (2010): 127-221. Web. 24 May
  2013.

Njeng, Eric Sipyinyu. "Achebe, Conrad, and the Postcolonial Strain." *CLCWeb: Comparative
  Literature and Culture* 10.1 (2008): n. pag. Web. 12 Dec. 2013.

Qin, Desiree Baolian. "The Role of Gender in Immigrant Children's Educational Adaptation."
  Current Issues in Comparative Education 9.1 (2006): 8-19. Web. 5 Jan. 2013.

Personal and Professional Websites

In the entry, *Uncle Tom's Cabin* is *not* italicized. Although it's a title that would ordinarily be italicized, since the rest of the website title is in italics, the book title is set off in regular type.

Railton, Stephen, ed. Uncle Tom's Cabin *and American Culture: A Multi-Media Archive.*
  Dept. of English, U of Virginia, 2007. Web. 9 Apr. 2013.

Blog

If a blog has no title, insert "Online posting" in place of the title, without quotation marks or italics. Note that in the second entry, the author's actual name, identifiable on the blog's website, is given in brackets after his screen name.

Waldman, Deane. " 'Care' Has Deserted Managed Care." *Huffington Post.* HuffingtonPost.
  com, 26 June 2008. Web. 18 Nov. 2013.

Joe [Joseph Romm]. "Should You Believe Anything BP Says?" Online posting. *Climate
  Progress.* Center for American Progress Action Fund, 17 May 2010. Web. 24 May
  2013.

Podcast

MLA does not give a specific format for citing a podcast. The following formats may be used.

Elving, Ron, and Ken Rudin, eds. "It's All Politics, May 27: NPR's Weekly News
  Roundup." *NPR.* NPR, 28 May 2010. Web. 5 June 2013.

Wiman, Christian, and Don Share, eds. "Iamb What Iamb." *Poetry Foundation.* Poetry
  Foundation, 1 June 2010. Web. 7 June 2013.

Postings to an Online Group

MLA does not give a specific format for citing a posting to an online group. The following format may be used for such a citation.

Zoutron. "Re: Geometry of Sound." Online posting. *Geometry.research.* Groups.Google.
  com, 30 Mar. 2007. Web. 21 Apr. 2013.

E-book on iPad, Kindle, Nook, or Another Device

Rowling, J.K. *Harry Potter and the Chamber of Secrets*. New York: Arthur A. Levine, 1999. Kindle file.

Posting on Social Media

UN Refugee Agency. "Please share! We're rushing in aid as 66,000 #Congolese refugees stream into western #Uganda." 15 July 2013, 4:22 p.m. Tweet.

MoMA. "Photo by Emilio Guerra." *Museum of Modern Art*. *Facebook*, 10 July 2013. Web. 17 July 2013.

Citing Sources Found Through an Online Database or Scholarly Project

Follow the format for "Citing Sources Found on a Website," but also specify the database or project. Do not include the URL or information about the library system used.

Scholarly Journal Found in an Online Database

After the publication information (volume, issue, date, and page numbers), give the title of the database, italicized, and the medium (*Web*). End with the date you accessed the information. See also the entry "Scholarly Journal Found on the Internet."

Weiler, Angela M. "Using Technology to Take Down Plagiarism." *Community College Week* 16.16 (2004): 4-6. *EBSCOhost*. Web. 17 Oct. 2008.

Book Found in an Online Scholarly Project

Franklin, Benjamin. *The Autobiography of Benjamin Franklin*. London, 1793. *Electronic Text Center*. Ed. Judy Boss. Web. 16 Jan. 2009.

Citing Other Common Sources

Include the medium through which you accessed the source, for example, *CD* for "compact disc" or *E-mail* for an e-mail message you received.

CD-ROM or DVD-ROM

Cite the following information (when available): author, title (italicized), version, place of publication, publisher, year of publication, and medium (*CD-ROM* or *DVD-ROM*).

World Book Encyclopedia. 2006 ed. Renton: Topics Entertainment, 2006. CD-ROM.

Visual Art

For a work of art, start with the artist's name and then give the title of the work (italicized). If you know the year the work was done, state it. Otherwise, use *N.d.* If you viewed the work in person (second example below), give the medium of the work, the place where you saw the art, and the location. If you viewed the work in a print source (first example), omit the medium of the work but give complete publication information and end with *Print*. If you viewed the art on the

Web (third example), omit the medium, add the title of the database or website, the medium you used (*Web*), and your date of access.

Blake, William. *A Vision of the Last Judgment.* 1808. Petworth House, Natl. Trust, UK.
    William Blake. New York: Abrams, 2001. 68. Print.

Cole, Thomas. *View from Mount Holyoke, Northampton, Massachusetts, after a Thunderstorm—*
    The Oxbow. 1836. Oil on canvas. Metropolitan Museum of Art, New York.

Cole, Thomas. *View from Mount Holyoke, Northampton, Massachusetts, after a Thunderstorm—*
    The Oxbow. 1836. Metropolitan Museum of Art, New York. *MetMuseum.org.* Web.
    24 May 2010.

Cartoon or Comic Strip

Alcaraz, Lalo. "La Cucaracha." Comic strip. *GoComics.com.* Uclick, 7 May 2010. Web.
    7 May 2010.

Byrnes, Pat. Cartoon. *New Yorker* 19 Apr. 2010: 44. Print.

Television or Radio Program

Give the network that carried the program, the call letters and city of the local station on which the program was seen or heard, and date of the broadcast. If, as in the example below, the program is an episode in a continuing series, give the episode title first (in quotation marks) and then the program title. You might also include additional information such as the director or narrator.

"A Matter of Choice? Gay Life in America." Part 4 of 5. *Nightline.* Narr. Ted Koppel. ABC.
    WPVI-TV, Philadelphia, 23 May 2002. Television.

Movie, Recording, CD, DVD, Videotape, Audiotape, Filmstrip, or Slide Program

Provide the author or composer; song title in quotation marks; album or film title (italicized); director, conductor, or performer; manufacturer or distributor; year of release; and medium (for example, *Film*). For a re-release, see the first and third examples below.

Dylan, Bob. "Visions of Johanna." *Blonde on Blonde.* 1966. Sony, 2004. CD.

The Hurt Locker. Dir. Kathryn Bigelow. Voltage Pictures, 2008. Film.

The Hurt Locker. Dir. Kathryn Bigelow. 2008. Universal Studios Home Entertainment, 2010.
    DVD.

Personal or Telephone Interview

Como, Anna. Telephone interview. 4 May 2010.

Langdon, Paul. Personal interview. 26 Jan. 2008.

Lecture, Speech, Address, or Reading

If there is no title, use a description such as *Keynote address* or *Lecture*. Include any series or meeting title.

Blacksmith, James. "Urban Design in the New Millennium." Cityscapes Lecture Series. Urban
    Studies Institute. Metropolitan College, Washington, DC. 18 Apr. 2005. Lecture.

E-mail Message

Start with the sender's name.

Mack, Lynn. "New Developments in Early Childhood Education." Message to the author. 30 Aug. 2006. E-mail.

Prepare the References List: APA Format

Researchers in the social sciences and in education use a citation format developed by the American Psychological Association (APA) and explained in the *Publication Manual of the American Psychological Association*. If you're writing an essay for a course in sociology, psychology, anthropology, economics, or political science, your professor will probably expect APA-style documentation. History, philosophy, and religion are sometimes considered humanities, sometimes social sciences, depending on your approach to the topic.

Parenthetic Citations in the Text

As in the MLA format, APA citations are enclosed in parentheses within the text and provide the author's last name. The main differences between the two formats are these:

- The year of publication appears after the name.
- Page numbers appear after the year only when a source is quoted or when specific parts of a source are paraphrased or summarized. (A citation without a page number refers to the source as a whole.)
- The abbreviation *p.* or *pp.* appears before any page number(s).
- A comma appears between the author's name and the year, and between the year and the page number.

Here are examples of APA parenthetic citations:

Education experts have observed that "as arts education funding dwindles in school systems, theatres of all sizes have assumed more and more of the burden of training young people and exposing them to the arts" (Cameron, 2004, p. 6).

If you use an attribution that gives the author's name, put the publication year (in parentheses) right after the author's name and put the page number at the end. The attribution is underlined in this example.

The social commentator Bob Herbert (2004) argues that middle-class Americans "are caught in a squeeze between corporations bent on extracting every last ounce of productivity from U.S. employees and a vast new globalized work force that is eager . . . to do the jobs of American workers at a fraction of the pay" (p. 20).

If a work has two authors, cite both, using *and* in a text attribution and an ampersand (&) in a parenthetic reference. For a work with three to five authors, name all authors in the first citation. In subsequent citations, name only the first author followed by *et al.* For a work with six or more authors, cite the first author followed by *et al.*

Dawn Newman-Carlson and Arthur M. Horne (2004) assert that schools must "explore the implementation not only of programs that assist bullies and aid their victims but also of those that strengthen the positive relationships between teachers, bullies, victims, and . . . bystanders to bullying" (p. 259).

Schools need to develop programs that work on improving the relationships between all parties to school bullying—bullies, their victims, bystanders, and teachers (Newman-Carlson & Horne, 2004, p. 259).

General Instructions for the APA References List

A double-spaced alphabetical list of sources, titled *References*, appears at the end of a research essay using APA documentation style. The citations include much of the same information as MLA citations do, but they are formatted in different ways. Notice that the first four items in the following instructions are the same as for a Works Cited list.

- Include only those works you actually quote, paraphrase, summarize, or otherwise directly refer to in your essay.
- Start a new page, with the heading *References* centered, at the top, and place the list at the end of your essay.
- Double-space the entries in the list, and don't add extra space between entries.
- Start the first line of each new entry at the left margin; if an entry extends beyond one line, indent all subsequent lines five spaces (half an inch).
- Place the publication date in parentheses directly after the author's name and follow it with a period.
- For two or more works by the same author, arrange the works by publication date, giving the earliest first.
- For two or more works by the same author that are published in the same year, differentiate the dates with lowercase letters—(1996a), (1996b)—and alphabetize them by title.
- For an item with up to seven authors, give the last names and initials for all authors. Use an ampersand (&) instead of *and* before the last author. If there are more than seven, list the first six, add a comma and an ellipsis, and end with the name of the last author. Invert the names of all authors.
- Invert all author names, and use only initials for an author's first and middle names.
- For an article, capitalize only the first letter of the title (and subtitle) and any proper names. Do not enclose the title in quotation marks.

- For a book, capitalize only the first letter of the title (and subtitle) and any proper names. Italicize the title.
- For a journal, give the full title, in capital and lowercase letters, italicized.
- Abbreviate publishers' names but include the word *Books*, *Press*, or *University* when it is part of a publisher's name.

Here's the general order of information for an entry:
- Author or other creative individual
- Relevant dates
- Title of a shorter work
- Descriptive information
- Larger work or source of a shorter work
- Place of publication
- Publisher or distributor
- Relevant identifying numbers or letters
- Medium (format)

Citing Print Sources—Periodicals

For a periodical in print form, you'll need to consult (1) the page with the journal title and copyright information and (2) all pages on which the article appears.

Basic APA Format for a Printed Periodical

Author's last name, author's initials. (date). Article title: Article subtitle. *Periodical Title, volume*(issue), pages.

- **Author.** See the guidelines on authors' names in "General Instructions for the APA References List." If the article is unsigned, begin with its title.
- **Date of publication.** Include the year, in parentheses, followed by a period. For newspapers and weekly magazines, include the year, followed by a comma, then the month and day.
- **Article title.** Give the article's complete title, with capitals for the first word of the main title and subtitle and any proper nouns. Do not put the title into quotation marks. End with a period.
- **Periodical title.** Supply the periodical's full name, in italics. Follow with a comma.
- **Volume and issue numbers.** For scholarly journals, give the volume number in italics. If the journal is paginated by issue, include the issue number in parentheses after the volume number with no intervening space. Do not italicize the issue number. Do not use the abbreviation *vol.* Follow with a comma.
- **Page numbers.** Give the page range (for example, 27–34). If the pages in an article aren't continuous, give all the page numbers separated by commas (for

example, 67–68, 70, 72). End with a period. Do not use *p., pp., page,* or *pages* before the numbers, except when citing a newspaper article.

Article in a Weekly or Biweekly Magazine

Leo, J. (2004, February 16). Campus censors in retreat. *U.S. News & World Report, 136,* 64–65.

Article in a Monthly or Bimonthly Magazine

Wheeler, J. (2004, September/October). Outsourcing the public good. *Utne, 124,* 13–14.

Article in a Daily Newspaper

Include the abbreviation *p.* or *pp.* before the page number(s).

Doolin, J. (2003, August 19). Immigrants deserve a fair deal. *The Boston Globe,* pp. A19, A25.

Editorial, Letter to the Editor, or Reply to a Letter

For an unsigned editorial, start with the title, add the word *Editorial* in brackets, a period, and then the date.

Baldwin, W. (2010, May 10). Sidelines: Defend yourself against tax torture [Editorial]. *Forbes, 185*(8), 10.

Playing fair with nuclear cleanup [Editorial]. (2003, October 5). *The Seattle Times,* p. D2.

Article in a Continuously Paginated Scholarly Journal

Include a Digital Object Identifier (DOI) at the end of your entry if one is available. For more information on the DOI, see page 502.

Morrison, G. Z. (2010). Two separate worlds: Students of color at a predominantly white university. *Journal of Black Studies, 40,* 987–1015. doi:10.1177/0021934708325408

Article in a Scholarly Journal That Paginates Each Issue Separately

Chew, C. (2004). Achieving unity through diversity. *Black Issues in Higher Education, 21*(5), 8–11.

Article by More Than One Author

Follow the format in the first example for a citation with up to seven authors. For a citation with more than seven authors, follow the format in the second example. (See the guidelines on authors' names in the "General Instructions for the APA References List" on pages 498–499).

Seamon, M. J., Fass, J. A., Maniscalco-Feichtl, M., & Abu-Shraie, N. A. (2007). Medical marijuana and the developing role of the pharmacist. *American Journal of Health-System Pharmacy, 64*(10), 1037–1044.

Troubleyn, L., Kinnaer, F., Ervynck, A., Beeckmans, L., Caluwé, D., Cooremans, B.,...Wouters, W. (2009). Consumption patterns and living conditions inside Het Steen, the late medieval prison of Malines (Mechelen, Belgium). *Journal of Archaeology in the Low Countries, 1*(2), 5–47.

Review of a Book

Chiasson, D. (2010, April 19). Forms of attention [Review of the book *Rain,* by Don Paterson]. *The New Yorker,* 116–118.

Citing Print Sources—Books

For a book, you'll need to consult (1) the title page and (2) the copyright notice on the back of the title page. You will also need to know the specific page numbers of any material you are citing.

Basic APA Format for a Printed Book

Author's last name, Author's initials. (year). *Book title: Book subtitle.* City, State (or Country): Publisher.

- **Author.** See the guidelines on authors' names in "General Instructions for the APA References List."
- **Year of publication.** Supply the most recent year of copyright in parentheses, followed by a period. Don't use the year of the most recent printing.
- **Book title.** Give the complete book title in italics. If the book has a subtitle, separate it from the title with a colon and a single space. Capitalize only the first word of the main title and subtitle and any proper nouns. End the title with a period.
- **Place of publication.** Give the first city of publication listed on the title page. Unless the state is mentioned in the publisher's name (as in a university press), give the state also, using U.S. postal abbreviations. For cities outside the United States, spell out the city and country. Separate city and state or country with a comma. Follow with a colon and a space.
- **Publisher.** Shorten the publisher's name, giving only key words and omitting the terms like *Co., Publishers, Inc.* However, keep the words *University, Press,* and *Books* spelled out. (For example, write *Norton* for *W. W. Norton and Company* but spell out *University of Chicago Press.*) End with a period.

Book by One Author

McDonnell, L. M. (2004). *Politics, persuasion, and educational testing.* Cambridge, MA: Harvard University Press.

Multiple Works by the Same Author

Repeat the author's name with each entry, and list the entries by year of publication, from earliest to latest.

McChesney, R. W. (1999). *Rich media, poor democracy: Communication politics in dubious times.* Champaign: University of Illinois Press.

McChesney, R. W. (2004). *The problem of the media: U.S. communication politics in the 21st century.* New York, NY: Monthly Review Press.

Book by Multiple Authors

Gunningham, N. A., Kagan, R., & Thornton, D. (2003). *Shades of green: Business, regulation, and environment.* Palo Alto, CA: Stanford University Press.

Revised Edition

Weiss, T. G., Forsythe, D. P., & Coate, R. A. (2001). *The United Nations and changing world politics* (3rd ed.). Boulder, CO: Westview.

Book With an Author and Editor or Translator

Use the abbreviations *Ed.* and *Trans.*

Douglass, F. (2003). *My bondage and my freedom* (J. D. Smith, Ed.). New York, NY: Penguin.

Anthology or Compilation of Works by Different Authors

Kasser, T., & Kanner, A. D. (Eds.). (2004). *Psychology and consumer culture: The struggle for a good life in a materialistic world.* Washington, DC: American Psychological Association.

Section of an Anthology or Compilation

Give the inclusive page numbers, preceded by *pp.*, for the section you are citing.

Levin, D. E., & Linn, S. (2004). The commercialization of childhood: Understanding the problem and finding solutions. In T. Kasser & A. D. Kanner (Eds.), *Psychology and consumer culture: The struggle for a good life in a materialistic world* (pp. 212–228). Washington, DC: American Psychological Association.

Section, Poem, or Chapter in a Book by One Author

Wolfson, E. (2004). Is marriage equality a question of civil rights? In E. Wolfson, *Why marriage matters: America, equality, and gay people's right to marry* (pp. 242–269). New York, NY: Simon & Schuster.

Reference Work

Temperance Movements. (2000). In *Columbia Encyclopedia* (6th ed.). New York, NY: Columbia University Press.

Book by an Institution (Corporate Author)

United Nations Department of Economic and Social Affairs. (2004). *Human development, health, and education: Dialogues at the Economic and Social Council.* New York, NY: United Nations.

Citing Sources Found on a Website

Citations for websites require much of the same information used in citations for print sources. To this, add retrieval information—an Internet address (URL) or a DOI (digital object identifier). The DOI, used primarily with scholarly materials, is a permanent, unique identifier for articles on the Web. For an online newspaper, magazine, or similar publication, use the publication's home page URL. For difficult-to-find sites, include the entire URL. To construct a citation, you will need information from

(1) the entire screen of the Web page you are citing, including the address bar, and (2) the home page of the website, if that is different from the page you are citing.

Basic APA Formats for an Online Source

Print publication information. doi: 10.xxxx/xxxxxxxxxx

Author's last name, Author's initials. (date). Item title. *Website Title* (version or edition, if any). Retrieved from [URL]

- **Author's name.** Give the author's name, as for a print item.
- **Title of the selection.** Give the title of the selection, as for an article title, followed by a period. To cite an entire website, see "Source" below.
- **Date of publication.** Give the date of publication as for a print item. If the date is not available, use *n.d.* (for "no date").
- **Source.** Give the title of the website, as for a book or publication title.
- **Version or edition.** List any volume, issue, and page numbers as for a print edition. Or list any relevant version, edition, or report number in parentheses after the source, followed by a period.
- **Sponsor.** Give the sponsor or owner in the retrieval information if a URL is cited.
- **Medium.** Include the retrieval information. If a DOI is available, use "doi:" plus the number. Otherwise, give "Retrieved from" plus the site owner's name (if different from the source) and the URL of the source's home page. Do not end with a period.

Newspaper or Magazine Article

The third citation is to an online-only magazine.

Restoring the wetlands [Editorial]. (2008, July 26). *Los Angeles Times*. Retrieved from http://www.latimes.com/

Orecklin, M. (2004, August 16). Stress and the superdad. *Time*. Retrieved from http://www.time.com/

Nachtigal, J. (2004, August 18). We own what you think. *Salon*. Retrieved from http://www.salon.com/

Online Reference Work

Salem witch trials. (n.d.). In *Encyclopaedia Britannica Online*. Retrieved from http://www.britannica.com/

Scholarly Journal Found on the Internet

For articles accessed from a website, follow the citation format for print articles (see pages 499–500) and end with retrieval information. If a DOI is available, as in the first example, include it. Otherwise, include the URL of the site's home page, or use the URL of the actual page cited if finding the document would otherwise be difficult. No retrieval date is needed for documents that are in final (published) form and unlikely to change. Note that some articles published on the Web do not give page numbers, as in the second example below.

Ensor, R., & Hughes, C. (2010, March/April). With a little help from my friends: Maternal social support, via parenting, promotes willingness to share in preschoolers born to young mothers. *Infant and Child Development, 19*(2), 127–221. doi:10.1002/icd.643

Njeng, E. S. (2008). Achebe, Conrad, and the postcolonial strain. *CLCWeb: Comparative Literature and Culture, 10*(1). Retrieved from http://docs.lib.purdue.edu/clcweb/vol10/iss1/3

Qin, D. B. (2006). The role of gender in immigrant children's educational adaptation. *Current Issues in Comparative Education, 9*(1), 8–19. Retrieved from http://www.tc.edu/cice/

Personal and Professional Websites

Railton, S. (Ed.). (2009). Uncle Tom's Cabin & *American Culture: A Multi-Media Archive.* Department of English, University of Virginia. Retrieved from http://utc.iath.virginia.edu/

Blog

If you are reasonably sure that you know the actual name of the author, include it in brackets, with a question mark, as in the second example. Otherwise, use the author's screen name.

Waldman, D. (2008, June 26). "Care" has deserted managed care. *Huffington Post* [Web log post]. Retrieved from http://huffingtonpost.com

Joe [Romm, J.?]. (2010, May 17). Should you believe anything BP says? [Web log post]. Retrieved from http://climateprogress.org/2010/05/17/bp-oil-spill-blame-bob-bea-60-minutes/

Winter, C. (2010, May 17). Re: Should you believe anything BP says? [Web log comment]. Retrieved from http://climateprogress.org/2010/05/17/bp-oil-spill-blame-bob-bea-60-minutes/

Podcast

Elving, R., & Rudin, K. [Eds.]. (2010, May 28). *It's all politics, May 27: NPR's weekly news roundup* [Audio podcast]. Retrieved from http://www.npr.org/

Wiman, C., & Share, D. [Eds.]. (2010, June 1). *Iamb What Iamb* [Audio podcast]. Retrieved from http://www.poetryfoundation.org/

Postings to an Online Group

Include an appropriate description (*Online forum comment; Electronic mailing list message;* and so on) in brackets.

Zoutron. (2007, March 30). Re: Geometry of sound [Online group comment]. Retrieved from http://groups.google.com/group/geometry.research/browse_frm/month/2007-03

E-book on iPad, Kindle, Nook, or Another Device

Rowling, J. K. (1999). *Harry Potter and the chamber of secrets* [Kindle ed]. New York: Arthur A. Levine.

Posting on Social Media

United Nations Refugee Agency. (2013, July 15, 4:22 p.m.). Please share! We're rushing in aid as 66,000 #Congolese refugees stream into western #Uganda [Twitter post]. Retrieved from https//: twitter.com/UNRefugeeAgency

MoMA. (2013, July 10). Photo by Emilio Guerra. Retrieved from https://facebook.com /MuseumofModernArt

Citing Sources Found Through an Online Database or Scholarly Project

Follow the format for "Citing Sources Found on a Website," but also specify the database or project. Do not include the URL or information about the library system used.

Scholarly Journal Found in an Online Database

If the database entry provides a DOI, include that in the citation. (See "Scholarly Journal Found on the Internet.") If there is no DOI, do not include the database name. Instead, find the home page of the journal and include its URL.

Weiler, A. M. (2004). Using technology to take down plagiarism. *Community College Week, 16*(16), 4–6. Retrieved from http://www.ccweek.com/

Book Found in an Online Scholarly Project

Include the date the book appeared online and, when available, the book's original publication date.

Franklin, B. (1995). *The autobiography of Benjamin Franklin.* Retrieved from http://etext .lib.virginia.edu/toc/modeng/public/Fra2Aut.html (Original work published 1793)

Citing Other Common Sources

Include the medium through which you accessed the source, for example, *CD* for "compact disc" or *E-mail* for an e-mail message you received.

CD-ROM or DVD-ROM

World Book Encyclopedia. (2006). [CD-ROM]. Renton, WA: Topics Entertainment.

Visual Art

The following formats are adapted from other APA citation formats. The first citation is to a work of art viewed in a book; the second, to a work viewed in person at a museum; the third, to a work viewed online.

Blake, W. (2001). *A vision of the Last Judgment* [Reproduction of a watercolor painting.] In *William Blake* (p. 68). New York, NY: Abrams.

Cole, T. (1836). *View from Mount Holyoke, Northampton, Massachusetts, after a thunderstorm—The Oxbow* [Oil on canvas]. The Metropolitan Museum of Art, New York, NY.

Cole, T. (1836). *View from Mount Holyoke, Northampton, Massachusetts, after a thunderstorm—The Oxbow* [Oil on canvas]. Retrieved from the Metropolitan Museum of Art at http://www.MetMuseum.org.

Cartoon or Comic Strip

The following formats are adapted from other APA citation formats.

Alcaraz, L. (2010, May 7). *La cucaracha* [Comic strip]. Retrieved from http://www.GoComics.com

Byrnes, P. (2010, May 19). [Cartoon]. *The New Yorker*, 44.

Television or Radio Program

Koppel, T. (Narrator). (2002, May 23). A matter of choice? Gay life in America (Part 4 of 5). [Television series episode]. On *Nightline*. Philadephia, PA: WPVI-TV (ABC).

Movie, Recording, CD, DVD, Videotape, Audiotape, Filmstrip, or Slide Program

Include the original date of release in parentheses at the end of the citation. For motion pictures, include only the country of origin.

Dylan, B. (2004). Visions of Johanna. On *Blonde on blonde* [CD]. New York, NY: Sony. (1966)

Bigelow, K. (Producer & Director). (2008). *The hurt locker* [Motion picture]. United States: Voltage Pictures.

Bigelow, K. (Producer & Director). (2010). *The hurt locker* [DVD]. Los Angeles, CA: Universal Studios Home Entertainment. (2008)

Personal or Telephone Interview

According to APA style, personal communications are not included in the References list. Instead, cite such communications only in the text. If your instructor asks for interviews to be documented in the References list, you may use the following format.

Como, A. (2010, May 4). [Telephone interview].

Langdon, P. (2008, January 26). [Personal interview].

Lecture, Speech, Address, or Reading

Blacksmith, J. (2005, April 18). *Urban design in the new millennium.* Presented in the Cityscapes Lecture Series, Urban Studies Institute, Metropolitan College, Washington, DC.

E-mail Message

See the comment under "Personal or Telephone Interview."

Mack, L. (2006, August 30). New developments in early childhood education [E-mail message].

Student Research Essay: MLA-Style Documentation

The sample research essay that follows was written by Brian Courtney for a composition class. In his essay, Brian uses the MLA documentation system. (On pages 518–519, excerpts from the research essay are formatted in APA style.) To help you spot various types of sources, quotations, and attributions, we've annotated the essay. Our marginal comments also flag key elements, such as the essay's thesis statement, plan of development, and concluding summary.

As you read the essay, pay special attention to the way Brian incorporates source material and uses it to support his own ideas.

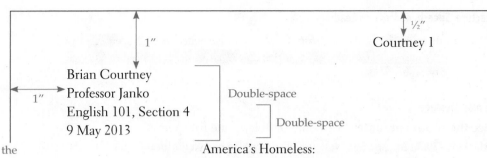

1"

½"

Courtney 1

Brian Courtney
Professor Janko
English 101, Section 4
9 May 2013

1"

Double-space

Double-space

Double-space the
heading.

Introduction

Thesis, with plan
of development

Parenthetic cita-
tion for informa-
tion that appears
in two sources.
Sources given in
order they appear
on Works Cited
list. First citation
indicates a work
with more than
three authors;
page number *and*
first author's name
given since author
is not cited earlier
in the sentence.
No author or page
number given for
the second source
since it is an
unsigned online
article.

Common
knowledge is not
documented.

America's Homeless:
How the Government Can Help

They rummage through trash cans and solicit spare change.
They lie on the floors of public restrooms. Seeking warmth, they
huddle over sidewalk steam grates. At the age of thirty, they look
fifty-five. "They" are the homeless, and they make up a growing
percentage of America's population. Indeed, homelessness
has reached such proportions that the private sector and local
governments can't possibly cope. To help homeless people toward
independence, the federal government must support rehabilitation
and job training programs, raise the minimum wage, and fund more
low-cost housing.

1

Not everyone agrees on the number of Americans who are
homeless. Estimates range anywhere from 600,000 to 2.3 million
at any given time (Link et al. 353; "Millions"). According to the
Economist, a study in the mid 1990s estimated that twelve million
Americans "have been homeless at some point in their lives" ("Out
of Sight"). Although the figures may vary, analysts agree on another
matter: that the number of homeless, particularly of homeless
families, is increasing. According to the National Alliance to End
Homelessness, families with children are the "fastest growing
group of homeless people," comprising about 40% of the homeless
population. A United States Conference of Mayors survey in 2003
found that requests for shelter access by homeless families increased
in 88% of twenty-five major US cities, an increase of 15% over the
previous year ("US Conference" i-ii).

2

Finding ways to assist this growing and changing homeless
population has become increasingly difficult. Even when homeless
individuals or families manage to find a shelter that will give them
three meals a day and a place to sleep at night, a good number have

3

Courtney 2

trouble moving beyond the shelter system and securing a more stable lifestyle. Part of the problem, explains sociologist Christopher Jencks in his now classic study, is that many homeless adults are addicted to alcohol and drugs (41-42). And psychiatrist E. Fuller Torrey adds that nearly one-third of the homeless have serious psychiatric disorders (17). Individuals suffering from such disorders and from addiction often lack the ability to seek and obtain jobs and homes, and therefore remain homeless for a longer period of time ("Mental Illness"). While not addicted or mentally ill, many others simply lack the everyday survival skills needed to turn their lives around. Reporter Lynette Holloway notes that New York City officials believe the situation will improve only when shelters provide comprehensive programs that address the many needs of the homeless (B1). As Catherine Howard, director of the Bronx-based Paradise Transitional Housing Program, wrote in a letter to the *New York Times*, "Identifying the needs of the homeless and linking them with services in the community is as important as finding suitable housing. Many homeless people return to the…shelter system and eventually to the street because of the lack of such support services." Far from seeking to assist the homeless, Leonard C. Feldman observes in *Citizens without Shelter*, many US cities have "turned to a more punitive approach," passing legislation outlawing the homeless lifestyle (2).

4   Luckily, a number of agencies are beginning to act on the belief that the homeless need "more than a key and a lease" if they are to acquire the attitudes, skills, and behaviors needed to stay off the street (Howard). In an effort to reduce homelessness in New York City, Mayor Michael R. Bloomberg sought in 2004 to implement more widely a "supportive housing" model. Originally applied to single homeless people, supportive housing was expanded to include families, "keeping the services tenants need close to their apartments"—often in shared buildings (Kaufman, "City " B1). Such a government initiative follows the lead of many nonprofit agencies. Besides providing shelter, nonprofit agencies such as New York City's Project Renewal and Boston's Pine Street Inn offer substance-abuse programs and intensive follow-ups to ensure that clients remain sober and drug-free (Holloway B1; United States 29).

Attribution gives author's name and area of expertise. Parenthetical reference at end of sentence gives just the page numbers since the author is cited in the attribution.

Parenthetic reference gives page but not author since author is cited in the sentences.

Full-sentence quotation is preceded by a comma and begins with a capital letter.

Quotation blends into rest of the sentence (no comma; quotation's first word is not capitalized).

For one of multiple works by the same author, include all or part of title, preceded by a comma, between author's name and page number.

Second source is a government publication.

Courtney 3

To help the homeless cope with psychological problems, New York City's Lenox Hill Neighborhood House and Boston's Community Action Now Program (CANP) provide in-house social workers and psychiatric care (Holloway B1; Van Meder). Joan Van Meder, CANP's cofounder and director, explained in an e-mail interview that her organization offers one-on-one and group sessions helping not only recovering substance abusers but also runaway teenagers (some of whom are pregnant) as well as individuals overwhelmed by personal traumas such as divorce, death of a family member, or loss of a job. Staff counselors refer individuals with more severe psychological disturbances to community health agencies.

In addition to providing psychological support, many   5
organizations instruct the homeless in basic survival skills. Adapting the principles of "Continuum of Care," a project sponsored by the Department of Housing and Urban Development, such agencies provide training in the everyday skills that clients need to live independently (Halper and McCrummen 26). New York City's Homes for the Homeless has established facilities called "American Family Inns." Functioning as "residential, literacy, employment, and training centers for entire families," these centers emphasize good nutrition, effective parenting, education, household-management skills, and job-search and interview techniques (Nunez 72). Boston's Project Hope also works to guide the homeless toward self-sufficiency, showing them how to apply for jobs and how to obtain disability compensation and veterans' benefits (Leonard 12-13). At St. Martin de Porres House of Hope, a Chicago shelter, homeless women and their children are assigned household jobs upon their arrival and learn the basics of domestic budgeting and home maintenance (Driscoll 46). Such increased responsibility teaches the homeless how to cope with life's everyday challenges—and prepares them for the demands of working life.

Since many of the homeless have little work experience,   6
it is not surprising that vocational training is a key service provided by broad-based agencies. According to Jencks's often-cited survey, 94% of the homeless lack steady work (50). The same survey shows that most heads of homeless families have never

---

Margin annotations:

No page number given for second source in parenthetic citation because source is an e-mail interview.

E-mail interview source is identified.

Parenthetic citation for a work with two authors

Parenthetic citation for a single-author source. Page number *and* author are given since the author is not cited earlier in the sentence.

Courtney 4

worked longer than six months (Nunez 28). Through challenging instruction that includes practice in writing a résumé and
interviewing for a position, CANP and other agencies coach the
homeless in getting and keeping a job. As a result of such intensive training, CANP has an outstanding job placement rate, with
75% of those completing its job-training program moving on to
self-sufficiency (Van Meder).

7   Unfortunately, organizations like CANP are struggling
to survive on dwindling allocations. Boston's Project Hope,
for example, served as a short-term way-station for homeless
families through the late 1980s, until the recession of the early
1990s. Then welfare and public-assistance policies of the mid
1990s reduced the program's operating budget. Fewer families
now meet the tighter eligibility requirements to stay at the
shelter, and those who do are forced to stay longer because
so few housing subsidies are available (Leonard 11-12). It's
apparent that government aid is necessary if suppliers of
comprehensive assistance—like CANP and Project Hope—are
to meet the needs of a growing population.

8   Besides funding local programs for the homeless, the government also needs to raise the minimum wage. Some homeless
people are employed, but their limited education locks them into
minimum-wage positions that make it nearly impossible for them
to afford housing. According to the Economic Policy Institute,
"real pay for the bottom 10 percent of wage earners rose less than
1 percent in adjusted dollars from 1979 to 2003"; meanwhile,
housing costs tripled in the same period (Kaufman, "Surge").
Dennis Culhane, professor of social welfare policy at the University
of Pennsylvania, explains that employed homeless individuals—who
typically receive the minimum wage—pay such a high percentage of their salary on housing that "their income doesn't cover
their housing costs" (qtd. in United States 12). For instance,
researchers studying the economics of Baltimore, Maryland,
determined that, per hour, the actual living wage is approximately $2.50 *more than* the minimum wage earned by workers

E-mail interview
source provided
in parentheses
since no attribu-
tion given in the
sentence.

Second title by
author of multi-
ple works cited
in this essay.

Where a secondary
source is quoted—
in a government
publication

Courtney 5

Attribution leading to a long quotation. Attribution is followed by a colon since the lead-in is a full sentence. If the lead-in isn't a full sentence, use a comma after the attribution.

in that city (Hess). Patrick Markee also points to this disastrous decline in minimum-wage buying power:

> Indeed, the causes of modern mass homelessness are a matter of little debate, and reside in what many academics and advocates call the affordability gap: the distance between the affordability (and availability) of secure, stable housing and the income levels of poor Americans. . . . The other side of the affordability gap has two elements, one of which is by now familiar to most Americans: the steep decline in real wages since the mid-seventies; the steady erosion of the minimum wage; the widening gulf between rich and poor during the past two decades; and the growing severity of poverty. (27)

Long quotation indented ten spaces. Double-space the quotation, as you do the rest of the essay. Don't leave extra space above or below the quotation.

The word *Americans* is followed by a period plus an ellipsis, indicating that some material has been deleted.

No author or page number is given since source is an unsigned one-page article.

Parenthetic citation for article obtained online; author provided but no page given since electronic text does not follow the pagination of the original.

Attribution naming book and its author

Quotation preceded by *that* blends into the rest of the sentence (no comma; quotation's first word is not capitalized).

The *Economist* concurs that this escalating affordability gap makes it difficult for poor people to find suitable housing. Even so, the magazine argues, eroding incomes and a lack of affordable housing aren't the only culprits in the homeless problem. For the *Economist*, homelessness results from a variety of social problems, including single-parenting, substance abuse, and mental illness—and a combination thereof ("Out of Sight").

Numerous studies dispute such an interpretation; they conclude, as does one urban researcher, that a lack of affordable housing—not "an enduring internal state" like addiction or mental illness—plays the critical role in putting people on the street (Shinn). In *Making Room: The Economics of Homelessness*, Brendan O'Flaherty points out that large-scale deinstitutionalization of the mentally ill occurred between 1960 and 1975; however, it wasn't until the 1980s—a period marked by sharp cuts in subsidized housing—that large numbers of the mentally ill wound up living on the streets (235). Shinn cites a study that supports the view that a lack of affordable housing is at the center of the homelessness problem. She conducted a longitudinal study of homeless families who received subsidized housing in New York City and found that "whatever other problems families may have had, an average of 5 years after entering a shelter, 61% were stably housed

9

10

Courtney 6

in their own apartments for at least a year and an average of 3 years. Only 4% were in a shelter." Shinn concludes, "Receipt of subsidized housing was both a necessity and a sufficient condition for achieving stability." Even Jencks, whose views are similar to those of the *Economist*, believes that more affordable "housing is still the first step in dealing with the homeless problem. Regardless of why people are on the streets, giving them a place to live . . . is usually the most important thing we can do to improve their lives" (qtd. in United States 7).

11   Clearly, the federal government must increase its funding of low-cost housing. Such a commitment is essential given recent developments in both the private and public housing markets. As Markee explains, affordable private housing has become increasingly scarce in the last several decades (27). The major problem affecting the private market is gentrification, a process by which low-cost units are transformed into high-cost housing for affluent professionals. Following the economic boom of the late 1990s, rents have risen across America, tempting landlords to gentrify their low-income housing ("Out of Sight"). As neighborhoods gentrify, housing that formerly trickled down to the poor is taken off the low-cost market, increasing homelessness (O'Flaherty 117). Also, in gentrified areas, many of the tenements and SRO (single-room occupancy) hotels in which the desperately poor used to live have been gutted and replaced by high-priced condominiums. And the tenements and SROs that remain generally demand more rent than the poor can pay (Halper and McCrummen 29).

12   Where can people turn to seek relief from these inflated costs in the private housing market? What remains of public housing can hardly answer the problem. As Markee notes, the 1980s saw the federal government cut spending on public housing and housing subsidies by 75%. In 1980, for example, federal agencies helped build 183,000 housing units. By the mid-1980s, that number had fallen to 20,000 (27). To counteract these reductions, many cities invested heavily in new housing in the late 1980s. In the 1990s, though, city budgets slashed such investments in half

No parenthetic citation is needed because author's name appears in text and because electronic text does not follow pagination of the original.

Courtney 7

(Halper and McCrummen 28). Municipal money now goes to constructing temporary shelters that can house only 2% of the cities' homeless population (Halper and McCrummen 27).

Conclusion provides a summary and restates the thesis.

In light of all these problems, one conclusion seems inevitable: the federal government must take a more active role in helping America's homeless. While debate may continue about the extent and the causes of homelessness, we know which approaches work and which do not. The government must increase its support of programs that make a demonstrable difference. Such programs do more than provide food and shelter; they also offer substance-abuse counseling, psychological support, instruction in basic survival skills, and job training. Finally, unless the government guarantees a decent minimum wage and affordable housing, even skilled, well-adjusted individuals may be forced to live on the street. The government can't continue to walk past the homeless, face averted. In doing so, it walks past millions in need.

13

Courtney 8

Works Cited

Driscoll, Connie. "Responsibility 101: A Chat with Sister Connie Driscoll." Interview by Bruce Upbin. *Forbes* 19 May 1997: 46-47. Print.

Feldman, Leonard C. *Citizens without Shelter: Homelessness, Democracy, and Political Exclusion*. Ithaca: Cornell UP, 2004. Print.

Halper, Evan, and Stephanie McCrummen. "Out of Sight, Out of Mind: New York City's New Homeless Policy." *Washington Monthly* Apr. 1998: 26-29. Print.

Hess, Robert V. "Helping People off the Streets: Real Solutions to Urban Homelessness." *USA Today Magazine* Jan. 2000: 18-20. *EBSCOhost*. Web. 6 Feb. 2013.

Holloway, Lynette. "Shelters Improve under Private Groups, Raising a New Worry." *New York Times* 12 Nov. 1997, late ed.: B1+. Print.

Howard, Catherine. Letter. *New York Times* 18 Nov. 1997, late ed.: A26. CD-ROM. *New York Times Ondisc*. UMI-ProQuest. Oct. 1998.

Jencks, Christopher. *The Homeless*. Cambridge: Harvard UP, 1994. Print.

Kaufman, Leslie. "City Is Gambling on an Old Program to Cure Homelessness." *New York Times* 19 July 2004: B1+. Print.

---. "Surge in Homeless Families Sets Off Debate on Cause." *New York Times* 29 June 2004: A18. Print.

Leonard, Margaret A. "Project Hope: An Interview with Margaret A. Leonard." Interview by George Anderson. *America* 2 Nov. 1996: 10-14. Print.

Link, Bruce, et al. "Lifetime and Five-Year Prevalence of Homelessness in the United States: New Evidence on an Old Debate." *American Journal of Orthopsychiatry* 65.3 (1995): 347-54. Print.

Interview published in a weekly magazine—interview's pages are consecutive

Book by one author—publisher's name is abbreviated

Article by two authors, in a monthly magazine; pages are consecutive

Article in a full-text online database. The title of the database and the access date are listed.

Article in a daily newspaper—section indicated along with pages; pages are not consecutive

Letter to a daily newspaper, obtained from a CD-ROM

Second work by the same author, listed alphabetically. Three hyphens and a period appear in place of author's name.

Article, by more than three authors, in a scholarly journal

Courtney 9

Book review in a
weekly publication

Unassigned
material accessed
on the Internet

Press release

Unsigned edito-
rial in a weekly
magazine obtained
through an online
database

Article in a
scholarly journal
obtained through
an online database

Government
publication

E-mail interview

Markee, Patrick. "The New Poverty: Homeless Families in
     America." Rev. of *The New Poverty*, by Ralph Nunez.
     Nation 14 Oct. 1996: 27-28. Print.

"Mental Illness and Homelessness." Factsheet. *National Coalition for
     the Homeless*. National Coalition for the Homeless, 18 Apr.
     2001. Web. 27 Apr. 2013.

"Millions Still Face Homelessness in a Booming Economy." *Urban
     Institute*. Urban Institute, 1 Feb. 2000. Web. 2 May 2013.

Nunez, Ralph da Costa. *The New Poverty: Homeless Families in
     America*. New York: Insight, 1996. Print.

O'Flaherty, Brendan. *Making Room: The Economics of
     Homelessness*. Cambridge: Harvard UP, 1998. Print.

"Out of Sight, out of Mind." Editorial. *Economist* 20 May
     2000: 27. *EBSCOhost*. Web. 27 Mar. 2013.

Shinn, Marybeth. "Family Homelessness: State or Trait?" *American
     Journal of Community Psychology* 25.6 (1997): 36-42.
     Expanded Academic Index ASAP. Web. 30 Mar. 2013.

Torrey, E. Fuller. *Out of the Shadows: Confronting America's
     Mental Illness Crisis*. New York: Wiley, 1997. Print.

United States. Cong. House. Subcommittee on Housing and
     Community Opportunity of the Committee on Banking and
     Financial Services. *Hearing on Homeless Housing Programs
     Consolidation and Flexibility Act*. 105th Cong., 1st sess.
     Washington: GPO, 1997. Print.

"US Conference of Mayors 'Hunger and Homelessness Survey,
     2003.'" *National Alliance to End Homelessness*. NAEH, Dec.
     2003. Web. 3 May 2013.

Van Meder, Joan. Message to the author. 18 Apr. 2010. E-mail.

Commentary

Brian begins his introduction with an evocative description of a typical street person's struggle to survive. These descriptive passages prepare readers for a general statement of the problem of homelessness. This two-sentence statement, starting with "'They' are the homeless" and ending with "the private sector and local governments can't possibly cope," leads the way to Brian's thesis: "To help homeless people toward independence, the federal government must support re-habilitation and job training programs, raise the minimum wage, and fund more low-cost housing."

By researching his subject thoroughly, Brian was able to marshal many compelling facts and opinions. He sorted through this complex web of material and arrived at a logical structure that reinforces his thesis. He describes the extent of the problem (paragraph 2), analyzes some of the causes of the problem (3, 4, 8–12), and points to solutions (4–6, 8, 11–12). He draws upon statistics to establish the severity of the problem and quotes expert opinion to demonstrate the need for particular types of programs. Note, too, that Brian writes in the present tense and uses the third-person point of view.

Beyond being clearly organized and maintaining a consistent point of view, the essay is unified and coherent. For one thing, Brian makes it easy for readers to follow his line of thought. He often uses transitions: "In addition" (5), "Besides" (8), and so forth. In other places, he asks a question (for example, at the beginning of the twelfth paragraph), or he uses a bridging sentence (for instance, at the beginning of the fifth, sixth, and eighth paragraphs). Moreover, he always provides clear attributions and parenthetic references so that readers know at every point along the way whose idea is being presented. Brian has, in short, prepared a well-written, carefully documented essay.

Student Research Essay: APA-Style Documentation

To give you an idea of how a research essay in APA style would look, we've excerpted Brian Courtney's research essay (pages 518–519) and reformatted those pages in APA style. APA papers may also require a title page and an abstract. The pages are numbered continuously, starting with the title page, and the References list starts on a new page. For additional specifics, see the APA *Publication Manual* or ask your instructor.

AMERICA'S HOMELESS   3

Center the title and
double-space it.
Indent the first line
of every paragraph
5 spaces. Double-
space the text.

In general, use
numerals for 10
and above.

For a source with
five or more
authors, give the
first author's sur-
name and "et al."
followed by a
comma and the
year. Alphabetize
two sources given
in the same citation
and separate them
with a semicolon.

For a source
listed by title in
the References list,
abbreviate the title
in the text citation.

For a source listed
by organization in
the References list,
give a shortened
form of the
organization name.

America's Homeless:
How the Government Can Help
They rummage through trash cans and solicit spare change.
They lie on the floors of public restrooms. Seeking warmth, they
huddle over sidewalk steam grates. At the age of 30, they look 55.
"They" are the homeless, and they make up a growing percentage
of America's population. Indeed, homelessness has reached such
proportions that the private sector and local governments can't
possibly cope. To help homeless people toward independence,
the federal government must support rehabilitation and job training
programs, raise the minimum wage, and fund more low-cost
housing.

Not everyone agrees on the number of Americans who are
homeless. Estimates range anywhere from 600,000 to 2.3 million at
any given time (Link et al., 1995; Urban Institute, 2000). According
to *The Economist*, a study in the mid 1990s estimated that 12 million Americans "have been homeless at some point in their lives"
("Out of Sight," 2000). Although the figures may vary, analysts agree
on another matter: that the number of homeless, particularly
of homeless families, is increasing. According to the National
Alliance to End Homelessness, families with children are the "fastest growing group of homeless people," comprising about 40% of
the homeless population. A U.S. Conference of Mayors survey in
2003 found that requests for shelter access by homeless families
increased in 88% of twenty-five major U.S. cities, an increase of
15% over the previous year (*U.S. Conference*, 2003).

AMERICA'S HOMELESS   10

References

Anderson, G. (Interviewer), & Leonard, M. A. (Interviewee).
    (1996, November 2). Project Hope: An interview with
    Margaret A. Leonard [Interview transcript]. *America*, 10–14.

Feldman, L. C. (2004). *Citizens without shelter: Homelessness,*
    democracy, and political exclusion. Ithaca, NY: Cornell
    University Press.

Halper, E., & McCrummen, S. (1998, April). Out of sight, out
    of mind: New York City's new homeless policy. *Washington*
    Monthly, 26–29.

Hess, R. V. (2000, January). Helping people off the streets: Real
    solutions to urban homelessness. *USA Today Magazine*,
    18–20. Retrieved from http://usatodaymagazine.net

Kaufman, L. (2004, June 29). Surge in homeless families sets
    off debate on cause. *New York Times*, p. A18.

Kaufman, L. (2004, July 19). City is gambling on an old program
    to cure homelessness. *New York Times*, pp. B1, B3.

Center "References" at the top of a new page and double-space to the first line. Start each entry flush left and indent subsequent lines 5 spaces. Double-space throughout.

Give the author's last name and initials, followed by the date.

For two authors, use an ampersand (&) between names and invert the second author's name.

Place the date in parentheses right after the author's name.

For journal, magazine, and newspaper articles, capitalize the first word of the title and subtitle and proper nouns. Use regular type.

Give all page numbers on which an article appears.

Items by the same author are listed in chronological order—earliest first.

ACTIVITIES: WRITING THE RESEARCH ESSAY

1. Imagine that you've just written a research essay exploring how parents can ease their children's passage through adolescence. Prepare a Works Cited list for the following sources, putting all information in the correct MLA format. When you are finished, reformat the list as a References list in APA style.

   a. "The Emotional Life of the Adolescent," a chapter in Ralph I. Lopez, M.D.'s *The Teen Health Book: A Parent's Guide to Adolescent Health and Well-Being.* The chapter runs from page 55 to page 70. The book was published by W.W. Norton & Company (New York, NY) in 2002.

   b. A radio broadcast in the series *Voices in the Family,* hosted by Dr. Daniel Gottlieb and produced by Laura Jackson. The broadcast, "Adolescents, TV, and Sex," aired on 27 September 2004, on WHYY-FM, Philadelphia.

   c. An article titled "Transmission of Values from Adolescents to Their Parents," by Martin Pinquart and Rainer K. Silbereisen. The article appeared on pages 83 to 100 in the Spring 2004 issue (volume 39, issue 153) of *Adolescence* (which paginates each issue separately).

   d. An unpaginated article, titled "Normal Adolescent Development," on the website *Adolescence Directory On-Line,* published by the Center for Adolescent Studies at Indiana University. The article appeared on 29 September 1998 and was accessed on 27 March 2007. The URL is <http://education.indiana.edu/cas/adol/development.html>.

2. Assume you're writing a research essay on obesity. You decide to incorporate into your essay points made by Robert Lustig, Laura Schmidt, and Claire Brindis in "The Toxic Truth About Sugar" (page 437). To practice using attributions, parenthetic citations, and correct punctuation with quoted material, do the following:

   a. Choose a statement from the essay to quote. Then write one or more sentences that include the quotation, a specific attribution, and the appropriate parenthetic citation.

   b. Choose an idea to summarize from the essay. Then write one or more sentences that include the summary and the appropriate parenthetic documentation.

   c. Find a place in the essay where the authors quote an expert or experts. Use this quotation to write one or more sentences in which you:

      • First, quote the expert(s) and
      • Second, summarize the ideas of the expert(s).

   Each of the above should include the appropriate attribution and parenthetic citation.

21

Writing About Literature

In this chapter, you will learn:

21.1 To identify the elements of literary works
21.2 To read a literary work
21.3 To write a literary analysis by viewing one student's annotated essay and reading a poem and a short story

Your purpose in **literary analysis** is to share with readers some insights about an aspect of a poem, play, story, or novel. (For the sake of simplifying a complex subject, we discuss literary analysis as though it focuses on a single work. In practice, though, a literary analysis often examines two or more works.) In a literary analysis, your thesis and supporting evidence grow directly out of your reading of the text. All you have to do is select the textual evidence that supports your thesis.

By examining both *what* the author says and *how* he or she expresses it, you increase your readers' understanding and appreciation of the work. Close textual analysis develops your ability to think critically and independently. Studying literature also strengthens your own writing. Finally, literary analysis is one way to learn more about yourself, others, and life in general.

Elements of Literary Works

Before you can analyze a literary text, you need to become familiar with literature's key elements.

Literary Terms

Theme: a work's controlling idea, the main issue the work addresses. Most literary analyses deal with theme, even if the analysis focuses on the methods by which that theme is conveyed.

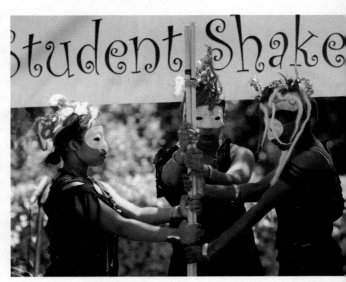

Plot: the series of events that occurs within the work.

Structure: a work's form, as determined by plot construction, act and scene divisions, stanza and line breaks, repeated images, patterns of meter and rhyme, and other elements that create discernible patterns. (See also *image, meter, rhyme,* and *stanza.*)

Setting: the time and place in which events unfold.

Character: an individual within a poem, play, story, or novel.

Characterization: the way an author develops an individual in the work.

Conflict: a struggle between individuals, between an individual and some social or environmental force, or within an individual.

Climax: the most dramatic point in the action, usually near the end of a work and usually involving the resolution of conflict.

Foreshadowing: hints, within the work, of events to come.

Narrator or **speaker:** the individual in the work who relates the story. The narrator is *not* the same as the author.

Point of view: the perspective from which a story is told. In the **first-person** (*I*) point of view, the narrator tells the story as he or she experienced it. The first-person narrator either participates in or observes the action. In the **third-person** point of view, the narrator tells the story the way someone else experienced it. The third-person narrator is not involved in the action. He or she may simply report outwardly observable behavior or events, enter the mind of only one character, or enter the minds of several characters. Such a third-person narrator may be *omniscient* (all-knowing) or have only *limited knowledge* of characters and events.

Irony: a discrepancy or incongruity of some kind. *Verbal irony,* which is often tongue-in-cheek, involves a discrepancy between the literal words and what is actually meant ("Here's some news that will make you sad. You received the highest grade in the course"). If the ironic comment is designed to be hurtful or insulting, it qualifies as *sarcasm* ("Congratulations! You failed the final exam"). In *dramatic irony,* the discrepancy is between what the speaker says and what the author means or what the audience knows. The wider the gap between the speaker's words and what can be inferred about the author's attitudes and values, the more ironic the point of view.

Satire: ridicule (either harsh or gentle) of vice or folly, with the purpose of developing awareness—even bringing about reform. Besides using wit, satire often employs irony to attack absurdity, injustice, and evil.

Figure of speech: a nonliteral comparison of dissimilar things. The most common figures of speech are **similes,** which use the word *like* or *as*; **metaphors,**

which state or imply that one thing *is* another; and **personification,** which gives human attributes to something nonhuman.

Image: a short, vivid description that creates a strong sensory impression.

Imagery: a combination of images.

Symbol: an object, place, characteristic, or phenomenon that suggests one or more things (usually abstract) in addition to itself (rain as mourning; a lost wedding ring as betrayal).

Motif: a recurring word, phrase, image, figure of speech, or symbol that has particular significance.

Meter: a basic, fixed rhythm of accented and unaccented syllables that the lines of a particular poem follow.

Rhyme: a match between two or more words' final sounds.

Stanza: two or more lines of a poem that are grouped together. A stanza is preceded and followed by some blank space.

Alliteration: repetition of initial consonant sounds ("A *b*utterfly *b*looms").

Assonance: repetition of vowel sounds (like the "a" sounds in "m*a*d *a*s *a* h*a*tter").

Sonnet: a fourteen-line, single-stanza poem following a strict pattern of meter and rhyme. The Italian, or *Petrarchan,* sonnet consists of two main parts: eight lines in the rhyme pattern *a b b a, a b b a,* followed by six lines in the pattern *c d c, c d c* or *c d e, c d e.* The English, or *Shakespearean,* sonnet consists of twelve lines in the rhyme scheme *a b a b, c d c d, e f e f,* followed by two rhymed lines *g g* (called a *couplet*). Traditionally, sonnets are love poems that involve some change in tone or outlook near the end.

How to Read a Literary Work

Read to Form a General Impression

The first step in analyzing a literary work is to read it through for an overall impression. Do you like the work? What does the writer seem to be saying? Do you have a strong reaction to the work? Why or why not?

Ask Questions About the Work

One way to focus your initial impressions is to ask yourself questions about the literary work. You could, for example, select from the following checklist those items that interest you the most or those that seem most relevant to the work you're analyzing.

✔ ANALYZING A LITERARY WORK: A CHECKLIST

☐ What *themes* appear in the work? How do *structure, plot, characterization, imagery,* and other literary strategies reinforce the theme?

☐ What gives the work its *structure* or shape? Why might the author have chosen this form? If the work is a poem, how do *meter, rhyme, alliteration, assonance,* and *line breaks* emphasize key ideas? Where does the work divide into parts? What words and images are repeated? What patterns do they form?

☐ How is the *plot* developed? Where is there any *foreshadowing?* What are the points of greatest suspense? Which *conflicts* add tension? How are they resolved? Where does the *climax* occur? What does the *resolution* accomplish?

☐ What do the various *characters* represent? What motivates them? How is character revealed through dialogue, action, commentary, and physical description? In what ways do major characters change? What events and interactions bring about the changes?

☐ What is the relationship between *setting* and *action*? To what extent does setting mirror the characters' psychological states?

☐ Who is the *narrator*? Is the story told in the *first* or the *third person*? Is the narrator omniscient or limited in his or her knowledge of characters and events? Is the narrator recalling the past or reporting events as they happen?

☐ What is the author's own *point of view*? What are the author's implied *values* and *attitudes*? Does the author show any biases? Is there any discrepancy between the author's values and attitudes and those of the narrator? To whom in the work does the author grant the most status and consideration?

☐ What about the work is *ironic* or surprising? Where is there a discrepancy between what is said and what is meant?

☐ What role do *figures of speech* play? What *metaphors,* if any, are sustained and developed?

☐ What functions as a *symbol*? How can you tell?

☐ What *flaws* do you find in the work? Which elements fail to contribute to thematic development? Where does the work lose impact because ideas are stated directly rather than implied?

Reread and Annotate

Begin a second, closer reading of the literary work. Look for answers to your questions. Underline striking words, images, and ideas. Draw connecting lines between related items. Jot down questions, answers, and comments in the margins. Of course, if you don't own the work, then you can't write in it. In this case, make notes on a sheet of paper or on your computer. We've marked the accompanying poem to give you an idea of just what annotation involves.

a   When, in disgrace with Fortune and men's eyes,

b   I all alone beweep *my* outcast state,

                            useless

a   And trouble deaf heaven with *my* bootless cries,

b   And look upon *myself* and curse *my* fate,

c   Wishing *me* like to one more rich in hope,

         good looks—

d Envy   Featur'd like him, like him with friends possess'd,

                  talent   *knowledge*

c   Desiring this man's art, and that man's scope,

d   With what *I* most enjoy contented least;

e   Yet in these thoughts *myself* almost despising ◄────────── Changes to increasing

         by chance   *(First time lover is mentioned.)*

b   Haply I think on thee, and then my state,

e   Like to the lark at break of day arising

b   From sullen earth, sings hymns at heaven's gate;

f   For thy sweet love rememb'red such wealth brings

         don't want to trade places

f   That then I scorn to change my state with kings.

Contrast between unhappy self-absorption ("beweep") and thoughts of "sweet love," between "outcast state" and "scorn to change my state."

Changes to increasing joy. Turns away from self-absorption.

Joyous images. New beginning. Healing power of love.

Modify Your Annotations

Your annotations will help you begin to clarify your thoughts about the work. Read the work again; make further annotations on anything that seems relevant and modify earlier annotations in light of your greater understanding of the work. At this point, you're ready to move on to the actual analysis.

Write the Literary Analysis

When you prepare a literary analysis, the steps you follow are the same as those for writing an essay.

Prewrite

Early in the prewriting stage, you should take a moment to think about your purpose, audience, point of view, and tone. Your **purpose** is to share your insights about the work; you assume that your **audience** is composed of readers already familiar with the work.

As you write, you should adopt an objective, **third-person point of view.** Guard against veering off into first-person statements like "In my opinion" and "I feel that." The **tone** of a literary analysis is generally serious and straightforward. However, if your aim is to point out that an author's perspective is narrow or biased or that a work is artistically unworthy of high regard, your tone may also have a critical edge. Be careful, though, to concentrate on the textual evidence in support of your view; don't simply state your objections.

Prewriting actually begins when you annotate the work in light of several key questions you pose about it (see pages 523–524). After refining your initial annotations (see page 525), try to impose a tentative order on your annotations. List the most promising of these points on a separate sheet; then link these points to your annotations. You could, for instance, simply list the annotations under the points they support. Or you can number each point and give relevant annotations the same number as that point. Another possibility is to color-code your annotations: Give each point a color; then underline or circle in the same color any annotation related to that point. Finally, prepare a scratch outline of the main points you plan to cover, inserting your annotations in the appropriate spots. (For more on scratch outlines, see pages 29–31 in Chapter 2.)

If you have trouble generating and focusing ideas in this way, you might *freewrite* a page or two on what you have highlighted in the literary text, *brainstorm* a list of ideas, or *map out* the work's overall structure (see pages 26–27 in Chapter 2). Mapping is especially helpful when analyzing a poem.

If the work still puzzles you, it may be helpful to consult outside sources. Encyclopedias, biographies of the author, and history books can clarify the context in which the work was written.

Identify Your Thesis

Formulate a **working thesis**. As in other kinds of writing, your thesis statement for a literary analysis should include both your *limited subject* (the literary work you'll analyze and what aspect of the work you'll focus on), as well as your *attitude* toward that subject (the claim you'll make about the work's themes, the author's methods, the author's attitudes, and so on).

Here are two effective thesis statements for literary analysis:

In the poem "The Garden of Love," William Blake uses sound and imagery to depict what he considers the deadening effect of organized religion.

The characters in the novel *Judgment Day* illustrate James Farrell's belief that psychology, not sociology, determines fate.

If your instructor asks you to include commentary from professional critics or other sources, try to formulate your thesis about the work *before* you read anyone else's interpretation. Then use others' opinions as added evidence in support of your thesis or as opposing viewpoints that you can counter. (For more on thesis statements, see Chapter 3.)

Thesis Statements to Avoid

Guard against a *simplistic* thesis. A statement like "The author shows that people are often hypocritical" doesn't say anything surprising and fails to get at a work's complexity. More likely, the author shares insights about the *nature* of hypocrisy, the *reasons* underlying it, the *forms* it can take, or its immediate and long-term *effects*.

An *overly narrow* thesis is equally misguided. You shouldn't, for example, sum up the theme of Hawthorne's *The Scarlet Letter* with the thesis "Hawthorne examines the intolerance of seventeenth-century Puritan New England." Hawthorne's novel probes the general, or universal, nature of communal intolerance. Puritan New England is simply the setting in which the work's themes are dramatized.

Also, make sure your thesis is *about the work.* Discussion of a particular *social* or *political issue* is relevant only if it sheds light on the work. If you feel a work has a strong feminist theme, it's fine to say so. It's a mistake, however, to stray to a non-literary thesis such as "Feminism liberates both men and women."

A *biographical thesis* is just as inappropriate as a sociopolitical one. Point out the way a particular work embodies an author's prejudices or beliefs, but don't, devise a thesis that passes judgment on the author's personal or psychological shortcomings ("Poe's neurotic attraction to inappropriate women is reflected in the poem 'To Helen' "). It's usually impossible to infer such personal flaws from the text alone.

Support the Thesis with Evidence

Once you've identified a working thesis, return to the text to make sure that nothing in the text contradicts your theory. Also, keeping your thesis in mind, search for previously overlooked **evidence** (*quotations* and *examples*) that develops your thesis. Consider, too, how *summaries* of portions of the work might support your interpretation.

If you don't find solid textual evidence for your thesis, either drop or modify it. Don't—in an effort to support your thesis—cook up possible relationships among characters, twist metaphors out of shape, or concoct elaborate patterns of symbolism. Be sure there's plentiful evidence in the work to support your interpretation.

Organize the Evidence

When it comes time to **organize your evidence**, look over your scratch list and evaluate the main points, textual evidence, and outside research it contains. Focusing on your thesis, decide which points should be deleted and which new ones should be added. Then identify an effective sequence for your points. That done, check to see if you've placed textual evidence and outside research under the appropriate points. If you plan to refute what others have said about the work, the discussion on pages 391–392 will help you block out the outline's refutation section. What you're aiming for is a solid, well-developed outline that will guide your writing of the first draft. (For more on outlining, see pages 51–54 in Chapter 5.)

When preparing your outline, remember that the patterns of development can help you sequence material:

Comparison-Contrast

In Mark Twain's *Huckleberry Finn*, what traits do the Duke and the Dauphin have in common? In what ways do the two characters differ?

Definition

How does Ralph Waldo Emerson define *forbearance* in his poem of that name?

Process Analysis

Discuss the stages by which Morgan Evans is transformed into a scholar in Emlyn Williams's play *The Corn Is Green*.

Notice that, in these assignments, certain words and phrases (*have in common; in what ways...differ; define;* and *discuss the stages*) signal which pattern would be particularly appropriate. For help in deciding which pattern(s) of development you might use in such circumstances, turn to page 60 in Chapter 6.

Write the First Draft

When preparing the draft, you should also take into account the following four conventions of literary analysis.

Use the Present Tense

The literary work continues to exist after its completion. Use of the past tense is appropriate only when you refer to a time earlier than that in which the narrator speaks.

Identify Your Text

Even if your only source is the literary work itself, some instructors may want you to identify it by author, title, and publication data in a formal Works Cited entry. For more about Works Cited entries, consult the most recent edition of the *MLA Handbook for Writers of Research Papers*.

Use Parenthetic References

If you're writing about a very short literary work, your instructor may not require documentation. Usually, however, documentation is expected.

Fiction quotations are followed by the page number(s) in parentheses (89); poetry quotations, by the line number(s) (12–14); and drama quotations, by act, scene, and line numbers (2.1.34–37). The parenthetic reference goes right after the quotation, even if your own sentence continues. If you use sources other than the literary text itself, document these as you would quotations or borrowed ideas in a research essay on your Works Cited page.

Quote Poetry Appropriately

If you're writing about a short poem, it's a good idea to include the poem's entire text in your essay. When you need to quote fewer than four lines from a poem, you can enclose them in quotation marks and indicate each line break with a slash (/): "But at my back I always hear / Time's winged chariot hurrying near." Verse quotations of four or more lines should be indented ten spaces from the left margin of your paper and should appear line for line, as in the original source.

Revise Overall Meaning, Structure, and Paragraph Development

After completing your first draft, you'll gain helpful advice by showing it to others. The checklist that follows will help you and your readers apply to literary analysis some of the revision techniques discussed in Chapters 7 and 8.

✔ REVISING A LITERARY ANALYSIS: A CHECKLIST

Revise Overall Meaning and Structure

- ☐ What is the thesis of the analysis? According to the thesis, which elements of the work will be discussed? In what ways, if any, is the thesis simplistic or too narrow? In what ways, if any, does it introduce extraneous social, political, or biographical issues?

- ☐ What main points support the thesis? If any points stray from or contradict the thesis, what changes should be made?

- ☐ How well supported by textual evidence is the essay's thesis? What evidence, crucial to the thesis, needs more attention? What other interpretation, if any, seems better supported by the evidence?

- ☐ Which patterns of development help shape the analysis? How do these patterns support the thesis?

- ☐ What purpose does the analysis fulfill? Does it simply present a straightforward interpretation of some aspect of the work? Does it point out some flaw in the work? Does it try to convince readers to accept an unconventional interpretation?

- ☐ How well does the analysis suit an audience already familiar with the work? How well does it suit an audience that may or may not share the interpretation expressed?

- ☐ What tone does the analysis project? Is it too critical or too admiring? Where does the tone come across as insufficiently serious?

Revise Paragraph Development

- ☐ What method of organization underlies the sequence of paragraphs? How effective is the sequence?

- ☐ Which paragraphs lack sufficient or sufficiently developed textual evidence? Where does textual evidence fail to develop a paragraph's central point? What important evidence, if any, has been overlooked?

- ☐ Which paragraphs contain too much textual evidence? Which quotations are longer than necessary?

- ☐ Where could textual evidence in a paragraph be more smoothly incorporated into the analysis?

☐ If any of the paragraphs include outside research, how does this material strengthen the analysis? If any of the paragraphs consider alternative interpretations, are these opposing views refuted?

Revise Sentences and Words

☐ Which words and phrases wrongly suggest that there is only one correct interpretation of the work?

☐ What words give the false impression that it is possible to read an author's mind?

☐ Where does the analysis fail to maintain the present tense? Which uses of past tense aren't justified?

☐ Where is there inadequate or incorrect documentation?

☐ Where does language lapse into needless literary jargon?

☐ If poetry is quoted, where should slash marks indicate line breaks? Where should lines be indented?

Edit and Proofread

When editing and proofreading your literary analysis, you should proceed as you would with any other type of essay (see Chapter 9). Be sure to check textual quotations with special care. Make sure you quote correctly, use ellipses appropriately, and follow punctuation and capitalization conventions.

Pulling it all Together

Read to Form a General Impression

The following short story was written by Langston Hughes (1902–1967), a poet and fiction writer who emerged as a major literary figure during the Harlem Renaissance of the 1920s. Published in 1963, the story first appeared in *Something in Common,* a collection of Hughes's work. Read the story and gather your first impressions. Then follow the suggestions after the story.

Langston Hughes

EARLY AUTUMN

When Bill was very young, they had been in love. Many nights they had spent walk-   1
ing, talking together. Then something not very important had come between them, and they didn't speak. Impulsively, she had married a man she thought she loved. Bill went away, bitter about women.

Yesterday, walking across Washington Square, she saw him for the first time in years. "Bill Walker," she said.

He stopped. At first he did not recognize her, to him she looked so old.

5   "Mary! Where did you come from?"

Unconsciously, she lifted her face as though wanting a kiss, but he held out his hand. She took it.

"I live in New York now," she said.

"Oh"—smiling politely. Then a little frown came quickly between his eyes.

"Always wondered what happened to you, Bill."

10   "I'm a lawyer. Nice firm, way downtown."

"Married yet?"

"Sure. Two kids."

"Oh," she said.

A great many people went past them through the park. People they didn't know. It was late afternoon. Nearly sunset. Cold.

15   "And your husband?" he asked her.

"We have three children. I work in the bursar's office at Columbia."

"You're looking very..." (he wanted to say *old*) "...well," he said.

She understood. Under the trees in Washington Square, she found herself desperately reaching back into the past. She had been older than he then in Ohio. Now she was not young at all. Bill was still young.

"We live on Central Park West," she said. "Come and see us sometime."

20   "Sure," he replied. "You and your husband must have dinner with my family some night. Any night. Lucille and I'd love to have you."

The leaves fell slowly from the trees in the Square. Fell without wind. Autumn dusk. She felt a little sick.

"We'd love it," she answered.

"You ought to see my kids." He grinned.

Suddenly the lights came on up the whole length of Fifth Avenue, chains of misty brilliance in the blue air.

25   "There's my bus," she said.

He held out his hand, "Good-by."

"When..." she wanted to say, but the bus was ready to pull off. The lights on the avenue blurred, twinkled, blurred. And she was afraid to open her mouth as she entered the bus. Afraid it would be impossible to utter a word.

Suddenly she shrieked very loudly, "Good-by!" But the bus door had closed.

The bus started. People came between them outside, people crossing the street, people they didn't know. Space and people. She lost sight of Bill. Then she remembered she had forgotten to give him her address—or to ask him for his—or tell him that her youngest boy was named Bill, too.

Ask Questions About the Work

Now that you've read Hughes's story, consult the questions on page 524 so you can devise your own set of questions to solidify your first impressions. Here are some questions you might consider:

1. How does *setting* help bring out the theme?

   Answer: Both the time of year, "early autumn," and the time of day, "nearly sunset" suggest that time is running out. The place, a crowded walkway in a big city, highlights the idea of all the people with whom we never make contact—that is, of life's missed connections.

2. From what *point of view* is the story told? How does this relate to the story's meaning?

   Answer: The point of view is the third-person omniscient. This enables the author to show the discrepancy between what characters are thinking and what they are willing or able to communicate.

3. What *words* and *images* are repeated in the course of the story? How do these *motifs* reflect the story's theme?

   Answer: The words *young* and *old* appear a number of times. This repetition helps bring out the theme of aging, of time running out. *Walking* is another repeated word that gives the reader the sense of people's uninterrupted movement through life. The repeated phrase *people they don't know* emphasizes how hard it is for people to genuinely communicate and connect with one another. *Love*, another repeated word, underscores the tragedy of love lost or unfulfilled.

Reread and Annotate

In light of the questions you develop, reread and annotate Hughes's story. Then consider the writing assignments that follow.

1. Analyze how Hughes develops the theme that it is urgently important for people to "take time out" to communicate with one another.

2. Discuss some strategies that Hughes uses to achieve universality. You might, for example, call attention to the story's impersonal point of view, the lack of descriptive detail about the characters' appearances, and the generality of the information about the characters' lives.

3. Explain how Hughes uses setting to reveal the characters' psychological states and to convey their sense of loss.

Student Essay

Student Karen Vais decided to write in response to the first assignment. After using questions to focus her initial impressions, Karen organized her prewriting and began to draft her literary analysis. The final version of her analysis follows. As you read the essay, consider how well Karen addresses both *what* Hughes expresses and *how* he expresses it. What literary devices does Karen discuss? How are these related to the story's theme? Because the story was assigned in class and everyone used the same text, she didn't need to provide a bibliographic citation. Similarly, her instructor didn't require parenthetic documentation of quoted material because the story is so brief.

Stopping to Talk
by Karen Vais

1   In his short story "Early Autumn," Langston Hughes dramatizes the idea that hurried movement through life prevents people from forming or maintaining meaningful relationships. Hughes develops his theme of "walking" versus "talking" through such devices as setting, plot construction, and dialogue.

Introduction

Thesis with plan of development

2   The story's setting continually reminds the reader that time is running out; it is urgent for people to stop and communicate before it is too late. The meeting between the two characters takes place on a busy walkway, where strangers hurry past one another. The season is autumn, the time is "late afternoon," the temperature is "cold." The end of the renewed connection between Mary and Bill coincides with the blurring of the streetlights. The chilly, dark setting suggests the coming of winter, of night, even of death.

First supporting paragraph: focus on setting

3   In keeping with the setting, the plot is a series of lost chances for intimacy. When they were young and in love, Bill and Mary used to "walk . . . [and] talk . . . together," but that was years ago. Then "something not very important . . . [came] between them, and they didn't speak." When she says Bill's name, Mary halts Bill's movement through the park, and, for a short time, Bill "Walker" stops walking. But when Mary hurries onto the bus, the renewed connection snaps. Moreover, even their brief meeting in the park is already a thing of the past, having taken place "yesterday."

Second supporting paragraph: focus on plot

4   Like their actions, the characters' words illustrate a reluctance to communicate openly. The dialogue consists of little more than platitudes: "I live in New York now. . . . We have three kids. . . . You and your husband must have dinner with my family some night." The narrator's telling comments about what remains unspoken ("he wanted to say . . . ," "she wanted to say . . . ") underscore Bill and Mary's separateness. Indeed, Mary fails to share the one piece of information that would have revealed her feelings for Bill Walker—that her youngest son is also named Bill.

Third supporting paragraph: focus on dialogue

5   The theme of walking vs. talking runs throughout "Early Autumn." "Space and people," Hughes writes, once again come between Bill and Mary, and, as in the past, they go their separate ways. Through the two characters, Hughes seems to be urging each of us to speak—to slow our steps long enough to make emotional contact.

Conclusion

Commentary

Note that Karen states her *thesis* in the opening paragraph; this first sentence addresses the *what* of the story: "the idea that hurried movement through life prevents…meaningful relationships." The next sentence addresses the *how*: "Hughes develops his theme…through such devices as setting, plot construction, and dialogue." This second sentence also announces the essay's *plan of development*. Karen will discuss setting, then plot, then dialogue, with one paragraph devoted to each of these literary elements. In the body of the analysis, Karen backs up her thesis with *textual evidence* in the form of summaries and quotations. The quotations are no longer than is necessary to support her points. In the concluding paragraph, Karen repeats her thesis, reinforcing it with Hughes's own words. She ends by pointing out the relevance of the story's theme to the reader's own life.

Writing Assignment on "Early Autumn"

Having seen what one student did with "Early Autumn," look back at the second and third writing assignments on page 533 and select one for your own analysis of Hughes's story. Then, in light of the assignment you select, read the story again, making any adjustments in your annotations. Next, organize your prewriting annotations into a scratch list, identify a working thesis, and organize your ideas into an outline. That done, write your first draft. Before submitting your analysis, take time to revise, edit, and proofread it carefully.

ADDITIONAL SELECTIONS AND WRITING ASSIGNMENTS

The two selections that follow—a poem by Robert Frost and a short story by Kate Chopin—will give you further practice in analyzing literary texts. No matter which selection you decide to write on, the guidelines in this chapter should help you approach the literary analysis with confidence.

Robert Frost

Best known for his poetry about New England life, Robert Frost (1874–1963) was born in San Francisco and moved to Massachusetts in 1885. His first two collections of poetry, *A Boy's Will* (1913) and *North of Boston* (1914), were published in England, where he went after failing to be published in the United States. These collections—and the distinctly American voice shaping them—eventually won Frost recognition back home, where he returned to publish *Mountain Interval* (1916), a volume containing some of his most recognized poems. Frost received four Pulitzer Prizes and presented the poem "The Gift Outright" at President John F. Kennedy's inauguration in 1961. The following poem first appeared in *Mountain Interval*. The title alludes to the words of Shakespeare's Macbeth on receiving news that his queen is dead: "Out, out, brief candle! / Life's but a walking shadow, a poor player / That struts and frets his hour upon the stage / And then is heard no more. It is a tale / Told by an idiot, full of sound and fury, / Signifying nothing" (*Macbeth* 5.5.23–28).

"OUT, OUT—"

The buzz-saw snarled and rattled in the yard
And made dust and dropped stove-length sticks of wood,
Sweet-scented stuff when the breeze drew across it.
And from there those that lifted eyes could count
5   Five mountain ranges one behind the other
Under the sunset far into Vermont.
And the saw snarled and rattled, snarled and rattled,
As it ran light, or had to bear a load.
And nothing happened: day was all but done.
10   Call it a day, I wish they might have said
To please the boy by giving him the half hour
That a boy counts so much when saved from work.
His sister stood beside them in her apron
To tell them "Supper." At the word, the saw,
15   As if to prove saws knew what supper meant,
Leaped out at the boy's hand, or seemed to leap—
He must have given the hand. However it was,
Neither refused the meeting. But the hand!
The boy's first outcry was a rueful laugh,
20   As he swung toward them holding up the hand
Half in appeal, but half as if to keep
The life from spilling. Then the boy saw all—
Since he was old enough to know, big boy
Doing a man's work, though a child at heart—
25   He saw all spoiled. "Don't let him cut my hand off—
The doctor, when he comes. Don't let him, sister!"
So. But the hand was gone already.
The doctor put him in the dark of ether.
He lay and puffed his lips out with his breath.
30   And then—the watcher at his pulse took fright.
No one believed. They listened at his heart.
Little—less—nothing—and that ended it.
No more to build on there. And they, since they
Were not the one dead, turned to their affairs.

Writing Assignments on "Out, Out—"

1. Because it tells a story, "Out, Out—" can be described as a narrative poem. Discuss the poem's various narrative elements, including its setting, plot, characters, conflict, climax, and resolution. Analyze how these narrative elements work to convey what you think is the poem's main theme.

2. Despite the concise language of the poem, Frost manages to provide clear descriptions of the boy and the men in the timber mill and of what each of them represents. Looking closely at how Frost depicts the boy and the men—known as *they* in the poem—write an essay analyzing the different views of human nature Frost conveys.

3. The buzz-saw plays a central role in Frost's poem—to such an extent that it can be considered a character in its own right. Analyze the ways in which the buzz-saw is characterized in the poem. Be sure to discuss what commentary Frost might be making about the relationship between people and their objects of labor in his depiction of the buzz-saw.

Kate Chopin

Fiction writer Kate Chopin (1851–1904) is best known for her novel *The Awakening* (1899). When first published, the novel shocked readers with its frank sensuality and the independent spirit of its female protagonist. The story that follows, first published in *Vogue* in 1894, shows a similar defiance of socially prescribed expectations and norms.

THE STORY OF AN HOUR

Knowing that Mrs. Mallard was afflicted with heart trouble, great care was taken to break to her as gently as possible the news of her husband's death.   1

It was her sister Josephine who told her, in broken sentences, veiled hints that   2
revealed in half concealing. Her husband's friend Richards was there, too, near her. It was he who had been in the newspaper office when intelligence of the railroad disaster was received, with Brently Mallard's name leading the list of "killed." He had only taken the time to assure himself of its truth by a second telegram, and had hastened to forestall any less careful, less tender friend in bearing the sad message.

She did not hear the story as many women have heard the same, with a paralyzed   3
inability to accept its significance. She wept at once, with sudden, wild abandonment, in her sister's arms. When the storm of grief had spent itself she went away to her room alone. She would have no one follow her.

There stood, facing the open window, a comfortable, roomy armchair. Into this she   4
sank, pressed down by a physical exhaustion that haunted her body and seemed to reach into her soul.

She could see in the open square before her house the tops of trees that were   5
all aquiver with the new spring life. The delicious breath of rain was in the air. In the street below a peddler was crying his wares. The notes of a distant song which someone was singing reached her faintly, and countless sparrows were twittering in the eaves.

There were patches of blue sky showing here and there through the clouds that had   6
met and piled one above the other in the west facing her window.

7   She sat with her head thrown back upon the cushion of the chair, quite motionless, except when a sob came up into her throat and shook her, as a child who has cried itself to sleep continues to sob in its dreams.

8   She was young, with a fair, calm face, whose lines bespoke repression and even a certain strength. But now there was a dull stare in her eyes, whose gaze was fixed away off yonder on one of those patches of blue sky. It was not a glance of reflection, but rather indicated a suspension of intelligent thought.

9   There was something coming to her and she was waiting for it, fearfully. What was it? She did not know, it was too subtle and elusive to name. But she felt it, creeping out of the sky, reaching toward her through the sounds, the scents, the color that filled the air.

10   Now her bosom rose and fell tumultuously. She was beginning to recognize this thing that was approaching to possess her, and she was striving to beat it back with her will—as powerless as her two white slender hands would have been.

11   When she abandoned herself a little whispered word escaped her slightly parted lips. She said it over and over under her breath: "Free, free, free!" The vacant stare and the look of terror that had followed it went from her eyes. They stayed keen and bright. Her pulses beat fast, and the coursing blood warmed and relaxed every inch of her body.

12   She did not stop to ask if it were not a monstrous joy that held her. A clear and exalted perception enabled her to dismiss the suggestion as trivial.

13   She knew that she would weep again when she saw the kind, tender hands folded in death; the face that had never looked save with love upon her, fixed and gray and dead. But she saw beyond that bitter moment a long procession of years to come that would belong to her absolutely. And she opened and spread her arms out to them in welcome.

14   There would be no one to live for during those coming years; she would live for herself. There would be no powerful will bending her in that blind persistence with which men and women believe they have a right to impose a private will upon a fellow creature. A kind intention or a cruel intention made the act seem no less a crime as she looked upon it in that brief moment of illumination.

15   And yet she had loved him—sometimes. Often she had not. What did it matter! What could love, the unsolved mystery, count for in face of this possession of self-assertion which she suddenly recognized as the strongest impulse of her being.

16   "Free! Body and soul free!" she kept whispering.

17   Josephine was kneeling before the closed door with her lips to the keyhole, imploring for admission. "Louise, open the door! I beg; open the door—you will make yourself ill. What are you doing, Louise? For heaven's sake open the door."

18   "Go away. I am not making myself ill." No; she was drinking in a very elixir of life through that open window.

19   Her fancy was running riot along those days ahead of her. Spring days, and summer days, and all sorts of days that would be her own. She breathed a quick prayer that life might be long. It was only yesterday she had thought with a shudder that life might be long.

20   She arose at length and opened the door to her sister's importunities. There was a feverish triumph in her eyes, and she carried herself unwittingly like a goddess of Victory. She clasped her sister's waist, and together they descended the stairs. Richards stood waiting for them at the bottom.

Some one was opening the front door with a latchkey. It was Brently Mallard who   21
entered, a little travel-stained, composedly carrying his gripsack and umbrella. He had
been far from the scene of the accident, and did not even know there had been one.
He stood amazed at Josephine's piercing cry; at Richards' quick motion to screen him
from the view of his wife.

But Richards was too late.   22

When the doctors came they said she had died of heart disease—of joy that kills.   23

Writing Assignments on "The Story of an Hour"

1. Show how Chopin uses imagery and descriptive detail to contrast the rich possibilities for which Mrs. Mallard yearns with the drab reality of her everyday life.

2. Argue that "The Story of an Hour" dramatizes the theme that domesticity saps a woman's spirit and physical strength.

3. Does Chopin's characterization of Mrs. Mallard justify the story's unexpected and ironic climax? Explain your response.

Writing Exam Essays

In this chapter, you will learn:

22.1 To identify the three forms that written answers can take
22.2 To prepare for an exam essay
22.3 To write an exam essay answer by viewing the exam essay answer given by a student

If you have trouble writing essays at home, the idea of preparing an **exam essay** in a test situation may throw you into a kind of panic. How, you may wonder, can you show what you know in such a short time? Indeed, you may feel that such tests are designed to show you at your worst.

Instructors intend such exams to reveal your understanding of the subject—and to stimulate you to interpret course material in perceptive, new ways. They realize that the writing done under time pressure won't result in a masterpiece; such writing may include misspellings and awkward sentences. However, they *do* expect reasonably complete essay answers, with focused, developed, and coherent responses.

Three Forms of Written Answers

There are three general types of questions that require written answers—some as short as one or two sentences, others as long as a full, several-paragraph essay.

Short Answers

One kind of question calls for a **short answer** of only a few sentences. Such questions often ask you to identify (or define) a term *and* explain its importance. Be prepared to write one to three full sentences.

Here are two examples (in italics) of short answers for an exam in modern art history.

Directions: Identify and explain the significance of the following:

1. "Concerning the Spiritual in Art": *This is an essay written by Wassily Kandinsky in 1912 to justify the abstract painting style he used. Showing Matisse's influence, the essay maintains that pure forms and basic colors convey reality more accurately than true-to-life depictions.*

2. The Eiffel Tower Series: *Done around 1910 by Robert Delaunay, this is a series of paintings having the Eiffel Tower as subject. Delaunay used a cubist approach, analyzing surface, space, and interesting planes.*

Paragraph-Length Answers

Questions requiring a **paragraph-length answer** may signal—directly or indirectly—the length of response expected. A successful answer should address the question as completely yet as concisely as possible. Beginning with a strong topic sentence will help you focus your response.

Following is a paragraph-length answer to a question on a political science exam:

Directions: Discuss the meaning of the term *interest group* and comment briefly on the role such groups play in the governing of democratic societies.

An interest group is an "informal" type of political organization; its goal is to influence government policy and see legislation enacted that favors its members. An interest group differs from a political party; the interest group doesn't want to control the government or have an actual share in governing (the whole purpose of a political party). Interest groups are considered "informal" because they are not officially part of the governing process. Still, they exert tremendous power. Democratic governments constantly respond to interest groups by passing new laws and policies. Some examples of interest groups are institutions (the military, the Catholic Church), associations (the American Medical Association, Mothers Against Drunk Driving), and nonassociational groups (car owners, television viewers).

Essay-Length Answers

You will frequently be asked to write an **essay-length answer** as part of a longer examination. Here is a typical essay question from an exam in an introductory course in linguistics. A response to this question can be found on pages 544–545.

Account for the differences in American and British English by describing at least three major influences that affected the way this country's settlers spoke English. Give as many examples as you can of words derived from these influences.

How to Prepare for Exam Essays

Spaced study throughout the semester gives you a sense of the *whys* of the subject, not just the *who, what, where,* and *when.* Try to avoid cramming whenever possible. It prevents you from gaining a clear overview of a course and a real understanding of a course's main issues. As you prepare for an exam essay, follow the guidelines listed here.

✔ PREPARING FOR AN EXAM ESSAY: A CHECKLIST

- ☐ In light of the main concepts covered in the course, identify key issues that the exam might logically address.
- ☐ With these issues in mind, design several exam essay questions.
- ☐ Draft an answer for each anticipated question.
- ☐ Commit to memory any facts, quotations, data, lists of reasons, and so forth that you would include in your answers.

At the Examination

Survey the Entire Test

Look over the entire written-answer section of a test before working on any part of it. Note which sections are worth the highest point value, and plan to spend the longest time on those sections. Follow any guidelines about the length of the response. When "a brief paragraph" is all that is required, don't launch into a full-scale essay.

Understand the Essay Question

Once you've selected the question on which you're going to write, examine it carefully to determine its slant or emphasis. Most essay questions ask you to focus on a specific issue or to bring together material from different parts of a course.

Many questions use **key directional words** that suggest an answer developed according to a particular pattern of development:

Key Directional Words	Pattern of Development
Provide details about	Description
Give the history of, Trace the development of	Narration
Explain, List, Provide examples of	Illustration
Analyze the parts of, Discuss the types of	Division-classification
Analyze, Explain how, Show how	Process analysis
Discuss advantages and disadvantages of, Show similarities and differences between	Comparison-contrast
Account for, Analyze, Discuss the consequences of, Explain the reasons for, Explain why, Show the influence of	Cause-effect
Clarify, Explain the meaning of, Identify	Definition
Argue, Defend, Evaluate, Justify, Show the failings or merits of, Support	Argumentation-persuasion

Write the Essay

The steps in the writing process are the same, whether you compose an essay at home or prepare an essay response in a classroom test situation. The main difference is that during a test the process is streamlined.

Prewrite

Prewriting begins when you analyze the essay question and determine your essay's basic approach. Underline key directional terms, circle crucial words, and put numbers next to points that you should cover.

Make notes for an answer. Jot down main points as well as facts and examples. Try brainstorming, freewriting, mapping, or another prewriting technique (described in Chapter 2) to get yourself going.

What to Avoid. You won't have time to generate pages of notes, so try using words and phrases. Also, don't spend time analyzing your audience (you know it's your instructor) or choosing a tone (exams require a serious, analytic approach).

Identify Your Thesis

Exam essays should have a **thesis**. Often, the thesis is a statement answering the exam question. For example, in response to a question asking you to "Discuss the origins of apartheid," your thesis might begin, "The South African law of 'separateness,' or apartheid, originated in 1948, a result of a series of factors that...." Exam essay thesis statements are somewhat informal. They state the *subject* of the essay but *not* the writer's *attitude* toward the subject. In a test-taking situation, less-structured thesis statements are perfectly acceptable.

Support the Thesis with Evidence

In the prewriting stage, you jotted down material needed to answer the question. At this point, you should review the **evidence** quickly to make sure it's *adequate*. Also, check that support for your thesis is *unified, specific, accurate,* and *representative* (see pages 43–45 and 61–63).

Organize the Evidence

Before you start writing, devise some kind of **outline**. You may simply sequence your prewriting jottings by placing numbers or letters beside them. Or you can quickly translate the jottings into a brief, informal outline.

Go back and review the essay question one more time. If the question has two or three parts, your outline should tackle each one in turn.

Also, focus again on the question's key *directional words.* If the question asks you to discuss similarities and differences, your outline should draw on one of the two basic *comparison-contrast* formats (see pages 284–289). Because many exam questions call for more than one task (for example, you may be asked both to *define* a theory and to *argue* its merits), you should make sure your outline reflects the appropriate patterns of development.

Many outlines use an *emphatic* approach to organize material. However, when discussing historical or developmental issues, you often structure material *chronologically.* In some fields (art history is one) you may choose a *spatial* approach—for instance, if you describe a work of art. Quickly assess the situation to determine which approach would work best, and keep it in mind as you sequence the points in your outline. (Turn to pages 49–51 for more on outlining and emphatic, chronological, spatial, and simple-to-complex plans.)

What to Avoid. Don't prepare a formal or many-leveled outline; you'll waste valuable time. A phrase outline with two levels of support should be sufficient.

Write the Draft

Generally, you won't have time to write a formal introduction, so it's fine to begin the essay with your thesis, perhaps followed by a plan of development (see pages 36–37). Write as many paragraphs as you need to show you have command of the concepts and facts taught in the course. Refer to your outline as you write, but if inspiration strikes, feel free to add material or deal with a point in a different order.

As you draft your response, you shouldn't feel hesitant about crossing out material. *Do* make these changes, but make them neatly.

When preparing the draft, remember that you'll be graded in part on how *specific, accurate,* and *representative* your evidence is (see pages 43–45 and 61–63).

Make sure, too, that your response is *unified*. Stay focused on the question. Using topic sentences to structure your paragraphs will help you stay on track.

Your instructor will need transitions and other markers to understand fully how your points connect to one another. Try to show how your ideas relate by using *signal devices* (see pages 65–66).

As you near the end of the essay, check the original question. Have you covered everything? Does the question call for a final judgment or evaluative comment? If so, provide it. Also, if you have time, you may want to close with a brief, one- or two-sentence summary.

What to Avoid. Your first and only draft should be the one written on the exam booklet or paper. Don't cast your answer as one long paragraph spanning three pages. If you've outlined your ideas, you'll have a clear idea where paragraph breaks should occur. Finally, don't cram your response with everything you know about the subject. Give focused, intelligent responses.

Revise, Edit, and Proofread

If you've budgeted your time, you should have a few minutes left to review your essay answer. Above all, read your response to be sure it answers the question fully. Make any changes that will improve the answer. If something is in the wrong place, use an arrow and a brief note to indicate where it should go. Instructors will accept insertions and deletions. Use the standard editing marks such as the caret (see page 119) to indicate additions and other changes.

As you reread, check grammar and spelling. Obvious grammatical errors and spelling mistakes may affect your grade. If spelling is a problem for you, request permission to have your dictionary at hand.

Sample Essay Answer

The essay that follows was written by Andrew Kahan in response to this take-home exam question:

> Account for the differences in American and British English by describing at least three major influences that affected the way this country's settlers spoke English. Give as many examples as you can of words derived from these influences.

Andrew started by underlining the question's key words. Then he listed in the margin the main points and some of the supporting evidence he planned to include in his answer. That done, he formulated a thesis and began writing his essay. The handwritten annotations reflect the changes Andrew made when he refined his answer before handing in his exam.

1) Maritime pidgin (Portug. influ.)

2) African pidgin (Slaves comm. with each other and with owners)

3) Native American pidgin (words for native plants and animals)

American English diverged from British English because those who settled the New World had contact with people that those back in England generally did not. As a result of ~~this~~ contact, several pidgin languages developed. A pidgin language, which

has its own grammar and vocabulary, comes about when the speakers of two or more
unrelated languages communicate ~~for a while~~ over a period of time. Maritime pidgin,
African pidgin, and Indian pidgin were three influences that helped shape American
English.

By the time the New World began to be settled, sailors and sea merchants of the [all]
European nations had traveled widely. A maritime pidgin thus ~~immerged~~ [emerged] that enabled
diverse groups to communicate.* Since Portugal controlled the seas around the time the
colonies were settled, maritime pidgin was largely influenced by the Portuguese. Such
Portuguese-derived words as "cavort," "palaver," and "savvy" first entered American
English in this way.

*and trade with each other

The New World's trade with Africa also ~~effec~~ affected American English. The
slave trade, in particular, took American sailors and merchants all over the African
continent. Since the traders mixed up slaves of many tribes to prevent them from
becoming unified, the Africans had to rely on [their own] pidgin to communicate with each
other. Moreover, slave owners relied on this African-based pidgin to communicate
with their slaves.** Since slaves tended to be settled in the heavily populated American
coastal areas, elements of the African pidgin readily worked their way into the language of the New World. Words and phrases derived from African pidgins include
"caboodle" and "kick the bucket." Other African-based words include "buckaroo"
and "goobers," plus words known only in the Deep South, like "cooter" for turtle.
African-based slang terms and constructions ("uptight," "put-on," and "hip," meaning "cool" or "in") continue to enter mainstream English from black English even
today.

[important]
Another influence on American English, in the nation's early days, was contact with Native American cultures. As settlers moved inland from coastal areas, they
confronted different indigenous peoples, and new pidgins grew up, melding English
and Native American terms. In particular, many words for places, plants, and animals have Native American roots: "squash," "raccoon," and "skunk" are just a few.
Another possible effect of Native American languages on American English may
be the tendency to form noun-noun compounds ("apple butter" and "shade tree").
While such constructions do occur in British English, they are [much] more frequent in
American English.

British and American English differ because the latter has been shaped
by contact with European languages like Portuguese, as well as by contact with
non-European languages—especially those spoken by Africans and Native
Americans.

**until they mastered English.

Commentary

Alert to such phrases as *account for* and *influences that affected* in the question, Andrew wrote an essay that describes three *causes* for the divergence of American from British English. The three causes are organized roughly chronologically, beginning with the influence of maritime exploration, moving to the effect of contact with African culture, and concluding with the influence of Native Americans.

Although the essay is developed mainly through a description of causes, other patterns of development come into play. The first paragraph *defines* the term *pidgin*, whereas the second, third, and fourth paragraphs draw on *process analysis;* they describe how pidgins developed, as well as how they affected the language spoken by early settlers. Finally, the essay includes numerous *examples*, as the exam question requested. Andrew's response shows a solid knowledge of the material taught in the course and demonstrates his ability to organize the material into a clear, coherent statement.

ACTIVITY: WRITING EXAM ESSAYS

In preparation for an exam with essay questions, devise four possible essay questions on the material in one of your courses. For each, do some quick prewriting, determine a thesis, and jot down an outline. Then, for one of the questions, write a full essay answer, giving yourself a time limit of fifteen to twenty-five minutes, whatever is appropriate for the question. Don't forget to edit and proofread your answer.

A Concise Handbook

Sentence Faults

Fragments

A full **sentence** satisfies two conditions: (1) it has a subject and a verb, and (2) it can stand alone as a complete thought. Although a **fragment** is punctuated like a full sentence, it doesn't satisfy these two requirements.[1] There are two kinds of fragments: phrase fragments and dependent clause fragments.

Phrase Fragments

If you punctuate a phrase as if it were a sentence, the result is a **phrase fragment**. Following are five kinds of phrase fragments and ways to correct such fragments.

Noun Phrase Fragment

I was afraid of my wrestling coach. *A harsh and sarcastic man.* He was never satisfied with my performance.

Added-Detail Phrase Fragment

Many people have difficulty getting up in the morning. *Especially on Mondays after a hectic weekend.* They wish they had one more day to relax.

Prepositional Phrase Fragment

After a long day at work. I drove to the bank that opened last week. *On the corner of Holly Avenue and Red Oak Lane. Next to the discount supermarket.*

frag

---

[1]For information on the way an occasional fragment may be used for emphasis, see page 101 in Chapter 8.

Present Participle, Past Participle, or Infinitive Phrase Fragment

Waiting [present participle] *to buy tickets for the concert.* The crowd stood quietly in line. No one cared that the box office would be closed until the morning.

The children presented the social worker with a present. *Wrapped* [past participle] *in gold aluminum foil.*

After years of negotiating, several nations signed a treaty. *To ban* [infinitive] *the sale of ivory in their countries.*

Missing-Subject Phrase Fragment

Every weekend, the fraternities sponsored a joint open-house party. *And blared music all night long.* Not surprisingly, neighbors became furious.

How to Correct Phrase Fragments

There are four strategies for eliminating phrase fragments from your writing. When using these strategies, you may need to reword sentences slightly to maintain smoothness.

1. Attach the fragment to the preceding or following sentence, changing punctuation and capitalization as needed. When attaching a phrase fragment to the *beginning of a preceding sentence,* place a comma between the fragment and the start of the original sentence:

Fragment	Environmentalists predict a drought this summer. *In spite of heavy spring rains.* Everyone hopes the predictions are wrong.
Correct	In spite of heavy spring rains, environmentalists predict a drought this summer. Everyone hopes the predictions are wrong.

To attach a phrase fragment to the *end of a preceding sentence,* change the period at the end of the preceding sentence to a comma and change the first letter of the fragment to lowercase:

Fragment	I spent several hours in the college's Career Services Office. *Trying to find an interesting summer job.* Nothing looked promising.
Correct	I spent several hours in the college's Career Services Office, trying to find an interesting summer job. Nothing looked promising.

To attach a phrase fragment to the *beginning of a full sentence that follows it,* change the period at the end of the fragment to a comma and make the capital letter at the start of the full sentence lowercase:

Fragment	*Overwhelmed by school pressures and family demands.* She decided to postpone her education. That was a mistake.
Correct	Overwhelmed by school pressures and family demands, she decided to postpone her education. That was a mistake.

2. Insert the fragment into the preceding or following sentence, adding commas as needed:

Fragment	The tests were easy. *Especially the essay questions.* We felt confident that we had done well.
Correct	The tests, especially the essay questions, were easy. We felt confident that we had done well. [fragment inserted into preceding sentence]
Fragment	*A robust girl who loved physical activity from the time she was a baby.* My sister qualified for the Olympics when she was seventeen.
Correct	My sister, a robust girl who loved physical activity from the time she was a baby, qualified for the Olympics when she was seventeen. [fragment inserted into following sentence]

3. Attach the fragment to a newly created sentence:

Fragment	Although I proudly call it mine, my apartment does have some problems. *For example, very little heat in the winter.*
Correct	Although I proudly call it mine, my apartment does have some problems. For example, *it has* very little heat in the winter.

4. Supply the missing subject:

Fragment	Although they argued frequently, my grandparents doted on each other. *And held hands wherever they went.*
Correct	Although they argued frequently, my grandparents doted on each other. *They* held hands wherever they went.
or	
Correct	Although they argued frequently, my grandparents doted on each other *and* held hands wherever they went.

Dependent Clause Fragments

Unlike phrases, which lack either a subject or a full verb, **clauses** contain both a subject and a full verb. Clauses may be **independent** (expressing a complete thought and able to stand alone as a sentence) or **dependent** (not expressing a complete thought and, therefore, not able to stand alone). A dependent clause (often called a **subordinate clause**) begins with a word that signals the clause's reliance on something more for completion. Such introductory words may take the form of **subordinating conjunctions** or **relative pronouns**:[2]

Subordinating Conjunctions

after	once	even though	when
although	since	if	while
as	so that	in order that	
because	unless	until	

---

[2]Dependent clauses introduced by relative pronouns are often referred to as *relative clauses.*

Relative Pronouns

that	which	whoever	whomever
what	who	whom	whose

If you punctuate a dependent clause as though it were a complete sentence, the result is a **dependent clause fragment** (identified by italics in the example):

Fragment	*Because my parents wanted to be with their children at bedtime.* They arranged to leave their late-shift jobs a few minutes early.

How to Correct Dependent Clause Fragments

There are two main ways to correct dependent clause fragments. When using the strategies, you may need to reword sentences slightly to maintain smoothness.

1. Connect the fragment to the preceding or following full sentence, adding a comma if needed:

Fragment	I thought both my car and I would be demolished. *When the motorcycle hit me from behind.*
Correct	When the motorcycle hit me from behind, I thought both my car and I would be demolished. [fragment attached, with a comma, to beginning of preceding sentence]
or	
Correct	I thought both my car and I would be demolished when the motorcycle hit me from behind. [fragment attached, without a comma, to end of preceding sentence]
Fragment	*Although the clean-up crews tried to scrub the oil-coated rocks thoroughly.* Many birds nesting on the rocky shore are bound to die.
Correct	Although the clean-up crews tried to scrub the oil-coated rocks thoroughly, many birds nesting on the rocky shore are bound to die. [fragment attached, with a comma, to beginning of following sentence]
or	
Correct	Many birds nesting on the rocky shore are bound to die, although the clean-up crews tried to scrub the oil-coated rocks thoroughly. [fragment attached, with a comma, to end of following sentence]

Guidelines for Using Commas with Dependent Clauses

- If a dependent clause with a subordinating conjunction (like *when* or *although*) precedes the full sentence, the dependent clause is followed by a comma (as in the first and third corrected sentences above).
- If a dependent clause follows the full sentence, it isn't preceded by a comma (as in the second corrected sentence above).
- The exception is dependent clauses beginning with such words as *although* and *though*—words that show contrast. When such clauses follow a full

sentence, they are preceded by a comma (as in the fourth corrected sentence above).

When connecting a relative clause to a full sentence, you set *off* the *relative clause* with a comma if the clause is **nonrestrictive** (that is, if it is *not essential* to the sentence's meaning):

Fragment	As a child, I went to the mountains with my parents. *Who never relaxed long enough to enjoy the lazy times there.*
Correct	As a child, I went to the mountains with my parents, who never relaxed long enough to enjoy the lazy times there.

Note that in the corrected version there's a comma between the independent and relative clauses because the relative clause (*who never relaxed long enough to enjoy the lazy times there*) is nonrestrictive. In other words, it isn't needed to identify the writer's parents.

Take a look, though, at the following:

Fragment	As a child, I went to the mountains with the family. *Who lived next door.*
Correct	As a child, I went to the mountains with the family who lived next door.

In this case, the relative clause (*who lived next door*) is needed to identify which family is being referred to; that is, the clause is **restrictive** (*essential*) and, therefore, is *not* set off with a comma. (For information on punctuating restrictive and nonrestrictive phrases, see pages 571–572.)

When a relative clause beginning with *that* is attached to a nearby sentence, no comma is used between the relative and independent clauses:

Fragment	My uncle got down on his hands and knees to rake away the dry leaves. *That he felt spoiled the beauty of his flower beds.*
Correct	My uncle got down on his hands and knees to rake away the dry leaves that he felt spoiled the beauty of his flower beds.

2. Remove or replace the dependent clause's first word:

Fragment	The typical family-run farm is up for sale these days. *Because few small farmers can compete with agricultural conglomerates.*
Correct	The typical family-run farm is up for sale these days. Few small farmers can compete with agricultural conglomerates.

Practice: Correcting Sentence Fragments

Correct any phrase and dependent clause fragments that you find in the following sentences. Be careful, though; some of the sentences may not contain fragments, and others may contain more than one.

1. Even though there must be millions of pigeons in the city. You never see a baby pigeon. It makes you wonder where they're hiding.

2. Children between the ages of eight and twelve often follow teenagers' trends. And look up to teens as role models. Mimicking their behavior in frequently disconcerting ways.

3. The student's dorm room looked like a disaster area. Heaps of dirty clothes, crumpled papers, and half-eaten snacks were strewn everywhere. Keeping the room neat was obviously not a priority.

4. My grandfather likes to send off-beat greeting cards. Like the one with a picture of a lion holding on to a parachute. The card reads, "Just wanted to drop you a lion."

5. About a year ago, my mother was unexpectedly laid off by the restaurant. Where she had been hired five years earlier as head chef. The experience made her realize that she wanted to go into business for herself.

Comma Splices and Run-on Sentences

cs
r-o

A **comma splice** occurs when a comma is used to join, or splice together, two complete thoughts, even though a comma alone is not strong enough to connect the two independent clauses. A **run-on**, or **fused, sentence** occurs when two sentences are connected, or run together, without any punctuation to indicate where the first sentence ends and the second begins.

Three Common Pitfalls

Following are three situations that often lead to comma splices or run-on sentences and ways to correct these sentence errors.

1. When the second sentence starts with a personal or demonstrative pronoun: The following are **personal pronouns:** *I, you, he, she, it, we,* and *they. This, that, these,* and *those* are **demonstrative pronouns.**

Comma Splice	The college's computerized billing system needs to be overhauled, *it billed more than a dozen students twice for tuition.*
Run-on	Lobsters are cannibalistic and will feed on each other *this is one reason they are difficult to raise in captivity.*

2. When the second sentence starts with a transition: Some common **transitions** include the words *finally, next, second,* and *then.*

Comma Splice	You start by buttering the baking dish, *next you pour in milk and mix it well with the butter.*
Run-on	The dentist studied my X rays *then she let out an ominous sigh.*

3. When two sentences are connected by a transitional adverb: Some of the most common **transitional adverbs** are shown on the next page.

Transitional Adverbs

accordingly	furthermore	meanwhile	still
also	however	moreover	therefore
anyway	indeed	nevertheless	thus
besides	instead	nonetheless	
consequently	likewise	otherwise	

Comma Splice   We figured the movie tickets would cost about five dollars, *however, we forgot to calculate the cost of all the junk food we would eat.*

Run-on   Fish in a backyard pond will thrive simply by eating the bugs, larvae, and algae in the pond *nevertheless, many people enjoy feeding fish by hand.*

How to Correct Comma Splices and Run-on Sentences

There are four strategies for eliminating comma splices and run-on sentences from your writing.

1. Place a period, question mark, or exclamation point at the end of the first sentence and capitalize the first letter of the second sentence:

Comma Splice   Our team played badly, *we deserved to lose by the wide margin we did.*
Correct   Our team played badly. We deserved to lose by the wide margin we did.

Run-on   Which computer do experts recommend for the average college student *which system do experts consider most all-purpose?* They seldom agree.
Correct   Which computer do experts recommend for the average college student? Which system do experts consider most all-purpose? They seldom agree.

2. Use a semicolon (;) to mark where the first sentence ends and the second begins:

Comma Splice   In the eighteenth century, beauty marks were considered fashionable, *people even glued black paper dots to their faces.*
Correct   In the eighteenth century, beauty marks were considered fashionable; people even glued black paper dots to their faces.

Run-on   Many men use hairstyling products, facial scrubs, and cologne *however, most draw the line at powder and eye makeup.*
Correct   Many men use hairstyling products, facial scrubs, and cologne; however, most draw the line at powder and eye makeup.

Note that when the second sentence starts with a transitional adverb (such as *however* in the last corrected sentence above), a *comma* is placed *after* the transition.[3]

---

[3]For information on punctuating transitional adverbs when they appear midsentence, see pages 571–572.

3. Turn one of the sentences into a dependent clause:[4]

Comma Splice	The camping grounds have no electricity, *however, people flock there anyway.*
Correct	*Although* the camping grounds have no electricity, people flock there anyway.
Run-on	The highway was impassable *it had snowed all night and most of the morning.*
Correct	The highway was impassable *because* it had snowed all night and most of the morning.

When using this strategy, refer to the list of guidelines on pages 550–551 to help you decide whether you should (as in the first corrected example) or shouldn't (as in the second corrected example) use a comma between the independent and dependent clauses.

4. Keep or add a comma at the end of the first sentence, but follow the comma with a coordinating conjunction. The following words are **coordinating conjunctions:** *and, but, for, nor, or, so, yet.*

Comma Splice	Well-prepared and confident, I expected the exam to be easy, *it turned out to be a harrowing experience.*
Correct	Well-prepared and confident, I expected the exam to be easy, but it turned out to be a harrowing experience.
Run-on	Last election we campaigned enthusiastically *this year we expect to be equally involved.*
Correct	Last election we campaigned enthusiastically, *and* this year we expect to be equally involved.

Practice: Correcting Comma Splices and Run-on Sentences

Correct any comma splices and run-ons that you find in the following sentences. Be careful, though; some commas belong just where they are.

1. Since the town appeared to be nearby, they left the car on the side of the road and started walking toward the village, they soon regretted their decision.
2. With unexpected intensity, the rain hit the pavement, plumes of heat rose from the blacktop, making it difficult to drive safely.
3. Plants should be treated regularly with an organic insecticide, otherwise, spider mites and mealy bugs can destroy new growth.
4. Have you ever looked closely at a penny, do you know whether Lincoln faces right or left?

---

[4]See pages 549–550 for a list of words that introduce dependent clauses.

5. The library's security system needs improving, it allows too many people to sneak away, with books and magazines hidden in their pockets, purses, or briefcases.

Faulty Parallelism

Words in a pair or in a series should be placed in parallel (matching) grammatical structures. If they're not, the result is **faulty parallelism**:

Faulty Parallelism   After the exam, we were *exhausted, hungry,* and *experienced depression.*

In the preceding sentence, three items make up the series. However, the first two items are adjectives (*exhausted* and *hungry*), whereas the last one is a verb plus a noun (*experienced depression*).

Words that follow correlative conjunctions (*either...or, neither...nor, both...and, not only...but also*) should also be parallel:

Faulty Parallelism   Every road into the city is either *jammed* or *is closed* for repairs.

Here, *either* is followed by an adjective (*jammed*), but *or* is followed by a verb (*is*).

How to Correct Faulty Parallelism

To correct faulty parallelism, *place words in a pair or in a series in the same grammatical structure*:

Faulty Parallelism   *After the car baked in the sun for hours, the steering wheel was hot, the seats were sticky, and there was stuffiness in the air.*
Correct   After the car baked in the sun for hours, the steering wheel was hot, the seats were sticky, and the air was stuffy.

or

Correct   After the car baked in the sun for hours, the steering wheel was hot, the seats sticky, and the air stuffy.

Faulty Parallelism   *Parents are either too permissive or they are too strict.*
Correct   Parents are either too permissive or too strict.
or
Correct   Parents either are too permissive or are too strict.
or
Correct   Either parents are too permissive, or they are too strict.

Practice: Correcting Faulty Parallelism

Correct any faulty parallelism that you find in the following sentences. Be careful, though; not every sentence contains an error.

1. The professor's tests were long, difficult, and produced anxiety.
2. Medical tests showed that neither being allergic to dust nor seasonal hay fever caused the child's coughing fits.

3. The hairstylist warned her customers, "I'm a beautician, not a magician. This is a comb; it's not a wand."
4. The renovated concert hall is both beautiful and it is spacious.
5. My roommates and I are not only learning Japanese but also Russian.

Verbs

Problems with Subject-Verb Agreement

A **verb** should *match its subject in number.* If the subject is singular (one person, place, or thing), the verb should have a singular form. If the subject is plural (two or more persons, places, or things), the verb should have a plural form.

How to Correct Faulty Subject-Verb Agreement

To deal with each of the following six problems, you must determine the *verb's subject* and make sure the *verb agrees with it,* rather than with some other word in the sentence.

1. When there are two or more subjects: When the word *and* joins two or more subjects in a sentence, use a plural verb.

Correct   A beautiful maple *and* a straggly oak *flank* [not *flanks*] the building.

However, when the word *or* joins the subjects, use a singular verb:

Correct   A maple *or* an oak *offers* [not *offer*] good shade in the summer.

2. When the subject and verb are separated by a prepositional phrase: Be sure to match the verb to its subject—not to a word in a prepositional phrase that comes between the subject and the verb.

Correct
One of the desserts *was* [not *were*] too sweet even for me.
To pass inspection, the *plumbing* in all the apartments *needs* [not *need*] to be repaired.

3. When the words *either...or* or *neither...nor* connect subjects: When *either... or* or *neither...nor* link two subjects, use the verb form (singular or plural) that agrees with the subject *closer* to the verb.

Correct
Neither the students *nor* the *professor likes* [not *like*] the textbook.
Neither the professor *nor* the *students like* [not *likes*] the textbook.

s-v agr

4. When the subject is an indefinite pronoun: Some **indefinite pronouns** (such as *anyone, anything, each, either, every, everyone, everybody, everything, neither,* and *nobody*) take a *singular verb*—whether they act as a pronoun subject (as in the first sentence that follows) or as an adjective in front of a noun subject (as in the second sentence).

Correct
> *Neither* of the libraries *was* [not *were*] open.
> *Neither* library *was* [not *were*] open.

Other indefinite pronouns (such as *all, any, most, none,* and *some*) take a *singular or a plural verb,* depending on whether they refer to one thing or to a number of things. In the following sentence, *some* refers to a single tutoring session, so the verb is singular:

Correct   The student reported that only *some* of her tutoring *session was* helpful.

In this next sentence, however, *some* refers to multiple sessions, so the verb is plural:

Correct   The student reported that only *some* of her tutoring *sessions were* helpful.

5. When there is a group subject: When the subject of a sentence refers to a group acting in unison, or as a unit, use a singular verb.

Correct   The debate *club* is [not *are*] on a winning streak.

However, when the subject is a group whose members are acting individually, rather than as a unit, use a plural verb:

Correct   The *debate club argue* [not *argues*] among themselves constantly.

If, in this case, the plural verb sounds awkward, reword the sentence so that the group's individual members are referred to directly:

Correct   The debate club *members argue* among themselves constantly.

6. When the verb comes before the subject: Words such as *here, there, how, what, when, where, which, who,* and *why,* as well as *prepositional phrases,* are apt to invert normal sentence order, causing the verb to precede the subject. In such cases, look ahead for the subject and make sure it and the verb agree in number.

Correct
> There *is* [not *are*] always a long *line* of students at the library's duplicating machine.
> What *are* [not *is*] the *reasons* for consumers' complaints about the car?
> Near the lifeguard station, looking for us everywhere, *were* [not *was*] our *parents.*

Practice: Correcting Problems with Subject-Verb Agreement

Correct any errors in subject-verb agreement that you find in the following sentences. Be careful, though; some sentences may not contain any errors.

1. Each of the children wear a name tag when the play group takes a field trip.
2. Next week, the faculty committee on academic standards plans to pass a controversial resolution, one that the student body have rejected in the past.
3. Neither the sales representative nor the customers were happy with the price increase, which is scheduled to go into effect next month.
4. The human spinal column, with its circular discs, resemble a stack of wobbly poker chips.
5. Both the students and the instructor dislikes experimental music.

Problems with Verb Tense

vt

A **verb's tense** indicates the time—*past, present,* or *future*—of an event. Here we show how to correct two common problems with verb tense: (1) inappropriate shifts in tense, and (2) faulty use of past tense.

How to Correct Inappropriate Shifts in Verb Tense

The sentence that follows switches from the past tense (*bought*) to the present (*breaks*), even though both events took place in the same (past) period of time. To avoid such inappropriate shifts, *use the same verb tense to relate all events occurring in the same time period*:

Inappropriate Tense Shift	The township *bought* a powerful new lawn mower, which *breaks* down after two weeks.
Correct	The township *bought* a powerful new lawn mower, which *broke* down after two weeks.

When writing, decide which verb tense will be most effective; then use that tense throughout—unless you need to change tenses to indicate a different time period.

Much of the writing you do in college will use the past tense:

Changes in the tax law *created* chaos for accounting firms.

However, when writing about literature, you generally use the present tense:

Twain *examines* the conflict between humane impulses and society's prejudices.

How to Correct Faulty Use of Past Tense

The following sentence uses the **simple past tense** (*finished, burst*) for both verbs, even though one event ("the plane finished rolling down the runway") *preceded* the other (the plane "burst into flames"). To distinguish one past event from an earlier one, use the **past perfect tense** ("*had* washed," "*had* gone," "*had* finished") for the earlier event:

Faulty Past Tense	The plane already *finished* rolling down the runway when it *burst* into flames.
Correct	The plane *had* already *finished* [past perfect] rolling down the runway when it *burst* [simple past] into flames.

Practice: Correcting Problems with Verb Tense

Correct any errors in verb tense that you find in the following sentences. Be careful, though; some tenses shouldn't be changed.

1. I parked illegally, so my car is towed and gets dented in the process.
2. We had already ordered a truckload of lumber when we decided not to build a deck after all.
3. Dr. Alice Chase wrote a number of books on healthy eating. In 1974, she dies of malnutrition.
4. By the time we hiked back to the campsite, the rest of the group collected their gear to go home.
5. In her poetry, Marge Piercy often pays tribute to women's strength and resilience.

Pronouns

Problems with Pronoun Use

Pronouns are words that take the place of nouns (persons, places, things, and concepts). Indeed, the word *pronoun* means "for a noun." As the following sentences show, pronouns keep you from repeating words unnecessarily:

After I fertilized the plant, *it* began to flourish. [*it* takes the place of *plant*]
When the students went to register *their* complaint, *they* were told to come back later. [*their* and *they* replace *students*]

When using pronouns, you need to be careful not to run into problems with case, agreement, and reference.

Pronoun Case

A pronoun's correct form, or **case**, depends on the way the pronoun is used in the sentence. A pronoun acting as a *subject* requires the **nominative case**. One acting as

case

a *direct object* (receiving a verb's action), an *indirect object* (indicating to or for whom the action is performed), or an *object of a preposition* (following a preposition such as *at*, *near*, or *to*) requires the **objective case**. And a pronoun indicating *possession* takes the **possessive case**. The list on the below page classifies pronouns by case.

Nominative Case	Objective Case	Possessive Case	
I	me	my	mine
we	us	our	ours
you	you	your	yours
he	him	his	his
she	her	her	hers
it	it	its	its
they	them	their	theirs
who	whom	whose	

How to Correct Faulty Pronoun Case

To correct any of these five problems, *determine whether the pronoun is used as object or subject; then put the pronoun in the appropriate case.*

1. Pronoun pairs or a pronoun and a noun: Use the nominative case when two pronouns act as subjects.

Correct   *He* and *I* [not *Him* and *me*] are different ages, but we have several traits in common.

Also use the nominative case when a pronoun and noun serve as subjects:

Correct   *She* [not *Her*] and *several transfer students* enrolled in the new course.

Conversely, use the objective case when a pronoun pair acts as direct object, indirect object, or object of a preposition:

Correct (Direct Objects)   My parents sent *her* [not *she*] and *me* [not *I*] to the store to buy decorations for the holiday.
Correct (Indirect Objects)   The committee presented *him* [not *he*] and *me* [not *I*] with the award.

Similarly, use the objective case when a pronoun and noun function as direct object, indirect object, or object of a preposition:

Correct (Object of Preposition)   The doctor gave the pills to the three other patients and *me* [not *I*].

A hint: When a pronoun is paired with another pronoun or with a noun, and you're not sure which case to use, imagine the sentence with only one pronoun.

For example, perhaps you wonder whether it's correct to write, "The student senate commended my roommates and *I* for our actions." "The student senate commended *I*" doesn't sound right, so you know *me* is the correct form.

2. A pronoun-noun pair acting together as subject or object: If a pronoun-noun pair acts as the subject, use the nominative case.

Correct   *We* [not *Us*] *dorm residents* plan to protest the ruling.

If the pronoun-noun pair serves as an object, use the objective case:

Correct   The dropout rate among *us* [not *we*] *commuting students* is high.

3. Pronouns following forms of the verb *to be*:   In formal English, use the nominative case in constructions like the following.

Correct
It is *I* [not *me*].   This is *she* [not *her*].

In such constructions, the objective case (*me* and *her*, for example) is so common that the formally correct nominative case may sound strange. However, before using the more colloquial objective case, check with your instructor to make sure such informality will be acceptable.

4. Pronouns following the comparative *than*:   Comparisons using the word *than* tend to imply, rather than state directly, the sentence's final word (placed in brackets in the following sentence).

The other employees are more willing to negotiate *than we* [are].

To determine the appropriate case for the pronoun in a sentence with a *than* comparison, simply add the implied word. For example, maybe you're not sure whether *we* or *us* is correct in the preceding sentence. As soon as you supply the implied word (*are*), it becomes clear that *we*, not *us*, is correct.

5. *Who* and *whom*:   When, as in the first example that follows, a pronoun acts as the subject of a sentence or clause, use *who* (the nominative case). When, as in the second example, the pronoun acts as the object of a verb or preposition, use *whom* (the objective case). You can test whether *who* or *whom* is correct by answering the question stated or implied in the *who/whom* portion of the sentence. The pronoun that answers *who/whom* will reveal which case to use.

"*Who/Whom* did you meet at the jazz festival"? → "I met *him* at the festival." → Since *him* is the objective case, use *whom*.

"The employees want to know *who/whom* will supervise the project." → "*She* will supervise the project." → Since *she* is the nominative case, use *who*.

Practice: Correcting Problems with Pronoun Case

Correct any problems with pronoun case that you find in the following sentences. Be careful, though; some pronouns are used correctly.

1. At this college, neither the president nor the dean automatically assumes that, on every issue, the faculty is better informed than us students.
2. Between you and I, each of the dorms should have their security systems replaced.
3. Neither of the boys impressed she or me with their musical ability.
4. After enjoying prosperity through most of the 1980s, she and him were unprepared for the rigors of the next decade.
5. To whom did the theater manager give the free passes?

Pronoun Agreement

pro agr

A pronoun must **agree in number** with its **antecedent**—the noun or pronoun it replaces or refers to. If the antecedent is singular, the pronoun must be singular. If the antecedent is plural, the pronoun must be plural.

How to Correct Faulty Pronoun Agreement

To deal with these four problems, either *change the pronoun so it agrees in number and person with its antecedent* or *change the noun to agree with the pronoun you have used.*

1. Compound subject: A compound subject (two or more nouns joined by *and*) requires plural pronouns.

Correct   Both the oak *tree* and the rose *bush* had trouble regaining *their* strength after the storm.

However, when the nouns are joined by *or* or *nor*, whichever noun is closer to the verb determines whether the pronoun should be singular or plural:

Faulty Pronoun Agreement   Neither the oak tree nor the rose *bushes* regained *its* strength after the storm.
Correct   Neither the oak tree nor the rose *bushes* regained *their* strength after the storm.
Correct   Neither the rose bushes nor the oak *tree* regained *its* strength after the storm.

2. Collective nouns: Collective nouns represent a collection of people or things. Some examples are *company, university, team,* and *committee.* If the collective noun refers to a group or entity that acts as one unit, use the singular pronoun.

Faulty Pronoun Agreement   The *band* showed *their* appreciation by playing several encores.
Correct   The *band* showed *its* appreciation by playing several encores.

If, in this case, the singular pronoun form sounds awkward, simply make the antecedent plural. Then use the plural pronoun:

Correct The band *members* showed *their* appreciation by playing several encores.

When the collective noun refers to members of a group who act individually, use a plural pronoun:

Correct *The band* disagreed among *themselves* about the songs to be played.

3. Indefinite pronouns: Here is a list of singular indefinite pronouns.

Indefinite Pronoun	Possessive Form		Reflexive Form
anybody	his, her	his, hers	himself, herself
everybody	his, her	his, hers	himself, herself
nobody	his, her	his, hers	himself, herself
somebody	his, her	his, hers	himself, herself
anyone	his, her	his, hers	himself, herself
everyone	his, her	his, hers	himself, herself
no one	his, her	his, hers	himself, herself
someone	his, her	his, hers	himself, herself
either	his, her	his, hers	himself, herself
neither	his, her	his, hers	himself, herself
each	his, her	his, hers	himself, herself
one	one's		oneself

In everyday speech, we often use plural pronouns (*their* and *themselves*) because such pronouns cause us to picture more than one person. For example, we may say "*Everyone* should bring *their* own computer disks." In formal writing, though, these indefinite pronouns are considered singular and thus take singular pronouns:

Correct
Each of the buildings had *its* [not *their*] lobby redecorated.
Neither of the ballerinas was pleased with *her* [not *their*] performance.

Using the singular form with indefinite pronouns may mean that you find yourself in the awkward situation of having to choose between *his* or *her* or between *himself* and *herself*. As a result, you may end up writing sentences that exclude either males or females: "Everybody in the mall seemed lost in *his* own thoughts." (Surely some of the shoppers were female.) To avoid this problem, you may make the antecedent plural and use the plural pronoun:

The *shoppers* in the mall seemed lost in *their* own thoughts.

4. A shift in person: Within a sentence, pronouns shouldn't disrupt pronoun-antecedent agreement by shifting person (point of view).

Faulty Pronoun Agreement

> To drop a course, *students* [third person] should go to the registrar's office, where *you* [second person] obtain a course-change card.

Such shifts are most often from the third or first person to the second person (*you*). In the preceding example, *you* should be *they*.

Practice: Correcting Problems with Pronoun Agreement

Correct any problems with pronoun agreement that you find in the following sentences. Be careful, though; some pronouns are used correctly.

1. We proponents of the recycling plan challenged everyone on the town council to express their objections.
2. All job applicants must call for an appointment, so that the personnel office can interview you.
3. The committee passed their resolution that each of the apartments was to be free of asbestos before occupancy.
4. Typically, one of the girls loses their schedule of upcoming games, so the coach always reminds the team of its next event at the start of each competition.
5. Neither the bank manager nor the bank officers admitted to their error in approving the risky loan.

Pronoun Reference

**pro
ref**

Besides agreeing with its antecedent in number and person, a pronoun must have a *clear antecedent*. A sentence that lacks clear **pronoun reference** is vague and ambiguous.

How to Correct Unclear Pronoun Reference

To make sure that each pronoun has an unmistakable antecedent, use the four strategies that follow.

1. Leave no ambiguity about the noun to which a pronoun refers:

Unclear Antecedent	The newcomer battled the longtime champion for the tennis prize. In the end, she won. [Who won? The newcomer or the longtime champion?]
Correct	The newcomer battled the longtime champion for the tennis prize. In the end, *the newcomer* won.

2. Replace a pronoun that lacks an antecedent with the appropriate noun:

Omitted Antecedent	In his talk on child abuse, the caseworker pointed out the number of *them* mistreated by day-care employees. [*Them* is meant to refer to *children,* but this word doesn't appear in the sentence.]
Correct	In his talk on child abuse, the caseworker pointed out the number of *children* mistreated by day-care employees.

3. Make sure a pronoun doesn't refer to the possessive form of a noun or to an adjective:

Omitted Antecedent	In *journalists' articles, they* often quote unidentified sources. [*They* refers to *journalists,* which is in the possessive case.]
Correct	*Journalists* often quote unidentified sources in *their* articles.

4. Place pronouns near their antecedents:

Unclear Antecedent	The *dancers,* performing almost daily, traveled by bus and train. The trip spanned several states. *They* returned exhausted and out of debt.
Correct	Performing almost daily, traveling by bus and train on a trip that spanned several states, the *dancers* returned exhausted. *They* were also out of debt.

Practice: Correcting Problems with Pronoun Reference

Correct any problems with pronoun reference that you find in the following sentences. Be careful, though; some pronouns are used correctly.

1. In Anne Tyler's novels, she gives us a picture of family life—at its best and at its worst.
2. To keep children away from dangerous chemicals, lock them in a storage closet.
3. Many patients' lawsuits against doctors end when they receive an out-of-court settlement.
4. All too often, arguments between a big and a little sister are ended by the younger one, when she threatens to blackmail her sister with some violation of household rules.
5. Since the old man's morning was planned around reading the newspaper, he became upset when it was delivered late.

Modifiers

Problems with Modification

mm

Misplaced and Ambiguous Modifiers

A **modifier** is a word or group of words that describes something else. Sometimes sentences are written in such a way that modifiers are **misplaced** or **ambiguous**. Here are examples of misplaced and ambiguous modifiers:

Misplaced Modifier	Television stations carried the story of the disastrous fire *in every part of the nation.* [The fire was in every part of the nation?]
Ambiguous Modifier	Singers who don't warm up *gradually* lose their voices. [What does the sentence mean: that singers who don't warm up will lose their voices gradually or that singers who don't gradually warm up will lose their voices?]

How to Correct Misplaced or Ambiguous Modifiers

Here are two strategies for correcting misplaced or ambiguous modifiers.

1. Place the modifier next to the word(s) it describes:

Misplaced Modifier	We scanned the menu *with hungry eyes.* [The menu had hungry eyes?]
Correct	With hungry eyes, we scanned the menu.
Misplaced Modifier	They *only* studied a few minutes for the exam. [Doesn't the word *only* describe a few minutes, not *studied?*]
Correct	They studied *only* a few minutes for the exam.

2. Rewrite the sentence to eliminate ambiguity:

Ambiguous Modifier	Giving money *frequently* relieves people's guilt about living well.

Writing the sentence this way could mean *either* that the frequent giving of money relieves guilt or that giving money relieves guilt frequently. Moving the modifier to the front of the sentence conveys the first meaning.

Frequently, giving money relieves people's guilt about living well.

The second meaning, however, can be conveyed only by rewriting the sentence:

Giving money *on a frequent basis* relieves people's guilt about living well.

Dangling Modifiers

An introductory modifier must modify the subject of the sentence. If it doesn't, the result is a **dangling modifier.** Here's an example of a dangling modifier:

dg1

Dangling Modifier	*Driving along the highway,* the blinding sun obscured our view of the oncoming car. [The sentence says that the sun was driving along the highway.]

How to Correct Dangling Modifiers

To eliminate a dangling modifier, you may *rewrite the sentence by adding to the modifying phrase the word being described* (as in the first corrected example that follows). Or you may *rewrite the sentence so that the word being modified becomes the sentence's subject* (as in the second corrected example):

Dangling Modifier	*While relaxing in my backyard hammock,* a neighbor's basketball hit me on the head. [The basketball was relaxing in the backyard?]
Correct	While *I* was relaxing in my backyard hammock, a neighbor's basketball hit me on the head.
or	
Correct	While relaxing in my backyard hammock, *I* was hit on the head by my neighbor's basketball.

Practice: Correcting Problems with Modification

Correct any misplaced, ambiguous, or dangling modifiers that you find in the following sentences. Be careful, though; not every sentence is incorrect.

1. While cooking dinner, the baby began to howl.
2. Swaying from the boughs of a tall tree, the children were intrigued by the ape's agility and grace.
3. When pondering her problems, it finally struck Laura that her life was filled with many pleasures.
4. At the end of the semester, I realized that I only needed tutoring in one course.
5. After swimming the entire length of the lake, the coach, much to his embarrassment, passed out.

Punctuation

p

Correct **punctuation** is no trivial matter. Notice how a single comma alters the meaning of this sentence:

Their uncle would be the only visitor they feared.

Their uncle would be the only visitor, they feared.

The first sentence suggests that the uncle's visit is a source of anxiety; the second sentence suggests that the uncle is, unfortunately, the only person to pay a visit. So choose your punctuation carefully. Skillful punctuation helps you get your message across; careless punctuation can undermine your credibility and spoil an otherwise effective piece of writing.

Period (.)

The most frequent misuse of the **period** is at the end of a *fragment*—a word or group of words that doesn't constitute a full sentence, only part of one. (For more on sentence fragments, see pages 547–551 of the Handbook.) The correct uses of the period are outlined here.

1. At the end of full statements: A period correctly completes any full sentence not worded as a question or exclamation.

> The campus senators asked when the college administrators would approve the new plan.

Although the preceding sentence reports that a question was asked, the sentence itself is a statement. For this reason, it ends with a period, not with a question mark.

2. With some abbreviations: A period is also used to indicate a shortened form of a word; that is, an abbreviation.

> Prof. (Professor) Dec. (December) p.m. (*post meridiem*, Latin phrase meaning "after noon")

When an abbreviation ends a sentence, only one period is needed at the sentence's close:

> They didn't place the order until 3 a.m.

Some abbreviations, though, have no period at all. These include the abbreviated titles of organizations and government agencies, as well as the official U.S. Postal Service abbreviations for state names:

> FDA (Food and Drug Administration)   ME (Maine)

In addition, it is becoming increasingly acceptable to omit the periods in frequently used abbreviations—for example, *mph* (miles per hour). If you're in doubt whether to include a period in an abbreviation, consult a recent dictionary. Many dictionaries have a separate section that lists abbreviations.

3. In decimal numbers: A period precedes the fractional portion of a decimal number.

> 5.38 (five and thirty-eight hundredths)

Because money is counted according to the decimal system, a period occurs between dollars and cents:

> $10.35

(For more information on writing numerals, see pages 585–586 of the Handbook.)

Question Mark (?)

1. At the end of direct questions: Just as a period concludes a statement, a **question mark** concludes a question.

> The panelists debated the question, "Should drugs be legalized?"

> Did the consultants name their report "The Recycling Crisis"?

Notice that in the first example above, the actual question occurs only within the quotation marks. Therefore, the question mark is placed *before* the final quotation marks (and no final period is necessary). In the second example, though, the whole sentence is a question, so the question mark goes *after* the final quotation marks.

2. In parentheses, following an item of questionable accuracy: Whenever you're unable to confirm the accuracy of a name, date, or other item, indicate your uncertainty by following the item with a question mark enclosed in parentheses.

> The fraud, begun in 1977 **(?),** was discovered only this year.

Exclamation Point (!)

At the end of emphatic sentences: An **exclamation point** is placed at the end of a sentence to indicate strong emotion.

> That's the worst meal I've ever eaten!

Use exclamation points sparingly; otherwise, they lose their effectiveness.

Comma (,)

The **comma** is so frequent in writing that mastering its use is essential. By dividing a sentence into its parts, commas clarify meaning. Compare the following:

> As soon as we had won the contest was declared illegal.

> As soon as we had won, the contest was declared illegal.

The comma shows the reader where to pause to make sense of the sentence. The following pages discuss the correct use of the comma.

1. Between sentences joined by a coordinating conjunction: When joining two complete sentences with a coordinating conjunction (*and, but, for, nor, or, so, yet*), place a comma *before* the coordinating conjunction.

> My father loves dining out, *but* he is fussy about food.

It's permissible to omit the comma, though, if the two complete sentences are very short:

They lied *yet* they won the case.

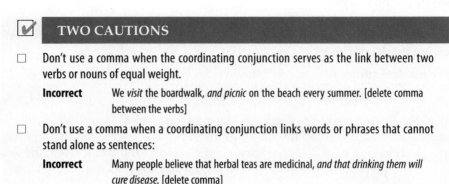

☑ **TWO CAUTIONS**

☐ Don't use a comma when the coordinating conjunction serves as the link between two verbs or nouns of equal weight.

Incorrect   We *visit* the boardwalk, *and picnic* on the beach every summer. [delete comma between the verbs]

☐ Don't use a comma when a coordinating conjunction links words or phrases that cannot stand alone as sentences:

Incorrect   Many people believe that herbal teas are medicinal, *and that drinking them will cure disease.* [delete comma]

2. Between items in a series: Use a comma to separate *three or more* items in a series.

It was a long, lonely, frightening drive to the cabin.

Notice that in the preceding example a comma appears before the last item in the series, whether or not this last item is preceded by *and* or *or*. (Although journalists and popular writers often omit the last comma in a series, its inclusion is expected in most other writing.)

However, if each item in the series is joined by *and* or *or*, do not place commas between them:

We didn't applaud *or* support *or* encourage the protesters.

3. Between adjectives of equal weight: A comma can substitute for the word *and* between adjectives of *equal weight* that describe the same noun.

Collecting exotic, colorful plants is one of my grandparents' hobbies.

In this sentence, the adjectives *exotic* and *colorful* contribute equally to the description of the noun *plants*. To test whether two adjectives have equal weight, reverse them or imagine the word *and* between them. If the sentence sounds fine, the adjectives have equal weight; thus, there should be a comma between them.

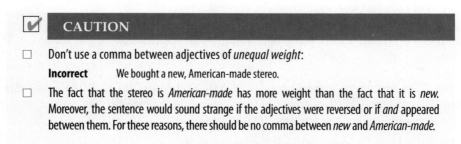

☑ **CAUTION**

☐ Don't use a comma between adjectives of *unequal weight*:

Incorrect   We bought a new, American-made stereo.

☐ The fact that the stereo is *American-made* has more weight than the fact that it is *new*. Moreover, the sentence would sound strange if the adjectives were reversed or if *and* appeared between them. For these reasons, there should be no comma between *new* and *American-made*.

4. Setting off nonrestrictive word groups: When a word, phrase, or clause describes a noun but isn't crucial for identifying that noun, it is *set off* from the rest of the sentence *with a comma.* Such a word or group of words is considered **nonrestrictive,** or **nonessential.**

> The professor asked the class to read Twain's *Pudd'nhead Wilson,* a novel both droll and dark.

Because *Pudd'nhead Wilson* identifies the novel sufficiently, the phrase *a novel both droll and dark* is nonrestrictive and, thus, set off with a comma. If the nonrestrictive phrase appears midsentence, it is preceded and followed by commas:

> The professor asked the class to read Twain's *Pudd'nhead Wilson,* a novel both droll and dark, by the end of the week.

In the next sentence, however, the book's title is *not set off by a comma* because the word group making up the title is **restrictive,** or **essential;** that is, it is needed for identification (Twain wrote more than one novel):

> The professor asked the class to read Twain's droll and dark novel *Pudd'nhead Wilson.*

(For a discussion of restrictive and nonrestrictive clauses, turn to pages 550–551 in the Handbook.)

5. Setting off words that precede the main body of the sentence: When introductory material precedes the sentence's main subject and verb, such material is usually followed by a comma.

> *Yes,* I'll be happy to read the report.   *Like most children,* my little sister loves animals.

If, however, the introductory material is very brief, you may often omit the comma:

> *Surely* everyone has an urge to see exotic places.

6. Setting off words that follow the main body of the sentence: Material attached to the end of a sentence—after the main subject and verb—is preceded by a comma.

> Many people think a walk is a waste of time, *like napping or daydreaming.*

7. Setting off interrupting words and phrases: Some words and phrases inserted into the body of a sentence can be removed without significant loss of meaning. Such *interrupting* elements are preceded and followed by commas when they occur midsentence.

> I told him, *when he mentioned the accident,* my version of what had happened.

> The snowfall was heavy; classes, *however,* were held as usual.

☑   CAUTION

☐   Note that a *pair of commas* must be used to set off interrupting words or phrases that occur midsentence. A single comma is *not* enough to set off interrupting elements:

Incorrect   The high school reunion, scheduled for Memorial Day weekend should be well attended. [comma needed after *weekend*]

Incorrect   The autumn day was surprisingly warm; we therefore, decided to go on a picnic. [comma needed before *therefore*]

☐   In the last sentence, the transitional adverb *therefore* should be flanked by commas because it occurs *within* an independent clause. But when a transitional adverb comes *between* two independent clauses, it is preceded by a semicolon and followed by a comma (see page 553 in the Handbook).

8. Setting off words in direct address: Use a comma before and/or after the name of a person or group being addressed directly:

Ladies and gentlemen, the meeting is about to begin.

9. Between a short quotation and the phrase that indicates the quotation's source: Use a comma between a short quotation and a reference to its source or speaker:

My roommate remarked, "You remind me of a hungry bulldog."

(For more on punctuating quotations, see pages 575–577 of the Handbook.)

10. Between the elements of a date or place: Use a comma to separate the non-numerical portions of a mailing address, as well as the numbers in a date:

The witness testified that the package was delivered to 102 Glendale Road, Kirkwood, New Jersey 08043, on January 23, 2014.

Also, place a comma after the year if the date appears before the end of the sentence:

They were married on June 28, 1974, in New York City.

When you reverse the day and month in a date or give only the month and year or the month and day, do not use commas. Also, don't put a comma between a state and a ZIP code:

February 14, 2014   14 February 2014   February 2014
New York, NY 10022

Practice: Correcting Comma Errors

Where appropriate, provide or eliminate commas in the following sentences. Be careful, though; some of the commas belong just where they are.

1. The local movie theater, despite efforts to attract customers finally closed its doors, and was purchased by a supermarket chain.
2. As a little boy, I dreamed about wearing a plaid flannel shirt and, like Paul Bunyan, camping out underneath towering trees.
3. Their parents, always risk takers divorced in August and remarried in February just six months later.
4. Shaken by the threat of a hostile takeover, the board of directors, and the stockholders voted to sell the retail division which had been losing money for years.
5. Despite my parents' objections I read Stephen King's novels *The Shining,* and *Carrie* when I was in junior high. The books terrified me; nevertheless, I couldn't put them down.

Semicolon (;)

1. Between independent clauses closely related in meaning: You may connect two independent clauses with a **semicolon,** rather than writing them as separate sentences. When you do, though, the clauses should be closely related in meaning. They might, for example, *reinforce* each other.

> Making spaghetti sauce is easy; most people can do it after only a few tries.

Or the clauses might *contrast* with each other:

> Many homebuyers harbor suspicious feelings about the real estate industry; most realtors, however, are honest and law-abiding.

Use of the semicolon is especially common when the *clauses* are *short*:

> Smile when you are introduced; nod or bow slightly to acknowledge applause; wait for silence; pause a second; then begin your speech.

You may also use a semicolon (instead of a period) between independent clauses linked by *transitions* (like *then* and *next*) or by *transitional adverbs* (such as *moreover* and *however*):

> We continually lost track of our sales; *finally,* a friend showed us a good accounting system.

Note that when the second independent clause starts with a transitional expression, a comma is placed *after* the transition. However, if a comma is placed *before* the transition, a *comma splice* results (see pages 553–554 of the Handbook on ways to avoid comma splices).

2. Between items in a series, when any of the items contains a comma: When individual items in a series have internal commas, another form of punctuation is needed to signal clearly where one item ends and another begins. For this purpose, use the semicolon.

> After dinner, we had to choose between seeing a movie classic, like *Casablanca, Rear Window,* or *It's a Wonderful Life*; playing Clue, Scrabble, or Monopoly; or working out.

3. Before coordinating conjunctions used to join independent clauses, when any of the clauses contains a comma: Ordinarily, independent clauses joined by a coordinating conjunction (*and, but, for, nor, or, so, yet*) have a comma, not a semicolon, between them. However, when any such clause has internal commas, a semicolon is needed between the clauses.

> The mist settled in the valley, hiding the fields, the foliage, and the farms; and the pleasant road became a menace.

Colon (:)

1. To introduce an illustrative statement or list of examples: Use a colon to introduce lengthy illustrative material—either a full statement or a number of examples—whenever that material is preceded by a full sentence.

> In the spring, the city has a special magic: Street musicians, jugglers, and ethnic festivals enthrall tourist and resident alike.

As the first example shows, when the material following the colon can stand alone as a complete sentence, it begins with a capital letter (*Street*). Otherwise, the material after the colon starts with a lowercase letter (*my*).

2. To introduce a long quotation: Use a colon when a complete sentence introduces a long quotation (five or more lines) that is set off in block (indented) form without quotation marks.

> The witness to the accident told the police:
>
> > I was walking to my car in the parking lot when I glanced over at the other side of the street. I saw the traffic light turn yellow, and a silver convertible started to slow down. Just then, a red station wagon came racing down the street. When the convertible stopped for the light, the station wagon kept going—right into the convertible's rear fender.

(See Chapter 20 for more information on the format for long and short quotations.)

3. After the opening of a business letter: Follow the opening of a business letter with a colon.

> Dear Ms. Goldwin:

Use a comma, however, in the salutation of a personal letter.

4. Between parts of certain conventional notations: A number of standard notations include colons. One example is time notation, with hours and minutes separated by a colon.

> 4:52 p.m.

In a ratio, a colon substitutes for the word *to*:

> By a ratio of 3:2, Americans prefer Glocko cleanser.

In a reference to the Bible, the colon separates chapter and verse numbers:

> Genesis 2:14

Titles and subtitles (of books, journal articles, short stories, works of art, films, and so on) are also separated by a colon:

> *Election Handbook*: *A Participant's Guide*

Quotation Marks (" ")

1. Direct quotations: A *direct quotation* reproduces exactly the wording, punctuation, and spelling of the source. It is also enclosed in *double* **quotation marks**.

> "Youngsters in elementary school should learn the importance of budgeting money," the psychologist said.

A quotation within a quotation is enclosed in *single* (' ') quotation marks.

> The psychologist said, "It was gratifying when my children told me, 'We're glad you taught us how to spend money sensibly.'"

✔ CAUTION

Indirect Quotations

- ☐ *Indirect quotations*—those referred to or paraphrased rather than reproduced word for word—*don't* get quotation marks:

  Correct The psychologist said that even young children should be taught how to manage money wisely.

- ☐ In the preceding sentence, the word *that* is often used to introduce an indirect quotation. There is *no comma* before or after *that* in this case.

Use a comma between a short quotation and an identifying phrase like *they commented* or *he said*. Such phrases may be placed before, after, or within the quotation:

She argued, "They won't reject the plan."

"They won't reject the plan," *she argued*, "if they understand its purpose."

When, as in the last example, the identifier interrupts the quotation midsentence, commas flank both sides of the identifier. But if the identifier comes between two quoted sentences, it is followed by a period:

"They won't reject the plan," *she argued*. "They understand its purpose."

☑ **CAUTION**

More on Punctuating Direct Quotations:

☐ Place a period or comma *inside* the closing quotation marks:

Correct   "You know what you meant to say," the instructor remarked, "but the reader doesn't."

☐ Place a colon or semicolon *outside* the closing quotation marks:

Correct   The article stated, "Rice is the major foodstuff of all Asian peoples"; in particular, the Japanese eat ten times more rice than Americans.

☐ Place question marks and exclamation points according to their context. If a quotation is itself a question or exclamation, the question mark or exclamation point goes *inside* the closing quotation marks. No other end punctuation is used:

Correct

"Who's responsible for this decision?" the chief executive demanded.
Each department head responded, "Not me!"

No comma is used when an identifying phrase follows a quoted question or exclamation.
    If the entire sentence, not just the quotation, is a question or an exclamation, the question or exclamation mark goes *outside* the quotation marks, at the end of the entire sentence:

Correct

Who taught you to ask for things by saying "Gimme"?

☐ Use no punctuation other than quotation marks when a quotation is blended (with or without the word *that*) into the rest of a sentence:

Correct

People who believe that "rules are made to be broken" only substitute their own rules.

Capitalization in Direct Quotations

☐ Start a quotation with a capital letter if it is a full sentence:

Correct

The author admitted, "**T**he classy-sounding pseudonym was a marketing strategy."

☐ Start a quotation with a lowercase letter if it is not a complete sentence, or if it is blended (with or without the word *that*) into the rest of your sentence:

Correct

Using a "**c**lassy-sounding pseudonym" was, the author admitted, "**a** marketing strategy."

(For information on adding to or deleting from quotations, see Chapter 19.)

2. Titles of short works: Put quotation marks around the titles of short works—book chapters, poems, stories, articles, editorials, essays, individual episodes of a television or radio program—that are part of a larger work or series.

> Kenneth Koch's poem "Mending Sump" parodies Robert Frost's "Mending Wall."

Titles of longer works are italicized (see pages 584–585 of the Handbook).

3. Calling attention to a word's use: To focus attention on a particular word or term, you may enclose it in quotation marks.

> People frequently say "between" when they should say "among."

Quotation marks also enclose words being used humorously or ironically:

> To celebrate their victory, the team members indulged in such "adult" behavior as pouring champagne over each other's heads.

(See pages 584–585 of the Handbook on highlighting words with italics.)

Ellipsis (...)

An **ellipsis**, consisting of three spaced periods (...), indicates that *words* have been *omitted from quoted material*. To use the ellipsis correctly, follow the guidelines presented here.

1. When to use the ellipsis: You may use an ellipsis to shorten a quotation, as long as you don't distort its meaning.

Original

> The judge commented, "It won't surprise you to learn that this has been the most disturbing and the most draining case I have tried in all my years on the bench."

With Ellipsis

> The judge commented, "It won't surprise you to learn that this has been the most disturbing...case I have tried in all my years on the bench."

When you drop words from the end of a sentence or omit an entire sentence, the period that ends the sentence appears in its usual place, followed by the three spaced periods that signal the omission:

> The judge commented, "It won't surprise you to learn that this has been the most disturbing and the most draining case I have tried...."

Notice that in this case, there is no space between the last word in the sentence and the sentence's period.

2. When *not* to use the ellipsis: When you omit words from the beginning of a quotation, do not use an ellipsis; just begin your quotation at the point you've selected.

> The judge commented, "This has been the most disturbing and the most draining case I have tried in all my years on the bench."

Apostrophe (')

1. In place of omitted letters: In standard contractions, an **apostrophe** replaces any omitted letters.

> can't, don't, I'm, it's, she's, we've

Apostrophes also replace any letters dropped for the purpose of reproducing casual speech or slang:

> "Keep singin' an' marchin'!" he shouted.

2. To indicate possession: To show the possessive form of most *singular nouns,* add *'s:*

> The singer**'s** debut was a disaster. The boss**'s** office was small and poorly lit.

For *plural nouns* ending in *s,* add only an apostrophe to show possession:

> Students' grades improved after computer-assisted instruction.

Plural nouns that do *not* end in *s* need both an apostrophe and an *s* to show possession:

> The children**'s** school was set on fire.

To show *joint possession* (two or more owners of the same thing), make only the last noun possessive:

> Lubin and Wachinsky's firm handled the defense.

To show *individual possession* of more than one thing, make each noun possessive:

> The girl**'s** and the boy**'s** parents urged them to date other people.

☑ CAUTION

☐   The possessive forms of personal pronouns do *not* include an apostrophe. Here are the correct forms:

   mine, yours, his, hers, its, ours, theirs

☐   Note that *its* (*without* an apostrophe) is the *possessive* form of *it*:

Correct
The theater closed *its* [not *it's*] doors last week.

☐   The word *it's* means "it is" or "it has" (the apostrophe takes the place of the omitted letters):

Correct

It's [meaning "it is"] cold today.

It's [meaning "it has"] been a difficult time for us.

☐   Similarly, *whose* (*without* an apostrophe) is the possessive form of *who*:

Correct

Whose [not *who's*] coat is on the table?

☐   The word *who's* means "who is" or "who has" (the apostrophe takes the place of the omitted letters):

Correct

We wonder *who's* [meaning "who is"] going to take her place.

They want to know *who's* [meaning "who has"] been tabulating the results.

Amounts (of time, money, weight, and so on) should also be written in possessive form when appropriate:

Employees can accumulate a maximum of a month's sick leave.

3. To indicate some plurals: When a letter, symbol, or word treated as a word is made plural, an apostrophe often precedes the final *s*.

I got mostly C's my first semester of college.

He uses too many *and*'s to connect one thought to another.

However, common abbreviations such as *DVR, ESP,* and *SAT* don't take the apostrophe in the plural:

The local television station reported that residents sighted three *UFO*s last summer.

When you refer to a decade, you may omit the apostrophe:

The 1960s were turbulent and exciting.

An apostrophe is required only to replace omitted numerals that indicate the century:

The '60s were turbulent and exciting.

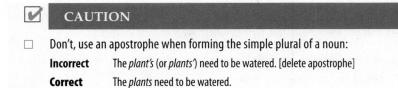

☐   Don't, use an apostrophe when forming the simple plural of a noun:

Incorrect   The *plant's* (or *plants'*) need to be watered. [delete apostrophe]

Correct   The *plants* need to be watered.

☐   Don't use an apostrophe when forming the third-person singular form of the verb:

Incorrect   The television *blare's* all day in many homes.
Correct   The television *blares* all day in many homes.

Parentheses ( )

( )

Parentheses enclose subordinate but related ideas, facts, or comments—items that would unnecessarily interrupt the sentence if set off by commas. A parenthetic remark may be located anywhere in a sentence except at the beginning, but it should immediately follow the item to which it refers. The presence of parentheses does not otherwise affect a sentence's punctuation. Here are some guidelines to follow when using parentheses.

1. A parenthetic sentence between two other sentences or at the end of a paragraph: If you place a parenthetic sentence between two other sentences or at the end of a paragraph, simply write the parenthetic sentence as you normally would; then enclose it in parentheses. The sentence in parentheses should begin with a capital letter and end with a period or other end punctuation.

> Writing home from summer camp is a chore most youngsters avoid. (Some camps have children write home once a week.) Most parents, though, eagerly await letters from their kids.

2. At the end of a sentence: Material that extends or illustrates a sentence should be inserted in parentheses at the end of the sentence *before* the closing period. Such parenthetic material shouldn't start with a capital letter. Also, the parenthetic material doesn't have its own period.

> It is a cruel irony that everything I am allergic to is wonderful (like chocolate, roses, and dogs).

3. A parenthetic sentence inside another sentence: When parenthetic material that can stand alone as a full statement occurs within another sentence, the parenthetic material should *not* begin with a capital letter or end with a period.

> Watering a garden the right way (yes, there's a wrong way) is important.

If, however, the parenthetic material is a question, do end it with a question mark:

> Watering a garden the right way (you didn't think there was a wrong way?) is important.

4. After a word that would be followed by a comma: When you insert a parenthetic comment after a word that would otherwise be followed by a comma, move the comma to the end of the parenthetic element.

Original   Without sufficient water, the trees started to lose their leaves in July.

Parenthetic   Without sufficient water (only half an inch the whole month), the trees started to lose their leaves in July.

5. Enclosing numbers or letters assigned to items in a series: Use parentheses to enclose the numbers or letters assigned to items in a series. The items in a series are followed by commas.

Before making a drastic change in your life, you should (1) discuss it with friends, (2) seek the advice of people who have had a similar change, and (3) determine whether a less dramatic change would be sufficient.

6. Enclosing inserted dates and organizations' abbreviations: When you add information such as dates and abbreviations to an otherwise complete sentence, enclose this information in parentheses.

Frank Lloyd Wright (1869–1959) was one of America's foremost architects.

Brackets [ ]

1. To clarify a quotation: When, for the purpose of clarification or correction, you insert your own words into a quotation, enclose them within **brackets**.

"Research done at that laboratory [Sci-Tech] is suspect," the physician testified.

Use parentheses, not brackets, to insert a comment within your *own* sentence or paragraph.

2. To signal a linguistic irregularity within a quotation: Quotations sometimes contain linguistic irregularities—such as colloquialisms or errors in spelling, grammar, or usage. In such cases, you may want to follow the irregularity with the Latin term *sic* in brackets, thus indicating that the questionable word or expression appears exactly as used by the quoted writer or speaker.

"None of the tenents [sic] complained about the building," the landlord wrote in a letter to the housing authority.

Note: When omitting words from a quotation, you should insert an ellipsis enclosed within brackets to indicate that *you*, rather than the original author, are inserting the ellipsis. (For information about the use of brackets when quoting material in a research paper, see page 480. For more on quotations, see Chapters 19 and 20.)

Hyphen (-)

A **hyphen** consists of one short line (and should not be confused with the dash— see page 583).

1. To break a word: A word that is too long to fit at the end of a typed line may be divided between two syllables, with a hyphen indicating the break. (Check the dictionary if you're uncertain where the syllables begin and end.)

> Once a clear contest between good and evil, between right and wrong, television wrestling now features stereotype-defying and ambiguous protagonists.

Most word-processing programs automatically either break long words at the end of lines or move them to the next line (called "word wrapping").

2. To combine words into an adjective or noun: When you combine two or more words to form a new adjective or noun, use hyphens between the original words.

> The question is whether this country should maintain first-strike capability.

The only exception is a compound adjective that contains an adverb ending in *ly*. In this case, don't place a hyphen after the *ly*:

> The poorly constructed DVD player jammed within the week.

In a series of hyphenated compound adjectives or nouns all having the same final word, write that word only at the end of the series:

> First-, second-, and third-year students must take one semester of gym.

3. Between a combined number and word: Hyphenate a numeral combined with a word:

> The new car has a 2.6-liter engine.

4. After certain prefixes: Compound words beginning with *self* or *ex* take a hyphen after the prefix.

> My ex-roommate is self-employed as a computer consultant.

Words that without the hyphen would be misread as other words also take a hyphen.

> A growing number of young professionals live in co-ops.

5. To write certain numbers: Use a hyphen when writing most numbers composed of two words.

> The zoning ordinance outlines twenty-one restrictions.

Note, however, that two-word numbers such as *one hundred* and *two thousand* don't take a hyphen.
A hyphen is required when a fraction is used as a compound modifier:

> The class was almost one-half empty.

(For more on writing numbers, see pages 585–586 of the Handbook.)

Dash (—)

A **dash** (—) is composed of two (or three) typed hyphens (-- or ---). Don't leave a space between the hyphens or between the words that precede or follow the dash.

To highlight a thought or idea: A dash *signals* an *added* or *interrupting thought* and, unlike parentheses, highlights that thought. When the added thought occurs at the sentence's end, it is preceded by a single dash.

> The package finally arrived—badly damaged.

When the added thought occurs midsentence, it receives two sets of two dashes, one set before the added thought and another after:

> The ambassador—after serving for more than two decades—suddenly resigned her post.

Practice: Correcting Problems with Punctuation

Correct any punctuation problems that you find in the following sentences.

1. The New Madrid fault, which lies in the central part of the country will be the site of a major earthquake within the next thirty years.
2. In the children's story, the hero carries a fresh, yellow rose rather than a sword.
3. "Branch offices, and drive-in windows," the bank president announced, "will be closed January 4, the day of the governors funeral".
4. The scientists said that "they wondered how anyone could believe stories of outer-space visitors."
5. On one of the office's paneled wall's the executive had a framed copy of the poem, "If."

Mechanics

Capitalization

Always capitalize the pronoun *I* and the first word of a sentence. Following are other **capitalization** guidelines.

cap

1. Proper names: Whether they appear in noun, adjective, or possessive form, proper names are always capitalized. **Proper names** include the following: names of individuals; countries, states, regions, and cities; political, racial, and religious groups; languages; institutions and organizations; days, months, and holidays; historical periods; product brand names; fully specified academic degrees (Master of Science in Chemistry); and particular academic courses. Here are some examples:

> *Representative O'Dwyer, a Democrat from the Midwest,* introduced several bills in *Congress* last *March.*

> All *Buddhists* are vegetarians.

584 Part VI · A Concise Handbook

Do not capitalize the names of ideologies and philosophies, such as *communism* and *idealism* (unless the name is derived from that of an individual—for example, *Marxism*). Similarly, avoid capitalizing compass directions, unless the direction serves as the name of a region (the *West*, the *Northeast*) or is attached to the name of a continent, country, or city (*North America, South Angola, West Philadelphia*).

Finally, don't capitalize the following: seasons; animal breeds (unless part of the name is derived from that of a place—such as *French poodle* and *Labrador retriever*); types of academic degrees (*bachelor's, master's, doctorate*); or academic subjects and areas (*sociology, mathematics*), unless they're part of a course title or department name (*Sociology I, Mathematics Department*). Here are some more examples:

On one side of the Continental Divide, rivers flow *east;* on the other, they flow *west.*

In San Francisco, there is little temperature variation between *spring* and *summer.*

2. Titles of literary and other artistic works: When writing a title, capitalize the first word and all other words, except articles (*a, an, the*), conjunctions (*and, but*), and prepositions (*on, to*) of fewer than five letters.

In *The Structure of Scientific Revolutions,* Thomas Kuhn discusses the way the scientific establishment resists innovation. However, Anna Stahl disputes Kuhn's argument in *The Controversy Over Scientific Conservatism.*

3. Official and personal titles: Capitalize official and personal titles when they precede a name or are used in place of the name of a specific person:

Only *Reverend* Zager could stretch a sermon to an hour and a half.

Weeks before Father's Day, the stores start featuring gifts for *Dad.*

Do not capitalize such titles otherwise:

The *reverend* encouraged the congregation to donate food and clothing to the poor.

His *dad* writes for the local paper.

Italics

ital

Italicizing (*slanted type*) serves the same purposes as underlining.

1. Titles of individual works: Italicize the titles of works that are published individually—not as part of a magazine, anthology, or other collection. Such works are often lengthy—entire books, magazines, journals, newspapers, movies, television programs, musical recordings, plays, and so on. They may, however, also be works of visual art, such as paintings and sculptures. Here are some examples:

When I was a child, my favorite book was *At the Back of the North Wind.*

The movie critic panned *Friday the 13th, Part 83.*

However, titles of certain historical documents and major religious writings, such as the books of the Bible, are neither italicized nor enclosed in quotation marks, but important words begin with a capital letter:

Bhagavad Gita	the Koran	Song of Solomon
the book of Genesis	Bill of Rights	Old Testament
the Bible	U.S. Constitution	Monroe Doctrine

(See page 577 of the Handbook for ways to designate the titles of short works like poems and short stories.)

2. Foreign terms: Foreign words not fully incorporated into mainstream English should be italicized.

> Before protesters knew what was happening, the legislation was a *fait accompli*.

3. For emphasis: Italicize words you wish to stress, but do so sparingly because too many italicized words actually weaken emphasis.

> The campaign staff will *never* allow the candidate to appear in an open forum.

4. Letters and numbers referred to as words: Italicize letters or numbers when they function as words.

> In the local high school, teachers give *A*'s and *B*'s only to outstanding students.

5. Calling attention to a word's use: To call attention to the way a word is being used, you may italicize it.

> Why use *conflagration* when a simple word like *fire* will do?

(See page 577 of the Handbook for another way to highlight words.)

6. Vehicles of transportation: Italicize the names of ships, planes, trains, and spacecraft.

> A design flaw led to the explosion of the space shuttle *Challenger*.

Numbers

1. When to use words: Generally, *words* instead of numerals are used for numbers that can be written out in *one* or *two words*. When written out, numbers between 21 and 99 (except round numbers) are hyphenated (*twenty-one; ninety-nine*). If the number requires *three or more words*, use *numerals*; a hyphenated number counts as one word. Also use words for any number that occurs at the start of a sentence.

> The store manager came up with *three* fresh ideas for attracting more customers.
>
> *Two hundred forty-eight* people were on the hijacked plane.

num

You may prefer to rephrase a sentence that begins with a long number, so that you can use numerals instead of words:

The hijacked plane had *248* people on board.

2. When to use numerals: Numerals are generally used to indicate measurements.

The office was approximately *10 feet, 8 inches* wide.

Dates, times, addresses, page numbers, decimals, and percentages are also usually given as numerals. When a date includes the day as well as the month and year, give only the numeral to identify the day (for example, write *March 4*, not *March 4th*; *May 2*, not *May 2nd*):

The builder claims that the wood delivered on *August 3, 2013,* was defective.

Use numerals when a time reference contains *a.m.* or *p.m.* or specifies the minutes as well as the hour:

We set the alarm for *5 a.m.* and left the house by *5:45.*

However, use words with *o'clock*:

My roommate has trouble getting up before *eleven o'clock* in the morning.

In addresses, the house or building number is always given in numerals:

Last weekend, I visited my childhood home at *80 Manemet Road.*

For a numbered street, use numerals unless the number is less than ten or the building and street numbers would be written next to each other—a potential source of confusion:

The shelter moved from 890 East 47th Street to *56 Second Avenue.*

Always give page numbers as numerals. It's also standard to give percentages and decimal amounts in numerals:

Sales increased *5%* last year.

More than *2.5 million* boxes of oat bran were sold last year.

Abbreviations

ab

1. Personal and professional titles: The **abbreviations** for some personal titles appear *before* the person's name.

Dr. Tony Michelin   *Ms.* Carla Schim

Others come *after*:

Houston J. Marshall, *Esq.*   Nora Rubin, *MD*

Professional titles such as *Professor, Senator,* and *Governor* may be abbreviated only before a full name:

Prof. Eleanor Cross   Rep. George M. Dolby

2. Common terms and organizations: Use the standard initials for common terms and widely known organizations.

DVR   FBI   NATO   CIA   URL   ESP   AT&T

Notice that these abbreviations do not include periods.

The first time you refer to a less familiar organization, give its full name, followed by the abbreviation in parentheses. Thereafter, you may refer to the organization with only the abbreviation. If the organization uses an ampersand (&) for *and* or abbreviations for terms such as *Incorporated* (Inc.) and *Company* (Co.), you may use them as well.

3. Time: Use the Latin abbreviations *a.m. (ante meridiem)* and *p.m. (post meridiem)* for time of day.

They started work at *4 a.m.* and got home at *6:15 p.m.*

Use numerals with the abbreviations *AD (anno Domini*—"in the year of the Lord"), *BC* ("before Christ"), *CE* (the common era), and *BCE* (before the common era), unless you refer to centuries rather than specific years. In that case, write out the century before the abbreviation:

The pottery was made around *AD 56,* but the tools date back to the *third century BC.*

Note that the year precedes *BC (684 BC)* but follows *AD (AD 1991).*

4. Latin terms: If you use the Latin abbreviations *i.e.* (for "that is") and *e.g.* (for "for example"), remember that they should be followed by a comma and used parenthetically.

Employees are enthusiastic about recent trends in the business world (**e.g.,** the establishment of on-site day-care programs and fitness centers).

Whenever possible, however, replace these abbreviations with their English equivalents.

In addition, try to avoid *etc.* ("and so on") by citing all examples you have in mind, instead of leaving them up to the reader's imagination.

5. Names of regions: Except in addresses, don't abbreviate geographic regions.

With a student rail pass, you can tour *Great Britain* [not *G.B.*] at discount rates.

Exceptions to this rule include *Washington, D.C.,* and *U.S.* when it is used as a modifier (*U.S. policy,* for example).

In addresses, states' names are abbreviated according to the postal designations—with two capital letters and no periods:

NY   RI   NJ

6. Units of measure: Don't abbreviate common units of measure.

> The bedroom was *15 feet, 9 1/2 inches* wide.

However, do abbreviate such technical units of measure as millimeters (*mm*) and revolutions per minute (*rpm*).
(Turn to page 590 for a practice exercise on mechanics.)

Spelling

Spelling

sp

Spelling need not be a mystery. For reference, always have on hand a current standard dictionary or a spelling dictionary. If you use a word processor, an automatic "spell-check" program may be valuable (though not always foolproof). Another strategy is to keep a personal inventory of the words you misspell or need to look up repeatedly. Finally, knowing about basic spelling rules and commonly misspelled words can help you minimize spelling errors. You should find the following guidelines on the next page helpful.

1. When *i* and *e* are adjacent: Do you remember the rhyme for spelling a word with an adjacent *i* and *e*?

i before e	*except after c*	or when pronounced like *a* as in *neighbor* and *weigh*
achieve	ceiling	beige
piece	conceited	freight
thief	deceive	reign
yield	receive	their

The rule does *not* apply if the *i* and *e* are in separate syllables: *science, society.* It also does not apply to the following exceptions:

caffeine	inveigle	seize
either	leisure	sleight
financier	neither	species
foreign	protein	weird

2. Doubling the final consonant: This rule applies to words that satisfy the following conditions.

- The word's last three letters must be consonant, vowel, consonant, *and*
- The word must be either one syllable (*plan*) or accented on the final syllable (*control*).

In such cases, double the final consonant before adding an ending that begins with a vowel (such as *-ed, -er, -al,* and *-ing*):

plan/plan**ned**   control/control**ler**   refer/refer**ral**   begin/begin**ning**

However, do *not* double the final consonant in the following cases:

- Words that end in a silent *e* (*pave/paved, mope/moping*)[5]
- Words ending in two vowels and a consonant or in two consonants (*appear/appearance, talk/talking*)
- Words whose accent is not on the final syllable (*develop/developing*)
- Words that no longer are accented on the final syllable when the ending is added (*refer/reference, prefer/preferable*). An exception is the word *questionnaire,* which does contain a double *n*.

3. Dropping the final silent *e*: For a word that ends in a silent (not pronounced separately) *e,* drop the *e* before adding an ending that begins with a vowel.

cope/cop**ing**   receive/receiv**able**   cute/cut**est**   guide/guid**ance**

But keep the *e* before an ending beginning with a consonant:

sincere/sincer**ely**   base/bas**ement**   definite/definit**ely**   nine/nine**ty**

Exceptions include the following: *truly, awful, argument; dyeing* and *singeing* (to avoid confusion with *dying* and *singing*); *changeable, courageous, manageable, noticeable,* and similar words where the final *e* is needed to keep the sound of the *g* or *c* soft.

4. Adding to words that end in *y*:   For most words ending in *y,* change the *y* to *ie* before adding an *s:*

city/cit**ies**   study/stud**ies**   story/stor**ies**

Change the *y* to *i* before all other endings, except *-ing:*

copy/cop**ies**   cry/cr**ies**   study/stud**ies**

The *y* remains when the ending is *-ing:*

cop**ying**   cry**ing**   stud**ying**

The *y* also stays when it is preceded by a vowel:

delay/dela**ys**/dela**yed**/dela**ying**

5. Words ending in *-f* and *-fe*:   Words ending in *-f* and *-fe* normally change to *-ves* in the plural.

leaf/lea**ves**   life/li**ves**   knife/kni**ves**   wife/wi**ves**

An exception is *roof,* whose plural simply adds an *-s*.

---

[5]An exception is *write/written*. Note, however, that the *-ing* form of *write* is *writing,* not *writting*.

6. Common spelling errors: Homonyms are words that sound alike but have different spellings and meanings. (A spelling dictionary will provide a complete list of homonyms and other commonly confused words.) If you're not sure of the differences in meaning between any of the homonym pairs listed, check your dictionary. Here are a few of the most troublesome:

accept/except	knew/new	their/there/they're
affect/effect	lose/loose	to/too/two
complement/compliment	principal/principle	whose/who's
its/it's	than/then	your/you're

Cognates are words with the same root. However, they may not always have the same spelling:

curious/curiosity   disaster/disastrous   generous/generosity   four/forty

Some words contain *silent* (or nearly silent) *letters* that are often erroneously omitted when the word is spelled:

environment	supposed to	government
February	sophomore	used to

Finally, avoid *nonexistent forms* of words. For example, there is no such word as *its'*; *a lot* is two words, not one; and few instructors consider *alright* an acceptable variant of *all right*.

Practice: Correcting Problems with Mechanics and Spelling

Correct any mechanics or spelling problems that you find in the following sentences.

1. "Emerging Nations in today's World," one of the supplementary texts in Modern History I, is on reserve at the libary.
2. Last year, while visiting my parents in central Florida, I took a disastrous coarse in Sociology.
3. The analysts of the election-eve pole concluded, "Its a toss-up."
4. For some reason, Spring tends to have a depressing affect on me.
5. Weighing in at 182 lbs. was Tim Fox, a sophmore from a community college in Ala.

Acknowledgments

Angier, Natalie. *The Canon: A Whirligig Tour of the Beautiful Basics of Science,* Houghton Mifflin Harcourt, 2008.

Appleton, Josie. "The Body Piercing Project" from *Spike Magazine* July 9, 2003. Reproduced by permission of Spiked Ltd.

Barry, Linda. "The Sanctuary of School" from *The New York Times,* January 5, 1992. Copyright © 1992 by Lynda Barry. All rights reserved. Used with Permission.

Borel, France. "The Decorated Body" from *Parabola 19* (Fall 1994): 74–78. Reproduced by permission of Parabola Magazine.

Bosker, Bianca. "How Teens Are Really Using Facebook" from *The Huffington Post* May 21, 2013. Copyright © 2013 AOL Inc. All rights reserved. Used by permission and protected by the Copyright Laws of the United States. The printing, copying, redistribution, or retransmission of this Content without express written permission is prohibited.

CDC/NCHS, National Health Examination Survey I 1960–1962; National Health and Nutrition Examination Survey (NHANES) I 1971–1974; NHANES II 1976–1980; NHANES III 1988–1994; NHANES 1999–2000, 2001–2002, 2003–2004, 2005–2006, 2007–2008, and 2009–2010. In Cynthia L. Ogden and Margaret D. Carroll, "Prevalence of Overweight, Obesity, and Extreme Obesity Among Adults: United States, Trends 1960–1962 Through 2007–2008," Health E-Stats, National Center for Health Statistics, Dept. of Health and Human Resources, June 2010.

Cohen, Patricia. "Clueless" From *Slate,* September 16, 2003, Copyright © 2003 The Slate Group. All rights reserved. Used by permission and protected by the Copyright Laws of the United States. The printing, copying, redistribution, or retransmission of this Content without express written permission is prohibited.

Fraser, Laura. "The Inner Corset" from *Losing It: America's Obsession with Weight and the Industry That Feeds on It.* Copyright 1997 by Laura Fraser. Reproduced by permission of the author.

Garibaldi, Garry. "How The Schools Shortchange Boys" from *City Journal,* Summer 2006. Copyright 2006 The Manhattan Institute. Reproduced with permission.

Goodman, Ellen. "Family Counterculture" from *The Boston Globe* 8/16/1991. Copyright © 1991 Boston Globe. All rights reserved. Used by permission and protected by the Copyright Laws of the United States. The printing, copying, redistribution, or retransmission of this Content without express written permission is prohibited.

Horton, Alex. "On Getting By" from *Blog, Army of Dude.* Reproduced by permission of the author.

Hughes, Langston. "Early Autumn" from *Short Stories by Langston Hughes.* Copyright © 1996 by Ramona Bass and Arnold Rampersad. Reprinted by permission of Hill and Wang, a division of Farrar, Straus and Giroux, LLC.

Hulbert, Ann. "Beyond The Pleasure Principle" From *The New York Times,* March 11, 2007. Copyright © 2007 The New York Times. All rights reserved. Used by permission and protected by the Copyright Laws of the United States. The printing, copying, redistribution, or retransmission of this Content without express written permission is prohibited.

Hymowitz, Kay S. "Tweens: Ten Going on Sixteen" from *City Journal,* Autumn 1998 Copyright 1998. The Manhattan Institute.

Johnson, Beth. "Bombs Bursting in Air" Reproduced by permission of the author.

Johnson, Keith. "Who's a Pirate? In Court, A Duel over Definitions" from *The Wall Street Journal.* August 20, 2010.

Kimmel, Michael S. "A War Against Boys" from *Dissent Magazine,* 2006. © Michael Kimmel, 2006. Reproduced by permission of the author. All rights reserved.

King, Stephen. "Why We Crave Horror Movies," Copyright © Stephen King. All rights reserved. Originally appeared in *Playboy* (1982). Reproduced by permission of Darhansoff & Verrill Literary Agents.

Lorde, Audre. "The Fourth of July" from *Zami: A New Spelling of My Name* published by Crossing Press. Copyright © 1982, 2006 by Audre Lorde. Used herewith by permission of the Charlotte Sheedy Literary Agency

Luscombe, Linda. "The Science of Romance: Why We Flirt" from *Time Magazine,* January 17, 2008.

Lustig, Robert et al. "The Toxic Truth About Sugar" From *Nature* February 2, 2012. Nature Publishing Group.

McClintock, Ann. "Propaganda Techniques in Today's Advertising." Pearson Education.

McDonald, Cherokee Paul. "A View from the Bridge" From Florida *SunSentinel,* February 12, 1989. Copyright © 1989 Florida SunSentinel. All rights reserved. Used by permission and protected by the Copyright Laws of the United States. The printing, copying, redistribution, or retransmission of this Content without express written permission is prohibited.

Marlow, Michael and Sherzod Abdukadirov. "Government Intervention Will Not Solve Our Obesity Problem" from *U.S. News and World Report,* June 5, 2012.

Murray, Joan. "Someone's Mother" from *The New York Times Magazine,* May 13, 2007. Copyright © 2007 The New York Times. All rights reserved. Used by permission and protected by the Copyright Laws of the United States. The printing, copying, redistribution, or retransmission of this Content without express written permission is prohibited.

Parks, Gordon. "Flavio's Home" from *Voices in the Mirror,* 1990. Copyright by Gordon Parks. Reprinted by permission of SLL/Sterling Lord Literistic, Inc.

Quinlan, Anna. "Driving to the Funeral." Copyright 2007 by Anna Quindlen. First appeared in *Newsweek* June 11, 2007.

Sanders, Scott Russell. "The Men We Carry in Our Minds." Copyright 1984 by Scott Russell Sanders; first appeared in *Milkweed Chronicle;* from the author's own collection, *The Paradise of Bombs;* reproduced by permission of the author and the author's agents, Virginia Kidd Agency, Inc.

Sherry, Mary. "In Praise of the "F" Word" from My Turn, *Newsweek,* May 6, 1991. Reproduced by permission of the author.

Shipley, David. "What We Talk About When We Talk About Editing" From *The New York Times,* July 31, 2005. Copyright © 2005 The New York Times. All rights reserved. Used by permission and protected by the Copyright Laws of the United States. The printing, copying, redistribution, or retransmission of this Content without express written permission is prohibited.

Suárez, Mario. "El Hoyo" from *Chicano Sketches* edited by Mario Suárez, Francisco Lomeli, Cecilia Cota-Robles Suárez, and Juan Casillas-Nunez. © 2004 The Arizona Board of Regents. Reprinted by permission of the University of Arizona Press.

Sutherland, Amy. "What Shamu Taught Me About a Happy Marriage" from *The New York Times,* June 25, 2006.

Weiner, Eric. "Euromail and Amerimail" From *Slate,* March 25, 2005, Copyright © 2005. The Slate Group. All rights reserved. Used by permission and protected by the Copyright Laws of the United States. The printing, copying, redistribution, or retransmission of this Content without express written permission is prohibited.

World Health Organization. Data from *The World Malaria Report, 2012.*

Wright, Alex. "Friending, Ancient or Otherwise" from *The New York Times,* December 2, 2007; Copyright © 2007 The New York Times. All rights reserved. Used by permission and protected by the Copyright Laws of the United States. The printing, copying, redistribution, or retransmission of this Content without express written permission is prohibited.

Photo Credits

P. 1: StepStock/Fotolia

P. 6: Ricardo Arduengo/AP Images

P. 14: Berc/Fotolia

P. 34: Jade/Blend Images/Getty Images

P. 41: Monkey Business/Fotolia

P. 48: Monamakela/Getty Images

P. 56: Monamakela/Fotolia

P. 78: WavebreakmediaMicro/Fotolia

P. 90: JupiterImages/Getty Images

P. 116: Vivek Prakash/Reuters

P. 125: Eco Images/UIG/AGE Fotostock

P. 155: Library of Congress Prints and Photographs Division [LC-DIG-fsa-8b29516]

P. 183: Advertising Archives

P. 216: Dann Tardif/LWA/Corbis

P. 249: Jack Hollingsworth/Getty Images

P. 282: ZUMA Press/The Advertising Archive

P. 313: Coco Robicheaux/Alamy

P. 336: Robert Kneschke/Fotolia

P. 349: Donald Miralle/Getty Images

P. 369: Brand X Pictures (top left), Gibson, Charles Dana, 1867–1944 (top right), Bain News Service (bottom)

P. 381: FDA.gov

P. 449: Janine Wiedel Photolibrary/Alamy

P. 471: Asia Images Group/Getty Images

P. 521: ZUMA Press, Inc./Alamy

P. 539: Robert Kneschke/Fotolia

Index